Portrait of an
AMERICAN
LABOR LEADER:
William L. Hutcheson

William Levi Hutcheson

SAGA OF THE UNITED BROTHERHOOD OF CARPENTERS AND
JOINERS OF AMERICA 1881-1954

Portrait of an

AMERICAN
LABOR LEADER:
William L. Hutcheson

by Maxwell C. Raddock

AMERICAN INSTITUTE OF SOCIAL SCIENCE, INC.   NEW YORK

5Y

To

Lillian, Richard, Carole, Franklin and Bruce

PREVIEW TO UNDERSTANDING

The subject of this book is the United Brotherhood of Carpenters and Joiners of America. Its activity fundamentally directed toward the economic betterment of its members, the U.B. of C. has undergone a remarkable metamorphosis in the seventy-four years of its uninterrupted existence. Growing steadily in size and power, it has in a large sense affected our economic life. That it has raised the living standards of the individual members, among other things, is a well-known fact as our story will attest.

The main object of this work is to inquire into the life, work, personality and character of William Levi Hutcheson — one of America's a-typical labor leaders to have emerged on the American scene in the past forty years. His story is part of a larger inquiry into the social, economic, organizational and political history of America, covering a period of eight decades.

Actually, the Brotherhood is here viewed as a case study of that striking movement in modern life which historians have described as the "organizational revolution". The Labor movement is part of it, as are the farm, professional and other voluntary economic groups. As part of the labor movement with 835,000 members, the U.B. of C. is a vital and salutary economic and political force in our democracy.

Along with the rise in the power of voluntary economic organizations, there has also been a great rise in the economic power of the national state. This movement is evident in its most extreme and malignant form in the Communist states, where the state virtually becomes the only economic organization, all other organizations being subordinate to the oligarchic state. Even in our own country, we have seen the national state assuming more and more economic responsibility, through the sponsorship of social security schemes, direct governmental aid to depressed industries, protective tariffs, the governmental regulation of industry and labor, and the trend to nationalized industry — the T.V.A., for example.

It is in this sense, I might point out, that a voluntary economic organization, such as the Brotherhood became a dependable bulwark against the drift toward totalitarianism under Hutcheson's stewardship. William L. Hutcheson saw this basic struggle more clearly than some of the labor leadership of today — that keeps demanding more governmental intervention without telling us how, at the same time, to avert resultant totalitarianism.

Much of our basic thinking still assumes a system which is composed of many small units. Even today, of course, many segments of our economic system—e.g., retailing, the service trades, agriculture—are still in the hands of small-scale units but are not somehow affected directly by the existing large economic organizations. Nevertheless, the rise of the labor movement (or other similar economic organizations) has profoundly affected our economic system — for the better, to be sure. A system which is affected by large economic organizations presents problems, both for economic policy on the part of the government and for standards of economic morality on the part of business, which are different from those of an unorganized society. It is doubtful whether our thinking in these matters has caught up with the changes that have taken place in our system, and we are in real danger of accepting principles, beliefs, nostrums and panaceas which were applicable to an earlier less complex system, but which do not really apply to the present

* * *

These preliminary but necessary observations out of the way, the United Brotherhood of Carpenters and Joiners of America, as I have stated, is here viewed as a *case study* of a large economic organization —the labor movement—operating during the second half of the twentieth century—the crucial era of makeshift and totalitarian panaceas. It is important, therefore, to understand something of the causes underlying this carpenters' movement if our attempt to shed light on the problems which it faced is to bear any fruit.

What, indeed, first brought men like the members of the U.B. of C. together into that compact movement or union now 835,000 strong?

Is the rise and growth of an economic organization such as the Carpenters the result of a more deeply felt need for it on the part of those who participate in it, or is it a result of an improvement in the technique of organization which makes it easier to develop and then to supply that "need"? Both these elements undoubtedly played some part in the growth of the Brotherhood. The obvious answer is that the U. B. of C. produced such results as advancing its members socially and economically.

Economic betterment of its members was by no means a negligible factor in explaining the attraction of the Brotherhood. There was a desire, too, for human status. The Carpenters' records point up these factors. Much of the drive which leads people to join labor unions is the desire to be able to look the boss squarely in the eye — an equal! — in addition to winning a fair wage for work done.

That there has been an intensification of these needs for organization in every industry during the past seventy years is certain. It is the logic of democratic society that implies dissatisfaction with any subordinate status. The labor movement especially has been regarded as an instrument for the rise of the "lower" groups as a whole. The emergence of numerically large, cohesive unions like the Brotherhood was of course the counteraction of labor to the concentration of control over capital and our economic resources. This came about in the second decade of our century. The U. B. of C. is thus a symbol of labor's reaction to the growth of giant corporations.

What is the organizational structure of the United Brotherhood of Carpenters and Joiners of America? What were the unfavorable influences to which it was subjected, technological, social, legal, governmental, political? What were the challenges it had to face? What type of leadership did it produce in the course of nearly eight decades of its turbulent existence?

Admittedly, the external environment often involves direct conflict with other organizations, and the fewer the number of competing organizations, the more acute that conflict becomes. Prudent leadership in human relations has in recent years done much to attenuate jurisdictional strife. A case in point is the recent "peace-pact" between the Carpenters' Brotherhood and the International Association of Machinists, which was brought about by Maurice A. Hutcheson, Al Hayes and co-officers of both labor organizations.

Union leaders are acutely sensitive to their constituencies and are generally in grave danger of losing their jobs if they do not fulfill their promise. Union constituencies are universally called upon to ratify their decisions, and not infrequently repudiate them. In other words, if a union leader does not "come through"—his career is short-lived. To an examination of these and other phases of the Brotherhood's work and that of its leadership I shall revert in the subsequent chapters of this book.

This book is a biography and an interpretation of the work, ideas and views of William Levi Hutcheson, the labor leader, the political catalyst, the human relations technician — in short, his personality. Related to the life and times of Hutcheson is the grim but highly dramatic chapter of labor's unconcealed bid for the gradual, increasing recognition and acceptance of its leaders and trade unions. It was part of a challenge to the American businessman and industrialist who achieved the most dominant position in the community, with labor always trailing far behind. Here was a "marginal" job to be done, and who but the "socially penalized" would do it!

Hutcheson, the son of a migrant, wandering worker, was "stimulated,"—to borrow a favorite phrase from historian Arnold J. Toynbee—

into the General Presidency of the United Brotherhood of Carpenters & Joiners of America at a time when labor's gains, moderate as these were then, gave way to the old law of supply and demand. And the supply of labor ran ahead of the demand, with the still heavy flow of helpless, impoverished and destitute immigrants who were accustomed to little and were indeed willing to work for just that. Born on the frontiers of Michigan, he was conditioned to a tough, hardy existence. Himself a "marginal" job seeker until the age of twenty-eight, and subjected to "penalization", he was prepared to challenge businessman and industrialist alike. He even matched powers with our reformer First World War President Woodrow Wilson, of whom he was no mean admirer. Recognition and status for his constituents was all he sought. It was his first trial battle, out of which he emerged the victor.

Soon a period of disillusionment and frustration followed, and invariably those experiences shifted his loyalties as well as intensified his aggressiveness. It was much later that this penalized labor leader sought to overcome his "social handicaps" by joining the Masons, Odd Fellows and other associations which occupy a very significant and increasingly strategic position in our total social structure.

There were, of course, others of that generation: John L. Lewis, Sidney Hillman, to cite two outstanding examples, who, like Hutcheson, sprang from the same "socially penalized" part of the population. This is clearly brought to our attention by Saul Alinsky and Matthew Josephson, recent biographers of Lewis and Hillman, respectively.

All three were dominant personalities, "other-directed," consumption-minded leaders, militant in their attitudes. All three served the constituencies of their respective unions—the United Brotherhood of Carpenters and Joiners of America, United Mine Workers of America and Amalgamated Clothing Workers of America — for more terms than is *normally* permissable, lest they be assailed with the opprobrium of autocrat. All were delegated great power, with fewer controls than might seem desirable in less intense times. All grew up in an atmosphere of struggle and conflict. But during that period of "organizational revolution," unions perforce became *imperium in imperio,* a state within a state, agencies of conflict. And, as in the national state at war, intense loyalty of the union members, backed by a highly centralized structure in the union itself, becomes a necessary pre-condition for *survival.* It is only when the unions and their leaders achieve recognition and have established their position vis-a-vis both the employers and society at large, that more democratic standards have a better chance of coming into their own. In the case of all three, their long tenure in office was simply the result of the leader's achievement for the rank and file and of an identity of mental processes between the leaders and the led.[1]

Yet comparatively few of the labor leaders were the subject of controversy and an ambivalence of feeling as was Hutcheson. But because he was controversial, the author has tried to understand him by tracing all the influences and conditionings of his early life and the *Zeitgest* upon him. I have tried to relate his personality and the experiences of his youth to the development of the labor movement. A socio-psychological approach may help us, I felt, trace associations in our protaganist's thoughts that might otherwise have escaped us.

I knew William Levi Hutcheson well. I first met him some twenty years ago, when I served my journalistic apprenticeship under the guidance of Abraham Cahan, best known as the author of *"Rise of David Levinsky"*, and one of the most distinguished daily newspaper editors in the country during the whole span of labor's rise. Here, I thought, is an extraordinary, vital man, with a flavor all his own. Strikingly different too from other labor leaders of his day and different, too, from the impression that some writers and publicists passed on to the American public mind for a quarter of a century. Bible-quoting, acid at times, eloquent and witty, he registered sharply. For a time I toyed with the idea of doing a book on Hutcheson, but it wasn't until 1953 that I found the time to begin it. When I got started, the difficulty of the task became apparent to me.

This difficulty lay in the nature of the evidence about him. In the first place, it was curiously scanty, and what there was—was uniformly repetitive. For once a suspicion arose in my mind that the motivation may not have been entirely that of the objective reporter, or historian, preoccupied exclusively with an objective recital of the facts. He himself had been somewhat reticent, unwilling to be interviewed or written about, although on frequent occasions he would talk to the writer into the early mornings after convention proceedings were over. This reticence is characteristic of his son Maurice, the General President of the United Brotherhood of Carpenters and Joiners of America, a gentle, soft-spoken and self-effacing man, who, although within the ranks of labor since the age of 14, does not conform to the generally accepted stereotype of a labor leader.

Moreover, most labor reporting during the first quarter of the current century was permeated with a strong emotional coloring derived mainly from a well-established scale of moral values. With few exceptions, the labor movement and its leaders were always pelted with a good deal of dust and pebbles, quarried from faulty facts, faulty logic and faulty

---

[1]For a more detailed analysis, see Professor Wright Millis' *The Men of Power: America's Labor Leaders* (Harcourt, Brace and Co. 1948), Chapter III.

statistics. The writers knew what they liked, to be sure. But what they didn't like was labor and labor leaders. They had no hesitation in giving their work a persuasive tone, and some of our contemporary labor chroniclers seem to relish their targets. There were tales and anecdotes in profusion. Most of them of questionable veracity. Finally, what evidence had accumulated about William L. Hutcheson was strikingly one-sided and even derogatory. Accounts of him, written and oral, by those who had been his co-workers and close associates in the American Federation of Labor were often revealing, but I could hardly take them at face value. I wanted to keep an open mind. On the other side were a number of books such as Bruce Minton's and John Stuart's *Men Who Lead Labor,* Edward Levinson's *Labor on the March,* Herbert Harris' *American Labor,* Charles A. Madison's *American Labor Leaders,* Harold Seidman's *Labor Czars,* and others. These seemed to me wholly unreliable as to the Hutcheson story *per se* and as to his total impact upon the American social scene. They had apparently been written on the assumption that if a labor leader became a Republican, opposed a blank check for "industrial unionism", and served long tenure in office, the duty of the labor historian was to ascribe it to any one of five evil motives, brushing aside all available evidence that pointed to the laudable intentions and lasting achievements of the subject.

William Hutcheson was a Republican, but his Republicanism was located in the heart of America where "the Protestant traditions are still alive and memories of the past are household words." Actually, his Republicanism "was in keeping with the Lincoln-Roosevelt traditions."[2] That he was no patron saint of financial success nor a devotee of the strong and the smug, will be amply documented elsewhere in this book. Similarly, Hutcheson did *not* oppose the organization of mass-production industries in the 'thirties. As a keen student of labor and its dynamics, he knew full well that mass unionism was a reflection of the rise of a growing populous stratum of permanent industrial workers—fathers and sons. He also knew that in the English-speaking countries the organization of specialized trades, or crafts, has fitted in ideally—and this in the light of American labor's own experience—with the American social structure. What Hutcheson opposed was the industrial catch-all, one big union, a conglomeration of craftsmen and the unskilled. That he was confirmed in this approach is attested to by the fact that the A. F. of L., whose very existence was challenged two decades ago, is now greatly bolstered, both morally and organically to formulate a basis for peace with its once rival, the CIO.

Had these publicists, textbook writers and historians employed their

---

[2]Andre Siegfried, *America Comes of Age* (Harcourt, Brace and Co. 1927), p. 278.

technical proficiency in which they are presumably grounded, they would have presented an array of historically verified and verifiable facts rather than relied on legend and embroidered gossip.

What concerns us here no less is to record the fact that such sentiments and perversions of fact, often accompanied by diatribes have been "transferred" unto the second generation of labor leaders. That there still persists such a marked tendency and paralyzing attitude among some of the present-day reporters of the labor scene, occasions no small concern to labor, its leaders and the interested public. Greater discernment and objective reporting would reveal that since his ascendancy to the office of the presidency of the U. B. in January, 1952, Maurice A. Hutcheson, the son of William L. Hutcheson, has in that relatively short time proven to be a stabilizing influence inside the labor movement and indirectly, on the conduct of our economic affairs. He has taken measures to rectify defects in the machinery, which more often than not intensified rather than checked oft-lamented jurisdictional and industrial strife. There is mounting evidence of his advanced social outlook, revealing a growing awareness of the interlocking interests between the labor standards of workers in the U.S., Canada, and every part of the free world. His role on the International Development Advisory Board under Foreign Operations Director Harold E. Stassen, in itself represents a major departure from the confining policy advocated by leaders of American labor throughout every period of economic crisis.

Propaganda disguised as history is of course not conducive to the clarification of socially significant issues, with which the above-mentioned writers claim to be concerned. Historical objectivity has no friends in a garrison state, or in any spiritually totalitarian regime. Fortunately, however, it is not a heresy in our democracy.

I believe that it ought to be possible to tell the truth about an important creative personality, whether he be a labor leader or master of capital, or a politician, without being wholly swayed for or against him. I believe especially that it would be a disservice to American history and the dynamic movement of labor, if I were to depict men of varying social, economic and political ideas as conflicts between saints and sinners. Common sense dictates that men are not, and should not be thus compartmented or pigeonholed. I have therefore tried, to the best of my ability, to remain scientifically objective, which of course in itself constitutes a moral judgment.

To me, Hutcheson represented a trend in social and human affairs that helped *neutralize* the ever-increasing powers of the new Leviathan state. He believed, as I do, that a healthy American society must seek to achieve the greatest possible equilibrium of power, the greatest possible social check upon the administration of power. "Power must be weighed out ounce by ounce," Sam Rutherford aptly said. And the labor movement in America constitutes such a repository of power in the community. Knowing him as I did, I am also convinced that he was a man great in character and force, whose immense influence was in most respects beneficent; that he and his successor and their co-workers unfalteringly advanced the welfare of the workers will be demonstrated with facts and figures. What I have tried to do, therefore, has been to show what sort of a man he really was; how his ideas developed out of his Scotch-Irish—New England background; his conditioning on the then "Northwestern frontier"; the ideas, personalities and experiences he was exposed to during his early manhood; and how he was influenced by the general stream of events in American history.

As to the facts in this book, I have been scrupulously careful — rejecting unverifiable legends, unsubstantiated tales of his life and work. As to the interpretation of Hutcheson's motives and ideas and actions, that is entirely my own. I did not allow much of the interpretation of others to get in the way of my direct access to the primary sources themselves. While I have talked with Hutcheson frequently and intimately, additional time has passed since work began, to afford me an added measure of detachment and objectivity.

William L. Hutcheson's extensive personal files and correspondence, extending over a period of forty years, have been at my disposal throughout. These were made available to me, and that for the first time to any writer without reservations, by Maurice A. Hutcheson, and by U.B. General Secretary Albert E. Fischer. Included are a great variety of socially and historically significant items, which shed much new light on the character and personality of our subject. The discoveries I have made therefrom will, I am confident, add much to the rounded picture of William Levi Hutcheson. Also made available to me in their entirety were the Executive Board's minutes of the Brotherhood, fortified by vital data from the "parent" American Federation of Labor. I have, of course, thoroughly examined the published proceedings of the union itself.

In a year spent on research, extensive travel and scores of interviews I have profited from the generous help of more people than a brief preface can mention. I should like to single out at least those who were able to supply information to me from their long and intimate association with Hutcheson himself and their experiences in the labor movement: John L. Lewis, President of the United Mine Workers of America; Frank Duffy, late General Secretary Emeritus of the U. B. of C. & J. of A; John P. Frey, President Emeritus of the A. F. of L. Metal Trades Department; Richard J. Gray, President of the A. F. of L. Building and Construction Trades Department; Matthew Woll, Vice-President of the American Federation of Labor; William McSorley, President

of the Wood, Wire & Metal Lathers International Union; Patrick
E. Gorman, General Secretary-Treasurer of the Amalgamated Meat
Cutters and Butcher Workmen of North America; Charles W. Hanson,
President, N. Y. City District Council of Carpenters; Ted Kenny, President and Daniel J. Butler, Business Representative of the Carpenters
District Council of Cook, Lake and Dupage Counties in Illinois; Peter
Terzick, Editor of "The Carpenter"; Joseph Plymate, personal secretary
to the U. B. General President, and C. Marshall Goddard, Superintendent of the Carpenters' Home in Lakeland, Florida. I wish to express my
warm thanks to all of them. For revealing insights into the life of William
L. Hutcheson, I am indebted to Mrs. Bessie Hutcheson, now nearing
eighty-five and residing with her children in Milan, Indiana; Bud Hutcheson, his youngest brother, Mrs. Minnie Bliss, his sister, and to
Dr. Reverend Logan Hall of the Methodist Church of Indianapolis, Indiana. Many leaders in law, finance, industry and politics, too, cooperated
by personal interviews and discussions. The writer is especially indebted
to Dr. John R. Steelman, formerly assistant to President Truman, Mr.
Samuel Ungerleider, Wall Street financier, Mr. Charles H. Tuttle,
renowned attorney and General Counsel of the Brotherhood, Mr. Louis
B. Wehle, distinguished lawyer, close confidant of President Woodrow
Wilson and of Franklin D. Roosevelt and special assistant to War Secretary Newton D. Baker, the Hon. Arch L. Bobbitt, Supreme Court Justice,
Indiana, Leon Keyserling, chairman of ex-President Truman's Council
of Economic Advisers, and others in the political circles of both parties.

I should like to single out at least a few of the officers of the
Brotherhood who were able to supply information from their unique
and rich store of experience in the United Brotherhood of Carpenters
& Joiners of America: John R. Stevenson, O. William Blaier, first and
second vice-presidents, respectively. I am immensely indebted to General
Executive Board Members of the U.B. in the United States and
Canada; Charles Johnson Jr., Raleigh Rajoppi, Harry Schwarzer, Henry
W. Chandler, R. E. Roberts, J. F. Cambiano and Andrew V. Cooper
whose alert, intelligent and helpful discussions contributed immeasurably
to the writer's effort. The author has profited from the help of Frank
Chapman, Treasurer, and the late Abe Muir, General Executive Board
Member from the Northwest Region. For general cooperation and technical and statistical details, the author is indebted to the U.B. Staff in
the Executive Department, librarians, archivists, technicians in the
photostat section and to the union's resident legal representatives in
Indianapolis.

Many libraries have been of assistance — particularly the directors
and staff of the Michigan Historical Society, Michigan State Library in
Lansing, Michigan Historical Commission, University of Michigan in

Ann Arbor, Historical Society of New York, the Saginaw Public Library, the New York Public Library, the Chicago Public Library, Chicago University, New York State School of Industrial Relations, Cornell University, the National Archives, the Franklin D. Roosevelt Library, Hyde Park, the Newberry Library, the Library of the U. S. Department of Labor and the Library of Congress, Canadian Historical Association in Ottawa, the Public Archives of Canada, Chicago Historical Society, International Labour Office in Geneva, Switzerland and New York, Ontario Historical Society, Methodist Historical Society and the Scots Ancestry Research in Edinburgh. Many thanks are due to Mr. Herbert Hoover, oldest living ex-President of the United States for his personal aid and cooperation, to the family of the late William Howard Taft, 26th President of the United States and former Chief Justice of the U. S. Supreme Court and the late Senator Robert A. Taft for permission to examine relevant papers at the National Archives of the Library of Congress.

Primary and secondary sources, inclusive of newspapers and periodical literature, are cited in the appendix, at the end.

I must also give honorable mention to Dr. I. A. Graeber, historian and sociologist, who, as the Director of Research, indefatigably collated the materials in this book and helped the author considerably with cool, dispassionate and valuable suggestions; to my devoted colleague and brother Mr. Charles Raddock, whose objectivity was most helpful. My deepest appreciation to Miss Rhoda Quasha, Lorraine Gratz, Mildred Bruchs and all other staff researchers and aids and above all, to my wife, who not only stimulated the writing of this book, but made it possible by her astonishing ability in carrying out our previous commitments to a community we learned to love.

I shall be gratified if judicious readers agree that this work promotes not only a better understanding of the man and labor leader Hutcheson and of the Brotherhood of Carpenters & Joiners of America of which it treats, but equally of the crowded epoch of which we have all been a part. The picture painted here represents the fairest judgement I can bring to bear upon an extraordinary man and upon the turbulent times on which he left a prodigious influence.

Maxwell C. Raddock

Mamaroneck, New York
September 25, 1955

CONTENTS

                Page

Preview to Understanding   VII

PART 1 — FOREBEARS and PIONEERS

Chapter I
    William Levi Hutcheson's Origins   3

Chapter II
    In the Land of Timber   17

Chapter III
    The Beginnings of a Career   56

PART II — CHALLENGE and RESPONSE

Chapter IV
    The Leader and the Led 65

Chapter V
    The Heroic Age 80

Chapter VI
    Birth of Labor Equality   109

Chapter VII
    The Era of Disillusionment   118

PART III — WE CAN MAKE OUR OWN FUTURE

Chapter VIII
    Alliance for Victory 129

Chapter IX
    The Struggle for Self-Approval 137

Chapter X
    Let My People Go   144

Chapter XI
    The Fifth Column   159

PART IV — RISE of the LEVIATHAN STATE

Chapter XII   *Page*
The Great Depression 169

Chapter XIII
American Standards vs. Doles 176

Chapter XIV
The Yawning Gulf: A. F. of L. and C. I. O. . . . 192

Chapter XV
Reliance on the State 210

Chapter XVI
Hutcheson Before the Bar 239

PART V — MYTH or REALITY

Chapter XVII
The Image of America 253

Epilogue 329

PART VI — THE NEW and the OLD

Chapter XVIII
The New and the Old: Maurice A. Hutcheson . . . 339

PART VII — THE SAGA of the BROTHERHOOD

Chapter XIX
A Chest of Tools 355

Chapter XX
Leadership in the Brotherhood 388

Chapter XXI
Protecting the "Job" 395

Chapter XXII
The Badge of Skill 406

Chapter XXIII
Where Old Carpenters Go to Live 416

PART | I

FOREBEARS and PIONEERS

CHAPTER | I

WILLIAM LEVI HUTCHESON'S ORIGINS

Among the many ethnic and cultural strains which have from our very pioneer beginnings enriched the American milieu, the "Anglo-Saxon" strain has been taken for granted. If we make this observation it is simply because the history of the British, Scottish and Welsh newcomers to America is most meaningful when played as counterpoint to the experiences of the great mass of immigrants of the time. Their dexterity with shuttle, pick or chisel raised British immigrants to the top of nineteenth century American trade unionism. What is not generally known, we believe, is that the Anglo-Saxon tradition particularly permeated the American labor movement.[1] And our protagonist — William Levi Hutcheson — is a case in point.

Even his colleague Samuel Gompers, co-founder of the American Federation of Labor, Jewish by birth and faith, served his union apprenticeship in London, where he was born. But it seems — though it is not pertinent here to elaborate on this generalization — that what has always distinguished trade unionism in English-speaking countries from the trade unionism which originated, say, in France or Germany, was its comparative conservatism: for whereas French or German trade unionism was grafted on to a revolutionary concept of labor organization, Anglo-Saxon (and Scandinavian) unionism consistently followed a middle of the road course, as it were, and confined itself to the fundamental function of the trade union — namely, the preservation of workers' rights and privileges and to a reconstruction of the industrial relationship away from a paternalistic benevolent dictatorship toward a more equalitarian democracy. American soil at the end of the nineteenth century somehow gave rise to American craft unionism, which followed the pattern of organization that had succeeded in England.

---

[1] Rowland T. Berthoff, *British Immigrants in Industrial America* (Harvard University Press, 1953), pp. 88-106.

3

Be this as it may, William Levi Hutcheson's antecedents were workers under the British crown, poor as only Englishmen, the Scotch and the Irish could be — and resenting it as Englishmen can resent sordid poverty; that is to say, by getting out — as their Jamestown and Plymouth kinsmen had done two centuries earlier when they found that the emasculated British Isles could no longer sustain them and that the grass was more fertile across the Atlantic. This is what the British, Scotch and Irish did, and this is what Bill Hutcheson's forebears did. Though the family finally wound up in Saginaw, Michigan, their peregrinations began back in Ulster County in Northern Ireland. You might describe this extensive and circuitous pilgrimage of the Hutcheson breed as a typical migrant exodus from an improverished Europe. But it was indeed more than that, for that giant of a man who was sprung from the vigorous loins of that prospecting family, and who was later to become an articulate and controversial leader of millions of American wage-earners, was always conscious of his origins — and never forgot the starvation and pestilence which forever haunted his childhood.

Before, therefore, we get on with the public life of William Levi Hutcheson — or "Big Bill Hutch," as he was fondly called, it might be interesting to devote some deserving pages to the humble folk whose name he eventually brought to public attention or, as many think, glorified by his indefatigable "paternal" championing of the cause of the "craft" worker.

Thus, our story really begins a century and a quarter ago — on January 7th, 1825, to be precise. It was Thursday when the boat, not much larger than a two-masted brig, sailed out of the Clyde with its human cargo bidding an uncertain and fearful farewell to the Old World.

Early that Sunday it had taken its last batch of passengers at Lough Foyle, Ireland. Emigrants all, the company was now complete, drawing together for human companionship on the deck — Scots, Irish, Ulstermen, Welsh — men, women and children. For six weeks, they were told, their whole universe would be this small wooden vessel. The captain, hungry for profit, had exploited every possible nook for improvised bunks, leaving little room for provisions or even an adequate supply of water. Cooped up in the ship's hole, these ill-fed and ill-clothed "pioneers" resigned themselves to the North Atlantic gales which numbed them into "ship fever" insensibility. Down there in steerage no one escaped the ravages of the winter crossing.

But they were a hardy lot—most of them under thirty, and even the younger ones were already married and encumbered with families. Steerage 4, for example, sheltered the young, attractive widow, Mary Campbell Hutcheson, barely twenty-seven, and her two tots, Daniel and David. Like most of the unmarried, poor Irish girls who dreamed of finding work in the States as domestics, Mary was bracing herself to assume a similar role — the only one to which she could profitably adapt herself.

For the most part, they were a quiet, orderly, well-mannered group of emigrants deriving from poor worker families, the unemployed and the idle by economic compulsion, dispossessed crofters, skilled artisans of all types, rural and urban laborers and, of course, some ambitious and competitive individuals who aspired to making fortunes in the new land of opportunity. Widow Hutcheson had no such ambitions. Her primary hope was that of finding a home for her orphaned sons.

As noted above, these men and women had sailed from their respective British homes at the beginning of the nineteenth century — as their kinsmen a century or two before had done before they settled Massachusetts Bay Colony and environs. The present crop did not venture forth, you might say, to a strange and unfriendly land whose language and customs were alien to them. For though America had already emerged from the status of British colonialism, most "native" Americans were British descended, scattered through all the colonies, including Welshmen who had peopled William Penn's province and Scots and Ulstermen who had pushed the frontier across the Appalachians.

At the dawn of the eighteenth century, 60 per cent of the white population was of English and Welsh stock, 8 per cent Scottish, and 6 per cent Scotch-Irish, while less than 4 per cent was Southern Irish. Of course, these Americans, having been settled for a century and a half in the New World, were no longer "pure" Englishmen, Welshmen, Scots, or Irishmen like the first English settlers. Furthermore, with immigration entirely blocked by the Napoleonic War, the next generation grew up indigenously American.[2] After 1815, and on through the 'seventies, immigrant officials counted some three and a half million men and women arriving from the United Kingdom to the United States.[3]

It was the largest movement of population from a nation which pioneered the Industrial Revolution, whose powerful industrial forces were soon to be released in the New World at a pace no country had since matched. Statistical vagaries notwithstanding, more Englishmen, Scots, Welshmen, Ulstermen and Irishmen came to America during the nineteenth century than had come during the preceding two centuries. It was not at all accidental that they came to the United States in that period and immediately found work in certain manufacturing cities, in industries and mining camps. Their talents, skills and experiences

---

[2] Marcus Lee Hansen, *The Atlantic Migration* (Harvard University Press, 1941), pp. 72-76.

[3] U.S. Commissioner-General of Immigration, *Report*, 1930, pp. 202-203; Bureau of the Census *Statistical Abstract of the United States*, 1951, p. 94.

were suited for a virgin, untapped, rich and burgeoning continent. America offered myriads of jobs at wages unmatched in the already crowded labor market of Britain. A man who deserved a good job in America hoped to earn a fatter pay packet and rise further and faster in a constantly changing, fluid, creative American society. If he could not become an Andrew Carnegie, like the fabulous British-born iron-master, there was room enough on the lower rungs of the industrial ladder. Rise or not, a man could sooner dine at a fuller table. "In America," gloated the English workingmen, "you can get pies and puddings!"

After two hundred years of emigration, the Englishman had more friends and relatives in America than in Yorkshire, Sheffield or Glasgow to post him on current conditions. Few British towns and villages did not know the States through the letters of their "Yankee" sons and daughters. Few of the stay-at-homes had not themselves thought of shaking the old-country dust from their worn-down heels.

The very name of America conjured up for Europeans a bright if hazy vision of a promised land. There was a charm connected with the word "America" which silenced the most ordinary dictates of caution. A sensible man would cross the Atlantic with less anxiety about his prospects than he would have had if he contemplated removal, say, from Kent to Yorkshire. Thus, since 1607 men and women had been led to abandon the Old World for the New.

From time to time political or religious oppression had also driven true believers to seek a land more tolerant, at least of their particular heresies. Others had been forcibly transported to America as convicts or slaves. Taxpayers had cheaply disposed of paupers by paying for their ocean voyage. Many fled outright oppression at home. And of course there have been nearly as many personal motives for emigration as there have been emigrants. Throughout three centuries however, humdrum economic circumstances and forces probably moved most of the venturers. All sought their share in the promise of a better life through emigration.

In the first quarter of the nineteenth century, when Mary had arrived, laboring men throughout Great Britain had sustained a prolonged and crushing series of blows. Depression in British trade drove out swarms of skilled artisans, farmers and peasants. Crises in agriculture, and the inauguration of scientific high-farming had upset English, Welsh and Scottish rural society. In the Highland glens recurrent potato shortages uprooted crofters. In overpopulated Ireland, the chronic potato blight now attained famine proportions — goading 54,338 in one year to flee across the ocean. Cholera, typhus and famine gave Ireland the highest mortality in Western Christendom, with less than one fifth of the population barely reaching the age of forty. Whole blocks of houses stood deserted in England's industrial cities, their cellar doors removed for firewood. Thousands of homeless men loitered at street corners, with their idle chests of tools at their feet. Factories were padlocked, and "unwanted" girls were starving. This, then, was the human stuff embarking on the Clyde — a company of the rejected, hungry, weak and prodigal; in short, all who had been unable to prevail against circumstances in their own land and were therefore now fleeing to another.

Mary Campbell Hutcheson, with the responsibility of a tiny family on her youthful shoulders, rendered helpless by the lash of economic need, was escaping virtual destitution. The typhoid epidemic and famine which struck Ulster and environs the year before, claimed her 29 year old husband Daniel, leaving her two young children fatherless.

Little Daniel, now 4 years old, took to sailing like a tar, but his nine-year old brother David and his mother, too, lay sick and prostrate in steerage as the decrepit vessel jumped on the sea like a catboat.

Unfortunately for Mary and the children, they were not included among the lucky ones who were sent to Canada by private or state aid. Wealthy benefactresses and private philanthropists had assisted slum dwellers and destitute Highlanders to the sparsely populated colonies, particularly Canada. The British government, even before its revival of interest in the Empire, had been experimenting with a rehabilitation project of placing its unemployed and displaced agricultural workers in Canada. Land and equipment would be provided for them upon arrival, but the expense of passage had to be borne by the emigrants. The British sent hundreds of such destitute crofters and workers and planted them in the colonies north of Lake Erie. Hordes of Irish paupers and crofters were thus driven to Canada during that particular decade.

As a widow, Mary was not qualified for the official bounty. A loan of a few pence would have enabled her to sail to London, where private charitable societies staked stranded families to three to five pounds for cabin passage. There was the Emigrant Aid Society of London, which held out the hope of passage to British North America and the New World on winnings from lotteries conducted for the benefit of the poor. But to obtain a direct loan or outright gift of charity on which to reach London was, for any one of Houston's twenty-five families, impossible. The town of Houston, with a population of one hundred and fifty, was typical of the many that had been reduced to the level of paupery,[4] and widow Hutcheson had no one to turn to back home.

It had been a year since Mary had written to her husband's rich Uncle Edwin, in Brighton, Canada, requesting passage for herself and the kids. Many poor Irish and Scotch-Irish often depended on such

---

[4]William F. Adams, *Ireland and Irish Immigration to the New World* (Yale University Press, 1932), pp. 64-65.

help from successful relatives or friends in Canada and America.[5] It was quite common in those days for groups of thirty or forty, sometimes an entire village, to sail together when their emigrant relatives and friends could contribute enough for a combined voyage.[5]

Hope for Mary was held out by the Gamble family, whose nearby residence was a turf hut without windows which had been shared by the six little Gambles, father, mother, and the pigs. They had sailed the previous June to Quebec on passage money provided by their cousin in Canada, promising to look up Mary's uncle Edwin on their arrival. And, indeed, Jessica Gamble had not forgotten! For on October 24, 1824, Mary was happily reading to her children Uncle Edwin's letter:

"Dear Mary,

"I think you was better get a little from the parish and set out for Canada while you have a chance to. If you don't come soon it is likely you will starve, and if you find a bite to eat your children won't, whilst if you was to come hither with David and Daniel, anyone would be glad to take one or even both and keep them as their own kind until coming of age, and give them 100 acres of land and give stock besides. I was agreeably surprised when I come here to see what a fine land it be. It be excellent land, which bear crops of wheat and corn for twenty years without dung. Here you will dwell in our home and help on the farm and cook. You can make soap, candles, sugar, treacle and vinegar. I am happy with the country and so is Kate, as we are so much respected here as any one of our neighbors, and so would you.

"You had better now set out for a vessel and make sure you have ascertained correct date of sailing. And then arrange the date on which you embark. This will avoid the costs of lodgings, and also of spending a big amount of money in public houses. The Captains and Agents always ask more money from a lone woman with children. But I have already booked you to Quebec. Remember, Mary, there must be on board fifty gallons of pure water and fifty pounds of bread, biscuit, oatmeal, for each passenger. A few medicines for the voyage will be necessary, especially the purgative kind, as a sea voyage is certain to produce costiveness. The medicines that Kate says you must take are Epsom Salts, a box of blue pills, castor oil, emetics made up in doses, rhubarb, and a little fever medicine. Take also an ounce bottle of sulphate of quinine which you will find a certain cure for the ague, if you should meet with it. And now having given you all the necessary cautions, I will take leave, me and Kate wishing you and the children health and a pleasant voyage, when we will be ready to embrace you with affection.

Uncle Edwin"

Two nights of the steerage had filled Mary, Daniel and David with horror. Their sleeping quarters were unsuitable, mother and children occupying but one bed with about fifteen inches of canvas to sleep on. The stench of so many human beings cooped up in these narrow confines

---

[5]"Third Report from the Select Committee on Emigration from the United Kingdom," *Parliamentary Papers*, 1826-7, V (550) (s2240); *Scottish-American Journal, May 4, 1867.*

without ventilation added to the general malaise. Meals were unbearable, even for healthy folk. The stinted portions of bread, porridge and soup evoked outcries from the passengers — "disgusting," "unfit to be set before human beings or even pigs." The only food Mary and her boat companions cared for was oatmeal, which could not spoil or turn rancid. Friendly seamen brought extra rations for Daniel and David, while Mary lived almost entirely on biscuit and oatmeal. Others among the passengers, who fortunately had their own provisions, occasionally shared them with the widow and her children.

Saturday night afforded Mary some pleasant hours. From steerage appeared fiddlers, and a native Welsh chorus. Hornpipe, reel and song helped those sober English, Scottish and Irish workmen pass the tedium of a rough winter crossing. Recitations were spiritedly rendered in Scottish brogue and quadrilles were danced to the music of the screeching fiddles. The impulse to sing was strong, and on rough nights the passengers gathered by the main deck-house, in a place sheltered from the wind and rain, the women clinging to ladders which led to the hurricane deck, or linking arms to make a ring against the violent lurching of the ship. They sang to their hearts content. The doggerel was the familiar music-hall fare of the day, of course, — like, "Go, someone, and tell him from me, to write a letter from home," a popular ballad of the day. Mary contributed her favorite,

> "My Name is Mary Leary,
> From a spot called Tipperary,
> The hearts of all the lads I'm a'thornin';
> But before the break of morn,
> Faith! 'tis they'll be all forlorn,
> For I'm off to Philadelphia in the mornin'.
> Wid my bundle on my shoulder,
> Faith! There's no lass could be bolder;
> I'm lavin dear old Ireland without warnin',
> For I lately took the notion,
> For to cross the briny ocean,
> And I start for Philadelphia in the mornin'."

Sabbath was piously observed by everyone. Like most humble British folk, they were a God-fearing lot in the main. It was on a quiet, holy Sunday — the eighth Lord's Day on board — that the cheering outlines of the coast of Quebec were sighted.

Mary Campbell Hutcheson's belongings were of course few, and what she possessed consisted of a square box with ropes tied about it and two packages done up in coarse homespun canvas, plus a string of kitchen ware. She was met by the agent of the Quebec Aid Society, a middle-aged Scotsman, whose practiced demonstration of paternalism and characteristic superciliousness of the "native" towards new arrivals, were in fact a conscious attempt to discourage pauper immigrants from remaining in the port. The fact that he had once been a destitute Highland crofter, who only a decade ago had himself arrived from the United Kingdom to seek virgin soil in the Maritime Provinces and Lower Canada, only served to increase his arrogance. A quick look at Mary, however, and her two young children, changed his attitude, it seemed.

For Mary and her children, apparently, belonged to that class of pauper immigrants upon whom immigration commissioners and welfare agencies somehow did not frown. Unattached and young, and with two young male children, she was regarded with favor as a welcome addition to a sparsely populated, loyal British outpost. Others, mostly middle-aged poor Irish crofters, seemed like a burden too large to handle for the colonial officials.

Mary was asked to await the arrival of her benefactor, Uncle Edwin, who would take her under his legal protection and shelter her in Brighton. In the meantime, she and her tots were given food and lodging by kindly women volunteers attached to the above-mentioned Aid Society.

*   *   *

Three hundred and fifty miles inland, north of Lake Ontario and Presque Isle Harbor, lay the village of Brighton, in the Newcastle district. It was a comparatively calm community. Occasional grumblings and battle cries on the part of its settlers against the "British yoke" had effected little change in its brief history of three decades since its original settlement early in the nineteenth century. The tempo of Brighton, as was typical of so many other surrounding pioneer communities, was geared to survival rather than to speed. In the 'thirties and 'forties, when bustling villages and rising cities sprang to life a short distance across the channel, Brighton moved at a well-regulated pace and with monotonous regularity. And Uncle Edwin, an early settler, kept slow pace with the tempo of his adopted habitat.

Not unlike the towns of Port Hope, Bowmanville, Newcastle, Grafton and Trent, which varied in ethnic inheritance from province to province and township to township, Brighton reflected the ethnic composition of its settlers. These were mostly Scotch tenant farmers and Scotch-Irish landless agricultural workers, Methodist and Presbyterian, who, uprooted from their native glens by agrarian reorganization in the early nineteenth century, had sailed to a broader and freer Canada in search of fresh soil. Not much later, a few families drifted in because they had friends and relatives in Brighton. It was an accepted practice of the Methodists to assist relatives in getting established, and no one expected praise for doing so. Homes and resources were shared with the newcomers as a matter of course. Initial material aid in the form of housing, clothing, equipment, as well as gratuitous advice and suggestions, were given these "green-horns" without any show of generosity. Mutual aid was one of the laudable, fundamental characteristics of the Methodist community of Brighton.

A farming community, Brighton, on Mary's arrival, had a population of approximately 250. Its child population was rather high, four to five children per family being the rule. Although sanctimoniously denied, there was a strong tendency to prize male children more highly than female children. Males would prove an economic asset to parents.

The township was well settled by 1825, its farms all cleared and in a good state of cultivation. Large quantities of wheat and other grain, all of excellent quality, were raised. The old log shanties and cob-roofed farms had been displaced by frame buildings, with orchards attached. The delay in building a traversable road was a constant source of grievance and dissatisfaction to the settlers, as was the small allotment for educating the young. In fact, Brighton offered no education to its children. Its monitorial system, by which one teacher, himself a mere initiate in the 3 R's, taught the lesson to the elder pupils, had proved ineffective. The pupils he was trying to teach would frequently absent themselves in the winter and help their fathers on the farm in the summer. The community's early education of its young, therefore, fell upon the mothers who taught them the rudiments of English reading, writing and arithmetic.

Still, the greater part of Brighton's population was literate. Most of them could read and write. While their schooling might have been rudimentary, the more vigourous nonconformist Methodist Sunday Schools instructed both child and great-grandmother in the reading of Scripture.

Brighton had one Methodist congregation. In the early years, when almost everyone was poor and families, struggling on bare subsistence levels, church services had been held east of Murray Township at the "oak plains". Five years later, the village church was completed by the cooperative participation of its parishioners, who, after eleven or more hours of labor in the fields, had spent their evenings renovating the church. The more the structure, interior and ritual resembled those of the "good Methodees" in England, the more fond of church did they become. Here, there was no class distinction. Economic tensions relaxed in time, and the children of the settlers grew to manhood and womanhood, and no discernible anxiety or worry over "social status" bothered them. Nobody looked down upon a newcomer. Uncle Edwin had written the truth to Mary when he boasted of how he was "respected here as anyone of our neighbors."

Mary Campbell Hutcheson was not baffled by her new environment. In many ways, Brighton seemed like the village of Houston, Ulster, where she came from. Her life and that of her children would, it seemed, be pleasant. Food was plentiful! With nine people to cook for, Mary cheerfully assumed her role of housekeeper in Uncle Edwin's household "until the children grow up."

Edwin Hutcheson was in affluent circumstances, with a ratable property of $8,000 inclusive of milch cows, oxen and horned cattle. His wife Kate, though hardly turned forty, bore signs of hard labor and looked much older than her years. She and Edwin were now regarded as among the "early settlers." Her habits of energetic industry and familiarity with privation gave Kate a hard, stern mien. She had been wife, mother and co-worker for twenty years. Two of the older sons were now married in Chicago, where they had settled two years ago. Both had chosen grain merchandising as their occupation. The two remaining children were still home, performing all sorts of chores required for running a successful farm. Mary's arrival afforded Aunt Kate more leisure than she had known since her marriage, and Mary learned to get along with her aunt despite the burden placed on her.

It wasn't difficult to administer the household. But the possibility of marrying again was far more desirable to the young widow. There was indeed one prospect — a local widower, with four young orphans, in the neighboring village of Coburg, a distance of twenty-six miles from Brighton. Until then, however, Mary ungrumblingly did her cooking over the primitive fire made against a log, hanging kettles upon iron hooks to swing over the flames. The roasted potatoes were made by covering them with hot ashes and coals, and she did her baking by setting a tin oven before the fire with the open side toward the fire. She was quite skilled with her fingers. Her crocheted doilies, afghans and other products of her nimble fingers pleased her aunt. Knitting stockings and mittens for Uncle Edwin and the boys occupied Mary's long winter evenings.

Mary even found time to teach David and Daniel the rudiments of the 3 R's during the winter months. In the one-room house which she occupied with the children, she would tell them grim stories woven out of her own experiences in Ulster. She told them of the famines and privations that the people in her native village underwent; and of the many children that went hungry "departing into heaven," never to return again. She told them of their own father David, who died of an incurable disease, "taking a long journey to heaven." Daniel hardly remembered his father, who had died when the boy was three.

In the summer, Daniel would help his brother cut hay with a scythe and wheat with a grain cradle. Though he became particularly fond of log-splitting and was quite handy in the use of the axe, Daniel had little interest in farming. He dreamed of the big city across the continental boundary. . . .

The Sabbath provided all the emotional fervor for Brighton's inhabitants. The Sunday School and the Bible Society supplemented the education of young and adult alike. Preparations for Sunday would begin from Saturday noon. It was expected as a matter of course that the whole family would attend church, getting an early start in the morning. There were no cushion seats, no pews, and no foot stools, and the restless feet of children dangled from the benches as they listened to the long and tiresome sermons and lengthy prayers of the Reverend Thomas Ward. Without an organ, communal singing at worship was the common practice. The congregational hymn-singing must have left an indelible impression on Daniel's mind, for years later he kept up the practice of reciting and chanting the psalms and snatches of Scripture for his American-born children.

Sunday was the day for leisure and recreation. Visiting friends, neighbors and relations was the thing to do. The twelfth of July, the anniversary of William of Orange's victory at the Boyne, offered an opportunity for celebration as did of course Halloween and Christmas. Picnics and excursions on the lake were not uncommon. "Surprise parties," where ten or twelve families suddenly descended upon the home of friends were a popular version of visiting in these rural communities. Pairing and quilting and domestic bees were particularly enjoyed. In addition, there were always benefit entertainments, dances and parties, occasions that they used to raise money for indigent friends and relatives in the Old World.

The men, on the other hand, frequently had occasion to visit the town, and their contact with the local officials, the merchants, and tradesmen was not only practical, but lessened the monotony of their existence. They also engaged from time to time in hunting and fishing, attended bees, fairs, horse races and, occasionally, a traveling circus from the States. There were the inevitable taverns and English-style "pubs," of which Brighton had two.

Bees were the most popular form of amusement in Brighton. Every settler would invariably hold two or three each year, provided he could furnish a good "pot pie," and plenty of grog, and never take objection to his guests' fighting. Feats of prowess, such as putting the stone and hurling the hammer, axemanship and skill in handling recalcitrant oxen or horses provided amusement for the young people at the contests. They spent the evening in dancing, while the older men and women concluded their day's work by discussing crops, prices, local politics and such news as had come from the Old World. Scotch and Irish reels, four-hand and eight-hand reels were the universal favorites.

Above the noise of the dancing could be heard the scraping sound of the fiddle, and the voice of the caller as he shouted "Salute your partner," "Promenade all," or "Grand chain."

Rural balls were the most attractive of amusements, and Mary somehow found time to put in an appearance. People would travel many miles through the bush to take part in them. A species of amusement once very common, and still to be found in some parts of Ontario, was the "charivari" or "chivari." It was typical of weddings that involved a match between a couple of a disproportionately unequal age, or in second marriages. The "chivari" party would appear at the home of the newlyweds, usually after midnight, with horse bells, "bull roarers," tin pans and copper kettles and surprise the bride and groom. If the bridegroom did not emerge and supply another round of drinks, the ear-splitting catcalls would continue the rest of the night.

Halloween was another festival religiously observed. It was celebrated in traditional style with a blazing fire in the open grate, and on the fire a huge pot full of potatoes, and round the fire a "wheen" — lads and lasses trying their fortunes by putting nuts on the live coals, with the younger members of the family "dookin" for apples in the dimly lighted background.

On Christmas Eve, all Brighton went midnight caroling through the village. Two local stores offered settlers "your Christmas beef and goose" and "the genuine English plum puddings", and the owners decked their stores with boughs. The church was trimmed by the children under the watchful glare of the parents.

The "Minister's Party" was another celebration which, while social was identified with the church. At this party he received useful gifts and some duplicates of things he already had. Not infrequently these offerings were articles which the owner was glad to part with and so passed them on to the minister. The latter's salary was notoriously small and these gifts were presented to him in order to supplement his meager wage. The community was served with a supper, all of which was contributed by those attending the party, each one bringing whatever he wished.

There were few marriages in Brighton, although spinsterhood and bachelorhood were frowned upon in the community. A girl unmarried by twenty-five was considered an old maid and at thirty she was beyond connubial salvation. Brighton had about thirty "old-maids," a condition which was of course a source of great anxiety to the parents. There were no bachelors, except for a few widowed farmers for whom there was an increasing demand. Brighton was a village without young men. All of them, on reaching maturity, would hop over in the Spring into the United States, where the vista was broader and opportunity greater. In the few marriages that had taken place, the disparity

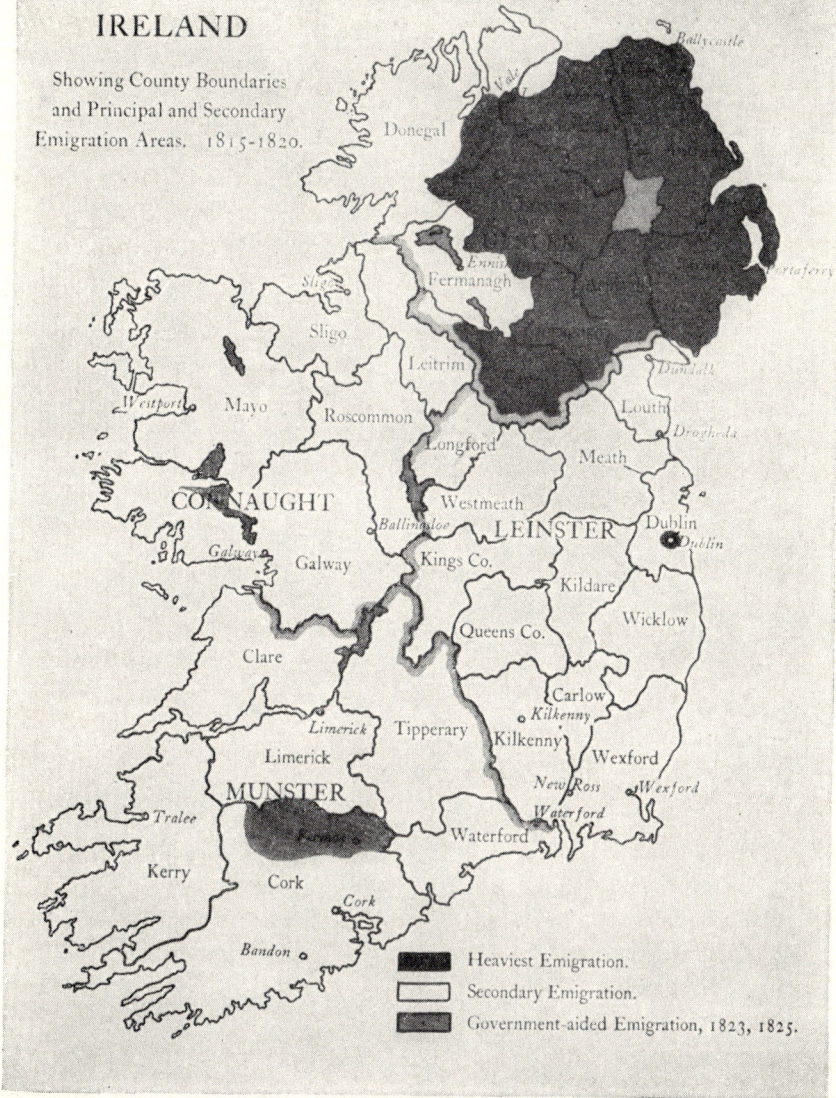

IRELAND

Showing County Boundaries
and Principal and Secondary
Emigration Areas. 1815-1820.

Ballycastle

Vale

Donegal

Ennis
Fermanagh

Sligo

Leitrim

Sligo

Portaferry

Dundalk

Westport

Mayo

Roscommon

Longford

Louth

Drogheda

Meath

CONNAUGHT

Ballinasloe

Westmeath

LEINSTER

Galway

Kings Co.

Dublin

Dublin

Galway

Kildare

Clare

Queens Co.

Wicklow

Carlow

Kilkenny

Limerick

Tipperary

Kilkenny

Limerick

Wexford

Limerick

New Ross

Wexford

MUNSTER

Waterford

Tralee

Waterford

Kerry

Cork

Cork

Bandon

Heaviest Emigration.

Secondary Emigration.

Government-aided Emigration, 1823, 1825.

*From the British Isles they fled to America and Canada—54,338 escapees from the
famines in the decade following 1820. Among them were William Levi Hutcheson's
paternal grandmother, Mary Campbell Hutcheson and her two tots, Daniel Orrick
(his father) and David.*

Artist's sketch showing Mary Hutcheson on her arrival in Quebec with her two orphaned children—on prepaid tickets that Uncle Edwin had sent her from Brighton, Canada.

in the ages between bride and groom was accepted as no hindrance to romantic love. Mary Campbell Hutcheson, at most, could hope for a middle-aged spouse.

Brighton and the neighboring communities seemed full of runaway sons of farmers and apprentices, always seeking to carve out their careers in the "land of promise" within easy reach across the channel. Nothing could deter these youths from seeking better jobs across the border.

Thousands of native British Canadians came to American industrial and urban centers in those days. In the middle of the last century, ending with the Civil War, their movement across the continental boundary assumed the alarming proportions of an exodus. Whether they staunchly trekked a hundred miles or engaged steamboats for a few dollars to ferry them to a new job, the goal was a *city*. Many choices lay before them. A short overnight journey would take them from Halifax to Boston. As the "Boston States" attracted young maritimers in quest of jobs and fortunes, so Chicago, Detroit and other rising mid-western cities drew immigrants from Ontario. The young people were not content to remain on the parental homesteads but instead sought the more exciting life of the city.

Since the provinces had no great cities to absorb them and no West (actually Northwest) to tempt them, many ambitious farmers' sons and daughters struck out for the cities which needed the girls as domestic servants and the lads in many skilled and unskilled jobs. Practically every home had at least one son and one daughter whose services were not in demand in the immediate household or the neighborhood. For them, reaching maturity involved emigration. And the movement, once under way, was not limited to farm workers. Some abandoned the farm for the rising American Northwest, where every town and township might become a city and where business was expanding to include a new empire to be exploited economically.

The emigration of the young people was not directed toward any one American community. Nor did they find employment in any single line of economic activity. Manufacturing in the East, lumbering and mining in Michigan, claimed their skills. In the lumber districts of Michigan, Wisconsin and Colorado, for example, Canadians were found in the woods, in the sawmills and in the field of merchandising timber products.

On the whole, the movement engendered a spirit of restlessness and adventure, and house-painters, blacksmiths, carpenters and shoemakers saw apprentices slip away as soon as their terms of seven years were over.[6]

---

[6]Marcus L. Hansen, *The Mingling of the Canadian and American Peoples,* (Yale University Press, 1940), p. 163; "Reports of the Industrial Commission," *House Document,* 57 Cong., 1 Sess., No. 184 (December 5, 1901). XV. 447-448; Hansen, *Ibid,* pp. 162-164, 205-206, 209-210; Eleventh Census of the U.S., (1890) II, 485.

In a sense, America offered even more to laborers than to skilled craftsmen. While the latter had their jobs and might rise in their own industries, any lad "with a willingness to take any work that presents itself,
and with a bit of luck, could go as high as any."[7]

Mary Campbell Hutcheson gradually realized that she would lose
her growing sons to the inevitable exodus, particularly the restless and
adventurous Daniel Orrick, who had a way with the axe, detested
farming and in general was eager for wider horizons. She did not
try to discourage him. After ten years in Brighton, she knew that Daniel
was a "grown lad" and would eventually be setting out for himself, as so
many other male teen-agers in those days did. At fourteen in the 1830's
a boy was a man, especially if he had a widowed mother and an orphaned
brother. . . .

So, at fourteen, Daniel decided to hire himself out as an apprentice
to Jared Irwin, a carpenter in the Township of Coburg. He was to
spend eight summers with him, for which he'd be paid three and one
third dollars per month. Small though the wage was, it afforded him
a valuable apprenticeship in the carpentry trade and, above all, a feeling of self-reliance.

Yet, that was Daniel's last summer in Brighton. Jared Irwin's induce-
ment of raising Daniel's wages proved to no avail. Daniel caught the
prevailing spirit as he joined the exodus of young men crossing the
northern border with the approaching thaw season. "You will do better
away, Dan," were the last parting words of Mary Hutcheson to her
boy. . . .

*   *   *

Daniel Orrick Hutcheson, as you may have guessed by now, was
the father of our subject, William Levi Hutcheson, who was his third
child — and Mary's third grandchild. If, as it may seem to some
readers, we have devoted too much time to antecedents and gone to
great and perhaps supererogatory lengths to provide the "background
to the background," it was primarily because Daniel's early peregrinations were contributory to the ultimate crystallization of William
Levi Hutcheson's character. To be sure, the original pilgrimage of the
Hutcheson forebears, which began from the Clyde, remained the family's epic — as were the Scripture narratives on which they were nurtured.

Here, then, is the sketchy, typical background of our protagonist, a
product, as we have seen, of Anglo-Saxon poverty, whose father's early
struggles and his own development, comprise the next chapters.

---

[7]Thomas Greenwood, *A Tour in the States and Canada,* (London, 1883), 158.

CHAPTER | II

IN THE LAND OF TIMBER

Detroit in the 1840's had already outgrown its earlier form of a small city. In the decades that followed, the city turned into a mushrooming metropolitan, industrial community, dotted with spires and towers against the sky, steamboats, schooners and canoes on the river, noisy docks, busy streets. . . .

Since 1837, the year of the great speculation fever, which was followed by a panic, the city had retained many of its boom features. The Great Lakes furnished an admirable means of commerce for the coasting and export trade. Wharves, piers and shipbuilders displaced the once comfortable dwellings and mansions of the affluent and influential French Canadians. As the lumber industry, like the fur trade a decade earlier, moved Northwest, Detroit became a leading port for the lumber trade. Here were gathered innumerable entrepreneurs from the East, commercial agents, prospectors, speculators, industrialists and fortune hunters, who arrived by boats coming from Buffalo to Detroit at a fare of five dollars or less. Arriving, too, were the immigrant transients—the Cornish, the Scotch-Irish, the Welsh and Irish. These loggers and copper and iron miners moved into the forests of Michigan lumber and the upper peninsula of Michigan, whence came most of the country's copper and iron ore. Trudging hundreds of miles from across the border were hundreds of ambitious lads in quest of jobs in the city. The twenty-two year old Daniel Orrick Hutcheson was one of these many lads who had thus made their way to Detroit.

This general migration was depicted in a song popular at the time, which ran as follows:

> *"Come all ye Yankee farmers who wish to change your lot,*
> *Who've spunk enough to travel beyond your native spot,*
> *And leave behind the village where pa and ma do stay,*
> *Come, follow me, and settle in Michigania,*
> *Yea, yea, yea, in Michigan-ia. . . ."*

17

Yankees direct from New England and the old pioneer stock from Ohio, Pennsylvania and Kentucky kept swelling the human streams racing towards southern Michigan. To what Alexis de Tocqueville dubbed the "real desert", vast numbers turned. Horace Greeley's counsel of 1837, "Go West, young man!", gained renewed vigor and meaning. The Northwest was in ferment all along the line. Towns were growing into cities. Michigan, which had a population of 31,000 in 1830, boasted 212,000 in the 'forties, ever swelling with a heterogeneous humanity. The impelling motive behind these hordes moving through the "Great Lakes Country", as it was called then, was the constant striving for economic betterment, for a share in the abundance of land and natural resources. To many, it meant the establishment of new homes and businesses. Success lured them and they hoped either to make a fortune or merely find a better job in the rising cities. Some did succeed in building empires. Considerably more ascended a few rungs in the ladder, gaining a livelihood and a surplus, neither of which they had hitherto possessed in great measure. Others, less enterprising, were left behind, somehow never possessing their world.

When he arrived in Detroit, Daniel Orrick was condemned to the status of a seasonal migrant worker, shifting from back-breaking labor as a deck-hand on a timber boat in the summer months to caulking in the winter months. He alternated between hewing of timber during the great lumbering era in Saginaw and farming in the summer. As a steersman manning the keelboats on the long upriver trips, he learned the topography of Michigan, an experience he later utilized as a mail carrier between the straits of Mackinaw and Houghton.

That he didn't marry until he had reached forty-two is testimony to the fact that none of these laborers could earn enough to provide for a wife and family even a minimum of subsistence, even if the wife was fortunate enough to earn fifty cents a week in domestic chores. Mathew Carey had estimated that of the rivermen, "five per cent returned to their families in the winter, with broken constitutions, by fevers and agues, one-half of whom are carried off to an untimely grave."[1] In his *Address to the Wealthy of the Land,* Carey concluded that these men did not average much more than 200 days' employment a year, and their wages were as low as $20.00 a month.[2] Outdoor workers conformed to the normal working day schedule — from sunrise to sunset.

As a caulker, Daniel was driven during the summer months from early in the morning until late at night, at a wage of $1.40 per day. Attempts to establish a ten-hour system for "mechanic" carpenters and

---

[1]Mathew Carey, *Address to the Wealthy of the Land,* (Philadelphia), W. F. Geddes, 1831, p. 6.
[2]Ibid.

caulkers in Detroit resulted in the discharge of all hands for adhering to their system.

Daniel Orrick Hutcheson's wanderings, migrations and quests, in which he was joined by thousands, (and somewhat later by millions) seeking a new dispensation of economic opportunity, became illustrative of a condition which the rising industrial giant brought in its wake during its process of formation, as well as in periods of intensive transformation. Anachronistic though it may appear, this first generation of workers, who only yesterday had tilled the soil and harvested the crops in towns and semi-rural communities, became exposed to the insecurities which arose from the seasonal and intermittent character of much of their employment. Technological unemployment, inevitable in a period of kaleidoscopic change in industry, commerce and transportation, further affected their position. Periodic crises temporarily paralyzed commerce and industry. The new city worker, whose low wages left him practically no margin for savings, more often than not turned to other available occupations. Both the skilled and the unskilled workers always hoped to escape from wage work. If they could not effect their leap, fluid as the class structure still was, they could find refuge in farms of their own, wherever the price of land was still low.

Daniel's homeless wanderings came to a halt in 1867, when he was married to Elizabeth Culver, in Bay City, at the head of the Saginaw Bay which was Michigan's chief lumbering outlet for four decades. "It was in the Saginaw Valley, seven years later, that the acorn, from which the oak, William Levi Hutcheson, the third child of Daniel Orrick, had sprouted."[3]

Elizabeth Culver was eighteen and Dan Orrick was forty-three, and despite all the hardships this couple endured from the very beginning of their fruitful union, they managed somehow to raise the two daughters and three sons born to them in Saginaw. Husband and wife, we might note, were no richer in 1880, when Daniel Oliver, the fourth, first saw the light of day, nor ten years later, when the youngest, Bud Amos, was born, or when the first child, Mathilda, was born, a year after their marriage, or when Minnie was born two years later. Nor on Feb. 7, 1874, when our subject William Levi first uttered his defiant cry at a world which had little to offer to his carpenter father.

It is to Minnie, now eighty-five, and to Bud, now sixty-five, that we owe the following recollections of Dan's role as a pater-familias, citizen, "farmer," lumberjack and bible-quoting pleader for lost causes.

---

[3] A Detroit Carpenter, "Extracts from the Diary of William C. King," *Michigan Historical Society*, Vol. 19:3, p. 69.

Interviews by the author with these survivors of Bill Hutcheson's generation revealed Ol' Dan as quite an heroic figure after his own fashion who — at seventy-eight, for example, white-haired and white-bearded, wielded a sharp axe over hard and stubborn timber, and at seventy-one thrilled with pride when he finally received his citizenship papers.

A domineering father, Dan would never resort to disciplining his children by corporal punishment, except on the one occasion, Bud recalls, when he left his father's buck-saw "sticking in the wood." "Apparently," Bud adds, "Dad meant to make a good carpenter out o' me."

As for Mother Hutcheson, she matched her Bible-guided spouse with her own piety and devotion. Elizabeth — whom everyone called "Bill" since her lumber-jack days at Skinner's — did not allow a playing card in her domicile. And except for dominoes, no "gambling" was permitted. Though neither the New Jersey nor Pennsylvania Dutch — and Elizabeth was both — were known for strictness, nonetheless Mrs. Dan O. Hutcheson chose to raise her children in an environment that witnessed no card-games, no rowdiness, plenty of hard work and serious responsibility. Her husband liked to cut a rug at times or recite from memory "Ol Mother Shipton's" verses and his favorite "Iron Will Float", or whistle a tune off-key — Dan could never carry a tune in his head and it bothered him! What dominated the Hutcheson farm were Dan's two inevitable tool chests, fifteen varieties of "ads" round and square, planes, axes, the big heater stove and the cooking oven. Add the steady routine of church-going, when every Sabbath morning Elizabeth and Dan marched off with their kids to worship, cutting a path through the thick Saginaw woods.

The church, apparently, was the only social outlet for the Hutchesons, the Culvers, the Clearys, and the Stevenses, the only white families in the region. Their neighbors were Indians, and it was at the church services and socials that the white neighbors found kinship. This, in short, was William Levi Hutcheson's boyhood universe in the Saginaws.

It was a universe crude, raw, surrounded by wild tumultuous beauty, unbridled individualism, hardiness and self-reliance. Soon it was to yield an abundance of land and natural resources, attracting pioneers of every race then pouring into the unsettled Northwest, in a quest unattainable for some, shot through with grim circumstances for others. And William Levi Hutcheson's own experiences were part of it from the very beginning. He was at home in its translucent waters as a child, and his youth spent at the source of that stream stayed with him to the very end.

Andre Siegfried, a keen student of America's national character, once observed "that it is in the tranquil backwaters of the old American towns that the men of sterling influence are created."[4] Into the making of William Levi Hutcheson somehow went the experience gathered by his hapless father, and the accretions of lore and symbols that then permeated the frontier town. No leader of men can be understood in isolation or apart from his environment, for he is himself a focal point and a product of the work of predecessors, lesser or greater, of forces favorable and unfavorable, and of cultural conditioning, it goes without saying. And William Levi Hutcheson, child of a seasonal migrant worker, subjected to the push and pull, the dionysiac and apollonian forces ever present in American industry, undertook subsequently to secure, protect, and extend the security of his workers with dogged determination. Bred and nurtured in the primeval Michigan forests, he recreated a castle surrounded by timber in Lakeland, Florida, for the superannuated and those suffering from occupational ailments. When he was a mere boy, he had never forgotten that his father was an old man — an octogenarian who toiled until the end came — at age 86. . . .

When William Levi Hutcheson was born, Bay County had a population of 39,000, having passed the first stage of its pioneering period. Today, Saginaw in Saginaw County is the fourth largest city in the State of Michigan.

In 1874, the year of William Levi Hutcheson's birth, Saginaw produced 573,632,771 feet of lumber. Today, Saginaw is entirely denuded of the forests of fine pine timber. If that lumber had all been sawed into two inch planks and if those planks had been laid on a sidewalk two feet wide, the walk would extend 8 million miles. This boardwalk would reach 320 times around the earth at the Equator.

For nearly four decades of the last century, beginning in the 1850's, Saginaw and its "twin," Bay City, were the chief outlets for Michigan's lumbering operations. During those years was begun and carried to consummation, without regard for conservation or the rights of future generations, the destruction of Michigan's white pine forests.

Wrote W. L. Clements, one of Michigan's historians and labor leaders:

"Saginaw Valley was the focal center of Eastern Michigan in this destruction; Saginaw River the confluent stream through which the logs passed to the mills. Along the river, mills were then in course of erection, commerce and population were increasing, which a little later were to make Saginaw and Bay City the busiest communities in the State, and to put an accelerated activity into twenty years, which, with

---

[4]Andre Siegfried, *America Comes of Age,* (Harcourt, Brace and Co., 1927), p. 278.

today's advanced ideas of conservation, should have been spread over a century."[5] That the Saginaw Valley enjoyed preeminence in the history of the lumber industry of the Northwest is generally conceded, in view of the fact that from the earliest days of the state's development, it was the central figure around which the lumber business of a large district of Michigan revolved.

Saginaw was one of the northwest's frontier towns at the middle of the nineteenth century. Into its virgin wilderness filtered the settlers, whose sole earthly possessions were found inside a clumsy chuck wagon; newly organized lumber syndicates and combinations of all types were followed by land cruisers, lumberjacks, speculators and adventurers and hordes of immigrants of heterogeneous origin. Here were the first sawmills established, featuring sort of a glorified cross-cut saw, a single gate as it was called, driven by a converted marine engine, and calculated to cut about 2000 feet of one-inch boards in a twelve-hour day. Saginaw and its twin, Bay City witnessed the first experiment in the use of the band-saw for cutting lumber, which James J. McCormick made in 1858. Not much earlier, in the 'forties, Saginaw carried the dust of the Chippewa Indians. Jacob Astor's American Fur Company had an agency established at the present site of the City of Saginaw. More ruthless business methods have rarely been known than those that were practiced by that German immigrant in this part of the country. Saginaw saw the first battle royal between independent Detroit fur merchants, represented by the shrewd French operator, Louis Campau, and the fur empire of Jacob Astor. In fact, the defeated Louis Campau was credited with plotting the original "Town of Sagina."[6]

Bela Hubbard's *Memorials of a Half-Century* had left an eye-witness description of the beginnings of Saginaw.

". . . Descending now a wider stream, with a smooth and gentle current, we passed, successively, the mouths of these long feeders to the great stream — the Flint, the Cass and the Tittabawasee — and on the twenty-third of September (1837) were opposite Saginaw City. The last few miles had presented to our view the first irreclaimable marsh we had seen, and here there was plenty of it. The "City" occupied what seemed to be the only considerable elevation for many miles, being about thirty feet above the river. . . .

"The oldest settlement for farming purposes was made about 1829, and the present site of Saginaw City laid out in 1835. This was just before the height of that mad fever of speculation into which so many plunged wildly, and which built in the wilderness many prospective

---

[5]Fred Landon, *Lake Huron*, (Bobbs-Merrill Co., 1944), p. 105.
[6]*Ibid*, pp. 68-69.

cities, most of them existing only in the privileged future or on paper plots. Saginaw was one of the few that had good foundation for its celebrity; though as yet there had been little realization of its dreams of future greatness.

"My notes record that the city comprised nearly fifty frame houses, four stores, one handsome dry goods and grocery store, on a large scale, two warehouses, and another in progress, a small church, two steam sawmills, and in the process of erection, a large edifice, to be called the "Webster House"; this already made a sightly appearance, being sixty by eighty feet. All were of wood. The stockades of the fort still remained; they were some ten feet in height, and surrounded about an acre. I believe the abandonment of this fortress was occasioned by sickness among the troops, in 1824, three-fourths of the garrison being ill at once of the fevers of the country. . . . Beyond the settlement, immediately about the "City", extended the untrimmed forest, as vast and almost as undisturbed as . . . real desert."[7]

This was the Saginaw that Bela Hubbard had seen in 1837, when he accompanied Dr. Douglas Houghton on the first expedition commissioned by the newly-constituted State Geological Survey, and this was the Saginaw where Daniel Orrick Hutcheson settled.

As yet the lumberman's axe had not been applied to the great northern primeval forests. Going overland from Detroit to the Shiawassee River, the surveying party would descend by the stream to the Saginaw River through extensive Chippewa reservations where native clearings extended for miles along the riverbank, many acres being covered by crops of corn, the chief food. But the Indians were still nomadic and the so-called villages were only resorted to at such times as cultivation and harvesting of their food supply required. Their chief occupation was trapping and hunting, and the presence of trading houses met with in the wilderness gave evidence of the barter that was carried on. Not much earlier, on September 24, 1819, the great tribe of Chippewa Indians signed the Saginaw Treaty, relinquishing vast acres of the Lower Peninsula, from lake to lake, to General Cass. At that time, there were perhaps fewer than 8,000 white inhabitants in the entire territory of Michigan, and the entire vicinity of Saginaw had no more than a dozen white men, mostly traders.

The Saginaw River marked the last of the occasional clearings that had been encountered on the journey from Detroit. Vessels made but semi-occasional voyages from Saginaw to Detroit. "The road through the woods" to Flint, was a little better than a wood road or Indian trail, and traversable at certain seasons only, with oxen, and sled, or on horse-

[7]Bela Hubbard, *Memorials of a Half-Century*, (G. P. Putnam's Sons, 1887), pp. 74-75.

back. In the open winter the passage from Detroit to Flint and Saginaw was frequently made in huge uncomfortable wagons, sometimes through water and deep mud. The whole country around Saginaw seemed like a vast swamp. Outside of Saginaw there appeared to have been no settlements, excepting very meager beginnings at the site of Bay City.

What gave the "Town of Sagina" its form and semblance of a town and county in embryo was the speculation mania, which seized Eastern and Detroit real estate operators who saw an opportunity to make fortunes in Michigan land speculation. Saginaw's lots cost as high as $2,000, while an acre lot within view of the river sold for $80,000. Nearly the entire county bordering on the east side of the Saginaw and Shiawassee Rivers to the south side of the Cass River and extending for a mile along the north bank of the Cass was plotted and brought into the Detroit market for sale. Little did the purchasers know that these plots covered acre upon acre of land submerged at all seasons of the year. Its only occupants were the muskrat, the bullfrog and wild fowl.

In 1838 the huge bubble of speculation burst. Saginaw went down as did the village of Owasso, the birthplace of former Governor Thomas E. Dewey of New York. Genesee, Shiawassee, Pontiac, and hosts of other village projects met with a similar fate. Then followed several years of widespread economic disaster. The country was paralyzed for a long time, finding but little relief until the passage of the Bankrupt Act of 1842. For several years little progress was made in the Valley of the Saginaw.

It was not until the late 1850's that Saginaw first emerged from early ruins — a New England City! For it was then that the restless, insurgent stream of New Englanders that had earlier peopled Ohio and Illinois began to push up as far north as the Straits of Mackinaw. They were to leave their indelible stamp on the new little city. It was, to be sure, a Western city, but it was also and was to remain, a New England city, and not even the deluge of immigrants who continued to pour in during the succeeding decades was to change its fundamental temper.

The western movement was now in full swing, having recovered its momentum after the hard times of the late 'thirties and 'forties. The great tide of emigration added thousands to the population, and in the ensuing decades it was augmented at the rate of 20,000 yearly. Day and night long lines of covered wagons slowly moved westward along the highways and the residents they passed called them "the Michigan movers."

The first line of settlement was along the Chicago Road, now U.S. 112, crossing the southern tier of counties. White Pigeon, the only town on this highway between Detroit and Chicago, became the goal of

settlers for the St. Joseph country, as Southwest Michigan and Northwest Ohio were called. Wagons loaded with household goods and sur-
mounted by "live freight" of women and children, the men trudging
on foot, were racing to make "an entry" of some splendid tract of land
in White Pigeon, one of the three government land offices in Michigan.

Joining in this race of "Michigan movers" was the Culver family,
which consisted of Sam and Eliza, husband and wife, two sons, Elias,
Linas, ages four and eight, respectively, and two daughters, Carolyn
and Elizabeth, twelve and fourteen years old. Four years later, incidentally, their oldest child, Elizabeth Culver, was to become the wife of
Daniel Orrick Hutcheson, whom she would meet in the northern forests,
bordering on Saginaw. But of that — later.

From Sandusky, Ohio, their place of origin, the Culver family,
William Levi Hutcheson's maternal grandparents, made their way to
a paradise in the New Eldorado. A little port on the fringe of civilization, Sandusky was a gambling town, with a reputation for horse-
racing. For years Sam Culver had been a struggling farmer, taking on odd
jobs during the winter at 75 cents a day to support his growing brood
of children. Flour, which was $7.50 a barrel, went up as high as $10.00.
Pork was thirty cents a pound. Potatoes, which grew in abundance in
Ohio, went up to $3.00 a bushel and were frequently impossible to
procure at that price. Most provisions had to be brought in from Buffalo. Sam Culver sold his possessions, and on September 12, 1858, he
and his family started out for the "woolly" country.

"Their outfit consisted of a covered wagon, two yoke of oxen, one
cow, bedding, and all the other articles for family use that could be
stowed away in the wagon, and still have room for the family," related
Mrs. Minnie Bliss, second child of Elizabeth and Daniel Hutcheson,
now 85, and a resident of Lakeland, Florida.[8] "There was a tin oven
latched on the back of the wagon ready for use and as soon as the camp
was pitched and a fire built, the oven was brought forward. Grandmother
Eliza had her kneading board and soon had a shortcake the size of the
dripping pan ready for the oven. There was plenty of milk from the cow.
The churn was handy to strain the milk nights and mornings and the
jostling of the wagon through the day would gather the butter. Elizabeth
did the churning, and the family had rich milk for the shortcake as well.

"A journey in this clumsy vehicle," continued Mrs. Bliss, "even on
this much-traveled road, was nothing less than an ordeal. As the wagon
swung along, the passengers were hurled against one another and shaken
up until the strongest suffered fatigue. In three days they went thirty-
one miles. It was no joy ride on the "corduroy" road! Once, the wagon

---

[8]Interview with Mrs. Minnie Bliss, April 12, 1954, at Lakeland, Florida.

fell into a bottomless swamp. Only by the combined efforts of the family, reinforced by the rails which they carried, were they able to pry out the wheels.

"The Culver family arrived in White Pigeon on October 3. The land office was besieged long before the hour arrived for opening. Crowds of anxious faces gathered about the doors and blocked up the windows, eager to make what they thought would be the first claim for the choice land. After much waiting, Sam Culver succeeded in "entering" a claim for forty acres on Section 26, located about 2 miles north of St. Joseph.

"A prolonged journey, lasting ten days, brought the hopeful Culver family to their destination, where they took up their land.

"The house was built of rough logs, covered with elm bark, with split rails or slabs of floor. The window was cut of logs and a sheet of foolscap paper was greased and pasted over the hole. They had but one board in the make-up of the house. It was used for a door and was some fifteen inches wide, fourteen feet long, and they carried it from a neighbor's, a distance of four miles. Men came from the neighborhood to help them lay up the house, bringing their dinner with them, for the supplies were two miles away. They cleared the spot, built the house, and the family moved in within a week.

"This pioneer castle had not twenty-five cents worth of hardware from cellar to garret, and no furniture except such as the family could make for themselves. In this condition many had the chills and fever.

"Among the suffering and bitternesses of pioneer life were the mosquitos, fleas, and bed bug pests. Millions without number were annoying and sucking the life's blood of the occupants. These flat infernals would get into the cracks and crevices of the pioneer 'castles', and nothing but hell fire and brimstone would remove them. They dared not resort to that extreme remedy for fear of burning the cabin.

"Toward the latter part of the year of 1864, throughout the country, nearly every pioneer was sick. Whole families were prostrated at the same time and those who escaped were weakened by care of the sick. Others were afraid to get near the sick or the dead.

"Grandmother Eliza, Elias, and Linas were overtaken with the shaking ague, Elizabeth and Elias having already had a few turns with the dumb ague. Grandfather Sam fired alarm guns for assistance, but no assistance came. In the morning Elizabeth brought Dr. Sanger. He was seemingly worse off than the patients. He dosed out some calomel, castor oil, and fever powders, and was barely able to ride home to St. Joseph. The castor oil was old and the stomach wouldn't have it. The stuff would grit between their teeth. They were very sorry that they were fated pioneers.

"In the night two of them died. Grandfather Sam was the undertaker, preacher and sexton and the funeral procession consisted of Eliza,
Sam, Elizabeth, and Caroline. So they buried their dead without a
funeral note or a gospel word spoken. The four remaining members of
the family looked more like escapees from a graveyard than a funeral
procession. Only six families remained in that vicinity. The Culver
family, now consisting of Sam and Eliza, Caroline and Elizabeth,
boarded up the cabin and left for the Saginaw Country in the fall
of 1865."

The little City of Saginaw had begun to prosper in earnest in the
1860's as the great flow of capital to the valley had stimulated investment
in timber lands and sawmills. Then in the 'seventies and on, the unlimited
demand for lumber created by the western migration and accelerated
by the urban movement changed the aspect of things. Towns and cities
were springing up overnight and throughout the county districts. Houses
and barns were clamoring to be built. The demand for lumber, at first
a weak call from far away, rose with ever louder and still louder cres-
cendo as the canny businessmen began to dream dreams and young men
to see visions. Lumber kings purchased vast acreages of virgin forests
from a beneficent government at the minimum price of $1.25 an acre.
The Chicago and Northwestern Railroad and others, which had been
given grant lands, sent out landcruisers to look their gift horse in the
mouth. Settlers were "filling up the oak openings". Everywhere men
filtered into the woods to find where the choicest stands were to be had.
There was no profit in lumbering until the late 'fifties of the last century.
There was no market for cull lumber which sold for $4.50 per M. feet
nor two or three grades of uppers at from $9.00 to $11.00.

Great wealds of valuable timber growing adjacent to the various
rivers rising on all sides in the interior were brought to Saginaw. The
vast acres of virgin forest bordering on Saginaw brought organized
crews of lumberjacks and sent millions of feet of logs tumbling down
the rolling Saginaw to the ravenous mills. These in turn sent the
lumber gliding along the highways of traffic to the ultimate consumer.
Saginaw had fourteen sawmills and nine others were underway on the
tributary streams. It was the central point, at which marked logs could
be separated for each owner to claim his own.

For thirty years the conquest was waged with ever increasing tempo.
Its axes and saws bit the wood and the great monarchs, chanting silent
prayers to the Almighty, came humbly crashing down in pain to the
echo of timber-z-z from the lusty throats of the woodsmen. The same
spirit of reckless exploitation which swept railroad lands, timber and
mineral riches into corporate grasp, with so little moral squeamishness,
began also to permeate employer policies toward workmen.

Into the woods flocked men like bees into a hive. Many had seen service in the Civil War and were drawn into the valley by the mushrooming prosperity of a growing city. Many others were recent immigrants who came eagerly to try the first chance that fortune offered in the new land of opportunity. Some were natural floaters dominated by an insatiable wanderlust. Occasionally one proved a fugitive from justice, and took to the friendly shelter of the forest. They were of varying ethnic stock, mainly West and North European: Scandinavians, with a sprinkling of French-Canadians, Irish, Scotch and English. Many mastered a variety of skills and were at home alike in forest as on farm and on stream.

This teeming and exploited Saginaw Valley was Daniel Hutcheson's last terminus, at which, he hoped, all his migrations would end. He was forty-one when he arrived there, yet he remained the same strong giant, never hesitating to undertake any kind of conquest. His virile physique could still cope with a merciless enemy, the woods.

For twenty-three years, since his arrival in Detroit, he had adhered religiously to the counsel of his British contemporary, Thomas Greenwood, who said, one with a willingness to work, to take the work which presents itself, and a bit of luck, could go as high as any. But somehow that "bit of luck" eluded him. Like the natives of the United States, he wished only for a fair deal, and no favor.[9]

Through the years he had trudged through the length of Michigan, as far north as the wilderness of Mackinaw, that primitive, picturesque little harbor, approximately 300 miles from Detroit. Here he was engaged as a mail carrier between Mackinaw and Houghton. Often he made this distance on foot, when the beastly critters refused to pull the sled. And, when President Abraham Lincoln made the first call for volunteers, in July 1861, Daniel Orrick Hutcheson promptly enlisted.

This great sectional struggle marked the beginning of Daniel's own political orientation. His committment to Lincoln's political creed reflected the interest configuration of the country. He was not unlike the native free-soil farmers and self-educated workers on the Northwestern frontier from whom the Great Emancipator drew his major source of strength. He felt intensely the scathing attacks and derision to which Abe Lincoln was subjected in the press. The description of "Black Republicans," who were charged with inciting and provoking the slave-owning South to rebellion and Civil War, was pregnant with meaning to the honest mind of this literate worker. It was an experience he never failed to recount to his progeny. That it had left its effects on the impressionable William Levi, of this there is little doubt. The

---

[9]See Thomas Greenwood, *op. cit.*

old man's manifest disapproval of his grandson, Maurice A. Hutcheson, peddling the *Detroit Free Press* on the streets of Saginaw during his school vacation, years later, sprang from the same source of anger. For it was that newspaper, of which Daniel Orrick had been a daily reader, which had taken a stand against Lincoln's administration. . . .

*   *   *

The wild woods welcomed Daniel as he flung himself at the mercy of fortune with a right good will. Inured to cold weather, he soon became intoxicated with the free, wild life. Despite the fact that he was forced to remain in only limited and marginal occupations for almost two decades, he changed in neither temperament, character nor bodily vitality. He laughed in the grim face of danger. He feared neither man, nature in the raw, nor the proverbial devil. It was these attributes that were characteristic of the behavior of his son, William Levi.

At Skinner's lumber camp were 600 men broken up into crews of sixty. The first task of the crew was to establish a base of operations. They selected a camp site, cleared the ground and built a series of shanties, bunk-houses, a cook's camp, a rudehouse and a stable. While the men busied themselves with this labor, the foremen scouted the surrounding forest and blazed the trails for a system of convoy roads, main thoroughfare, skidways and banking ground.

The main road was laid out along the creek bed, so that it could be easily iced down during the traffic of the winter. Each man was set to the work for which he was best fitted. Some were axe men, some teamsters, others sawyers. The pick and shovel men did the necessary grading. Daniel was a sawyer.

Then, one bright morning when all was in readiness, the wholesale slaughter of the majestic pine would begin. The glint of axes was in the air, the whine of the saws and the aroma of fresh sawdust and the loud bellow of timber-z-z, everywhere and all at once, assailed the senses.

The proud monarchs came tumbling to the ground amid the uproar in rapid succession. They were sawed into logs, dragged down the convoy roads and piled on the skidways, later to be sledded down the iced roadway to the banking grounds, to await the Spring thaw.

The day began with the whanging of the chore boy's alarm at four in the morning. The lad would roll out of his blankets with his clothes on. He would jerk on his boots, his mackinaw, and his cap, and rustle about starting the fires. He would begin at the cook's camp, hurry to the men's shanty, and then on to the camp's office. The cook would bounce out, and whip up breakfast. As soon as the stoves were aglow, he would return to the men's shanty, and shake the teamsters, axemen and sawmen out of their stupor. They would quietly dress and disappear down the lane of the new-fallen snow with their lanterns aglimmer. The teamsters would open the stable, feed and harness the horses.

At five o'clock "Gabriel" again blew his horn. This was a gruff and hardy signal, often seconded by a gruffer, hardier call, "come and get it." The men tumbled into the cook's camp, and crowded along the puncheon benches facing the crude oilcloth-covered table.

The hungry mouths were opened to vast quantities of baked beans, fried ham and bacon, potatoes, hash, prunes and buckwheat flap-jacks, followed by a constant stream of steaming coffee. The hurried meal was punctuated by a series of remarks on the quality of the cooking.

Elizabeth Culver was the cook. She was the sole woman on the camp. Her "cookee", or assistant, was a male. Here in this environment, the cook occupied a special status. She was a personage of some importance. In the four months until the operation was completed, Daniel succeeded in exchanging words with Elizabeth, and on occasions when the sawing was within reach of the cook's camp, he would return there for his mid-day "chat."

When the afternoon had worn away, and darkness was quickly closing in, the men returned to the cook's camp for the only square meal of the day.

After the evening meal, the men returned to their bunk shanty, tugged off their heavy, wet, German socks, hung them on the drying line over the stove, pulled on dry footwear, and sat down on the "deacon's" seat outside the bunks to "chaw terbakker" and to swap yarns and sing songs.

It was here that Paul Bunyan first drew the breath of life, and here also that the lumberjack ballads came into their own. Often there were coarse jests and salty anecdotes, and tales of adventure that lighted the eye and set the heart aflame. Imagination and fancy set the stage and supplied the actors, and satisfied the hunger within for the life of the great world, not too far removed from the sheltering walls of the great forest.

Logging and timber-making had their dangers. Few were free from cuts and gashes due to the slipping of axes on the frozen timber. To be pinned hopelessly under rolling logs or be crushed to death was not an infrequent occurrence.

Life in the timberland moved on with its steady grimness, hardness, crudity and exhausting toil that only the strong could survive. The only respite from labor was afforded on Sunday, and on that day some would grind their axes, repair their saws or set the camp in order for operations during the week. Daniel would rather read the marked passages from the Scriptures, a family heirloom with which his mother had parted on his exodus to the States.* Without homiletics, his delivery was in the same natural tone of voice with which he addressed his fellows in the forest or on the street.

By the time the Spring thaw arrived, the Saginaw was piled high with logs, as were the Cass and Shiawassee Rivers. While the "jacks" were getting out the logs, other crews would be making the river ready for the drive. A reservoir of water would be held at the head of the waters of the stream, and at intervals of a few miles each, sluice gates would be thrown across the river and storage reservoirs prepared, so that the logs could be floated down from point to designated point on the roaring flood waters.

The "jacks" would discard their heavy winter clothing for cotton overalls, flannel shirts and sharply calked leather boots. Armed with freshly pointed peaveys, they were ready for the hard battle. The logs had to be run through the tortuous channels, over rapids, where often they lodged in unmanageable jams. Each "jack" knew that, before the fray was ended, he would be in and out of the water constantly, under it as likely as not. It was no wonder that many of these jacks became as hard-fighting, hard-drinking a crew as ever trod on "neat's leather."

The logs were rolled into the water from banking grounds, and fed into the smother of the foaming, boiling stream, end jostling end, and bark chafing grating bark. Upon the constantly shifting pattern of tapestry made by the logs, the wary riverman set his calks and his unerring peavey, and labored by corkscrewing the logs this way and that, to keep them moving smoothly. If any of the logs "struck a snag" and impeded the flow, the jack had to be on the job constantly. With unerring judgement born of experience, he had to free the log and set it joyously on its way.

Driving tried the steadiest nerve and the strongest will. Always a jam was imminent and the sucking, swirling current was ever ready without a second's warning to pull the sturdiest jack to instant death. The hours were unmercifully long, and the meals irregular, to be snatched, a bite at a time, whenever the opportunity offered. The weather was changeable, and feet and legs usually sopping wet, and chilled.

It was no wonder that many jacks waxed fatalistic. When one of his mates suddenly went to a muddy death, a jack drew a deep breath, vowing to be a bit more alert. When a near accident passed and a jack had by a hair's breath escaped disaster, he would laugh bitterly,

---

*This bible, well over a hundred years old, is now owned by Mrs. Minnie Bliss — older sister of our protagonist and second child of Daniel Orrick Hutcheson, Eighty-four years old, she was helpful and gracious during our interview at her home in Lakeland, Fla.

prod the offending log with his peavey, and shout after it: "Hell, no! You ain't got my name writ on your dastard bark. Get along with yer, scoundrel!" No accident was ever too discouraging or dangerously long to halt the flow of the drive. The logs were kept moving at whatever hazard.

On quitting the camp, the lumberjacks were paid off in camp orders drawn on the lumber company, for the net sum due each one, and payable at the company's office in the Saginaws. No money circulated in the camps, for the simple wants of the men were supplied them from the company's store and charged to their accounts. Beyond these necessities there was no way of spending money in the depths of the forest, and the men who remained through the long winter came out with orders drawn for fifty to a hundred dollars. The teamsters drew as high as two hundred dollars.

In the good old lumbering days of the 'seventies and 'eighties, and even 'nineties, when all was bustle and boom on the river, the "red sash brigade" of lumberjacks was one of the picturesque features of the border towns. Upon breaking up the lumber camps in the Spring, these hardy woodsmen came to town in droves, bedecked in mackinaw coats of many colors, red sashes, pacs and hurons, and with rolls of money, the earnings of a winter's toil, which they spent freely in revelry and dissipation. Saginaw and its twin, Bay City, was one of the bawdiest places in the Lower Peninsula. It was a wide open town that welcomed the many reckless woodsmen with outstretched arms, a condition that was naturally to their liking — and they did just about as they pleased.

At the time, a Captain Naigly kept a hotel in the low, two-story brick building on the west side of Jefferson Street, near Tuscola. He was the "father" of a large number of lumberjacks who stayed at his house and enjoyed his hospitality. He knew how to handle them, too. The wiser ones who realized the pitfalls of the city made him their banker. He would cash their camp orders at no charge, either handing out a generous roll of bills, or retaining the greater part in his safekeeping. This preliminary arranged, he would look after their physical comfort. A visit to Jerry's Barber Shop on Lapeer Street relieved them of a winter's growth of hair and whiskers, and a hot bath made them tolerably presentable. Next, a call at Jack Seligman's clothing store refitted them with new, clean outfits, including the inevitable red sash, and at Lenheim's with new boots or pacs.

After some minor purchases had been made, interspersed with a few drinks, the lumberjacks were ready to take in the sights of the town, and this they proceeded to do in characteristic fashion. Water Street, from the depot on Potter Street to Sears and Holland's Mill near Bristol Street, was the principal trail, one of the favorite haunts, the Riverside House, being situated at the corner of McCorsky Street. The main streets of the town were rendered indescribably gay and fantastic by the fighting woodsmen, though the lives of peaceful citizens were often jeopardized by their murderous outbreaks. Many reckless spirits lost their "wads" in one night by theft; others spent their all in a week or ten days, while a few wiser ones still kept part of their hard-earned wages. Truth to tell, the tradesmen were eager to take away the woodsman's earnings in an incredibly short time. The rougher element got most of it, from Warren Bordwell's show house, on Washington Street, to the ever-open row of resorts on Franklin Street. Those who tarried too long at the taverns and those who had to be intoxicated to be conquered, were alike dragged in the back room by the "bouncer," robbed of any money they still possessed; and when they finally recovered from their stupor, were cast out like worn-out shirts.

Those were the roisterous, rough days in the Saginaws — but also the heyday of much wealth, when substantial fortunes were made in trading, generally at the expense of the dwellers of the North Woods.

Twenty miles from the Saginaws, within the boundaries of the 32 townships constituting Saginaw County, Bay City looked attractive to Daniel. It had a river harbor, a mushrooming lumbering industry and a shipbuilding trade. Here, amidst the annual frolicking and revelry, and the uninhibited exuberance of the "jacks," he was proceeding to carry out his cherished plan of making a fresh start for himself.

The draining experience in the immense forest north of Saginaw had left no debilitating effects on him, although he was in his early forties. His cheeks were pink and his blue, deep-set eyes shone bright. He was seasoned and robust. The clear, cold air and vigorous exercises filled him with ever-renewing vitality.

Within the limits of Saginaw County there was the Township of Williams, which was credited with giving birth to the first two white children in the Valley. The settlement of Williams had begun in the middle 'fifties, and the few expectant home-seekers who saw the rich land in the "oak openings" went no farther.

There was no underbrush. The land was covered with a heavy scattering of timber of different varieties of oak, hickory, hazel-brush and willow with a heavy coat of prairie grass. The grass was so tall that, when the early settlers went after their cows, guided by the sound of their tinkling bells, they could lap the grass over their heads as they followed the trail. It was here that the remaining members of the Culver family had made a home for the first time since they left Sandusky, Ohio.

*   *   *

Sam Culver, his wife and his two daughters, Catherine and Elizabeth had arrived in Williams June 28, 1866 and located on Section 24.

Their nearest neighbors, Ambrose Stevens and James Cleary, lived in log shanties on Sections 28 and 26, three and one half miles from the Culvers. In 1867 the first town site was laid out in Williams, named after Mrs. Gardner D. Williams, who gave birth to the first white child in the Saginaws. There was no road in the Township of Williams at the time. Its residents made roads as they came to need them. All followed Indian trails as much as possible. As late as 1867 there was no road from Bay City to Williams Township.

The Culver log castle was twenty feet square inside, one and a-half stories high, roofed with shingles. There were four of them to occupy it. But there was still room left for a little furniture, which the Culvers bought from one Savery, who was leaving the country for Texas.

Elizabeth Culver, the elder of the two sisters, now reaching eighteen, managed the domestic life of the family in the summers. Upon arriving in the Saginaws, she was engaged as a cook at Skinner's lumber camp, which was somewhat of a departure from the prevailing practice, for only male cooks were permitted on the lumber camp. As tedious and exhausting as the work was, she felt compensated by the boisterous, noisy surroundings while the food was being served. Her own feelings of loneliness, lack of friends, her rootlessness, resulting from a continuous search for a home by her parents, were now greatly assuaged. Her childhood experiences, the battling with hardship by her parents, gave her more than a familiarity with privation. There had been days of poverty, cornbread, coarse food, and sometimes shoeless feet. She had endured the fever scourge which had taken two members of her family.

There was but a distance of nine miles that separated Daniel Orrick Hutcheson from Elizabeth Culver. Nine miles of Indian trail proved no deterrent to Daniel, nor did the marked disparity in their ages.

Elizabeth Culver reached the age of marriage when Daniel was completing his forty-second birthday. She was of medium height, robust, with chestnut brown hair and gleaming brown eyes. In her veins flowed the strains of two virile peoples, fusing the tempestuousness of the Scotch-Irish with the proverbial asceticism of the Pennsylvania Dutch. Daniel Orrick was a tall, muscular giant, with a swaggering gait, as he strutted the streets of Saginaw. Among the loggers, Elizabeth Culver would spot him by the mutton-chop cut of his whiskers, and his tweed sack suit.

Daniel's exuberant manner and laughing eyes pleased the "marriageable" Culver lass. His adventures in the new country in the north had a romantic appeal for her. His swaggering gait and booming voice gave her a feeling of assurance. A girl aspiring to a family of her own could do worse than being courted by this giant of a man.

He had found a **dollar-a-week** room and "a perfect" eating place on

McClasky Street. It had the best buy in food in town: a large plate of beans, two slices of bread, a big chunk of apple pie and coffee—all for ten cents. He ate the same meal twice a day—and occasionally invited the Culver girl to share his daily fare.

Elizabeth's and Dan's courtship was brief. They were married on March 10, 1867 — and from that union issued five children over a span of twenty-three years!

It might be interesting to note, by the way, that our authority for this portion of the story — Bud Amos Hutcheson, youngest of the Hutchesons — was born on February 17, 1890, when Daniel Orrick had reached three score and five and his wife Elizabeth was only three months past forty-one.

All through those years Daniel barely succeeded in earning enough for his family — certainly never a surplus. Often the Hutcheson larder ran very low, and potatoes constituted its *piece de resistance*. On one such occasion some years later when Dan, saying his Grace, asked for the blessing from the Heavenly Father, his son Will, with characteristic causticity, commented impiously, "a very poor blessing indeed . . ."

The month of February, 1874, was a bitter one in the Saginaws. The weather was very disagreeable with its sudden alternations of intense frost, snows and storms. At the beginning of February the weather improved slightly, but starting February 6, the cold struck again and was followed by a five-inch snow. In the saloons, men drinking their liquor straight tarried. They could speak of nothing but the precautions they had to take in driving their horse-carts and sleighs over the snow-driven countryside, where they were looking for coal and timber. They drank a toast to Daniel Orrick, whose wife had just given birth to another child.

A son had just been born to Dan Orrick, the ship caulker at the Davidson Shipyards in Bay City, "a big fella" whom he christened William Levi. Born on the seventh, Saturday, William Levi would be lucky. His parents had him baptized a month later in the neighboring church, thus adding one more Methodist to the city. The drinkers laughed in whispering that "old Dan O.", as he was called in late years, "wasn't leading a dull life," for Dan O., they agreed, was "a man who had not forgotten his studies." He had already had two children in an interval of eight years. But the first two, Mathilda and Minnie were "only" girls.

Saginaw was expanding as its population continued to increase from 39,097 in 1870 to 47,000 the following year. The manufacture of lumber from the log by the Saginaw mills was now united with the making of salt. For the first time means was found of utilizing the surplus refuse material as fuel for the manufacture of salt, thereby enhancing the profits of both branches of industry. More recently, coal deposits underlying the surface of the Valley had been tapped, notably the Sebewaing Mines. Bay City was also developing into an important shipbuilding center.

Daniel Orrick had not conquered the world. His lot, in fact, had not improved much. His manual skills as a logger and sawyer were valuable enough for four months in the year in a city where the manufacture of lumber from logs reached the phenomenal figure of 736,106,000 feet cut in one year. Because of the transient nature of the lumbering industry and the abundant supply of unskilled workers, the wages never did go higher than ninety-six dollars per season. An attempt, for example, by the Knights of Labor to organize the unskilled workers in that lumbering area in the year 1879 resulted in failure, partly because many of the lumberjacks were immigrants who had not been so gainfully employed previously, and also because others, mostly laborers from the rural regions in Michigan, opposed unionization.

In the summer, Daniel worked as a ship-caulker in the neighboring Davidson Shipyards, earning two dollars a day for twelve hours of work. With three children on hand, ages four and six, and a newborn infant, his hardships often compelled him to be away from home, working as a coal miner.

Among the Jewitts, Williams brothers, the Littles, Charles Richman, the Swarthouts, the Jennisons, the Elmers, all of whom owed their newly acquired importance to their newly-acquired riches from lumber, Daniel was destined to remain the transient, seasonal worker and the plebian to boot.

But he was not unhappy. His jobs, his wife, sufficed for him. For the future, his son William would be his triumph. The girls in these regions, as elsewhere where the men outnumbered the women, would be asked in marriage continually, especially when they were strong and pretty.

William Levi Hutcheson was ushered into this world with only the aid of a neighbor midwife—a Mrs. Faith Williamson. The home in which he was born was comprised of a log structure of fourteen by sixteen feet, with a roof slanting one way. It was six feet high on the lower side. Through the chinks in the logs came all the fresh air the family needed, and on awakening on cold winter mornings they found the bed covered with snow. Nevertheless, the home was rather well equipped for almost any emergency in a medicinal way, with bunches of dried herbs, consisting of catnip, saffron, sage, peppermint, hoarhound and the ever-ready, indispensable bottle of goose oil. There was no boiled water for the children, but just good clear fluid from the nearby spring. The food was coarse and the diet rough, but the house was free from actual want.

When he was not away, Daniel's small world centered around his cabin. His three healthy children, an affectionate though quarrelsome band, were held with firm discipline. The Bible, the rules he had learned in his Uncle Edwin's house, the maxims and stories once related by his mother and those of their friends and neighbors who had come to share the frugal meals, made up the substance of his instruction. Daniel developed in his children first, a religious sense, which he often described as "Wesleyan social service;" secondly, hard common sense, which he defined as a taste for work and for simplicity. An aggrieved spirit, nurtured by courage and religious fatalism, was part of the Hutcheson legacy, it appears.

Of all the three children Dan preferred his third, William Levi, a lanky fellow with bright eyes and inexhaustible vitality. Everything that went on around him impressed him irresistibly and stimulated him curiously. Indeed, during those years Saginaw County offered lessons and sights to a little boy.

There was the vari-colored, multi-lingual "red-sash brigade," an annual event which attracted the crowds of Saginaw. Mostly they were Finns, French-Canadians, Scotch-Irish, Swedes and Irish, whose giant bodies sought to conquer the world of men as easily as they conquered the inanimate, cruel forests. Although few of the lumberjacks had ever risen to the heights of "Bill" Callam, an Irish lumberjack whose ingenuity brought him into the sudden possesssion of valuable timber and rich veins of ore, he was part of the lore and legend which continued to feed the fertile imagination of these forest dwellers. They continued to consume vast quantities of whiskey as an antidote to their exhausting labor. Others were lured by the lurid promises of the "bunco-steerer," who would treat them to a drink or two, to prove his generous nature. Once he had them started, they were at his mercy. Robbed of the money they still possessed, they were frequently cast out into the gutter . . .

William never forgot those childhood scenes. They were engraved on his mind. For, years later, he consistently counseled his constituents against the excessive use of liquor.

Playing in front of his father's cabin, fascinated by the colors of the mackinaw coats, pacs and red sashes which adorned the woodsmen and by the salty talk, he revealed a quick intelligence and ready tongue. At five years of age he had already memorized the Ten Commandments, and at seven was enrolled in South Williams School. He was always happy at the return of his father, who would read to him the familiar passages marked on pages 489 and 532 of the family Bible. He told them stories of the picturesque tough lumberjacks, who "could whip an army," of Chase Benjamin, Jimmy Gleason, Jim, Pat, Tom and Jack Roach, giants and great fighters. There was Tom Hayes, the conductor of the Jackson, Lansing and Saginaw Railroad. Tom was a strong and fearless man, the right man for his job. For railroading, particularly the part of the conductor, was tough in those days. He had to be able to handle all men, with fists if necessary. "I have seen him," recounted his father, "walk down a string of flat cars and demand fares from six lumberjacks who he knew did not have fares. They would not pay or get off the train, so he cleared the cars with a peavey. They were tough. He was tough. They showed fight. And he fought!" These stories of physical prowess absorbed William immensely.

Later, old Daniel chuckled inwardly when he saw William fight in the dust with his little comrades, whom he never spared the finishing blow. He rejoiced to see him take charge of the games, though he found it necessary to show him paternal anger sometimes. One day, William amused himself catching small fish left on the beaches by the receding waters. He had the idea of pilfering bricks from a house under construction nearby to erect a little dike which would make it possible for his playmates to catch the fish without wetting their feet. This was too much for Bible-spouting old Dan O. He invoked the seventh Commandment with deep conviction, in a memorable scene William Levi never forgot.

South Williams was a large school house built a mile and a half from the Hutcheson house, its interior quite primitive and rough. Seated upon the splinter-edged bench and at the rustic desk, William studied his first lessons in reading, writing, arithmetic and good manners. He made rapid progress, except in arithmetic, which presented nothing concrete to this realistic mind. The child's instinct turned toward concrete things, guiding him always in that direction. There was, however, the taste for reading, particularly history books. From the beginning, he found time to satisfy it, especially during the long winter evenings when his father was away. The difficulty lay in finding books. Daniel Orrick had little besides the *Workingmen's Advocate* and sermons on Protestant theology, and a collection of poems attributed to Clarence H. Pearson, the lumberjack. "Silver Jack," the hero, fascinated William. He tried Bunyan's "Pilgrim's Progress," "Robinson Crusoe." Better still, he liked James Fenimore Cooper's "Oak Openings," with whose subject he was quite familiar. The hardy pioneer battling rugged nature and savage natives, the raw material of great epics, filled his childish dreams, as did the beauty of Michigan oaks. The oak tree had, since July 6, 1869, become Michigan's symbol of opposition to slavery, a fact which impressed itself early on the mind of William.

William Levi had a strong desire to work. The growth of the town, with new buildings springing up everywhere amidst booming prosperity, heightened that feeling. Activity reigned everywhere. Saline deposits and iron brought new riches to already opulent lumbermen, whose sudden wealth rivaled the fairy tales of old. The son of a Scotch-Irish immigrant felt in his veins the harsh invitation to life tendered by Michigan's seasons, which killed off the weakest but toughened the rest.

William would sit for long hours watching the fire in the oven, and musing. He was ten. The life of his wandering father loomed as intolerable. He could not resign himself to such a cruel, hapless role. The affection which his father and mother gave him no longer sufficed. The value of work and hope of improving one's lot, which had driven his father to the New World, had been repeated to him continually. Must that bright vision of promise remain a chimera? He was eager to do something and above all do better than his father.

The eighty-five year old Minnie Bliss, William's surviving sister, to whom we owe much of the previously detailed account of their parents' life, still remembers how she and her younger brother William, whom she always called a "sassybrass," found their playmates among the Indian children who lived near their farm.

These red-skinned playmates were familiar visitors to the log-cabin which housed the Hutchesons on those hardscrabble acres which the children called their farm. She remembers her junior brother as a gaunt and lanky lad, "big and strong for his age," with whom she'd play hide-'n-seek among the numerous stumps of pine trees felled by their father and how the energetic William would help Daniel O. pile up and burn heaps of brush and clear the land for sowing, put up stalls for the pigs and barns for the corn. Even then, she relates, William showed pride in his building prowess as he participated in the building "bees" held in the rural community every spring.

William, she recalls, may have been proud of his "buildin' " talents, but he was prouder still of the notions he carried in his young brain. He was quite opinionated even then, she remembers, and though their parents didn't think it proper for children to talk back to their elders, William wouldn't hesitate "to speak right out" when a discussion arose at home or when the neighbors came in for a talkfest with Ol' Dan. After listening patiently for as long as an hour, William would suddenly hop up from his chair and take issue with a garrulous visitor whose remarks didn't "sit right" with the youngster. "Bill," relates Minnie, "always spoke out. He was a sassybrass — but when he spoke up he always made sense."

Her "lanky and bony" kid brother, she relates, had a gift for debate. After a day spent doing odd jobs for neighboring farmers, Bill would come home and spend the evenings reading. If he wasn't working, he was reading—or arguing, she recalls. Regardless, though, of his contentiousness and argumentativeness, she remembers, Bill never used cusswords or profanity to make a point. Even at fourteen, when boys thought it a feat of masculinity to spout lumberjack eloquence, Bill could resort to his knowledge of history—a subject he loved—and to example and analogy to illustrate an argument. Their neighbors liked to provoke him into one—and amused to behold the lanky lad dressed in the home-made trousers which always revealed his gaunt, blue shins as he stood up to make his point vociferously.

Mrs. Minnie Bliss still recalls how, when the snow was deep in Bay County, old Daniel would put Bill behind a rigged-up washtub into which Minnie was tucked in, and off they'd slide to school, a mile and a half through snowbound forest, with Daniel pushing the tub most of the way. Their mother had prepared a lunch for the boys, and ad-monished Bill to watch over Minnie. But she was fonder of her boy, or so it seemed, remembers Minnie, because Bill "was good with the his-tory books."

William also liked to read the papers which his father brought home from the general store from time to time.

He was growing up, for Daniel realized that his son could drive a nail with his left hand as well as with his right. It was therefore time for the boy to be launched in some trade. Since the boy didn't care for farming, there were other useful occupations. "Will," Daniel used to say, "has a good head on his shoulders." He was more inquisitive and better informed, it seemed, than most boys of his age. At thirteen, it was time, thought Dan, for the lad to get started.

In April, 1886, Dan made it a point to take Bill with him around town and show him the workmen at their various trades. He observed that this interested the boy, distracted him, and won him over, but he tried in vain to discover which of all those trades the boy would choose as his vocation. William Levi seemed to be as pleased with one as with the other, and was not carried away by any. He was deliberate and hestitating. Perhaps he might be made a carpenter and be entered as an apprentice at the Wheeler Shipyards in Bay City. But what of the insecurity and precariousness of the construction trades, thought Daniel. Had he not himself been at the mercy of seasonal employment and periodic idleness inherent in that industry! Daniel's life was the case history of a drifting, seasonal, migrant worker, a toughened but patient victim overawed by these very pressures and tensions. His frequent absences from home during the long winters resulted in misunderstand-ings between Elizabeth and himself, and he didn't wish such a future for his Will.

He had been reading in the *Workingmen's Advocate* of the devices employers practiced when confronted with labor shortages or strikes. They would advertise in the British or Canadian newspapers, or send industrial agents to hire bricklayers, carpenters or other skilled tradesmen, who would often undercut union wages in cities such as New York or Boston. In the event of strikes by carpenters, their employers sometimes hired "strike breakers"—Scots, English Canadians, and immigrants hardly out of Castle Garden, in New York's port of debarkation.[10]

American unions objected to the Scots because their sudden mass appearance each Spring would dash hopes of labor shortages and resultant high wages. In March and April crowds of Scotsmen would land wherever new buildings were going up and not a few drifted into Michigan, where they worked through the season, and went north to the lumber camps in the winter. "This sort of thing is repeated year after year until the term of 'greenhorn' is a by-word and a reproach among Scotsmen who work here all year," Daniel gleaned from the *Scottish-American,* a newspaper which he read habitually.[11]

American workers, not a few of them likewise Scottish immigrants, complained that these interlopers worked for "whatever wages they can get. They boast in Scotland of the big wages they got in America, but which they certainly never received nor had the courage to demand."[12]

Finally Daniel Orrick hit upon the right idea. Perhaps to be a master-carpenter would be right for William. Carpentry, combined with the boy's obvious predilection for leadership, plus the Hutcheson temperament, might ultimately enable his Will to climb as high as the industry allowed. He would take William to Detroit, an adventure the lad certainly looked forward to.

Richard F. Trevellick, Cornish-born head of the International Union of Ship Carpenters and Caulkers, and close friend and collaborator of Andrew Carr Cameron, editor of the *Workingmen's Advocate,* was scheduled to address the National Labor Union, a reformist utopian organization in Detroit.

Richard Trevellick was a typical Scotsman, strong, full of life, and quarrelsome. In oratory he was terse and direct. He was an indefatigable worker and for a time served as organizer for the Knights of Labor. As chairman of the Eight Hour League, he pleaded for the support of labor activities. He crusaded for producers' cooperatives, the abolition of convict labor, Chinese exclusion, the sale of public land only to actual settlers. In the late 1870's and 1880's, Trevellick presided over the Greenback Party conventions and other labor reform movements. He remained a brilliant organizer throughout his career and was on friendly terms with the important political personalities. Daniel had developed

---

[10]Importance of Contract Laborers, "House Miscellaneous Documents," 50 Congress period, 1 Sess., No. 572, Pt. 1, (1888, pp. 138-148); "Report of the Select Committee on Immigration and Naturalization," II, pp. 271-272, 280-281.

[11]*Scottish-American,* Sept. 14, 1887.

[12]Rolland T. Berthoff, *op. cit.,* p. 87 seq.

sympathies for the Greenback Party through reading Andrew Cameron's *Workingmen's Advocate,* which spoke for that party and other important national liberal movements.[13]

Hearing him was a novel experience to young William Levi. He listened intently to the speaker's matter-of-fact presentation of issues that were meaningful and agitating to an audience estimated at six hundred. Eight hours a day, enough wages for roast beef, forbidding the employment of children under the age of 14, were subjects easily absorbed by William's alert intelligence. He had heard those identical debates and discussions at the house from his father's friends. The Detroit trip proved fruitful.

William Levi Hutcheson left South Williams school with a creditable record. He had been at school for six and one-half years, and that was enough for the son of a migrant worker. Daniel's fourth child, Daniel Olivier, was only eight and it was now time for William Levi, the oldest son, to augment the family income. He was entered as a carpenter's apprentice. While Will didn't mind the work, he was reluctant to remain at home. He had a craving for adventure outside of Saginaw. His mother's entreaties prevailed and Will yielded. He was industrious and prudent. He meditated long before making decisions, now applying a resourceful mind to his two major problems: how best to pursue the craft of carpentry and how to secure more money — at the same time helping to lift the heavy burden from the shoulders of his aging father.

There was little he could do to really solve the latter, and his growing young body soon felt the initial effects of a ten-hour day's work, at fifty cents a day. But weekly contributions of three dollars towards the upkeep of the family gave him a sense of pride and achievement.

The image of his fifty-four-year-old drifting father, seeking refuge at the homes of strangers during the cold winter months when he was away, had a disturbing effect on the life of this boy. It was this, incidentally, that in later years impelled him to establish an "approximation" of a home for the carpenters of the United Brotherhood in Lakeland, Florida.

Among the newspapers which his father obtained on his visits to Detroit were old issues of the *Detroit Unionist.* William found much to glean from these pages after a day's work. One piece, provocatively entitled, "Whither are we Drifting?" in the Sept. 4, 1882 issue, struck him particularly by its tone of defiance, extravagant language and sermonizing:

"Eastern capitalists are becoming alarmed of the magnitude the labor movement has assumed, and are now besieging the authorities at Washington

---

[13]*Dictionary of American Biography,* III, pp. 433-434; XVIII 640-641.

to interpose the military arm of government in their behalf. A large delegation visited the Secretary of War a short time ago and asked what troops he had east of the Mississippi available for the protection of property in case of labor disturbances. "One regiment of infantry and three artillery," was the reply.

"We have read, time and time again, the old blue laws of Connecticut, and each time with increased disgust and contempt for the authors of that black record, and blessed our soul that we lived in the age of enlightenment and Christianity; but the reading of only a few published clauses of the New York Penal Code convinces us that the boasted civilization in the East is rapidly sinking into a whirlpool of ignorance, superstition and barbarity!

"Turn your charitable institutions into penitentiaries; build scaffolds at every cross-roads; add another story to the wretched tenement houses; do what you will, and for a time the people will acquiesce. But let your army alone—it belongs to the whole country; and the very moment the attempt is made to use troops to shoot free American citizens, there will be kindled such a fire that fluids thin as water will not quench . . ."

Here was a new language for a boy nourished on the strict and pious words of Methodist sermons and the Scriptures. Here was also a lot to think about for an apprentice, a fourteen-year-old, anxious to make his mark in the world, imbued with the spirit of adventure, and eager to make some money for himself. It set his mind on fire. He followed labor events with a curiosity remarkable for a boy of his age.

Late in December, 1888, Samuel Gompers, first President of the American Federation of Labor, arrived in Saginaw. The young apprentice listened attentively to the simple, democratic language of this self-taught, erudite "East Side" cigar maker who, despite the fact that his trade of cigar making was not one which many English-speaking immigrants or Americans entered, had a shrewder insight into the needs and thinking of the American worker than most of his contemporaries. Gompers had not neglected to heap praises on one of Saginaw's most active labor leaders, John Dutcher, a member of the Executive Committee of the newly-organized Michigan Federation of Labor. He was introduced by Joseph A. Labadie, a printer with literary proclivities, one of Michigan's outstanding champions of the labor cause.

Gompers spoke of the need for a cohesive local labor organization which would harmonize the interests of all laborers working in the same trade. "It is the weaver for the weaver and the carpenter for the carpenter who will fight for his own immediate welfare, rather than that of the mass of laborers." he exclaimed. He also pointed to the failure of "mixed" labor organizations, and the nondescript followers of the Knights of Labor, which included in its ranks the "scavenger alike with the most expert craftsman. . . ." William soon caught the enthusiasm that agitated the receptive audience.

Michigan and its growing industrial cities of Detroit, Lansing, Jackson, Flint, Muskegan, Bay City, and Saginaw Valley have, since the 1860's, been fertile grounds for "labor reformers," itinerant lecturers and "philosophers" of every hue. Here, the National Eight Hour League was given its first breath of life and impetus in the late 1870's. Richard F. Trevellick reached large audiences in his plea for the support of labor activities. John Francis Bray lived out his last fifty years on a hardscrabble Michigan farm, of which the principle crop, it was said, was Socialist polemics. No national movement escaped the attention of that Northwestern state.

Early attempts to organize the artisan "working class" in the industrializing city of Detroit were made before the admission of the State into the Union. The Detroit Mechanics Society, informally organized in 1818, was incorporated two years later. Ypsilanti claimed a Workingmen's Society at an early date. The Carpenters Society was organized in 1830. A formal trade union, established by the Printers in 1848, served as the model for other groups. The Iron Molders organized on a similar basis in 1860, while the Machinists followed their example during the next year. The year 1864 marked the origin of three large groups: the Cigar Makers Union, the Carpenters Union, and the Operative Engineers Union.[14]

"Animated by a progressive spirit, members of the local trades unions early came to the conclusion that their interests would be better protected by the formation of a central trades organization, or the Detroit Trades Assembly." Michigan's first central trade union body was formed in 1865. However, its life was short, having yielded to the Panic of 1873.[15]

The increase in membership did not lead to the results anticipated. Friction between trade union followers and proponents of industrial units such as advocated by the Knights resulted in schisms. Rural-urban rivalries caused cleavages. Quarrels among rival personalities produced factionalism, and weakened the numerical strength of Michigan's organized wage earners.

More fundamental as a source of friction was the issue of political action. One group desired to serve as the nucleus for a liberal third party, and varying degrees of semi-official endorsement were given to the various third parties which flourished successively during the growth of the Knights. Others frowned upon this affiliation, and controversies ensued. The factors mentioned resulted in a rapid decline in membership of the Knights, which, in April, 1880, gave way to the Detroit

14John J. Scannell, "Early History of the Labor Movement," *Historic Michigan,* II: 50 (National Historical Association), p. 830.

15Labor's Annual Souvenir Journal, Sept. 7, 1891.

Council of Trades and Labor Unions, which was formed on a new basis.

It was during a period of sporadic decadence in trade unionism that the Knights of Labor had appeared on the scene. Founded in Philadelphia in 1869, it had emphasized the inclusion of all workers, trade union and otherwise, in one large order. Although the original plan suggested a secret fraternal order, the organization abandoned this characteristic and was stressing cooperatives and policies of economic reform.

The "industrial" catch-all of the Knights had made rapid progress in numerous localities of Michigan. Within a short period of seven years it was able to claim eight thousand members, including many farmers.

The dramatic entrance of the Knights into the Saginaw Valley had furnished young William Levi with his first visible experience of a labor strike. The picture in his mind of that strike, an imbroglio that he had witnessed one torrid summer day, always remained vivid. The arrival of twenty companies of State militia, reinforced by two-hundred and fifty armed Pinkerton "detectives" dispatched from Chicago, both fascinated and awed him.

The Saginaw Valley lumberjacks and rivermen, numbering 5,500, about 550 of whom were child laborers, went out on a strike, demanding a ten-hour day with no reduction in pay. Under the slogan *"Ten Hours or no Sawdust,"* the strikers chartered a steamboat and a barge and steamed upriver from Saginaw. Stopping at every mill town, they paraded behind a brass band and an American flag, resuming their journey only after every lumber and sawmill worker had stopped his work and the mill fires had been banked. Thus, all the seventy-eight mills and fifty-eight salt blocks in the Valley were shut down. The strike leader, Thomas Barry of Saginaw, was arrested repeatedly, until his bail aggregated the unprecedented amount in those days of $25,000. Barry was released, the lumberjacks emerging the victors.

William had now come to the point where a moral crisis was unavoidable. He was restless and dissatisfied, for new influences and experiences had begun to occupy his mind and touch his sensibility. The sermons he had read by the dozens in his father's house and the endless inspirational readings of Scripture began to irritate instead of calm him. One day, when his father concluded reading to him, *"Yea, they are greedy dogs which can never have enough, and they are shepherds that cannot understand: they all look their own way, everyone for his gain, from his quarter,"* William wanted to know the reason for people's greediness. His father's answers did not allay his doubts. William thought religion was useful when it improved the conduct of men. He was a "fundamentalist" from the start!

William was intimate with another apprentice, Collins, who had a lively mind and expressed himself with more facility than he. Following the fashion of the age, the two boys were extremely fond of discussion, held long debates on every subject, and of course talked a lot about girls. One day, the foreman objected to the quarrelsome apprentice who, weary of discussing the Saginaw strike, had taken recourse to blows, the better to impress his ideas on Collins. Collins, less belli- cose, was reduced to silence though not quite persuaded.

More than once their quarrels wound up with Old Dan O. as the arbiter. Though wishing to keep an equal balance between the two, Dan was apt to take William's side, and Collins was even less persuaded than before.

William was displeased with his situation as an apprentice, and proud of his "superiority" over Collins in reasoning. It inflamed his desire to convince, to influence, perhaps to command. His instinct for leadership was profound and irresistible. He loved politics, though he never quite regarded his interest in that field as an end in itself. Nothing could satisfy him entirely but the feeling that he was leading men by serving their causes in a common objective. His natural traits forced him to want to be a chief, responsible for his becoming one.

The situation at the Wheeler Shipyards was daily becoming more delicate. William's repeated involvements with Collins in discussions and fisticuffs did not augur well for either one of them.

Collins did not share William's ideas. He thought a laborer could not impose his wishes on his employer. If a worker disliked his boss or conditions of work, he could either quit or turn his hand to some new calling. It was always best to look out for "Number One." Besides, Collins hoped to become a boss himself. Yet, among William's many friends, none was superior to Collins, whose friendship he wished to retain despite all the bickering.

Actually, Collins reflected the general temper, thinking and attitudes of the times. A legacy, which had been deeply embedded in the fluid American social structure since industrialization, was transforming American society from about 1880 to 1919. Collins' thinking was individualistic, stressing equality of opportunity, individual responsibility, and advancement through personal effort. Even second generations of raw recruits who entered industry hoped to escape soon from wage work. Employers on the other hand, always refused to grant workers high wages lest they "pamper them with the idea of still obtaining more." It took William more than a decade, culminating with his own initiation as a union business agent and organizer for a Saginaw local of the United Brotherhood of Carpenters & Joiners of America, to learn the reasons why unionism developed slowly and with great difficulty.

Meanwhile, William sensed that many of the workers were disturbed

Seventy Years of Life and Labor by Samuel Gompers:
(E. P. Dutton & Co., Inc.)

*A rare photo of Samuel Gompers as he appeared in the late 1880's, when
William Levi Hutcheson met up with the President of the newly-formed
American Federation of Labor for the first time at a Saginaw labor rally.*

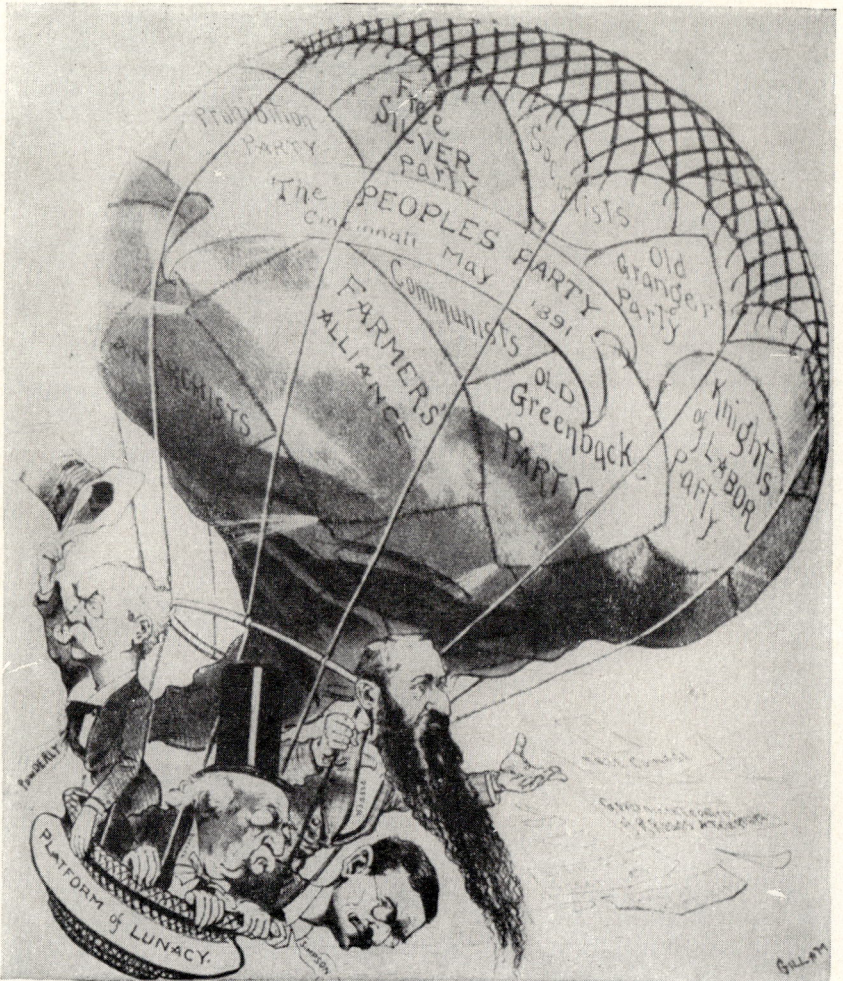

(Judge Magazine)

"Judge" comments on the formation of the People's Party in 1891, during Will Hutcheson's formative years in Michigan.

"*In the Land of Timber*": *Raping the forests of white pine in Michigan in the 1880's.*

"Ten Hours or No Sawdust," cried Saginaw Valley's lumber and sawmill workers among them 550 child laborers, as they halted their work, banked the mill fires, in response to their union's general strike call in 1885.

"Long Timber Days"—no clock-punching then. Teamsters started day's work around 3 a.m. Sawyers, axemen, swampers and skidders were in the woods at the break of dawn, ready to tackle their back-breaking jobs, working until dark. Wages ranged from $10.00 per month up, depending on the lumber market.

The Lumberjack's "antidote" to exhausting labor—time off for a slug at a local pub near a logging camp on the Tawas River on Saginaw Bay during the 1880's.

The Hutcheson Family in 1885. Front, (l. to r.) Mother Elizabeth, Oliver and Father Hutcheson, "lord of a farm"—ship caulker, laborer, axeman. Back, 11-year-old William, and his sisters Minnie and Mathilda.

Proud Addition—Dan O. Hutcheson reached three score and five and Mother Elizabeth only forty-one when Bud Amos (on father's knee) was born. Others in picture are 16-year-old Will and his brother Oliver.

The "formal" wedding picture of William Levi Hutcheson and Bessie King taken Oct. 10, 1893. Bride and groom were only nineteen.

At the turn of the century William Hutcheson would be returning sporadically from his job-hunting safaris—in quest of work as a journeyman carpenter, miner, well driller or farmhand—whatever chore presented itself during long layoff stretches. Son Maurice age 7, was already aware of his sire's employment problems.

Times were hard, but a load of second-hand lumber plus his own skill, enabled business agent "Big Bill" Hutcheson of the Saginaw Carpenters Union, to build this house for his growing family. On porch are "Ma" Bess and the 2 girls, Myra and Stella.

about his noisy quarrels and discussions. His lassitude and discontent were also beginning to show. All this was disagreeable to an ambitious seventeen year-old boy, who was anxious to come up in the world. Assuredly, Daniel Hutcheson was a good father and proud of his young son. But he could not favor him openly, as he had promised to maintain discipline between the two apprentices. His father was thus helpless, and William could not count on him.

After William had been looking for work among the sawmills of Saginaw and found that the Wheeler Shipyards had taken care to warn them in advance, thus closing the mills of the city to him, he realized grimly that he could count only on the resources of his imagination, ingenuity and physical strength to secure a future. To establish himself as a journeyman in Saginaw was, plainly, out of the question.

To be true to himself and to become a leader he would have to leave the city. It was a form of filial treason, but there was nothing else to do. He felt rejected and alone. God was a distant image for him then and morality a personal matter. There was nothing to hold him back, except his devoted father and patient mother. He would leave — if only to help them. Good Mother Elizabeth, how she had suffered in the past, as well as for the future of her William. . . .

For the winter months, William joined his father as a sawyer at the Saget McGraw Mill at Portsmouth. He was not the worse off for it. He learned much about the evolution of the sawing machinery — from the sash to the mulay saw, which was superseded by the rotary, or circular, as it was commonly called. The circular saw was capable of cutting more than one thousand feet an hour.

The end of the winter passed. Towards the middle of April, in the midst of the noisy, irrepressible red-sash brigade, the apprentice silently slipped away to Auburn, Michigan.

William was seventeen and a half years old and was already leaving his family and his past. He knew no one in Auburn or in the rest of the world. But he knew what he wanted; he was conscious of his physical force, his endurance, the vivacity of his mind and the ardor of his ambition.

He was directed to a little inn in Auburn, where he found lodgings for the night. The following day, refreshed, he made the long stretch of two miles to a farmer who did grain-growing, dairying and canning. There were other young men who worked there for one dollar a day — clearing land, cutting down wood and digging roads and ditches, the common work of laborers. Some expected to acquire experience in stock-farming. Most of them, however, deserted the place within the year.

William's was the routine, tedious job of dairying, hardly suitable for one so vigorous and alert. Yet whatever happened pleased him whether it was pleasing or not, simply because it had happened and because he was young.

When he no longer had the example, the presence and conversation of his father to restrain him, William became more and more impervious to the call of the pealing Sabbath bells. At first he regretted not going to Church, but he felt he could not spare the time from his reading on Sundays. However, his loneliness soon revived his habit of attending church every Sabbath with commendable regularity.

At a church party in Freeland's only Methodist Church, 3 miles distant from his place of employment, William soon met Bessie King — an attractive daughter of a local farmer. The first time they met, Will drove Bess home in his horse and buggy.[16] "We dated every two or three weeks thereafter and each time out we went to Church." After a courtship lasting almost a whole year, Bess and Will were married on October 10, 1893. Like his father's nuptials, Will's were celebrated in the above-described "chivari" style, although Will and Bess were both only nineteen. Will's 72-year-old father, Daniel Orrick, "dreamed the whole idea up — bull-roarers, tin cans, pots and pans, anything we could lay our hands on — and we gave Will a chivari treatment a la Brighton," Bud Hutcheson gleefully confided to us.

Auburn's backwoods farming techniques sapped William's initiative and heightened his restlessness. Back home in Bay City, his father Daniel had fulfilled a long cherished ambition, one that to him signified rank. He had acquired a small farm and was now the "lord" of his own acres. He invited Will and Bess to "come and let us work the farm together, share and share alike." After pooling their savings, father and son still didn't possess enough money to buy the expensive equipment which the commercialization of agriculture then required. At its best, the land could give only a hard living. The farm supported cattle, but few men, still Daniel held on to it with the "old Scotch tenacity that never yields."

As more and more capital became necessary, William took off for the wheat fields of the Dakotas where it was said that "the land was more fertile and opportunities boundless," leaving behind his wife Bessie and his year-old daughter Myra, "until I can earn enough money to buy us some decent equipment."

When he arrived in the Dakotas he found that there were as many mortgages as there were farms in that area. He headed back for home. En route he encountered sharecroppers by the truckloads traveling on the road. He became intimately acquainted with the crop-lien system under which the share-cropper tenant pledged his crop to country merchants for groceries or petty cash advanced during the growing season.

---

[16]Interview with Mrs. Bessie Hutcheson on her farm in Milan, Indiana, November, 1954.

The prices of goods thus furnished ran from fifty to one hundred per cent above prices prevailing elsewhere, and interest rates from forty to one hundred per cent above average.

When he returned home, he turned to part-time farming and such odd jobs as he could find, constructing barns and drilling wells, that supplemented his meager earnings but little. He was comforted by the hearth of his family and that of his devoted parents, but not enough to attenuate his frustrating experiences in the West Northcentral states. His own ambition, the image of the landless proletariat, the share-croppers and tenants whom he learned to know, the drifting armies of the unemployed, rejected by the wide-spread economic distress, heightened his agitation and morbid anxiety.

At any rate, it became increasingly obvious to William that if he pursued a farming career he would always continue to be dependent upon store credit and the landlord in order to carry on from year to year. What was happening was that tenancy was increasing in the nation and that owner-operator farming was declining. And, while it was true that tens of thousands laboriously climbed the ladder to ownership, more descended the ladder than climbed it. Large-scale tenancy and rapid descent were particularly high during the depression of the 1890's; for the increasing cost of land and farm equipment was making the climb to ownership most difficult. A second thing he learned was that the good American land was filling up. Traditionally, when the American working man's position became intolerable, as it did during the depression, he could always go west — even if he could hardly raise the cash to go. The west had been the land of new hope, not only for men adventurous and ambitious, but also for the discards of America's Iron Age, and of industrialism. But the new frontier was rapidly closing, and the chances to find escape and new opportunity dwindled.

Another thing that was happening was the depression of 1893, of which William Levi Hutcheson, his wife and daughter were the tragic victims. He was one of nearly two million who were idle four to six months out of the twelve, otherwise earning something like ten dollars a week, working ten hours a day, six days a week, and devoting the remainder of the year towards seeking employment as a journeyman carpenter. To the census of 1900, William, as the head of his household, was but one out of six and a-half million workers who were jobless, and quite without income. In the 'nineties, hundreds of thousands tramped the roads like vagrants or professional hoboes. Like William, they were for the most part earnest, thoughtful men, skilled workmen. "They were expert machinists, miners, and practically every kind of craftsman," reported Samuel Gompers, President of the American Federation of Labor.

"General stagnation of business which followed the financial storm was terrific, and was manifest in industry, construction and in all employing concerns, which slowed down if they did not stop. All kinds of people were without work. There was a curious money scarcity. There seems to have been plenty of everything but money. Those of us who had no Wall Street connections were somewhat blindly sure there was a money trust somewhere and that we were its victims. Our whole economic structure was paralyzed. Working men all over the country found themselves without work or money. They were hopeless in the clutches of some invisible power," wrote Gompers.[17]

In the west, where there had been rapid building of railroads, unaccountable thousands found themselves adrift. There was nothing to do anywhere, so the men determined to come east. "Men traveling the road without money naturally fell into step together. They shared the benefits of their ingenuity as well as their misfortune. Outwardly they were bands of homeless vagabonds roaming the country. There was a picturesque element in the situation that lent itself to publicity. The newspapers gave it much space. Someone conceived the idea of utilizing the eastward movement of the unemployed as a national demonstration to focus attention on the need for relief measures."[18]

That these personal painful memories were never banished from his mind, but indelibly, burned themselves into his consciousness, was clearly apparent as William Hutcheson unfolded the story of his life to this writer, in the Fall of 1952, at the Columbia Club, in Indianapolis.

William was already past twenty, and not unlike the uncountable thousands of others who traveled the road penniless, in search of work. Although neither of them met on the road, both William Levi Hutcheson and his junior by six years, John Llewelyn Lewis, were gnawed by the same constant lurking fear of worse things to come, because what was happening to them seemed without rhyme or reason. Here on the road were failure, defeat and want visiting the ambitious and energetic. They found their fortunes interlocked with those of great numbers of like workingmen in a pattern complex beyond their understanding, and apparently brought on by unreason and injustice. But soon the "sufferings of their own flesh" were to be channelized into a hazardous but constructive effort: to improve the position of the "lower" groups in a society which had abandoned them temporarily, if it did not entirely discard them.

The hideous depression of the mid-nineties brought much suffering to William L. Hutcheson. It marked him inwardly as the panic of 1873-4

---

[17]Samuel Gompers, *Seventy Years of Life and Labor Vol. I.* (E. P. Dutton and Co., 1925), p. 9.
[18]*Ibid,* pp. 9, 10.

had marked his father exactly two decades previously. Daniel's personal distressing failure sought expression at the age of 73 in the Greenback and Granger parties. In William the transformations were much more painful, accompanied as they were by great strains and emotional discomfort. Brought up in a roaring industrial town, his sordid experiences during that period did more to chart his career than anything else that ever happened to him. Dr. Bakke, social scientist of a later day, has described for us the effects those bitter experiences had on millions of youths who were similarly marked for the rest of their lives during the Great Depression of the nineteen-thirties.

His career broken, unable to find steady employment, he was forced into intermittent wanderings and travels, to take on "marginal" jobs to support his wife and their daughter, Myra. His journeys carried him to the rich Coeur d'Alene forests in Idaho, where he sought employment as a miner.

Hutcheson made the journey to the Coeur D'Alene forests in response to a help-wanted call by nearby industrial agents. This job, he was told, would "pay well." On arrival, he found that the entire region was strikebound, with federal troops in command. U. S. soldiers were posted with bayonets poised, arrayed against workers as if they were a foreign enemy engaged in battle!

President Harrison had ordered the miners' strike suppressed. As martial law was established, striking union men, who were arrested and herded into bull pens, lost their jobs to strikebreakers.

Indictments charging all sorts of trumped-up offenses came thick and fast. One of the men arrested, a forty-year old unemployed bystander, was charged with actively aiding the strike. The next day the police shipped him, together with the families of the strikers, out of town. Hutcheson was deeply stirred by this incredible spectacle. This was the first time that he saw the federal arm of Government abuse its power in a local labor dispute.

At the same time, another big strike broke out at the Carnegie Steel Works at Homestead, Pennsylvania, the men demanding a revision of the wage scale and recognition of their union. Steel was heavily protected in the tariff on the plea of protection of the American workmen, but the steel plants had been consistent opponents of the unions, and the demands were rejected. Three hundred Pinkerton detectives were engaged to guard the works, and a clash occurred with the men in which ten were killed and sixty wounded. With the aid of eight thousand State troops the strike was won for the company.

There were other strikes in 1894, which impinged upon the mind of Hutcheson, involving about three-quarters of a million workmen, adding still more to the huge army of six million unemployed.

The most serious one was at the Pullman plant in Chicago after the Democrats elected Grover Cleveland President and Adlai B. Stevenson Vice-President. Pullman had built a so-called "model village" in which he housed his workmen, and then cut wages so low as to leave them nothing above the rents that he demanded. The American Railway Union, led by the fiery Eugene V. Debs, supported the Pullman strikers by refusing to haul trains with Pullman cars attached. The Railway magnates refused to consider arbitration. For the first time in our history, in a labor dispute, the government secured a blanket injunction under Section IV of the Sherman Act to prevent the strikers from interfering in the movement of the trains. The court issued a preliminary order restraining "any persons from interfering with, hindering, obstructing or stopping any mail train, express train or other trains, whether freight or passenger, engaged in interstate commerce . . . . And from, in any manner, interfering with, injuring, or destroying any of the property of any said railroads engaged in, or for the purpose of, or in connection with, interstate commerce . . . . Or from using threats, intimidation, force or violence to induce employees to quit the service of the railroad, or to prevent persons from entering the employment of the railroads."

When the workers ignored the court order, President Cleveland, despite the protests of Governor John Altgeld of Illinois, who insisted that he had the situation well in hand, dispatched federal troops to Chicago, and after considerable violence the strike was crushed by superior force. The men lost the strike. Cleveland's wish to preserve law and order as he saw it, had played into the hands of the Railway managers, and by the use of the injunction had involved the courts in labor disputes. Debs and other union leaders were arrested and charged with contempt of court for their refusal to obey the injunction. The presiding judge of the Circuit Court for the District of Chicago ruled that the injunction was authorized by both the Sherman Act and the common law prohibition against unlawful conspiracy, and the defendants were sentenced to six months in prison. The case was then carried to the Supreme Court which sustained the lower court's ruling. The Supreme Court refused to pass on the acceptability of the Sherman Act, and based its decision on the grounds that the government had authority over transportation of the mails and interstate commerce and that an injunction could be issued to prevent persons from jeopardizing this authority.[19]

This was the beginning of William Levi's practical education. Return-

[19]Harry J. Carman and Harold C. Syrett, *History of the American People*, (Alfred Knopf, 1952), p. 175 seq; Peddleton Herring, *The Government of Democracy*, (Norton & Co., 1950), pp. 171-172.

ing to Freeland, his thoughts centered on the weird, broad chasm between boss and worker. He thought about its implications ever after.

Widespread rumors and popular fears that the strong men of Wall Street and the trusts of the East might ultimately take over the United States, monopolize business and the sale of the necessities of life and control the lives of the ordinary small citizens, penetrated Freeland, as they did almost every town in the west. The dreary events, the bitter outcry of the "little people" who had been hurt, more than confused him. Comforts, conveniences and wealth had so piled up, reasoned William, that it almost seemed as if the whole world had been invented for a select few to play in. What was happening that prevented this new wealth which the millionaires were so happily raking in (and from which millions of Americans in the middle economic ranks were directly or indirectly benefiting) from flowing all the way down to the lower levels of American society? Neither he, the wage earner, nor his father, the farmer, was sharing in the prosperity promised them by President Cleveland and the protected trusts and manufacturers.

His father's farm in Freeland, which William shared with his wife and daughter was now under heavy mortgage. Chances of regular employment for William had not improved. As a matter of fact, they grew slimmer as employers manifested a decided tendency to import new immigrant labor at reduced wages.

For nine bewildering years after his marriage in 1893, Hutcheson used all the ingenuity at his disposal to eke out a living at a multiplicity of "marginal" jobs, varying farm work with mining and drilling water wells and intermittently constructing farm barns. For nine years he was barred from fully pursuing his chosen craft of carpentry. For nine years still, he kept trying, although by no means successfully, to overcome this cruel "penalization" and handicap. During those nine years it became necessary for his family to move from North Williams to Freeland and from Freeland to Midland. Then for intervals he was completely inactive. But during the enforced slacks his thoughts centered on how the trend of the times could be reversed, a matter of personal concern to him, affecting as it did his family's fortunes. Although the misery of 1893 had now run its full course, and prosperity returned with a rush four years later, he, Bess and the children continued to feel the heavy effects of poverty.

In 1896 William Hutcheson became eligible to cast his first vote during the McKinley-Bryant presidential campaign, the hottest, and perhaps the most furious in the whole history of the United States. The issue of using federal troops in labor disputes became an explosive one. To be sure, William was excited by the Presidential campaign and argued with the best in Freeland that Bryant, the Democratic candidate, was unsound. Hutcheson's caustic criticism of the Democratic party and its candidate on election day reportedly created an untoward incident. "A party which invoked military force to suppress the Pullman strike in Chicago is not fit to administer the American people," shouted Will Hutcheson, the six foot two inches of him towering over his listeners. "It was not radical," he persisted, "to demand that the rights of man should go hand in hand with the rights of property, lest profit should cease to be a benefit and become a menace to all Americans."

"This is Americanism, as I understand it," he exclaimed.

William's restive mind and pent-up emotions found little comfort in the Republican Party of Harrison and McKinley. He recalled with bitterness and chagrin his Idaho experience, when Republican President Harrison, like Democratic President Grover Cleveland after him, crushed the strike of miners by the use of Federal troops.

Can the promises of politicians be taken seriously, wondered William? For or against Harrison, the successful Republican candidate was elected on the main issue of the tariff. Of course, it was said to be necessary to maintain the high standard of living of the American workmen. In the same year the McKinley Bill was served up for the protected manufacturers, while a sop was thrown to the discontented in the form of the celebrated Sherman Anti-trust Act, which was supposed to make illegal the evils complained of by the people by firmly curbing the trusts. It riled Will considerably that not a single one of the accused officers of the great corporations had been imprisoned for violation of this Act.

Hutcheson's cynical view of politics was further enhanced by the experiences Eugene V. Debs had with Grover Cleveland. Here was a man who stirred Will Hutcheson's imagination, and in the contest between capital and labor, Debs — who not until a half dozen years later identified himself with the Socialist movement — stood out in William Hutcheson's mind as a reformer in behalf of labor. To Debs, the issues of the campaign between Harrison and Cleveland in 1892 seemed clear. The Republican party, firmly controlled by the business interests, had nominated Benjamin Harrison of Indiana, a combination corporation lawyer and senator who had been exceedingly hostile to the wage earners. On the other hand, the Democratic incumbent, Grover Cleveland, was a man of great personal integrity who had shown some respect for labor's rights and had been instrumental in setting up a board of voluntary arbitration for labor disputes on the railroads. So Debs agreed to share the platform with Senator Vorhys at a Democratic rally on behalf of Grover Cleveland in Terre Haute. Debs attacked Harrison and the Republicans. "I believe," he exhorted his listeners, "that when this campaign will have closed, the workingmen throughout the country will have dignified and glorified themselves and their cause by showing the people of the country that he who volunteers to organize a company of soldiers to shoot down the workingman when they are striking for their rights never can become President of this country."[20] Debs had good reason to regret his oratory when in 1894, only two years later, the Democratic President of the United States, Grover Cleveland, used federal troops to crush the Pullman strike in Chicago, and did not intervene when the outspoken Debs was sentenced to a prison term of six months on a contempt of court charge.

This was a lesson from which Hutcheson profited. A seed had been sown, and as time went on, it sprouted into a full-grown social outlook of the role of the wage earners in American society.

---

[20]Ray Ginger, *The Biography of Eugene V. Debs,* (Rutgers University Press, 1949), p. 58.

CHAPTER | III

THE BEGINNINGS OF A CAREER

On Sunday night, May 3, 1902, William came home a grim and determined man. It occurred to him then that something was wrong with the system and somebody must do something about it or one day there would be a terrific social explosion that would change the political complexion of the country. The broad chasm between employer and worker must be bridged so that the George Pullmans and George Baers (bosses of the Pullman Company and the anthracite mines, respectively) could not deny jobs to men merely because they dared to form themselves into a union. William Hutcheson felt a union was a God-given right.

Four years passed and the misery of 1893 had run its full course. Born on May 7, 1897, Maurice A. Hutcheson, like his father and grandfather before him, was then brought into the world, at the tail end of an economic depression. Eventually, there were four children, the last, Stella, born in 1900. During Will's intermittent migrations, it became necessary for Bess and the children to move in with Will's folks and later with hers —from North Williams to Freeland and again from Freeland to Midland, a radius of approximately twenty miles.

William started to look for work, now turning instinctively to his craft. He hurried, as if driven by a sense of urgency. He had no money and went directly to the Dow Chemical Company, which sprawled across the southeastern end of the city.

This chemical empire, founded by Dr. Herbert A. Dow, not only influenced Midland's physical appearance, creating a well-planned city of neat streets and distinctive architecture, but molded and shaped the social, religious, cultural and economic life of the community as well.

Founded in 1890 as the Midland Chemical Company, it was, after the lumbermen withdrew from the section, following the green frontier northward, perilously close to bankruptcy during the panic of 1893, for Dr. Dow had always needed money for his experiments and he borrowed heavily. At the turn of the century, when consolidations were in the air and assumed threatening proportions, the Midland became the Dow Chemical Company, the world's largest supplier of aspirin.

Midland had some seven thousand people. There were a few more women in its population than there were men. Slightly over sixty per cent of Midland's residents were born near or around Midland; approximately one-fourth were foreign-born, mainly Slavs, Germans, French and Scotch; the remainder had been born elsewhere in the United States. The first impression one gained of the town was that of a model company community.

More than three-quarters of the employable population were maintained by the wages and salaries of the Dow Chemical Company, the rest being farmers. The semi-skilled, constituting about one-half of the employables, were making seventeen and one-half cents an hour; the top rate for skilled artisans such as carpenters, building tradesmen, and those engaged in transportation, was twenty cents an hour with "time lost." Boys and girls between the ages of ten and fifteen, as well as common laborers, worked for twelve and one-half cents an hour when work was available. No one was very happy about working for Dow.

For twelve years no man would dare attempt to organize the Dow plant for fear of losing his job, although there were rumblings of discontent among the workers. It was an organizer's nightmare, what with the dissensions and antagonisms between the unskilled Poles and the highly skilled Germans, in addition to the company's highly effective system of ferreting out trouble-makers.

It was at the Dow Chemical Company that William Hutcheson was baptized into unionism. At first, organizing was done underground, but by 1904 a new local union was successfully launched and dared to come out in the open in Midland proper. Then the tragic mistake occurred. Those workers reported by spies as taking part in union meetings were summarily fired for "unsatisfactory service." Altogether, about 100 people were discharged, most for union activity. Yet the movement among the employees to band together and do something about their lot had caught fire and the company couldn't stop the tide. The company, however, steadfastly refused to recognize the union or meet with William Hutcheson, who had collected an enormous number of grievances from individual employees.

William's pleas to the superintendent that there must be something wrong with management, or the workers would not find themselves in the position that they were in, were rudely rebuffed with the retort that new recruits from the east and south would replace the fired "trouble makers." Two days later, Hutcheson and two of his close associates found themselves without jobs and on the blacklist.

William Hutcheson always remembered his initial unhappy experience in unionism at the Dow Chemical Company. Forty years later, on January 25, 1944, when A. F. of L. Organizer H. A. Bradley applied to the Executive Council of the American Federation of Labor for an international union charter embracing the entire industry, Hutcheson took occasion to inquire on the extent to which the Dow Chemical plant in Texas was organized. Bradley replied that, "the application is now in for Dow Chemical of Texas."[1] Then and there Hutcheson urged his fellow members on the Executive Council and President William Green to grant Bradley the charter.

To be blacklisted in a community like Midland meant almost total isolation for the Hutcheson family, as well as for William to be condemned to unemployment. It was a new experience and a strange and painful situation. But William had also learned his lesson. First, if organized labor was to succeed, it must have internal unity, good sense in its leadership and it must temper the hotheads in its ranks. In order to confront the boss, workers must first learn how to get along together. The union must appeal to collective self-interest, and a pride in workmanship.

The time had now arrived for William to abandon Midland and move his family to the Saginaws.

News of William's daring and organizing ability had already seeped through the labor fraternity by word-of-mouth of his dismissed confederates who had already abandoned Midland for Saginaw. The pilgrim's return to Saginaw was a timely one. The two carpenters' locals, 334 and 59, had, since their inception, been competing with each other, despite the fact that neither had impressive memberships. A revealing fact about these two locals was the constant ebb and flow, the persistent departure of the old, established carpenters to other jobs elsewhere, and the arrival of new ones, especially Slavic, Germanic and some English, to take their places. Also, precious energy, that might have been used in building one strong local to improve working conditions, hours and wages, was misdirected on local loyalties between east and west Saginaw. The empty treasuries of both were factors in their failure to organize. William's experience, missionary zeal and articulateness would prove invaluable to fledgling, disunited carpenters' locals in a community flexing its industrial muscles. Hutcheson knew Saginaw and the satellite communities as the surveyors knew the timber forests.

Hutcheson became business agent of both locals in 1906 at a weekly

---

[1] Interview with Louis V. Winiecke of Saginaw, Michigan, Sept. 17, 1954. Winiecke, a member of Carpenters Local 334 since Sept. 4, 1913, is now its president.

salary of $16.80. While business agent, he also acted as treasurer, his wife Bessie keeping the books for him. Riding his bicycle to cover his list of union "prospects," Will Hutcheson stirred both laughter and admiration on the part of Saginaw's residents.

Oldsters around Saginaw still chuckle as they recall a then familiar sight on the streets of Saginaw: the "lanky business agent of the Carpenters Union," his knees scraping the handle-bar and his long legs dangling clumsily from his two-wheeler, while making the rounds of the area, enroute to prospective members.

"Big Bill" covered his territory for a whole year on bicycle, until he had signed up a reasonable number of new recruits.

He then convened the union's executive board. In his characteristic straightforward manner, Bill explained to them that it wasn't fitting for a union representative to confront the boss on such unequal terms, "I on a two-wheeler and they in their handsome flivvers," as he put it.

Will made his executive board this modest offer: "If you'll pay for the oats and the axle-grease, I'll use my horse and buggy to cover the territory." After due deliberation, the board came up with a counter offer:

"Since you have to feed your horse anyway, the union oughtn't be asked to pay for anything but the axle-grease." Bill immediately recognized the justice of their counter-proposal, the wear and tear on his chariot notwithstanding, and compromised on the board's terms.

In the evening, Bill Hutcheson would make door-to-door canvasses. Not a few householders were suspicious, while others were afraid to do anything about joining. He would explain to them the whole story of the Carpenters Union, the conditions in the industry and the benefits to be derived from affiliating. Sometimes, William, tired of discussions, would not hesitate to impress his ideas on his cowardly prospects in firmer fashion. More often than not, they were persuaded and calmed. Others had no idea what a union was about, demanding to know what good it could do them! A few turned out to be good prospects. William concentrated on them, hoping that others would emulate them.

Hutcheson found himself comfortable in this environment. He instructed his prospects on the virtues and objectives of collective action, an inclination he had had since the age of seventeen, though without the chance of trying it out. He set himself to the task with an iron will, and aided by his sharp sense of realism, he soon got into step with his co-workers. His own nature served him in every way, as did the strength of his sincerity.

On the whole, Hutcheson was proud of the results of his methods. From 1906 on, he succeeded in energizing the Carpenters Local 334, markedly increasing its number of recruits. From a weak, amorphous local with a membership of approximately ninety-five, Saginaw's Carpenters Local 334 became a model for Southern Michigan, with a loyal membership of three hundred.

The Carpenters' desperate necessity to win "something" strengthened Hutcheson's determination to "bring home the bacon." This he achieved locally through the same methods he later employed most successfully on a national scale.

Hutcheson's objectives, as expressed by Louis V. Winiecke, the local's incumbent president, an erstwhile police judge of Saginaw, "were to avoid strikes and settle differences with employers by arbitration. It was not Hutcheson's policy to interfere with management, but simply to reform and improve the working conditions and hours and wages of his constituency." For the first time, Saginaw's carpenters secured an eight-hour day, at forty cents an hour and the right to observe four legal holidays in the year with pay. The standard week was six days for as long as ten hours a day.[2]

But that did not suffice him. His first act, as a delegate to the sixteenth biennial convention of the United Brotherhood of Carpenters and Joiners of America, held in Des Moines, Iowa, September, 1910, was to formulate a plan of action in Michigan designed to strengthen the organization of the unorganized, the implementation of which would require the resources of the Brotherhood in addition to the Building Trades of the A. F. of L. Thus it was that "the General President was instructed to continue the work of organization until the unions now established are strong enough to carry on the work themselves."

The State of Michigan had been among the most poorly organized in the country. The history of its union activities had been marked by political factionalism, competing unions, strikes, scabbing and violence. In 1910, the State's forty-five Carpenter locals had a total membership of 4,808, leaving five thousand unorganized.

Hutcheson's second concern was with the effects of industrialization on the health of the carpenters. This he revealed in another resolution, which was submitted to the same convention. He called for the appointment of a committee, the object of which was to consider means, with the view of "establishing mineral baths, maintained by the U. B. for those of our fellow workers who are afflicted with rheumatism and kindred diseases, resulting from exposure, while working at the trade." That year the Brotherhood paid out to its membership $24,800 in disability benefits, 23.5% of whom suffered from fatal industrial accidents; 15.5% of the recipients were adversely affected by complications of all types; 13.5% suffered from nephritis; 5% from pneumonia; 3% had typhoid fever; 4% had apoplexy; 3% hemorrhage. Hutcheson's own

---

[2]*Saginaw News, May 13, 1912; A.F.L. Weekly News Service,* June 1, 1912.

fledgling local in Saginaw was a beneficiary in the amount of six hundred dollars.

This was the extent of the practical service that this thirty-six year old initiate attempted to render to his fellow unionists. His ideas had their source in suffering, the evils of casual work, and ambition. Very soon his projects were to become as precise as a plan of battle. To make his ideas triumph was a matter of conquering the world. He needed, first of all, an intensely loyal constituency of militant co-workers, with himself as general, who would make battle and serve the cause of the carpenters.

During the five years between 1910 and 1915, Hutcheson was engaged in as arduous a battle as he had so far attempted, in order to make his place in the sun.

Following the advice of his constituency, he accepted the nomination for the post of General Executive Board Member from the Third District of the United Brotherhood of Carpenters, an office for which the holder received "the sum of four dollars a day for such part of their time as is used in the service of the U. B." Hutcheson lost that race to John H. Potts of Cincinnati, a delegate older in years and in tenure.

But William Hutcheson did not declare himself beaten as quickly as all that, although he was pleased with his appointment to the Finance Committee instead. In the meantime, his objective was to organize the carpenters of Saginaw. This he was to achieve after a short-lived strike of 48 hours duration, in June, 1912, when both east and west Saginaw became unionized. The Carpenters Union won recognition, as well as a raise in wages, from forty cents to forty-five cents an hour, a rate higher than that prevailing in larger urban areas throughout the United States.

But the son of the migrant worker prepared to win the second lap. Almost half of his life had been telescoped into a relatively brief period of intensive transformation. Saginaw had not been sufficiently challenging for one who had been subjected to generating movements and influences. With the aid of the loyal friends who came to know him in the U. B., he was able to effect his first leap on January 20, 1913, when he was elected by ballot to the office of the Second General Vice-President, which was created in September, 1910. Not much later, when Arthur A. Quinn of New Jersey resigned as First General Vice-President, Hutcheson filled his position, on May 1, 1913.

Accompanied by his sixteen year-old son Maurice, who forty-two years later succeeded him to the General Presidency of the United Brotherhood of Carpenters & Joiners of America, William Hutcheson boarded the train for Indianapolis, leaving Bess and the children behind in Saginaw "until Maurice and I find a comfortable place to live.[3]

[3]Interview with Maurice A. Hutcheson, Indianapolis, Ind.

PART II

CHALLENGE and RESPONSE

CHAPTER | IV

THE LEADER AND THE LED

William Hutcheson's rise to the presidency of the United Brotherhood of Carpenters and Joiners of America, on October 8, 1915, was
more than an accident, albeit his elevation to that office was the result
of a *vis-major*, the death of President James Kirby. Hutcheson was past
the age of forty-one, which was the average age of his thirteen predecessors, two of whom, John D. Allen and W. J. Shields, were each thirty-
two years old when they assumed the office of the presidency. Hutcheson's emergence as a major labor leader was illustrative of an era, when
labor, on the one hand, had been in almost constant retreat, fighting a
continuous rear-guard action for its survival, and on the other hand,
the dawn of a new era, during which labor challenged the existing order
of things, seeking rather consciously and aggressively an improved status
for its group. This was the period of the "consumption-minded," other-
directed personality labor leader, rather than the "inner-directed" mor-
alizer of the not-too-distant past.[1]

This was the period that gave us John L. Lewis of the United Mine
Workers of America, and contemporaneously William Levi Hutcheson
of the United Brotherhood of Carpenters and Joiners of America. Their
emergence at that time was labor's reaction to industrial authoritarianism,
which reached its peak before World War I. It was labor's reaction to
the martial vices so skillfully developed by the employers at that time.
Their arrival coincided with labor's determination to match by aggressive
collective action the centralization of power inherent in the industrial
giants and combines.

That America needed aggressive leadership was amply proved by
the dismal conditions such as prevailed at the concluding decade of the
last century on to World War I.[2] The worker's need to compensate

---

[1]David Riesman, *The Lonely Crowd.* (Doubleday Anchor Books, 1935), p. 203.
[2]Harold V. Faulkner, *The Decline of Laissez Faire, 1897-1917* (Rinehart & Co.,
1951), pp. 289-309.

for, as well as to balance, the unbalanced disproportion of power introduced into modern life by large-scale production and distribution, became a necessary pre-condition to his survival and welfare. This desire for balance became necessary only because the great disparities and disbalances of power between the giant corporation and the worker prevented competitive bargaining from being free and equitable. The worker's economic weakness, compared with the strength and financial resources of the company, not only made it difficult, but well-nigh impossible to bargain at all. The development and pressure of large-scale industrial units, with their inevitable centralization of power, thus created the need for another type of organization, as an offset. The growth, then, of the modern giant corporation and the concentration of economic power created the growth of the larger national union, acting as an offset to the former. Furthermore, these national unions could survive only by developing such leaders as were able to impose their authority by autocratic methods.[3]

The character of a labor union, also the personalities who led it, depended to a great extent on the nature of the opposition which it met and the industry in which it operated. Scientists concerned with the behavior of human individuals and human institutions have frequently called our attention to the fact that unions that grow up in an atmosphere of struggle are, like national states, agencies of conflict.[4] Because of this, more power must frequently be delegated to officials, with more secrecy and fewer controls than might seem desirable in organizations that do not live in an environment of conflict.

Many of the moral problems involving the relations of the individual to his union, or the responsibility of a union official to his constituency, or the autocratic structure of the union itself, have risen out of the fact that unions grew up in an atmosphere of struggle and tension. And, in order better to defend themselves in the struggle with the "outsider," they necessarily depended on the twin supports — intense loyalty of the constituents, and agressive leadership.

It took twenty years more for the community to realize that the violence used by business and industry were incompatible with the general cultural framework in which it operated, and it was not until the 1930's that these tactics brought down upon it the almost universal condemnation of society and the law.

The key position of the leader in our own time arose, not merely because he occupied a central position in the chain of the control mechanism of his union, but also because he set up a new mechanism or

---

[3]Frank Tennenbaum, *A Philosophy of Labor*, (Knopf, 1951), pp. 114-137.

[4]Kenneth E. Boulding, *The Organizational Revolution*, (Harper and Bros., 1953), p. 105.

modified the old. The new labor leader, in order to "right wrongs" and obtain economic and "psychological" advantages vis-a-vis the highly efficient, large-scale industrial organization, was necessarily an organizer, a creator of organization, rather than an "executive." Organizational weaknesses or defects in the union's structure had to be reduced to an absolute minimum. "Social distance" between the organizer, members of the General Executive Committee and the rank and file receivers at the end of the line tended to prevent the national union from fulfilling those functions which it intended to serve.

Neither Hutcheson, nor Lewis, Hillman or Dubinsky were executives. All four were innovators, creative entrepreneurs, who organized, created new structures, new combinations of factors, or modified those that tended to slow the progress of the organization. As leaders of four major unions, they created roles rather than filled them. They were the square pegs in a round hole that did something to square the hole. Each came to a major role and did something to change it. It was the impact of their leadership and of their dominant personalities that provided their respective unions with collective social power and prestige, without which they could not obtain justice in the new technical era.

For thirty-six years, William Levi Hutcheson served in the role of leader-organizer of the Carpenters. For those thirty-six years, he sought not simply to maintain his own power and personal integrity, but to offer policies that had the most meaning to his followers. During those years he was the Carpenters' fighting spokesman and single-minded champion.

At forty-one, when he succeeded to the key position of the presidency, the Brotherhood had an extended, unwieldly structure, threatened by internal breakdowns in its communications system. Extending its *lebensraum* to fourteen sub-divisions of the woodworking trade, the Brotherhood grew to a membership of over 261,000, with 2,015 local unions, 132 district councils and 14 state and provincial councils. The existing gaps between the national union and the large metropolitan district councils required correction. Powerful local leaders opposed "outside" interference in local affairs of the local unions and autonomous district councils. Small local unions created for a pre-big industry era made for inefficient, unbusinesslike government. Heterogeneity was accentuated by the existence of French, German, Swedish, Hungarian and Jewish local unions; as late as 1918 the Brotherhood's official monthly, *The Carpenter,* printed German and French sections. Inadequacies of leadership, evinced by a preference to function within the framework of the existing organizational structure, did not hasten the process of amalgamation and centralization.

The need to strengthen and centralize this unstable structure of the Brotherhood had already been apparent during the administrations of William D. Huber and James Kirby,[5] Hutcheson's predecessors, and a series of steps to correct its defects had been taken. But it was not until the nineteenth convention, in 1916, that the streamlining process was instituted in earnest.

Constitutional changes devised to strengthen as well as extend the authority and powers of the chief officers of the Brotherhood were easily effected.[6] In addition to extensive control over organizing and administration, the new incumbent General President was voted authority to intervene in the affairs of local unions and district councils, or "suspend those which either willfully or directly violated the Constitution, laws or principles of the Brotherhood with the consent of the General Executive Board." The General President was also given power to merge two or more local unions and "to enforce consolidation provided such course received the sanction of the General Executive Board." Authority to try members who were found guilty of offenses against the union laws was also granted to him. Further, the Brotherhood's constitution made it mandatory that "no member shall hold an office unless he is a citizen of the United States or Canada." Henceforth, all union business was to be conducted in the English language.

Section 58 of the amended Constitution granted the General President authority to supervise trade movements, i.e., strikes and lockouts, on the ground that since many contractors did work of an interstate character, "such movements would involve the members in districts other than the one directly affected." No trade movement "was to become effective until such time as the General President had been notified and given an opportunity to make an effort, either in person or by representative, to bring about an adjustment of the controversy." This meant a diminution in the power of the district councils. It meant also that the Brotherhood as a universal bargaining agent was seeking a much greater degree of uniformity in wages and working conditions in the bargaining area.

To make laws and adjustments in conformity with new needs in a changing industry, or amend the union's constitutional procedure, was one thing. But to compel obedience on the proud, powerful, and parochial district councils was another. These local unions and the District Council clearly wanted both: to eat their cake and have it too; to gain all the benefits of a large national union, the Brotherhood, but not to subordinate themselves to its procedures, or surrender an ounce of their

---

[5]*U.B.C.J.A. Proceedings Seventeenth Convention,* (1914) pp. 637-692.
[6]*U.B.C.J.A. Proceedings Nineteenth Convention,* (1916) pp. 252 seq.

freedom of action; to help pass laws giving the chief officer authority over local affairs, but to raise an enormous clatter when he enforced them. And no group of carpenters needed taming more than did the New York locals.

The New York City Building Trades were a law unto themselves, not only in their relations with other New York City unions, but also in their dealings with their respective international bodies, with the A. F. of L., and later the Building Trades Department. To be sure, their negative character and behavior mirrored the environment which surrounded them. Even as mere fledglings at the close of the last century, they demanded special consideration.

New York building techniques were more than a decade in advance of other cities, and New York building activities involved more capital than those of any other city in the continental United States. With this early advantageous beginning, the institution of building trades came to maturity earlier in New York City than elsewhere. Consequently, independent local unions of various building trades were strongly entrenched in New York years before "national" unions were formed. The communication-executive-effector chain between the New York Carpenters and the United Brotherhood was loose, and at best, nominal.

In 1908 the employers organized themselves as the Building Trades Employers Association, and the various building trades unions, through their business agents, as the Board of Business Agents, which consisted of all the business agents of each of the various building trade unions. They had met as a group, elected their officers, and acted together on strikes, lockouts, and collective bargaining negotiations. Together, these two groups, the Employers' Association and the Business Agents, regulated New York City building and construction to their own satisfaction and to the exclusion of the various national unions. They settled jurisdictional matters in their own way without consulting national union officers, banned sympathetic striking and practiced rigid control over skills.

The Board of Business Agents refused to accept a Building Trades Council charter from the Building Trades Department of the A. F. of L. because the Department's laws prohibited agreements such as they had with the Building Trades Employers Association. At the 1913 convention of the Building Trades Department the presidents of the various unions showed increasing concern with the reckless autonomy of their New York locals.

In 1915, when Hutcheson assumed the presidency, New York City with its five boroughs had 73 local unions, comprising a membership of under 17,000 Carpenters. Of these, no less than 40 percent of the locals were organized on the basis of ethnic origin. There were German-speaking locals, Norwegian, Swedish, Hungarian and Jewish, each promoting its own rather than the common interest. Claims to jobs and jurisdictions were borough-wide. Carpenters, in search of work in boroughs other than their own were barred. Exorbitant initiation fees and assessments frequently restricted the job-seeker to his own borough.[7] A contemporary building trades' delegate reports "it was not at all an uncommon practice for the business agent to favor members of his own local with jobs in preference to others. . . . And as for favors, the business agent surely would not think of wasting his generosity on strangers whom he had to face only once a year, during city-wide elections. . . . It was a hard fight to try and break down the traditional system of favoritism. My early struggle for centralized control so as to minimize the practice of favoritism and discrimination was not popular with the 'active' members. . . ."[8] Multiple localisms, parochial, sectional interests and even ethnic divisions did not make for unity in the New York Carpenters family.

This, in brief, was the situation when Hutcheson rose to the presidency.

In such circumstances, it wasn't surprising that Hutcheson's career as general president had started on the organizational and technical level, a grave responsibility that no chief officer in the annals of trade unionism had ever been eager to assume.[9] He had not been in office more than seven weeks when a dispute arose between the United Brotherhood, its officers, the general executive committee and the New York District Council. Actually, the controversy reached back to May, 1914, when President Kirby, Hutcheson's predecessor, had shown considerable reluctance to intervene in the affairs of the District Council. At that time, Oliver Collins, secretary of the New York District Council, requested permission to strike. The general executive committee of the Brotherhood refused to sanction a strike on the ground that only about forty percent, or 7,187 of the District Council's membership of 16,500 voted in its favor. On July 31, secretary general Duffy explained to Collins the reasons why the Brotherhood could not sanction such movement:

> "Owing to the lack of thorough organization, the large number of men out of work and the fact that fifty-one percent of the members involved did not vote in favor of the demand, the Board cannot see its way clear at this time to grant official sanction desired . . ."[10]

[7] For the above information, the writer is indebted to Messrs. Charles W. Hanson, president and Daniel Quigley, vice-president of the District Council of Carpenters of New York & Vicinity.

[8] Philip Zausner, *Unvarnished, The Autobiography of a Union Leader* (Brotherhood Publishers, 1941), pp. 97-98.

[9] Phillip Taft, *The Structure of Government of Labor Unions.* (Harvard University Press, 1954), Chapter IV.

[10] U.B.C.J.A., *Proceedings* (1914), pp. 764-769.

When the New York District Council appealed the ruling of the General Executive Board to the 1914 convention, the delegates backed the ruling of the Board as part of the centralization program and wrote it into the Constitution.

The New York Carpenters had been restive for several years, having failed to obtain a pay increase from their employers for nine consecutive years. Largely responsible for this condition was the inefficient and inept leadership of the District Council.

The New York District Council leaders had failed sadly. For 2 years, no new members had been recruited for the union to maintain its position, although there was an increase in building construction activity. Eight thousand floating, unorganized carpenters in New York and environs sapped the strength of the unions, thereby keeping wages continuously low. Much bickering, and weak leadership not only affected the efficiency of the union in collective bargaining but even permitted the rise of corrupt practices among the agents, injurious to the members' economic welfare.

Nor was the relationship between the Carpenters' Council and the Building Trades Employers' Association a friendly one. The attitude of the old-timers in the District Council toward the Employers' Association was one of hostility. "The building trades unions of that era almost without exception had nothing but contempt for the Association and for arbitration or mediation as a substitute for avoidable strikes. The old building trades' concept was that the bosses couldn't be trusted, that the only purpose for which they combined into an association was to fight and oppress labor, that arbitration and mediation were the bosses' ruses to deprive labor of the opportunity for its rights.[11]

"This new form of relationship (employers' association) between the union and the employers tended to weaken certain of the powers of the council and the business agents. The old custom of placing a number of bosses on the unfair list on the council meeting night and restoring them to good standing within a short time for reasons which aroused suspicion received a terrific blow . . . The larger and more substantial employers could no longer be placed on the unfair list, often on flimsy grounds, to be restored to the fair list the next day on equally questionable grounds."[12]

But the contractors affiliated with the Building Trades Employers' Association controlled the greater part of New York's building construction work. They built New York's rising skyscrapers, factory buildings, wharves, and the transit system. Not a few operated on a nationwide scale. On the whole, these building contractors employed large crews

[11]Philip Zausner, *op. cit.*, pp. 97-98.
[12]*Proceedings*, supra, p. 99.

of building tradesmen. There was also an unaccountable number of so-called "lumpers", or subcontractors or independent contractors, a considerable number of whom were former union foremen. In the main, they gave spotty employment to "green hands", at less than the prevailing union wage-scales, as compared to the more "legitimate" and stable contractors who were affiliated with the Association.

In the spring of 1916, building was looking up, and the New York Carpenters wanted a raise more than ever. Secretary Elbridge Neal of the New York District Council appeared before the General Executive Board and requested permission to turn out on May 1, 1916, if necessary, to gain a fifty cents per day increase in four of the boroughs and sixty cents a day advance in Manhattan. After a long session, the Board gave reluctant consent and agreed to give financial aid in, "such sums as the funds will warrant to any strike which ensues," with the understanding that the New York District Council reduce the initiation fee to five dollars, and an organizing drive be gotten under way among the eight thousand non-union carpenters, and that a fund be created for the protection of the men who may be called out.[13]

On March 3, 1916, Neal opened negotiations with the representatives of the Building Trades Employers' Association. The best offer of the Employers' Association was a thirty cents a day increase to go into effect October 1, 1916. The District Council representative proposed that the increase take effect August 1, 1916. The Employers' Association refused, maintaining that "the unions know fully well that, unlike the lumpers, we are right in the middle of big construction jobs which were undertaken by us on the old wage rates."[14]

Neal's failure to reach a settlement with the Building Trades Employers' Association was once again considered at the regularly-scheduled second quarterly meeting of the General Executive Board, on April 10. On that day the Board invoked the ruling that if an agreement "could not be reached before May 1, our members (Carpenters) must not be called on strike until the General President or his representatives have an opportunity to bring about a settlement."[15] At this time, the Board moved rather slowly. Meanwhile, Neal continued negotiations, which had started on March 3, with the employers. The best offer of the Employers' Association was still 30 cents a day raise, to go into effect October 1, 1916. Neal again responded by accepting the offer if that date were moved up to August 1. The Employers' Association refused.

---

[13]*The Carpenter*, Vol. XXXVI: 2 (February, 1916), p. 28; *N. Y. Times* May 2, 1916, pp. 20, 23.

[14]Interview with Christian G. Norman, late Chairman Emeritus of the Building Trades Employers' Association.

[15]Frank Duffy, *Hist. of the U.B.C.J.A.* (MSS), p. 398.

Ten days later, on April 20, Secretary General Frank Duffy wrote Elbridge Neal "not to remove the men from work until such time as the General President had been notified and given an opportunity to make an effort . . . to bring about an adjustment . . ."[16]

Indianapolis, Ind.,
April 20, 1916

Mr. E. H. Neal, Secretary
New York Carpenters' District Council
142 East 59th Street
New York, New York

Dear Sir and Brother:

At a meeting of our General Executive Board held at this office on April 18th General President Hutcheson brought to the attention of that body the situation regarding the proposed trade movement for an increase in wages in New York and vicinity. After the most careful consideration of all the facts in the case it was decided that if an agreement could not be reached before May 1st, our members must not be called on strike until the General President has an opportunity, through a representative, to bring about a settlement.

With best wishes and kindest regards, I am,

Fraternally yours,
FRANK DUFFY, General Secretary

The proud and arrogant New York District Council ignored these instructions. Its business agents called the men out on strike on May 1, to enforce the demands.

Roughly, ten thousand men turned out on May 1.

The "lumpers" and independent contractors capitulated as they usually did in boom times. The spring of 1916 witnessed considerable construction in the apartment-house field. Speculative builders were putting up rows of houses in one single operation. "The subcontractors were pitted against each other in merciless throat-cutting competition. The chief aims of most of these contractors seemed to be more and still more contracts, regardless of price. Since the wage element was as high as seventy percent of the contract price, the entire competitive structure rested on labor costs, and these, in spite of nominally prevailing union-scales, were actually anything from the union rate down to next to nothing."[17]

While the "lumpers" and speculators promptly acquiesced to Neal's original demand for a fifty cent a day increase, it was the going practice to make any temporary concession contingent upon the ultimate scales set in the final settlement with the powerful B.T.E.A. In actual practice the majority of these independent contractors seldom adhered to the letter of their union agreements, which were hardly ever reduced to writing. "The actual wage paid these men was less than $3.00 a day and

---

[16]UB.C.J.A. Proceedings (1916), p. 399.
[17]Philip Zausner, op. cit., pp. 74-75.

some as little as $2.00 to $2.25.”* Under this arrangement approximately ten thousand carpenters went back to work. The Building Trades Employers' Association proclaimed its determination to resist the District Council's "pressure tactics."

Hutcheson arrived in New York four days later to apprise himself of conditions and to attempt to bring about a wage settlement. He closeted himself with the officers of the District Council, who frankly confessed that they were "helpless". They could neither get further wage increases from the Employers' Association nor protect the United Brotherhood's jurisdiction in New York.[18]

The national union had spent considerable sums of money to protect and maintain its jurisdiction in New York, but the District Council officers had not proved capable of fulfilling their primary obligations both to the constituency and the Brotherhood.

Although Hutcheson had his share of misgivings about the New York Employers' Association, desperate necessity, economic considerations and those of tactic required that he promptly meet with their representatives in an effort to settle the strike. Mr. Christian Norman, the late President Emeritus of the B.T.E.A. whom we had interviewed thirty-eight years later, on October 17, 1954, well recalled the fierce displeasure, condescension and arrogance to which the Brotherhood's new president was exposed. They "wielded a big stick". They accused the Carpenters' District Council of creating moral tensions between the employers of the association and the workmen. But Hutcheson did not retreat. He pointed out that members of the Association had violated their commitments to the carpenters, that the wages were pitifully low, that they hadn't received a single raise in nine consecutive years; that a detailed agreement would be carried out with rigidity.[19] He was bent on establishing bona fide collective bargaining procedures with the more "legitimate", powerful contractors, who, by the practiced customs of the trade, set the wage-scale for the unwieldy and highly competitive construction industry.

After several conferences, Hutcheson effected a settlement which provided that the striking carpenters in all five boroughs were to get fifty cents a day increase, half of it to take effect on July 1, and the other half on August 1. Under this settlement, Hutcheson succeeded in getting twenty cents more per day for the carpenters, to take effect

---

*In speaking of the building trades, Zausner has pointed out that whenever a business agent came on the job to examine the cards to determine whether or not the men were in good standing and to ask them what they were getting, all men, regardless of their ability to understand or speak English, were rehearsed in the one important answer: "Four dollars." (Philip Zausner *op. cit.*, pp. 75-76.)

18*U.B.C.J.A. Proceedings* (1916), p. 43.
19*Ibid.*

August 1, than Elbridge Neal was willing to accept on either March 3 or April 30, when his negotiations with the Employers' Association collapsed. At that time, the best offer of the B.T.E.A. Employers' Association was a thirty cents a day raise, to go into effect on October 1. The raise in wages per day under Hutcheson's agreement was uniform in all five boroughs of the city. Hutcheson stated that he made the settlement "in order to eliminate the levies that the Manhattan locals placed on Brooklyn brothers who were tempted to Manhattan by higher scales."**

Hutcheson's gains exposed the ineffectiveness of the District Council's leaders. From the very beginning, Neal had demonstrated an unwillingness to abide by the rules and instructions of the national officers. To be sure, he was strongly opposed to "outside" interference in his local affairs. The history of unionism has been replete with instances in which local leaders and their followers have come into conflict with the international officers of large centralized organizations.[20]

Before leaving New York, Hutcheson and his aides, despite the obstruction of the District Council officers, proceeded over the weekend to communicate with the striking carpenters. On Monday, May 6, he called a mass meeting at Cooper Union. Although it was short notice, 800 carpenters showed up in the afternoon of that day. Hutcheson announced the terms of the settlement, advising the strikers to return to work on Tuesday, May 7. The leaders of the District Council and their followers who attended the meeting denied Hutcheson's right to make terms for the union.*** they announced that they would hold a

---

**For a very illuminating and objective study of the highly ramified workings governing the industrial relations in the building industry, see William Haber, *Industrial Relations in the Building Industry*, (Harvard Univ. Press), 1930, pp. 250 seq.

[20]Philip Taft, *op. cit.*, pp. 128-134.

***Describing the behavior of labor unions, their government and union discipline, Professor Taft makes the following pertinent comment: . . . "In addition to extensive control over organizing and administration, the Chief Executive frequently is given authority to intervene in the affairs of local unions, and, if necessary, appoint an administrator. Locals may be operated inefficiently or they may be led by corrupt and oppressive leaders who are willing to sacrifice the interests of the membership. Chief officers are given the power, in many unions, not only to intervene in the affairs of the local unions under certain circumstances, but to try members who are guilty of offenses against union law. This type of clause is necessary, for local members may refuse to take action against a popular or powerful figure guilty of violating the rules and practices of the union. In some unions Executive officers are given wide grants of power, but usually this is the result of some earlier action being challenged successfully in the courts. In other words, a narrow interpretation by the courts of the rights of the heads of unions over their locals compels the organizations, if they are to have the means to handle inefficiency, corruption, and oppression to extend the powers in this area of their chief executives. It is erroneous to assume that whenever intervention in the affairs of locals takes place the locals usually are in the right or that intervention is against the interests of the members. Like the medieval king's court, the central organization is often the guardian of the rights of members against powerful local "barons." (Philip Taft, *The Structure and Government of Labor Unions*. Harvard University Press, 1954, p. 127).

meeting on May 8 as a protest.

On May 8, leaders of the District Council held their own protest meeting and rejected Hutcheson's settlement. In response to the defiant attitude of the carpenters who refused to accept the terms reached in the agreement between the General President and the Employers' Association, the chief officer of the Brotherhood telegraphed James Morrissey, chairman of the New York Carpenters District Council, cautioning that suspension would follow if the members would not immediately return to work.

Four days later, on May 12, Hutcheson called an emergency meeting of the General Executive Board. At that time, he was instructed to leave for New York and make one last attempt to persuade the rebel locals and the District Council to accept the settlement.

It was at this time that Hutcheson invoked the authority of the Brotherhood's constitution, which granted the chief officer of the union the authority not only to make settlements with employers but to enforce them as well. Members of 63 local unions, on the wishes of their entrenched local business agents, had refused to abide by the agreement. The penalty for violating the constitution and union law was suspension.

Just so that members of the suspended local unions would have an opportunity to retain their standing and benefits of the Brotherhood, they were notified by the national union that they could transfer their memberships to non-suspended locals. But Neal applied for and obtained a temporary injunction which restrained the Brotherhood and the General President from enforcing the union laws that were "made by referendum vote of the entire membership."

The temporary injunction was granted to attorney Morris Hillquit, well-known Socialist leader, at a hearing on August 7, 1916, before Judge J. A. Mullen of the New York State Supreme Court in Bronx County.[21] It restrained Hutcheson as chief officer of the Brotherhood, from exercising the constitutional power granted him under Section 30 of the General Laws of the constitution. This section empowered the General President to place under trust and in safe-keeping . . . "all property, books, charter and funds held by, or in the name of, or on behalf of said (suspended) local unions . . . until such time as they shall reorganize."

This is not the place to discuss the wisdom or unwisdom of Judge Mullen's restraining order, although the judiciary had not infrequently demonstrated a lack of sympathy with or knowledge of union procedure and behavior.

What was at issue now was the broad problem of union discipline:

---

[21]Neal Hutcheson v., 106 N.Y.S., 1007-1010, (1916).

the refusal of locally entrenched leaders to accept the rules of the national union which they helped to formulate; localism versus centralized rule; a constitutionally strengthened leader who refused to permit the existence of small, weak and divided local unions and the perpetuation of an inefficient local "barony" which for years operated without concern for its members who supported the organization.

The procurement of a permanent injunction by the New York District Council, the resort of the rebel leaders to the civil courts, understandably provoked Hutcheson. It was "a weapon that has been used by those who opposed labor." The Brotherhood had been subjected to many costly actions in the civil courts at the hands of open shop employers over the years, and the litigation instituted by the U.B.'s own members in the New York District against their parent organization aroused in him a feeling of "loathing and contempt" for the recalcitrants. It was that action on the part of the rebels that ultimately led to the final expulsion of the sixty-three locals.[22] This sentiment was likewise expressed by the committee of five elected by the five hundred delegates attending the nineteenth convention of the Brotherhood.

". . . We find that more injurious than all this to trade unionists, was the action of the said suspended Local Unions and District Council in applying for and securing an injunction against William Hutcheson individually and the United Brotherhood, its officers, representatives . . ."[23]

The New York District Council not only resorted to the civil court, but created a football atmosphere, which was accompanied by an immense amount of palaver, histrionics, game playing, recriminations, and general emotional hysteria. Determination of wages was all but forgotten with the football field free-for-all. Dethroned local leaders and aggrieved business agents circulated appeals among the members of the Brotherhood. To win "rooters", they distributed circulars in which they subjected the chief officer of the International to calumnies and diatribes designed to incite the membership against him.[24]

The suspended local unions sent sixty-one delegates to the nineteenth biennial convention on September 18, but they were not recognized by the Credentials Committee. On the second day of the convention, a special trial committee of five, selected out of eighteen nominees, opened its hearings, which lasted seven days. The trial committee heard the testimony of the accused and of witnesses and examined whatever documents were submitted. On the eighth day, at the conclusion of the hearing, a motion to hear a report of the committee was brought to a

---

[22]E. E. Cummins, "Political and Social Philosophy of the Carpenters' Union," *Political Science Quarterly*, Vol. XLII (1924) pp. 404-408 and passim.

[23]*U.B.C.J.A. Proceedings* (1916), p. 399.

[24]Appeal of Local Union 376 of N.Y.C. of U.B.C.J.A., p. 25.

roll call and lost by thirty-nine votes. On September 28, the last day of the convention, delegate Howet read the decision of the trial committee. The committee recommended that the suspended unions be rechartered by the Brotherhood; that the "consolidation of the rechartered local unions should not exceed twenty-five"; that these unions should "become affiliated with a new District Council of New York and vicinity", and to be formed by and under the authority of the General Executive Board or by such agents as the General President may designate. The trial committee further recommended that the "benefits of the members, as far as donations from the General Office were concerned, be resumed and therefore continue uninterrupted after proper financial settlements have been made . . . by the suspended local unions."[25]

A quick application of the brakes was in order.

The time had come for strong leadership to intervene in the inevitable conflicts between "localism" and centralized rule. One "bad" variation would upset a number of significant variables in the organizational structure of the Brotherhood. Rambunctious, "tough" New York was not to be permitted to defy the rules of the organization. "Without rules and the power of enforcement, unions could neither defend their own standards from erosion, nor could they compel the acceptance of terms agreed upon with the employers whenever obedience was unacceptable to a minority of the membership."[26]

Could a weak leadership have compelled obedience of local unions found guilty of violating their obligations?

"As one examines the instances in which local unions were taken over by the international, it is obvious that . . . intervention may be in defense of all or part of the local members, or because of the refusal of a local union to accept the rules of the international or contract negotiated on a regional level. In large organizations, occasional conflicts between "localism" and centralized rule are inevitable. The large power granted in some international unions exists to enable the international to intervene in local situations in the general interest of the union . . . There is no evidence that unions in which the central organization has considerable power intervene freely in local affairs . . . In fact, the opposite seems to be true. Failure of the international to supervise the locals effectively can lead to serious abuses. The ideal situation is one in which a large measure of autonomy exists in practice, but the international union can, if necessary, intervene. Extreme localism does not necessarily lead to democratic or even efficient organization."[27]

25*U.B.C.J.A. Proceedings* (1916), p. 400.
26Philip Taft, *op. cit.*, p. 123.
27*Ibid*, pp. 133-134.

At no time since 1916 has the Brotherhood found it necessary to suspend local unions or invoke international supervision. In fact, in the last several years, very few locals have been taken over by the International. "Out of 2,104 locals functioning in the Carpenters' Union in 1946, two were suspended under the jurisdiction of the President," reports Professor Taft.

It has been the mark of a good organizer to find a final solution for a problem rather than juggle it. That Hutcheson faced and corrected this unwanted deviation during the first six months of his presidency rather than tread softly as his predecessors had done previously, was characteristic of the virile leadership he manifested throughout his 36 years in office. The exigencies of the times required that William Hutcheson display courage in order to emerge the "bonnie fechter" to his entire constituency as well as to his opponents across the bargaining table.

It was largely due to this decisiveness that New York's District Council of Carpenters has grown into one of the Brotherhood's vital outposts with a membership of thirty-two thousand. In bold contrast to the year 1916, the Council now boasts of setting the wage pattern for other construction unions in the world's largest metropolis.

CHAPTER | V

THE HEROIC AGE

The very conditions that placed the confused, inefficient and narrow New York locals under receivership had now been eliminated by Hutcheson. As head of the Brotherhood he was forced to assume jurisdiction of the 63 locals until their officers agreed to abide by the rules of the organization. Sixty-three out of seventy-four locals, less than three percent of the Carpenters' local unions, cut across by various national lines and reducing the solidarity of the whole, were now welded into a tightly-knit vital outpost of twenty-two local unions, adding to the over-all strength of the Brotherhood. The attitude of the General President on reclaiming the New York locals was set forth in his report to the nineteenth convention. Hutcheson noted:

"To my knowledge such a condition as has been created in New York has never been paralleled in the history of the organization, as the former District Council saw fit to go into the Civil Courts and ask for an injunction. . . . In every well regulated institution or organization it is necessary to have laws, rules and regulations for the Government of such bodies, and in the laws of our Brotherhood we have outlined a course our members who have a grievance may follow, and whether it be an individual member, local union or District Council should make no difference."[1]

The relative emphasis which Hutcheson placed upon *organization* during the initial period of his administration was, in fact, a recognition of the new forces that were pressing for a change in an increasingly technical age. Hutcheson felt most acutely, that if the Carpenters' union were to become a unit of autonomous power and strength, it was his responsibility as a leader to eliminate the segregative characteristics,

[1]UBCJA, *Proceedings* (1916), p. 44.

make it into a smooth, cohesive and responsible instrument for the protection of the interest and rights of his constituents. Hutcheson wanted more than a transitory victory. In justifying his intervention in the New York conflict, he sought to appeal to the intelligence of the delegates, gathered at the convention in 1916, in Fort Worth, Texas. Like an educator in the broadest sense of that term, he explained that the General officer of the central union can approach the task before him in a "calm, dispassionate manner, and usually knows and has at his command statistics showing conditions in cities in which the trade movement is contemplated; he is ready with argument to convince the employers of the justness of the demand of our members. These means, thus employed by our general officers have tended to prevent ill-advised movements and to increase the interest of our organization and to teach the employers that we are not a body of irresponsible men who do not keep agreements made, but that we are an organization of mechanics who believe in justness and fairness."[2]

"Leadership cannot be spasmodic," Hutcheson often reiterated to this writer. "I have in the course of my career as a labor leader insisted upon being myself and refused to truckle to people." John L. Lewis, in speaking of Hutcheson, whom he knew intimately for nearly four decades, remarked: "He [Hutcheson] was a strong man. He was never an inconsistent man. He met his problems head-on. He was always forthright in his advocacy of any issues in which he took a stand."[3]

But Hutcheson's real "challenge" that was to test his leadership qualities was yet to come. It required the application of all his accumulated experiences, a guiding social-political philosophy of the role of labor, courage and foresightedness. His "response" came as Hutcheson confronted a series of new developments and conditions literally unique in American history. For the first time the American wage earner had it in his power to gain measurably in status as well as advance unionization under uniquely favorable conditions of wartime scarcity. These clearly emerging signs that bode well for American labor had not escaped him, though they seemingly eluded labor's leadership.

As the tempo of the war was gaining momentum in Europe, Hutcheson observed the mere beginnings of a social awakening. He observed, also, that these were the outgrowths of an economic situation, rather than an improvement of the conscience of employers. In 1914 when Henry Ford established the five dollar-day-minimum wage, it was considered by most people to be extreme radicalism. Most business men were indignant: Ford was ruining the labor market, he was putting crazy

---

[2]*Ibid*, p. 42.

[3]Interview with John L. Lewis, on Tuesday, June 15, 1954, in headquarters of the United Mine Workers of America, Washington, D. C.

ideas into workmen's heads, he would embarrass companies, which couldn't possibly distribute such largess, he was a crude self-advertiser. People with tenderer minds hailed Ford for his generosity and said that he was showing what a noble conscience could achieve in the hitherto unregenerate precincts of industry. Meanwhile the Ford plant was mobbed by applicants for jobs.

At that time the going wage in the automobile industry averaged two dollars and forty cents per nine-hour day. What Ford had actually done — in his manufacturing techniques, his deliberate price-cutting, and his deliberate wage-raising—was to demonstrate with unprecedented directness one of the principles of modern industrialism: the dynamic logic of mass production. This is the principle — that the more goods you produce, the less it costs to produce them; and that the more people are well off, the more they can buy, thus making this lavish and economical production possible. In brief, it was the first time that the idea of the worker as a consumer began to take hold.

There was also a marked decrease in the importation of European labor. Before 1914, immigration had provided a large and continual source of new workers. By 1916, the need of Europe for its own manpower and the wartime restrictions on travel had reduced the excess of those arriving in the United States over those departing to 264,000. By 1917, the excess had shrunk to 81,000. To that shrinkage of immigration was added the effect of the withdrawal of over four million men for the armed forces. Unemployment in manufacturing and transportation declined from nearly thirteen per cent of the labor force in 1914 to what may be considered an absolute minimum of 3.5 per cent in 1917.

The demand for labor had already become insistent before April, 1917, because of the war orders of the allies and the stimulus that they provided to the American economy in general.

For once in three long generations, the iron law of supply and demand was reversing its cycle, when the demand of labor was running ahead of the supply. Hutcheson, who fifteen and twenty years earlier felt the harsh effects of this oppressive "law," began to see visions in 1916. He would lead his large army of carpenters into the Promised Land.

Meanwhile the orders for goods flowed from overseas like tidal waves. From 1914 to 1916, our exports of explosives rose from six million dollars to four-hundred and sixty-seven million dollars. The exports of steel and iron doubled. Wheat at high prices flowed from the West in an endless stream. By July 1916, we had bought back, chiefly from England, about 1 billion 3 million dollars worth of securities sold to her when we needed capital for development. Farms and factories were busy as never before, and prices were going steadily up. The most hectic gold rush of frontier days had been nothing compared with this rush from Europe to give us dollars.

Before the war, established trade unions had included only a small percentage of the workers of the country and were largely concentrated in a relatively few occupations, such as building, transportation, printing and clothing. New conditions now combined to increase manifestations of labor unrest, not only among those who were organized, but also in establishments where unions had not been recognized. The demand for labor strengthened the worker's bargaining power while the enlarged profits of business tended to aggravate conditions still further. Prices and the cost of living began to shoot upward. At the same time, the pressure for production led to long hours, speed-up, and other working conditions that aggravated discontent.

The United States Commission on Industrial Relations, reporting in 1915, found that between one-fourth and one-third of the male workers eighteen years of age and over, in factories and mines, earned less than ten dollars a week; from two-thirds to three-fourths earned less than fifteen dollars, and only about one-tenth earned more than twenty dollars a week; from two-thirds to three-fourths of women workers in industrial occupations generally, worked at wages of less than eight dollars per week. There were still many industries in which the normal working week was over seventy-two hours. The rule was still twelve dollars for a seven day work-week in a substantial number of places. A large part of the industrial workers were still prevented from joining unions by the unyielding opposition of their employers and were denied the benefits of collective bargaining.[4] In 1915 organized labor totaled 2,607,700, of whom the Carpenters numbered 263,395. In the year 1915 on through 1917, the number of strikes increased from 1,405 to 4,359, involving 1,213,000 people.

The story of how planning and organization became necessary and of how the wild horses of economic and governmental particularisms were bridled and driven as a team is a truly fascinating one. Agencies of control were created in confusing array, altered, brought into conflict with one another, coordinated and recoordinated, until finally, when the war was over, something like a semblance of order had emerged. These agencies covered almost every sphere of economic life and were more numerous than anyone could have ventured to predict at the beginning.

The germ of the idea of industrial coordination had arisen in 1915. As a result of President Wilson's message to Congress of December 7, 1915, America started building "a Navy second to none" and a huge

---

[4]Alexander M. Bing, *Wartime Strikes and Their Adjustment,* (E. P. Dutton & Co., 1921).

merchant marine. A Naval Consulting Board, previously created to deal with the industrial requirements of the contemplated program, consisted of two members each from various scientific societies and was headed by Thomas A. Edison the inventor. This board in turn set up in August, 1915, a committee on Industrial Preparedness that included in its thinking the possible requirements of the Army as well as the Navy. Its chief work was to draw up an inventory of manufacturing plants that could make munitions. The chairman of the committee, Howard V. Coffin of Detroit, was trained by his experience to see the need for more industrial preparedness and was one of those who was instrumental in creating a Council of National Defense. This was composed of Cabinet Ministers — the Secretary of War, Secretary of the Navy, Secretary of the Interior, Secretary of Agriculture, Secretary of Labor, and Secretary of Commerce, who, under the military Appropriations Act, were given authority to coordinate industries and resources for national security and welfare. But the main work was performed by an advisory commission of seven, consisting of leaders outside the government. Among the seven dollar-a-year men to have been appointed to the advisory commission of industrial experts was Samuel Gompers, President of the American Federation of Labor.

Gompers' participation in the survey of manufacturing plants that could make munitions started in December 1915.[5]

A mere glimmer of understanding that "only labor, the labor of men as well as women could overcome the shortage of materials" became apparent at that time. But who could speak for labor as a whole? "No individual or group except as self-appointed volunteers, for the pick-and-shovel men. . . . But skilled labor had generals of its own choosing. . . . For the government to deal directly with these would have brought 854 leaders into a convention of much the same kind as though every railroad president and every maker of tools . . . were assembled every time a contract that concerned them was assigned or a policy determined."[6] Perhaps the wisest action of the Council of National Defense, when it appointed an advisory commission of industrial experts had been to make Samuel Gompers the member to represent labor. He, too, had become a dollar-a-year-man in the company of millionaires and specialists, many of whom he had met before in his battles for shorter hours and higher pay.[7]

The United States faced an unprecedented production program. The war created an emergency in which it was necessary, besides recruiting

[5]Samuel Gompers, *Seventy Years of Life and Labor* (E. P. Dutton & Co.) Vol. II p. 350 seq.

[6]Frederick Palmer, *America at War*, Vol. I (Dodd, Mead & Co., 1931), p. 259.

[7]*Ibid*, p. 260.

and drilling an enormous army in building up to the required war strength, to embark on a ship-building program for commercial and military reasons, hastily to construct cantonments each of which was as large as a city and to produce quantities of munitions on a scale that dwarfed into insignificance the former activities of the Government.

To meet it successfully required a greatly augmented supply of labor. Interruptions of production resulting from industrial disputes had to be avoided as far as possible. The health and good will of the workers had to be safe-guarded in order to stimulate productiveness. Conditions creating a high labor turnover, constituting a terrific waste of human resources, had to be removed; it was absolutely essential to remove every factor that would interfere with production and to take advantage of every factor that would promote it. All these considerations were important for the military objective of the nation, wholly aside from questions of social justice or long-term reform. Their importance, however, was not recognized by employers or government purchasing agencies. Production quotas were filled in spite of, and not because of, the Federal Government's labor policy, by a process of extended muddling through. Although the administration was liberal in its tendency and early called to its assistance the President of the American Federation of Labor, Samuel Gompers, the government failed to establish a national labor program, or to develop a sound labor relations policy. The government's plans for labor administration and adjustment were developed during the entire course of the war by a process of improvisation.[8]

The old habits of many employers and of the production-minded industrialists, who administered the government agencies, persisted until the United States declared war on Germany and were difficult to eradicate even during the ensuing period. All of them, whether or not they had dealt with unions, had had their thinking on labor relations conditioned in an over-supplied labor market, and had at no time given adequate thought to the problem of labor management. They saw only the "production" problem and were content, as they had been in the past, to allow both the labor supply and labor problems to take care of themselves. In truth, "capital and labor were inclined to regard each other as natural enemies. Labor had seen capital as only what labor could force by organization, and capital had seen labor as holding a strike in threat at periods when it had the employer at a disadvantage." ". . . Gompers looked a little askance at his dollar-a-year comrades, and they returned the scrutiny. It was fortunate that they were to have time to share together in their numerous pre-war meetings . . . Capital

---

[8]George Soule, *Prosperity Decade: From War to Depression 1917-1929* (Rinehart and Co.), p. 66.

and labor were bound to say to each other, "now are you going to show that *you* are more patriotic?"[9]

To be sure, Frederick Palmer, Newton Baker's biographer, was right. For soon in the months following the declaration of war and on, cynical management, who knew better, conveniently unfurled the American flag, challenging America's wage earners to a patriotic contest as if to test which of the two was the better American. It was an irresistible, timely stratagem whose disguised aim was to repress the urges and moderately just claims of a "lower" section of the American community. Actually, labor's wholehearted support of the war had already been pledged even before America's declaration of war on April 6, 1917.

A general trade-union conference called by Gompers on March 12, 1917 adopted a declaration expressing American labor's position in peace and in war. "It was an offer of service by labor and a statement of conditions which would make possible fullest cooperation with the administration."[10] The declaration pointed out that the national effort would be weakened if labor's interests were sacrificed under the guise of national necessity. The government must enlist the wholehearted cooperation of wage earners by checking economic exploitation. The cornerstone of national defense, read the declaration, was economic justice, and the government should recognize the organized labor movement as the agency through which cooperation with the wage earners must be carried on. Safeguards of labor standards were demanded, as was direct representation on national boards, "co-equal with that given to any other part of the community." Labor believed that to "establish at home justice in the relation of men" was a fundamental part of the preparedness of the nation; that "wage earners in war times must keep one eye on employers at home, the other on the enemy threatening the National Government."

For the first time in seventy-nine years, labor leaders were in a *classically* advantageous position: they were operating in a sellers' rather than a buyers' market, as the demands for labor continued to increase. However, most of them were torn between patriotism and a sense of trade unionism. Rather than exploit this unique opportunity and advantage in behalf of America's wage earners, increase their share in the total product, help in the establishment of sound labor relations and ultimately gain greater collective social power, which labor required for the achievement of justice,* most American Federation of Labor leaders

---

[9]Frederick Palmer, *op. cit.* Vol. 1 p. 260.

[10]Samuel Gompers, *op. cit.* p. 358-359.

*Professor Reinhold Niebuhr comes to this conclusion . . . "The development of the modern machine also makes collectivization of power in industrial management a technical necessity and the subsequent organization of labor power a necessity of justice." (Kenneth E. Boulding, *The Organizational Revolution*, Harper & Bros., 1954, p. 233).

plunged into the government production program with a zeal of devotion and loyalty equalled by none. Curiously enough, while our British cousins, closest to us in trade unionism, had given labor its properly assigned role during the war — a fact which had not escaped Gompers[11] — most American labor leaders had not profited from this experience, nor had they crystallized their own position. American labor leaders confined their demands to such conservative claims as improvements in working conditions, increases in wages, the eight-hour day, and the right to collective bargaining and of organization into trade unions.[12] Of course, they conducted a highly successful series of organizational forays designed to unionize as many workers as possible and to get the best possible conditions for those already unionized.

Doubtless, it was the sensitiveness and morbidity that settled over all "lower" minority movements in times of duress, that enabled the directors and managers of governmental agencies connected with the war to successfully promote the stereotype of labor — that it was incapable of demonstrating the same habits, loyalties and patriotism as the larger community.

As for the majority of American labor leaders, it was a case of myopia coupled with the conviction of their own helplessness which constrained them from attempting to win a "station" for labor in a war for democracy.

To be sure, labor and its leaders were subjected to considerable pressure, and moral suasion. Even the highly sympathetic, public spirited Secretary of War Newton D. Baker and his special counsellor Louis B. Wehle, were not adverse to the use of cajolery, threat and intimidation.** Even President Samuel Gompers, whom Newton Baker described as "the Statesman of Labor . . ., who knew labor human nature better . . . and employer nature as well or better," was not immune from pressure and outright intimidation at the hands of the Secretary of War and his counsellor Wehle.

---

[11]Samuel Gompers, *op. cit.* p. 359.

[12]Bing, *op. cit.* p. 236.

**He (Newton D. Baker) always had one final appeal to both capital and labor; their duty to the U.S. and its soldiers, and back of that the call upon public opinion to turn its wrath upon the hesitant . . . One day, one of the two big leaders of the building trades, a giant who had been used to giving and taking hard knocks, wrote a letter to Wehle saying that the building trades would withdraw from the cantonment agreement which was only fattening the contractors. Wehle allowed him a little time to cool off and then requested him to come to a personal conference. "Did you get a letter from me?" he asked Wehle after silence, "No." "That's funny." Then Wehle made the appeal, the same appeal that so often won with labor . . .: "the delay in building the cantonment might mean the loss of lives or of a battle. Would any man want such a letter held up against him in the future? Really, the letter had not been received officially. It was then and there returned to the writer who promptly tore it up and did the same with a carbon copy in his files." (Frederick Palmer, *op. cit.,* p. 264).

Hutcheson, in the meantime, had been watching from the sidelines. With a knowledge of the terrain, and the given advantage of the "law of supply and demand," he conceived a plan for labor to occupy its New Jerusalem. He knew no fear, to begin with; nor was he afflicted with temporary myopia. Whereas other labor leaders fought a mild, hesitant, rearguard action, he came out with a precise, carefully planned war labor policy predicated upon labor's becoming a "co-equal" in the American community. To achieve this objective, Hutcheson saw the "union shop" as the very foundation upon which all other "union conditions," inclusive of labor responsibility, rested. Hutcheson defined the "union shop" as "our right under the law; that we will refuse to work with him (non-union man), and we recognize that he has the same right to refuse to work with us. He is free to choose his own company at work; so are we." "Employers" he explained, "are forever telling us that non-union men are more numerous than union men, therefore, if that be true he has greater power to refuse to work with union men."[13]***

Hutcheson's plan, if implemented, would permit the United Brotherhood, in close cooperation with the Emergency Office of the Department of Labor and various other war labor agencies, to train, examine, requisition, and furnish all trained mechanics in the carpentry trade for the war effort. It would give the Brotherhood the right to bargain collectively with the Government and industrial managers to establish a "mutual understanding" and conditions of work for the labor his union supplied.[14]

Twenty-four hours after the Declaration of War by the United States against Germany, the Council of National Defense held its first war meeting. President Gompers renewed labor's pledge of loyalty and cooperation. The Counsel of National Defense, in turn, announced several weeks later that "prevailing standards" of labor would be observed pending a fuller study of the question of labor in wartime. In the Spring of 1917, the Government had still to enunciate the specific details of its labor program. In the meantime Congress criticized the War Department for "surrender-

---

[13]UBCJA, *Proceedings of the Twentieth General Convention* (1920), pp. 26-32; pp. 167-170.

***"We also desire to call to your attention the error made by many of our members in the use of the term "closed shop," when they really mean the "union shop." A closed shop is a shop that is closed to any person who is a member of a labor union. While we disagree with the principle of the closed shop, nevertheless, we must admire its advocates for being on the level and honest with employees and the public in stating the truth of their position, so that "he who runs may read" and reach a just conclusion as to why the shop is closed to union men. The "closed shoppers" are honest-to-God angels in comparison with the "open shoppers," (Ibid, p. 170.).

[14]See "Memorandum", (Proceedings of the Twentieth General Convention of the UBCJA (1920) pp. 28-32.

ing to the capitalists, while industrialists regarded Secretary of War Baker as too friendly to labor."[15]

The Carpenters were especially skeptical. In their official organ, *The Carpenter,* doubt was expressed "respecting the offer of labor to participate on the loyal and generous basis" set forth in the manifesto, a reference to Gompers' declaration underwritten by the Executive Council of the A. F. of L. "Should it (the Government) do otherwise we may look for the inefficiency, the blundering, the want of coordination which followed the entry of other belligerents into the war."[16] In its May issue it approvingly quoted the *New Republic* article, in which Gompers was cautioned lest the press magnify "this recommendation into a guarantee against strikes and all forms of industrial unrest."

"But patriotic manifestoes," it continued, "unsupported by definite administration plans, offer no such guarantee. Existing standards are changed day by day through the rising cost of food. Workers cannot do efficient work on a diet of *loyalty. (Emphasis* ours). The government has entered into contracts with certain manufacturers to deliver munitions at a fixed price. These prices are based upon existing rates of wages."[17]

Subsequent events proved that the Brotherhood's skepticism was well justified. The Government and industrial managers not only ignored the trade unions' offer to recruit labor, "give it the same consideration and recognition as was given associations of financial interests and manufacturing establishments," but it [Government] also failed to establish even the semblance of an over-all labor program. "But as this was not done," stated Hutcheson in retrospect, "it was therefore necessary that constant attention be given to matters as affected our membership in order to maintain the standards we had established and to retain unto ourselves the rights, benefits and privileges as guaranteed to us under the laws of our country."[18]

Immediately after the declaration of the war the construction of cantonments was commenced. The War Department's Construction Division planned to construct sixteen cantonments for training the new National Army that was to be drafted. The cantonments were scattered over the country, and each was to handle a division of thirty-six thousand men with additional units. The ground had to be stripped, graded, drained, and prepared, the water supply brought in, the sewage system built.

---

[15]Louis B. Wehle, *Hidden Threads of History: Wilson through Roosevelt* (Macmillan Co., 1953), p. 6.

[16]"Where Union Labor Stands," *The Carpenter* Vol. XXXVII: 4 (April, 1917), p. 26.

[17]The Carpenter, Vol. XXXVII: 7, (May, 1917), p. 4.

[18]Report of William L. Hutcheson, General President, "Proceedings of Twentieth Convention," (1920), p. 22.

Among the essential structures were the barracks or tents, messes, kitchens, officers' quarters, hospitals, warehouses, refrigeration, laundry and sewage disposal plants, electric-power plants, garages, stables, repair shops. One over-all general contractor was to be selected for each project.

The Government began dispensing contracts profusely. Contracts were awarded on cost-plus basis which had long been in business use, especially for work that could not be specified for the contractor in advance. An unregulated scramble among contractors for labor and material began in the Summer of 1917. Contractors and Government officials, in their eagerness to get their particular pieces of work done, disregarded the effects of their actions on other government work, and the stealing of men, from one cantonment to another, was freely indulged in. Many non-union or unfair builders received government contracts and, hiding behind the war effort, were able to foster anti-union programs. While the owners had been making huge profits, the working men had genuine grievances.[19] The war psychology, unsanitary housing conditions, the great increase in the cost of practically every article that entered into the workingman's budget, with luxury rampant, as was always the case in such a period, gave the wage earners a feeling they had not been getting their share. Furthermore, the enormous increase in the earnings of large corporations, which seemed fairly bursting with assets piled up by war business was well known. No single factor, however, caused more unrest and dissatisfaction among the workingman than the cost-plus-method. Viewed from the point of view of the worker, with the rise in the cost of living playing serious havoc on his wages, the war for democracy, became a "rich man's war."[20]

Labor difficulties developing into stoppages had more than correspondingly intensified. Early attempts to remedy the *status quo* in the handling of labor disputes were promptly rebuffed by Major General Goethals and the civilians on the General Munitions Board, a creature of the National Defense Council. The fear prevailed that the liberalism in Washington "would sanction the picket line, restrict court injunctions."[21] More recently, the Government had forced the enactment of the eight-hour law for railroads. By June, 1917, Samuel Gompers' ringing patriotic manifesto, labor's symbolic act of devotion to our country in an hour of emergency which also forecast the "establishment of justice at home in the relation of men," had been emptied of all meaning. He was burdened with the complaints of union Presidents, chief among them the Presidents of the Building Trades Unions. For cantonment con-

---

[19]*The Carpenter*, Vol. XXXVII: 7, (July, 1917), pp. 15-16.
[20]Bing, *op. cit.* p. 8.
[21]Louis B. Wehle, *op. cit.* p. 19.

struction, shipbuilding, and plant expansion were the first tasks before the Government. Important, too, was the fact that the building industry in the large cities had been strongly organized.****

On June 18, when labor disturbances had grown into a grave threat to the Army's construction program, Louis B. Wehle, legal expert for the Council of National Defense and the Munitions Board, was requested by Secretary of War Baker to submit a draft of an agreement that would lay the groundwork for "prompt, centralized, and consistent policy in handling labor disputes." The draft as drawn up by Wehle required that: "All disputes ought to be submitted for decision to an adjustment board of three members, one representing the Army, one labor, and the third the public." It was Wehle's belief that in the light of Gompers' declaration, "that he (Gompers) would be willing to have organized labor controlled by such a board, and that he would concede the open shop to the Government in war emergency construction in exchange for the Government's concession that the Board could use union scales of hours and wages in effect at some past date." Such basic scales of wages would be modified by changes in the cost of living. Mr. Wehle emphasized that construction projects "would have to be wide open." On June 19, 1917, Gompers went into conference with Secretary of War Newton D. Baker. Out of that conference emerged the Baker-Gompers Agreement which set the pattern for a multitude of adjustment bodies that followed during the war.[22]

June 19, 1917.

"For the adjustment and control of wages, hours and conditions of labor in the construction cantonments there shall be created an Adjustment Commission of three persons, appointed by the Secretary of War; one to represent the Army, one the Public, and one labor; the last to be nominated by Samuel Gompers, member of the Advisory Commission of the Council of National Defense, and President of the American Federation of Labor.

"As basic standards with reference to each cantonment, such Commission shall use the union scale of wages, hours and conditions in force on June 19, 1917, in the locality where such cantonments are situated. Consideration shall be given to special circumstances, if any, arising after said date which may require particular advances in wages or changes in other standards. Adjustments in wages, hours or conditions made by such boards are to be treated as binding by all parties."

(Signed) Newton D. Baker

Samuel Gompers

****Hutcheson was the first to realize the importance of Government contract placement to the Carpenters, and in the Spring of 1917 stationed three General Representatives in Washington to influence the placement of war contracts among unionized contractors.

[22]Louis B. Wehle, op. cit. p. 20.

This agreement was simply an isolated and specific pact made to regulate the treatment of craftsmen engaged on the construction of War Department cantonments. It provided for the organization of the first War Labor Adjustment Board and the Cantonment Adjustment Commission. The Commission was to use as basic standards the union wages, hours and conditions in force in the various localities and was to make such adjustments as were required by circumstances.

In the course of events, the Baker-Gompers Agreement became the master agreement upon which all subsequent war labor agreements were patterned.

But the crucial question of the open shop was not yet formally resolved. Orally, the Baker-Gompers Agreement specifically exempted the union shop from "prevailing conditions" even in localities where the union existed, but it had not been stated in the memorandum.

Gompers proceeded with a great deal of caution, especially because in signing the Baker-Gompers memorandum he was assuming authority that only the international union Presidents in the building trades possessed. In addition, the point of the open shop was loaded with dynamite. However, the necessity for expressly clarifying the word "conditions," so long as there was a possibility that anyone could misunderstand the intention of the memorandum in connection with the question of the union shop, continued to plague Wehle. On the twenty-third of June, Samuel Gompers agreed to clarify the memorandum by wire addressed to Wehle:

"Your understanding of the memorandum signed by Secretary Baker and me is right. It had reference to union hours and wages. The question of union shop was not included."[23]

In insisting on the open shop instead of the union shop, the Government took the position that the enormous volume of work and the short time in which it had to be done precluded dealing only with the unions. On the contrary, the project would have to be wide open, and many thousands of unskilled men would have to be trained to do the work as it progressed.

On June 25, 1917, the Executive Council of the A. F. of L. met. On the twenty-seventh, after two days of deliberation, the Council demanded "direct representation by workers, co-equal with other interests, upon all agencies, boards, committees and commissions entrusted with war work." "These Boards," the Executive Council added, "are now composed almost entirely of business men . . . War contracts must not be allowed to be an opportunity for private gain and the accumulation of war profits . . . Therefore, we, the Executive Council of the A. F. of L. urge the Council of National Defense that you endorse the principle of

---

[23]For a comprehensive recital of events surrounding this chapter of labor history during World War I, See Louis B. Wehle, *op. cit.* pp. 19-26.

accrediting representation for Labor on all agencies, committees, boards or commissions organized under the Council of National Defense."[24]

The Federation appeal to the Council of National Defense was ignored. The Government representative sitting on each of the boards maintained by the separate departments of the Government was usually an industry man. There were practically no labor men sitting on the various industry control committees set up by Bernard Baruch of the then War Industries Board to regulate each industry. Yet, it was these various committees which doled out the valuable war contracts.

Hutcheson and the Carpenters cautioned Gompers in the Summer of 1917. "Mr. Gompers must have learned by this time that mere representation of the workers on the various boards and committees of the Advisory Commission will be insufficient either to protect the interest of the workers or to make the experience and machinery of their organizations effective as instruments for the speeding up of production and the prevention of strikes. The time has come when the Government should lay aside its equivocal attitude toward organized labor and openly give preference in the placing of contracts to industries where the men are organized. The effect of such policy would be to restore the injured prestige of Mr. Gompers . . . Moreover, it would immediately put at the Government's disposal a machinery for the prompt adjustment of grievances such as years of trial and experience are generally required to develop."[25]

Thus, from the very beginning since America's entry into the war, William Hutcheson was the only one among the union leaders who charted and pursued a clear-cut, logical and consistent policy. Its formulation spelled out for labor the achievement of a respectable status under conditions of full employment and joint responsibility of industry, labor and government for the maintenance of uninterrupted production.

Whether Samuel Gompers intended it or not, the Baker-Gompers Agreement, elucidated on June 23, was a bargain for union scale of wages and hours in exchange for the open shop. Although, he was without authority to sign this agreement, the feeling was general that the memorandum "would exert the necessary leverage for subjecting the building-trades unions and their members to its undertakings." Subsequent moves by Gompers to apply basic union standards to non-union or open shop construction jobs resulted in fierce arguments and conflicts between Wehle and the harrassed labor leader. When Gompers

24Hutcheson's Private Papers covering A F of L meetings, June 25-27, 1917: . . . "This was clearly understood between Mr. Gompers and myself this morning when we agreed that it would not be legally possible at this time to insert in an understanding . . . even so much as a provision that preference be given to members of organized labor."

25The Carpenter. Vol. XXXVII: 8, (August, 1917), p. 34.

insisted that if, in a given locality, a plant had, say, on July 15 been non-union or open shop, a labor dispute in that plant should neverthe-less be settled by applying such union standards as had been obtained in the district, the government pronounced it as "a violation of the Baker-Gompers agreement, because it would have automatically trans-formed open shops into union shops." "This," inveighed Wehle, "was profiteering on the emergency."[26]

The effect that the Baker-Gompers Agreement has had on the Car-penters was described by Hutcheson himself at the Twentieth Conven-tion of the United Brotherhood on September 20, 1920:

"The interpretation placed thereon [Baker-Gompers Agreement] was circulated by the War Department to the various representatives who were in charge of Government construction, and they were in-formed that President Gompers had agreed that members of trade unions would work with non-union men, thereby establishing a con-dition contrary to that observed by our members whereby they do not work with men of our craft unless they are members of our Brotherhood, which caused a great deal of trouble for our members and involved them in many controversies."[27]

In the face of the Baker-Gompers Agreement, Hutcheson's program for the solution of the labor problem, inclusive of the union shop and union responsibility, had no chance of being realized. Its acceptance by the government administrators would be a brilliant admission of their incompetence. It would invite examples for other unions to follow Hutcheson. As for the Carpenters' President, he was made the subject of popular spontaneous combustion and cast in the role of an evil spirit among a group of vacillating, confused labor leaders.

Before the year 1917 was over, the field of war time labor relations was so encrusted with tripartite boards that it is futile to attempt to list them. Actually, they numbered 18, and together they set competing wage rates for the existing supply of labor. Practically every division of every bureau of every Government department and agency had its own separate little adjustment board. No one agency existed to coordinate the efforts of these boards. Union leaders were confused. They knew little of the Government's labor standards and of the yardstick for measuring them. The result was still more confusion, which in turn brought on serious localized labor shortages during the summer of 1917.

This rash of tripartite labor boards brought into existence, by August 1917, the three War Labor agencies with which Hutcheson was to deal. There was the Cantonment Adjustment Commission, the first govern-

[26]Wehle, op. cit. p. 23.
[27]UBCJA Proceedings of the Twentieth General Convention, (1920), pp. 24-25.

mental agency created during the war to deal with the labor situation. It was organized on the basis of the Baker-Gompers Agreement, with a jurisdiction extending to cover all Navy land construction, repair work and construction of all stores and warehouses. The Arsenal and Navy Yard Wage Commission was established on August 15, to settle wage matters relative to work done on these. On August 25, the Wage Adjustment Board of the Emergency Fleet Corporation (E.F.C.) of the United States Shipping Board was established. It was specifically with the latter agency that William L. Hutcheson chose to test his formula of the labor aims as he conceived them.

Here was an industry with a labor problem which for sheer difficulty has hardly been surpassed. To grapple with it required more than mere courage and ambition; it required toughness of spirit and the moral conviction that the things he set out to do were right.

The shipbuilding labor problem contrasted strongly with the relatively simple one that had been handled through the Baker-Gompers Adjustment machinery of the Cantonment Adjustment Commission. Instead of there being one temporary employer, that is, the over-all contractor, at each camp site, there were scores of employers, few old and mostly new, where the shipyards were under construction. Businessmen rushed into the shipbuilding industry, lured on by the prospect of high profits, who knew no more about shipbuilding than Gilbert and Sullivan's immortal First Lord of the Admiralty knew about the "Queen's Navee." While most of the old yards were under efficient management and some few even operated union shops, the great majority of the new yards built during the war were owned and managed by men who were not familiar with the technical problems of shipbuilding and these yards were managed on the whole inefficiently. Without exception, all operated open shops.

However, not only were the majority of the yards inefficiently managed, but each employer was intent only upon fulfilling his own contract and was not concerned with the success of the shipbuilding program as a whole. The truth of the "Invisible Hand" doctrine of Adam Smith, that every man sought his own best interests, ruled supreme. To add to these difficulties, the relations between the workmen and employers was in many sections one of either open or ill-concealed hostility. There was no clear-cut national labor policy and many employers, both old and new did not recognize the principle of collective bargaining, refusing to deal with any organization of their men. The general prejudice of workmen against the owners was heightened by the fact that the owners had reaped huge profits from the sale of requisitioned ships to the Shipping Boards and expected liberal sums from the new contracts let by the Fleet Corporation.

When war was declared, the United States had about sixty ship-yards with 215 ways, and all of these were busy. The Government's building of cargo ships, both of steel and wood, had been promptly be-gun under the Act of September 7, 1916, with its huge appropriations, which later were greatly enlarged. The United States Shipping Board, created by the Act, confined itself to ship operation and had in April 1917, organized the Emergency Fleet Corporation (E.F.C.) for con-structing ships. After E.F.C.'s orders to existing shipyards had filled to capacity, it made contracts for additions to old plants and for construc-tion of new yards. This expanded capacity on the three coasts and Great Lakes was quickly absorbed by new ship orders.

In August, 1917, the E.F.C. had under projection, construction, or repair in American shipyards, about 1,500,000 tonnage in steel and wood-en ships under cost-plus fee contracts. It was also completing or repairing about 700,000 tons of seized German and Austrian ships. Moreover, the Navy, with its own yards overtaxed, was having many vessels built in private yards.

Strikes in shipyards on the Delaware river and at Portland, Oregon, and Seattle were in progress even before August; the situation in the East was rapidly deteriorating. Grievances mounted as employers per-sisted in their open shop ways, flatly rejecting union overtures for recog-nition and the "union shop." There were also genuine wage complaints, in addition to the unplanned mass transfer of thousands of workers, who, lured far from their homes, looked askance at the huge profits of the employers when they compared them to their own wages and the rising cost of living.

The aforementioned Wehle, Harvard-trained government "trouble-shooter," a crafty and erudite negotiator, once again appeared on the scene.

The crucial task of calming the aggrieved shipyard workers, lest they go out on a general stoppage of work in the yards, was assigned to him by President Wilson himself. Wehle's recent performance with Gompers, in negotiating the Baker-Gompers' Agreement had been a success, at least theoretically. Time now, was of the essence, and to work out a wage-adjustment machinery in shipbuilding similar to what he had carried through for the Army land construction, was Wehle's immediate objective.

On August 14, 1917, Wehle called on Gompers, and together they agreed that there should be an Adjustment Board similar to that for the cantonments. But they quickly reached a sharp difference. Sharp words were followed by threats and challenges, but Gompers was not moved. Gompers took Hutcheson's "hunch" quite seriously; his proposal to Wehle would, in effect, eliminate the open shop. Wehle left in anger, Gompers was exceeding his official authority, he added. He was going to "try to negotiate this agreement with some of the international union Metal Trades presidents." And, stated Wehle, when "I have the signatures of two or three of them, I'll come back to you, and then I'll expect you to back it up and enlist other necessary signatures."[28]

Wehle made good his threat. He secured the signatures of the international presidents of the International Association of Machinists, International Union of Boilermakers, Iron Shipbuilders and Helpers of America, and the Secretary and President of the Building Trades Metal Trades Department of the A. F. of L. It was approved and signed by Franklin Delano Roosevelt, then Acting Secretary of the Navy and by the Secretary of the Navy, Josephus Daniels.

Victorious Wehle returned to Gompers, requesting that he enlist other international presidents. This he did. In the presence of Wehle, Gompers obtained long-distance phone authorizations from a number of international presidents whose names he signed "per S. G. " Among the signers of this Agreement were: Edward N. Hurley, Chairman of the Shipping Board and Admiral W. L. Capp, General Manager of the E.F.C. However, missing from the list was the President of the United Brotherhood of Carpenters and Joiners of America, who was also Fifth Vice-President of the Building and Construction Trades Department.

Gompers wrote to Hutcheson on August 15, asking him to sign the pending Agreement, which was modeled after the Baker-Gompers Memorandum. Hutcheson refused.

The President of the Carpenters contended that since the Agreement reached between Secretary of War Daniels, Assistant Secretary of War Roosevelt, the Shipping Board and Gompers, was patterned after the Baker-Gompers paper, his signature would imply acquiescence with the open shop principle conceded in the latter agreement. "I declined," Hutcheson explained, "to become a party to the Memorandum . . . believing that as an organization we were entitled to some consideration in the way of maintaining unto ourselves the conditions that we had established . . . as has been clearly demonstrated by some few employers doing the work for the Government, that they will not overlook an opportunity to take advantage of the workman and ignore whenever possible the conditions established in the various localities and districts of our organization. Therefore, I did not believe it was to the best interests of our membership to enter . . . into any understanding."[29] Hutcheson firmly maintained that, "While we have every desire, intention and thought of assisting the officials of the government in the crisis we are now passing through, yet at the same time we have no thought or intention of waiving

[28]See Wehle, *op. cit.*, pp. 40-44.
[29]*The Carpenter,* Vol. XXXVII: 11; (Nov., 1917), pp. 25-26.

or giving up our rights to maintain for ourselves the conditions we have established."

The Agreement was drawn up between August 19 and 20 without Hutcheson's commitment.

The next step was to organize the Shipbuilding Wage Adjustment Board. Its three regular members were to be representatives, first, of the Government's Production Agency, the E.F.C. (or the Navy, if the dispute concerned work on Naval vessels) ; second, of Labor; and third of the public, to be appointed by the President. As in the Baker-Gompers Agreement, the Shipbuilding Wage Adjustment Board provided for an open shop, with permission for the unions to organize those workers they could. This tripartite, government-labor-public board was also created to hear grievances and to set-up wage scales, hours, and working conditions which were enforced at such plants on July 15, 1917. Increases in the cost of living were to be the basis for altered wages. Under it, the three members of the Board were to be augmented by two from the District where the dispute existed: one local man to be designated by the shipyard employers, the other by shipyard labor. When disputes involving shipyard carpenters were to be heard, it was provided that Hutcheson appoint a representative of the Brotherhood.

On August 20, President Wilson appointed V. Everitt Macy as the public's member. President Gompers appointed A. J. Berres as the board's labor member. Hurley nominated E. F. Carry, a Chicago manufacturer as a third Board member. He was soon displaced by L. A. Coolidge. Louis B. Wehle was designated as Counsel for the Adjustment Board.

Friction developed quickly at top government level. Hurley and Capps, co-signers of the Memorandum that laid the foundation for the Shipbuilding Adjustment Board, did everything they could to wreck it. Both objected to labor representation, and attempted to prevent already loosely drawn and ambiguous provisions of the Agreement "concerning wages, hours or conditions of labor" from being put into effect. Hurley and Capps refused to reimburse the contractors for any advances in their labor costs resulting from the Board's action. This had already been impliedly given by Hurley and Capps when they signed a memorandum, which dovetailed into the E.F.C.'s Shipbuilding Agreement. Mr. Edward M. Hurley, the President of the E.F.C. was a Chicago manufacturer, who interestingly enough was a great supporter of President Wilson in his 1912 and 1916 campaigns. But this not-too-representative admirer of Wilsonion democracy also "believed in the stiff arm for dealing with organized labor."***** His anti-labor maneuvers, as demonstrated by his

---

***** "Mr. Hurley is playing with dynamite; he is jeopardizing the honor of the Government in its dealings with organized labor." (Louis B. Wehle, *op. cit.* p. 46).

desire to evade or "welch" on the Adjustment Board had caused much concern to Secretary of War Baker and to co-signer Franklin D. Roosevelt.

The Board had not been formed a moment too soon. In the absence of a clear-cut, coordinated and centralized labor policy, many of the shipyard owners with cost-plus contracts had refused to bargain collectively with the workers. Ship labor disturbances on both east and west coasts mounted alarmingly. Strikes over wages, hours, use of "fair" material, the union shop and general working conditions were rapidly materializing on the west coast. When the Board arrived on the coast, on October 7, more than 60,000 shipyard workers were on strike. The settlement of these disputes therefore was the first task which confronted this newly-created agency. After a series of hearings on the three coasts of Portland, Seattle and San Francisco, the Board handed down its decision on November 4. As the result of the investigation carried on by members of the faculty of the University of Washington, the Board decided that the cost of living had increased 31 percent since July 1916, and the wage rates were accordingly increased by that amount and were made effective for all the yards on the Pacific coast. In Portland, where the open shop was the issue, "trouble shooter" Wehle pressed the workers to withdraw their demands for a union shop in exchange of a "shop committee system" to handle employee complaints. Willingly they agreed to give up their boycotting of the use of "unfair material."

The wage increases created by the Board were unsatisfactory to Coast labor because the shipyard owners in their scramble for the labor supply had overtopped in many yards the pay fixed by the Board. Upon the complaints of the workers in other yards, the E.F.C. granted a ten per cent war service premium based upon the minimum rate for eight hours straight time, to be paid to every worker in the Pacific Coast shipyards who should work the full time of forty-eight hours in any consecutive six days. After February 1, 1918 this was to be converted into a permanent increase of ten per cent, thus placing the daily wage for basic trades at $5.75.

Hutcheson was greatly distressed by the principles involved in the West Coast settlement. As the price of settlement, A. J. Berres and the West Coast labor leaders, following the Baker-Gompers Agreement, had traded the union shop for a thirty-one per cent wage raise. Furthermore, the Adjustment Board had decreed a lower wage rate for house carpenters working in shipyards than for ship carpenters.

Hutcheson felt that these two moves were interrelated, and that if the Government allowed the United Brotherhood to train and recruit labor, he could prove that qualified house carpenters were as proficient in the building of ships as were the ship carpenters; and in order "to show the Government that the Brotherhood is willing to assist in this work," Hutcheson at once proceeded with the mechanics of making an inventory of "those in the carpentry craft who desired to take this task" [constructing wooden ships], assuring the Government that there would be no work interruptions. Consequently, he advised all members that "they should demand a minimum wage as established, whether they were shipwrights, ship joiners or house carpenters."[30]

Throughout November and December of 1917, Hutcheson reiterated his demand for one wage scale for carpenters, at the same time requesting that a representative of the Brotherhood sit in on the Wage Adjustment Board to arbitrate differences affecting the hours, wages and conditions of work of carpenters.

For the first time, Hutcheson felt compelled to deal with the E.F.C. President, Mr. Edward N. Hurley. The latter quickly dispensed with Hutcheson, advising him to take the matter up with the Adjustment Board. In the meantime, the situation in the shipyards had become more acute, and the carpenters were becoming more restless not only in New York but in Baltimore as well.

Hutcheson arrived in Washington early in January, 1918, and accompanied by Board member Tim Guerin, sought to present the grievances of the Carpenters to Mr. Blackman, a representative of the Shipping Board, to whom Mr. Hurley referred them. After discussing the conditions under which the carpenters were working, Blackman suggested that Hutcheson submit in writing a statement he considered "fair and equitable for the membership of the Brotherhood." Actually, the memorandum was Hutcheson's solution to the labor supply woes which had beset Hurley and his aides. The woes themselves stemmed from the lack of any clear-cut Shipping Board policy for recruiting, training and dealing with a skilled labor force.

Carpenters were recruited by individual contractors through newspaper advertisements. After travelling many miles, they often found no jobs awaiting them, or were refused jobs because of their union membership. Men who were lured to a distant locality by the promise of high wages often found wages to be lower than in their own districts. In some instances large numbers of skilled carpenters answered the Government's call only to find that there was no work awaiting them. Private contractors in each instance had been left free to hire and discharge men as they saw fit, and to pay them whatever wages they pleased. In many instances, the carpenter was put to work at common labor; in other instances he was forced to accept employment at his trade at wages less than those prevailing in that district.[31]

[30]*The Carpenter,* Vol. XXXVIII: 2, (February, 1918), p. 18.
[31]"Mr. Hurley and Labor," *The Public,* (New York, Feb. 23, 1918), p. 3.

The rate of labor turnover was, consequently, higher than that of any other industry in the United States. Three men had to be hired in the course of a year to keep each one-man job filled. Between April and October of 1917, 17.1 per cent of all possible shipyard working hours had been lost in disputes, strikes, and 6.5 per cent of all firms had been affected by strikes.

Since the United Brotherhood was the sole national agent representing carpenters, it was held responsible for labor shortages and work stoppages.

This was Mr. Hurley's perverse logic.

Hutcheson's "memorandum" submitted to Hurley on February 7, 1918 was a precise blueprint for the maximum utilization of carpenters' skills and the training of newcomers. Hutcheson's plan provided that the Department of Labor assume the role of a central clearance agency, rather than have the contractors and shipyard employers carry on cut-throat competition for the labor supply and thus bring about paralysis of any adjustment machinery.

Hutcheson asked for a conference with Hurley early in February in order personally "to explain to him the feeling of unrest that prevailed among the carpenters in the shipyards in Hog Island and Baltimore." Hurley refused to listen, let alone negotiate a settlement with Hutcheson. Instead he sent two aides to talk with Hutcheson on February 5. Hutcheson submitted a "memorandum" designed to ameliorate the grievances of the workers and to solve the labor supply problem. These demands accurately reflected the grievances of the men and Hutcheson's plan to settle the labor supply problem.[32]

The demands were taken to Hurley through the medium of Charles Piez, General Manager of the E.F.C. and Blackman. Hurley rejected them flatly, insisting that Hutcheson become a party to the agreement which established the Wage Adjustment Board (or the Macy Board). Hutcheson again refused, repeating that such commitment on his part would, in effect, mean the acceptance of the whole structure of the war labor program pursued by the Government and the A. F. of L., and as favoring the *open shop* of the Baker-Gompers Agreement, after which the Board was patterned.

Hurley now entered the situation with a personal demand that Hutcheson sign the Agreement. Hutcheson now receded from his former position, attempting once again to arrive at "some understanding whereby . . . he could keep the members of the organization satisfied, contented and at work."[33] He then suggested to Hurley that "the Brotherhood would

---

[32]*The Carpenter,* Vol. XXXVIII: 5, (May, 1918), pp. 4-5.
[33]*Ibid.,* p. 5.

agree to submit to the Wage Adjustment Board the proposition of considering hours and wages with the understanding that when such matters are to come up for consideration that a member of our organization, who would be familiar with the conditions prevailing throughout our jurisdiction, sit on the Wage Adjustment Board." Clearly, Hutcheson agreed to sit with the Board only if its representatives sat as a collective bargaining agent empowered to discuss only wages and hours, thus exempting the Carpenters from the open shop.

Again Hurley refused, advising Hutcheson that he take up the matter with the Wage Adjustment Board.

Hutcheson met with the Macy Board on February 11. To that conference he was accompanied by Secretary Frank Morrison of the A. F. of L. and General Secretary Frank Duffy of the U.B. Again he reiterated his demands, which were identical with those he had submitted to Hurley, namely that the Brotherhood would readily participate on the Board *in the role of a collective bargaining agent only,* but refused to subscribe to the open shop as epitomized by the Baker-Gompers Agreement. Mr. Everitt Macy did not reply. Gompers, who had interceded as the situation deteriorated, presented Hutcheson's "proposed memorandum" to Everitt Macy on February 13.

PROPOSED MEMORANDUM

In order to bring about a closer cooperation between the United States Emergency Fleet Corporation and the United Brotherhood of Carpenters and Joiners of America, the following is proposed:

When matters pertaining to hours and wages in reference to construction of wooden ships or work affecting the woodworking craft are being considered by the Wage Adjustment Committee of the United States Emergency Fleet Corporation, a representative of the United Brotherhood of Carpenters and Joiners of America shall sit on said committee with full authority and voting power, the same as other members on the committee.

The next day Macy replied that the Agreement excluded the union shop, and that the Carpenters would not be granted "special concessions."

Macy declined in these words:

"Mr. Samuel Gompers, President
American Federation of Labor
Washington, D. C.

My Dear Mr. Gompers:

Your letter enclosing proposed memorandum from Mr. Hutcheson has been received. The matter has been discussed by our Board and we have unanimously voted that the Board cannot extend privileges to one craft that have not been granted to others. You are a party to the Agreement under which we are working, and if any changes are to be made therein we believe that they should be made by those who created the Board. To accede to Mr. Hutcheson's request that the functions of the Board should be limited to questions involving hours and wages would leave this organization free to establish closed shops, etc., which privilege has been waived by the organizations signing the agreement. To accede to his demand that a representative of his organization should sit on our Board would result in the Board being composed of four members, two of whom would represent labor as against one for the Navy and Fleet Corporation.

These changes are so fundamental that they could only be adopted by those creating the present Board. It is our belief that should it be necessary to grant these concessions to the Carpenter's organization, it would be better to ask for a separate Board, so that all organizations coming before our Board may be given equal consideration.

Hoping that you will understand our position in the matter,

Yours very truly,

(signed) V. Everitt Macy, Chairman

Hutcheson was indignant. His own compromising position was treated with contempt and cynicism. Both Messrs. Hurley and Macy arbitrarily refused to accept the Brotherhood as a sole bargaining agent for its 50,000 carpenters engaged in the war effort. Instead they demanded that he subscribe to the open shop provisions of the Baker-Gompers Agreement. Here was a basic principle, which Hutcheson refused to surrender at any price.

Actually, behind Hutcheson's adamant refusal to accept the open shop lay his logical solution to the larger problems confronting labor. His position was that unless the union shop were uniformly provided for, the labor leader would have no power of compelling the workmen to obey the rulings of the Board, since they would have no control over non-union men. Union leaders would consequently be bound before the public and the employer to keep labor in line and yet not furnished with the authority to do that effectively. Hutcheson's demand to represent his own constituents was nothing more than a labor leader's request for authority that would be commensurate with the responsibility which he was already forced to shoulder. But this was also labor's unique opportunity to organize the unorganized at a time when the demand for labor was greater than the supply.

There can be no doubt that, if granted the union shop, Hutcheson could have regulated the labor force he supplied.

Hutcheson's memorandum to both Hurley and Macy did not demand the union shop. He simply asked that union carpenters be used for as long as the United Brotherhood could provide capable, trained men. When it could no longer supply qualified mechanics, the United Brotherhood of Carpenters would agree to work beside any man who "could drive a nail." He was never taken up on his offer.

For all of these causes, both immediate and otherwise, a strike situation arose in February on the east coast. While Hutcheson was dickering with the Macy Board, the ship carpenters in Baltimore and in Staten Island, N. Y. took the situation into their own hands. On February 11, they walked off the job. Three days later, as Hutcheson was vainly trying to see the Chairman of the United States Shipping Board in Washington, Hurley sent the following telegram to Hutcheson in Indianapolis:

Washington, D. C.
February 14, 1918

William L. Hutcheson, General President
United Brotherhood of Carpenters and Joiners
of America
Indianapolis, Indiana

While the people of this country are mourning the loss of brave young Americans in the Tuscania horror — while the thousands of American homes are anxiously watching the list of survivors slowly coming in to make certain that another precious life has been snatched from the Atlantic Ocean, a telegram comes — and with it the grim announcement that the Carpenters in shipyards are now on strike. Before any Government agency is given an opportunity to act, and despite the good record of our Adjustment Board's promptness and fairness in dealing with all labor matters, you attempt to paralyze the shipbuilding industry at the Port of New York.

Do you realize that you are adding to the fearful danger our soldiers already face, the danger of starvation and the danger of slaughter if food and ammunition are not sent over in ships and many ships at once? Do you think the fathers and mothers whose sons are making this sacrifice will sit patiently by and permit this paralyzing of the lifeline between us and the Western front to go on?

Will you take my friendly suggestion and go back to work at once? The machinery for dealing with all your demands and with the right of labor is at hand. You will be well advised to follow the methods of well-managed and patriotic organizations, at least until you have tested whether or not your Government, for which our ship-builders are now working can be fair. I advise you to end the paralyzing of the shipyard work now. I'm sure you did not deliberately imperil the lives and safety of brave fellow-citizens. I'm sure you believe with me that those whose sons are now giving their blood that you and I and our children may be safe and free, will not long permit either you or me to invite destruction of heroic lives and disaster to a great world cause.

(Signed) Edw. Hurley
Chairman U.S. Shipping Board.[34]

Hurley's patriotism, compounded of imperial arrogance, demagoguery, and contempt for labor, cleared the underbrush for the heavy artillery with which he could make a direct assault upon the lone intransigent labor leader.

---

[34]*The Carpenter,* Vol. XXXVIII: 5, (May, 1918).

"Death to traitor Hutcheson and his slacker Carpenters," "Long live patriot Hurley," verbalized the American press, both enlightened and otherwise.

Never was greater opprobrium brought down upon the heads of American workingmen so blatantly. Never had the bloody shirt been waved so conspicuously.

"The fathers and mothers . . . mourning the loss of brave young Americans in the Tuscania horror," were moved. And, as if by design, the press, its spokesmen, and "special correspondents" immediately made themselves the most important factor in the bargaining between Hutcheson and Hurley, preventing any reasonable settlement of the shipyard muddle. Cartoonists of *The Globe*[35] and the *Evening Mail*[36] sharpened their pencils, projecting Hutcheson as the Prussian drill Sergeant and killer of American youth. Even Pulitzer's crusading *New York World* joined in the chorus, singing hosannas to "patriot" Hurley.[37]

Even Billy Sunday, when he mounted the pulpit of the famed Marble Collegiate Church to address the ministers on "Liberalism," denounced Hutcheson as a traitor and the Carpenters as slackers.[38] In Baltimore, the Reverend Charles Eaton identified the strikers with "Germans," and "to give in to the demands of the Carpenters and Joiners would be suicidal." The Carpenters, hearing that, refused to listen. Altogether, the picture of Hutcheson as conveyed in the press, was one of a "dangerous man" who bears watching, lest he turn over American democracy to the bloody hands of the Kaiser. He was un-American, to say the least. He alone among American labor leaders, put the brand of Cain upon the head of patriotic American labor, shouted Hurley through the pages of the fourth estate. Accordingly, both labor and its leadership must condemn him and reject him. With the heathens, he belonged to the "massa perditionis."

Hutcheson, the son of a migrant worker and carpenter, whose father had abandoned his chest of tools at the call of President Lincoln, overnight became a public menace.

The chorus of denunciation that descended upon Hutcheson in the month of February, 1918, was not unlike the storm of abuse that was heaped at John L. Lewis in the fall of 1941, when he closed the "captive" mines briefly in September and again on October 27. Neither Hutcheson during World War I, nor his friend Lewis in World War II, saw danger to the national welfare by workers voluntarily joining the union; and

---

[35]*The Globe,* Feb. 18, 1918, p. 1.
[36]*The Evening Mail,* Feb. 16, 1918.
[37]*The World,* Feb. 16, 1918.
[38]*The Globe, op. cit.* p. 1.

no amount of opprobrium, scorn and abuse, such as had seldom been visited upon Americans by their fellow-citizens, could obscure that fact. That they were the "whipping boys" of the two World Wars, few will deny. Conceivably, few have enjoyed such a role in a climate which was asphyxiated by Government demagogues, the press and management. Yet, both remained firm in their conviction — that labor unions must not be denied the right of normal growth and legitimate aspirations, and that the traditional open shop policy of the anti-labor employers backed by anti-labor government managers must not prevail. In the case of Hutcheson during the First World War, labor was still in the "lower" group of the American community, and to win some semblance of recognition for it in the American economy and in American life was his sole objective.****** There was no basis for the charge that Hutcheson took advantage of the national emergency for organizational purposes. Or that Hutcheson, any more than Lewis, betrayed America.

At best, the granting of the union shop by the Government meant in no way control of the labor supply available to employers. Companies were still to do the hiring. Hurley's and Billy Sunday's shameless epithets of "betrayal" directed at Hutcheson in 1918 were the very ones which the extreme left-wingers and the committed communists threw at the face of Lewis in 1941.[39] Both fought for a principle, which, had it not been perverted and reduced to the level of demagoguery, would have resulted in a greater participation of labor in government war efforts. All he sought, emphasized Hutcheson, was a semblance of recognition for labor and the Carpenters, "a feeling that would heighten their sense of responsibility." Lewis was merely seeking to consolidate the Miners' position, requesting the union shop in the normal course of its development. Whereas Dr. John Steelman, during World War II, joined Lewis in granting the United Mine Workers a union shop in the captive mines, Hurley, the Wilson Democrat, chose the way of the "patriot."

More restrained and even cordial was Hutcheson's reply to Hurley, assuring him that the U.B. was composed of loyal and patriotic citizens simply trying to redress their grievances.

Mr. Hurley, Chairman,
U.S. Shipping Board,
Washington, D. C.

Dear Mr. Hurley:

Copy of your telegram of the fourteenth inst., addressed to me at Indianapolis, is at hand.

******"We will establish the union wherever we can," said Hutcheson, "for it lifts itself above the gaseous welter of speculation and stands out honestly and firmly for a higher standard of citizenship." (See *Proceedings*, U.B.C.J.A., 1920, p. 168).

[39]Joel Seidman, *American Labor From Defense to Reconstruction* (Chicago University Press, 1953), pp. 64 seq.

In reply thereto, beg to inform you that I have endeavored to my utmost to prevent the cessation of work now being done by members of our organization on ships undergoing construction for the United States Shipping Board and now that they have ceased to work, it will be impossible for me to influence them to return unless I have some definite proposition to give them pertaining to their working conditions.

You will recall some few days ago I took up with you the matter of reaching an understanding affecting the membership of our organization and you are familiar with what transpired at that time, and you have no doubt been informed by your representative whom you referred the matter to of the fact that nothing was accomplished looking towards arriving at some understanding.

The United Brotherhood of Carpenters and Joiners of America is composed of patriotic and loyal citizens, thousands of whom are now serving their country, many others have sons who are in the service. Millions of dollars have been invested by our organization and our members in the purchasing of Liberty Bonds to assist the Government in the prosecution of the War. We stand ready and willing to further show our patriotism by renewing the memorandum as presented to your Mr. Blackman on the date of February 7, 1918, where the services of our entire organization was offered to the United States Shipping Board to assist in carrying out their program of shipbuilding. And I, personally, stand ready and willing to assist in bringing about a condition that will be satisfactory and just for our membership.

I beg to remain,

> Yours most respectfully,
> Wm. L. Hutcheson, General President,
> United Brotherhood of Carpenters and
> Joiners of America.

But the Chairman of the United States Shipping Board would have none of this, fully confident in his position that both the public and the press had been sufficiently aroused and would thus bring down wrath and damnation on one so unpatriotic in their midst. On February 15, the walkout of the Carpenters spread to Baltimore, and Hurley once again released a telegram in which he protested that the Carpenters were "as loyal as members of other crafts" . . . and "to go back to work and trust their Government through the Labor Adjustment Board to deal fairly with them. . . ."

Realizing that he could get nowhere and that some further effort would have to be made to bring a quick adjustment of the controversy, Hutcheson called on President Woodrow Wilson to intervene.

Hon. Woodrow Wilson, President
U.S.A.

My dear Mr. President:

The situation now existing in the shipyards is of a nature that requires immediate attention. I, as President of the United Brotherhood of Carpenters and Joiners of America, endeavored to reach an understanding with the offi-

cials of the United States Shipping Board, but was unable to do so. I feel that
if given the opportunity to lay the matter fully before you, that a solution
could be quickly arrived at. I desire to inform you, my dear Mr. President,
that I, as a patriotic citizen, am desirous of rendering every assistance to you
and our country to carry on the work necessary to bring about a successful
conclusion of the World War in which we are engaged.

> Yours most respectfully and sincerely,
> Wm. L. Hutcheson, General Pres.
> United Brotherhood of Carpenters and
> Joiners of America.

President Wilson replied the next day, advising Hutcheson that if
he conferred with the Macy Board, a settlement could be arranged. On
February 19, Hutcheson induced the Carpenters to return to work with
the promise that their grievances would be given immediate consideration.

From February 19 to February 21, Hutcheson bargained with the
various members of the Macy Board. On the twenty-first, Piez, General
Manager of the U.S. Shipping Board, agreed to take up the question
of special consideration for the United Brotherhood of Carpenters and
Joiners of America if the other signatories of the Agreement approved.

Hutcheson met with the full Macy Board on March 5. Both Franklin
D. Roosevelt, representing the Navy, and A. J. Berres, representing the
Metal Trades Department, declared themselves satisfied with the Board
as it was then constituted. However, Berres made it plain that if the U.B.
got special consideration and was granted conditions which the other
trades had not received, the other unions which had signed the original
Agreement would press for similar demands. Here matters stood.

As a parting note at this conference, which was Hutcheson's last, he
reiterated: ". . . that we propose to retain that right of citizenship so long
as there was permitted to exist between us and our Government a
profiteer who was paid a percentage on labor performed by our members,
but that if we worked direct for the Government we would raise no question as to whom we work with."[40] The United Brotherhood never became a party to the Agreement, and the Agreement was never changed.

---

[40] *The Carpenter,* Vol. XXXVIII: 5, (May, 1918), pp. 11, 12.

CHAPTER | VI

BIRTH OF LABOR EQUALITY

Alone among the A. F. of L. union leaders, with Samuel Gompers as President, Hutcheson had had the courage and foresight to press in a war for democracy for "co-equal" representation, participation and responsibility of labor together with the "other associations of financial and manufacturing establishments." From the very beginning he spoke out against a loose, confusing war labor policy under which all of the A. F. of L. union leaders chafed. The sole union leader, not a signatory to the Agreement, who recognized Hutcheson's position, was W. J. Bowen of the Bricklayers. He told the delegates to the 1918 Building Trades Department Convention that, "I want to have it clearly understood that at the time he [Hutcheson] was under fire (February, 1918), men high in the affairs of organized labor in America ought to have made it clear why he made this stand." Bowen went on to say that while Hutcheson was struggling for the principle of the union shop which all the trade union leaders wanted and felt entitled to, the other leaders had deserted him, afraid to face public censure, Bowen concluded his remarks:

> "I am opposed to the efforts of those who condemned Hutcheson's efforts to make a condition prevail. I take my stand with Hutcheson. Those who would distort what the man attempted to do, either did not fully understand or they designedly took advantage of a situation that might make them stand good with somebody else. Mr. President, I hold to wit: that if the unionism that you and I understand and that has been instilled into us is good in any direction it is best suited where an application of it can be made to apply. This is going to be given expression to on the floor of the Convention that begins next week, I presume, because if I were in that position that certain men are it would occupy the attention of the delegates."[1]

[1]*The Carpenter,* Vol. XXXVII: 8, (August, 1918), pp. 44-45.

The Carpenters' strike not only exposed the imperious arrogance of bureaucratic managers in charge of Governmental agencies and the anti-union attitudes of employers, but the inadequacies of the Government's whole labor program. It pointed up the fact that no coordinated, centralized over-all labor policy existed and that the tripartite Boards developed piecemeal through the Baker-Gompers paper, had not solved the mediation problem, and had not even dealt with the labor supply. Hutcheson, in exposing the sins and half-way makeshifts of America's War labor policy, forced President Wilson's hand in dealing with the problem squarely. In point of fact, out of these aggravated, "bad" conditions of the Carpenters' strike, labor as a whole was to make an enormous gain in the moral position of unionism. For the first time in its stormy career, and a full year after war was declared, labor was given an important voice in the direction of war agencies, and protected against unfriendly acts by employers. The anti-union employer suddenly found himself the disturber of public order instead of its professed defender. The community and its presumed spokesman, the press, accepted it as a salutary and desirable development. The position labor had thus gained temporarily in 1918 became a permanent acquisition with the passage of the Wagner Act in 1935 and set a precedent for World War II. It marked the birth of labor equality in action, and Hutcheson had no small share in its conception.

The agreement between management and labor for the settlement of disputes by a Board on which both parties would have equal representation was soon to become a fact. This was what Hutcheson had been clamoring for all through the war in disputes with Hurley. There were hopes, on the part of Hutcheson as well as of many others, that the war-time success in working together peacefully would lay the groundwork and carry over into the post-war period and permit the reaching of an agreement under which the danger of strikes could be minimized. These hopes proved impossible of attainment. Once hostilities were over, management fought bitterly to take determination of employment conditions back into their own hands. As we shall soon see, the iron law of supply and demand reversed its short-lived cycle.

There was no doubt but that the President's position was a difficult one. For a whole year, he tolerated Hurley's profanities and sanctimonious flag-waving, of which Hutcheson, incidentally, was not the sole target.[2] Hutcheson's telegram requesting a personal interview with the President sprang from his conviction that he was friendly toward labor. "We people of this country can thank our good stars that Woodrow Wilson is in the Presidential chair instead of some of his recent Republican

---

[2]Louis B. Wehle, *op. cit.*, p. 61

Union "Volunteers", among them his big son Maurice, helped Bill Hutcheson build a larger and more modern house in 1913. Hardly had the family set foot in it, when the call came from the Brotherhood to "take up your duties as resident Vice-President in Indianapolis."

N. Y. American, Feb. 27, 1918

"We'll match the shipbuilders 'sacrifice for sacrifice'" the General President of
the United Brotherhood of Carpenters assured Woodrow Wilson.

Members of the National War Labor Board of World War I, as they assembled on March 14, 1918 to discuss principles and policies governing relations between worker and employer "for the duration." Establishment of the WLB was an outgrowth of Hutcheson's crusade for labor equality. Left to right: B. L. Worden, W. H. Van Dervoort, Loyal A. Osborne, L. F. Loree, Frank J. Hayes, T. A. Rickert, William L. Hutcheson, former president William Howard Taft, U. S. Secretary of Labor Wilson, C. Edwin Michael, Frank P. Walsh and Victor Olander.

In Manchester, England, 1924 — William L. Hutcheson, (right) General Secretary F. Wolsencroft (center) of the Amalgamated Society of Woodworkers and George H. Lakey, Vice-President of the Brotherhood discuss the fusion of both labor organizations.

predecessors," said he a year before America's entry into the war.[3] To him, Wilson was the authentic voice of American democracy, of that hope of a better and richer life for the mass of humble and ordinary folk who make up the American nation. To Hutcheson, Wilson's was the voice of the Democratic frontier, of Abe Lincoln, and Teddy Roosevelt.

On January 4, 1918, after a series of conferences with the members of the Council of National Defense, President Wilson appointed the Secretary of Labor as War Labor Administrator. Later, on January 28, on President Wilson's authority, the Secretary of Labor called together the War Labor Conference Board for the purpose of formulating in advance a series of principles to be applied in labor management disputes during the war. On it sat five labor men appointed by the American Federation of Labor, and five industry men chosen by the National Industrial Conference Board. These men, in turn, chose two public members who alternated as Chairman. Hutcheson participated in these conferences.[4] His "plan of mediation and arbitration" became the model upon which labor-management relations were based for the duration of the war and, but for certain departures, were substantially followed in World War II.

On March 29, 1918, Hutcheson submitted his plan to the Secretary of Labor Wilson which established the National War Labor Board. The latter endorsed it enthusiastically and on April 3, Hutcheson received simultaneous acknowledgements from the Secretary of Labor and the President of the United States:

April 2, 1918

My Dear Mr. Hutcheson:

I am in receipt of the report of the War Labor Conference Board outlining a plan of mediation and arbitration for the period of the war. It is a splendid piece of work which gives us the assurance of industrial peace at home while we are combating the common enemy from abroad. Accept my sincere congratulations.

Sincerely yours,

W. B. Wilson,
Secretary of Labor
Washington, D. C.

In appreciation of Hutcheson's contribution to the creation of the National War Labor Board, President Wilson wrote:[4]

---

[3]*Dallas News,* June 20, 1916, p. 1, *Hutcheson's Private Papers* (1916).

[4]Those representing labor besides Hutcheson were: Frank J. Hayes, President of the United Mine Workers of America, J. A. Franklin, Pres. of the Brotherhood of Boilermakers, Victor Olander, representing Seamen's Union and T. A. Rickert, Pres. of United Garment Workers.

April 2, 1918

The White House, Washington

My Dear Mr. Hutcheson:

I have been so much and so deeply gratified, in common I believe with the great body of our fellow-citizens, by the outcome of the conference of the War Labor Conference Board that I cannot deny myself the privilege and pleasure of writing you at least a line to say how highly serviceable I believe the result attained will be to the country and how fine an example it is of the spirit of cooperation and concession which is drawing our people together in this time of supreme crisis.

Cordially and Sincerely yours,

Woodrow Wilson

On the fifth of April, Hutcheson replied to the President's letter, in which he expressed "gratification of the results attained," reassuring the President, that, "it is my desire in the future, as I have in the past, to put forth the best thought and effort I possess for the services of our country and its citizens."[5] By proclamation, on April 8, 1918, President Wilson created the National War Labor Board, later known popularly as the "Taft-Walsh Board," to promote and carry on mediation and adjustment in the field of production necessary for the effective conduct of the war. . . . "The two chief appointees were former President William Howard Taft and Frank Walsh, who had headed the Joint Congressional Commission on Industrial Relations of 1915. Management and organized labor were equally represented on the new Board.

The establishment of the National War Labor Board was the first recognition by the government that the labor problem in times of war was basically a mobilization problem, and should henceforth be handled by labor relations experts; moreover, its creation represented a mighty step forward: labor had recognition of its rights to organize and bargain collectively — rights which it did not possess before.

Three days before President Wilson's official proclamation, creating the N.W.L.B., Hutcheson sent out a special circular addressed "To the Officers and Members of all Local Unions," in which he announced the formation of the Board, its purposes, personnel, scope, and the manner in which a local union is to proceed on a controversy.

Although the charter of the National War Labor Board exhorted vaguely against wartime strikes or lockouts, it definitely did not extract a no-strike pledge from labor! While the founding documents asked that there be no strikes or lockouts, they provided no effective penalties against striking workers. "You will note," stated Hutcheson in his printed circular, "that there *should* (his emphasis) be no strikes or lockouts during the war." "This the representative of labor could readily agree to be-

---

[5]*Hutcheson's Private Papers.* April 5, 1918.

cause of the fact that at all times we contend that there should be no strikes, and owing to conditions confronting our country we can maintain unto ourselves our rights as citizens of the U.S. and as trade unionists. This, however, would not mean, that as a last resort we could *not strike,* (ours) but it signifies our willingness to agree that all methods of mediation and conciliation should be exhausted before resorting to ceasing work."[6]

In return for its cooperation, labor received everything which the Carpenters' leader had been demanding. Through Hutcheson's dramatic demonstration, the continued existence of the union shop where it is prevailed and all other superior union labor standards were guaranteed. Labor received the right to organize defense workers, provided only that no coercion was used. Eight hours were declared the basic day and the cost of living was declared the yardstick for fair wages. Finally, the Department of Labor was declared the official labor mobilizing agency and was ordered to use the facilities of the trade unions in its recruiting activities. This was as Hutcheson had demanded since the advent of the war.

The leaders of the United Brotherhood greeted the National War Labor Board with unqualified enthusiasm. It was expressed by Hutcheson in a telegram to President Wilson four days after the Board's creation:[7]

". . . We are in hearty accord with the principles, functions and powers of the National War Labor Board as set forth . . . Under date of March 19, 1918, and approved. We hope that all Departments of the Government will cooperate with the Board, so that basic conditions under which labor shall be employed on Government work, direct or through contractors, may be established and thereby bring contentment among the workers, which has not existed up to this time. . . . A few days after war was declared we offered the services of the members of our organization in whatever way they were most needed. We take this opportunity to assure you that we have never deviated from that position and we again offer you . . . the services of our membership of 308,000 men . . . (and) the entire machinery of our organization . . . so that the war may be speedily won, freedom proclaimed and worldwide democracy established . . ."

Three days later, President Wilson congratulated Hutcheson and the Brotherhood for the "action" they had taken.

"Your telegram of April 12 conveys a most welcome message. The action taken by the U.B.C.J.A. . . . does them the highest credit and speaks a spirit of patriotism which I am sure will meet the applause and approbation of all public-spirited men."

---

[6]*Hutcheson's Private Papers,* June 7, 1918.

[7]"The War Labor Board," *Proceedings of Twentieth Convention,* U.B.C.J.A. (1920), p. 283.

Throughout the rest of the war, Hutcheson actively participated in the Board, and the United Brotherhood cooperated closely with it.

While ex-President William Howard Taft's appointment to the National War Labor Board was greeted with plaudits and considerable exuberance by the National Industrial Conference Board, that of Hutcheson and Frank P. Walsh was viewed with anxiety and misgivings. With unconcealed brazenness, this otherwise respectable body of industrialists not only sought to influence Taft but also to prejudice him against Walsh, Hutcheson and other labor men on the Board. Its "communiques" to Taft simulated kindness, respect and exaggerated flattery but never once neglected an opportunity to deride and express contempt for the labor men who served with Taft. It might be that the National Industrial Conference Board had good reason to remember Taft, the President, who although weak and pliable, was not a reactionary himself. He did little to resist the reactionary forces from regaining headway, and the United States Chamber of Commerce had remembered with fondness his guiding hand.

Self-righteous Ralph M. Easley, with his patriotic business executives of the National Civic Federation was another anxious correspondent who tried to tempt Taft into an alliance with the five employer representatives "selected by our Conference Board." This paragon of "Americanism" lost no time to write Mr. Taft on April 18, 1918:

"Dear Mr. Taft:

As I predicted to you that no agreement could come out of a committee on which you, Frank P. Walsh, Hutcheson and Van Der Voort (representing the employers) were lined up . . . the two dangerous problems, vis, the Closed and Open Shop and compulsory arbitration, have been solved in the only practical way in which they could be solved. . . . Of course you will have to be prepared for attempts to violate the contract by the disloyal members of the union. . . ."[8]

Melancholy evidence at hand reveals that the effectiveness of the National War Labor Board was entirely due to the cooperation of the Government, the five labor representatives and their alternates and the confidence that was created among the workers by its decisions. The Board had acted in more than 11,000 industrial controversies and had handed down 200 awards and recommendations involving hundreds of thousands of workers and hundreds of millions of dollars in wages. "All this was accomplished in spite of the fact that even during the period of hostilities there was no effective cooperation on the part of the five employer members appointed by the National Industrial Conference Board. On the part of certain of them there was not only no cooperation

[8]William Howard Taft Papers, Yale Series 37, Feb.-April (Library of Congress).

but active attempts to hinder effective functioning of the Board and destroy its usefulness."[9]

This experience with the recalcitrant employers inside the War Labor Board was not entirely lost on ex-President Taft. Initially, his designation distressed Hutcheson as much as it did Frank J. Hayes of the United Mine Workers and Frank P. Walsh, all of whom were not entirely unaware that Taft had treated labor's appeals for legal redress throughout his administration with rank indifference. Samuel Gompers, who only once in his thirty-seven long year career as president of the American Federation of Labor had deviated from his non-partisan political policy, derided Taft and the Republican Party so bitterly as to become an ally of the Democrats. Only two years earlier, Hutcheson himself had spoken deprecatingly of Taft as he addressed his first union convention in the role of General President of the Brotherhood, when he thanked the "stars for President Wilson." This in no wise deterred Hutcheson and Taft from developing a quick and lasting friendship.

While hard-headed Hutcheson was indulgent with the harshness of labor's criticism of Taft, he undertook despite it, to woo the ex-President and win him over to labor's side. If there was an admitted change of attitude in Taft toward labor during the war it was due to Hutcheson's wooing of Taft. Taft's "submissiveness to the constant stimulus" of William Hutcheson, who served with Taft on the National War Labor Board spelled the difference between the ex-president's conservatism in the White House and his liberalism in the Supreme Court of the United States. Unfortunately, Frank P. Walsh's role on the Board was rendered innocuous by the many antagonists, among them the employers' representatives, who hated Walsh and his well-known pro-labor sympathies. Even Taft's own son, Charles P. Taft, the "liberal" in the Taft family, sought to discredit that well-known liberal in missives to his father.[10]

The Taft-Hutcheson friendship began with their common interest in conservation and reforestration. Hutcheson himself had seen a whole generation of Americans despoiling the land of Michigan while subduing it, forests were hacked to pieces, farm land misused, natural resources plundered right and left.

Taft was fascinated by Hutcheson's matter-of-fact narratives of the rape of the forests in the north country. Often they were seen together walking the streets of Washington during the war, busily engaged in a serious talk. Hutcheson's bluntness and demeanor were a refreshing ex-

---

[9]William Howard Taft Papers, Yale Series 42, Jan.-Feb., 1918 (Library of Congress).

[10]*New Republic Vol. XXVII* (July 27, 1921), p. 230; See also Alan E. Ragean, "Chief Justice Taft" *Ohio State Archeological and Historical Society,* Vol. VIII (Columbus, 1938).

perience to the portly professor who had been persuaded to take a leave of absence from Yale Law School and serve as co-Chairman to the National War Labor Board, a post he had hesitated to accept because "labor would be displeased" with his appointment. Hutcheson's alert intelligence impressed Taft. His adroit handling of the employer members on the Board provoked amusement and concealed admiration from Taft.

It was more than a source of pride to the Carpenter's President to have been accepted in the ex-President's household, where he made his first acquaintance with young Robert Alonzo Taft, the "conservative," with whom he was to hobnob years later in Washington after the latter was elected U. S. Senator from Ohio. Hutcheson always looked ahead. His eighteen-month-old association with the ex-President was an experience that he never failed to retell to his intimates. For a whole year and more Taft drew heavily on the resources and experience of the Carpenters' President. If Taft now seemed to atone for his reactionary "sins" through a liberal record as co-chairman of the National War Labor Board, a measure of it was due to his association with Hutcheson.

With the dissolution of the War Labor Board early in 1919, Hutcheson continued his friendship with the ex-President, writing him terse notes, inquiring of his health. And when William Howard Taft was appointed Chief Justice of the United States Supreme Court in the summer of 1921, Hutcheson congratulated him. Taft replied:[11]

Pointe a-Pic, Canada
July 26, 1921

William L. Hutcheson, Esq. Carpenters Bldg.
Washington, D.C."

"My dear old Hutch:

     I have your kind letter of July 20th, and thank you very much for your warm congratulations upon my appointment to be Chief Justice. I thank you, too, for thinking that I will try and do the fair and impartial thing. With warm regards and pleasant memories of our associations in the National War Labor Board, believe me, as always,

Sincerely yours,
William Howard Taft[12]

The Carpenters' President did not see eye-to-eye with Samuel Gompers, who opposed Taft's appointment.

An attempt to coordinate the numerous labor activities of the Government was now made in May, 1918 by the appointment of a War Labor Policies Board in the Department of Labor. Felix Frankfurter was chosen Chairman, and the Board included representatives of all the various departments and agencies dealing with labor matters. It did not under-

---

[11]Taft Papers, *Supreme Court Series,* July 2, 1921.
[12]*Taft Papers* Yale Series 37 (May-June, 1918), War Labor Board, April 3, 1918.

take detailed administration, but served as a clearing house through which policies might be unified. It investigated such matters as central recruiting of labor, a project that Hutcheson advocated from the very beginning of the war; standardization of wages, conditions of work, dilution and training employment of women and children, and other current problems.

American workers were disturbed during the summer of 1918 as skyrocketing living costs sent their real wages plummeting. Profit-hungry businessmen nullified Frankfurter's program of wage stabilization by sending the price spiral spinning mercilessly upward. In a determined effort to set this unwanted condition in balance, Frankfurter called a hurried conference of the various adjustment agencies on September 9. All representatives in attendance unanimously agreed not to make any changes without the initial approval of the committee. Fully five weeks later, on October 14, Frankfurter presented his stabilization plan to President Wilson.

But the war came to an abrupt end before the President formally gave Frankfurter's stabilization program his attention. Thereafter, he took no further action, leaving the disbalanced domestic peacetime economy to shift for itself.

What were the actual effects of the war on the United Brotherhood? There can be no doubt that the United Brotherhood made enormous gains. With a membership of 263,395 in 1916, the Brotherhood rose to well over 300,000. It went up steadily until 1920, becoming the largest union in the building trades with a membership of 402,778.[13] It was through Hutcheson's knowledge of the economic power relationships in a democratic America, coupled with conscientious planning, that the Brotherhood attained a degree of national recognition, power and status it had never possessed before.

[13]Leo Wolman, *The Growth of American Trade Unions* (National Bureau of Economic Research, N. Y. 1929), pp. 46-49, *U.B.C.J.A. Membership* (1881-1953).

CHAPTER | VII

THE ERA OF DISILLUSIONMENT

From the colonists hoping to establish a Biblical commonwealth in New England, to nineteenth century reformers planning the abolition of sin, the Americans have always exhibited a strain of millennial thinking. This trait persisted with the twentieth century. During the World War, dreamers who were busy reconstructing the social and economic order and the architecture of the Versailles Treaty aspired to inaugurate a "permanent and just peace." And in the post-war period, a supposedly disillusioned generation adopted as a creed the possibility of material abundance for all men.

But during the decade that followed the Armistice the torch of idealism that had kindled the revolt of the American conscience at the dawn of our own century seemed to have pretty well burned itself. People were tired. In particular their public spirit, their consciences and their hopes were tired. The returning soldiers were disillusioned about the crusade they had been sent off on. The newly formed American Legion became one of the chief exponents of the identification of patriotism with opposition to social, political or economic reform of any kind. In some cases its members were even used against strikers. Foreigners began to seem a dubious lot anyhow; those from east and southeastern Europe were almost completely barred in 1924; American enthusiasm for the League of Nations petered out. People felt it was time to relax; to look after their own gardens, rather than after other people and the world in general; and to have a good time.

In the United States, there was neither a revolutionary movement nor a political party representing labor. The Socialist party, whose influence had been growing for many years, notwithstanding the fact that it seemed foreign to the nature of Americans, suffered considerable defections when it decided not to support the war. The split with the Communists further weakened it. Eugene V. Debs, who was renominated for the Presidency in 1912, gathered a vote of 897,000 and found himself jailed. Nevertheless, there was a good deal of discussion of economic and social reconstruction. The brief unemployment crisis that accompanied demobilization and the abolition of war controls, including much of the labor adjustment machinery, gave rise to a feeling of insecurity. The cost of living went on rising more rapidly than ever, and the patriotic inhibition on strikes no longer affected labor.

In 1919 the first serious strike in many years was launched to organize labor in the steel industry, which was traditionally anti-union and had broken the only labor organization in its field a generation earlier in the violent Homestead strike of 1892-1893. Over one-third of the steel workers had a twelve-hour day. Another large fraction of the steel workers still had the ten-hour day, while a small minority had achieved the forty-eight hour week then prevalent throughout the country. The regular labor movement, as represented by the A. F. of L., was poorly prepared, at least financially,* to challenge this industrial giant whose treasury was filled to overflowing from fat war contracts. No single organization held undisputed union jurisdiction over the steel industry, but twenty-four crafts and trade unions claimed the right to enroll the various occupations in it. No one of them had the resources to carry on a successful strike of the small minority of workers over whom it had jurisdiction.

In order to cope with this situation, the Federation's convention in 1918 passed the resolution introduced by William Z. Foster to form a steel workers organizing committee, consisting of the presidents of twenty-four international unions claiming jurisdiction in the industry. The chairman of the committee was John Fitzpatrick, an honest veteran labor leader, and president of the Chicago Federation of Labor.

One of the central body's potent influences, William Z. Foster, then posing as a regular trade unionist, was in fact a believer in Syndicalism, who thought that by this method of organization the Federation might be induced to accept at least an approach to industrial unionism. The committee started its organization work in September 1918, with a high degree of success in the Chicago District, Indiana, and Ohio,

---

*Only three years previously, on Oct. 16, 1916, President Gompers proudly announced that the A.F.L. had at long last realized one of its great dreams: it had purchased its own building, which stands at the corner of 9th St. and Massachusetts Ave. N.W., Washington, D.C.; and that it had an additional trunk telephone line now connecting it with the outside world.

where the National War Labor Board prevented the discharge of union members. Later, when it went up to the Pittsburgh District it encountered much greater difficulty, for the National War Labor Board had ceased functioning. Yet, because of the spontaneous interest in the movement on the part of the workers themselves, it made more headway than the employers suspected. On July 20, 1919, the committee asked the United States Steel Corporation to confer about its demands, chief among which were the abolition of the twelve-hour shift, one day's rest in seven, wage increases, and an eight-hour day. Judge Gary refused to confer with their leaders or discuss the matter. He insisted that there was no issue except communism and the confiscation of property. His position was backed by other executives in the mass production industries. It was clear that the unionization of steel would open the way for unions in the rubber, automobile, and other assembly line plants. The result was the calling of a strike, which began on September 22.

Despite the pleas of President Wilson and Samuel Gompers that the steel strike be suspended, William Z. Foster went ahead with his plans, effectively shutting down the steel districts. The companies replied by the use of every device of industrial warfare. Their full-page newspaper advertisements, aided by friendly editorial opinion, labeled the strike leaders as Reds. Local police officials broke up the union meetings. In Gary, Indiana, Negro strike-breakers were called into the steel plants; when the strikers rioted, federal troops moved to establish martial law. Under these circumstances, defeat was inevitable. The unions themselves fumbled their strategy; skilled workers remained indifferent to the plight of the unskilled "hunkies," who for the greater part consisted of southeast European immigrants; and an adequate strike treasury was lacking.**

The struggle over, changes were grudgingly made in the more blatant abuses, the low wage scale and the twelve-hour shift, but the citadel remained impregnable to organization. There was a moral victory, however. The Industrial Relations Department of the Inter-Church World Movement thoroughly investigated (1922) the strike, supported the steel workers, and exposed the rough tactics of the steel companies. Not much later, the steel workers won an eight-hour day

---

**The problem of financing the steel strike was uppermost in the mind of President Gompers and the Executive Council of the A.F.L. on October 6, 1919. The National Committee for organizing the Iron and Steel Workers started its activities with but $1,000, whereas the "actual strike payroll was over $200,000 a month for the past three months." President Tobin of the International Brotherhood of Teamsters said "their organization was in no position to place additional burdens on their membership." "The Miners have helped by giving organizers, and since the strike they have placed 16 additional organizers in the field to assist to win the strike," reported John L. Lewis. (Hutcheson's Private Letters, Oct. 5-22, 1919, Washington, D.C.).

through the pressures applied by William Levi Hutcheson and the church leaders upon President Warren G. Harding.[1] But unionization of the mass industries had to await a more favorable climate with the coming of the New Deal era. Unfortunately, it was this large group which felt the full force of the industrial policy of exploitation of labor, and was in need of any help they might receive through unionization.

The failure and financial inability of the American Federation of Labor and its affiliates to organize the unskilled and the semi-skilled in the mass production industries, due in large measure to the unyielding opposition of the all-powerful industrial groups and the mounting anti-union climate following the war, encouraged the small revolutionary wing in labor to carry their propaganda among the unorganized. Yet, it was the self-interest of the craftsmen, particularly the carpenters, printers, cigar-makers, and the highly-skilled metal tradesmen, that spurred on the American labor movement despite the fact that recurrent panics and managerial opposition had wiped out many flourishing trade unions. This motivation undoubtedly accounted for the Federation's making great strides during the war, provided it with a high degree of solidarity and equipped it to fight more effectively for its existence.

Ironically enough, management regarded the Federation as dangerously radical, along with the Communists and the "Wobblies" who were closely akin to the Russian Bolsheviks. They associated all unionism with collectivism. The object of all three, the Communists, the International Workers of the World, and the American Federation of Labor, was the over-turn of free enterprise. They had been jarred by the abortive strike in steel. They believed the unions had no business in their plants .They were determined, at all costs, to keep the unions out, and one way of doing it was to inaugurate the American Plan.

As for William Z. Foster, he emerged shortly as a militant Communist leader, whose ultimate revolutionary objective tended to undermine the American labor movement as well as to discredit its leaders.

While the steel strike was in its last stages, the soft coal miners also walked out. The miners complained about unemployment and the high cost of living and asked for a sixty per cent wage increase and a thirty-hour week. The mine operators declined to negotiate with the union at all, on the ground that a strike order had been issued to go into effect if no agreement could be reached, and they would not bargain under threats. The union therefore set the last day of October for the beginning of the strike.

President Gompers of the American Federation of Labor, on October 29, telegraphed John L. Lewis that if the strike was postponed

---

[1] William Hutcheson, *Private Papers* (August, 1919).

a conference with the operators would be possible. Simultaneously, the Attorney General of the United States, A. Mitchell Palmer, made a public statement that the Act creating the Fuel Administration was still in force and that under it a strike would be illegal because of clauses forbidding combinations to restrict production and transportation. At the time of the passage of the Act in question, President Wilson had assured labor that these clauses were not intended to cover union activity. Nevertheless, Attorney General Palmer threatened that all resources of the government would be used to prevent cessation of mining operations. If it had not been for that threat, the strike might have been postponed, but the union decided that the rights of labor were at stake and that they could not compromise them by retreating before what they had regarded as an unfair procedure.

A day later, on October 30, President Wilson renewed the wartime regulation of coal prices, and on this legal basis, Attorney General Palmer persuaded Federal Judge Albert Anderson to issue a drastic and detailed restraining order preventing the union or anyone else from doing anything in aid of the strike. Judicial interdiction of union liberty could scarcely have gone further. Nevertheless, on the following day, over 400,000 miners failed to report for work. On November 8 the court order made permanent the restraining order and compelled the union to cancel its strike on November 11. The executive council of the American Federation of Labor denounced the Government for breaking faith with the Miners in its interpretation of the law and urged all affiliated organizations to support the Miners union. The strike continued for several weeks until December 14, when the renewed Fuel Administration granted a fourteen per cent wage increase to the union and, per the President's proposal, created a commission to adjudicate the Miners' other demands.

The steel and coal strikes together caused a temporary drop in the curve of industrial production and probably contributed something to the increase of prices already resulting from the excess of demand over supply. They also frayed the nerves of the industrial leaders, to whom the spectacle of the Bolshevist overturn of capitalism in Russia was frightening. Lenin and his fellow-revolutionists were a far distance from American shores, but the basic theory of Marxism was one of world revolution and already there were stirrings of unrest of labor on this continent. Strikes by hundreds of thousands of textile workers, telephone operators, and others made 1919 a critical year. Worst of all was the Boston police strike, which came as a result of the city's failure to remedy a low salary scale that began at $1100 a year. Even President Wilson denounced the strike as "a crime against civilization." Bay State Governor Calvin Coolidge declared in a politically astute reply to Samuel

Gompers, "there is no right to strike against the public safety by any-body, anywhere, anytime." This statement was so widely acclaimed that it helped to send him to the White House.

Among the labor radicals there was a perceptible sentiment for the creation of a National Labor Party. As in the past, its leaders were mainly enthusiasts and crusaders. Now, their small ranks were reinforced by cadres of militant communists who were out to convert the world to their point of view. Local labor leaders were stimulated in Chicago, New York, in the Northwest, and other cities, although the officers of the national unions in the American Federation of Labor were opposed to independent political action and did their best to discourage it. While communist Russia was relatively weak in 1919 and offered no threat to the United States, it succeeded in establishing a Fifth Column in the American trade unions and the United Brotherhood of Carpenters was not wholly immune from it.

Gompers and the executive council of the American Federation of Labor were thus subjected to a formidable push and pull from three sides. On the one hand, they had been rebuffed by a formerly friendly administration, which had given labor status and recognition, even if only for the "duration of the War." Wilson's half-hearted concern with do-mestic ferments, his incapacity to work out an industrial policy in the critical year of 1919, tended strongly to disillusion and alienate labor; his initial refusal to appoint a labor representative in the person of Gompers to the Peace Commission added insult to injury.*** On the other hand, there were the successive assaults of the die-hard employers on trade unionism itself that engendered both fear and resistance on the part of labor leadership. Finally, there were the articulate, aggressive radicals within the labor movement who threatened to capture it for in-dependent political action and to reorganize the federation on the lines of industrial unionism. There was a flood of reconstruction programs. For instance, the Chicago Federation of Labor called for an International League of Labor to complement the League of Nations, a broad program of public ownership of industry in the United States, and the stabilization of employment through a flexible program of public works.

Loath to surrender the vision of a better day so prevalent during the war, the Federation convention in June, 1918, appointed a committee to draw up a reconstruction program of its own. This program, approved by the executive council on October 28 of the same year, concentrated on trade-union gains, and endorsed the Plumb Plan of the Railroad Brotherhoods for government ownership of railroads and the nationaliza-

---

***The President initially appointed Mr. Louis Brandeis to represent American labor at the Peace Commission, but overwhelming pressure brought to bear by the A. F. of L. resulted in the appointment of Samuel Gompers.

tion of the mines and of all public utilities. Its legislative demands included a law making it a criminal offense for employers to interfere with the right to organize; protection of women and children in industry, guarantee of the right of public employees to organize; federal regulation of corporations; tax reforms; public housing; public employment exchanges; limitation of the power of the Supreme Court to declare legislation unconstitutional; guarantees of freedom of speech; and a two-year suspension of immigration. It favored a living wage, an eight-hour day, and a five-day week with prohibition of overtime, all to be achieved by trade-union action.

The storm on which trade unionism was being tossed did not subside. As an aid in riding it out, the Federation called a union conference in Washington in September 1919. The conference adopted a report entitled "Labor's Bill of Rights." This declaration, besides reiterating labor's traditional program, demanded deflation of the currency and publicity for corporate accounts, endorsed scientific management and supported the League of Nations and the International Labor Organization (ILO).

On June 7 of the same year, the Fortieth Convention of the A.F.L. elected William L. Hutcheson and President Hynes of the Sheet Metal Workers as delegates to the British Trades Union Congress and as co-delegates to the Amsterdam meeting of the International Federation of Trades. Hutcheson could not accept. The Brotherhood's campaign to counterattack the employers' vigorous assault on the building trades and trade-unionism "made it imperative that I remain in the United States."[2] Hutcheson's own disillusionment with President Wilson's futile attempt to establish a basis for co-operation between capital and labor under peacetime conditions, was reflected in his unwillingness to serve as labor's representative at the National Industrial Conference.

"Due to circumstances and occurrences I fail to see wherein I would be justified in accepting appointment to the Industrial Conference now being held,"[3] he wired Samuel Gompers on October 15, 1919. Hutcheson's displeasure over Gompers' unauthorized war-time activities which came to plague him for the greater part of the war was demonstrated at the thirty-ninth annual convention of the American Federation of Labor, on June 19, 1919. His resolution to "cancel the Baker-Gompers Agreement on or before July 1, 1919" was adopted at that convention.[4] He supported John L. Lewis at the fortieth convention, when the latter

---

[2]American Federation of Labor, *Proceedings, Fortieth Annual Convention,* (1920), p. 130.

[3]William Levi Hutcheson, *Private Papers* (1919).

[4]American Federation of Labor, *Proceedings, Thirty-ninth Annual Convention* (1919), p. 383.

entered into a campaign to dethrone Gompers and become President of the A. F. of L.****

The proposal to improve relations with labor, that the big companies of the country establish liason with Gompers and the American Federation of Labor, received a very cold reception on the part of industry; a fact which Hutcheson correctly interpreted as preliminary to a declaration of war on trade-unionism; a development which proceeded with increased momentum in the 'twenties.

President Wilson called a National Industrial Conference consisting of seventeen representatives of employers' organization and bankers, twenty-one individuals supposed to represent the public (a group which, strangely enough, included John D. Rockefeller, Jr., and Elbert H. Gary, Chairman of the United States Steel Corporation), and nineteen representatives of unions. The conference split on labor's demands that the steel strike be arbitrated, and could not reach an agreement on collective bargaining with autonomous labor organizations. The employers wished to leave the door open to employee representation plans and "company unions" that were not affiliated with the national labor movement. Labor delegates left the conference and it dissolved without reaching any conclusions.

Even Herbert Hoover was at that time regarded as "radical" by persons less conservative than the frequenters of the Union League Club. At that time, Hoover was working on the Industrial Conference of 1920. It was months prior to his appointment as U.S. Secretary of Commerce in the Harding Cabinet. In fact, he was regarded as presidential material by the Democrats, and not much later by the Republicans. It was the plan of the Democratic National Campaign Committee to nominate Herbert Hoover of California for President and Franklin D. Roosevelt of New York for Vice-President.[5]

****Lewis' biographer, Saul Alinsky writes:
"I ran against Gompers for the Presidency of the A.F.L. in 1921 because a number of unions were sickened by Gompers' dependency upon the Federal Administration. They could not stomach the reverent awe which he had in his heart for Presidents. I want to tell you that at that convention I did not campaign for a single vote . . . I never asked for a vote in my life for anything. When the count was completed I got one-third of the votes of the Federation body against Gompers." (See Saul Alinsky, John L. Lewis. An *Unauthorized Biography*, Putnam's Sons, 1949), pp. 22, 23, 24. Mr. Lewis' statements have been disputed by Frank Duffy, general secretary of the Brotherhood and then vice-president of the American Federation of Labor. Our informant revealed to the writer that Lewis did campaign for the support of Hutcheson and other Presidents of International Unions after Frank Duffy of the Carpenters turned a deaf ear to Lewis plea that he run for the Presidency of the Federation. Lewis' espousal of Industrial unionism was another reason for his break with Samuel Gompers. That Lewis' idea of "an all-inclusive union that would embrace all members of an industry regardless of skills or lack of skills," was premature was proved by subsequent developments in the 1920's.
[5]Louis B. Wehle, *Hidden Threads of History: Wilson through Roosevelt* (Macmillan, 1953), pp. 81-88.

Mr. Hoover was greatly concerned with developments in the labor relations field, particularly with the left-wing groups like the Communists and "Wobblies," and the signs pointing to outright industrial war.

He had known Gompers intimately during World War I, from 1915 to 1919. Gompers and the American Federation of Labor were in fact responsible for his appointment to head Belgian Relief, the Food Administration, and the two served together on the American Delegation to the Peace Conference in Paris. He admired Gompers, particularly his staunch opposition to the then emerging Communism.

Attempting to save the situation, Mr. Hoover called several meetings of business men at the Metropolitan Club in New York. He cautioned those present against setting up of management and labor as separate classes, believing as he did that both are producers, and not classes. He supported the organization of labor and collective bargaining by representatives of labor's own choosing.

The company officials couldn't conceive how Gompers could speak for their employees unless the employees were members of American Federation of Labor unions. The mere suggestion of establishing a better means of communication between labor and management was regarded by management as "Bolshevism."[6]

It is interesting to speculate how the Hoover Plan might have changed the whole history of labor relations in America had it met with the approval of a large segment of industry. To be sure, it would have led to the immediate unionization of the companies accepting it. Instead, labor was forced to redirect all of its energies toward a more immediate task—that of resisting the American Plan campaign, which William L. Hutcheson undertook to lead in the strategic building trades and effectively defeated in the late 'twenties. One wonders now, if the violence and bloodshed of the 1930's could have been avoided, had the dominant classes of the 'twenties not been as stupid as the nobles of France before the revolution.

---

[6]Cyrus S. Ching, *Review and Reflection* (B. C. Forbes & Sons, 1953), pp. 28-29.

PART | III

WE CAN MAKE OUR OWN FUTURE

CHAPTER | VIII

ALLIANCE FOR VICTORY

If a National Labor Party had become established in this country it would have been the product as much of die-hards as of radicals. British experience told the story for all to hear. It was very largely the end product of a series of repressive acts. Not until the existing parties had clearly indicated a stubborn refusal to compromise with trade union leaders did the latter turn to independent political action. Through harsh experience the British workmen were driven to the conclusion that as one editor expressed it, "the difference between Liberal and Tory is pretty much that between upper and nether millstone."*

By contrast the flexibility of the American system in cushioning violent movements and gradually responding to labor's plea might be of the utmost significance. Our system of government itself condemned the third party to a position of unimportance. It was Hutcheson's point of view that a leader of a third party must necessarily be satisfied with playing the role of an agitator. No regular way whereby he might enter into the governmental process has been provided. The minor party, as one writer said of the Socialist Party, "has the unique if somewhat gloomy prospect of being always a bridesmaid but never a bride in the matter of national policy. It is dead right about the fact that a marriage is taking place that is never found in the double-bed of practical politics on election night." Drawing on his own early experiences in Michigan, where labor's forays into the political field gave it many an uncomfortable hour, Hutcheson was unalterably opposed to the establishment of a third party. "A third party" he maintained "must fight where the pressure groups bargain."

*The gravity of the problem as it pertained to the 1920's was admirably stated by Walter Lippman: "Confronted with the deep insurgency of labor, what do capitalists and their spokesmen do? They resist every demand, submit only after a struggle, and prepare a condition of war to the death. When farsighted men appear in the ruling classes—men who recognize the need of a civilized answer to this increasing restlessness, the rich and the powerful treat them with scorn and a hatred that are incredibly bitter." (Walter Lippman, *A Preface to Politics*, Macmillan Co., 1933 Edition, pp. 282-283).

The call for a national party "One Big Union" came largely from enthusiastic radicals with a background of semi-feudal countries, and of native followers who made "scientific socialism" into a fundamental theology.

Actually, the facts as they obtained after the first World War did not fit into the procrustean formula of the Communists nor of the radicals. Organized labor was divided by issues both economic and psychological. Before the wage earners could be successfully organized and their purposes envisaged, many psychological factors had to be taken into account. "American workers have accepted the rags-to-riches philosophy," Hutcheson reiterated, as he privately recalled his boyhood friend, Collins. Whether or not the worker abandoned this point of view in the course of economic development is highly debatable. A National Labor Party's success would almost certainly depend on increased class-consciousness and there are no classes in the United States.

The American Federation of Labor derived its strength chiefly from craft unions—skilled workers forming the aristocracy of labor. The conflict of interests between such wage earners and their less skilled fellows had not been lessened. By its very nature, craft unionism could never embrace the whole of the working class, and for industrial unionism to win complete control of the labor movement would require not only time but also basic changes in the attitudes of the skilled workers. Assuming that labor could have reached agreements within its own ranks and the increase in wages would have had a stimulating rather than a contrary effect upon unionization after World War I, it did not follow that a distinct national labor party could have been formed. Organized labor was certainly not strong enough to succeed. The strength of union labor was estimated at 5,000,000 and its ranks continued to diminish.

Organized labor's reaction to the bewildering events of the postwar period expressed itself in the formation of the Non-Partisan Political Committee, on December 13, 1919. It reflected "Labor's Grievances, Protests and Demands," and a determination to apply "every legitimate means and all of the power at its command to accomplish the defeat of Labor's enemies who aspired to public office."

President Gompers and the Executive Council of the A. F. of L. opposed the building of a "National Political Labor Party." Gompers assumed that the State was a neutral power; the possession of which was open to all citizens in equal degree. The U. S. labor movement had not been led by men who thought in terms of class struggle, nationalization of wealth, and the like. It focused on ways and means. The movement had need of all of its intelligence and skill to attain tangible gains for wage earners. It had conjured up no imaginary ideological battles and paid scant heed to the soothsayer.

As a minority movement, labor had in the past reacted sporadically and intensely against the status quo. Since the war, however, it had greater significance, owing not to the protests of the movement but rather to the spirit of quiet conviction. "Labor had achieved one conquest, the precious right of recognition, for which I fought," argued Hutcheson. And it was only for the duration of the War.

"My approach had given workers in wartime more than they could have won by direct share of political power as a party. Through the establishment of the National War Labor Board, labor obtained an enhancement of its position with the government; the Taft-Walsh Labor Board marked that advance."

While postwar labor had been subjected to strains and stresses from all sides, a realistic appraisal of its own position, buttressed by a unique American environment hinted at above, logically led the Federation to retain its "non-partisan" character. But this "non-partisan political action" did not envisage non-partisanship but aggressive bargaining with the dominant political party. Through its lobbying activities, labor could participate in the task of adjusting conflicting interests and of constructive devices for management. A third party, however, was not a device suited to achieve this end. Third parties have been primarily concerned with advertising their wares on the national market, rather than with adjusting immediate and urgent conflicts.

"In the 1920's organized labor needed fighting spokesmen and tested champions," stressed Hutcheson. How could such men work most efficiently? "The answer is that labor leaders had greater scope if they remained outside political parties. The labor movement could not be ignored by the politicians, so long as it remained uncommitted to either party." As a pressure group, the movement was a force that might shift for or against the Democratic or Republican candidates.

The methods of politics in the United States have also suggested a division of labor between the professional party man and the special interest representative. The latter filled the very useful function of organizing and clarifying the views of persons having definite but limited common interests.

When Hutcheson joined the Harding-Coolidge team in 1920, he viewed himself in that role. His first chance came when, on the morning of August 23, 1920, there arrived a letter from Senator Warren G. Harding, Presidential candidate of the Republican party, inviting him "to add to the dignity of the occasion," meaning Labor Day. The Carpenter's General President was profoundly moved. Partly a Hoosier himself on his maternal grandmother's side, William L. Hutcheson accepted the invitation, though never forgetful of the fact that the Brotherhood of Carpenters' came first in the scheme of things.

United States Senate,

WASHINGTON, D. C.

Marion, Ohio
August 21, 1920.

Mr. Wm. H. Hutchinson,
International Carpenters &
Joiners of America,
Carpenters' Building,
Indianapolis, Indiana.

My dear Mr. Hutchinson:

I am going to participate in
the Labor Day program here in my home
City of Marion,.September 6th, and it
would be a very great compliment to me
and a satisfaction as well, if you
could somehow arrange to be present on
that day and add to the dignity and
importance of the occasion and perhaps
find opportunity to becomingly say a
word.

I recall your expressions sometime back when you expressed a wish to
be helpful and I should like you to
know that this occasion is one in which
I think you can be of considerable
assistance. Moreover, it will be a
pleasure to meet and greet you personally
once more.

Very sincerely yours[1],

WGH-L

W. G. Harding

---

[1] William L. Hutcheson, *Private Correspondence* (August, 1920).

August 25, 1920

Mr. Warren G. Harding
Marion, Ohio

My dear Mr. Harding:

Yours of August twenty-first at hand and in reply thereto would advise
that I had made no arrangements to participate in a Labor Day celebration
due to the fact that the Twentieth General Convention of our Brotherhood
convenes in this city on September twentieth and there are many pre-con-
vention matters demanding my personal attention; however, nothing unfore-
seen happening, I will accept your invitation and make arrangements to be
in the City of Marion on Labor Day.

I would appreciate if you would inform me as to the time the program
begins so that I may time my arrival in accordance therewith.

Very truly yours,
William L. Hutcheson[2]

WLH
JMS

The setting up of a research division in the National Republican
Committee headquarters in 1919 provided Hutcheson with an opportunity to channel labor intelligence, as well as to place recommendations
before the 1920 resolution committee.

For twenty-four years thereafter, including periods of suspended ani-
mation and avowed conservatism favored by the general climate of
opinion during the 'twenties, Hutcheson chose to fight his political battles
in behalf of labor within the Republican Party.[3] He influenced its labor
planks for eight successive Presidential elections, gave it other moral
assistance and on occasion, made personal token contributions to the Indiana State Republican Committee. For a quarter of a century, Hutcheson was the only labor leader of any consequence who goaded the
Old Guard into accepting a more "liberalizing" affirmative program. In
periods of economic distress, its pedestrian pace and outcome distressed
him. Nonetheless, there arose many indications that Republicans read
a lesson from history. Certainly, since 1936 Republican leaders vied in
showing how to be liberal and conservative at the same time. True to his
role, Hutcheson always worked for immediate and concrete advantages,
focusing upon ways for advancing the strength of the carpenters by gaining wages and other concessions rather than preaching loyalty to the
kind of a social order that would be best in the future.

Hutcheson's own political belief was expressed in the following
terms:

[2]*Ibid.*
[3]Peddleton Herring, *The Politics of Democracy, American Parties in Action*
(W. W. Norton & Co., 1936), p. 242.

". . . No one will gainsway or deny the importance of political action on the part of wage earners in their constant struggle to right the wrongs and to secure to the workers a full and equal opportunity to life and liberty and the pursuit of happiness. Differences arise not on the principle of political action, but to the extent of which economic trade union determinism should be supplemented by political power and influence of the wage earners should be manifested.

"That there is room for improvement in the efficient exercise of the political power of the wage earners is freely admitted. *The dangers of exercising this power from a purely partisan political standpoint* (emphasis ours) is convincingly portrayed in the report of the Executive Council . . . With the increasing tendency to place employees in public and semi-public utilities under public and governmental control there is an increasing need of more closely solidifying the forces of labor in all their varied manifestations and in such a manner as not to interfere with the workers' freedom of choice and freedom of action. To render ineffective, or to hamper in any degree, or to lessen the importance and value of trade union economic determinism merely to attain possession of political authority, to place into dominance political parliamentarism will not have been a gain but a loss to the advancement of the workers to a fuller, a freer, a better and nobler life."[4]

As the leader of the second largest voluntary economic organization in the "non-partisan" American Federation of Labor, Hutcheson had now come of age. Harding, the presidential nominee and standard bearer of the Republicans, had persuaded his party that it was good politics to accept a labor leader into the fold, providing both with a means of playing at the game of politics in a way that would enable the party politician and the labor leader to profit from each other's support and views.

Neither the Democratic party nor the Republican party offered significant choices in the election of 1920. Weary of striving onward and upward, the electorate favored a "return to normalcy." The great creative period of the progressive era was over. Even the Wilson administration, once consecrated to reform, lapsed into lethargy. For two years it fumbled the pressing problem of labor and industrial relations. It sought to cure ills by exhortation, and even resorted to violence by invoking military force to settle a steel strike. In December, 1918, President Wilson announced the relaxation of government control and looked forward to the "ordinary normal process of private initiative." Organized labor, once profoundly grateful to the Wilson administration and vigorously supporting the Democratic ticket, withdrew into neutral isolation, bidding for the sturdy hand of the farmer to strengthen its ranks in its Non-Partisan political campaign. The Cox-Franklin D. Roosevelt team was as colorless as it was dull. Furthermore, Hutcheson's resistance to the open shop in Army and Navy land construction under

---

[4]*U.B.C.J.A. Proceedings of the Twentieth General Convention,* (1920), pp. 352-353.

the Baker-Gompers Agreement, and his altercations with Assistant Secretary of the Navy, Franklin Delano Roosevelt, were reasons enough to dislike the Vice-Presidential nominee.[5]

The retreat became a route in 1920. Warren G. Harding was elected President by a popular majority of 6,000,000. He was the Senator from Ohio whose great assets, aside from his charm and good looks, were his kindliness, folksiness and humility. An amiable man of no lofty intellectual or moral stature, he had no urge to improve anything. "America's present need is not heroics but healing; not nostrums but normalcy," meaning normality. Naturally, he was disturbed by the greed displayed by America's businessmen and industrialists.

If Hutcheson needed a little persuasion to accept the cabinet post of Secretary of Labor under President Harding, there were no ways of proving it. He was independent, he wouldn't stay tethered and the Secretary of Labor had in the past been chosen from retired union men who had never been a real power in the ranks of organized labor. The Carpenters' General President couldn't be tempted. "I don't mind telling you," he reminisced, "that while I viewed this offer as a compliment to me personally, it was, I believe, a recognition for labor by a Republican President; I felt that I could never serve as a rubber stamp for anybody, not even for the President of the United States. It was not yet in the cards for a Secretary of Labor to have full freedom of action that I would require to be able to administer this office. I could not think of accepting this cabinet post, serve labor, and at the same time remain free to exercise my judgment and abilities."

Hutcheson's unwillingness to accept the Secretaryship of Labor under three successive Republican administrations was predicated upon his knowledge that labor and its leadership had never been close confidants of government; that labor's position was not yet sufficiently advanced to be able to associate its economic welfare with its influence on government. It was his view, that labor unions, not unlike great industrial organizations are depositories of power. Depending on the size and strength of these power-units, they could use political instruments as a way of fighting their economic battles.

He was satisfied with his role as personal labor confidant of Harding and Coolidge, and later of Hoover. The appointment of James J. Davis to fill the vacancy of Secretary of Labor was in no small measure due to the advice and influence of William Hutcheson, in return for favors, past and future. "Davis, a good Bull Moose, he was a man whose decisions could be counted upon."

---

[5]Arthur S. Link, *Woodrow Wilson and the Progressive Era, 1910-1917* (Harper & Bros., 1954), p. 241.

Throughout the Harding administration, Hutcheson was more than *persona grata* with the White House. Frequently, one would see him enter the White House with a box of cigars under his arm. These he brought for George Christian, Harding's private secretary. The pardon of Debs, on Christmas of 1921, was not without the promptings of Hutcheson. It was deeply appreciated by the Carpenters' president. It was a link in the solidarity which existed between them.

President Harding's Conference on Unemployment did not provide the unemployed with jobs when there were none to be found, but it had the singular virtue of a wider understanding — that it was no longer possible to identify unemployment with a congenital unwillingness to work. Hutcheson was impressed with the generosity and sincerity of President Harding. Harding's proud display of Typographical Union Label 673 in the composing room of his newspaper, *The Marion Star,* always gratified the Carpenters' president. "The Chief thought a great deal about Hutcheson; he always gave him good and honest counsel," George Christian told President Harding's broker, Samuel Ungerleider.[6]

---

[6]Interview with Samuel Ungerleider, May 25, 1954.

CHAPTER | IX

THE STRUGGLE FOR SELF-APPROVAL

Hutcheson was now 54 years of age. The Brotherhood, with a membership of 402,778, now ranked second among the largest unions in America. Having finally achieved considerable power as a labor leader and a degree of public acceptance, and even employer respect, given him by reason of his identification with Republican political personages, his future actions were now propelled by two main drives: to utilize his newly-acquired position for advancing the welfare of the Carpenters and at the same time, to concentrate on his own social status in the community. He joined the Elks, later the Masons, and the Indiana Chamber of Commerce, where he sought the formal fruits of a feeling of social accceptability. This was not a desire to travel in "high society," as much as it was an urge to be received and accepted uncondescendingly as an individual at the more staid places of his community, though he was quite comfortable in his old familiar environment.

This led to extra-curricular activity. His concern and generous impulses for the starving children in the Near East helped to save many an orphan in that impoverished, ravaged area. His post as delegate to the Near East Relief Committee, on which he served together with John L. Lewis, John McParland and AFL Secretary Frank Morrison, was one of the most satsifying experiences in the life of this Saginaw woodsman.[1] His membership in the Knights of the Road, to which he contributed yearly a hundred dollars, he retained.

Hutcheson never ran the danger of union criticism for hobnobbing and palavering with industrialists, financiers, and others in the business and political world, although not a few of them sought to influence him or to curry favor of one kind or another, especially in the late 'forties and 'fifties. As will be seen further, he never "sold" labor to the "opposi-

[1] American Federation of Labor, *Proceedings, Forty-first Annual Convention,* (1921), pp. 254, 442.

tion" despite a steadily growing friendship with the latter. Actually, it was Hutcheson's notion that the social "weight" and influence of a labor leader representing 402,778 men was surely comparable with that of an employer who had only 1,000 employees. Neither a Chamber of Commerce, a Rotary Club, a church group, nor a Community Chest invited a labor leader to become active in its activities and campaigns. Being head of a large labor union had an odium of unsavory potency and in some way was an indictment against him. The sophisticated notion that capitalism is a partnership of *management and labor* was then unthinkable.

Taking color from its environment and the conditioning of new capitalism, Hutcheson sought co-operation with management. Recalling in retrospect, perhaps, that this era marked the brief triumphal march of American industry and business during the seventeen fat years from 1913 through 1929 — or, to be more precise, until October 1929; that the new capitalism willingly abandoned its practice of obtaining employees' services at the lowest possible cost, embracing, as it were, the belief that the wage earner is to be regarded not only as producer but as consumer, it should occasion no surprise that labor and its leadership hastened, in practice, either to imitate or co-operate with ownership over the carcass of profits.

These were booming years, and for this fact there was ample basis. For one thing, there was rapid growth of the automobile industry — which meant expanding business not only for the automobile manufacturers and parts' manufacturers, but also for dealers, garage men, filling station operators, trucking companies, bus companies, roadside businesses, and so on, indefinitely. There was the incipient but blooming radio industry after Dr. Frank Conrad put on the first scheduled broadcast in 1920; by the end of that decade, radio sales totaled over three-quarters of a million dollars a year. There was the lively rise in the construction industry, in which the Carpenters' President was particularly interested. Confident business called for bigger and better buildings in a more and more congested urban population. A nouveau-riche middle class, arising from World War I, called for new apartment houses and private homes, and the motorized suburbs and booming resorts called for new real estate developments. Better still, manufacturers had been learning what new machines and a careful planning of production could do to increase output. During the years between 1922 and 1929 the physical production of the agricultural, manufacturing, mining and construction industries, increased by thirty-four per cent — an astonishing figure — and between 1920 and 1930, output per man hour increased by twenty-one per cent!

So far, so good. It seemed, the stuff could be produced all right. The question was whether it could be sold. The consensus was that a brisk enough salesman could sell it. And so the 1920's saw the canonization of the salesman and the business man as the brightest hopes of America. But where were the consumers? Sinclair Lewis' "Babbitt" was on the march — but where was "babbitry's" customer?

One of the most interesting developments of the time was the elaboration of the new wage theory, the general thesis of which was that the purchasing power of the workers should be increased because productivity was rising. Later in the decade it was accepted by some employers and took a firm hold on popular discussion. In retrospect, this was a fundamental change in the American attitude toward the production and "division" of wealth. Whereas in the past, the employers had looked upon their employees merely as aids in production, whose services should be obtained at the lowest possible cost, now, the new ideas began to spread that these seemingly simple formulae were no longer operating. If businessmen were to grow and sell an increased volume of products, the obvious answer was that this could occur only through an increase in the purchasing power of the people who already existed. Wage earners began to be regarded both as producers and consumers as well. Henry Ford expressed this belief — that it was to the advantage of the employer to pay high wages in order to provide the market for his product.*

Thus the theory of the economy of high wages now became a prominent article in the creed of business spokesmen as well as of labor unions. There was truth to that theory; there still is. But there are many reasons to doubt that it ever was deliberately practiced by many individual employers, or that it can consistently be practiced in a noncollectivist economic system, at least without strong and sustained collective action by labor. The larger part of the growth and purchasing power of wage earners that was noted at this time had actually occurred as a result of the postwar deflation, when wage rates had fallen less rapidly than the cost of living, in consequence of the bitter resistance offered by Hutcheson and the few less-relaxing labor leaders to wage deductions that employers had been doing their best to effectuate in the building trades.

The emphasis on the gains to be expected from increased productivity naturally led unions to attempt to convince employers that, instead of being a barrier to this improvement, they could offer positive

*President Samuel Gompers and his successor, William Green paid homage to the five-dollar-day and five-day-week, instituted by Henry Ford. In actual operation, "these two gifts" fell short and below the immediate high expectation of the two labor leaders. "For the new concession, meaning the five-day-week, like the five-dollar-day, was a qualified gift. It was ringed with reservations. If the meaning of these qualifications had been clear at the time, capital and labor might well have interchanged their first appraisals of their innovation." (See Keith Seward, *The Legend of Henry Ford* Rinehart and Co., 1948, p. 175 seq).

assistance. The Baltitmore and Ohio Railroad shopmen system put into effect on the railroads reduced grievances and wastes, and Sidney Hillman's Amalgamated Clothing Workers of America, organizing shops for employers, was so efficient that they increased wages of those at work and reduced the number of jobs available for their members.[2] While the officers of the Brotherhood of Locomotive Engineers were establishing labor banks and financial holding companies with a zeal, if not with the skill of Wall Street speculators, other unions were offering to co-operate with management in order to obtain labor efficiency and discipline. "During the ineffectual organizing campaign in the automobile industry in 1926 and 1927, labor representatives spent almost as much time in trying to convince employers that collective bargaining would be to their advantage as they did in organizing the employees. Union-management co-operation was endorsed in 1926 by the American Federation of Labor.[3]

The effort to spread organization by conciliating employers and favoring positive aids to efficiency was, of course, greatly stimulated by the competition of "work councils" or company unions under the domination of employers. One of the earliest models of these plans was that installed by the Rockefellers in the Colorado Fuel and Iron Company after a brutal war in 1914, between the miners and the company. Eleven children and two women had been killed during an attack on a tent colony of strikers by State militia, who poured machine gun bullets into it and set fire to the tents. "Let us abolish the industrial conflict, for at bottom the interests of employer and employee are one," declared John D. Rockefeller, Jr. The first step toward this utopia was a conversion. He became a devotee of the new gospel and prescribed the "introduction of a new spirit in the relationship between the parties in industry — the spirit of justice and brotherhood." This spirit, once present, he felt, had been lost through the complex growth of industry. The plan involved welfare work of various kinds, the choosing of representatives of employees by secret ballot, conferences with company officials three times a year, and a provision for referring deadlocked disputes to the State Industrial Commission.

These plans were widely initiated, with variations. The United States Steel Corporation, for instance, conducted safety campaigns among the workers, established emergency and base hospitals, improved the sanitary conditions of the mills, built dwellings for its employees, constructed club houses, and laid out athletic fields and playgrounds. There were glee clubs, basketball teams, bowling leagues. Many com-

[2]Morris L. Cooke and Philip Murray, *Organized Labor and Production,* (Harper and Bros., 1940) pp. 109-122.
[3]*Report of the Proceedings of the 46th Annual Convention, AFL, (1926)* pp. 51-52.

panies went further than this derisively labeled "toilet policy." They established pension funds for the superannuated employees mostly in metal working establishments, railroads, and public utilities. Many companies encouraged their employees to buy stock in the firm by offering them shares at low prices. Rarely did employee ownership come even close to majority control, but here was another incentive device to insure labor co-operation. A decade later more than 300 concerns had employee stock purchase plans and their roll-call was that of the industrial giants. In the depression that followed the 'twenties stock ownership alienated rather than won the affections of employees.

Other methods as well, were tried to bind the workers to the employers and prevent unionization. The forms and functions of such organizations defied categories. One aspect of that drive was the sponsorship of company unions that were little more than recreational clubs. Company unions were more common in the larger than in the smaller establishments, and at their height, in 1928, nearly 400 companies had them. Bethlehem Steel, International Harvester, Standard Oil of New Jersey and the Pennsylvania Railroad were corporations that sponsored this device. The motives that lay behind this manifestation of the "new capitalism" varied all the way from a sincere desire to introduce a new day in industrial relations to a desire to smash unions. The latter was the more compelling motive. Certainly company unions have smoothed the path of labor management by acting as a safety valve for grievances. But they were a travesty of collective bargaining, however much they might adopt a protective coloration of its forms. Thus "new capitalism" made palatable the revival of the labor injunction and the yellow-dog contracts (which the courts upheld) and hastened the decline of trade-unionism.

Never before had American businessmen and even economists been so confident that the erratic fluctuations of the business cycle had come under control and that severe depressions were a thing of the past. The ringing slogan of that era was "stabilization of business" and statesmen and economists believed that the end of poverty was in sight. Will Hays popularized the businessman's slogan, "Less Government in business, more business in Government." Income taxes were cut, war debts were largely retired, and politicians were elected who believed that the real initiative and leadership in American society belonged to the businessman. Party differences did not seem too acute to the millions who ceased to go to the polls. As long as prosperity continued, the "booster spirit" of Kiwanis prevailed and the solidarity of businessmen was affirmed. "Rugged individualism" was the keynote of the new business civilization.

Alas, this business civilization did not stand the test of time. The sincerity of its utterances, that, "wage earners constitute the majority of our population . . . that these people are the spenders of the nation . . .," was belied by their deeds. It profferred the olive branch with one hand, while wielding the court injunction in the other.

Hutcheson's growing social status as a labor leader wielding tremendous power did not deceive him. Of course politics offered him an avenue toward public acceptance. He lunched at the respectable club of the Chamber of Commerce and, on occasions was invited out in "upper" social circles, either because of a host's desire for novelty or simply out of curiosity. Mostly it was the latter. Condescending invitations were more distasteful to him of course than a "social" rebuff. As far as Hutcheson was concerned, his desire for social position was all in keeping with our American ideals about equality and hence needed no sanction or apology.

Whereas his total annual income reached a maximum of $7,500, the social boons and usufructs of that income were not too evident, except for custom-made tailored suits and a homburg. William Hutcheson was a big man, and standard size clothes couldn't fit him. He did not move into the fashionable area of Indianapolis in order to raise himself, and particularly his family, to the status of employers. He, his wife Bessie, and his family of four grown-up children continued to occupy the same simple three-bedroom house on Forty-Second Street since their arrival in Indianapolis, in 1913. He did purchase a farm in Milan, Ohio which he tilled as relaxation and refuge, especially when he had been under tension all week. A quiet card game, reading, fishing and hunting were his main hobbies. His wife frequented the sewing circles at the Rebecca Lodge or the Brotherhood's social functions.

Myra, the eldest of the children, aimed no higher; she was comfortable in the environment in which she was raised. Her suitor was a charming, upright chap, who lived in the old city neighborhood. Nor was Stella elbowing for a social position among the daughters of the businessmens' families. She did persevere to "make" the Junior Club, but her fond dream was still to come true.

Maurice, now twenty-six years of age and second oldest in the Hutcheson family, returned to Indianapolis after an absence lasting five years. It took much persuasion and eloquence on the part of Secretary-General of the Brotherhood Frank P. Duffy to induce Maurice to accept the job of auditor and statistical clerk at $45 a week. A previous visit to the union hall of Local Union 75, Maurice's alma mater, which certified him as a master carpenter, was hardly reassuring and he departed more hastily. Although his father wanted him to rise to a professional level, introverted Maurice inclined toward the individualistic occupation of carpentry. From childhood on, he was exposed to a magnificent collection of carpenters tools which were jealously guarded and preserved by his grandfather, Daniel. His father's tools, of later vintage, were also there, though neatly tucked away in the basement.

On his seventeenth birthday, Maurice heeded the latter's counsel. The time for selecting a vocation had arrived — Maurice took the first step toward becoming a carpenter. This was made possible by "Spurge" Meadows, who enrolled him as an apprentice carpenter in Local 75. Meadows was the business agent of that local. Prior to entering the union, Maurice attended vocational high school in the evenings, while working as a clerk in the records department of the Brotherhood at $13 a week.

For three years, from 1915 to 1918, he applied himself to the carpentry craft. A dollar an hour, plus overtime lured him to the Quantico Marine Training Camp in Virginia. He then drifted to Youngstown, Ohio, where Carpenter's Local 171 assigned him to a housing project intended for war workers. Here he contracted poison oak sleeping out in the bunks. At twenty he came to New York. Joining Local Union 1456 of the Dock Builders and Pile Drivers, he was assigned to defense work in Port Newark. It was here that he first met the ebullient George Meany, who in 1952 became President of the American Federation of Labor. Both worked side by side (Meany as a plumber) at their own particular crafts until May 7th, 1918, when Maurice enlisted in the United States Navy. With the increasing demand for technicians repairing "flying boats," the son of the General President of the U. B. of C. & J. A. was transferred to the Aero-Marine School in Keyport, New Jersey, to supplement his training.

There was Delos, the youngest of the four in the Hutcheson family. A youth of delicate health, his father enrolled him in a private military school. After graduation, he pursued his studies in business administration and accountancy at Purdue University. His proud father hoped to utilize his training, but Delos died at the premature age of thirty-three of tuberculosis.

CHAPTER | X

LET MY PEOPLE GO

It was a bleak morning indeed when Hutcheson, the labor leader, enjoying social "position" soon began to have misgivings. Notwithstanding the soothing and mellowing protestations about the importance of labor, the greater part of management had been employing every device to block the real yearnings of the wage earners. Reporting to the Twenty-first Convention, on September 22, 1924, disillusioned Hutcheson cautioned his own carpenters:

"There have been attempts made to disrupt not only the morale of the membership of our organization, but the conditions that have been established. These attempts were made by different forces, and from different angles. In some localities the endeavor was made by the employers, backed by the Manufacturers' Associations, the Chambers of Commerce, etc. These attacks took various forms; the one that was the most catching was where they attempted to put into effect what they were pleased to term the "American Plan" of employment, but which really meant putting into effect a condition whereby men of our organization could not procure or secure employment by any other means than under the rules and conditions as laid down by those who were advocating that system of employment."[1]

Nothing galled him more than the "American Plan," a device implying that anyone not in favor of open-shop stood for something un-American. It was a psychologically propitious time for anti-union management to label its crusade "American." Here was an old method of return to the ruthless free hand in exploiting labor. Labor, of course, was free too — to accept their wages or go without.

The decade from 1919 to the eve of the Great Depression has been aptly named the "Roaring Twenties." It was a delirious, fabulous period of low morals and easy money. Many employers thought the unions pampered and wages too high. They were irritated by the growing power of unions during the war and anxious, as always, to rid themselves of the

[1] U.B.C.J.A., *Proceedings, Twenty-first General Convention* (1924), p. 3.

restraints placed upon their labor policies by outside negotiators and collective bargaining. The series of strikes in coal and steel gave them the chance for a test of relative power. Superficially, the initial advantage seemed to rest with the workers. Never had the number of organized men been so great. But a large segment of the unions was new, unacquainted with union difficulties and unschooled in patience and discipline. Unions were torn apart by radicals, and faction fought faction.

In this new era employers dissipated none of their advantages. To begin with, the World War had created a natural propensity to violent emotions *en masse*. For years the people had been exhorted to hate the Germans and to exalt the American way; this urge, checkmated by the armistice, was now easily diverted against enemies, fancied and real, of American institutions. It was an age of recklessness, red and xenophobic hysteria. Labor outbreaks of a novel sort strengthened this delusion. The collapse of Czarist Russia, the fear of Bolshevism and the breakout of strikes all over the country and in numerous industries convinced millions that the social structure was endangered by organized labor. Undoubtedly, employers believed so, and were willing that others should not forget the lesson. The stratagem might now be applied to labor as a whole. The movement was given unusual coherence by the American Plan, whereby "it is recognized as fundamental in this country that all law-abiding citizens . . . have the right to work when they please, for whom they please, and on whatever terms are mutually agreed upon between *employee* and employer and without interference or discrimination upon the part of others. We express our purpose to support these fundamental principles of the American Plan of employment by the maintenance of the open shop." It should be noted that in the resolution the word "employee" is singular. These principles, greeted by hosannas from trade associations, chambers of commerce, and associated industries from East to West, dotted the nation with "open shop" plants, industries and towns. On the surface the American Plan did not object to American unions; it only prohibited the "un-American" closed shop. Actually the movement was a movement to smash all unions. "The only good Indian is a dead Indian."

Gompers and Hutcheson profoundly sensed what had happened, and they forecast what was going to happen. Early in 1920, Hutcheson started to educate the Carpenters' delegates in earnest so that they could cope better with the forces that were soon to press them on all sides. "This term, 'open shop' has been coined by employers of labor who are opposed to all labor unions and was brought into general use in an attempt to deceive the public", warned Hutcheson. "The term as applied by employers relates to a factory . . . where labor of any kind is performed by laborers or artisans who work for hire and where such working people cannot collectively present to the employer their conviction as regards wages, hours of labor, or sanitary conditions . . . finally, 'the open shop' is a denial of the right of individual liberty . . ."[2] He upbraided the delegates and the members of the Brotherhood for being "careless with the way the term (open shop) is used."

". . . We feel we should call it to your attention that the employers who advocate this so-called "open shop" are telling the public that the non-union man is not willing to be placed on an equality, industrially or politically, with other workmen. They are telling the public that the non-union man insists upon being treated as a prize property, and that the property belongs to employers. They are telling the public that the non-union man insists upon being the ward of the employers, as the employer is insisting upon the right to represent the non-union man . . ."[3]

The open-shop drive was fostered by employers' associations that had a long record of opposition to organized labor. These included the National Metal Trades Association, the National Erectors Association, the National Association of Manufacturers, and the National Founders Association. And, there were "citizens' committees" galore. Large companies, engaged in labor espionage, participated in the drive, in which nation-wide advertising and publicity were employed. Offices set up under such names as the National Open Shop Association, enlisted the co-operation of local employers' organizations. According to the *Iron Trade Review* of November 11, 1920, open shop associations were active in 240 cities of 44 states.

The objective was not merely to limit the power of unions but also to invade their strongholds. Labor organizations in the building trades were among the oldest and best organized in the country. The drive for the open shop, disguised as the American Plan, had been conducted with special vigor in the building industry because these workers had always been extraordinarily successful in attaining organization, and also, because of the housing shortage and the high rents, the building trades were particularly vulnerable to an attack that needed the support of public opinion. In city after city across the country the pattern was identical. By the time 1922 came around, the National Association of Manufacturers could boast that building under open-shop conditions had risen by five percent since 1921, when it constituted thirty-one percent of all cities in the United States.[4]

"There has never been any doubt at to what is back of the 'open-shop' movement," wrote Samuel Gompers in the *American Federa-*

---

[2]U.B.C.J.A., *Proceedings* (1920), p. 169.

[3]*Ibid*, p. 170.

[4]National Association of Manufacturers, *Open Shop Bulletin*, No. 23, (Nov. 12, 1928), p. 6.

tionist of February, 1921. "It is backed by the powerful enemies of labor and fostered by an artificial propaganda. What experience has taught the workers, recent unimpeachable testimony and admissions have made clear to the whole world."[5] President Gompers had reference to Eugene G. Grace, President of the Bethlehem Steel Corporation who was quoted in an Associated Press dispatch in the *New York Times* of December 16, 1920, as follows: "The Bethlehem Steel Corporation will refuse to sell fabricated steel to builders and contractors in New York and Philadelphia districts to be erected on a union shop basis." On being questioned, Mr. Grace asserted that his decision would not be altered even if building operations were suspended entirely because of this action. He further declared that even if ninety-five percent of his employees belonged to a union, he would not recognize them as union men.

The open-shop drive was vigorously prosecuted in scores of important cities, such as Seattle, Indianapolis, Milwaukee, Detroit, Los Angeles, Dayton, Louisville and New Orleans. In Tucson, Phoenix, Yakima and Spokane, Billings and Helena, Sioux Falls, Idaho Falls, Utica, and Duluth, self-constituted "citizens' committees," and "Industrial Associations," formed by the business community, forced the American Plan upon unions and contractors alike. They were strengthened by the National Merchants and Manufacturers Associations, whose teams coerced local merchants and industrialists to adopt the American Plan. By the end of 1923, the National Association of Manufacturers reported that thirty-nine percent of all communities were building on the American Plan basis, and they were substantially correct.[6] In Chicago and San Francisco, the Carpenters entered into a struggle with self-constituted open-shop groups which was to last for the balance of the 1920's.

Among the organized building tradesmen, few of the unions were in a position to ward off the unscrupulous, well-organized, well-subsidized activities of the American Plan. The United Brotherhood, although it sustained losses of 36,862 "war babies" since 1920, still remained numerically the largest union, with 365,916 members. It had a full treasury and even a surplus of three-quarters of a million dollars. Above all, its chief officer was quick to realize the nature of this movement whose unconcealed purpose it was to smash all unions. Again, Hutcheson decided to lead his army of carpenters in the defense of the union shop, and before the decade of the 'twenties was over, the Brotherhood had spent $683,189.00 to defeat the American Plan.

Hutcheson's first testing ground was Seattle, Washington, where the business community instituted the American Plan. Here was an oppor-

---

[5] *American Federationist,* Vol. XXVII, Part 1, (Feb., 1921), p. 109.
[6] *Open Shop Bulletin,* No. 23, p. 6.

tunity to assault the building trades unions which suffered more severely from postwar readjustment. Thirty thousand shipyard workers, recruited from all parts of the country, were rendered jobless. The rallying cry of the anti-union employers was the American Plan. The Mayor of Seattle, Ole Hanson, won short-lived fame by his determination to destroy the unions and replace them by the Industrial Association of Seattle. A general strike was called which tied up the entire city. Abe Muir, Hutcheson's aide, crusaded behind the scenes. Soon a breach was opened by the election of Hugh Cauldwell, public-spirited Mayor of Seattle. Negotiations were begun; endless conferences were held with community leaders and heads of construction unions on all points at issue. The Industrial Association melted away under the hot wrath of an aroused public, which derived no advantages from the open-shop, claims of the Association notwithstanding.

As 1921 dawned, Seattle returned to normal. Union agreements were renewed to the satisfaction of labor and management. "This was not an easy task. Passions ran high; invectives against union leaders were retracted, and the building tradesmen were rehabilitated," reported Abe Muir.* In city after city across the country, the pattern, with slight variations was the same.

Hutcheson's next move was in Salt Lake City, where the building trades were under a sustained attack. Again the Brotherhood undertook to bear the entire brunt of the conflict. Here, the general contractors were given no choice to decide for themselves whether or not to affiliate with the movement. They were bluntly told by the chairman of the Industrial Association that unless they adopted the American Plan system, they would be barred from buying basic materials for the construction of a building. The contractors were favorably inclined toward the unions, doubtless for the reason that they desired to retain their skilled mechanics. The Industrial Association took the opposite view. Nevertheless, the friendly contractors decided to meet with the representatives of the Brotherhood, and after a conference lasting several hours without the benefit of a drink of water, the meeting was adjourned.

As Hutcheson and his aide, Abe Muir, were leaving, three of the principal contractors requested a private conference. "At the final hour of the conference, they agreed to employ union carpenters and building tradesmen if they would be permitted to post the Industrial Association's bulletin on the job." To this, neither Hutcheson nor Muir would agree. Both argued straight facts and statistics, pointing to the damage and financial anarchy the American Plan system had brought in a succession of cities.

---

*The late Abe Muir was an undeviating champion of the union shop, and devoted aide to Hutcheson as U.B. general representative.

"If you want to see grass growing in the streets of Salt Lake City, you follow this American plan of destruction and you will see just that, and much faster than you think," Hutcheson warned them. They did not listen. Not much later, the enterprising builders left the city. Skilled mechanics were directed to go to southern California, where they were provided with construction jobs.

Assaults were also made on newly-rising communities, on Phoenix, Arizona, Billings and Helena, Montana. All construction work ceased. Contractors were driven to desperation; others joined building trades unions to earn their livelihood. The sole survivor of the Phoenix shambles was Dale Webb, one of the owners of the New York Yankees.

The war of extermination against organized labor in the building trades had not abated. By the mid-'twenties advocates of the American Plan claimed forty percent of all cities. Unionism languished; total trade-union membership was dwindling from over five million in 1920 to less than four million in 1927. One reason for this decline was that the incumbent union leadership was slow to appreciate the calamitous effects of the American Plan. As the tom-tom of Americanism was beaten, nation-wide publicity and some respectable monthlies continued to exhort the lower and new middle classes to hate the unions, and above all, the building tradesmen, the carpenters, the bricklayers, plasterers, painters and electrical workers and their leaders. They, it was alleged, were responsible for the high rents, housing shortages, and the high cost of building.

"What it (the American Plan) has done, is to revive and restore to healthy activity a moribund industry that was in its virtual death throes on account of long-continued class control," wrote Warren Ryder in the *American Review of Reviews*.[7] "This is accomplished through granting to every man the right to work, regardless of whether or not he belonged to a trade union."

San Francisco was operating almost entirely under the American Plan. Since July, 1921, contractors and builders were smarting under the iron rule of the self-constituted Industrial Association. Recalcitrant builders and contractors who continued to practice collective bargaining or employed union tradesmen did so at the risk of being hard hit or losing to a rival. They would be denied cement, plaster, lumber, concrete aggregates and building materials unless they agreed to hire nonunion labor. The half-hearted employers who were in the midst of a construction job were subjected to intimidation and rowdiness at the hands of the hired toughs who were supervised by "Black Jack" Jerome, whose feats of brash violence were chronicled in the better San Fran-

---

[7]Warren Ryder, "The American Plan in San Francisco," *Review of Reviews* (Jan.-June, 1923), p. 187.

cisco Press. On October 13, 1923, the American Federation of Labor
called upon the Department of Justice to "proceed at once to prosecute
those responsible for illegal and unlawful acts carried on by the Industrial
Association of San Francisco to prevent fair employers from reaching
a settlement with the organizations in the building trades."

The villains now sought to exonerate their labor policies through
the agency of skillful public relations counsel. To that end the Industrial
Association published the *Independent* in order to carry a "message" to
the San Francisco populace.

A strike was called of all the building tradesmen. But the intransigent Industrial Association had no intention of permitting union men
in construction work. Strike-breakers were imported, a back-to-work
movement was solemnly chronicled as a fact at the moment of the
strike's effectiveness. The Carpenters held on. The battle raged. Hundreds were wounded and hospitalized, but no one was sucessfully
punished. It was an industrial battle with all its attendant evils.

Hutcheson arrived in San Francisco in May of 1926. At once he
met with J. F. Cambiano, President of the Bay Counties District Council
of Carpenters and Abe Muir, the Brotherhood's general representative.
His first step was a request for peaceful mediation. But the Industrial
Association flatly declined mediation on the basis of any modification
of the American Plan.[8] "The United Brotherhood is equally deter-
minded to establish its principle. So far as we are concerned," wrote
the *Independent,* "our sympathy is entirely with the Industrial Association."[9] Subsequent attempts by Hutcheson at peaceful settlement which
would give the Carpenters the right to bargain collectively with their
employers failed. A number of contractors were willing, but the pressure wielded by the Association was more decisive.

In the meantime, skillful Mr. Ryder went so far as to spread the rumor
that Tom Mooney was Vice-President of the United Brotherhood of
Carpenters and Joiners of America. The charge was delirious and utterly
careless of the evidence available. Mooney had neither been an officer
of the Brotherhood nor even its member.

At this time Hutcheson revealed his strategy: to weaken the intransigent Association by causing defections among the half-hearted contractors. The Brotherhood agreed to import cement from Belgium.
Lumber was purchased from independent mills throughout the Northwest. It bought and operated gravel beds to supply rock, sand and
gravel to builders employing union carpenters. By February, 1927,
the number of defections was large enough for the Brotherhood to effect

---

[8]*The Independent* (July-December, 1926), p. 60.
[9]*Ibid.*

a complete settlement. The Association's appeal for a "few hundred thousand dollars" drew less than a moderate response from the business community. The American Plan was now disintegrating and condemned to defeat. "Previous to the Carpenters' strike, the American Plan was well established," wrote Mr. Warren Ryder.

The Carpenters sold their mills, the aggregate plants, their holdings in gravel beds, and disposed of the imported cement.

In Chicago the building trades entered into a struggle with self-constituted open-shop groups which was to last for the balance of the 1920's. Nineteen principles were laid down by forty-six open-shop associations officially adopting the name "American Plan."** Another "Citizens Committee to Enforce the Landis Award" was created to enforce these principles. Here, as in San Francisco, Hutcheson employed the identical strategy to defeat the American Plan.

In the spring of 1921 a concerted movement of "industrial freedom" was started by the Employers' Associations. Their slogan was "back to normalcy", aiming at a reduction in wages to almost pre-war levels. Most of the building trades unions agreed to arbitration. The Carpenters' Chicago District Council took the position that the proposal to reduce wages was unwarranted and refused to be a party to the arbitration. Judge K. M. Landis rendered his award, reducing the wages for all building trades, including those that were not parties to the arbitration. The Carpenters' Union was branded an outlaw organization by Judge Landis for refusing to accept the terms of the Landis Award; all the members were denied employment unless they were willing to accept the terms of the award. The Carpenters resolutely accepted the challenge and quit their jobs.

Non-union carpenters were imported from other cities by the thousands, through the "Citizens Committee's" privately operated employment agency. Contractors were urged to dismiss union carpenters, and hire non-union artisans through the Citizens Committee employment office, and when urging failed, the contractors were coerced and threatened. Millions of dollars were raised and used in a frantic effort to subdue the Carpenters. On April 29, 1922, the Carpenters decided to take the initiative against the Citizens Committee. The District Council published 200,000 pamphlets explaining the "Carpenters' side of the controversy with the Citizens Committee,"[10] On that day Chicago witnessed a parade of 12,000 Carpenters and building tradesmen.

However, when the Citizens Committee had been incorporated to set up shop for meddling in union affairs, the Carpenters "decided to

---

**The name "American Plan" was officially adopted in Chicago, in January, 1921.
[10]Chicago District Council, *Minutes,* April 18, 1922 to May 5, 1922.

use the weapon so frequently used against organized labor." Through
its attorney, Hope Thompson, the Council filed a bill of injunction
against the Citizens Committee in the Superior Court. The application
for an injunction was denied on the grounds "that two non-union men
had been assaulted," and the Court held that because of this alleged
assault the District Council did not come into court with clean hands
and was not entitled to relief; this notwithstanding the fact that there
was no evidence that the union had anything to do with the alleged
assaults.

In March, 1924, the Brotherhood's counsel, Joseph Carson, filed an
amended bill of complaint. This was not called to trial until the latter
part of 1925.

On Monday, June 19, 1924, Hutcheson arrived from Indianapolis.
Never one to give in without a fight, he harassed the members of the
Citizens Committee, submitting seven reasons why Judge Landis' find-
ings were unjust, dangerous and corrupting. At the same time, he
pushed his strategy with the same audacity he applied in San Francisco.
He called on seven of Chicago's largest contractor members of the
Building Construction Employers' Association, whom he had never
seen before, but who remained his only hope. On Wednesday, June
11, the officers of John Griffith and Son, of Thompson and Starret,
of George A. Fuller, Hageman and of Harris, R. C. Wieboldt, Blome
and Sinek and of Avery Brundage agreed to meet Hutcheson. They
were confronted by a few embarrassing questions and adverse speeches
about the American Plan. He was a firm believer in Peter getting
a relatively large slice of a much larger pie; but what about Paul,
who was also an American?

On Friday, June 13, an agreement was negotiated in behalf of
20,000 carpenters. It marked the end of a three-year struggle against
the "open shop" in Chicago and the Citizens Committee to enforce
the Landis Award. The agreement fixed the "minimum scale at $1.25
an hour for the first twelve months." It also provided that the "scale
for the second year shall be set prior to February 1, 1925 to permit
the contractors to bid on Spring and Summer construction."[11] The agreement dated from July 1, 1924, and expired May 31, 1926.

Hutcheson pointed out that with the "signatures of its largest members on the new agreement, the pact was virtually made with the Building
Construction Employers' Association." The non-union carpenters who
were imported by the Citizens Committee to Enforce the Landis Award
were invited to join.

[11]Agreement as drawn up between Hutcheson and the seven building contractors,
dated June 13, 1924; The New Majority, Vol. 2: 25 (Chicago), June 21, 1924,
p. 3; The Daily Worker, Chicago (April 13, 1924), p. 2.

Behind Hutcheson's quarrels with the National Board of Jurisdictional Awards lay his strenuous opposition to the American Plan. "Employ none but union building trades mechanics throughout," Hutcheson warned the constituent members of the National Board.[12] As soon as the Carpenters reaffiliated, the open-shop movement in the building trades started to lose its vigor. Its high water mark was maintained in 1926 in San Francisco, and then the percentage of cities building on open-shop basis began to decline. In 1928, the National Association of Manufacturers complained that the open-shop gains of the 1921 to 1927 period had been all but wiped out.[13]

In his report to the 1928 Convention, Hutcheson announced that ". . . while there are still periodical attempts made by employers to put into effect the 'American Plan,' our membership has been able to combat these efforts so that the system has not become anything other than what might be termed local. The struggle was a particularly strenuous one in San Francisco."[14]

The postwar hysteria, which fostered chauvinism, intolerance and xenophobia, brought about an amazing revival of the Ku Klux Klan, growing from a few thousand in 1920 to an estimated 2,500,000 members in 1924. It captured entire counties and even state governments, as in Indiana, Hutcheson's own home state. Practical politicians, among them a number of southern and midwestern Democrats, thought it wise to carry a Klan membership card. Klan night riders intimidated critics, whipped and tarred opponents. They harassed labor leaders and organizers.

The Carpenters Local Union 55 in Denver, Colorado was "captured" by a cell of Klansmen, secretly operating in the union. Its secretary-treasurer, Charles Logan, mulcted the members for Klan membership cards and hooded uniforms. Encouraged by the response, Logan proceeded to expel the local's president, a critic of the Klan.

Hutcheson, apprised of this development, warned the Klansmen to dissociate themselves from the hooded Order, or be liable to suspension. The Klansmen refused. Expulsion of 18 known Klansmen followed. A lawsuit for damages in the amount of $360,000 was instituted against Hutcheson, himself, and the Brotherhood, by Col. William J. Simmons of the Invisible Empire. Joseph O. Carson, attorney in charge of the Brotherhood's legal department and Wayne C. Williams, Sr., lawyer for Carpenters Local Union 55, argued the case.

---

[12]Building Trades Dept., *Convention Proceedings* (1928), p. 102.
[13]*Open Shop Bulletin*, No. 23, p. 6.

[14]U.B.C.J.A., *Proceedings*, (1928), p. 46.

The suit was settled to the satisfaction of the Brotherhood. The 18 plaintiffs were reinstated after signing an affidavit to the effect, that "our constitution bespeaks the victory of freedom and tolerance. . . . That as members of the Brotherhood we will seek to keep the local union free from either religious or racial bigotry and disputes. . . . Any other course would long since have shattered our ranks, if indeed they could ever have been mustered in the beginning. . . ." Hutcheson, a member of the committee on report to the Executive Council of the American Federation of Labor, was co-author and co-signer of the declaration entitled "Ku Klux Klan," which was printed in pamphlet form and distributed among the central bodies of the Federation.[15]

Hutcheson's attitude towards accepting Negro carpenters as members of the Brotherhood was a forthright one. The Brotherhood was one of forty-six unions affiliated with the A. F. of L. that accepted Negro workers to membership since 1919.[16] In 1920, when three delegates from Georgia, Florida and Mississippi complained that Negro carpenters had been turned away from membership in Southern locals, Hutcheson was rudely jarred, proclaiming with further emphasis, . . . "That the color line was never recognized in dealing with applications for charters, or in any other connection in the work of the organization, and that there were cases where charters have been granted over the objections of existing local unions and district councils, where the facts showed that the issuance of such charters was for the best interests of the organizations." He concluded by reminding the delegates that the "constitution draws no line insofar as creed, color or nationality is concerned."[17]

While Hutcheson was all for union-management co-operation so raucously proclaimed by the converts to "new capitalism" in the 'twenties, he was a fierce opponent of "fake partnerships" and "piece work systems."

He was more than a moderate advocate of an industrial *marriage between the unions and the employers*. A wedding between the two was not without mutual convenience and even an advantage to both parties, thought Hutcheson. The worker would gain status, a sense of dignity and protection from the arbitrary use of management's power; and in return, management would gain freedom from trouble, better morale, better discipline and higher productivity. None the less, he was an opponent of the utilization by management of the various devices, such as recreational clubs, group insurance plans, old-age pension programs, "industrial democracy" schemes, the "works councils," and other attractions.

---

[15]A.F.L., *Proceedings Twenty-third Annual Convention*, (1923), pp. 12, 270, 271.

[16]A.F.L., *Proceedings Thirty-ninth Annual Convention*, (1919), p. 305.

[17]U.B.C.J.A,. *Proceedings of the Twentieth General Convention*, (1920), pp. 437. 442-443.

The employers' open-shop movement and the promotion of company unions weakened the Brotherhood, as well as other unions. During 1920-29 the number of organized workmen affiliated with the A. F. of L. had declined from nearly 5,000,000 to 2,750,000. Men ceased to pay dues or attend meetings, and even faithful union men soon encountered an undignified struggle for jobs that were being grabbed by younger men under forty. Also, machines displaced men in the race for economy and efficiency.

It had taken Hutcheson ten years of agonizing struggle and frustration to tackle the most intractable American Plan and to drive home the point — that unions are not only useful but necessary adjuncts as part of modern industrial government, and their role will be an increasingly vital and salutary one in modern technical society so long as they remain autonomous and independent of both management and the state. "There can be no substitute, in advancing the best interests of both workers and employers, for intelligently run unions, operating apart from the cloak of management," Hutcheson reiterated. The advocacy and the introduction of frills such as group insurance, old-age pension programs, "free" clinics and cafeterias; the "plant committee plan" and "factory council" by welfare capitalism of the 1920's aimed at undermining the labor movement by a process of erosion, he reasoned.

That the Brotherhood itself was seriously affected by a decade of paternalism practiced by the magnificoes of industry was clearly demonstrated by its own membership rolls. In 1928, 36,384, or approximately 8 per cent of the total membership were in arrears in paying their dues. Whereas in 1924, U.B. members in good standing totaled 327,574, their number dropped to 295,250 in 1928.[18]

Hutcheson's attitude toward the various efficiency schemes was succinctly stated in 1924: "Every brother should be his own keeper in this matter, a reference to the speed-up system. . . ." At the same time, he urged the carpenters to "awaken to the opportunity and arrange to see that Congressmen and Senators from their various districts are either communicated with, or interviewed . . . so that in the future, on all government work, the conditions in the locality where the work is being done will be recognized and observed." Hutcheson had reference to building contractors who procured contracts for the erection of government buildings, but disregarded entirely the established conditions of building tradesmen.[19]

Hutcheson viewed with suspicion the "so-called labor banks" and the "Union Labor Life Insurance Company." Unlike the supporters of the labor banking movement who entertained romantic ideas concern-

---

[18]U.B.C.J.A., *Proceedings Twenty-second General Convention,* (1928), p. 137.
[19]*Ibid* (1928), p. 61.

ing the possibility of labor's venture into finance, the Brotherhood "refused to be influenced in any way by those soliciting its patronage in behalf of institutions of this character." It had religiously and consistently adhered to the policy of directing the depositing of funds in national banks where the deposits are protected by guarantee. As for group insurance, it refused to violate its own "principles, rules . . . to take out labor insurance," even though the head of the Union Labor Life Insurance Company was the Fourth Vice-President of the American Federation of Labor.

The Brotherhood's own benevolent system had paid out in a period of four years (1924-1928) $2,842,407.54. Hutcheson's approach to old-age programs was the dedication on March 12, 1929 of the Home for Aged Carpenters, in Lakeland, Florida, at a cost of $775,548. It was a dream whose fulfillment he had sought when he was a fledgling Saginaw business agent, at the age of 32. Nothing that either "welfare capitalism" or imitative labor had tried to do for its superannuated had matched the magnitude of the program and services the Brotherhood of Carpenters extended to its own over-aged, and infirm in the roaring 'twenties.***

How did the Brotherhood figure in the Federation's endorsement of the LaFollette-Wheeler ticket in 1924? How did Hutcheson reconcile his own active participation in Republican politics with the "non-partisan" stand of his union?

It was not too difficult for a leader of a minority pressure group to reconcile what in effect were dual political roles. On the one hand, there was Hutcheson in the role of General President of the union who tirelessly reiterated the idea of "non-partisanship." On the other, there was Hutcheson the "private citizen" and member of the Brotherhood who, although enjoying in full, the symbols of prestige and power of his office, brooked no interference with his independent religious and political opinions. His political philosophy did not permeate his relations with the Brotherhood nor his industrial relations. In 1940, 1948 and 1952, respectively, however, a conjunction of events carried him so far from his moorings that he took the unusual step of asking the Brotherhood's membership to vote against Roosevelt and later, to "punish" Taft, the father of the Taft-Hartley Act. He was consistent enough not to have "interfered" with those of the Carpenters who subscribed $923.52 to the National Non-Partisan Political Fund of the American Federation of Labor, which promoted the candidacy of the LaFollette-Wheeler ticket in 1924.

This political dualism also became the stock in trade of the members of the Executive Council of the American Federation of Labor. Mr.

***See final chapter, *"Where Old Carpenters Go To Live."*

William Green, an enrolled Democrat and a delegate-at-large from Ohio to the 1920 Democratic convention, expressed a willingness to "do anything he could to help the program of the A. F. of L.," at a time when the Federation itself was chilled by the Cox-Roosevelt ticket. In 1924 Vice-President James Duncan and William Green strongly dissented from the Federation's position with a "feeling that they could not abide by the decision that endorsed the LaFollette-Wheeler ticket by name." Yet on February 15, 1925 the newly-elected President William Green asked for and received "authorization" from the Executive Council of the Federation to dine and confer with Franklin Delano Roosevelt on his household boat, LaRocco, in Miami Florida.

The one member of the Executive Council who from the very beginning of the discussion steadfastly opposed the endorsement of the LaFollette-Wheeler ticket and who cast his vote against it, was Frank Duffy, Second General Vice-President of the Federation and General Secretary of the United Brotherhood. Duffy, an enrolled Democrat, bitterly denounced the taking of such action as a departure that could do nothing but harm to the labor movement. He declared that the labor vote could not be "delivered" and that even if it could be delivered, neither the Federation nor any of its affiliated unions nor any group of labor officials should tell the members how to vote. Once the action had been taken, however, neither Hutcheson, nor Duffy, nor any member of the Brotherhood's General Executive Board, fought it. On the other hand, they did not actively support it. The Brotherhood's non-partisan policy was followed to the letter during the 1924 presidential campaign.[20]

After the 1924 elections, when John W. Davis, the Democratic nominee, was defeated by Coolidge, the Brotherhood undoubtedly improved its position by taking this stand. It clearly strengthened Hutcheson's bargaining position at the Republican administration, especially after organized labor had alienated itself from both the Democratic and Republican parties.

Senator Robert M. LaFollette's 5,000,000 "protest" votes proved far from sufficient to encourage continuance of the effort to build a third national party. Although the Federation disclaimed any responsibility for the policies advocated by other adherents of the third party, it was inevitable that public opinion would associate it with Socialists and other radical and liberal supporters. Hutcheson and the general officers of the Brotherhood considered themselves justified in having taken the stand they did. Both Hutcheson and Duffy were among the staunchest supporters of the Federation's resolution. George T. Walker, John Howatt, Alex Kelso, J. P. Wyler, Harry Schwarzer and James Gould, the

---

[20]Interview with William Levi Hutcheson, in Indianapolis, January, 1951.

Brotherhood's delegates to the A. F. of L., equally supported it. It read: "Resolved, that to accomplish such purpose the A. F. L. will sponsor no new party at this time, but will continue as in the past, upholding the right and condemning the wrong, aiding its friends wherever they may be found."

The policy of the Brotherhood was thus in entire accord with that of the A. F. of L. Even when the American Federation of Labor itself was wavering, tentatively abandoning its "non-partisan" allegiance, the Brotherhood stood staunchly by its traditional policy.[21] In other words, whatever success has been attained through adherence to this policy has been due in no small measure to the steadfast support of the Brotherhood. The general officers had been absolutely unwavering and among them the opinion prevailed that the Brotherhood would not support a labor party in the foreseeable future. One could not say that this was the unanimous view of the Brotherhood's delegates to the A.F.L., nor of the membership. Among the six delegates elected to represent the Brotherhood at the 1924 A.F.L. Convention, three were known to have been Democrats, two were Republicans and one was a Socialist. A sampling of the membership in the 1924 elections revealed that the great majority intended to vote the Democratic or Republican ticket, but that all of these expressed disapproval of the Federation's commitment to the Progressive ticket, and were in full accord with the official attitude of the Brotherhood and even firmly convinced of the inadvisability of forming a separate labor party. A minority stated that they intended to vote for the LaFollette-Wheeler ticket. Of these a small minority approved the action of the Federation, expressing the opinion that members of the U. B., as well as of other trade unions, should vote as individuals and not according to the direction of any labor organization. The general opinion, insofar as it was ascertained, opposed the formation of a separate labor party and predicted that the Brotherhood would adhere to its non-partisan policy. While the Amalgamated Society of Carpenters contained a considerable number of Socialists who were absorbed through the merger with the U. B. in 1913, it broke with them in 1917 over the pacifist and pro-German policy of the party.[22] There was a very strong tendency among the Furniture Workers to urge independent action in politics. For the most part they were German Marxist Socialists. More recently, however, they have been actively opposed to a third party. Pressure of the environment, Americanization, and better wages have had their effects on these new arrivals.

---

[21]E. E. Cummins, "Political and Social Philosophy of the Carpenters Union," *Political Science Quarterly*, Vol. XLVI (1924), p. 412.

[22]See Roland P. Berthoff, *British Immigrants in Industrial America*. (Harvard University Press, 1953), pp. 100-104.

CHAPTER | XI

THE FIFTH COLUMN

While Hutcheson threw himself headlong into fighting the American Plan, planning trips from coast to coast, the Communists, full of fresh proletarian vigor, prepared to attack him from within the organization of the Brotherhood. The situation had come to a head in September of 1924.

> . . . "The attack has been made in many instances by men who have been misled into believing that the propaganda that has been spread by men like Foster and his kind was more in keeping with organized labor than the principles of our organization. What should be kept in mind is the policies and the principles upon which the U.B.C.J.A. was founded, by that man whom we all reverence—P. J. McGuire. Every member of our organization should remember that the U.B.C.J.A. is a trade union, and that at any time any member advocates anything that pertains to Industrialism, Communism or any other 'ism', there is no place in our organization for that kind of man. There are only two kinds of 'isms' that should enter our organization—that of trade unionism and Americanism."[1]

Since 1920, the United Brotherhood became the Communists' prime target for conversion to Marxist "messianism." Fired with remarkable zeal and fanatic devotion, doubtlessly stimulated by the new Soviet, the American converts proceeded in a variety of guises and shapes to set up shop in the Carpenters' union; and early in the 1920's they launched a carefully planned assault upon it and upon its General President.

From the very beginning, it was the aim of the newly organized American Communist Party to capture the reformist unions, drive out their leaders, and use them as weapons in the war upon capitalism. For this purpose the Communist apostles in Russia's Mecca decided to organize the Red Labor Union International and pursue its campaign of conversion in the unions of the world. American trade unionism was among the types considered at the Congresses of the Red Labor Union

[1]U.B.C.J.A., *Proceedings* (1924), p. 4.

International. "In America, as in no other country, the labor unions and their leading elements play the part of direct agents of capital," read the holy pronouncements of the Muscovites. The "A. F. of L. serves as a most reliable tool in the hands of the bourgeoisie for suppressing the revolutionary movement . . . Therefore the question of creating revolutionary cells in groups inside the American Federation of Labor and the *independent unions is of vital importance*," declared the First International Congress of Revolutionary Trade and Industrial Unionism.[2]

The labor situation in the United States during that time was more fluid and more unsettled than usual. Membership in the labor unions had increased quite rapidly during the first World War, but within a period of three years the ranks of organized labor had been reduced by approximately sixty percent. The postwar period, as previously described, witnessed a wave of strikes, unparalleled in extent and intensity. There was considerable dissatisfaction with the traditional views of the labor movement, with organization and political policy. Moreover, the dissatisfaction manifested itself in opposition to international officers, Hutcheson being one of them. There were demands for political action, through the medium of a National Labor Party.

Into this situation stepped William Z. Foster, who now saw an opportunity for building a broad opposition within the American Federation of Labor. Hiding his Communist views and affiliations, Foster proposed that the more militant workers organize themselves so that they could muster the strength to reform and take over various trade unions and eventually the A. F. of L. itself.

Foster, as the leader of the steel strike, was for a time able to pose as a "pure" progressive trade unionist. The big issue that he raised was the amalgamation of the trade unions. Instead of the A. F. of L. allowing several craft unions or semi-industrial unions to function in an industry, Foster preached that the several unions in an industry amalgamate and form one big union. He repeatedly scolded the new converts who left the conservative trade unions and formed dual organizations. But until his exposure as a Communist during a secret meeting of Communist leaders in the woods at Bridgman, Michigan, Foster simulated a moderate attitude. He was thereby able to gain a substantial following among trade unionists who believed that the A. F. of L. and its affiliates ought to be reformed. Resolutions favoring Foster's program were enacted by several internationals and by a number of State Federations of Labor, and city central bodies. Among those favoring amalgamation was the Chicago Federation of Labor, then the most vociferous city central body in the country.

[2]*Resolutions & Decisions adopted by First International Congress of Revolutionary Trade and Industrial Unions,* pp. 19, 33.

In pursuit of his program, Foster decided to launch a new organization, ostensibly "purely educational" — the Trade Union Educational League (T.U.E.L.), whose announced objective was to reconstruct the labor movement from stem to stern. In 1922 the elaborate plans of T.U.E.L. went awry when it was discovered that Foster had been a participant at the above-mentioned secret conclave of leading Communists. Many leading progressive trade unions which favored a reform of the American labor movement hastily dissociated themselves from Foster and his Communist supporters. The Trade Union Educational League then became the battering ram with which the Communists sought to subdue the labor movement of the United States and convert it to a Communist auxiliary. They failed completely to achieve their major aim. But in many unions they carried on a relentless, unscrupulous war against the officers, a war which was sometimes both troublesome and quite destructive.

The Communists, operating through the Trade Union Educational League, planned to invade all unions, but the affiliation of their adherents determined which unions were to feel the brunt of the pressure. Factions were organized in the unions of all important industries, coal mining, metal, building, transport and the needle trades. "The trade union factions are important, for they are the instruments through which the Party carries out its policies in the union . . . Our Party must always act as a unit in the unions. This can only be done through the faction system," wrote Foster.

The Trade Union Educational League sought to set up shop in the United Brotherhood of Carpenters.[3] As the League's attempt to penetrate the Building Trades Union got under way in 1922, its leaders published a small sheet, *The Progressive Building Trades Worker,* and opened headquarters in New York, Chicago, Philadelphia and Detroit from which the drive to capture the United Brotherhood was directed. They worked to implement a long-winded, eighteen-point platform, ostensibly designed to make the Brotherhood into a more "democratic organization," a plan for the "amalgamation" of all building trades unions into "one big union," a labor party and finally, affiliation of the Brotherhood with the Red Labor Union International.

The Communists, through the Trade Union Educational League, were able to establish a few active, vociferous units boring from within the Brotherhood. They captured two local unions in New York, and succeeded in penetrating six others in Chicago, Detroit, Los Angeles, Portland, Philadelphia and Cedar Rapids. In the 1924 elections, Willis K. Brown of Local Union 183 in Illinois and Morris Rosen of Local Union

---

[3]*William Z. Foster, "Party Trade Union Factions," The Workers Monthly, July,* 1925, pp. 424, 415.

376 of New York ran against General President William L. Hutcheson, polling almost 13,000 votes, which represented about .03 percent of the total. Hutcheson won by a walk away. This was the high water mark of the influence of the Communists in the United Brotherhood.

At the same time, the borers-from-within Communists, through the Trade Union Educational League, conducted an elaborate campaign of vilification in widely circulated pamphlets, circulars, cartoons and monographs, in which Hutcheson and the Brotherhood were savagely denounced and ridiculed; a campaign, incidentally, which set the tenor and pattern for the more serious labor historians, "experts" of all types, and even doctoral candidates in the 'thirties, 'forties and 'fifties, who were not averse at parrotting the "writers" of the League of the 1920's.

Through the mediation of the Trade Union Educational League and the *Progressive Building Trades Worker,* writers like Dr. Herbert Harris, Charles A. Madison, Edward Levinson, Harold Seidman, Stuart, Minton and many others, a downright antipathy against the Carpenters Union and its General Officers intruded itself into the American labor world, in public opinion forming agencies of varying colorations. "What's Wrong in the Carpenters' Union," authored by Morris Rosen, a Trade Union Educational League "plant" in the Brotherhood, and his "Appeal of Local Union 376 to the Membership of the United Brotherhood to the 22nd General Convention From the Decision of General President William L. Hutcheson, and the General Executive Board," have since become the "J'accuse"-like documents, from which the above-mentioned writers and labor journalists have prolifically and repeatedly quoted. This will be verified in short order in another part of this book.

But Hutcheson was not their sole target. There was John L. Lewis of the United Mine Workers of America, and David Dubinsky of the International Ladies Garment Workers Union, who, not unlike Hutcheson, were subjected to calumny and diatribes at the hands of the Trade Union Educational League.[4]

To be sure, Hutcheson was able to overcome Communist opposition by either expelling or disciplining their adherents. First he expelled F. W. Burgess of Local Union 8, Philadelphia, a writer of scurrilous literature directed at Hutcheson and the Brotherhood. General Secretary Duffy, Vice-President Cosgrove, Neale and Arthur Martell led the Executive Board members to Philadelphia to correct the condition. Burgess was heard, admitted his affiliation with a Communist front — the Philadelphia Labor Defense Council. He was expelled at the end of the

---

[4]Philip Taft, *The Structure and Government of Labor Unions,* (Harvard University Press, 1954), pp. 6, 11.

month. With his departure, the Communist plants in Philadelphia were rendered ineffective.

The Brotherhood turned to Detroit on January 9, 1925 and ordered William Reynolds expelled. William Reynolds, a member of the Trade Union Educational League, was Morris Rosen's campaign manager in Detroit. Reynolds obtained 41 votes for Rosen in the 1924 election. He managed to capture his own Local Union 2140 and the Vice-Presidency of the Wayne County District Council. Duffy informed the members of Local Union 2140 by mail, on January 10, that they were to expel Reynolds. On January 19, the District Council requested further information on the Reynolds case. The General Executive Board of the Brotherhood instructed its Secretary to refer to a circular letter which it issued on April 18, 1919, "that any member . . . affiliating with a body or organization whose principles are in conflict with the principles of the United Brotherhood shall be expelled." William Reynolds was dropped.[5]

In Chicago it was Frank Stahl, a "progressive," who was strongly supported by the *Daily Worker,* against the administration of Harry Jensen, President of the Chicago District Council Carpenters and Joiners. Here the militants captured Locals 81 and 62.[6] The charge was "scurrilous literature," in which Hutcheson was described as an "open-shopper," "scab" and "sell-out." A left-wing pamphlet characterized the trial as a "star chamber affair." However, each of the accused signed statements pledging to sever connections with the Trade Union Educational League and apologize publicly for vilifying Hutcheson. They were reinstated on probation.

Finally, Hutcheson leveled his sights on the agitator who led the Trade Union Educational League drive on the Brotherhood. Morris Rosen captured Local Union 376, converting all its members to the League. He joined the local early in 1923 and within the year led a "Progressive" slate which wrested control of the union "from the old gang that was loyal to Czar Hutcheson."[7] He had been in the organization but a year and ten months when he ran against General President Hutcheson. The embezzlement of $1000 from the Local Union treasury, Rosen charged to Meyer Rudinsky, the old treasurer. After his local expelled him, Rudinsky went to Hutcheson. Hutcheson sent Tom Guerin to take possession of the books. Rosen refused to turn them over to Guerin. The latter stood on Section 10, Paragraph B of the Constitution which allowed a "deputy to take possession of all books, papers and financial accounts of any local union." Guerin left without the books.

5U.B.C.J.A., *Proceedings* (1924), p. 356.

6*Daily Worker,* June 1, 2, 3, 14, 1924.

7U.B.C.J.A., *Proceedings,* (1928), p. 250.

Duffy went off to New York, accompanied by a trial committee which consisted of John Cosgrove, Thomas Neale, J. W. Williams and John Potts. Rosen again refused to surrender the books in order to conceal the fact that the local's funds had been given to the Trade Union Educational League. Rosen was found guilty as charged, for refusal to surrender the books to (sic!) "this sly dog of a Hutcheson." Local 376 was suspended and several of Rosen's adherents in Local 1164 were ousted. In this final swoop, Rosen, the man who exposed himself to ridicule by running against Hutcheson, soon ended his maneuvers.

Yet, Hutcheson allowed Rosen, the leader of the camouflaged Trade Union Educational League and others of the opposition to appear at the 1928 convention. Rosen was still under suspension subject to convention appeal for violating Section 10, paragraph B, which "authorized the General President or his deputy, to take possession of all books, papers and financial accounts of any local unions . . ." When delegate Timmer objected strenuously to giving Rosen the platform to appeal his case, Hutcheson insisted he be allowed to speak and give his side. "Our rules provide for certain procedure," said Hutcheson; "it will require a vote of the delegates to give the brother the right to the floor."[8]

Said Delegate Weyler, L.U. 64: "I move, Mr. Chairman, should this Brother of this Local desire the floor that we grant him the privilege." The motion was seconded. A dramatic exchange followed.

Delegate Flynn, L.U. 13: Is this brother a delegate to this convention?

President Hutcheson: He is not. Therefore, it will require a vote of the delegates.

Delegate Flynn, L.U. 13: I move that we adhere to our procedure and allow only delegates to have the floor.

Delegate Johnson: In view of the delegate having acknowledged authorship of the scurrilous literature, on behalf of the local I represent, I most seriously object to him having the floor.

Secretary Duffy: As a special request coming from your General Secretary for twenty-eight years, I ask you that he be given the floor and given all the time necessary to tell his story.

President Hutcheson: So do I. Let him have the floor.

The motion to extend the floor to the representative in question was carried.

President Hutcheson: Please come to the platform and stand here beside the flag, the one you don't think so much of.

Morris Rosen: Mr. President . . . the fact that you have given me

---

[8]*Ibid*, p. 240.

the floor is, in my opinion, a great victory for the democratic and progressive principles which I fought for when I was a candidate for General President during the last election. To my mind the manner in which we have conducted the fight, the publicity which we have given it shows that the General Executive Board has had to take note and has had to give me the floor. Perhaps the General Executive Board and the General Officers think that they may discredit me thereby, but I assure you that I am ready to stand and defend our case. How much I will be allowed to say will depend on the decency and fairness of President Hutcheson.

President Hutcheson: You have the floor and you may proceed as you see fit. I will take care of it afterwards. Go as far as you like.

Rosen was permitted to say all he wanted to say.

He launched into a tirade against Hutcheson, ostensibly on trade union grounds. Rosen charged Hutcheson with "unscrupulousness," "chicanery," and "persecution" of "all progressive members who dare to oppose, to challenge his almighty rule of the Brotherhood." Hutcheson was a "fakir," a "misleader," "autocrat," "bureaucrat," "czar," Rosen quoted prolifically from his unacknowledged writings. He then summed up with a direct challenge: "I ask you," he addressed the delegates, "to pass judgment on the actions of the General President, favorable action on our appeal may not only win the case for us, it will have the effect of putting a stop to Hutcheson's irresponsible moves."[9]

Duffy, in rebuttal, centered his attack on Rosen's undoubted Communist affiliation. He exposed Rosen's unsubstantiated charges, which, in addition to all else, accused Hutcheson of "aiding and establishing an open shop" in the building trades, and of Hutcheson "serving the capitalistic class." Leveling an accusing finger at Rosen, Duffy told the hushed delegates that Rosen had at no time "preferred charges against the General President along these lines." Rosen's charge of nepotism against Duffy, was then disproved by the General Secretary on the floor. Duffy went into a lengthy, documented recital of Rosen's maneuvers against Hutcheson and the Brotherhood. Duffy himself was rather mild when he stated: . . . "all the committee recommended was that the local union be reprimanded, let them go, perhaps after this things will be different. The General Executive Board accepted the decision. We thought after that that we would have no more trouble . . ."

After presenting an exhaustive array of facts which Rosen could not refute, Duffy stated: . . . "mind you, they reprimanded them once. We thought that would be enough, but they took little or no notice of reprimand."

---

[9] *Ibid.* (1928), p. 245. seq.

President Hutcheson: You have heard the statements made by General Secretary Duffy. Inasmuch as the action in revoking the charter of Local Union 376 was an act of the General Executive Board and not an act of mine . . . and due to the fact that Duffy served on the sub-committee . . . and he having given you a history of the case, I don't feel that it is necessary for me to make any reply to the remarks made by the man sitting in the chair. You have heard the report of the Appeals and the Grievance Committee. The motion before the House is to accept the report of the Committee.

The motion to adopt the report was unanimously carried.

Delegate Tierny, L.U. 9: In view of the evidence that has been offered here today, I move that Morris Rosen be expelled from this organization.

President Hutcheson: Please get out of this building and off the Brotherhood's property as quickly as possisble.

The appeals committee heard from eleven others, three of whom were ousted as Communists. Eight of them were disciplined. Two of these were proved blameless and six were put on probation.

The wayward members stayed on probation, while the committed Communist faction was squeezed out of the Brotherhood. The little influence they had was completely dissipated. Their adherents were left with mimeograph machines, faded cartoons, and a few memories to solace them. Their publications were left for the oncoming labor historians and researchers. They were discovered in the famed Astor Library, in the year 1937, when Bruce Minton and John Stuart of the *New Masses,* decided to collaborate on *Men Who Lead Labor.*[10] Its treatment conformed to the "new line" of the American Communist Party.

---

[10]Bruce Minton and John Stuart, "The Success of a Bruiser," *Men Who Lead Labor,* (Modern Age Books, Inc., 1937), Chapter II.

PART | IV

RISE of the LEVIATHAN STATE

CHAPTER | XII

THE GREAT DEPRESSION

Eight years of Harding and Coolidge prosperity had ridden Hoover into the Presidency in May, 1929. Already unemployment was disquieting. The Federation itself "conserved a strict adherence to a nonpartisan political policy," although it promoted George L. Berry of the International Printing Pressmen's Union as team-mate to Governor Alfred Smith. The Federation's recommendation was unacceptable to the Democratic leaders. Persistent demands by William Green that the Democrats accept Senators Robinson, Barkley or Congressman Rainey as vice-presidential candidates were unavailing. Herbert Hoover defeated Alfred E. Smith by 444 electoral votes to 87.

With the election of Hoover, Hutcheson continued as frequent guest of the White House. As a special interest representative in the Republican party, his activities had been confined for the most part to educating its leaders on such controversial topics as public works at the going union rates, social security, labor relations and employment. Realizing however, the relative ineffectiveness of these efforts at that time, Hutcheson chose a more direct way to aid the Republican presidential candidate. He set up within the structure of the National Republican party a "labor division," which was headed by Sturges Meadows, representative of Indianapolis Carpenters' Local 75, and later General Treasurer of the Brotherhood.

Hutcheson had known Hoover since 1922, when, as Secretary of Commerce under President Harding, he had been the chairman of the Unemployment Conference. Hoover's pronounced views of the role of the wage earner in the American community dovetailed with those of Hutcheson. Yet, while he differed with Hutcheson on the union shop, Hoover recognized collective bargaining with organized labor, and in the past, had issued a plea urging that course. Both Hutcheson and Hoover agreed that every effort should be made against setting up management and labor as distinct classes with opposing interests. It was far from "rugged individualism" and ultra conservatism for Hutcheson to advocate among the Republicans that wages should be maintained for the present, that construction work should be maintained by industry, and that governmental agencies should increase construction to give as much employment as possible at union scales, and that the available work should be spread among all employees by shortening the work week to five days.

On November 18, 1929, President Hoover took the first step to apply the idea practically, and arranged with Treasury Secretary Mellon that he propose to Congress, as soon as it should convene, an immediate increase in the Federal Public Building Program of $423,000,000.

Hoover proceeded to point out that the immediate duty was to consider the human problem of unemployment and distress; that the second problem was to maintain social order and industrial peace; the third was orderly liquidation and the prevention of panic. He explained that the immediate "liquidation" of labor had been the industrial policy of previous depressions; that his instinct was opposed to both the term and the policy, for labor was not a commodity. It represented human homes. Moreover, from an economic viewpoint, such action would deepen the depression by suddenly reducing purchasing power and, still worse, bring about industrial strife, bitterness, and fear. That he had failed to follow through with a series of bold steps was most unfortunate for the country.*

On the afternoon of November 21, the President held a conference with the "outstanding labor leaders" and secured their adherence to the program. Among the leaders who met with President Hoover were William Levi Hutcheson, William Green, Frank Morrison, William J. McSorley, John P. Frey, B. M. Jewell, A. F. Whitney and E. B. Curtis.

Two days later, the President called a second conference of the building construction industries and secured from Hutcheson and others an understanding to *aid, maintain and stimulate those industries.* At the same time the President telegraphed the governors and mayors throughout the country not to decrease public works, but to cooperate with him in expanding them in every practical direction, to take up the slack in employment. But once again business leadership resisted.

There were few, if any, in responsible power with both the will, vision and ability to check the onrush. Even the liberal Democratic presidential nominee of 1932 criticized Hoover for failing to balance

---

*Legally, however, labor won two important victories in the Hoover Administration. The Supreme Court in the Texas and New Orleans Railway case in 1930 unanimously decided that an employer's attempt to force a company union upon his workers constituted interference with their rights. And in March, 1932 Hoover signed the Norris-LaGuardia Anti-injunction Act, which also outlaws "yellow-dog" contracts.

the budget. The gay summer of 1929 ran to its end, and the gray Autumn began . . .

Then came the worst economic debacle in American history, for which no one was prepared.

On the morning of October 29, 1929, the towering structure of American prosperity cracked wide open. To the discerning, the spectacular crash of security values in the Wall Street panic was the signal that the upswing of the past seven years was not invulnerable. Gradually it became clear that economic activity was contracting and that the decline, once started, was accelerating at dangerous speed. All this was a familiar aspect of the business cycle. But in spite of the thoughtful books written on the subject, there was still no agreement as to the precise nature of the impulses that unloosed, periodically the upturns and downturns in the world of enterprise. Monetary and non-monetary causes, under-consumption and over-investment, psychological factors, all wove a tangled mess of theory. Data for the era were so abundant as to furnish selective evidence for almost any diagnosis.

But until the mid-'thirties, in the United States, the notion of the grave depression was not only foreign to the accepted systems of economics but its admission was largely barred to analysis. Unemployment, which was sufficiently a fact so that it could not be ignored, was generally associated with the activities of unions. Unions, it was said, restrained the worker from getting himself employed by preventing him from reducing the wage at which he offered to work and so making it worth the while of an employer to hire him. This was not the dogma of mossbacks. As late as 1930, Sir William Beveridge, a modern symbol of unorthodoxy, firmly asserted that the effect, at least potentially, "of a high wages policy in causing unemployment is not denied by any competent authority."

Be that as it may, the prosperity of the 'twenties, which led many to believe that the economy distorted by war had been successfully reconstructed, actually concealed abrupt maladjustments arising from the war and enhanced in subsequent years.

By 1932 the national income had fallen below that of 1912 when the population was less by 30,000,000 people. By the middle of the year 1932 — more than two-and-a-half years after the crash of 1929 — American industry as a whole was operating at less than its maximum 1929 volume. Unemployment in proportion to population almost doubled that of Britain and exceeded that of Germany, two countries that the United States had considered in fundamental decline since World War I. During this year of 1932, the total amount of money paid out in wages was sixty percent less than in 1929. In that year over 12,000,000 Americans were unemployed. As the depression deepened, the Com-

munists and Fascists were not alone in their glib manifestoes that capitalism was doomed. In Germany the world-wide depression brought Hitler
to power and in other lands many people loudly sounded the death knell
of capitalism. In the United States, the Great Depression brought an
epidemic of proposals for economic panaceas — the cult of technocracy,
the physiocrats, Upton Sinclair's EPIC, the Townsend Old Age Revolving Pension Plan; it brought the dictator-like Huey Long to brief regional power; it brought riots at farmers' bankruptcy sales, a Communist-
led march on Washington, and the briefly ominous Bonus Army march
of 1932. It also saw a rapid growth in the influence of Communists in
the labor unions — though not in their voting strength, which remained
extremely small.

In 1932 and 1933, the worst years of the long depression period,
approximately one-fourth of the labor force in the United States was jobless, and the number diminished very slowly as the decade of the 1930's
wore on. In 1933 the number of unemployed averaged 12,830,000, and
not until three years later did it fall below 10,000,000 to surpass that
figure again in the recession year of 1938. Between 1929 and 1933 the
American Federation of Labor lost 452,200 members, falling to 2,317,500.
Among the sharpest declines were those in building construction.[1]

The large number of unemployed intensified the downward pressure
on wages exerted by other depression influences. While unionists faced
threats from those without work, union employers were further jeopardized by competition of non-union firms which could operate with sorely
underpaid labor. It was impossible to sustain wages and union conditions
in the same economy with mounting millions of unemployed dramatized
tragically by the beggar, the bread line, the extemporized shack colonies
and "Hoovervilles." Between 1929 and 1933, labor income fell from
$50,964,300,000 to $26,386,000,000 or 48 percent. Because of pay cuts
and part-time work, average weekly earnings were reduced from $25.03
in 1929 to $16.73 in 1938. The index of the cost of living declined from
99.5 in 1929 to 75.8 in 1933, but that was less than the decline in wages.

Confronted with such discouraging economic conditions, the organized labor movement was weak and dispirited in this period of the
Depression, as it witnessed the collapse of standards built up so pain-
fully over many years. Unemployed union members could not pay dues.
Union scales became nominal; employers refused to make new union
agreements, or made them on worse terms.

From December, 1929 through June, 1932, fully one-third of the
Brotherhood's membership, or 100,013 members could not pay dues.
"Less than 30 percent of the Brotherhood's 300,000 members had been

[1] Leo Wolman, *The Ebb and Flow in Trade Unionism*, (National Bureau of Economic
Research, 1936), pp. 138-139.

employed."[2] The sharp decline in building construction tore into the Brotherhood's ranks, although it still remained the numerically largest international union in America.[3] President Hutcheson and all other general officers, down to organizer, took a reduction in salary. Unemployed members, unable to pay dues, were granted dispensation until June 30, 1936. For financial reasons, and because "many locals would be denied representation," the Brotherhood postponed its twenty-third General Convention, after a referendum taken March 27, 1932.

In August of 1931, as the Brotherhood entered the second-half of its first century and despite its growth for fifty years, it was now forced to lead a defensive, desperate struggle for the retention of union scales, reported Hutcheson. "On every hand wage cuts were demanded by employers. Our members resisted these efforts to tear down their established conditions to the limit of their ability. Many changes were forced upon us, but few were conceded. Our members refused to believe that low wages would create work . . . While sheer poverty made it impossible for many thousands of our members to pay dues, they never lost or surrendered their union principles."[4]

While the deadly totals of the unemployed carpenters continued to mount, and as the employers refused to make new agreements or made them on worse terms, the Brotherhood continued to use its defensive weapons to withstand the relentless onslaught of the depression. In 1929 alone, it conducted 95 trade actions, resisting wage deductions.[5] In the following year, it conducted 130 unsuccessful and successful strikes; and for the period ending June 1936, the Carpenters' Union carried out 223 trade movements, effective and otherwise. During that same period, the Brotherhood chalked up $56,598 toward strikes and lockouts. In pensions and benefits it paid out $2,803,635 in six uninterrupted years. Beginning June 1930, the Brotherhood authorized its officers to pay each pensioner $15 a month.

Obviously, there were many difficulties which the Brotherhood had to overcome. Paramount in the mind of Hutcheson was the problem of unemployment, which in the case of the building trades was particularly aggravated by a further threatening technological unemployment, in addition to the stagnant economy which failed to absorb the displaced craftsmen. There were the recurrent jurisdictional disputes between the International Association of Machinists and the Brotherhood, which both Hutcheson and President A. O. Wharton sought to solve amicably, so

---

[2]Frank Duffy, *History of the U.B.C.J.A.* (MSS).

[3]*Ibid.*

[4]*U.B.C.J.A., Proceedings,* (1936), p. 95

[5]*Ibid,* pp. 80-85; 182-183.

that "both organizations have better conditions in the work claimed by each."

In May, 1930 there began an almost interrupted two year decline, not only in security prices, but also in an infinitely more vital area — in the volume of American business. A vicious circle of ebbing sales was followed by declining corporate income, and attempts to restore that income by cutting salaries and wages and laying off men, which caused increased unemployment and further reduced sales, and led to increased business losses, which led to further cutting and further firing of men, and so on toward disaster. Little remained, but an undignified struggle for the remaining jobs in the jungle spirit of survival at any price.

The Federation's and Hutcheson's advocacy of the thirty-hour week was given a luke warm reception at the hands of management.[6] President Green's challenging call to management, that "so long as one workman is unemployed, the hours of labor are too long," was drowned out by the noisy and thoughtless opposition of the American Newspaper Publishers Association. It was then that the leaders of the American Federation of Labor turned to the Federal Government: to set the example for industry of a five-day, thirty-hour week.

For eight years the Republican party jubilantly assumed responsibility for existing prosperity. Now, confronted with a dismal change of economic conditions, neither it nor its spokesman, Herbert Hoover, could avoid completely the need for action. But President Hoover acted on the principle that the role of government in bringing the country out of depression must be secondary to that of private business initiative. In this he was a Jeffersonian liberal, whose doctrine of less government which most agrarian Democrats had prized at one time, had already been borrowed during the early 1920's by Republican businessmen. Now the party could neither admit that the prescription had failed nor muster enough imagination to attempt another cure. So for a year or two the depression was asserted to be a transitory phenomenon; the American business structure was at heart, sound, they argued. Hoover summoned business executives to Washington, at the urgent request of Hutcheson, to declare that there should be no wage cutting. It was futile. A modified program of self-liquidating works was devised.

Then the Reconstruction Finance Corporation was setup to bring federal aid to hard-pressed banks and business — while as a matter of principle, the government refused to put federal funds at the disposal of individual persons who were in trouble. The charge was made that the administration moved to vigorous action only when its favored big businesses were endangered. Naturally, Hoover did not regard the effort in

[6]*Hutcheson's Private Papers* (1932); *The Carpenter,* Vol. L: 3 (March 1930), pp. 20-21.

that light. Rather, the Corporation by aiding banks and other enterprises would enlarge credit and ensure confidence; business and industry would revive; men would be put back to work. Thus the shower of gold at the top of the pyramid would eventually enrich its lower levels.

Hutcheson's tireless efforts to promote Bill H. R. 9232 introduced in the House of Representatives bore no fruit. The bill provided that contractors or sub-contractors engaged in public works of the United States shall not pay less than the existing wage rates established for such services in private industry.

To describe Republican depression policy in terms of official government policy would be unjust. Hoover had little faith in salvation by statute. Instead he relied upon voluntary action under his own direction and organization. Business had been allowed to govern itself; now it was permitted to save itself. "Rugged individualism" was no more than a catchword, an empty phrase. So, as the President waved his baton, an interrupted stream of committees and conferences were marshalled in the capital. At first, when the reverberations of the stock market crash were stilled, Hutcheson and his labor confreres were summoned to the White House and invited to continue their plans of expansion and construction and building projects, preserve existing wage levels, and avoid industrial strife and aggressive demands. Hutcheson agreed in principle, but with reservations; business and industry, on its part, must keep its own promises made to the President. This they first failed to do.

Two years later the relief to the destitute and hungry was declared to be an obligation of "individual generosity" and "voluntary giving" through the Red Cross and committees of citizens or local governments. The Federal Government "must not set up" any organization for direct relief; such a policy was apt to weaken local responsibility and increase corruption and fraud. Finally, in 1932, Hoover was still appointing committees, studded with big names, to combat hoarding and convince business men they should borrow from the banks. The President regarded himself as the leader of a people, not as the head of a government. Since he abjured the sanction of power, he consequently relied upon co-operation.

But good will could hardly be expected to stand the strains of greed and self-interest. Business and management constantly broke their agreements with labor. In moments of irritation the administration petulantly complained; the rest of the time it presented a tragic appearance of seeking to cure the depression by prophecy, exorcism, and exhortation. An able and highly intelligent President, imprisoned by economic theories which were generally considered enlightened, had become the tragic culprit of the collapse of the going system.

CHAPTER | XIII

AMERICAN STANDARDS VS. DOLES

A biographical history of William Levi Hutcheson must note his ideological growth in these years. From advocating a laissez faire capitalism, and "less government in business" which strangled the Brotherhood, his labor plank for the Republican national committee included proposals for the expenditure of hundreds of millions of dollars for necessary and productive public works; urged higher wages, fewer hours and unemployment insurance, all of which were accepted by the Republican party. His proposals reiterated freedom in wage contracts, the right of collective bargaining by free and responsible agents of their own choosing. As for injunctions in labor disputes, Hutcheson reminded his Republican colleagues, that their "abuse should give rise to a serious question for legislation." Through Hutcheson, the Republican party pledged itself "to continue its efforts to maintain this present standard of living and high wage scale."

That the Republican national committee could not ignore the symbols of "liberalism" was entirely due to Hutcheson's vigorous stand. Actually, both major political parties had identical programs, but Democratic national headquarters proved able to put on a great show. Charles Michelson of the Democratic national committee did everything he could to criticize and embarrass the Hoover administration. Michelson directed timely darts at Herbert Hoover and Jouett Shouse toured the nation arousing party leaders to greater activity, intensifying the President's discomfiture. By the time of the Democratic national convention, although the candidate selected by the party was one intensely disliked by those in control of national headquarters, there was much less to explain away in a candidate such as Roosevelt than in Alfred E.

Smith. That latter had various political handicaps that added to the burden of local politicians in 1932, and the persistent attacks on the G.O.P. were showing results. It was then that Hutcheson stepped into the fray.[1]

On October 19, 1932, he addressed a communication to President William Green of the American Federation of Labor, in which he urged the Executive Council to "go a little deeper into the records of candidates before closing its books on the 1932 campaign." The letter implied that while Charles Michelson was attacking the record of President Hoover on labor matters, Governor Roosevelt's record itself was open to question. He urged an investigation of Governor Roosevelt's labor record.

Michelson countered with "Putting Labor on the Spot," a circular declaring that fourteen prominent labor leaders among thirty whose names appeared in Hutcheson's Republican circular had repudiated the attempt of the Republicans to represent them as opposing the Democratic tariff plank, and by implication, the election of Roosevelt.

Hutcheson said that the Republican circular had not represented the labor leaders mentioned in it as being opposed to the Democratic tariff plank as such, but had shown that either by personal appearance or through briefs they had asked committees of Congress to maintain protection for their respective trades. Hutcheson added that thirteen of the fourteen representing a large section of the American Federation of Labor had asked for such protection from Congress.[2]

Franklin D. Roosevelt's labor record as Governor was attacked by William L. Hutcheson in the following language:

> I here and now respectfully ask that the Executive Council, now in session, immediately proceed to investigate not only the labor record of President Hoover, but the labor record of his Democratic opponent, and to determine, if possible, where the Democratic candidate actually stands on vital issues of the day.
>
> I ask that this be done now, so that the information secured may be spread before the voters before going to the polls, and that the inquiry be open to the public and the press.
>
> The Democratic manager in question has mentioned many things he wished investigated. I ask that the Council investigate these phases of the Democratic candidate's position on labor matters:
>
> First I ask, is it true, as indicated in a recent speech, that the Democratic candidate agrees with the railroad managers, now seeking a 20% cut in wages, that the railroads should only be called upon to pay "what they can afford?"
>
> Is is true, as reported in Wall Street, that he has assured the railroad managers of his sympathy with their desire to reduce their labor costs?

---

[1] Pendleton Herring, *The Politics of Democracy* (W. W. Norton & Co., 1940), pp. 208-9.
[2] *New York Times,* October 26, 1932, p. 13: 2.

Secondly, I ask that the Council seek to determine the reason for Governor Roosevelt's failure over a period of more than three years, to enforce the labor laws of the State of New York against favored contractors. Specifically, I ask why favored subway contractors in New York City were permitted to pay as little, in some instances, as one-half the prevailing rate of wages in that city?

Third, I further ask that the Council seek an explanation of Governor Roosevelt's failure, for more than three years, to make the slightest endeavor to secure relief for the 40,000 traction workers in New York City now compelled to work seven days per week.

Fourth, I ask that the failure of Governor Roosevelt to make any move to secure relief for the thousands of employees of State institutions now compelled to work twelve hours or more per day and seven days per week be inquired into.

Fifth, I ask that the Council investigate the validity of Governor Roosevelt's claims for credit for labor laws based on a Republican legislature in both branches.

Sixth, the Democratic platform calls for immediate legislation to permit the brewing of real beer. The Democratic candidate says he stands on that plank.

Seventh, I respectfully ask that the Council seek to determine what he understands by "immediate." Does he approve of the defeat by Democratic voters, of the attempt to make that plank effective in the next session of Congress; if effected, will he force the fanatical dries in the party to make good that declaration?

Eighth, is the Democratic candidate for fiat money and abandonment of the gold standard, thereby automatically cutting American wages?

Ninth, is the Democratic candidate for the restriction of immigration as demanded by the American Federation of Labor and ignored by a convention which he controlled?

Tenth, at the behest of the anti-union South, the Democratic convention, controlled by the Democratic candidate's agents, refused to declare for collective bargaining. Does the Democratic candidate approve that action of his agents?

Eleventh, at the behest of the anti-union South, the Democratic convention controlled by the agents of the Democratic candidate refused to declare for the shorter work week.

Does the Democratic candidate approve that action of his agents?

Twelfth, Labor is vitally interested in a pure milk supply for the children of workers.

How does the Democratic candidate explain his unconditional pardon of Clougher — "the baby poisoner" — sent to Sing Sing for flooding the tenements of New York with doped milk?[3]

Fraternally,

William L. Hutcheson
Director Labor Bureau
Republican National Convention.

In July 1932, the American Federation of Labor had issued a decla-

3Ibid. October 22, 1932, p. 11: 8.

ration of "non-partisanship" as between the Republican and Democratic parties. In early fall, Hutcheson and the Building Trades Department of the American Federation of Labor declared themselves in support of President Herbert Hoover. His opposition to the Governor of New York had its origins in an old feud dating back to 1917-1918, when Franklin D. Roosevelt was in charge of labor problems for the Navy and private shipping yards. At that time, it will be recalled, Hutcheson led a daring campaign against the open shop which was established in Navy construction. He distrusted Roosevelt, who begrudged him an appointment with President Wilson which could have saved Hutcheson from considerable embarrassment. The Carpenters' General President never could gloss over lightly his encounter with the Government. His victory, however, extended his influence far and wide—to make it national. He now used that influence to aid the Republicans.

The Republicans ignored the protests of the unemployed, since they already had a dependable combination of sectional interests. The Democrats, in casting about for a successful sectional alignment of an urban-labor-consumer coalition, were forced to give heed, since their hope of victory lay in attracting voters away from the Republican party. The Democratic party accordingly alternated between the appeals to the West and forays into these urban Eastern regions where the Republicans were entrenched. Labor's vote was large, and it seemed important in a battle of margins to woo the labor mugwumps, and the voter outside would be influenced by their actions. Hutcheson was the labor leader of the Republican mugwumps. It was therefore "good politics" to reckon with that element.

On July 26, the New York Governor and his lieutenants maneuvered to induce the American Federation of Labor to reverse its "non-partisan declaration." As in World War I, Roosevelt and his confidant Louis B. Wehle turned to Joseph A. Franklin, one of the fifteen signatories of the Baker-Gompers Agreement and President of the International Brotherhood of Boilermakers. All three agreed that the process for obtaining an official A. F. of L. statement abandoning neutrality would be too slow to "justify trying to set it in motion." Instead, they drafted a statement form for signature by executives of international unions announcing their support of Roosevelt. On October 7, Franklin on his official letterhead, urged each international union president to endorse Roosevelt for President.

"During these discussions Roosevelt, Franklin, and I," reports Wehle, "had overlooked the fact that Daniel J. Tobin, President of the Teamsters' International was head of the Labor Bureau at the Democratic national headquarters in New York . . . Tobin resented Franklin's activity. . . . Tobin, by long-distance, phoned to Franklin . . . endorsed Franklin's action, reassuring him by wire, 'Proceed as per your schedule with my fullest approval.' However, a few days later, Tobin reversed his position." But by that time the A. F. of L's neutrality front had broken. The effect of Hutcheson's and the Building Trades Department's pro-Hoover statement was seemingly ineffectual.[4] Roosevelt's popular majority was more than 7 million votes.

In the winter of 1932, as President-elect Roosevelt was preparing his first "fireside chat" in Albany, a committee of two, consisting of Matthew Woll and Otto Weber, Vice-Presidents of the American Federation of Labor and New York residents, came to see Roosevelt. At the request of President Green, both argued for the appointment of Daniel J. Tobin as Secretary of Labor in the Roosevelt cabinet. President-elect Roosevelt had known Tobin since World War I, and had in fact relied on him for labor support during the Presidential campaign as chairman of the Labor Bureau of the national democratic committee. Roosevelt was non-committal. He appointed Frances Perkins as Secretary of Labor. She had been Industrial Commissioner of New York when Roosevelt was Governor.[5]

Franklin Roosevelt proposed a New Deal. Fundamental to its details was the diagnosis formulated to explain the existing prostration of the nation. Accepting the thesis that wealth had drifted into the hands of the few and that the many lacked purchasing power, Roosevelt asserted that the country was entering an era in which the rate of future expansion would necessarily be slower. The immediate necessity therefore, was to arrange more satisfactorily the existing order. "Our task . . . is the soberer"—of meeting the problem of underconsumption, distributing wealth and products more equitably, of adapting existing economic organization to the service of the people." At least this was the Roosevelt doctrine at the outset of his first administration. In his second, however, the emphasis given to increasing national income was explicable only in terms of a modification of his original assertion that "we are going to think less about the producer and more about the consumer."

To attain his objectives, Franklin Roosevelt did not propose the destruction of capitalism. But he did advocate alterations. These were to be accomplished by "planning." Although completely to plan and regulate economic conditions "is as impossible as it is undesirable," industrial planning was required to prevent the wasteful duplication of plans, premature obsolescense of machinery, and epidemics of bankruptcies; agriculture called for a "planned use of the land" and public

---

[4]Louis B. Wehle, *Hidden Threads of History: Wilson through Roosevelt,* (Macmillan Co., 1953), pp. 107-108.

[5]*William Hutcheson's Private Papers covering AFL Executive Council Meeting,* (Nov. 20-Dec. 2, 1932).

utilities and banking also needed plans. On analysis, planning differed little from the old idea of regulation. What agency should assume the task of planning and which classes should be benefited, were more vital questions. Washington, and not Wall Street, was to be the planner. The beneficiary of the planning was to be the "forgotten man of the 1932 campaign, the one-third of the population which was 'ill-housed, ill-fed, and ill-clothed' of the latter 'thirties" It was at least different from that of President Hoover. The bottom, not the top of the pyramid was Roosevelt's concern!

In formulation and application the Roosevelt program inevitably involved contradictions. Men have usually been inconsistent in propounding purely political philosophies. For Roosevelt journeyed through American history picking up intellectual luggage. Jefferson and Jackson provided aims; the Populist tenets contributed a currency program; the Progressive era of the first Roosevelt provided for "a planned use of the land;" the Hoover administration gave objectives and agencies to a Democratic successor. But undoubtedly the most formative influence was the Wilson administration, with its avowed sympathy for laborers, farmers, and small business men. Ideas came from overseas; mostly they were social reforms that had been approved decades before by British Tories, and in Scandinavia.

There is no need to rehearse here in detail the now familiar story of the New Deal. The country was cheered and galvanized by Roosevelt's convincing and contagious confidence in the spring of 1933; how in his first "fireside chat" over the radio, when the banks were still closed, he conveyed a serene assurance that they could be successfully opened — as they shortly were; how, during the first hundred days he jammed through Congress, at record-breaking speed, a jumble of hastily improvised legislation; how he gathered about him two successive "braintrusts" composed of intellectuals, social workers, liberal lawyers, college and university professors—undismayed idealists, who furnished him with economic ideas and oratorical ammunition.

Basically, the New Deal marked a reassertion and extension of the ideals of the earlier progressive movement which had suffered shipwreck when America entered the European conflict in 1917. "In striving to give effect to these ideals, the Roosevelt administration applied to the peacetime crisis many of the methods which the Wilson administration had used to mobilize the country's economic resources during the World War.[6] The New Deal was new only insofar as it was the first effort of the Government to set up agencies for control in so many directions at

---

[6]See Arthur M. Schlesinger, *The New Deal in Action, 1933-1939* (Macmillan Co., 1940); Emanuel Stein, Carl Rausenbush, *Labor and the New Deal*, (F. C. Crofts & Co., 1934), p. 5.

the same time. However, Roosevelt was far more adventurous in experimenting with unorthodox theories, some of which turned out to be failures; but the tempo of the early 'thirties demanded quick and heroic experimentation. Roosevelt responded.

"To put people back to work" was the main justification for the passage of the National Industrial Recovery Act (NIRA) signed by the President on June 16, 1933. Undoubtedly, it was the most important piece of legislation turned out by the Seventy-Third Congress. This bill was the product of many minds, for senators, cabinet officials and others were all busy in the hectic months of Roosevelt's first term inventing a plan for recovery. Actually, the law was born in the United States Chamber of Commerce and blessed by the President of the General Electric Company. President Roosevelt had at all times stressed the point that the New Deal was a cooperative venture between employers and workers, with the Government a coordinating, advisory agency to see to it that the rules of the game were carried out for the best interests of society as a whole.

Briefly, this "partnership" was to be worked out through "codes of fair competition" for each industry. The Act instructed the administrative officers to see to it that the codes are presented by employers, or by trade organizations representing them. It was in the codes that the rules of fair competition were stated. They were intended to put firms on a competitive equality, and they were divided into two general sorts, rules about production and sales competition, and rules about conditions of labor. First of all they were to limit the hours of labor. "The idea is simply for employers to hire more men to do the existing work by reducing the work-hours of each man's week," announced the President. This share-the-work movement, which the A. F. of L., Hutcheson and Hoover advocated, was to be different, inasmuch as wages were not to be reduced at the same time. Rather the codes were to establish minimum wages. Finally, child labor was to be prohibited, not only for humanitarian reasons, but also to clear their jobs for adult workers. Thus with one sudden stroke, the central government assumed the responsibility, however indirectly, of regulating the conditions of labor on a national scale. Never before had the state attempted such a broad interference with the right of employers to operate their businesses as they pleased. Never before had any governmental agency in the United States undertaken such a fundamental abrogation of the traditional doctrine of freedom of labor contract.

Into the nine months that followed, was crowded the formulation of measures for this immense and intricate task. By April, 1934, when the revision of the model code appeared, over 20,000,000 workers were covered by codes, an increase of 4,000,000 since July, 1933. By this time the conflict between codes and within codes, and the demands for exemption and reclassification, had become formidable. Yet acting with accustomed haste, the President invited individual employers to sign a reemployment agreement. This document set a rather uniform pattern for most of the subsequent codes. The labor of children under 16 years of age was, with certain exceptions, prohibited. "White collar" workers were to have a forty-hour week; although some elasticity was permitted, factory and mechanical workers or artisans were to have a maximum week of thirty-five hours. "White collar" employees were to secure minimum weekly wages ranging from $14 to $15 in places of over 2500 inhabitants, and wages in smaller places were to be raised; with certain exceptions, manual workers were to have forty cents an hour. Employers agreed not "to reduce the compensation for employment now in excess of the minimum wages . . . and to increase the pay for such employment by such an equitable readjustment of all pay schedules." By preventing the minimum from becoming the maximum, this provision was to protect the skilled and semi-skilled workers.

The codes hardly met these exalted standards. To begin with, the Presidential recommendations were often too elusive for practical use and too uniform for application to a multitude of industries in various stages of irregular historical development. Besides, most codes were bargains forged by the pressures of employers, government agents, and workers. But most codes, with the significant exception of the newspaper and retail trades, successfully barred employment under 16 years of age. As for hours, only about seventy percent of the workers covered by the codes achieved a forty-hour week. Wages were mired in a swamp of confusion and conflict. As for minimum wages, higher levels or differentials were permitted for whites over Negroes, men over women, workers in larger over smaller places, in the North over the South, in the East over the West. In the large cities in the North, nearly fifty percent of the employed covered by the codes had a minimum wage of forty cents an hour for a maximum of thirty-five hours. In the small towns of the South only a little over twenty percent of the employed reached this minimum and over fifty percent received less than thirty cents an hour. Actually, the businessman had enjoyed sufficient prestige to be offered a senior partnership in the New Deal, particularly in the writing of the National Recovery Act. Dominant corporations wrote the codes that fixed the prices, intended to stabilize business. In effect, immunity from anti-trust laws was conferred upon these firms in Section 5 of the N.R.A. period, just as Theodore Roosevelt had granted similar immunity to the United States Steel Corporation during the Panic of 1907.

If smaller business units were under-represented on code authorities, labor and consumers were practically not represented at all. Only three codes provided for voting members speaking for interests of consumers, and under only 37 codes were "labor members allowed and these not always with the right to vote."[7]

One of the most vigorous protests made by organized labor had been the urging that labor be directly represented on each authority. But the protest had brought little results. The position of the N.R.A. was that responsibility for enforcement lay with the industries themselves. The industries, too, had resisted labor representation; some of them gave as their reason the danger of including outsiders who might divulge trade secrets. Others complained that their privacy had been ruthlessly invaded and that hereafter (as J. P. Morgan had said:) "Business must be conducted in glass houses under constant public scrutiny."

Thus, in many ways the New Deal permanently altered the nature of the American economy. It had brought about profound economic, social and political changes. It unleashed new forces as well as initiated a series of far-reaching reforms. One of these, Section 7A of the National Industrial Recovery Act, set in motion forces which altered the entire complexion of United States management-labor relations. As far as labor conditions were concerned, Section 7A of the Act soon overshadowed the others in importance. It wiped out past barriers to union growth. For the first time in history, the United States Government affirmed the right of employees to organize into unions of their own choosing and to bargain collectively with employers, free from employer interference. In the Spring of 1933, that was a radical doctrine. Indeed, in an ordinary economic climate, its adoption by Congress would have been vastly more difficult. But, in view of the panic sweeping the country, and because Section 7A was only part of a package statute aimed at starting the wheels of business turning again, the opposition of industry to the Section was not as great as might have been expected.

According to its provisions, every code had to include the following conditions: "(1) That employees shall have the right to organize and bargain collectively through representatives of their own choosing, and shall be free from interference, restraint, or coercion of employers of labor . . . In the designation of such representatives or in self-organizations . . . (2) That no employee and no one seeking employment shall be required as a condition of employment to join any company union or to refrain from joining, organizing or assisting a labor organization of his own choosing . . . (3) That employers shall comply with the maximum hours of labor, minimum rates of pay, and other conditions of employment approved or prescribed by the President. . . ."

The language of Section 7A had produced more argument and disputation, more industrial conflict and even bloodshed, and more

---

[7]See Broadus Mitchell, *Depression Decade: From New Era to New Deal, 1929-1941*, (Rinehart & Co., 1947), Chapter III, pp. 228-250.

varied interpretation than all the other Sections of Title 1 put together. To begin with, Item 1 in paragraph (a) employed practically the same language as that contained in the "declaration of policy" of the Norris-LaGuardia Anti-Injunction Act of 1932. This meant, that this part of Section 7A became important because of the codification of almost all business under the national emergency; in other words, this language had no meaning, practically, until given force by the New Deal. It also meant that certain employers' associations like the N. A. M., realizing that this Section would furnish a decided impetus to unionization of non-union workers, tried to have a qualifying clause, the sense of which was that where satisfactory labor relations already existed between employers and individual workers or company unions, these should not be disturbed by anything in the Act. Labor, however, voted the proposal down. In any case, the wording represented the wishes of the American Federation of Labor.

To be sure, President Green had relied a great deal on the advice of Hutcheson, whose experiences on the National War Labor Board had proved invaluable. The War Labor Board in 1917-1918 had similar functions to those that the N. R. A. had in the early 'thirties. In many ways, the structure of the organization and the methods of work were so similar as to have suggested that the N. I. R. A. was cut from the old pattern.[8] On the other hand, in the N. I. R. A., the position of labor as a bargainer was much weaker than it was during the War.

The Recovery Act gave great impetus to union organizing activities, to unionization of unorganized workers, and strikes to force union recognition from employers. In their response to the invitation to form independent unions, workers were encouraged by the optimism engendered by the new administration, by the pick-up in employment, and by the removal of penalties on union membership and activities. Of less importance was the fact that relief was available to strikers. Not only was prompt expansion of unions spectacular, it gave labor a lease on life, having risen from virtual impotency to the position of an undisputed social, economic and political power. During the 'thirties, the American labor movement developed and expanded in a manner unprecedented in history, and the attendant growing pains were manifested in the turbulence which beset the country's industrial relations. In six years following 1933 when the N. R. A., particularly its Section 7A, came to its rescue, nearly 6,000,000 workers had joined unions. By the end of the decade, total union strength had been recruited to some 8,500,000, almost evenly divided between the American Federation of Labor and the C. I. O. This growth was not accomplished by a single

---

[8]Carroll H. Dougherty, *Labor Under the N.R.A.*, (Houghton Mifflin Co., 1934), pp. 7-8.

stroke. Nor was it achieved without great effort, violence and bloodshed.

Prior to the establishment of the National Recovery Administration, American Trade Unionism was in the doldrums. During the "roaring 'twenties" unionism had been weakened; the onset and progress of the Great Depression demoralized it. Before the N. R. A., membership in the Federation declined to 2,317,500; in 1934 it grew to 3,608,600, and to an estimated 3,888,600 in 1935. The last figure included 1,022,100, who in 1935 constituted themselves into the Committee for Industrial Organization, but nearly three-fourths of whom were drawn from the Federation. Still, the latter's membership rose 300,000 between 1934 and 1935.

The International Ladies Garment Workers Union, the United Mine Workers of America and the Amalgamated Clothing Workers had benefited extraordinarily from the early labor measures of the Roosevelt administration. Before the N. R. A., all three were literally reduced to a state of impotence and financial bankruptcy. Within two months the International Ladies Garment Workers Union emerged as a major union adding 100,000 to its remnant of 50,000; in a year it doubled its membership to 200,000; the United Mine Workers of America, at last cracking the non-union strongholds of West Virginia and Kentucky, enrolled 300,000. Before the N. R. A., its membership had been reduced to less than 60,000. "President Roosevelt wants you to join the union," was Mr. John L. Lewis' slogan of the day.

During the early years of the Depression both unions, the United Mine Workers of America and the International Ladies Garment Workers Union, sought relief from the payment of per capita tax to the already financially burdened Federation. John L. Lewis was authorized by "the Executive Council to 'make an appropriation' from the funds of the American Federation of Labor," lest the distressed miners lose their standing in that body.[9] Mr. Benjamin Schlesinger of the I.L.G.W.U. was hard put to repay a $5000 note for taxes that were due to the Federation for the year 1926-1927 To retain his standing, he made a partial payment of $1,000 due for the fiscal year of 1928.[10]

Under Hutcheson, the United Brotherhood of Carpenters remained solvent. Although its monthly income had been reduced by more than one-third, it continued to pay its full membership per capita tax to the Federation until the fiscal year of 1931. In October, 1932, when the Carpenters themselves experienced great financial strains, resulting from increasing unemployment existent among its members, Hutcheson did not regard it as "reasonable for the Federation to request that it pay on

[9]*Hutcheson's Private Papers* (Labor History file, July, 1928).
[10]*Ibid*, May 2, 1928.

its full membership." President Green's plea to Hutcheson that the Brotherhood "help the Federation meet its expenses," was carefully considered. To make sure, however, that the Executive Board of the Brotherhood approved, Hutcheson requested a detailed statement of the economy measures introduced by the Federation. This President Green did to the satisfaction of Hutcheson and the General Executive Board.[11]

Almost as soon as the Act was passed, there was a wave of strikes throughout the country, some of them in unionized industries, and some in newly organized ones. Some strikes were called to enforce code wages and hours, some for wages above the code minima. Many spontaneous walkouts took place. In some of them the workers believed that the employers were not living up to the code, and to go out on strike to force upholding of the law, was a meritorious action on their part, quite in line with the wishes of the Government. Under the N. R. A., conciliation of disputes had been stressed. This suggested that strikes were undesirable, no matter for what purpose they may be called. However, in spite of repeated pleas from the President and considerable public opinion against strikes, they continued to occur.

By the end of 1933 and early 1934 the scheme of industrial self-government seemed to imply a betrayal. President Green reiterated the Federation's position that the strike, as a weapon of last resort, must not be jeopardized. "The right to strike is fundamental; it is legally and morally right. The workers must not be called to surrender the right to strike. It is an absolute and unqualified right." At its 1933 convention the A. F. L. expressed extreme dissatisfaction with the operations of the Recovery Act. Labor had not been represented on every Board under the Act; and the directing authorities of the N. R. A., in declaring their "perfect neutrality" between types of organizations, interpreted 7A to permit employers to negotiate with every group of workers in an industrial unit rather than to compel them to deal with representatives of the majority. This decision heightened the administrative chaos so characteristic of the N. R. A. Employers could divide and rule. The result was that in many instances the chosen representatives turned out to be an agent of the company. A series of strikes, despite warnings by General Hugh Johnson, Administrator of the Act, led the government to the creation of the National Labor Board, on which equal and "genuine" labor representation was again conspicuously missing.

Promptly Hutcheson undertook to lead in the attack on the Recovery Administration. He charged, without giving quarter, that attempts were being made with the approval of the N. R. A. authorities "to lower wage scales already agreed to in direct negotiations between the Brotherhood

---

[11]*Hutcheson's Private Papers,* (October, 1932).

and the employers."[12] He criticized the low wages allowed relief workers on the ground that the government's course tended to encourage private employers to hold down pay. Actually, the annual earnings in the construction industries, which had been about $1,367.00 in 1929, fell to $874.00 in 1933.[13]

Since the building construction industry occupied a position of central significance in the American economy, utilizing materials produced by a myriad of industries, the National Industrial Recovery Act appropriated $3,000,000,000 for public works and direct relief. Need was dire, for private building had shrunk 95 percent from the middle of 1928 to the Spring of 1933, and the impoverished owners of dwellings neglected even essential repairs.

Hutcheson clamored for federal aid to building and construction not only as a means of keeping his members off the jobless rolls, but also to foster their self-respect and enable them to practice and retain their occupational proficiency. He vigorously opposed any effort on the part of Washington to set up and maintain a system that tended to depress the ranks of the skilled artisans. Hutcheson felt that it was the government's task to encourage skilled workers to apply their respective skills so that in the event of pressing need, it could be quickly met in a time of national emergency. He insisted that all work connected with the program shall have union standards as to wages and hours and that management should be turned over to general contractors, who are equipped to do the work more efficiently. In bringing this matter forcibly to the attention of Secretary Ickes, Hutcheson asked that the W. P. A. place on all future work, "union skilled mechanics as foremen and supervisors to whom it rightfully belongs. Then and only then will the intended results be obtained."[14] "I feel," said Hutcheson, "that under the present system, the politicians control this situation and Tom, Dick and Harry get most of the foremen and supervising jobs regardless of their ability." He felt that since the prevailing rate of wages was obtained "through efforts of the union mechanic, he should enjoy the fruits of his efforts and not the nonunion man, who seems to get all the privileges to the exclusion of the men who made wage rates possible."

He riled over the fact that carpenters had been classified as "handymen, hatchet and saw men, form setters, categories that no one ever heard of. . . ."

Again, a year later, when the sum of $4,888,000,000 was voted for relief and public construction projects, Hutcheson bore down upon the ad-

---

[12]*New York Times,* October 19, 1933, p. 1: 2.

[13]*U.B.C.J.A. Proceedings* (1936), p. 364.

[14]*U.B.C.J.A. Proceedings* (1940), p. 172.

ministration, by launching an attack upon "the President who took it upon himself to set up what he termed a sustenance or security wage; a wage so ridiculously low, as compared to the wages in the majority of localities, that it was through strikes and refusals of the workers to accept the wage that it was, in some instances, changed."[15]

Hutcheson saw much merit in the institution of the Civil Conservation Corps (CCC), a project aimed to carry on extensive work of protecting America's natural resources — always a favorite theme with him. Unemployed youths, from one-quarter to one-half million, congregated in 2,600 camps, secured healthful, productive work, which sought not only to counteract the corroding effect of enforced idleness but, by the same token, delayed their entrance into the already overcrowded labor market. All this was meaningful to Hutcheson. But he resisted any effort to exploit these unemployed young men and treat them as "beggars." .·. ."There isn't a camp I know in the country that has come anywhere near paying the established wage scale. We have hundreds of cases where we are told the scale has been set at sixty cents an hour, and the men are being told that they will have to take a reduction of 15 percent because they are government employees. . . . In Virginia they are paying mechanics 45 cents an hour. It is easy for them to say that they will adjust it, but if the work is completed before they pay it, what good will it do?"[16] The paychecks of these young men averaged $13.50 per man for a thirty-hour-week.

A year later, when Roosevelt decided to run for re-election, Hutcheson delivered a stirring appeal to the Carpenters, in which he attacked the President openly, holding him responsible for this new, hybrid American system.

The year 1935 was a memorable one for Hutcheson. At sixty-one, he felt like a robust, brisk man in his forties, still ready to lavish his energy. His face was now fuller, but not too large for his huge body, and an almost balding pate, and serious penetrating eyes and a determined chin. He looked like the dynamic figure who could evoke both respect and fear. The mere shaking of his hand would reveal an irrepressibly warm, friendly, simple man. Age and overwork, however, had brought on an obese condition.

At sixty-one he was solidly established among the major labor leaders of the Federation, who duly acknowledged his influence. He had been Tenth Vice-President of the Federation since October, 1934. And the A. F. of L. made full use of him immediately. Many of his confreres on the Executive Council envied his assurance and inde-

---

[15]*U.B.C.J.A. Proceedings* (1940), p. 172.

[16]American Federation of Labor, *Proceedings,* (1933), p. 415.

pendence. Hell, fury and vilification could not affront him; nor could the President of the United States palsy him.

He was firmly established in the Republican national committee. He was personally acquainted with all of its members, who consulted him on labor matters. He was friendly with many politicos, both Progressives and Conservatives. Many solicited his favors, but he detested the tatterdemalion political climbers and told them so.

Of course, he had his son Maurice to aid him, and Maurice accomplished his tasks intelligently and after his own fashion. He had no desire to fall back upon his father. He was perfectly willing to take on tedious assignments, requiring detailed analysis of vocational guidance in the carpentry trade. Part of the time he devoted to the auditing department of the Brotherhood, a work which was less than satisfying to the imaginative Maurice.

Two months after the United States joined the International Labor Office (I.L.O.), the Executive Council of the American Federation of Labor appointed William Levi Hutcheson to represent American labor at the conference in Santiago, Chile. At once the administration's opposition sprang up against him. Hutcheson's appointment as a representative of organized labor was personally "offensive" to President Roosevelt, and "shocking" to Secretary of Labor Madame Frances Perkins, "because Mr. Hutcheson had been an outspoken opponent of the New Deal, having led the Republican Labor Committee in the Hoover campaign."[17] There were rumors in some circles, reported the national press, "that the appointment was a reprisal by the craft unionists against the industrial unionists . . ."

President William Green, in a statement to the press, denied that "politics either national or trade union was concerned in the appointment." To reassure the administration and Madame Frances Perkins that no politics or reprisals in the labor union world were connected with the appointment of William L. Hutcheson, he issued the following statement:

> "The officers of the American Federation of Labor never understood that political considerations of any kind entered into the designation of labor representatives to International Labor Organization conferences . . . Recommendations of workers' delegates for attendance at these International Labor Organization conferences have been made without regard to politics or political consideration . . . It has never been understood that anyone connected with the affairs of the United States Government, set up any political qualifications for any representative of the workers who might be appointed to attend conferences of the International Labor Organization."[18]

17*New York Times*, Nov. 4, 1935, p. 6: 1.
18*Ibid.*

Hutcheson went to Santiago, as the Federation's representative, despite the stern opposition of President Roosevelt and his Secretary of Labor.

Dr. Harold Butler, Director of the I.L.O., who was responsible for the United States joining the International body, reported to the Executive Council of the Federation on January 15, 1936. He spoke of the effect that American labor would have on "reinforcing the Democratic forces . . . and the force making for labor organization . . . What actually struck me at Santiago as the fruitful part of that conference was that it gave a platform for the first time to representatives of labor to stand up and say what they thought. . . ."

Hutcheson followed Dr. Butler.

". . . . There were only two subjects of any consequence on the agenda and they were the forty-hour week in the textile industry, as submitted by the United States Government representative and social security laws. The conference was a regional one. There were no delegates from European countries. All others were representatives of countries in the Western Hemisphere . . . At the afternoon session, various groups, representing employers, government and workers convened separately to select a chairman for each group. I was nominated in turn as Vice-Chairman and Secretary of the Workers Group but declined, one reason being that I did not speak Spanish, and while they had a man who was supposed to be a translator, he was in fact an interpreter and not a translator . . . One of the delegates who spoke Spanish informed me that the translator was not giving what the speaker said but what he thought the speaker intended to say . . . Ambassador Phillips expressed himself as being pariticularly anxious to have the workers' representatives present.

"Most chaps have not had the experience in the labor movement we have had. They are timid. The Chilean representative made a very able address, not in any way radical. He said it was the first time he had an opportunity to get up and express his opinion. Dr. Butler heard later that the Chilean representative was arrested for making seditious statements . . . My idea is that much good would come from contact with those people in South America. While suspicious of one another, they would view favorably any contact between the North and South American countries. Moreover, there is great opportunity for exchange of commerce between South America and the United States . . ."

Along with his report Hutcheson described the economic conditions of the South American workers. "The difference is that we earn seven—eight times more—they get one-eighth of what our mechanics receive. They work eight hours. They do not appear to be very ambitious. Their living conditions, even under present conditions, could be improved. It would indeed be beneficial if the Pan-American Federation of Labor became more active and rendered them some help."[19]

---

[19]*Hutcheson's Private Papers, covering AFL Executive Council Meeting,* (October 1935 to June, 1935).

CHAPTER | XIV

THE YAWNING GULF: A. F. of L. and C. I. O.

The end of N.R.A. in 1935 marked a new period. The great significance of Section 7A, however, had not been lost in labor's long fight for freedom to organize; it laid the foundation for permanent legislation. Next year Congress enacted the Wagner Act, named for its persistent proponent, the Senator from New York. In this statute, Congress firmly recognized that collective bargaining was good for the country and enumerated legal restraints against employer interference with such organizing.

The leaders of the Executive Council of the American Federation of Labor had too often been blamed for the tardy maturity of their understanding, or for failure to respond to the tempo of the times. Both the partisan and the well-meaning accused them of being the complacent prisoners of the past rather than oracles who peer into the future. In the light of available evidence however, credit should be given to the Council for the role it played in the enactment of the Wagner Act and the Social Security Act. Records reveal that the Council of the Federation,* not only helped draft the Wagner Labor-Relations Bill with the full knowledge of the President of the United States and Secretary of Labor Madame Frances Perkins, but labored successfully for its passage.

Immediately upon the collapse of the N.R.A., the Executive Council quickly moved in to fill the breach. The Wagner Act was gone over very carefully with Senator Wagner. A. F. of L. Council members appeared before Congressional Committees, "appealed, argued and entreated." In addition to going before Committees in the Senate and the House, "each and every Council member, including Hutcheson, personally buttonholed as many lawmakers as they were able to contact and kept up the fight in other ways."

The A. F. of L. fought for the Federal Subsidy Plan as against the Credit Plan, proposed by the National administration. It helped draft the

---

*Members of the A. F. L. Council included Duffy, Rickert, Woll, Coefield, Wharton, Bugniazet, Harrison, Tobin, Hutcheson, Dubinsky, Bates, Gainor, Morrison, Weber, Berry, and John L. Lewis.

measure. "Its legislative committee and all the legislative representatives in Washington were active."

Soon after the Schechter case decision on June 5, 1935, the Executive Council of the Federation undertook "to lead the movement having for its objective and purpose, an amendment to the Constitution of the United States, so that social justice legislation could not be set aside by a Supreme Court decision. "I feel we could do that," President Green reported to the Council, "because we are a non-partisan movement. It occurred to me that we could assume the leadership without political considerations. But since that time the whole subject of constitutional amendment has assumed a political tinge . . . Nevertheless, it is very close to the hearts and minds of the masses of the people . . . We cannot be charged as being in opposition to the government in asking for a change; the Constitution is flexible, it has been changed. You will recall that in conformity with the opinion of our late Samuel Gompers . . . we withheld action on unemployment insurance, but finally the tide was so strong we had to reverse our position. The Social Security Law has passed Congress, it has been approved by the President, it provides money for the care of children and health projects. It will go to the Supreme Court and I believe it will be held unconstitutional, based on the same reasoning as the Railroad Act" . . .[1]

There was much concern about the Supreme Court. Hutcheson's view was that the Executive Council should promote a constitutional amendment, "that the Supreme Court as at present constituted can declare acts of Congress unconstitutional only on a six to three or two-third vote." But he believed that "Congress should not be given power to fix wages and hours in private employment. That is economically unsound."[2] While early in 1932 the American Federation of Labor put itself on record as opposed to statutory unemployment compensation, in 1935, it doggedly pushed this reform program as the accumulative lesson of the Depression had set the tide strongly in favor of social reform. The late Senator Robert F. Wagner frankly acknowledged the Federation's part in the Wagner and Social Security Acts, in the following telegram:

October 8, 1935

Mr. William Green, President
American Federation of Labor
Washington, D. C.

Congress has reaffirmed and reinforced the right to bargain collectively. Security steps have been taken to check the hardships of orphanhood, of

---

[1]*Hutcheson's Private Papers covering AFL Executive Council Meeting*, (June-August, 1935).
[2]*Ibid.*

unemployment and old age. New legislative measures to safeguard wage and hour standards . . . have been auspiciously commenced. Not one of these gains would have been even thinkable without the initiative and cooperation of the A. F. of L., including its wise leaders . . . Because of their active participation in social reform the nation owes them a debt . . ."[3]

Robert F. Wagner

The Wagner Act presented a concept which was extremely difficult for the business and industrial community of the nation to accept in 1935. Businessmen and their spokesmen of the press found no statute of the administration more difficult to comprehend, and labor relations of the mid-'thirties were marked by a series of legal battles. Flushed with victory, in the recent invalidation of the N.R.A., opponents of the administration were primed to discredit the Wagner Act. A report issued by fifty-eight prominent lawyers allied with the American Liberty League who analyzed the Wagner Act, stated that is was unconstitutional. On the basis of such advice, many employers chose to defy the law. A sort of guerilla warfare prevailed on the industrial relations front until the validity of the Act was upheld by the Supreme Court, in April 1937.

Actually the purpose of the Wagner Act was a simple one. In order to promote the flow of goods in interstate commerce, defined circumstantially by the Act, it was the policy of the United States to encourage the "practice and procedure of collective bargaining." The Act accordingly reaffirmed the right to organize and bargain collectively; it implemented these rights against employers' aggression by specifying five unfair labor practices such as: "Interference with employees in the exercise of guaranteed rights; financial or other support of a company union; use of hiring and firing to encourage membership in a company union or encourage membership in an independent union; discrimination against a worker because he complained to the Board; refusal to bargain collectively with the representatives of the employee; finally, representatives selected by a majority of the employees in a unit "appropriate for collective bargaining" should be the exclusive representatives of the workers for the purpose in hand.

A National Labor Relations Board of three members was appointed to administer the Act. This new body confronted the same sort of opposition as its predecessors. Many employers did not mind dealing with their employees, but they strenuously objected to dealing with an "outsider," who frequently knew nothing about the company, who was not an employee of the company, and who was, in fact, the representative of another "business" — a union organization. For counter-attack they

---

[3]*Hutcheson's Private Papers, covering AFL Executive Council Meeting,* (October 8, 1935).

opposed trade union activity with spies, guards, and discharges, and sponsored company unions.

The Government's encouragement of unionism spurred the drive towards organization and raised blunt questions as to the form such unionism should take. Historically, the labor movement had quarreled over the advantages and possibilities of industrial as against "craft" unionism. Whatever the theoretical considerations, the latter triumphed after 1890, and undoubtedly its victory meant a strong union movement —and a limited one. With the coming of Section 7A, the outpouring of pent-up emotions so long repressed by millions of under-paid and insecure workers was accompanied by a surge toward unionism. Although Section 7A proved a slender reed on which to lean, the unorganized workers in the mass production industries accepted its promise avidly, and literally stormed the American Federation of Labor. The Federation responded by organizing and forming 1,273 federal and local unions in such mass industries as automobiles, rubber, steel, radio, cement and textiles. By May 1935, the Federation had organized 54 federal labor unions in the major rubber plants of Goodyear, Goodrich, Firestone and Seiberling; 174 in the automotive industry, 17 unions of aluminum workers, 26 unions among cement workers and 16 unions among radio workers. Membership in that group of unions grew from 10,396 in 1933 to 111,489 in 1935. The number of federal unions grew from 307 in 1932 to 1,788 in 1934.

Labor unrest of those years also swept thousands of workers of other mass production industries either into existing unions or into federal unions jubilantly organized by the Federation. In line with the Federation's policy adopted by its Fall convention of 1933, these latter organizations were to serve as reservoirs of members from which later the International unions could siphon off the "crafts" to which per precedent they were entitled. On the other hand, large numbers of workers in the federal unions over whom craft unions claimed jurisdiction, were only nominally "craftsmen," whose industrial identification was really a single product, rather than with a process or a particular skill. These workers had not served apprenticeships, could not handle the traditional tools of the trade, but had been subject to the rigid and detailed discipline of mechanized, repetitive operations. These preferred mass unionism or industrial unionism covering entire industries instead of specialized trades.

In 1934 a conference of all union presidents was called by the American Federation of Labor further to consider the problem. This conference met in January, and decided to place the main emphasis on an organizing campaign and to allow the question of jurisdictional safeguards to mark time. In the meantime the Federation was to issue

charters on an industrial basis to workers in automobile, cement, aluminum and other mass production industries and to undertake a campaign
to organize the steel industry. Divergencies of opinion and policy soon
developed. President Tighe of the Amalgamated Association of Iron,
Steel and Tin Workers, whose A. F. of L. charter gave him sole jurisdiction, opposed the organization of steel workers by any newly-
chartered Federation group. "The backbone of the industry is the skilled
man in the tinplate and sheet mills," argued Tighe. He complained that
the so-called younger element who do not belong to the Amalgamated
are impatient with the leadership; that the industrial climate "up to the
present time" made it impossible to organize successfully. William Hutcheson was stirred. He pleaded for a compromise, explaining:

> "It seems to me we should consider and give this thought to this situation.
> It behooves us not to give too much consideration to dissatisfaction expressed
> . . . We all admit that there is an opportunity for larger membership in this
> organization. They have apparently only given thought to the more skilled
> membership in the trade. It seems to me this Council could be helpful to this
> organization by helping them organize and getting these men interested in the
> organization. Perhaps we could show the men who are dissatisfied that the
> legal way is for them to affiliate with this [the Amalgamated] and if they
> then feel the laws are obsolete to go about changing them."[4]

Tighe was in no position to organize the iron and steel workers. The
union's funds were exhausted; the structural defects and past failures of
the organization made affiliation unattractive to great numbers of steel
workers.

Hutcheson agreed with President Green that the steel workers "in the big
plants of these powerful companies be organized on an industrial basis."[5]
Remembering, however, the fiasco of 1919 and the Homestead strike of
1892, Hutcheson wanted to make sure whether the "Federation had sufficient funds to carry on such a campaign." John L. Lewis agreed. He volunteered to take the steel workers under his protective wing, claiming that
they needed the protection of the United Mine Workers of America.

On Tuesday, February 12, 1935, the Executive Council of the
Federation considered Mr. Lewis' motion as regards the issuance of
an international charter to the automobile industry. Lewis motioned
that a charter for a national or international union of automobile workers
be issued at once; that an active organizing campaign be inaugurated
by this international union in the automobile industry under the direction of the President of the A. F. of L.; and, finally, that all questions of
over-lapping jurisdiction in the automobile parts and special crafts

---

[4]*Hutcheson's Private Papers covering AFofL Executive Council Meeting,* (February,
1935).

[5]*Ibid.*

organizations encountered in the administration of this policy be referred to the Executive Council.

William Green and Hutcheson agreed with Lewis — but with one or two reservations. Neither of them were the blind, narrow "protagonists" of the craft point of view, as so many of the writers had suggested in defense of "industrialism."

President Green stood his ground unwaveringly when he expounded industrial unionism as the most fitting union structure for the automobile workers. He hit the nail on the head when he described the hash which modern machinery had made of craft distinctions. "The automobile industry presents the most perfect and highest development in mass production. The workers are brought into this industry in large numbers *en masse,* they are employed *en masse,* they work together as cogs in a great machine. . . . They think in mass terms. I am convinced because of the psychological, economic and industrial conditions established in the automobile industry, it is impossible to attempt to organize along our old lines. In the Rubber Workers we have been fortunate. In the erection of new buildings the workers should not be compelled to join the Automobile Workers Union. The rights of organizations that have jurisdiction over men engaged in building construction must be protected.

"I feel that our American Federation of Labor rests upon a sound basis. It has shown by experience that we are right, that we are pursuing the right lines. But I have always understood that our whole policy is so flexible as to enable us to meet any situation that might arise and in my judgment this is a situation in which we must be sufficiently elastic."[6]

"I take it," William L. Hutcheson replied, "that you recognize the fact that the American Federation of Labor has been brought up to its present strength as a result of craft organizations. If it is an admitted fact that the A. F. of L has been brought to the point it has, through following the lines of craftsmanship, I think we should adhere to that with the thought in mind of protecting these craftsmen and *at the same time give these men an opportunity to organize. I think that can be done, but I do not believe we should give them a charter so broad that* they can go out and claim any employee that might be employed by these automobile manufacturers."[7]

Hutcheson cited his experiences in the building trades organizations, and by way of illustration pointed to the automobile manufacturers who use their employees not only to maintain building equipment but on new construction, and at far less than the building trades' pay scales.

---

[6]*Hutcheson's Private Papers covering AFofL Executive Council Meeting,* (February 12, 1935).

[7]*Hutcheson's Private Papers covering AFofL Executive Council Meeting,* (February 17, 1935).

Lewis recognized the validity of Hutcheson's arguments. Said he: "To meet what you have in mind, I drafted Section Seven which reads that all questions of over-lapping jurisdiction on the automobile parts and special crafts organizations encountered in the administration of this policy be referred to the Executive Council. . . . After all, the fundamental obligation is to organize these people. If an injury has been done in the estimation of any organization they would have the right to take it up with the Executive Council, after we had accomplished organization and not before, after the fact of organization has been accomplished not to tie on reservations that will in themselves deter an effective campaign."[8] While Hutcheson clearly persisted on protecting the "job" of the Carpenters, he simultaneously yielded to Lewis when the latter assured him that the jurisdictional rights of the Carpenters and of others in the construction trades unions would be protected.

When the Fifty-fifth Annual Convention of the Federation met in Atlantic City in the Fall of 1935, the rough hewn and dynamic President of the United Mine Workers, scoffed at the Executive Council's "Progress of Organization in Mass Production Industries," a report describing the headway made by the Federation in organizing federal labor unions in mass production industries.[9] Derisively and with dramatic eloquence unmatched by any labor leader, he pointed to the meager results achieved since 1933, and especially since the San Francisco declaration in 1934, when the Federation arranged a compromise to issue charters on an industrial basis to workers in automobile, cement, aluminum, and other mass production industries and to undertake a campaign to organize the steel industry. But craft union rights were to be safeguarded and the Executive Council of the Federation was to determine the jurisdictional limits of the new unions. "On that basis, I submit," thundered Lewis, . . . "that it will be a very long time before the A.F.L. organizes those 25,000,000 workers that we are all anxious to organize. There are others among us who believe that the record indicates a need for a change in policy. This convention is teeming with delegates from those industries where those unions (federal labor unions) had been established and where they are now dying like grass withering before the autumn sun, who are ready to tell this convention of the need for that change in policy."

". . . There has been a change in industry," Lewis continued. "A constant daily change in the process, a constant change in its employment conditions, a great concentration of opposition to the extension and the logical expansion of the trade-union movement. Great combinations of

---

[8]*Ibid.*

[9]American Federation of Labor, *Proceedings* (1935), pp. 93-98.

capital have assembled great plants . . . And they are almost 100 percent effective in opposing organization of the workers under the policies of the American Federation of Labor. . . .

" . . . If you go there with your craft union they will mow you down like the Italian machine guns will mow down the Ethiopians in the war; they will mow you down and laugh while they are doing it and ridicule your lack of business acumen; ridicule your lack of ordinary business sagacity in running your affairs, because of the caviling in your own councils and the feebleness of your efforts."[10]

Lewis then closed his denunciation of craft unionism with a burst of oratory, and with his penchant for the sweeping and dramatic phrase, he said threateningly: ". . . Whereas today the craft unions . . . may be able to stand upon their own feet . . . defy lightning, yet the day may come when this changed scheme of thinking . . . will not be able to withstand the lightning and gale. . . . Heed this cry from Macedonia that comes from the hearts of men. Organize the unorganized."[11]

Lewis' words were part of the speech opening up an enormous struggle, the reverberations of which are still resounding under the impact of two comparative neophytes, Messrs. George Meany and Walter Reuther, both of unequal strength and marked intellectual disparities, with the maestro having retired into solitary. But Mr. Lewis was never one to sulk in his tent when there is work to be done. At this writing, fifteen million members of the A.F.L. and the C.I.O. are being subjected to what may turn out to be one rigid hierarchy instead of two. To what extent democratic "flexibilities" will actually prevail against the many forces tending toward hierarchy only the seer could say.

The President of the Metal Trades Department, John P. Frey, leader of the majority resolutions committee of the 1935 convention, was greatly disturbed. "I am of the opinion," he said, "that this does mark a definite turning point, that from now on our Federation of Labor will never be just what it was. I will confess that in all my years of experience I have never known exactly what was meant when anyone used the words 'craft union' or 'industrial union.' All I know about the term 'industrial union' is that it was not applied by trade unionists to any form of organization; it was an exotic importation from groups who do not believe in the A.F.L. . . . We have had for fifty-five years so-called industrial unions which never, by the wildest stretch of the imagination, covered the entire industry; and we have had the so-called craft unions, many of which are more industrial than those so-called. We have worked together with them side by side, and I want to ask

---

[10]*Ibid*, pp. 534-535.
[11]Saul Alinsky, *John L. Lewis: An Unauthorized Biography*, (G. P. Putnam's Sons, 1949), pp. 74-75.

of those who have had more of an industrial form of organization than others whether their form of organization has enabled them to show a better record of accomplishment than the so-called craft-unions which are now accused of standing in the way of progress. . . ."[12]

The lines were tighter drawn at the 1935 convention. John L. Lewis, President of an industrial union, took the lead in espousing the cause of industrial unionism as a more effective method of organizing the mass production workers. He had proposed such an organizing drive at the American Federation of Labor convention in 1934. He was especially eager for an industrial organization of the closely related steel workers. At that convention in San Francisco, Lewis seemed to have won his point. The declaration of the San Francisco convention provided that the "workers classified as mass production employees" should be granted charters in the mass production industries which would include all the mass production workers employed in such industries. So that there might be no misunderstanding and for the purpose of differentiating between craftsmen and mass production workers, the declaration adopted that year included the following language:

> "The American Federation of Labor is desirous of meeting this demand. We consider it our duty to formulate policies which will fully protect the jurisdictional rights of all the trade unions organized upon craft lines and afford them every opportunity for development and accession of those workers engaged upon work over which these organizations exercise jurisdiction. Experience has shown that craft organization is most effective in protecting the welfare . . . of workers where the nature of the industry is such that the lines of demarcation between craft is distinguishable."

So that there might be no infringement upon the rights of the national and the international unions affiliated with the Federation, provision was made in the Declaration to protect those rights.

> ". . . And safeguard the members of such national and international unions as are chartered, the A.F.L. shall for a provisional period direct policy . . . in the newly organized unions.

The convention could not have done otherwise than reaffirm the rights and the jurisdiction given the national and international unions which had been chartered by the A.F.L. many of which had become unions before the Civil War.[13] This, in short was the position of a majority of the A. F. of L Executive Council.

In the other corner stood John L. Lewis and his already organized wing of unions, which were disquieted by the "circumscribed and narrowly conceived philosophy" of Samuel Gompers and that of his successors, who climbed the ladder of the Federation.

---

[12]See *Proceedings, op. cit.,* pp. 552, 554.
[13]*Ibid,* pp. 552-554.

When the convention met, although Lewis preserved the fiction of organizing through the A.F.L., he was determined to organize the millions of potential members in the steel, automobile, rubber and other big mass production industries into a single "industrial" union of all employees in plants regardless of craft, whatever the means and price. Only his tactics remained to be revealed. The majority of the Executive Council was equally determined to stop Lewis. The immovable met the irresistable.

The clash came on Saturday morning, October 19.

On that day Lewis set the stage for the climactic act signalizing, as it were, the contest between "craft" and "industrial" unionism. He had used every tactic at his command, on and off the convention stage. He could not refrain from performing in Shakespeare, in which he is quite proficient. He quoted liberally pointed passages from Prophet Micah of Judah. His frontal attack failing, Lewis utilized other tactics. The same question on industrial organization came before the convention in at least nine different guises, consisting of resolutions on industrial unionism. One concerned an ambiguous quarrel over the Mine, Mill and Smelter Workers over whom the United Mine Workers started to extend jurisdiction beyond the original jurisdiction recognized by themselves and by other organizations affiliated with the A.F.L.

William L. Hutcheson was to speak on Thursday, the ninth day of the convention. He had sat, relaxed, as he listened intently to the controversies develop. Shrewd Lewis had not changed the usual seating arrangement, adjacent to the Carpenters' President. In years past, whenever a controversy was afoot, Lewis would either walk across the aisle to confer with Hutcheson or vice versa. The convention would usually watch these "conferences" in silence, knowing that a deal was being made to settle an issue.

Now no deals were to be made. Lewis, confident and belligerent, spoke again, addressing the conciliatory President of the Federation. "There is justice, and there is justice—justice to the weak and justice to the strong. The United Mine Workers of America happens to be strong. It is perfectly safe. The Mine, Mill and Smelter Workers happen to be not quite so strong. They are in jeopardy." Lewis sought to "protect" them from Hutcheson's Carpenters Union.

"I tell this convention that I regard it as a raid, as a thrust at the jurisdiction of the United Mine Workers of America, because if the Mine, Mill and Smelter Workers can be emasculated with impunity, then the U.M.W. of America can be raided with equal impunity."[14]

But Hutcheson, too, was determined to protect his own organization.

---

[14] *Ibid*, p. 627.

". . . Listening to the previous speaker," [Mr. Lewis], said Hutcheson, "you would imagine that all of the craft unions . . . were a set of pirates. He referred to records which he says are records of the action of the A.F.L., but in no case did he refer to written consents of any of the craft organizations giving to the Miners . . . jurisdiction over *all craftsmen employed by any company* (emphasis ours). . . . He didn't tell you that the Mine Workers as well as the Mine, Mill and Smelter Workers are now claiming all men that are employed by any particular mining company, whether it be in work on mine building or on a building in the city owned by these particular companies. . . .

". . . Now, just imagine the Mine, Mill and Smelter Workers having jurisdiction over Musicians, Motion Picture Operators, Service Employees, and all of the various building crafts that would be required for the erection, maintainence, alteration or repair of buildings! Visualize, if you can, and say what kind of an organization he is talking about and what kind of jurisdiction he is asking this convention to assign to the Mine, Mill and Smelter Workers. . . .

". . . I just want to call these few facts to your attention, and further call to your attention that the issue we had up here yesterday afternoon and the last evening is only being brought up again in a different form. Are we who represent craft organizations going to allow this abridgement of our rights? I, for one, am not going to do it. The gentleman was very magnificent when he said in his proposed amendment to take the place of the Report Committee, that the agreements entered into by the Anaconda Copper Company might be continued to their termination. That is very kind of him to grant that privilege, but as far as I'm concerned, any contract we have will continue without asking the consent of delegate Lewis. . . ."[15]

Actually, this was a prelude to the act, which Lewis was to play on that Sabbath morning, the last day of the convention when the minds and bodies were exhausted, nerves frayed. Delegate William Thompson of Rubber Workers Union No. 18321 was pleading for an industrial charter as the only basis on which Rubber Workers could be organized.[16]

The following dialogue was exchanged:
Delegate Hutcheson, Carpenters: Mr. Chairman, I rise to a point of order.
President Green: State your point of order.
Delegate Hutcheson: My point of order is that the industrial union proposition has been previously settled by this convention, that is all this resolution provides.
Delegate Thompson: (continuing) This is not calling for an industrial union. It is calling for jurisdictional rights.
Delegate Hutcheson: Read your resolution.
Delegate Thompson: The fight was made on the question of industrial unionism, and this is on the question of jurisdictional rights.
Delegate Frey, Secretary of the Committee: The resolve reads: "Re-

---

15*Ibid*, pp. 628-629.
16*Ibid*, pp. 725-726.

solved that the fifty-fifth convention of the A.F.L. formulate an industrial Rubber Workers Union, whereby the organization shall have full jurisdiction over all employees in and around the respective factories without segregation of the employees in the industry." The Committee recommends non-concurrence in the resolution.

Delegate Hutcheson: I would like to have the Chair give us an interpretation.

President Green: The committee recommended non-concurrence in the resolution.

Delegate Hutcheson: Are we going to sit here and listen again to the argument we have had with reference to industrial unionism?

President Green: (interposing) It would appear that this question has already been settled by the convention, after hours of debate.

Delegate Howard, Typographical Union: A question of information, Mr. President—

President Green (continuing):—And for that reason the Chair is inclined to sustain the point of order raised by delegate Hutcheson.

Delegate Howard: A question of information, Mr. President. Did not the San Francisco convention in adopting the report of the Resolutions Committee, direct the Executive Council to organize and grant a charter of the Rubber industry?

President Green: Yes, sir. That charter has been granted.

Delegate Howard: Does the charter that was granted conflict with the resolution, or does the resolution conflict with the charter? Was a restricted charter granted, or was an unrestricted charter granted in the rubber industry?

President Green: The charter was granted by the Executive Council, and the Executive Council, acting under the direction of the San Francisco convention defined the jurisdiction of the Rubber Workers International Union.

Delegate Howard: And it was not restricted, then?

President Green: Well, it was defined by the Executive Council.

Delegate Howard: The difference is, of course, on the interpretation of the word "defined" and "restricted," Mr. President.

Delegate Lewis, United Mine Workers: On a point of order, Mr. Chairman, this organization introduced a resolution bearing on specific matters. They are calling the attention of this convention to the specific problem in the hope that it had influenced the minds of the Executive Council. It does not deal entirely with the question of industrial unionism as decided by this convention. It deals with a problem in Akron, Ohio and elsewhere, and certainly in my judgment this organization and these delegates who introduce a resolution here have a right to tell this convention their own particular problems in relation to it. This thing of raising points of order all the time on minor delegates is rather small potatoes.

Delegate Hutcheson, Carpenters: Mr. Chairman, I was raised on small potatoes. That is why I am so small. Had the delegate who had just spoken about raising points of order given more consideration to the questions before this convention and not to attempting, in a dramatic way, to impress the delegates with his sincerity, we would not have had to raise the point of order at this late date, we would have had more time to devote to the questions before the convention.[17]

Lewis walked up the aisle and approached Hutcheson. As usual, the convention became quiet. Lewis muttered a profanity sotto voce to Hutcheson which caused the Carpenters' chief to reply in kind. At this point, Lewis unleashed a right to Hutcheson's jaw, and took a stinging right in return. A few more blows were exchanged and Hutcheson and Lewis grappled and went down amidst collapsing chairs and tables. With the delegates in an uproar, President Green pounded his gavel futilely, as the leaders of the two most powerful and largest unions in the land rolled about on the floor. Newspapermen were frantically wiring what everyone knew would be the top news story of that day. The blow Lewis landed on Hutcheson's jaw was timed with the careful precision of a choreographer pirouetting his dancing partner on stage.

"There is evidence that more than suggests that Lewis' physical attack on Hutcheson was premeditated and deliberate. First, there is the fact that any study of Lewis' own personality and behavior shows that he has with rare exception taken any action except in accordance with a carefully pre-conceived and thought-out plan," admitted friendly biographer, Dr. Saul Alinsky.

". . . All I will say," Lewis confessed to Alinsky, "is that I never walked across an aisle so slowly and grimly as I did that day in the 1935 convention. An act of some kind, an act dramatic to the degree that it would inspire and enthuse the workers of this country was necessary. Did I say necessary? It was essential. With this in mind, I laid my plans. The 1935 convention of the American Federation of Labor was to be the scene and Bill Hutcheson, unknowningly, was to be one of the main actors of the cast. . . .[18]

Herein lies the essential tragedy of Lewis, otherwise a most imaginative and brilliant leader of men. Lewis' aggression on Hutcheson, the friend, with whom he had so many elements in common, savored of a mission which raised him to the level of apostleship, nay, a second Moses. In the history of American trade-unionism he had become the most

---

[17]*Ibid*, p. 727.
[18]See Saul Alinsky, *op. cit.*, pp. 76-78.

dynamic figure, on its record. In the 'twenties the Leftists scolded him as unprogressive and reactionary, as they did William Levi Hutcheson; ten years later he was acclaimed as a labor statesman, while Hutcheson became the lightning rod against progress and a focus of antipathy for the agents of frustration. In the 'twenties, Lewis was probably more guilty of irrelevant professional Red-baiting than Hutcheson. And in 1936 Lewis was regarded by some as a radical. But for the short interval, during which he sojourned in President Roosevelt's New Deal camp only to have been rebuffed in 1940, both Lewis and Hutcheson "played" Republican politics. Both Lewis and Hutcheson assumed that our economy was one of plenty, and that the workers, if denied, have but to make their demands in sterner tones.

Actually, Hutcheson was not an exponent of the "craft" union philosophy of trade unionism. His own union was living testimony to it. For over four decades the Brotherhood had been expanding its structural equipment as to include in its jurisdiction nearly seventeen subdivisions of the woodworking trade. At the time when Lewis was preparing his planned bolt from the American Federation of Labor, he set out to organize the lumber and sawmill workers, whom Hutcheson regarded as "closely allied with the erection of buildings." The Brotherhood made no claims to being a craft union. Rather, its leaders recognized it as "a craft union, taking in all the branches of the industry." The policy of the United Brotherhood, in the 1930's was one of *craft-industrialism.*

No evidence can be adduced from the records that Hutcheson espoused the cause of craft unionism to the exclusion of organizing the unorganized in the mass production industries. A close inspection of the minutes fails to reveal that Hutcheson was the major stumbling block to Lewis' cause. What Hutcheson sought was the protection of his own constituency, the jobs of his own Carpenters, which, as will be observed in Part VII, is the driving power behind all unions, be they "Industrial" or "Craft."

> "I am perfectly willing to help organize any group of workers along reasonable lines so long as it does not infringe on our organization that has helped build up the labor movement to what it is today," Hutcheson reiterated on February 12, 1935.

On the other hand, we are persuaded that the Messrs. Bugniazet of the International Brotherhood of Electrical Workers, Coefield of the Plumbers and Wharton of the Machinists, all members of the Executive Council, felt greatly disturbed, if not menaced by the continued existence of Federal unions; that they, rather than Hutcheson or even William Green, adhered to a circumscribed, narrowly conceived approach. Mr. David Dubinsky, a member of the Executive Council, whose Interna-

tional Ladies Garment Workers Union felt the weight of craft considerations, at no time expounded the "industrial" philosophy of Lewis.
Finally, we are reminded, that ". . . Lewis had already decided to bolt
the American Federation of Labor and was operating according to
plan."[19] That zealous Lewis had planned to challenge the dominant
group in the Federation, defying all opposition and take prompt action
to set up a revitalized 1935 version of the Knights of Labor under the
encouragement of the administration can be inferred. Lewis' motivations had been covered by the father of the C.I.O. himself, in April
1946. In a magazine interview with William Hutcheson, the latter was
quoted as saying: ". . . I have asked John why he ever started with the
C.I.O. He told me that he did it because he was tired of the coal operators telling him, whenever he tried to raise the wages of his Miners,
that he was asking for more than the workers of steel, auto, and rubber were getting. I told John that if he had only come to me and explained it that way, things would have been different. I asked him why
he hadn't, and he said he wished he had; it was just one of those things
he'd forgotten."[20]

That such explanation should be made by Lewis is perhaps natural
and understandable since his formal break with the C.I.O. came in
October, 1942. Yet, he saw little need of expiation and atonement for
his sins. . . .

A month following the bout, on November 10, eight unions, representing, among others, miners, garment workers, and textile, oil, and re-
finery workers, formed the Committee for Industrial Organizations. This
C.I.O. was "to encourage and promote organization of the workers in
the mass production and unorganized industries of the nation," but
planned to remain in the fold of the American Federation of Labor. However innocuously phrased, it was a challenge to the Federation.

The A.F.L. chieftains early rejected as insincere the claim of the
C.I.O. heads that they sought merely to organize within the framework of the Federation. As early as January, 1936, the Executive Council of the Federation reported a growing conviction that the C.I.O.
activities constituted a "challenge to the supremacy of the American
Federation of Labor and will ultimately become dual in purpose and
character to the A. F. of L." The following August the unions comprising the C.I.O. were summoned to a hearing before the Executive
Council on charges of dual unionism; upon their failure to appear, they
were found guilty of "rebellion" against convention decisions and were
suspended for "fostering, maintaining and supporting this dual movement

---

[19]See Alinsky, op. cit., p. 78.
[20]Fortune, April, 1946, pp. 278-281.

and fomenting insurrection within the American Federation of Labor."

Hutcheson counseled caution against suspending the "rebels," who defaulted on their per capita tax to the Federation. "I think we should be sure of our grounds. If there is a possibility that the court will say we did not do everything, we should give that consideration; so if they take us into court we can show we have done everything reasonable before we suspend them. . . ."[21]

There was no end to hard words, that were soon followed by inevitable bitterness and strife. Nevertheless, the founders of the C.I.O. persisted, and under the militant leadership of John L. Lewis launched drives in the steel, automobile, rubber, and radio and electrical industries. The drives captured the imagination and won the loyalties of hundreds of thousands of workers in these industries, hitherto frustrated in their efforts to win collective bargaining; and a series of dramatic strikes made newspaper headlines in the following year and a half, as one after another open-shop citadel surrendered. By September 1937, membership in its thirty-odd assorted unions was, according to its own figures, approximately 3,718,000. Such an achievement surpassed the stampede to the Knights of Labor in the early 'eighties.

In 1937 the Executive Council of the A. F. of L. asked for and received from the convention authority to revoke the charters of the C.I.O. affiliates that had been suspended in September, 1936. At the same time the Federation accepted an invitation from the C.I.O. in an effort to bridge the deepened schism, and committees representing the two groups convened late in October, 1937.

At that session, the C.I.O. proposed that industrial unionism be made basic policy in mass industries and that a C.I.O. department be established within a united movement. The A. F. of L. countered with proposals that all C.I.O. unions chartered by the A. F. of L. return to the Federation, that conferences on jurisdiction be held between the newly-formed C.I.O. unions and conflicting A. F. of L. organizations, and that remaining questions be referred to the next A. F. of L. convention. Clearly the original proposal was completely unacceptable to the rival group.

In 1937 the growing sentiment of both the Federation and the C.I.O. was for a basis of agreement. Lewis recognized this. He proposed to the Federation convention that a committee of 100 from the C.I.O. meet with a committee of the same size from the Federation to conclude the peace. William Green, for the Federation, answered that such a large conclave could not be fruitful. The result was that much smaller committees, three from the Federation and ten from the

---

[21]*Hutcheson's Private Papers covering AFofL Council Meeting,* (July, 1936).

C.I.O. met in Washington in October. Divergent demands were composed, with the Federation making more concessions. All unions of the C.I.O. — the original Federation affiliates and the new C.I.O. unions later — were to re-enter the Federation together. Industrial unionism would exist in a list of industries to be agreed upon, and the A.F.L. conferees would urge their organization to vest in its convention exclusive authority to suspend or revoke the charters of affiliates. Phillip Murray, head of the C.I.O. conferees, agreed on this settlement.

The outlook for unified progress in the labor movement was bright. However Lewis stepped in, condemned the agreement reached and disrupted peace plans. Murray then issued a statement saying that negotiations were off. The Executive Council of the Federation charged that Lewis, "the supreme ruler of the C.I.O.", had cancelled the agreement reached between the Federation and the C.I.O. conferees.

Thereafter, understanding became increasingly difficult. "Dualism" became definitive in May, 1938 when the C.I.O. took organized form as the Congress of Industrial Organizations. The split was made absolute. C.I.O. leaders had matured to the point of insisting on jurisdictional claims, resulting in a wasteful duplication of effort and program and consequent confusion in collective bargaining.   ,

The rivalry of A. F. of L. and C.I.O. stimulated organizing efforts and vastly increased membership. The split was the price that had to be paid in order to focus efforts in mass production industries. The C.I.O., addressing itself to the unskilled and the semi-skilled developed a program that expressed a new ambition for unionism.

In his efforts to expand the C.I.O. as rapidly as possible, Lewis made use of whatever resources were available. These included the Communists, whom he had fought bitterly in the 'twenties within his United Mine Workers, and, like Hutcheson, barred them from membership by constitutional provision. For their part, the Communists having liquidated their Trade-Union Unity League in 1935 and being without hope of influence in the craft unions of the A. F. of L., were eager to seek refuge as well as work in the C.I.O. organizing drives in the hope of winning a strategic position in the resulting industrial unions.

Lewis had need of their organizing ability in steel, and felt confident that he could oust them whenever he found it desirable. As a result, the Communists became entrenched in high places in the United Electrical Radio and Machine Workers, the National Maritime Union, the Transport Workers Union, and other lesser C.I.O. unions. In addition, they already controlled the leadership of the International Fur and Leather Workers Union, and they exerted considerable influence within the United Automobile Workers. Though Communists and their fellow-travelers were a small minority within any of these unions their energetic

members, their disciplined cells, and their astutely led caucuses gave
them an influence far out of proportion to their membership. The Communist minority in the C.I.O. feared unity lest it diminish or nullify its
influence. In the early 'forties the issue of industrial versus craft unionism
was no longer the chief, or even a serious, cause of hostility though dual
unionism, in its most aggravated manifestations, had widened the rift.
It was this fierce contest which affected Hutcheson when he set out to organize the lumber industry in the Northwest.

Actually, this abrupt destruction of historic barriers to organization
was not entirely due to the adoption of novel or even "exotic" tactics of
industrial warfare, the sit-down or the stay-in strikes. Undoubtedly this
was an effective instrument, for strikers' possession of employers' property could hamper its seizure by police or deputies and its operation by
strike breakers. Any army inside the factory walls was tactically stronger
than a picket line outside. But in the last analysis, the C.I.O. won because
at last labor had the support of the State and the State no longer automatically and universally put the power of its courts and its other
law-enforcement agencies at the call of the employers.

Judges were more chary in issuing injunctions; sheriffs did not enforce
them; Governors on occasion called out militia because its presence would
aid the strikers; the relief funds of the State supplemented the strikers'
treasury; and the National Labor Relations Board, in the background,
compelled employers to bargain collectively in good faith. Thus the C.I.O.
was naturally in politics. The businessman could do little to halt the
rise of a rival power in industrial unions which used political as well as
economic weapons against him.

In the ultimate sense it was the power of the mass production industries, not the organizing abilities of John L. Lewis and Phillip Murray,
that brought new powerful unions into being. "The economic power that
the worker faced in the sale of his labor — the competition of many sellers
dealing with few buyers — made it necessary that he organize for his own
protection."[22] As a general rule, strong unions and strong leaders have
come into being only where markets were served by strong corporations.

The advent and rapid growth of the C.I.O. was more than a
checkerboard move in labor's struggle for power. When Lewis and the
industrial unionists insisted that entire industries and shops must be
organized as a unit regardless of the claims of well-recognized crafts, they
thus stressed the common interests of workers, and affirmed the principle
of labor solidarity. It was a short step from this to the decision of the
C.I.O. to contribute financially to New Deal campaign funds in gratitude
and hope. The days of the first Roosevelt had seen nothing like this.

---

[22]See John K. Galbraith, *American Capitalism: The Concept of Countervailing Power*
(Houghton Mifflin Co., 1952), pp. 120-122.

CHAPTER | XV

RELIANCE ON THE STATE

The 1936 presidential campaign came around, and the American Federation of Labor pursued its traditional non-partisan policy, publishing the labor records of the leading candidates and the labor planks of their party platforms but making no recommendations. William Green, however, personally endorsed Roosevelt for re-election and praised the Democratic labor program, and Jim Farley appointed Daniel J. Tobin of the A. F. of L. Teamsters, chairman of the Democratic Party's Labor Committee.* The C.I.O. formed Labor's Non-Partisan League, drafting George Berry, head of the A. F. of L. Printing Pressmen, who a short time later was elected United States Senator from Tennessee, as president, John L. Lewis chairman of the executive board, and Sidney Hillman as treasurer and fund-raiser. The name "Labor's Non-Partisan League" was chosen to indicate, that it was non-partisan, only in that it sought the support of the two wings of labor. But not all agreed with regard to the election of the New Deal President. However, the setting-up of Labor's Non-Partisan League was announced "as if from Administration circles in Washington, to the great vexation of Farley, Tobin, and William Green."

A constantly recurring motif in Hillman's career "was his preoccupation with the idea of putting American labor into politics through its own political organization, as in England, instead of leaving everything to the professionals. For Lewis, a life-long Republican, who had once felt himself flattered at the passing attention of a Harding or a Herbert Hoover, the venture was a novel one. Nonetheless, he threw himself into it with his characteristic ardor, proclaiming that "labor has

---

*Tobin's appointment as Democratic Labor Chairman was plainly a scheme to hold the conservative AFL close to the throne, while keeping the CIO element at a distance, says Matthew Josephson, Hillman's friendly biographer. So, "at once Hillman spoke to Lewis of the need for putting the CIO into the 1936 campaign and forestalling the Tobin-Farley arrangement." (See Matthew Josephson, *Sidney Hillman, Statesman of American Labor*, Doubleday and Co., 1952, p. 394).

gained more under President Roosevelt than under any President in memory. Obviously it is the duty of labor to support Roosevelt one hundred percent."[1]

Among the leaders of the C.I.O. were a number of men with progressive or moderately socialist leanings, who believed that only through favorable governmental policy could the economic interests of labor be protected. The new League, unlike LaFollette's Progressive party in 1924, "was to function mainly through one of the two major parties, and particularly the Democratic party in order to insure Roosevelt's re-election." A change in the administration raised a definite question whether the Amalgamated Clothing Workers of America would have to fight completely on its own and not get the support which it enjoyed under N.R.A."[2]

At a general Executive session of the Amalgamated held in Chicago, (April, 1936), Hillman "disclosed that he had been informed of the President's intention, if re-elected, to find ways of curbing the "power of review of the Supreme Court." The President had also promised Hillman that he would support the proposed Minimum-Wage Bill which Senators Black and Wagner were preparing. . . . "I believe if the demand is strong enough a way will be found to pass new legislation. . . . The N.R.A. was not repassed because labor was supine. The usefulness of this legislation had not been sufficiently explained to the workers, argued Hillman."[3]

Hillman believed that "there must be political power to safeguard labor's rights. If you are permitted by the police and court to picket, you will win a strike sooner than otherwise," he pointed out. "Or if you had the minimum wage, you wouldn't have to fight to get at least a miserable twenty-five cents an hour. . . ."

What Hillman advocated now was a distinctly *opportunistic approach*. But one also that suggested that the state can usefully have a part in buttressing labor's bargaining position. Some left-wing unionists had their doubts about President Roosevelt. Some of the Amalgamated's own doctrinaires on the executive board opposed formal support of the Democratic Party, but finally yielded to Hillman's arguments. Like Hillman, John Lewis believed in enlisting the support of the State. Of labor's donation of $770,000 to the Democratic cause in 1936, over fifty percent or $486,288.55 came from the United Mine Workers of America. In August, 1936, Lewis took the stump in behalf of Roosevelt, as he warned that: "When the people once become convinced that the economic and financial masters of America have no intention in logic . . . to make

---

[1]Matthew Josephson, *op. cit.*, p. 395.
[2]*Ibid*, pp. 396-397.
[3]*Ibid*, p. 397.

reasonable concessions and accord fair treatment to those who make it possible for them to assemble wealth, then it is a safe assumption . . . that the people of the country will do something about it."[4] In that heated election season the President earnestly counted upon the aid of the Lewises and Hillmans and Tobins and Greens.

Labor's Non-Partisan League seemed well suited to Lewis' self-proclaimed mission. He treated the League "as if it were his own affair and staffed it mostly with "loyal Lewis men," and even gave numerous hints that a political realignment for 1940 was being kept in mind." As of 1936, the League would develop as a future instrument for labor's "independent" political action, reasoned Lewis. The labor vote, which went overwhelmingly for Roosevelt, played an important part in his impressive victory over the Republican nominee, Alfred M. Landon, the League's New York branch, called the American Labor Party, polled nearly a third of a million votes. In pivotal New York State the thought was to channel the "regular" Socialists into the Roosevelt camp. Principally at the initiative of Messrs. Hillman, Dubinsky of the I.L.G.W.U. and Alex Rose of the Millinery Workers, who were subsequently joined by Joseph P. Ryan President of the New York Central Trades and Labor Council and of the International Longshoremen's Association and George Meany of the New York State Federation of Labor, the American Labor Party included the moderate Socialists, and a host of A. F. of L. and C.I.O. unionists, as well as Republican fusionists and New Deal Democrats.

As head of the C.I.O. and prime mover in Labor's Non-Partisan League, Lewis took credit for Roosevelt's labor vote. The average American assumed that Lewis would be in enormous favor with the administration and "on a pragmatic basis would be repaid by strong support in his activities." With this as his background, Lewis then proceeded to try to manipulate events to the advantage of the C.I.O. With cool assurance that the State could knuckle under to his will, he publicly called upon Roosevelt, at a tense moment, to ask him to repay labor for its political support. While the sit-down strikes in General Motors plants were at their peak in the early part of 1937, with its president angrily shouting "will a labor organization own the plants of GM Corporation or will the management continue to do so?", Lewis advised Roosevelt, through the Secretary of Labor, Madame Perkins, that "for six months the economic royalists of General Motors contributed their money and used their energy to drive this administration out of power. The administration asked labor for help to repel this attack, and labor gave its help. The same economic royalists now have their fangs in labor.

---

[4] See Saul Alinsky, *op. cit.*, p. 163.

The workers of this country expect the administration to help the workers in every legal way, and to support the workers in General Motors plants."[5]

The C.I.O. broke the opposition of the automobile industry by effective strikes against General Motors and Chrysler and won from the United States Steel Corporation and its subsidiaries, "Big Steel and Little Steel of Morgan and Gary," a collective agreement.

Lewis' ill-advised statement greatly embarrassed and antagonized the President and strained relations between the administration and the C.I.O. The President's "plague on both your houses" rejoinder appeared to Lewis ungrateful, not to say traitorous. Lewis' Labor Day radio address later that year emphasized the growing rift between him and the President. "It ill behooves one who has supped at labor's table and who has been sheltered in labor's house to curse with equal fervor and fine impartiality both labor and its adversaries when they become locked in deadly embrace," he declaimed.[6] Relations between Lewis and Roosevelt not only became cool thereafter, but played their part in returning Lewis to his lifelong Republicanism.

Whatever the vicissitudes of politics, it was a noteworthy trend of the era that the industrial workers had become active participants in elections, eager to use the fulcrum of government for attainment of their ends. The New Deal, aware of its commitment to a pro-labor policy and grateful for "working-class" support, manifested great reluctance to lay a restraining hand upon the unions, however irresponsible their zealous leaders might become.

The position of this new movement, however, was seemingly far from secure. At best, reliance upon the state was precarious, a fact which pragmatic Hutcheson had learned since the days of President Wilson. Lewis, now rebuffed by the "impartial" government and in personal pique, returned to his place of origin, where he once again encountered William L. Hutcheson, who was engaged in "liberalizing" Republican politics. In the 1940 Presidential campaign, Lewis, over the widest hook-up ever used by a labor leader of that time, appealed to C.I.O. members to vote for Wendell Willkie, and promised to resign from the leadership of C.I.O. if Roosevelt were reelected. Following Roosevelt's victory, Lewis had no choice but to fulfill his pre-election pledge and resign as C.I.O.'s head while retaining his leadership of the Miners.

The rock upon which the American Federation of Labor rested was not entirely submerged. True, the defections had been many, the

---

[5]*Ibid,* pp. 164-165.
[6]*New York Times,* January 22, 1937.

Federation's membership having dropped from 3,400,000 before the suspension of the C.I.O. unions in 1936 to 2,800,000 the following year as a result of the split. Two years later, the Federation was replenished with 800,000 new industrial recruits, who compensated for the losses that it had sustained in 1935 when the Committee of Industrial Organization was born. Which of the two organizations had the larger membership in 1938 and 1939 is a matter of debate, though the American Federation figures, based on per capita payments by affiliates, are far more reliable than the membership claims of the C.I.O. What is beyond doubt, regardless of membership figures, is that the A. F. of L. organizations, with their solid core of union-conscious craftsmen, were more cohesive, disciplined, and powerful than the newer and more volatile industrial unions of the C.I.O. Zealots in the C.I.O. might brush aside its fault-finding as querulous and its charges of "insurrection" as ridiculous; among them were some who sought to "renovate" it in their own image and even overwhelm it, while the Leftist critics, reinforced by a Communist minority, retaliated with vindictiveness in the name of new-old party line preachments.

But the Federation still had determined leaders. While some thought of waiting out the storm, believing that the C.I.O. would be one with the Knights of Labor, Hutcheson sought to grapple with it and to control it. He saw through the designs of those who sought to delay formal suspension of the defecting unions — while they were in fact consolidating their own ranks. Hutcheson was tough with David Dubinsky, who was on record as repeatedly urging a reunion of the Federation and the defecting intransigent unions that constituted themselves into C.I.O. He was the only one among the eight Executive officers of the defected unions who appeared before the Executive Council session of the Federation on the morning of August 5, 1936.

Dubinsky argued that in his judgment, "better results can be obtained, a serious split could be avoided if this Council should not act drastically at this moment and if the matter would be referred to the next convention. . . I would make the most hearty appeal to you that you should show the world you are above prejudice, that although you have the right to act you are willing to be patient to avoid calamity in the labor movement."[7] Hutcheson asked of Dubinsky: "Do you think this Council has not been patient?" Mr. Dubinsky replied: "The Council has been patient but I urge a little more patience."

Hutcheson: "This was considered last January. Efforts have been put forth since to get the organizations that comprise the Committee for Industrial Organization, to dissociate themselves from this committee. Vice-

---

[7]*Hutcheson's Private Papers covering AFL Executive Council Meeting,* (August, 1936).

President Dubinsky pleads now for further time. 'You can do it in No-vember.' "If you can do it in November, why not do it in August?"

Dubinsky admitted that he had been a participant in the C.I.O., that he had attended a number of sessions of that body from its in-ception. The President of the International Ladies Garment Work-ers Union denied, however, that "it is the determined and fixed policy of those in charge of the C.I.O. to organize an independent move-ment rival to the A. F. of L. "These are rumors. On the other hand, if there is a suspension of these unions, definitely yes. . . ." Dubinsky insisted that he be given two or three months till the convention . . . "or you will probably find our union in the other camp."[8]

The Committee for Industrial Organization was an incontrovertible fact. Evidence was overwhelming that all plans for its formation had been made prior to the convention in 1935. Dubinsky denied it, pleading for delay.

The Executive Council of the Federation rejected as insincere the claim of the C.I.O. heads that they sought merely to organize within the framework of the Federation. Early in January, 1936, the Execu-tive Council reiterated the growing conviction that C.I.O. activities constituted a "challenge to the supremacy of the A. F. of L. and will ultimately become dual in purpose and character to the A. F. of L." On the 3rd of August the unions comprising the C.I.O. were summoned to a hearing before the Executive Council on charges of dualism. Upon their failure to appear they were found guilty.

Hutcheson felt that the charges against the seceding organizations were sustained. "That," added Hutcheson, "places Vice-President Dubinsky (he was Vice-President of the Executive Council) now as having been convicted on the charges and I concur in the thought at least put forth by Coefield (Plumbers) that Vice-President Dubinsky has no right to sit in here in the further deliberations of the Council due to the fact of the indictment and evidence presented and the action of the Council declaring the charges were substantiated and they are guilty. . . ."

As alert as he was to the growing menace of Communism, Hutcheson was to the tactics of American nascent Fascism. He took an upright, unequivocal position against the National Union for Social Justice of Father Charles F. Coughlin. The erratic Father of the Shrine of the Little Flower, whose ambition it was to organize a Fascist movement by "driving the money changers out of the temple" sought the affiliation and representation of the American Federation of Labor on his Board of the "National Union." He promised organizer F. J. Dillon, in charge

---

[8]*Ibid.*

of organizing workers in the automobile industry, to "help and assist the Federation in its work." On May 1, 1935 the Executive Council of the Federation had reviewed organizer William Collins' report of Father Coughlin's meeting in Detroit. "At that meeting," reported Collins, "Father Coughlin had us, the Federation, on the spot to the extent that he asked if the A. F. of L. would support his program. . . ."** Hutcheson moved "that the invitation be rejected with thanks. In my opinion labor organizations for years have been working for social justice. The term used there is entirely a catch term. The principle in back of the trade union movement is to better the condition of the workers. In the last analysis, that is what that means. We have never attempted to take care of the spiritual welfare of the members of the labor organizations. We leave that to individuals. After we have been going on for fifty-odd years, I cannot see why we should become a part of that movement. If he has any ideas, he thinks he should put over let him come here." Hutcheson's motion was put to a vote and adopted unanimously. In the meantime, the Brotherhood of Carpenters and the Building Trades placed Father Coughlin on the unfair list when he built his Shrine of the Little Flower with non-union labor. Similar action was later taken by the Detroit Federation of Labor.[9]

No less significant was Hutcheson's attitude regarding the modification of racialism in the A. F. of L. locals which had shown little enthusiasm for Negro workers in their midst. Hutcheson was convinced that the economic bargaining power of the white workers would remain weak unless all workmen, regardless of race, were part of the labor movement. Well-meant exhortations were no substitute for practical equalitarian day-to-day contacts on the job. Inevitably the A. F. of L. felt his influence and eased the racial restrictions within the unions.[10]

This did not deter Hutcheson from viewing with melancholy and apprehension the elements that were now surrounding the C.I.O. The C.I.O. "would take the labor movement back to the days of the Knights of Labor. History will show that in attempting to organize the workers under the banner of the Knights of Labor the workers soon came to realize that that was the wrong form of organization, and from the failure of the Knights of Labor came the American Federation of Labor. . . ."

**Professor Broadus Mitchell, as well as a host of other American scholars, all staunch friends of the labor cause, have pointed to the Federation's concern with the Communist threat and "less apprehension of incipient Fascism of Coughlin." This attitude was in accordance with the old history of minorities, which generally fought harder against friends on the flanks than against foes on the front . . ." Professor Mitchell concludes that the Federation was "due for renovation." (See Broadus Mitchell, *The Depression Decade,* Rhinehart & Co., p. 29).

[9]Hutcheson's *Private Papers covering AFL Executive Council Meeting,* (May 1, 1935).
[10]See AFL *Proceedings* (1936), p. 75.

That Hutcheson opposed the one-big-union idea, of that there is no doubt. "If that policy is pursued and all workers were organized on an industrial basis it would mean the elimination of our organization, as under that procedure and plan all building workers would belong to one organization, and even then that would not give them control of all building for the reason that under the plan as proposed by the C.I.O. any buildings that would be erected by a company employing workers in their manufacturing plants, such as automobiles, rubber, steel, etc., those who would be engaged and employed to erect the buildings would have to belong to the Industrial Union covering the workers employed in the ordinary manufacturing of the product put out by that company, and it should be apparent to all members of our Brotherhood that the proposal of the C.I.O. would mean the elimination of craft organizations. . . ."[11]

Hutcheson viewed with disfavor the administration's implied encouragement of the "sit-down" strikes by the C.I.O. He knew of President Roosevelt's approval of, or acquiescence in Lewis' cause, when the latter swiftly followed-up his advantage by sit-down strikes that brought settlements with Firestone Tire, Goodrich Rubber, Chrysler Auto, Jones & Loughlin Steel, Pittsburgh Plate Glass, and many other nationally important manufacturers. Hutcheson had subscribed and had in fact practiced the theory of "countervailing force" in the American economy, a force which, acting in opposition to business managements, served not only to bring about a redistribution of national income downward to those in lower income brackets but enhanced labor's status as well.

But for labor to act as a "countervailing force," it must rely on its own organized efforts. He viewed with dismay the trend that "the Secretaries act in their Bureaus for you, not you from here for them." As a Midwesterner, it seemed to him, that it was getting to be a great temptation to those in control of Government to utilize their power to perpetuate themselves in office. There are limits, Hutcheson argued, to what government in democracy can undertake. If men are to be free and democracy to prevail, the functions of the Government must be shared by many political and economic divisions and functionaries, as well as non-Governmental bodies such as trade unions. Hutcheson assumed that two distinctive parties are essential to the functioning of the American party system, and in order for each to survive, both the Republican and Democratic parties must make continuing adjustment to economic conflicts. Unlike Lewis, Hillman, and

---

11"The Committee of Industrial Organization," Twenty-Third General Convention, U.B.C.J.A. (1936), p. 495.

Dubinsky, he was not attracted to independent political action on the part of labor for its own sake.

He decided to leave the Executive Council of the Federation, not without some sadness and no amount of pressure brought to bear by William Green caused him to change his mind. Quietly he watched the maneuvers of his confrere on the Council, Daniel J. Tobin of the International Brotherhood of Teamsters, whose ambition alternated between the presidency of the American Federation of Labor and United States Senator. He had already been turned down by Roosevelt as a Secretary of Labor in 1932. He now wooed James Farley, who in his role as Roosevelt's campaign manager, had arranged to have Tobin as chairman of the Democratic party's Labor Committee. He eyed George L. Berry, who far from being a model New Dealer, cleverly disguised his performances as president of Labor's Non-Partisan League. He was an unprincipled man, politically to the right of Hutcheson, who learned to keep shrewd silence, while aiming high politically. As soon as he became United States Senator from Tennessee, he anxiously sought out Hutcheson to press his hand again, despite the fact that he had muddied his name in the White House. Executive Council Member David Dubinsky resigned on the same day with Hutcheson, October 7, 1936, though for different reasons. Hutcheson's friend Lewis, who made a great commotion, resigned from the Federation on November 23, 1935. Although his beautiful project of the new labor empire to-be demanded all of his effort, he found time to sound off on his old friend. At first Hutcheson was frozen and abashed at the act of Lewis, but he speedily regained his composure. It was only a little incident in the busy life of two friends, an incident which has been exaggerated beyond proportion by the sport-loving labor writing fraternity.[12]

Hutcheson left the Council feeling that "the Brotherhood of Carpenters would be criticized as being the only organization having two members on the Federation, and that since Lewis resigned, it did not seem right, although it was all right under other circumstances." He would not go along with the expedient, opportunistic moves of certain members of the Executive Council. He did not approve Roosevelt's known political-social-constitutional views. He found stimulus in what he thought was a useful function of special interest representative in the Republican national committee. It was even pertinent to his own life, for his ambition goaded him to constant action, while his experiences with his friends on the Federation were a source of light. As a formulator of the labor program of one of the two major parties, Hutcheson saw himself performing an educational

---

[12]Quoted from Author's interview with John L. Lewis, Tuesday, June 15, 1954.

service. He felt that by constantly projecting on the inside the symbols of "liberalism" that influence party policy, that need for a picture of what should be would be given a chance. As a practical man he believed that neither party can corner the market on new and attractive ideas. Once a winning program is discovered it is equally attractive to both parties. Republican Presidential candidate Alfred Landon vied in showing how to be liberal and conservative at the same time. "True and traditional Republican liberalism can save the country from the false liberalism of Roosevelt. The Republican platform of 1936 did not look to the past and the other to the future."[13] Hutcheson dismissed the rationalized viewpoint of those that held that the struggle between the Republican and the Democratic parties was one between the spokesmen of wealth and the champions of the people.

His activities in the Republican National Committee and his promotion of Landon's candidacy brought him censure and criticism from the Carpenters Local Union 943 in Tulsa, Oklahoma. But those who demanded that Hutcheson desist received little encouragement from him and the General Executive Board of the Brotherhood. His pride was touched to the quick. He answered bluntly, setting forth the reasons why he opposed Franklin D. Roosevelt. He upheld the integrity of his office as President of the Brotherhood, reiterated the assurance which each member is given on joining the union.

In his reply to the local union, he wrote:

". . . In the years that I have served the Brotherhood as the General President I have followed what might be considered political ideas in handling the affairs of our organization, and the success of that policy I will not attempt to set forth, leaving it to the records in our organization as to what the accomplishments have been.

"I have always endeavored to put forth every possible effort for the advancement of our organization. I am for the election of Governor Landon as President of the United States because of his concepts of principles of government as set forth in the Constitution of the United States.

"I do not believe, as a citizen, or as a member of the Brotherhood, that it is to the best interests of the workers of the United States, or of our Brotherhood, to have a President who has shown by his attitude that he has but little regard and respect for the Constitution of the United States.

"That was clearly shown when he, the President, advised Congress that whether the proposed Guffey Bill was constitutional or not he desired them to enact it into law.

"Other acts by the President had shown that his interest in the workers was not what it should have been.

"In no time in the history of our country have we had a President who attempted to set himself up as a dictator in reference to the conditions under which people should transact business, as the present President.

---

[13]Interview with William Levi Hutcheson, Columbia Club, Indianapolis, Indiana, April 17, 1952.

"When the Bill to appropriate $4,800,000,000 was before Congress for consideration, through the efforts of representatives of the labor movement we were able to get Senator McCarran to introduce an amendment to the Bill to provide that the prevailing wage scale of the locality be paid on work being done under the appropriation. That amendment passed the Senate by a majority of two votes, but a few days later, through the activities of the President, it was called up for reconsideration and was defeated, and the President took it upon himself to set up what he termed a sustenance or security wage; a wage so ridiculously low, as compared to the wages in the majority of localities. . . .

"I cite the above to show why I have affiliated myself with the National Republican Committee in an effort to elect Governor Landon as the next President of the United States.

"I have done so not only as an American citizen, but as a member of the Brotherhood, feeling that if he, Governor Landon, is elected President of the United States he would have more regard for the principles of Americanism, as set forth in the Constitution of the United States, than does the President.

". . . As an American citizen, and as a member of the Brotherhood, I contend that I have every right to be for or against the election of Governor Landon, President Roosevelt or any other candidate for President of the United States, and in doing so I'm in no way attempting to involve our organization in any way, manner, shape or form. What I am doing and what I shall do, is done voluntarily because of my beliefs that in doing it I am performing a duty as an American citizen, and also that I am performing a duty for the members of the Brotherhood.

"I desire to inform you, and all other members of our organization, that I have no intention of desisting in what I am doing, and if the members of any local union of our Brotherhood object, the procedure is to prefer charges against me and send same to the General Executive Board."

Hutcheson was not intimidated. Nor were the members of the Carpenters local afraid to protest the conduct of their chief officer. The important thing was to mold public opinion to his way of thinking.

He denounced President Roosevelt's entente with John L. Lewis, from whom the Democratic party accepted in cash and services more than a half million dollars, of which only $50,000 was repaid. Hutcheson denied that Roosevelt would get anything like a united labor vote. "The workers of the country were beginning to realize that a vote for Roosevelt was a vote for the Committee of Industrial Organization. . . . The workers are getting educated now; they know what it is all about."[14]

Hutcheson termed the union led by John L. Lewis, a group very much in the minority, that it had tried for years to force the Federation to become "entangled in the spider web of politics," a reference to the 'twenties, when the leftists and extreme radicals tried to organize a distinctive militant third party. He called on labor to stand against "the un-American theory advanced by the radicals," and asserted that "these

---

[14]*New York Times,* August 14, 1936, p. 11.

evil influences never became a menace until the last three years."[15]

On November 28, Hutcheson voiced his opposition to the "fair labor standards." At a press conference on that day he declared: "If the Federal Government can establish a six-hour day, it can direct some future Congress to enact an eight or ten-hour day. . . . What we can get by law can be taken away by law. It is all right for the Government to fix hours for Government employees, but not private industry. *We should establish the shorter work day by our economic strength. . .*"[16]

The difference between Labor's Non-Partisan League, C.I.O.'s political adjunct and Hutcheson, primarily involved an issue of tactics. Unlike the League, which aimed at favorable governmental policy and seemingly ignored the gusts of popular opinion that changed the complexion of political administrations, the Carpenters' President consistently sought to make the welfare of labor its own concern. At no time, however, since his assumption of the Presidency, did he commit his ever-increasing army of carpenters to the Republicans; nor did the Brotherhood contribute to the Republican purse.

While Hutcheson was busily engaged in the Presidential campaign of 1936, a hue and cry was raised against him. It sprang from the William Z. Foster variant of the 'twenties, but slightly refined by his new rivals, the C.I.O. affiliates. Their pamphlets, penned by fictitious "rank and file committees of the United Brotherhood of Carpenters and Joiners of America," were flooded with abusive language. His life was searched for scandal; he was held up before the public as the "tzar," "diehard," "enemy of union democracy," "an opponent of organizing the unorganized," and similar reprehensible invective that the press and the books of tendentious writers repeated as fact. To discredit him further, he was declared to be the highest paid President of an international union, drawing an annual salary of $25,000. Actually, it was two-fifths of that amount as late as 1940.

There was the little White House intrigue indulged in by Major George L. Berry of the Printing Pressmen's Union, who brought "tall tales" to Roosevelt as far as these served to advance his political ambitions. As a practitioner in duplicity, Major Berry resorted to the use of Labor's Non-Partisan League, whose labor program he openly opposed as soon as he was elected United States Senator from Tennessee. He was cunning enough to disguise his views from powerful John L. Lewis and Sidney Hillman, who for reasons still obscure awarded him with the presidency of their militant political organization operating within the Democratic party.

---

[15]*Ibid,* September 7, 1936, p. 7.
[16]*Ibid,* p. 1.

Thus, while he was "climbing the steps of the White House together with Hillman and Lewis to confer with the President" on action to support the Wage and Hour Bill, Berry not only solicited Hutcheson's views on this proposed legislation but sought his help to defeat it as well. To be sure, Hutcheson did utter some harsh words about the President during the election campaign and criticized some of the New Deal legislation, but never once did he characterize a piece of federally-sponsored legislation as a "species of Fascism" in the manner of Major Berry.[17] Similarly, Berry's ardor to play the role of peacemaker and thus ingratiate himself with the White House, had not restrained him from joining in the campaign of vilifying Hutcheson's name.

In his memoranda addressed to the President and reproduced below, Berry identified Hutcheson as the sole major impediment to labor unity. Hutcheson's "influence," wrote Berry, "was responsible for failure of the A.F.L. to give Mr. Harrison (President of the Railway Clerks) and his associates the authority to sign "the peace agreement between the Federation and C.I.O." The following is the text of the memorandum between Senator Berry, President Franklin Delano Roosevelt and the latter's notations:

October 29, 1937

"Memorandum for the Secretary of Labor for preparation of reply for my signature, Franklin Delano Roosevelt. Letter from Senator George L. Berry 10/26/37 to the President: In re difference between the A. F. of L. and the C.I.O. encloses copy of an agreement, which he has prepared, and presented to Mr. George Harrison, Chmn. of the Peace Committee of the A. F. of L., and to Messrs. John L. Lewis and Sidney Hillman of the C.I.O. last December 1936. At the time this agreement was acceptable to the C.I.O. but the Committee from the A. F. of L. could not secure authority to sign, and thus the matter has been protracted. States he is reliably informed that Mr. W. Hutcheson influence was responsible for the failure of the A. F. of L. to give Mr. Harrison and his associate the authority to sign. Because of the possibility of the matter reaching the President, the Senator felt he should be in possession of the facts set forth in letter as well as the proposed agreement.

(Penciled notation), Sec. Labor "Prepare reply."[18]

Hutcheson was powerless to prevent the signing of such a proposed pact, for he was no longer on the scene of the Federation since December of 1936. Evidence supplied by Mr. Lewis and Hillman's biographers belied such hopes for peace in the divided "houses of labor." Instead of coming together, the C.I.O. was determined to drift farther apart. The respective views of both the C.I.O. and the A.F.L. had been so much discussed that they became as obscure as ancient mythology with its numberless gods.

---

[17]William L. Hutcheson, *Private Correspondence,* (1936 to 1937).
[18]Roosevelt Archives, Hyde Park, New York.

In 1936 it was not so much the principle of craft versus industrial unionism that caused the split; it was power among labor leaders, based on jurisdictional domains. Power based on jurisdiction — that has been the main issue which had kept the A. F. of L. and the C.I.O. apart. It has remained a point of disagreement throughout the several formal attempts which, since 1936, have been made to get the two federations together.[19]

It was not Hutcheson who blocked labor unity in 1936, aside from the fact that no unity was in the offing. Major Berry was far more verbose than factual and analytical, as his correspondence to President Roosevelt clearly indicated.

Hutcheson's struggle with the C.I.O. was limited to one industry, but what it lacked in breadth it made up in bitterness. It was fought with the leaders of Sawmill and Lumber Workers, and it was among the most violent of A. F. of L. — C.I.O. disputes. The roots stretched beyond March 1935, when the lumber workers were assigned to the Brotherhood's jurisdiction. Actually, the jurisdiction of all the lumber workers was awarded to the United Brotherhood by the Federation convention of 1911. In those days, however, lumbering and carpentry were distinctive trades; the lumber worker made lumber and the carpenter fashioned it into different products. Carpenters had little in common with lumber workers, so the carpenters made no serious effort to organize lumber workers at that time. But as the years rolled by, more and more of the work which carpenters performed on the job with their hand tools was transferred to power tools in the mills.

By 1934 the situation was ripe for a change. The lumber workers had no real organization to speak for them, the I.W.W. having been hounded out of existence during the war years and the A.F.L. Federal Lumber Unions being unequal to the job facing them. On the other hand, more and more carpentry work was gravitating toward the mills. Both lumber workers and carpenters were unhappy in their insecurity. Thus it was natural that in 1935 the American Federation of Labor should once more reaffirm its position of 1911, giving jurisdiction of the lumber workers to the United Brotherhood of Carpenters and Joiners of America.[20]

Hutcheson, who knew lumber and the lumber workers since his childhood, when Saginaw, Michigan was still a frontier lumbering town, explained to the delegates at the Twenty-Second General Convention of the Brotherhood, in December, 1936, the reasons why he

---

[19]Wright Mills, *The New Men of Power* (Harcourt, Brace & Co., 1948), p. 60.
[20]Frank Duffy, *History of the U.B.C.J.A.* (MSS.).

"decided to request of the A. F. of L., that the Brotherhood be given jurisdiction over the Lumber and Sawmill Workers."

". . . To most people there would seem to be but little, if any, connection between the men who go into the woods to cut down the trees and the men who erect finished products in a building, but it should be called to mind that while today there is a large number of employees performing the various operations involved in preparing the materials for use, nevertheless they are closely allied and therefore should be together in one organization for material benefits. . . . Years ago it was the custom of the workmen when erecting buildings to go into the woods, select the trees out of which they would construct the building, and they would not only select them but would shape and fashion and put material in place. Not only would they erect the walls in that manner but they would also put on the roof, making out of the rough logs what in those days was referred to as shakes, now known as shingles. . . . As time went on the inventiveness of man brought into use tools with which workmen could shape and fashion the materials needed. . . . Into use was brought the whipsaw and various types of hand planes for making of flooring, ceiling, moldings, trim, etc.

"As demands grew and the population increased it became necessary that more buildings be erected and there came about a system whereby one group of men felled the trees and when they were conveyed to the sawmill another group sawed them into lumber, and another group employed in what is referred to as trim mills made them into sash, doors, trim, etc., and still another group that is usually referred to as construction carpenters did the erection and installation of the material in the buildings. . . . That procedure and system has grown up to the present time until we now find there are large groups employed on each operation, or, as you might say, each division of the industry, in preparing the timber from the time the tree is felled until the finished material is installed in the buildings. . . ."[21]

This time the Carpenters were receptive to the idea of making the United Brotherhood an organization embracing all woodworkers. Under the leadership of Hutcheson, an active campaign was undertaken to organize the Pacific Coast lumber industry. The 130 A. F. of L. Federal labor unions with a membership of 7,500 welcomed the opportunity of tieing themselves to a stable and permanent organization. President Hutcheson placed Abe Muir and four additional representatives in the field, who began organizing hundreds of new local unions.

For nearly a century the loggers and lumbermen whom we described in Part I, were a picturesque race of their own. Through the boom days of Michigan, the loggers were a hard working, hard drinking, hard fighting lot. As reported by Stanley S. Horn, they were "real he-men, with hair on their chests; they chewed snuff. . . and drank their hooch. . . and made no pretense at being tin angels." Many were rough and tumble direct-actionists, with an I.W.W. background and possessed of a dem-

---

[21] *Ibid.*

ocratic tradition reminiscent of earlier frontiersmen. They were the most exploited migratory laborers in America. They seldom owned anything more than the shoes on their feet, clothes on their backs and an extra pair of socks. Seven or eight months of the year they spent in camps deep in the snow-covered woods. When they emerged in the spring their meager accumulated winter's wages were soon taken from them in the bars and saloons.[22]

The operators, like the men who worked for them, were hardy men. They earned, or borrowed enough money to get together an outfit. They bought timber when they could, pirated when they could not, and often built up tremendous fortunes.

As the timber stands in the Lake States petered out, the operators moved to the West Coast. With them they took many of their men. On the Pacific Coast they picked up where they had left off in Michigan, Minnesota and Wisconsin. Pigs under the bunkhouses and pine bows in the mattresses were standard equipment in the West Coast lumber camps up 'till World War I. But a change was coming over the woodsmen. They no longer wanted to live like animals. They wanted homes and families and decent wages and working conditions. They wanted steady jobs and safe working procedures. They wanted security, and a sense of permanency in an age of large-scale organizations.

Many abortive attempts at organizing a lumber union had taken place in the years before World War I. None of them, however, made any real progress. The only group actually organized on a functional basis was the Industrial Workers of the World (I.W.W.). Its methods of sudden and aggressive strikes and its resort to sabotage — "strike on the job" — enabled workers who had little money, or none at all, to coalesce quickly into unions and participate in wage and industrial conflicts. Its emphasis on industrial unionism appealed to the unskilled worker, the migratory and seasonal laborer, and the exploited Northwest Europeans and Canadians. The I.W.W. injected itself into the lumber picture. Conditions being what they were, it was not too difficult for it to enlist a hard core of adherents in the lumber industry. From 1910 to 1920 the I.W.W. was an organization to contend with on the West Coast.

Often its methods were crude and even brutal, but the I.W.W. did accomplish a little good in cleaning up intolerable conditions. However, any good the organization achieved in improving conditions, was offset by the extreme radicalism and revolutionary rhetoric of many of its leaders. When local authorities, shivering at its revolutionary doctrines, attempted to prevent organization and street speaking, "wobblies" would

22Stanley F. Horn, *The Fascinating Lumber Business,* pp. 75-76; Peter Terzik, Editor,

descend upon the community from every direction, exercise their "rights" and crowd the jails until officials grew tired of the burden of support. The World War brought a debacle. Popular hostility, court prosecution, and local vigilantism drove the leaders and the members into exile, put them into jail, or summarily dispatched them by lynch law.

To counteract the I.W.W. and unionism, the lumber industry during the war instituted an organization known as the Four L's, the Loyal Legion of Loggers and Lumbermen. It was stimulated by the Spruce Production Division, a "left arm" of the United States Army. Its head was Colonel Bryce P. Disque, who somewhat later was promoted to General. The Four L's was a company union pure and simple. Membership was compulsory and voluntary spying on suspected union members was properly rewarded. The dues, if any, were very small but the benefits to anyone but the employers were non-existent.

During World War I when the A. F. of L. decided to organize the loggers and lumbermen, A. F. of L. organizer Abe Muir of the Idaho State Federation of Labor, as dedicated and generous a Scot as we ever met, was assigned to the North Woods, to organize those highly exploited laborers.

It was from historic Coeur d'Alene, with its inexhaustable supply of logs, that organizer Abe Muir tried to lead the "weary and aching" loggers. His headquarters was a funeral chapel, which he was able to secure as a meeting place from a local undertaker. But no sooner had he arrived, when Lieutenant Burkholtz, of Colonel Disque's staff appeared, demanding "in the name of the United States Army to disband his union of loggers." He also demanded his records and all papers, which were hidden inside the piano. Had it not been for the restraining hand of Idaho's first Jewish Governor, Moses Alexander, a scene similar to that which was enacted in 1892 by the order of President George Harrison, would have been reenacted in the mid-year of 1918. Hutcheson's refusal to build wooden ships out of ten-hour lumber doubtless highlighted the plight of the lumberjacks in the Northwest. This, together with President Samuel Gompers' efforts in behalf of these last of American frontiersmen who lived outside the pale of civilization, resulted in an order being issued by Secretary of War Newton Baker for Disque and the Spruce Production Division to establish an eight-hour day.

Muir succeeded in extending the organization of loggers and lumbermen until the signing of the armistice, when the Four L's came into their own again. The ten-hour day was re-established. Union men were blacklisted and wages were reduced to the barest minimum of ten cents an hour. The A. F. of L.'s federal locals were too weak to withstand the onslaught.

In 1935 the famed Blue Eagle, symbolizing fair practices within industry and minimum wages for employees, changed the outlook of the loggers from despair to hope.

Abe Muir, now an organizer for the United Brotherhood of Carpenters, was sent by Hutcheson into the towering forests which were ablaze with discontent. "Workers responded in droves. Not even the hundreds of hired goons with their machine guns and tear gas could stem the tide of organization. In short order, 70,000 workers in the Fir lumber industry walked out in response to the union's strike call, their hearts set on winning a living wage."*** The strike was a long and bitter one. Violence, riot clubs and tear gas were used by the State Police. Direct actionists traded axes for picket signs. Only the National Guard prevented bloodshed. In the end the workers obtained an agreement. Wages that had been twenty-five cents to thirty cents an hour before the advent of the Brotherhood were raised to a fifty cents minimum. Time and a half pay for overtime and union recognition were also accorded the workers, but no "sole bargaining rights." Two other raises to bring the minimum wage to sixty-two and a-half cents an hour were won in short order in the next eighteen months.

But about this time the A. F. of L. was torn asunder by internal differences regarding the organization of mass production industries. This schism, which ultimately ended with the formation of the C.I.O., was felt throughout all organized and unorganized labor. Not even the Pacific Coast lumber industry was immune. Throughout the latter part of 1935 and the early part of 1936, zealous missionaries of the C.I.O., some of whom were either direct actionists or Communists, were all over the Pacific Coast lumber industry.

The matter came to a head at the Twenty-third General Convention of the Brotherhood, which was held at Lakeland, Florida, beginning December 7, 1936. Twenty-seven delegates, representing seventy thousand lumber workers, appeared before the convention. They had, they said, a set of demands. These included, "trade autonomy," two representatives on the General Executive Board of the United Brotherhood, full voice and vote in all matters affecting the lumber industry and three-fifths of their twenty-five cents per month per capita tax returnable to them. While the delegates from the lumber industry expressed themselves as being satisfied that the lumber workers belonged in the United Brotherhood, they at the same time saw themselves as being "bid for" by two rival unions, they constituting one corner of a triangle.

They were not happy with their "non-beneficial status" in the Brotherhood, which exempted them from paying to the General Office the regular per capita tax of seventy-five cents per month. Instead,

---

***Interview with Abe Muir, General Executive Board Member, U.B.C.J.A., in Indianapolis, a month prior to his passing, on May 30, 1954.

they were permitted to become non-beneficial members, paying twenty-five cents per month tax. Hutcheson explained, that "granting them this dispensation we were rendering them a great assistance by giving them an opportunity to become affiliated with the United Brotherhood of Carpenters and Joiners of America, and, in my opinion, we are the one group of organized workers that can give greater assistance and more help in bettering their working conditions than any other organization," or than they themselves could get "by their efforts alone."[23]

In granting them a dispensation to affiliate as non-beneficial members, Hutcheson explained, "I had the thought in mind that when they desired to become beneficial members they would do so by paying the full per capita tax, as per law, rules and regulations set forth in the General Constitution."[24]

In less than a year the Brotherhood organized 70,000 to 75,000 loggers, timber and sawmill workers. The Brotherhood "spent thousands of dollars for organizing these lumbermen, loggers and sawmill workers ". . . We spent the Carpenters' money in order to organize them, so that we could control the trade, not only those in the finished products, but from the cutting down of the tree until it becomes the finished product;" explained Frank Duffy, General-Secretary of the Brotherhood. ". . . When they got into trouble in Seattle, . . . and they sent us bills amounting to $7,500, they had paid $3,500, and there was a balance of $4,000 yet to be paid. They did not have the funds to pay that bill, and at that time our General Executive Board appropriated $2,000 to help pay the $4,000. The General Executive Board did not need to do that if they adhered strictly to the terms and conditions under which these men were granted a charter."[25] The sawmill workers, unable to pay the full per capita tax, were non-beneficial members. However, "the Brotherhood wanted the delegates present at the convention so (they) . . . may become acquainted with us and with our method of doing business."

The delegates were discontented. They wanted to be seated as full beneficial members. They next met with a sub-committee of the General Executive Board which consisted of T. M. Guerin, William J. Kelly and A. W. Muir. The delegates were granted concessions, to wit: (1) That a sub-committee of the Executive Board make a first hand survey of the complex nature of the industry and "make recommendations to cover all questions at issue and this to be done as speedily as possible,

[23]Frank Duffy, *op. cit.*
[24]*Ibid*, p. 482.
[25]*U.B.C.J.A., Proceedings* (1936), p. 25.
The per capita tax for all members was 75c a month. The Lumber workers who earned 50c an hour at this time, paid only 25c a month, hence the dispensation.

(2) to use the Brotherhood label on all logs so as to identify them from non-union products of like nature, (3) nine lumber firms now on strike be placed on the "we don't patronize" list, (4) that an organizing campaign be continued with organizers who speak the language of and understand the industry.

Delegate Dan Perillard told the convention: "I want to say in reference to the organizers in our District that Brother Muir and Brother Cameron have given us yeomen service and we are doing splendidly down there. But please let us go along with the way we are for the time being."

Delegate Don F. Helmick: ". . . But we have come here in our status and we hope that from this convention this relationship that I have spoken of will be built into a foundation. We belong with you. We realize very definitely and appreciate most sincerely the value of being members of this great Brotherhood."[26]

Hutcheson assured the delegation that the "members of the Brotherhood throughout the jurisdiction of our organization will give you every help and assistance possible."

At the convention's end, the delegates immediately journeyed north to closet themselves with John L. Lewis in Washington. At first Lewis refused to charter the lumber workers on the ground that he was interested in organizing the unorganized. However, when they returned to the Northwest camps, there, as well as across the country, the C.I.O. was bidding for the allegiance of the Loggers and Sawmill Workers. Hartung and Helmick were now advocating that the Lumber Workers leave the United Brotherhood to became a part of the C.I.O.

Day by day the number of agitators for secession from the United Brotherhood in favor of the C.I.O. increased. Harold Pritchett, a Canadian, suddenly appeared to lead the secession. He had $50,000 at his disposal, given him by the C.I.O. to disrupt the Lumber and Sawmill Workers. By June, 1937, when the Federated Woodworkers convened, Lewis was openly raiding the Brotherhood. He sent two of his chief lieutenants, John Brophy and Harry Bridges, to address the delegates. Hutcheson was invited but refused to appear. However, Muir did address the delegates. He denounced Lewis and the C.I.O.

Brophy and Bridges then harangued the delegates about their "second-class" membership in the United Brotherhood, and invited them to join the C.I.O. On July 20, 1937, approximately 35 percent of the membership seceded from the Brotherhood to become affiliated with the International Woodworkers of America, C.I.O. On the same day, the first convention of the International Woodworkers of America met with Lewis' blessings.

---

[26]*Ibid,* p. 317.

Since August of 1937, the Brotherhood sought to combat this dual movement. Through special circulars, the General Executive Board cautioned its members "not to handle any lumber or mill work manufactured by any operator who employs C.I.O. or those who hold membership in an organization dual to our Brotherhood."

". . . C.I.O. has challenged us," Hutcheson wrote in a specially-prepared bulletin during the second half of 1937. "We must meet that challenge without hesitation. Therefore appoint a committee to inform your employers and the lumber dealers that our members will refuse to handle any dual or C.I.O. products."[27]

With the issues laid down and the sides chosen, another phase of the struggle opened. It was characterized by a bitter, knock-down, and drag-out struggle for the allegiance of the Lumber Workers between the two rival unions. At its height, from 1937 to 1940, the struggle between the Brotherhood and the C.I.O. was the most extensive and bitter one. It had repercussions in the lumbering community of Oregon. It led to a complete anti-labor law enacted by referendum. It made union action virtually impossible until Supreme Court decision held such statutes unconstitutional. The dispute raged from 1937 to 1939, then gradually simmered down to a defensive campaign of denunciation. By 1940, although much bitterness still existed, the two unions were cooperating on a limited scale. In that year the Brotherhood had 35,000 lumber and sawmill workers laboring under closed shop agreements. "We were handicapped in our efforts due to the fact that shortly after the last convention (1936) a group that was affiliated with the Brotherhood left the organization and set up what they purported to be an International Organization, and affiliated with the C.I.O., and called themselves the International Woodworkers of the World . . . While for a time, they caused our members a great deal of annoyance and inconvenience, it is gratifying to inform you that we are making very material and substantial progress, and that the group which seceded . . . is gradually diminishing."[28] The International Woodworkers of America, and its President Harold Pritchett, claimed 100,000 members, virtually including all the forest workers. Actually, according "to the best opinion available, the I.W.A. had approximately 25,000 members."[29]

The secession of thousands of loggers from the jurisdiction of the United Brotherhood was a loss that inflicted a blow at the Brotherhood. The Brotherhood now felt itself surrounded by an imperialist "Alsace-Lorraine," against which it had to defend itself. A less determined man

---

[27]*The Carpenters,* Vol. LVII:9 (Sept., 1937), p. 17.

[28]U.B.C.J.A. *Proceedings* (1940) p. 42.

[29]Benjamin Stolberg, *The Story of the C.I.O.* (Viking Press, 1938), p. 240.

than Hutcheson might not have troubled much about this new "imperialism" and, doubtless would have given up attempts to organize the Pacific Coast lumber industry.

In spite of the fact that it opened up an area of severe jurisdictional strife between them, Hutcheson's dislike of Communism was only matched by his will to build a strong, inseparable union of "all woodworkers" in the U. S. and Canada. Harold Pritchett was a "blind follower" of the Communist Party line as were a number of others who successfully infiltrated into the C.I.O.[30]

Every reverse suffered in the Northwest Lumber industry only increased Hutcheson's determination to organize the unorganized lumber and sawmill workers. For the next ten or twelve years he spared neither time, effort or money in helping those lumber locals that remained loyal to the Brotherhood. In the course of two years, from July 1940 through 1942, the Brotherhood spent $79,750 toward organizing and protecting the sawmill and lumber workers in the Pacific Northwest. In 1950 Hutcheson again emphasized the importance of "completely organizing the unorganized" in the logging and sawmill industry.

With the financial backing and experienced leadership of the Brotherhood, the lumber workers were able to improve working conditions steadily. From the lowest wage mass production industry in the nation, the Brotherhood elevated wages in that industry from 45 cents an hour to $1.85\frac{1}{2}$ an hour (1954) minimum. Lumber workers were since raised from the status of semi-civilized bushmen to full-fledged "workers." As they will advance in educational level, and security of employment and wages, in measure of respect, self-direction, and accountability accorded them in the general community, they will become increasingly "quasi-professional." On the other hand, the lumber operators are beginning to accept notions of responsibility that allow the loggers and lumber workers a measure of self-government. Similarly, the Brotherhood's present President, Maurice A. Hutcheson is forcefully coming to grips with the specifically industrial as well as labor problems. The Brotherhood has actively interested itself in the production problems. The highly competitive nature of the industry which has pitted every operator against every other operator, is gradually being eliminated. The production and marketing of lumber are becoming more orderly procedures, thereby terminating the more violent fluctuations which made or ruined the operators.

Over this metamorphosis, which continues to change the industry from a savage jungle to a stable industry paying a living wage and

---

[30]*Ibid*, p. 239; Sidney Lens, *Left, Right and Center* (Henry Regnery Co., 1949), p. 395.

providing decent conditions, loomed the figures of William L. Hutcheson and his son, Maurice.

*   *   *

President Roosevelt's landslide in 1936 had brought no wailing to Hutcheson or gnashing of teeth. Soon after the President's re-election, he and the Brotherhood's attorney J. O. Carson, lost no time to "pressure" the White House for the appointment of Hon. Sewall Myer of Houston to a judgeship in the newly-created Southern District of Texas. With his customary graciousness the President thanked him "very much for his interest in writing him about this matter."[31] The letter was signed by Assistant Secretary to the President, M. H. McIntyre. To Hutcheson, politics seemed at times something futile, but he persisted in the political circus because he was caught in its harness, and because of an irresistable instinct that would not let him acquiesce in Roosevelt's "trial and error" experiments. He thought Roosevelt's attempt to raise the number of judges in the Supreme Court would "replace representative government with an autocracy;" that the President's proposed law early in February, 1937, would "violate our established constitutional order and enable Congress and the President in any time of stress to distort the character of our institutions."

Hutcheson denounced Labor's Non-Partisan League, as "non non-partisan." He strongly opposed the droping of union scales from work relief projects. On the whole, Hutcheson refused to treat as a partisan doctrine the whole process of distribution which the New Deal sought to achieve through political channels, but rather as the inevitable consequence of the functioning of popular government. His criticism of the New Deal aides was directed mainly at the way W.P.A. projects "are forcing the citizens to declare themselves paupers and beggars and on relief in order to get employment on W.P.A. projects. We will continue to enter protests, but I want you to know that the trouble is not with us as we did not formulate the rules and regulations governing the W.P.A. work."[32]

The New Deal did not and apparently could not, solve the basic recovery problem. Some of its works seemed actually to retard revival.

Roosevelt himself and the majority of his adherents saw nothing radical or revolutionary — in the pejorative sense — about the New Deal, arguing indeed that it promoted individual enterprise and free competition precisely because it favored small business over big business, the average citizen against monopoly, collective bargaining against con-

---

[31]Roosevelt Archives (Hyde Park Library, New York, Feb. 1, 1937).
[32]Hutcheson's letter addressed to Charles Weinscott, Secretary, Local Union 365, April 29, 1938.

centrated managerial power. Beyond any question, government intervention strengthened labor's hand.

Business, on the other hand, noted a new arrogance of labor, sit-in strikes and law-breaking tactics. Moreover, the quasi-judicial National Labor Relations Board appeared to overstep its professional impartiality in assuring C.I.O. unions an opportunity to redress old grievances by swinging to the other extreme. Even in the shadows of the war economy, radical C.I.O. leaders created the impression that labor's exclusive goal was a large share in the national income, not a due share in a larger national income. Many persons friendly to the labor movement turned sour at the same time of the sit-down strikes of 1937 and thenceforth tended to criticize the Federal Government against pampering C.I.O. unions, just as some had disapproved a contrary tendency during the prosperity era.

Hutcheson warned against such developments. "Business leaders called on the leaders of the C.I.O. to act. The C.I.O. was helpless. It had mushroomed hastily and not too well. It had opened its ranks to Communists and other crackpot labor theorists. They had swarmed in and were spreading their radical views," wrote the Brotherhood's official Journal, *The Carpenter*. "Business gave up. The long shut-downs in key industries had been costly . . . The majority of us are neither business nor economic experts beyond our pay envelopes, but when these pay envelopes stop we are justified to know what's wrong. And the answer? Business blames Washington and wants a hands-off policy. Washington blames business and there we are — in the middle . . . Even Mr. Lewis has admitted that his $500,000 was a bad investment. . . ."[33]

Roosevelt's "pump-priming" as a method for revival finally ended in July, 1939. At that time, the Works Projects Administration (WPA) took care of 3,325,000 people. Roosevelt launched his new $3,000,000,-000 Bill of indirect or "lending-spending" project. Apparently, expecting by speed and adroitness to reach his goal "through a broken field of dangers," he counted on support from liberals because the program would insure another army of men against idleness, and from the balance of power conservatives, because it excluded a prevailing union wage.

The $3,000,000,000 Bill was introduced on July 10, 1939. On the 28th, the Administration forces in the Senate defeated by only two votes a proffered amendment to require prevailing union wages on the projects. On July 31, under the influence of Senator Byrd, Roosevelt's program moved swiftly to its doom. The House by a vote that included 47 Democrats refused even to consider the Bill.

This last "lending-spending" episode, coming toward the end of

---

[33]*The Carpenter*, Vol. LVIII:5 (May, 1938), p. 25.

Roosevelt's second term, might well have made it his last term. With other current developments, it greatly reduced his prestige. But throughout history, wars or threats of war have kept many a chief magistrate and executive in power. Within about a month after Roosevelt's defeat in Congress, Hitler and Stalin overran Poland, and Europe was plunged into war. Roosevelt's dimmed star came back again into the ascendant.

In May 1940, the European war was eight months old.

Democratic leaders had made overtures for the presidential election, but Roosevelt was holding back. The tradition was wholly contrary to a third term, and there were other reasons why he should not challenge it. The weaknesses and strengths of Roosevelt almost faded before the stark issues that confronted the America of 1940. The need for domestic stability seemed to reinforce the call for leadership by the Republicans; but the realities and possibilities of war were uppermost in the public mind.

On October 11, 1940, Hutcheson resumed his post of special interest representative in the Republican national committee with greater ardor then ever. He was horrified, irritated, shocked, disapproving of the Roosevelt administration, which turned its tables against him and the Brotherhood of Carpenters. He published an indignant open letter, circularized it to the entire union membership and the labor movement, denouncing Roosevelt and "his" Department of Justice. It was straight from the shoulder, vehement and indignant. Labor and Roosevelt's opponents applauded it.

> "... It is the purpose of this open letter to convey to the members of our organization information in reference to the present conditions prevailing due to the activities of representatives of the Attorney General of the United States, who is appointed by the President of the United States, in persecuting, not prosecuting, members of the Brotherhood through obtaining indictments alleging that members have committed acts that were in violation of the Sherman Anti-Trust Law.
>
> "... It seems strange indeed that although the law referred to has been on the statute books for fifty years no Administration prior to the New Deal Administration ever attempted to say, or even inferred that men exercising their rights as trade unionists and as free Americans would be violating the provisions of said law. The acts of representatives of the New Deal Administration clearly show that they are not friends of our Brotherhood. Therefore the members should remember and follow the long practice ... of the American Federation of Labor; namely, assist your friends and defeat your enemies."[34]

"This communication," Hutcheson emphasized, "is not intended in any way to infringe on the political opinion of any member of the Brotherhood." He assured the membership, that "I will in no way inter-

---

[34]U.B.C.J.A., *Proceedings* (1940), p. 233.

fere with religious beliefs, political opinions, and domestic duties."

Harassed Hutcheson was stumping for Wendell Willkie as presidential candidate of the Republican party; he could scarcely do otherwise. He personally urged the candidacy of Senator Arthur Vandenberg during the high tide of the Democratic party's success; but the party machine thought otherwise. Vandenberg, like Hutcheson, appealed for the liberalization of Republican party policy through support of unemployment insurance, retirement pensions. Like Vandenberg, he concluded with the thought, "as Lincoln said, we must lean upon the heart of the great mass of the people, satisfied to be moved by its mighty pulsations." Hutcheson demanded the purging of reactionary elements from the Republican party and the preparation of an affirmative program. Yet, he recognized that the elements which forced Willkie's nominations were not old line Republicans.

Hutcheson hailed Willkie's campaign as "the fight of the common man against the forces which would deprive him of his Democratic rights. Perpetuation of tenure in office through exercise of political power," he said, "has destroyed popular government time after time. The two-term tradition was more vital to our national freedom than even the Constitution," he added, "since the Constitution can be set aside by the Executive with the support of the Supreme Court at any time."[35]

At no time, throughout the period of the New Deal, did Hutcheson find himself more comfortably situated — in his forward role of clarifying his views on labor inside the Republican party. Willkie's labor speech in Pittsburgh before an audience largely composed of labor men contained Hutcheson's labor program — that labor traditionally wanted. Willkie would approve the labor laws and their administration. He would appoint a Secretary of Labor directly from the ranks of organized labor — "and it will not be a woman either." This was sure of a big hand, as Hutcheson, not unlike other labor leaders, believed that the post belonged to them. On the night of October 25, Hutcheson continued to scold Roosevelt. Over WOR, he charged that the President had given labor "the most contemptuous snub in the nation's history, and by using the techniques of dictatorship had alienated the public against reform." The administration had tied itself to members of the Communist Party and fellow travelers, Hutcheson said; and "labor does not want these elements to lead America with the help of Government funds. The promises made by Wendell L. Wilkie have been fair to labor," Hutcheson declaimed, "and in his dealings with the A. F. L. unions Wendell L. Willkie as President of Commonwealth and Southern Corporation had always kept his agreements."[36]

[35]*N. Y. Times,* October 12, 1940, p. 11:1.
[36]*N. Y. Times,* October 26, 1940, p. 13:4.

A source of happiness to Hutcheson was the fact that John L. Lewis, the chief architect of the C.I.O., supported the Republican candidate. If, ostensibly, his opposition to the late President Roosevelt was based on his dislike of a break with the two-term tradition, only a little closer scrutiny was needed to see that, his vanity apart, Mr. Lewis' opposition was based, above all, on the fact that he regarded the support of the C.I.O. as the consideration in a contract between himself as the President of the C.I.O. and President Roosevelt as the leader of the Democratic party in which he traded votes for concessions. But when the Federal Government refused to knuckle to his will, Lewis turned to the Republican party. Hutcheson welcomed Lewis' support of Wendell L. Willkie. His own radio address, sponsored by the Independent Willkie advertising campaign was timed with that of Lewis'. On October 25, 1940, Lewis endorsed Willkie. "I recommend him to the men and women of labor, and to the nation, as well worthy of their support."[37]

Both Hutcheson and Lewis urged twenty-five million listeners to defeat Roosevelt. "The reelection of President Roosevelt for a third term will be a national evil of the first magnitude. The present concentration of power in the office of the President of the United States had never before been equalled. Personal craving for power, the overwhelming, abnormal and selfish craving for power is a thing to alarm and dismay. America needs no supermen. It denies the philosophy that runs to the deification of the State. Are we now to cast away the priceless liberty which is our heritage? It is obvious that President Roosevelt will not be re-elected for the third term unless he has the overwhelming support of the men and women of labor. If he is re-elected it will mean that the members of the Congress of Industrial Organizations have rejected my advice and recommendation. I will accept the result as being equivalent to a vote of no confidence, and will retire as President of the Congress of Industrial Organizations at its convention in November."[38]

Lewis made good on his pledge to retire as C.I.O. president if Roosevelt were returned to the White House, refusing to be a candidate for reelection. In his place, the convention chose Philip Murray, for long Lewis' right-hand man in the Miners' organization and more recently the head of the Steelworkers Organizing Committee.

"Deep national necessity" elected Roosevelt by a majority of nearly five million votes in the 1940 election, an electoral majority of 449 votes out of 531.

Although Lewis' and Hutcheson's opposition to Roosevelt doubtlessly sprang from different motives, both played the role of the "English Nonconformist" in American political life. Both Lewis and Hutcheson

[37]*Ibid.*
[38]*Ibid.*

tended to regard the political authority of the State with suspicion, as the reserve power which hampers their freedom and was even the main source of their "persecution." This was brought home with particular cogency to Hutcheson, who was "capriciously and irresponsibly" being "persecuted" by Professor Thurman Arnold, Assistant Attorney General of the Department of Justice in charge of the Anti-trust Division, as violating the Sherman Act. Both Hutcheson and Lewis thought the path of wisdom was to trade "votes" with a dominant political party in return for the maximum of protection of job control as the empire in which the unions would be sovereign. The one thing neither wanted was the invasion of their "interest aggregate" by the state power, for they were convinced that state action was only too likely to be hostile action.

Both Lewis and Hutcheson insisted that they must retain their power to pick and choose between friends and enemies by an *ad hoc* judgement about each candidate in each election. As was hinted above, the only difference in principle between the outlook of Hutcheson and Lewis and, say, Sidney Hillman, in 1940 was "the principle of maneuvre," on which American trade unionism relied.[39] This division of method, or what Laski calls, "the politics of policy," Hutcheson strongly defended and applied as General President of the Brotherhood of Carpenters. He incurred ill feeling, however, when a number of local unions felt that he violated this "principle of maneuvre." They refused to follow the reasoning of Hutcheson's "open letter." Their disapproval of the General President's act was vehemently expressed in resolutions passed by several Carpenters local unions and copies of which were addressed to The White House, to Hutcheson, and to Wendell L. Willkie.

Dear Mr. President:

This is to advise that members of the American Federation of the United Brotherhood of Carpenters and Joiners, Local 448 do not object to President Hutcheson, or anyone else supporting any candidate or party they wish, but do object to him using his office for the purpose of promoting some candidate for office. This activity has caused the United Brotherhood to lose all influence in Government affairs.

". . . The membership of Local Union 448 goes on record condemning the partisanship of President Hutcheson and agrees that our right to vote as our conscience dictates is an inviolable right to all American citizens. . . .[40]

Much more indignant in tone were the resolutions of the Lumber and Sawmill Workers local unions. It was not too difficult to detect the guiding hand of the C.I.O. and of the Communist opponents of Hutcheson and the Brotherhood.

---

[39]Harold J. Laski, *The American Democracy* (Viking Press, 1948), p. 227.
[40]Roosevelt Archives, Hyde Park, New York

A little excitement was caused by a delegate to the Twenty-Fourth convention on December, 1940. Williams, a union agent in Cleveland, rose at the convention and argued with the chairman to "reconsider" his political allegiance. "I know you will. I know the great work you have done with all the criticism you have received. Even though I don't agree with a man, I am willing to give him credit for what he has done."

Hutcheson, somewhat under strain but by no means on the defensive replied: "If the delegate wishes to renounce his rights of citizenship, I don't. I feel highly honored to have represented the Brotherhood for a quarter of a century. But in all those years and in the years to come I do not intend to give up my rights as an American citizen in expressing my views on issues affecting not only the members of the Brotherhood, but all the people of this country, merely because I am General President.

"I will not renounce my Americanism, because in all these thirty-eight years I have been a member of the Brotherhood I have been a union man unreproached. . . . It was proven by the remarks of our learned attorney . . . the other day, that the letter (open letter) I was criticized for sending out was only information to the members. His remarks verified the statement in that communication, and let me say again that as long as I have the breath of life in my body to express myself, I will remain and try to remain a good American and at all times a good and, a damned good trade unionist."[41]

41U.B.C.J.A., *Proceedings* (1940), p. 274.

America's Delegates at Pan-American Labor Conference in Santiago, Chile, January 1936. Seated at conference table are (left to right): Miss Frieda Miller, Chairman; Joseph Molamphy, Employers' Delegate; U. S. Ambassador Hoffman Philip, Government Delegate and William L. Hutcheson, representing Labor. Latter's appointment jarred political "sensitivities" of Madame Perkins, Labor Secretary in the Roosevelt administration.

For the first time in Indiana's political history, Republicans in '38 chose a labor man to chair GOP convention. Here Chairman William L. Hutcheson (left) poses with Supreme Court Justice Arch L. Bobbitt of the Hoosier State.

National labor spokesman William L. Hutcheson returns for a sentimental visit to the little old schoolhouse, in South Williams, where he studied the three R's.

It's Election time and the late "One World" Wendell L. Willkie, Republican presidential candidate in 1940, asked Bill Hutcheson over for a talkfest at his Rushville, Indiana farm.

CHAPTER | XVI

HUTCHESON BEFORE THE BAR

There was a vast historical irony in the fact that one of the most liberal, pro-labor governments ever possessed by the United States, embarking on an anti-monopoly drive which had its roots in the reformist zeal of the veritable Grangers of sixty years ago, should have chosen labor as its target. It was a curious paradox that the "Roosevelt Revolution," which consciously sought to strengthen the collective power of labor as never before, was in effect making an about-face vehemently accusing labor unions of violating the Sherman Anti-trust Law passed in 1890. Why the sudden evangelism for the "free flow of commerce," this surprising reversion to a law which had brought nothing but consternation, deep resentment and even imprisonment to labor since 1894? It was hardly consistent of the New Deal administration which, while avowing its faith in the "free enterprise system," failed to enforce the Anti-trust statute against business monopoly, directing it instead, against unions and their defenses. The whole episode of attempted reversal to 1890 was not only futile and aggravating from the first, but was hypocritical on the part of government, in view of its own steps by which it strengthened labor immeasurably.

One guess would be that this campaign against Hutcheson, and the United Brotherhood of Carpenters in particular had both psychological and even political overtones; and that trust buster Thurman Arnold who had been intimately involved in this campaign of *laissez faire* knew, to his embarrassment, that he was damning what the New Deal tried and successfully corrected. But for one who analyzed the uncritical economic "folklore" of America and was no less involved in the "Investigation of Concentration of Economic Power" since December 1, 1938, not to have drawn a mark of distinction between the "originators of power" achieved by industry and the subsequent development of a "countervaling power" stimulated by the New Deal, could not be "excused on the ground that he was ignorant of the facts."

To be sure, he and his Monopoly Committee paraded 552 witnesses, consuming 775 hours, published 31 highly revealing volumes, 6 supplements and 43 monographs. The Committee x-rayed the familiar manifestations of business combinations, patent pools, market controls and many others. In its Final Report to the Executive Secretary, it detailed unlimited evidence that "monopoly has greatly increased in American industry during the last fifty years because of the lax enforcement of the Anti-trust Laws . . . The tremendous development of trade associations during the 'twenties which increased price-fixing . . . in those industries which appeared to be competitive, competition is constantly breaking down."[1]

With a greatly bolstered appropriation of $1,325,000, trust-buster Thurman Arnold set out to conduct a full-dress inquisition against labor unions affiliated with the A. F. of L., lasting more than three years. In September, 1939 and June, 1940, eleven Grand Juries rained indictments on the heads of 81 unions, by no means all of which were in the building industry. Although the announced inquisition was directed against the building industry, the United Brotherhood of Carpenters and Joiners of America bore the main brunt of the auto-da-fe, as its national and local leaders were placed under indictments, spread across the whole continental United States, from Pittsburgh on the East to San Francisco on the West, from Chicago in the Midwest and New Orleans in the South. In a November 20, 1939 press release, Arnold announced that the ultimate goal of his drive against unions was to implement laissez faire by prohibiting "unfair" labor practices by employees, and the weapon which he proposed to use was the familiar weapon of the Sherman Anti-trust Act. What Arnold sought first through the use of the Federal Administrative agencies, the Justice Department and the Federal Courts, was to bring about amendations in the Wagner Act so as to inject himself into the internal affairs of trade unions. The Executive Council of the American Federation of Labor set Labor's clarion call against the court assault, saying that it would ". . . resist with all the power at its command the present reactionary efforts of the Department of Justice to control organized labor." Joseph A. Padway, General Counsel for the American Federation of Labor, held the attack to be "the most reactionary, vicious, outrageous attempt in the last dozen years on the part of any department of government to bring labor unions under the provisions of the Anti-trust Laws. Labor stands aghast and horrified at this bold attempt."[2]

But a much more disturbing aspect of Arnold's campaign against

---

[1]See U. S. Temporary Economic Committee, *Final Reports of the Executive Secretary* (Washington: Government Printing Office, 1941), p. 26.
[2]*Labor Relations Reference Manual*, Vol. B, p. 1148

trade unions was his move to limit their liberty of action. General surprise became fear as organized labor watched with dismay the destruction of free, independent unions in Europe. If the problem facing Thurman Arnold was one of curing minor ailments which were due to labor's growing pains and long years of corruption by business interests, his obvious remedies were apparently designed to destroy the rights of organized labor. This threat was the most serious one, in view of the fact that Congress was considering bills that aimed at impairing the democratic rights of association and collective action.

With this new approach to political and economic issues, the Assistant Attorney General and his fellow-lawyers of the Anti-trust Division set out to cure trade unions. He secured anti-trust indictments against hundreds of union leaders, starting with the International Brotherhood of Teamsters, International Longshoremen's Association, International Association of Marble, Stonecutters, Painters, Decorators, Paperhangers, Plasterers and Cement Finishers, Wine, Liquor and Distillery Workers Union, the Typographical Union, embracing no less than fifteen trades. Greater frankness, or even a better sense of humor, would have required Arnold to pursue his crusade with a touching quality of faith in the "new way of life." Instead, he used the familiar Machiavellian tactics of intimidation, cajoling labor leaders to enter consent decrees or plead guilty. The weak and the discouraged chose to make a clean escape because they could not bear up under the load.

Hutcheson refused to yield to these blandishments that were "literally spread in his path at luncheons that the Justice Department arranged for him and his chief attorney, Charles H. Tuttle, in Washington." At one of these luncheons in the summer of 1939, which was his last, Hutcheson sat calmly before eager Arnold. For two hours he answered questions in a staid tone of voice, always brutally frank. Trust buster Arnold gave him occasion to beat a retreat and declare *nolo contendere,* not to make a defense. But Hutcheson denounced him and the administration with such vigor and violence that the questioner seemed like an insulted buffoon.[3]

For his part, Hutcheson shrewdly gauged the extent and importance of Arnold's assault. Thinking of the effect of his action on labor as a whole, Hutcheson warned that:

> ". . . He, Mr. Arnold is endeavoring to bring about a condition so that he might act as a referee or arbiter in any dispute which arose. What the representatives of this administration were trying to do is to place labor organizations directly under their direction, so that they might tell us what we could do and when we could do it."[4]

3Interview with Charles H. Tuttle on March 3, 1954.
4U.B.C.J.A., Proceedings (1940), p. 234.

Came September 1939, Hutcheson was haled into Federal Court. This was hardly an invitation to tears for the hard-headed leader of the United Brotherhood of Carpenters and Joiners of America.

The application of the criminal sections of the Sherman Anti-trust Act against trade unions was a blow which moved Hutcheson, on the recoil, to rise against Thurman Arnold and the administration when President Roosevelt was renominated for a third term. The court assault on the Brotherhood and its officers demonstrated to Hutcheson the extent to which a State, and in this instance a supposedly friendly State, can go to intervene in union activities and practices. The assertion by a government official that the Sherman Anti-trust Act of 1890 applied to labor union activities and defenses in 1939 was considered by Hutcheson an *ukase* which must make itself felt throughout the entire labor movement.

Seven Grand Jury indictments were handed down against Hutcheson and the Brotherhood for restraint of trade under the Sherman Act. Each indictment attacked a different "unfair" practice, which the Assistant Attorney General thought in violation of the "American system of free enterprise." One group of indictments was directed against the boycott, or secondary boycott because it restrained trade by "building a tariff wall around a locality." Indictments lodged against Hutcheson and the Brotherhood in Pittsburgh on February 23, 1940, named eighteen national officers, inclusive of the Lumber Institute of Allegheny County, and the Master Builders' Association. The indictment alleged, among other things, interference by members of the Brotherhood with the shipment into Allegheny County of stock millwork made outside of Allegheny County. It also alleged that the Brotherhood denied permission to millwork manufacturers to use the label because they had labor agreements with the International Woodworkers of America, a labor union affiliated with the C.I.O.; and the making of agreements by the Brotherhood with independent contractors, which in part provided that all millwork should bear the label of the United Brotherhood of Carpenters and Joiners of America.[5]

The Chicago indictment returned February 1, 1940 charged the Brotherhood and its officers with violation of the Sherman Anti-trust Act. The indictment alleged that the defendant called strikes to "assist in the carrying out of an alleged conspiracy to interfere with a shipment of cut stone from outside of Chicago into the City of Chicago." Another indictment returned against the Brotherhood on that day alleged that the defendants entered into a conspiracy to prevent the Harbor Plywood Corporation from selling Douglas Fir Plywood in the State of Washing-

---

[5]*Ibid*, p. 48.

ton for shipment into other states of the United States for the "purpose of destroying Local 2521 of the International Woodworkers of America"; and it further alleged that Hutcheson called strikes of employes of purchasers and users of the products manufactured for the Harbor Plywood Corporation in order to carry out the alleged conspiracy.[6]

The San Francisco indictment alleged that the Bay Counties District Council and Local Unions 42, 550, 1956, 262, "have control of the supply of workmen available for the installation of millwork and patterned lumber in the San Francisco area, and that they have engaged in a conspiracy to exclude millwork and patterned lumber manufactured out of the San Francisco Bay area and shipped into that area."[7]

Of the seven indictments that encircled Hutcheson, none expressed Arnold's reliance upon "legal realism," more than the St. Louis indictment Number 21231. Arnold was determined to stand or fall on this indictment against Hutcheson and the Carpenters. The indictment also included three officers of the Carpenters District Council of St. Louis. They were charged with criminal conspiracy to restrain interstate commerce. In addition to this, the indictment charged that the defendants by their boycott appeal in the Brotherhood's official monthly, *The Carpenter*, "to refrain from the purchasing or using the products of the Anheuser-Busch Company," intended to keep the Anheuser-Busch beer from moving out of Missouri; that the boycott of the Borsari Tank Corporation kept it from shipping material into Missouri; and that the acts of the defendants were calculated to cut off manufacture and consequent shipping of beer and other products in interstate commerce."[8]

In the summer of 1939 the United Brotherhood of Carpenters and Joiners of America and the International Association of Machinists had been engaged in an old-fashioned jurisdictional dispute over which of the two should erect and dismantle machinery at the Anheuser-Busch plant in St. Louis. Both unions had separate collective bargaining agreements with the same employer for the work of its respective craft, but their crafts were overlapping and were not clearly defined. Both labor organizations were affiliated with the American Federation of Labor. At that time the brewing company planned an expansion of facilities. The Borsari Tank Corporation which was engaged to do the job assigned the work to the members of the International Association of Machinists. The brewing company rejected the Carpenters' claims and offered to arbitrate the dispute in accordance with the arbitration provision of its collective bargaining agreement. The Carpenters refused

---

[6]*Ibid*, p. 49.

[7]*Ibid*, p. 50.

[8]*The Carpenter* Vol. LIX: 8 (August, 1939), p. 1.

and declared a strike. The Gaylord Container Corporation, a tenant of Anheuser-Busch in St. Louis, also was engaged in construction work and its contractor was L. O. Stocker Company. The Carpenters refused to work for the contractor as well as the Borsari Tank Corporation, and picketed the Gaylord as well as the Anheuser-Busch Company. The defendants pleaded not guilty, asking for a dismissal of the indictment on the ground that the facts alleged in the indictment were insufficient, as a matter of law, to hold them criminally liable.

Judge Charles B. Davis of the Federal District Court for the Eastern District of Missouri at St. Louis handed down his decision on March 29, 1940. The court concluded that the indictment did not set forth a crime. It sustained the defendants' demurrers. The case was dismissed. Thereupon the Department of Justice appealed this judgment and took the case directly up to the Supreme Court of the United States.

Whatever the Department's specific and immediate aims, the appeal raised legal issues of paramount and far-reaching importance to the organized wage earners of America. The problem facing the Supreme Court was whether or not the activities and defenses of labor organizations came under the Sherman Anti-trust Act. If they did, the Justice Department could proceed with the rest of its case load, assured of a high percentage of victories. If they did not, the rest of the cases would have to be abandoned. More important perhaps, if labor unions did come within the scope of the Sherman Anti-trust Act, the Government would have the right to regulate the practices of labor unions as well as those of the employers, although the courts have in the past been for all "practical purposes, the agents of Big Business."

The quarrel between William L. Hutcheson and the Assistant Attorney General became a battle of Goliath and Goliath. Arnold had already taken advantage of his official position by "advising" nine union leaders to declare *nolo contendere*. Six unions had been compelled to pay approximately $130,000 in fines. This was but a small fraction of the total expense to them. Since Arnold's incumbency, thirty-eight indicted unions had spent well over $2,000,000 to resist the Anti-trust Division.

Hutcheson prepared for such eventualities. For two years, seven Anti-trust indictments cast a heavy shadow over the Brotherhood with the ever present threat of triple damages, which would have wrecked the financial structure of the union. He hired a battery of lawyers headed by the above mentioned Charles H. Tuttle, a former Federal District Attorney of New York. He assessed the membership fifty cents each per month for a period lasting six months. But he also paid back the Assistant Attorney General in his own coin. Arnold delivered an address at a dinner of the New York County Bar Association, and in

bold language pointed out the bottlenecks in business and the "bottle-
necks of business in labor." He even had much sport with "Big Bill"
Hutcheson, who stood exposed as a traitor to the basic doctrines of
American capitalism.

"What is wrong? Labor Analyzes Management's Immediate Duties,"
was the subject Hutcheson discussed over the National Broadcasting
Company, on April 23, 1940:

> "It is my purpose tonight to bring a charge against the executives of Ameri-
> can industry.It is a charge that I make, dispassionately, and in the spirit of
> helpfulness. And it is a charge that is written large in the hearts of millions of
> workers, who stalk unemployed through the streets of the United States.
>
> "Long before that (1900) labor had been working and planning to improve
> the lot and prospects of the average workers. Labor was striving for better con-
> ditions of employment, for a saving wage, for shorter hours, and for the general
> recognition of collective bargaining.
>
> "Management, too, had a goal that it was seeking. It was thinking in terms
> of more efficient production through new tools that were being placed in
> its hands. . . .
>
> ". . . In the past decade . . . labor has seen the establishment of reasonable
> standards of hours and wages on government contracts. It has been courted and
> comforted by those in power. . . . In spite of all this, labor has held fast to its
> independence. For it has known that what government gives, government can
> take away. . . . Today labor is openly challenging the theory that government
> can cure America's industrial ills.
>
> "Where government has failed, labor and industry can succeed, today, just as
> they did in the past, in spite of every handicap that government may place in
> the way.
>
> "The first responsibility of labor and management is to remove the handicaps
> under which they are laboring. After all, the basis of the American Government
> is that government is the servant and not the master of the citizen . . ."

At last, the time for the decisive legal battle had arrived. The case
of United States v. Hutcheson was argued before the high court on
December 10, 1940.

The Government contended: (1) That the object of the defendants
was not the protection and advancement of the rights of labor; no question of collective bargaining, wages, working conditions was involved,
and the defendants' acts were merely an attempt to win by force a jurisdictional dispute with another union. (2) This was not a local dispute
between employer and employee but a jurisdictional struggle between
national unions, resulting in various strikes in many different places,
imposing a direct and unreasonable burden upon interstate trade. (3)
The defendants had tried to stop interstate commerce of four companies,
with only one of which they had relations and against none of which they
had a real grievance. (4) They had attempted to make Anheuser-Busch
their partisan in their dispute with the Machinists or otherwise drive
that company from the interstate market. (5) There had been direct

physical restraint in interstate commerce on the goods of Anheuser-Busch and the Gaylord Container Corporation by the interference with delivery of materials for both the construction companies and Anheuser-Busch, and the defendants had *intended* to restrain interstate commerce. (6) The conduct of the defendants' interference with competition in every direction therefore came within the prohibitions of the Sherman Act. (7) The present case was distinguished from the Apex case and other cases in which the Court had held that the Sherman Law was not applicable to unions because in those cases there was an actual industrial dispute between unions and employers. But in this case the defendants had no real dispute with the employers, and nevertheless were trying to drive from the market an employer against whom the unions had no real grievance. Such exclusion from the market was in restraint of trade under both the common law and the Sherman Act. (8) The action of the defendants could not be justified under the rule of reason since jurisdictional strikes directed against an employer were essentially unreasonable because the employer was powerless and had no control or means of settling such strikes. (9) The Norris-LaGuardia Act was not applicable to this indictment. That Act merely limited the equity powers of the federal courts in the issuance of injunctions, but it did not change the rules of civil or criminal law. If the defendants as a matter of law, had committed a crime, the Norris-LaGuardia Act did not extend them protection.

The attorneys for Hutcheson argued: (a) That the Norris-LaGuardia Act did not differentiate between strikes conducted for jurisdictional reasons and other strikes. (b) The Apex case held that strike activities could not be prosecuted under the Sherman Act, and that unions under the Norris-LaGuardia Act were given immunity for their lawful strike activities; that holding was applicable to the case at bar. (c) Even assuming that the Sherman Act which was designed to curb business monopolistic practices was also applicable to industrial disputes involving suppression of competition, nevertheless it was not applicable to the case at bar. In this case the competition, if any, was among the *labor unions themselves* not involving any *business* monopolistic practices. A jurisdictional labor dispute could not be termed a "crime" under the Sherman Act. (d) The indictment was contrary to the immunity given to labor in Section 20 of the Clayton Act and the Norris-LaGuardia Act. The Government's contention that the Norris-LaGuardia Act was merely a regulation of equity procedure in federal courts was erroneous. On the contrary, the Act was a declaration of policy concerning the right of labor to strike, which right must be held to be a normal and legitimate act of labor unions. Since the indictment sought to make the strike criminal, it was in violation of the specific rights granted by Section 20 of the Clayton Act and by the Norris-LaGuardia Act. (e) The indictment did not cite any facts which would show that the defendants were engaged in a secondary boycott.

There was nothing illegal in asking people not to patronize Anheuser-Busch Beer; nor was the Carpenters' refusal to work a crime, since the Carpenters were not morally or legally bound to submit to the employer's choice giving the Machinists the exclusive right to do the disrupted work.

In the background of these legal disputations spread the panorama of the American labor movement in its utter harshness. It unfolded with Attorney General Richard Olney who issued a "blanket injunction" against Debs and the American Railway Union officials on July 1, 1894. Olney, emphasized anew the doctrine of criminal conspiracy, but supplemented these theories with the assertion that the Sherman Anti-trust Act applied to labor activities. The first section of that statute declared, "Every contract combination in the form of a trust or otherwise, or conspiracy in restraint of trade or commerce among several states, or with foreign nations, is hereby to be declared illegal." Forty-five years later, Hutcheson faced a similar threat of imprisonment and triple damages. Although Congress had never intended to proscribe labor union activity by an Act designed to curb trusts and monopolies, Grover Cleveland's Attorney General, like Roosevelt's Assistant Attorney General, utilized the Sherman Anti-trust Act for that purpose.

For twenty years the standard bearers of labor looked wistfully over the water to Great Britain, where courts rarely hampered activities with injunctions and where Parliamentary legislation specifically rejected the doctrine of criminal conspiracy as applied to combinations of employees and authorized peaceful picketing and exempted the agents and members of unions from suits for unlawful acts claimed to have been committed in behalf of the union.

Without similar protection American organized wage earners were vulnerable. Between 1902 and 1907 three cases brought American labor leaders to the verge of panic. The first was the Danbury Hatters case. A hat manufacturer of Danbury, Connecticut brought suit against 197 members of the United Hatters of North America. Alleging that the nation-wide boycott waged by the union against his hats was a conspiracy restraining interstate commerce, the latter sought criminal damages — $240,000 — under the Sherman Anti-trust Act. The defendants, many of whom never heard of the boycott, had their homes and savings accounts attached solely because they were union members. When the damages were eventually sustained by the Supreme Court, the Hatters Union and the American Federation of Labor raised the money and restored the houses but not the bank accounts to the unfortunate union members.

Most notable was the anti-boycott case involving the Buck Stove and Range Company of St. Louis. As if by design, it was revived by Arnold in an identical setting in September of 1939. The owner, J. W. Van Cleve secured an injunction (1906) against the officers of the American Federation of Labor because the *American Federationist,* the organization's organ, published the company's name on its "We Don't Patronize" list and thus furthered a boycott against Buck's Stove and Range Company products. When Samuel Gompers and two other officials ignored the injunction, they were sentenced to one year in jail or fines, from which they escaped only on technicalities. Finally in the Hitchman v. Mitchell case, involving the attempt of the United Mine Workers to organize West Virginia coal fields, a district court declared that union activities were in the "interest or betterment of mine labor in the state" but were a "far-reaching, unreasonable conspiracy in restraint of trade" and a "direct violation of the Sherman Anti-trust Act."

Labor's appeal for legal redress fell on deaf ears until 1914 when Congress passed the Clayton Anti-trust Act. It dealt not only with business but with the status of unionism. One article asserted, "the labor of a human being is not a commodity or an article of commerce," and hence declared that nothing in the Anti-trust Law shall be construed to "forbid or restrain individual members from lawfully carrying out the legitimate objects" of labor organization. Another section forbade the issuance of injunctions in disputes between employers and employees "unless necessary to prevent irreparable injury to property or to a property right" and then specifically forbade their issue to prohibit the quitting of work, a refusal to patronize, paying strike benefits, peaceable assembly, and peacefully persuading others to quit work or cease patronizing. Gompers hailed this enactment as "labor's Magna Charta." Cooler voices pointed out that several "weasel words" — for instance, "lawfully" and "legitimate object" — had been inserted into its provisions and that the statute might be interpreted as simply declaratory of already existing law.

The history of the Clayton Anti-trust Act again demonstrated that it was one thing in the United States to pass legislation and another to put it into effect. In every instance the judiciary had to determine whether the legislature had acted within the limits imposed upon it by constitutions.

It was not until 1920 that the Clayton Act was reduced to the proportions of a farce. Labor's "Magna Charta" vanished as a result of the decisions of the Supreme Court in the *Duplex* and *Bedford* cases. The Supreme Court, in substance, used a higher law of its own making by which to read into an act of Congress an intent which was exactly opposite to the announced purposes of the men who passed the statute.

With the growth of pro-union sentiment among large masses of the public, the violation of common decencies by employer groups, especially through the use of "stool pigeons," the use of the "yellow dog contract," and overt violence, Congress enacted the Norris-LaGuardia Act. In this manner Congress counteracted the unfavorable decisions of the Supreme Court. The Norris-LaGuardia Act sought first to prevent abuses in the issuance of injunctions; then, in order to further the process of collective bargaining, a procedure the Act regarded as desirable, it exempted certain forms of labor activity from injunctions and forbade their issue until every effort had been made to settle the dispute through negotiation or governmental mediation. Finally, yellow dog contracts were declared unenforcable in Federal Courts. But the Clayton Act had earlier attempted the regulation of the injunction.

February 3, 1941 was a great day for Hutcheson. The Supreme Court of the United States by a majority opinion dismissed the indictment against Hutcheson and the Brotherhood. Justice Felix Frankfurter delivered the majority opinion.[9] He traced the history of the Anti-trust laws with respect to labor unions and pointed out:

(1) After the Supreme Court had held that the Anti-trust Laws were applicable to labor, the Congress in 1914 enacted the Clayton Act, which included Section 20 extending certain immunities to labor.

(2) After the Supreme Court had held that the immunities contained in Section 20 of the Clayton Act were intended to apply only to controversies between an employer and an employee directly, the Congress in 1932 enacted the Norris-LaGuardia Act.

(3) The Norris-LaGuardia Act finally clarified the public policy of the United States in regard to industrial conflicts and broadened the allowable area of union activity to include all labor and not merely those involving immediate employer-employee relationships to the local strike against a company doing interstate business.

Justice Roberts, with Chief Justice Hughes concurring, dissented.

This momentous decision reversed two decades of legal precedence and "virtually took organized labor entirely out from under the Sherman Act. This in effect repealed that Act as far as labor was concerned on the strength of the Norris-LaGuardia Act. Under it labor "not only received protection against the abuse of the injunction but could no longer be prosecuted as a conspiracy under the Sherman Act."[10] This decision stands at the time of this writing as the definitive decision on labor and the Sherman Anti-trust Act.

---

[9]United States vs. Hutcheson, 312 U. S. 219 (1941).
[10]Elias Lieberman, *Unions Before the Bar* (Harper Bros., 1950), pp. 241 seq.

The significance and scope of this victory which Hutcheson and the Carpenters had won for organized labor was breathtaking. Hutcheson did not exaggerate when he said on Tuesday, April 23, 1944:

"This was a signal victory. It was and has been the first case and forerunner of all decisions affecting labor, on the right to Picket, the right to Boycott, the right to circulate statements, the right to assume and maintain jurisdiction, the right to persuade other trades to quit with us, the right to call strikes on other jobs and the right to enforce our laws as made by the membership of the Brotherhood."[11]

Thus by upholding the broader "self-help" trade union practices, the Supreme Court held to be legal the secondary consumption boycott which was practiced by the United Brotherhood of Carpenters and Joiners to win their jurisdictional struggle with the machinists. The Court also "acknowledged that rival union factions are free to fight out the inter-union dispute — a struggle between conflicting economic issues and ideologies — with channels of interstate commerce as their battleground." In making this decision, Justice Frankfurter limited the immunities under Section 20 of the Clayton Act to, "so long as a union acts in its self-interest and does not combine with non-union groups, the licit and illicit under Section 20 are not to be distinguished by any judgment regarding the wisdom or unwisdom, the rightness or wrongness . . . of the end of which the particular union activities are the means."[12]

Charles H. Tuttle, the Carpenter's chief counsel who was well informed on the situation added this tribute on Thursday, April 25, 1946:

"Suppose your General President had felt that rather than run the risk of jail and heavy personal fines, he [Hutcheson] would make peace with the Government, represented by the Anti-Trust Division and would have accepted a consent decree, just as other Unions did. He would have sold out the inheritance of organized labor for a mess of pottage and in exchange for his own personal safety. But he took the risk, and the decision which is now known as the United States versus Hutcheson has been very vital to those who boast of the freedom of organized labor. And I venture to believe that as long as our country stands free and progressive and relies on the power and strength that free men by virtue of their freedom give to the building up of the greatest nation on earth, that decision will continue to be over the archway of the approach to freedom."[13]

---

[11]*U.B.C.J.A. Proceedings* (1944), pp. 181-182.
[12]Charles O. Gregory, *Labor and the Law,* (W. W. Norton and Co., 1946), pp. 277-278.
[13]U.B.C.J.A., *Proceedings* (1946), pp.5-6.

PART | V

MYTH or REALITY

CHAPTER | XVII

THE IMAGE OF AMERICA

America's "Middletown" as depicted by the Lynds in the late 'thirties consisted of businessmen who were whistling in the dark and feigning optimism, but were frightened by the downward economic trend. By the end of the decade (1940) Americans still had faith in the reality of the ballot and their ability to elect a President and Congress of their choice. Popular books on the alleged power of "America's Sixty Families" and similar themes of predatory businessmen interested many thousands of readers but seemingly converted few outside the Left to any sense of urgency in combating the "robber barons." Hard times did deflate the prestige of businessmen who offered no abiding principles to cope with the perplexities of the time, and put the reins of national leadership in the hands of reformers. As a result, American economic individualism yielded to more collectivist tendencies and the philosophy of social security replaced the adventurous competitive spirit of nineteenth century America. Before World War II ended, the prestige of the businessman revived. His extraordinary record of production became the envy of the world. And American labor, despite the heat of conflict engendered by its bid for power, did not actually lose confidence in the creative powers of capitalism, nor in the unique abilities of the industrialist. To millions of people still in the throes of the Depresssion, nothing seemed so urgent as survival in a world of unemployment, insecurity and economic collapse. While they stood unnerved by the dismaying sequence of events abroad, as the "master race" appeared to be overrunning western civilization, Americans seemed lethargic in attitude. To be sure, "The Irresponsibles" were few, and those who promoted the "Wave of the Future," the notion that somehow social developments are inevitable and that the insistence upon ideals is fruitless and antiquated elicited a widespread protest even among people who were noted for their skeptical outlook of democratic values.

The American labor movement and its leaders who were bitterly opposed to Fascism and Nazism, saw unions crushed in dictator countries, labor leaders imprisoned or exiled, democratic rights suppressed, and civilian living standards lowered as an ever-growing proportion of the national income in Fascist countries was siphoned off to the military establishment. Labor watched anxiously as Hitler marched to Austria in March, 1938, and occupied the Czech Sudetenland in the Munich settlement in the fall of that year. The next spring he brazenly occupied the rest of Czechoslovakia, and Mussolini invaded Albania. The A. F. of L. and the C.I.O. alike gave both sympathy and money to save European labor leaders from sure death. On August 23, 1939, a stunned world heard that the German Nazis and the Russian Communists, supposedly deadly enemies, had reached an agreement. The Nazi-Soviet Non-Aggression Pact gave Hitler assurance that the Red army would be benevolently neutral in the fighting about to begin, permitting Nazis to crush Poland and then wage a one-front war against the democracies of Western Europe. A week after the pact was signed the German armies crashed across the Polish border, and the frightened and bewildered peoples of the earth faced the beginning of the Second World War.

When France collapsed in the Spring of 1940, the United States was beginning to step up its defense production very sharply. On the desperate need of the country to arm itself almost everyone could unite. Within a few weeks thereafter, Roosevelt was offering guns and fifty over-age destroyers in exchange for leases of some naval and air bases in the Atlantic. Quickly fitted with new British submarine detectors, they helped keep the crucial convoy lines open until Britain's new destroyers could be launched from her shipyards. By the early autumn of 1940, the American draft law was going into operation. Yet in that very season the two Presidential candidates — Roosevelt, breaking precedent by running for a third term, and Wendell Willkie, the last-minute choice of the Republicans — though they agreed upon aid to Europe, were both insisting that they oppose taking the United States into war. The orators of the "Fight to Defend America by Aiding the Allies," were vehemently opposed by the equally positive orators of the "America First Committee." During the following year, as Hitler desolated British cities with bombs, overran the Balkans, and invaded Russia, and as the Japanese began to threaten the subjugation of the Far East, opinion swung toward more and more direct intervention; the Lend-Lease Act went through Congress with a strong majority, American warships began convoying American supplies part way to England, and the United States changed the whole current of the war. Yet as the month of December 1941, arrived, the country was still sharply divided emotionally.

The reaction of American labor groups to the European fighting varied with their political orientation. On the whole, labor sympathized with the Western democracies in their struggle against the Nazis, at the same time insisting that the United States stay out of the war. Many in labor's ranks emphasized the dangers of reduced living standards and loss of freedom at home should America become involved in the shooting war. Shortly after the fighting began, William Green expressed the prevailing sentiment of the A.F. of L. in favor of avoiding entanglements in the war. In his opening address to the A.F. of L. convention in October, 1939, he opposed entry into the war, arguing that this would bring regimentation at home and wipe out many of labor's gains overnight. He suggested, instead, that the United States might serve as mediator in the conflict.

John L. Lewis took a very similar position, stressing in his report to the C.I.O. convention, the loss of real wages to which labor was subject during wartime. Lewis told the convention that labor was fundamentally opposed to any participation in the war; our safety and security lay in our non-participation in the conflict and in addressing ourselves to the major task of healing our scars left by the Depression. The collapse of French resistance in June, 1940, when the "phony war" suddenly erupted into a lightning war, carried down with it the comfortable illusion that America was secure from Fascist attack. To the labor movement, conscious of its fate in a Fascist society, the world situation looked bleaker than it did to most other groups. The reaction of labor was particularly important, since the most pressing task of the moment was to manufacture and ship to Britain the arms needed for the defense of that outpost of Democracy in Europe.

The decision to aid Britain and to strengthen America's defenses carried with it many implications for labor on the domestic front. One immediately favorable result would be the creation of jobs that were badly needed by an economy still struggling to emerge from a decade of depression. This quickening of the nation's industrial pulse, however, would not be an unmixed blessing, since along with it, prices would almost certainly rise as shortages of critical materials developed and as government agencies, supplied with authorized defense expenditures of twelve billion dollars, competed with civilians for a limited quantity of goods and services. Unless wages also rose, the living standards of workers would fall; yet if strikes broke out to protect living standards, or to win recognition or other concessions from employers, democracy's power to resist Hitlerism would be weakened. On the other hand, it would be folly to seek to protect democracy abroad by sacrificing essential rights at home. Despite these dangers, the bulk of the non-Communist labor movement favored maximum aid to Britain, short of entering the war ourselves, together with the strengthening of America's military defenses.

The A.F. of L. would do its full part in the national defense program, William Green declared, because it realized that the consequences of the war would not be confined to Europe, and that the "fate of our free labor movement is bound up with the fate of democracy." The C.I.O., while pledging its cooperation in the defense effort, emphasized its desire to keep the United States out of the war, at the same time insisting that labor's rights be preserved and that the labor movement be given adequate representation on agencies concerned with the defense program.

As for the American Communists, they once again illustrated that they were tied hand and foot with the Soviet Foreign Office; they could not permit even sympathy for the opponents of Hitlerism so long as the Nazi-Soviet Pact of 1939 remained in force. In unison they condemned "politicians who are bringing us closer to European war and are advocating conscription." As defense measures, the needs of the people and extensions of social services were given first place. But after the invasion of the Soviet Union in June, 1941, the tune changed. The Communist-dominated unions approved the policy of the Government in declaring that the defense of this country requires all possible aid to be given to Great Britain, China, the Soviet Union and other nations resisting Hitlerism, and urged the Government to put this policy into effect with all possible speed and energy. The only significant change was that now Hitler's legions were racing across Soviet soil. In 1942 Communist-dominated unions offered their advice to the Joint Chiefs of Staff, and urged "immediate opening of a western front so that the war can be brought to a more speedy conclusion." After the war ended, these unions reversed their position, so that it would coincide with that of the Communist Party.

During that time, two months after its formation in October, 1940, the America First Committee sought to stimulate labor opposition to the war. Hutcheson was among the labor leaders who were solicited to "serve as a member of the National Committee."[1] Acting chairman of the Committee was General Robert E. Wood, who supported Roosevelt in 1932 and again in 1936. By 1936 the General's ardor for the New Deal had begun to cool and his vote in that year was cast "doubtfully." In 1940 he supported Wendell Willkie ostensibly in opposition to the third term and the President's foreign policy. The America First Committee, wrote its national director, Mr. Stuart, "consists of conservatives and liberals, Democrats and Republicans, who maintained a non-partisan

---

[1] Wayne F. Cole, The Battle Against Intervention: 1940-1941 (University of Wisconsin Press, 1953), p. 169.

position throughout the political campaign. We devote ourselves to placing the simple facts of the international situation before members of all parties."[2]

On this National Committee was the daughter of John L. Lewis, Kathryn Lewis, who insisted that the union label be on all printed America First literature. Oswald Garrison Villard, a professional pacifist, was a member of the Committee as was Norman Thomas, perennial Socialist candidate for president, who spoke at America First meetings, and Senator Robert M. LaFollette. Jewish labor leader Sidney Herzberg of Chicago did his best to rally labor against intervention. Lewis J. Taber, master of the National Grange, Ray McKaig of the Grange in Idaho, and George N. Peek, former head of the First Agricultural Adjustment Administration, were all on the America First National Committee.[*]

A majority of those with political affiliations on the Executive Committee were Republicans. Hanford MacNider, Vice-Chairman, had been an active Republican. His services to the Republican Party were rewarded with political appointments by both Presidents Coolidge and Hoover. Mrs. Janet A. Fairbank, member of the Executive Committee, had been a member of the Democratic National Committeewomen from 1924 to 1928. She supported Willkie in 1940. Alice Roosevelt Longworth, daughter of Theodore Roosevelt, was a member of the Board of Counsellors of the Republican National Committee. Among other members of the America First National Committee were: William Castle, Mrs. Florence Kahn, Charles Francis Adams, Thomas N. McCather, and Charles Lindbergh.

William Levi Hutcheson took more than a month to appraise Stuart's request, and on December 30 he advised his correspondent:

Dear Mr. Stuart:

I have not as yet taken time to read the address by General Robert E. Wood, but in reference to the contents of your communication, I agree with the thoughts expressed therein, but in view of the fact that all my life I have been very positive in reference to my ideas I would not like to become a member of your Committee and have some statement go out from the Committee, to which I might take exception, and not being in a position to confer with other members of the Committee I hesitate to comply with your request in reference to becoming a member of your Committee.[3]

Very truly yours,
William L. Hutcheson
WLH-JP   General President

---

[2]Hutcheson's Private Papers, October 3, 1940.
[*]By September 1941, Oswald V. Garrison, Kathryn Lewis, Norman Thomas, Robert M. LaFollette and Sidney Herzberg resigned from the Committee.
[3]*William L. Hutcheson Private Correspondence*, December 30, 1940.

Entreaties by General Robert E. Wood, soliciting Hutcheson's "advice and cooperation as to the best way to present our program to Labor," were of no avail. Not until the 24th of September, 1941, did Hutcheson agree to join the National Committee of America First, writing General Wood as follows:

Dear General:

This will acknowledge yours of September 22nd, in reference to the accomplishments obtained and the efforts put forth by the America First Committee.

In regards to your request that I serve on the National Committee, will say I have no objections to rendering my support and assistance to help maintain and continue the principles of government as set forth in the Constitution of the United States and enunciated in the Declaration of Independence.

I'm sure you realize in looking after the affairs of our organization that there are numerous demands that require a lot of time. Therefore, anything I might do to assist the Committee in act or time would be rather limited. However, if under those circumstances, you think I could be helpful I would be glad to join you, and others, to help carry on, so that we, the people of this country, may maintain our rights and liberties as heretofore enjoyed.

Very truly yours,
William L. Hutcheson
General President

WLH-JP

He turned down Raimund S. Wurlitzer's request to address an America First mass meeting in San Francisco, on October 15, 1941.[4]

Then, on December 7, 1941, events moved, ending all of Hutcheson's doubts and emotional misgivings. The die was cast. The attack on Pearl Harbor was a challenge to the United States that had to be met. Hutcheson reacted quickly and decisively to the Pearl Harbor attack and lost no time to declare himself to the President on the 8th of December:

Hon. Franklin D. Roosevelt,
President United States,
White House,
Washington, D. C.

My dear Mr. President:

Heretofore, I have opposed sending an expeditionary force overseas. Now that our country has been attacked, it is the duty of every American to help in every way he can to supply and produce the necessary munitions of war so that we can speedily overcome our enemies and show them that we cannot be ruthlessly attacked without retaliating. There should not now be any need for Congress to give consideration to anti-strike legislation as I am sure that members of the various labor organizations, regardless as to their affiliation, will show their patriotism as real Americans by refraining from committing

---

4*Ibid,* Dec. 16, 1941.

any act or taking any action that would in any way handicap or slow up the progress in preparing and manufacturing the necessary munitions of war and to that end I desire to offer for myself and the members of the Brotherhood our cooperation and services in any way that they may be needed.

Respectfully submitted,

William L. Hutcheson

As for the America First Committee, it decided to dissolve itself on January 13, 1943.

American labor responded quickly to the attack on Pearl Harbor. At the special meeting of the A. F. of L. Executive Council, on December 15, the A. F. of L. at once pledged, on behalf of its five million members, a "no-strike policy" in all war and defense production industries. The C.I.O., similarly pledging all its resources to the nation's struggle against the Axis called for the enlisting of labor's "brains" to insure maximum production and the defeat of coercive and punitive labor measures such as the Smith "Slave Labor" Bill.

Almost subconsciously, Hutcheson rose to advocate the revival of the National War Labor Board, with the creation of which he had been conspicuously identified during World War I. Pointing to its successful functioning during the previous war, Hutcheson had urged the Executive Council of the Federation, back on February 11, 1941 to make this labor adjustment machinery part of its "declaration, so that we could clarify the situation by stating that so long as established union conditions are recognized, we as a labor group will recommend to our members that there be no strikes called on defense projects."[5]

The Board proved aggressive enough to force its solutions, usually impartial ones, upon labor and capital, Hutcheson declared. "If that could be made the policy of the Board which could be set up similar to the old War Labor Board without enactment of legislation, the Board would be fair in most instances."[6]

At that meeting the Council threw its support to the Hutcheson idea. "The history of the last war proves the effectiveness of this method. Industrial unrest was practically abolished and both the employer and labor cooperated with the Government in its production and war program. There is no reason for adopting any different method with respect to the present defense program. In such a program, the Government would have the whole-hearted support of the A.F. of L. and its affiliated organizations." At the same time, Hutcheson cautioned the members of

---

[5]Hutcheson's Private Papers based on the *Minutes of the Executive Council of the A. F. of L.*, February 10-20, 1941.
[6]*Ibid.*

the Executive Council against anaesthetizing labor into an unquestioned acceptance of the status quo idea. "We must endeavor to lay before the public that the pledge (no strike) was given with the thought in mind that so long as our established conditions are recognized we would not strike." Hutcheson was frank to admit that "understanding of our action does not seem to be known to the public. They think that no matter what is done we should not strike."[7]

The need for reviving the National War Labor Board, which Hutcheson advanced since February 11, 1941, was not recognized by President Roosevelt, although he had good knowledge of its first World War namesake. It took more than a year of trial and error, duplication and industrial strife in strategic defense industries to confirm the soundness of the Carpenters' General President's approach to the settlement of labor disputes. The issue of union security, for which Hutcheson argued, was another. This emotion-laden issue of union security stood out as the core of labor-management relations, though it did not comprise the whole story of industrial relations in that period. Instead, the President established in March of 1941 the National Defense Mediation Board.

The National Defense Mediation Board was, in fact, designed to supplement the already existing United States Conciliation Service, which was headed by Dr. John R. Steelman. The latter aided the parties in working out peaceful settlements of their collective bargaining problems, and thereby avoided or settled strikes. Except to perform these limited functions, the government remained largely aloof from the field of industrial relations. This government policy, satisfactory during normal times, proved inadequate during the crisis, when uninterrupted production of military equipment was essential. The National Defense Mediation Board had been handicapped by a lack of agreed-upon principles as a basis of its work, although such principles might have been established had the opportunity for an early representative conference been grasped. After Pearl Harbor, the President called a conference of industrialists and labor leaders from the NAM, the United States Chamber of Commerce, the A. F. of L. and the C.I.O.

The labor-management conference which met on December 17 had shown how vital the protection and extension of union security was to the nation's schooled labor leaders. It was certainly the most explosive problem with which employers, unions and government had to grapple. Then, as now, the disagreements and differences over the question were basic and fundamental, and the matter of freedom of individuals to work where they were qualified and acceptable to the employer was intertwined in the argument. All agreed readily on a no-strike, no-lockout

---

[7]Hutcheson's Private Papers based on the *Minutes of the Executive Council of the A. F. of L.,* January 17-27, 1944.

policy for the duration of the war, but they failed to agree on a policy as to union security. Labor was unwilling to freeze the status quo, and employers opposed any extension of the union shop. Instead of insisting upon a resolution of this issue, the President rather abruptly announced that agreement had been reached on policies to avoid interruption of operations.

The Defense Mediation Board began its life under circumstances somewhat less than promising. The President, choosing to establish an eleven-man National Defense Mediation Board by executive order rather than by Congressional action, could not confer upon it greater authority than he himself possessed. Since the country was not then at war, he had only the limited peace time powers of the Presidency at his disposal. The Defense Mediation Board, entering the area of mediation and the reduction of the number of stoppages, actually repeated the work of the Conciliation Service, though the greater prestige of the board members as Presidential appointees and in their own right may have helped them obtain settlements that evaded the Conciliation Service. Nevertheless, the number of workers involved in strikes increased from 2.3 to 8.4 percent in 1941.[8]

This Board, a tripartite organization of equal public, industry and labor membership, was set up to mediate such labor-management disputes and to get them settled without stoppage of production. The late Clarence A. Dykstra, then President of the University of Wisconsin was the first chairman of the Board. Cyrus S. Ching was a member of the employers' team which included Roger D. Lapham, chairman of the Board of the American-Hawaiian Steamship Company; Eugene Meyer, publisher of the Washington Post; and Walter C. Teagle, Chairman of the Board of Standard Oil Company of New Jersey. Labor was represented by George M. Harrison, President of the Brotherhood of Railway and Steamship Clerks; Thomas Kennedy, Secretary-Treasurer of the United Mine Workers; George Meany, Secretary-Treasurer of the A. F. of L.; and the late Philip Murray, President of the Congress of Industrial Organizations. Besides Dr. Dykstra, the public members were William H. Davis, prominent New Deal attorney; Frank T. Graham, President of North Carolina University and Charles E. Wyzansky Jr., attorney and a Federal judge in Massachusetts.

The Board represented a reasonable approach to the settlement of labor disputes during its less than nine-month span of existence, despite the difficulties under which it operated. Astonishingly enough, the Board's decisions were not binding on the parties to the dispute. Its functions were not clearly defined. It also gave both labor and manage-

[8]U. S. Bureau of Labor Statistics, Chart Series III, No. 1, (March, 1941) p. 37.

ment veto power at any time, and a resignation by either party would render the Board ineffective.

The Board was useful but not long-lived. Its downfall was caused by a "principle," which John L. Lewis defended, interchanging roles with Hutcheson whose performance in World War I had enhanced labor's status. Union security was the issue which proved the Mediation Board's undoing. John L. Lewis, whose Mine Workers were then part of the C.I.O., wanted the union shop—under which an employee has to join the union, usually within thirty to sixty days of his employment—extended to the so-called "captive" mines owned by the steel companies. The Board held many meetings on this case and a majority voted against the union shop in "captive" mines.

It was at this time that President Roosevelt declared himself against the union shop. The C.I.O. members promptly resigned from the Board and left it inoperative insofar as C.I.O. disputes were concerned. It continued to function for a time, but, being unable to handle C.I.O. cases, it could not be very effective and ultimately went out of business. Mr. Lewis, however, subsequently got the union shop in the "captive" mines by a two-to-one vote of an arbitration panel appointed by Roosevelt and composed of John R. Steelman, on leave as Director of the U. S. Conciliation Service; John L. Lewis and Benjamin Fairless of U. S. Steel. The decision, incidentally, was released for publication on the Sunday of the attack of Pearl Harbor.

When the Board ceased to function, there was an immediate clamor in Congress for some kind of restrictive legislation, a development which Hutcheson anticipated in his declaration to President Roosevelt on December 8, 1941. Failure on the part of the Administration to prepare adequately and wisely appropriate machinery for the settlement of industrial disputes in the war and postwar periods, doubtless played their part in developing the complicated situation out of which came the new labor legislation of 1947.[9]

Finally, on January 12, 1942, President Roosevelt issued an Executive Order creating the National War Labor Board of twelve members, four of them to represent employers, four labor, and four the public. Unlike the Defense Mediation Board, however, the role of which was that of a mediator, the War Labor Board was a tribunal for arbitration of all disputes, both sides agreeing to be bound by its decisions.

As Chairman, the President named William H. Davis, who likewise headed the old National Defense Mediation Board, the case load of which was now transferred to the new agency. The National War Labor Board bore the stamp of Hutcheson's thinking on labor relations since World

9Harry A. Millis and Emily C. Brown, *From the Wagner Act to Taft-Hartley,* (Chicago University Press, 1950), p. 296.

War I. Of the fifteen members on the Executive Council of the Federation, the Carpenters' President was best equipped to spearhead the idea. Although, he was appointed to serve on a panel of twenty of the administration of the War Labor Board, Hutcheson was far from enthusiastic. The National War Labor Board of 1918 differed from the W.L.B. of World War II, in that the former started its career with a set of principles formulated in advance rather than having its principles evolve, as was the case in the later war, from case decisions. One of the "principles" formulated in 1918 was that all workers were entitled to a "living wage." Despite some serious clashes of interest and opinion within the Board, it held together with its management, labor, and public membership and was able to carry on its important public service all through the war years.

The union security question was ever present in the Board's deliberations during the early part of its existence. In searching for a solution to the problem, the Board finally evolved the principle of maintenance of union membership and adopted it over the strenuous and continuing dissent of its industry members. This was the wartime compromise on the union security question. Maintenance of membership was almost automatically granted by the W.L.B. in any case where the union demonstrated that it represented a majority of the employees in a plant.

This principle, although far short of the closed or union shop prevalent in the building trades, was a wartime compromise on the part of Hutcheson, as well as of labor in general. It preserved an uneasy peace on the union security problem during the war and saved the War Labor Board from the fate which had befallen the War Mediation Board. Hutcheson, as well as all representatives of labor, threw all their weight and influence into the effort to prevent crippling defense strikes, and only in coal was there an industry-wide shut-down by an international union.

What happened to the national standard of living when the federal government poured into the national economy war orders by the billions, and then by the tens of billions and then by the scores of billions? Roaring prosperity.

During the 1930's the New Deal had been conscientiously trying to "prime the pump" by government expenditures of a few billions a year; what they had done with a teaspoon was now being done with a ladle. Who was getting the money?

As from a tomb in the blackout came the voice of Boris Shishkin, the American Federation of Labor's economist, who asserted that net profits of corporations in 1941 had climbed to a total of $7,200,000,000, equalled only in the dying boom year of 1929. He quoted official figures to show that in 1941 over 55 percent of the American families received an annual income under $1,500, the minimum subsistance figure for a family of four. Admitting that wage increases could add to inflationary dangers if not properly handled, the Federation proposed voluntary pay allotment plans throughout industry to divert a billion dollars of labor's buying power to defense bonds, combined with arrangements, where recipients were willing, to pay wage increases in the form of defense stamps and bonds. The Federation's executive council also called for increased social security taxes to finance expanded benefits, higher corporation taxes to prevent profiteering, and rationing of scarce goods at reasonable price levels.

The Executive Council of the Federation returned to their theme in an effort to avert a wage freeze, which would have, it declared, a devastating effect on America's war effort. Pointing to a rise in living costs in the last year of at least 12 percent, as reported by the Bureau of Labor Statistics, the Federation asserted that the rise had been far greater in most war industry towns. The resulting "economic disaster" to war workers was blamed squarely on the failure of the Office of Price Administration (OPA) to enforce price ceilings. The Executive Council argued that there had been no general or substantial wage increases in any basic war industry.

The Federation's assertion that "real wages" were falling were justified, especially with regard to those workers who remained on the same job for the past year. That this was true of a large number of workers could not be denied.

Somewhat sedate but determined was Hutcheson's demand for wage rates stabilization on all construction projects throughout the country. "This problem was made more pressing by the rising cost of living and by the necessity of equalizing wage rates in isolated areas as well as populated areas, in order that an adequate supply of men could be guaranteed to those projects which were located far distant from a natural source of skilled mechanics."

He was obliging and tactful to respond to Madame Perkins' invitation to "work out an understanding whereby machines in war production can be operated on a seven-day basis." Hutcheson had not forgotten the formidable clamor and violent protest which the Secretary of Labor had raised over his appointment to the International Labor Office (I.L.O.) conference held in Santiago in 1936. What she hadn't known was that the Federation had refused in turn to extend its urbanity to her, when she anxiously sought an opportunity to address the 1941 A. F. of L. convention.

Early Saturday morning, on January 17, 1942, Hutcheson hurried from the Willard Hotel to confer with Mrs. Perkins, Under-Secretary of War Patterson, and Assistant Secretary of the Navy Bard. With a few well chosen words, he repeated the voluntary no-strike pledge by labor during the war. Labor volunteered to give such pledge provided a mutually satisfactory agreement could be reached on machinery for settling disputes and the achievement of wage stabilization on all construction work, financed by the government; that the War Labor Board serve as an independent agency, a court comprised of representatives of labor, industry and the public, clothed with authority to render decisions in wage disputes; that production can be operated on a seven day week basis with employees working only six days, with time and a half over six days. In other words, a forty-eight hour week with time and a half over 8 hours daily.[10]

One of the aims of Hutcheson was to arrive at an agreement with Madame Perkins on a program to stabilize wage rates in the construction industry. The simple fact was that contracting agencies, or private contractors on fixed price contracts, in order to secure workers on particular projects, were departing from contract rates or Davis-Bacon* predetermination wage rates to higher levels as the urgency of particular projects dictated. The result could only be uncertainty, labor shortages and unrest in an industry which had traditionally operated in a sector on the basis of a single rate for a locality for each of the approximately fifty classifications. The Carpenters' General President was genuinely concerned over the prospect of getting wages too high that they would have to be sharply reduced later. He had lived through the period of wage reduction after World War I and did not wish to see it repeated. It was already becoming increasingly evident that a wage stabilization program would be required if inflation was to be avoided. Hutcheson, like his confreres, Harry Bates, President of the Bricklayers and John Coyne, President of the Building Trades Department, preferred to have machinery for wage stabilization on which they were represented to be confined to their industry rather than to take chances on a general law. Clearly all conditions specifically characteristic of the construction industry warranted that some orderly procedures be worked out to prevent wage demands from being lost somewhere between the contractors and procurement agencies.

Secretary of Labor Perkins was persuaded and thanked him for guiding her in these matters. Facing Undersecretaries Bard and Patterson,

---

[10]*Hutcheson's Private Papers,* January 12-17, 1942.

*The Davis-Bacon Law, originally enacted in 1931 and as amended in 1935, provides that the Secretary of Labor shall predetermine wage rates of laborers and mechanics in federally financed construction contracts in excess of 2000. These rates are to be determined according to the standard of those "prevailing for corresponding class of laborers and mechanics employed on projects of a character similar to the contract work in the city, village, or other subdivision of the state in which the work is to be performed."

he could not abstain from repeating, that the "Brotherhood prides itself on being one of the first organizations to support the government in these times of emergency." He was a man of principles, he added, and the "Brotherhood will cooperate with government officials, particularly those charged with the responsibilities for and prosecuting the war effort, in the building of army camps, air fields, shipyards, and all other projects requiring the services of our members."

During the week of May 10, President Roosevelt called in Hutcheson and the members of the Executive Board of the Building and Construction Trades Department and expressed similar concern over rising prices and wages. On April 27, the President had presented to the country a seven-point program to curb inflation. He proposed to the building trades the stabilization of wage rates as of May 1, 1942. Hutcheson and his associates objected to this date on the ground that many agreements had not, by that date, been concluded for the next year. They pointed to the fact that the expiration dates of agreements in the industry were concentrated in the first half of the year and proposed July 1, 1942 as a substitute date. Finally, an agreement was consummated on May 22, 1942, when the Wage Adjustment Board was established for the purpose of adjusting any wage rates which proved to be inadequate as of July 1, the date on which this agreement stabilized all building and construction wage rates. The Wage Adjustment Board remained in effect for one year, subject to annual renewal of the agreement for the duration of the war. It operated within a stable and certain political setting. Unlike other industries, there were virtually no strikes seeking to compel the WAB to change a decision. The voluntary origin of the Board lent a private flavor to its operations throughout its existence, and was significant in determining its membership on the union side.

The top union leaders in the industry were not only members of the Board but they were daily active in its meetings. There were no "messenger boys" among the regular members. They all enjoyed authority and prestige and were thus able to act quickly, make compromises and avoid dissents. Among the regular members of the W.A.B. were: Lt. Col. C. D. Barker, War Department; Lt. Commander Charles D. Pennmaker, Navy Department; Morton MacArtney, Defense Plant Corporation; Harry C. Bates, Bricklayers, Masons and Plasterers International Union; Robert Byron, Sheet Metal Workers International Association; John T. Coyne, Building and Construction Trades Department. The alternate members were: Arthur D. Hill, Jr., Acting Assistant Solicitor of Labor; Lt. Col. James T. O'Connoll, War Department; Comd. J. R. Perry, Navy Department; B. H. MacNeal, Defense Plant Corporation; Edward J. Brown, International Brotherhood of Electrical

Workers; John E. Rooney, Operative Plasterers' International Association of the U.S. and Canada. A third alternate Labor Member of the WAB was Maurice A. Hutcheson, who during the brief period of one year, had proved himself to be an expeditious conciliator, tactful, and with a knowledge and grasp of a highly complex industry. Here were no private interests to satisfy, but a goal whose attainment was to prevent labor disputes from interrupting vital military output. In October, 1943, Hutcheson appointed O. William Blaier as the Carpenters' labor member on the WAB, while Maurice Hutcheson became his father's intermediary, performing his tasks with vigor and skill.[11]

*   *   *

William Levi was born a Greenbacker, reared as one. When in his thirties and forties, his sympathies lay with the Progressive movement under Roosevelt, Taft and Wilson. And now at the age of sixty-eight, he pervaded with a spirit of Republicanism and Masonry. But no act of William's could erase completely the impressions of the past. The present and the future are alike, the prisoners of the past. And not once had he wished to return to the imagined utopia of an earlier day. The reluctance of the Republican caucus to forget the identity of Hutcheson made it harder for him to forget it. The rebuke accorded him in 1944 by the GOP when he sought acceptance as Vice-Presidential candidate annoyed the Carpenters' President. At the same time, he held to the faith that the American people can order their affairs with the ideal of freedom and Protestant individualism. It seemed right to him that the system itself was not to blame. William Levi celebrated temporizing and moderate alterations. He never lost confidence in the unique entrepreneurial ability of the American businessman.

Hutcheson was a studious observer of technological developments which he knew would profoundly alter the working and living conditions of the American wage earners. He fiercely disagreed with those who in the 1930's had come to the conclusion that the United States had arrived at a "maturing economy." The *"Future of Television,"* a paper he delivered before the thirty-sixth annual convention of the Building and Construction Trades Department, was in fact a blue-print for the practical application of television to the building industry after the war.[12]

Above all, he was a perfect friend, cheerful, a story teller and fond of sending boxes of oranges and grapefruit as Yuletide gifts to friends of the Brotherhood. His old friend, John L. Lewis was never neglected. They had forgiven each other in 1940 and Hutcheson was soon to serve as an

---

[11]John D. Dunlop and Arthur Hill, *The Wage Adjustment Board,* (Harvard University Press, 1950).

[12]William L. Hutcheson, "The Future of Television," *The Carpenter* vol. LXII: 12 (December, 1942), pp. 8-17.

intermediary between Lewis and the American Federation of Labor.

"This is a splendid yuletide gift and entirely in character with your generous traits," Lewis wrote to "Dear Bill." U. S. Conciliator and Assistant-to-President Truman, Dr. John R. Steelman was a regular recipient of Hutcheson's box of oranges and grapefruit as a Christmas gift, as was the Florida Democratic Governor Spessard Holland.

He took time out vigorously to promote the re-election of Senator Styles Bridges of New Hampshire.[13] Senator Bridges' friendship was useful to Hutcheson as he was Chairman of the powerful Appropriations Committee and a "middle-of-the-road" Republican Presidential contender. At the same time, Hutcheson sponsored New Dealer Leon H. Keyserling for the vacancy of Administrator of the U. S. Housing Authority with the White House, a post, which he landed.

February 24, 1942

My Dear Mr. Hutcheson:

The President has asked me to thank you for your letter of February 20 with reference to filling the existing vacancy of Administrator of the U. S. Housing Authority and urging consideration of the name of Mr. Leon H. Keyserling. He appreciates your letting him have the benefit of your comments on behalf of Mr. Keyserling and you may be assured that what you say will be kept in mind.[14]

Very sincerely yours,
M. H. McIntyre

Dr. Keyserling, New Deal economist and friend of labor, was the major draftsman of the National Labor Relations Act, the Full Employment Act of 1945, and the U.S. Housing Act of 1937.

In political circles Hutcheson had found many precious and powerful friends. He needed them to keep in touch with the political situation and to find his bearings, and to promote the interests of the Carpenters. He was still more firmly established among the leaders of the Federation, having been elected First Vice-President in October of 1939.

In January, 1942, Hutcheson had been cast in the role of a peacemaker. It had fallen to him, who had been made the symbol of intransigence to the idea of industrial unionism, to champion, as gracefully as he could, the reconciliation between the A. F. of L. and the C.I.O., and John L. Lewis. By now, both Lewis and the Carpenters' General President had resolved that there should be an end to their quarrels, and to renew the old pledges and conversation which had been excellent tonics for their minds and health. They both had many tastes in common, thrived on political discussions, hated disputes, and loved a good joke.

---

[13]Hutcheson's Private Papers, Oct. 10, 1942.
[14]Roosevelt Archives, Hyde Park, New York.

They passed long hours together with mutual friends at the Washington Hotel, discussing labor unity, and especially restrictive legislation aimed at labor.

On January 17, both A. F. of L. President William Green and C.I.O. President Philip Murray received an impressive communication from Lewis. Couched in the colorful language of an educated man, Lewis called for a cessation of "rivalry and conflict" in the "public interest." "Heretofore, this has not been possible. Previous conferences between the representatives of both organizations failed to coalesce. Conditions have now changed. America needs unity in every phase of its national economy. I address this letter to each of you in my capacity as a member of the Standing Negotiating Committee of the Congress of Industrial Organizations, acting under authority of its Third Constitutional Convention."

Hutcheson smiled, when Secretary-Treasurer George Meany read Lewis' letter to the members of the Executive Council of the Federation. His mind was already made up. There was nothing ambiguous in Lewis' letter. Hutcheson moved that the "President notify Mr. Lewis that the Committee (Peace) of the A. F. of L. stands ready to meet at any time."[15]

President Philip Murray discouraged any effort to achieve immediate unity, suggested instead collaboration on issues connected with the war, including higher production, political aid to candidates supporting Roosevelt and the war effort, and increased labor representation in government. The A. F. of L., for its part, found this response evasive, and asked that the C.I.O. answer directly and courageously the question as to whether labor should be united.

In mid-summer the attitude of the C.I.O. softened. In a peace bid for which President Roosevelt's influence was widely thought to be responsible, Philip Murray proposed that a discussion looking to organic unity be undertaken and at the same time a joint committee be established to decide jurisdictional disputes. The talk, held on December 2, 1942, at the Willard Hotel, resulted in an agreement to "hear and determine the disputed jurisdictional differences." Both committees agreed to "establish joint action on all issues directed toward and intensified prosecution of the war . . . anti-labor legislation, organizing the unorganized." The signatories to this agreement were William L. Hutcheson, Daniel Tobin, Harry C. Bates for the A. F. of L. and Philip Murray, R. J. Thomas and Julius Emspack for the C.I.O. Even ratification of the jurisdictional agreement remained in doubt until the Executive Council of the Federation took that action in mid-January, for by that time the

---

[15]*Hutcheson's Private Papers,* (January 12-17, 1942).

Federations' temper was aroused by the C.I.O.'s raiding of the Kaiser Shipyards in the West. Furious over this raid, Hutcheson urged an appeal to the President as Commander-in-Chief of all forces, for the C.I.O. and the National Labor Relations Board to "refrain from interfering in the situation existing in the Kaiser Shipyards for the simple reason that there are no C.I.O. members employed in these yards; that if there were the situation would be different."

The forty-one national or international unions chartered by the C.I.O. clashed and overlapped at a variety of jurisdictional points with 122 similar affiliates of the American Federation of Labor. Raids had been suffered by many unions, feelings were bitter, and the problems themselves were not easy of solution. Also, inside C.I.O. leftist union chiefs kept to themselves.

By May 17, 1943, Hutcheson gave up hope of bringing about unification of the labor movement. He had, he said, "come to the conclusion that there is no sincerity among the C.I.O. representatives; that they do not ever intend to come into the Federation for the simple reason that the activities of some of them are what we would call subversive." He made sure not to include Philip Murray, who was a most courageous opponent of Communism. He was convinced that "no matter what would happen, the C.I.O. would never come over as a unit." President Roosevelt's maneuver on May 7, 1943 to bring Philip Murray and Green together by suggesting a short trip to Great Britain, ostensibly to attend the British Trade Union Congress, was politely turned down by the Federation's President. The A. F. of L. sent its representative Daniel J. Tobin of the International Brotherhood of Teamsters instead.

John L. Lewis, frustrated and rebuffed by Murray, who opposed the merger of the two federations, was quick to express his displeasure by blandly asserting that the C.I.O. was indebted to the United Mine Workers to the amount of $1,665,000. During the organizational period of the C.I.O., Lewis asserted, the Miners' Union had extended $7,249,000 in financial aid to the C.I.O.; of this, he said, $1,685,000 had been in the form of a loan, of which only $20,000 had been repaid. Consequently, the Miners requested that their current per capita tax of $60,000 representing two months payment, be deducted from this loan. The Miners' Executive Board, in addition, condemned the C.I.O. actions with regard to the U.M.W. as "sabotage of union principles," and charged Murray with "false, malicious and defamatory matters" against Lewis and the Miners Union. In late May, Lewis declared Phil Murray's vice-presidency in the U.M.W. vacant and the latter promptly moved into the presidency of the United Steel Workers of America.

Immediately, the C.I.O. denounced Lewis as "hell-bent on creating national confusion and national disunity." Other C.I.O. unions joined in the fray. John L. Lewis, his daughter Kathryn and brother Denny, they asserted, "constituted themselves as a dynasty of labor; monopolists over a cartel of workingmen's bodies."

The formal break came in October, 1942, when the U.M.W., following Lewis' leadership, voted to withdraw from the ungrateful, unregenerate offspring, which had been conceived, nurtured, guided and maintained by the miners. And, like the father on the Trobriand Islands, the father of the C.I.O., Lewis was now rejected and unrecognized. As a climactic gesture, he extended the Miners' jurisdiction, formerly confined under the U.M.W. Constitution to the coal and coke industry, to cover "any industries" designated by the union's Executive Board. His union was in the midst of a series of stoppages that inflamed public opinion and embroiled him in bitter controversy with the Roosevelt administration. Perplexed and rejected, Lewis turned to his friend Hutcheson.

Throughout January and May of 1943, Lewis and Hutcheson continued their discussion about the chief sinners who had opposed their "accouplement" which both felt could have been achieved with unified and competent leadership. With the exception of Sidney Hillman and Philip Murray, who were astonished at Lewis' "performance," acting as a committee of one for the reunion with the A. F. of L., everyone was surfeited of the subject. Hutcheson and Lewis gave up the task and let events take their natural course. There is no evidence of the "secret bargain" which Lewis had allegedly made "with 'Big Bill' Hutcheson and others of the A. F. of L. executives, including Tobin, Woll, Meany and David Dubinsky, that Lewis through his new alliance, expected to dominate the councils of the combined federation of 10,000,000 workers." A close inspection of Hutcheson's private papers covering the proceedings of the Executive Council of the Federation betrays signs of intensive antagonism toward the Miners' president. Hillman's account to President Roosevelt of the "scheme that Dubinsky, Hutcheson and Woll negotiated," a maneuver to wrest control of the CIO from Philip Murray was baseless.[16]*** Any "accouplement," or merger, involved considerations of personal power which few in the CIO — particularly those with White House connections — were inclined to surrender. In addition,

---

[16]See Matthew Josephson, *Sidney Hillman: Statesman of American Labor,* (Harcourt, Brace & Co., 1952), p. 570.

***Hillman's biographer, Josephson has to say of this "conspiracy": "On Hillman's warning that labor unity at such cost should not be encouraged now, the President quickly moved to block the scheme. Green was called to the White House, as was Murray, whom Roosevelt gave assurance that he would back him up with all his influence in opposition to the Lewis-Hutcheson plan. Though the idea itself was a laudable one, none believed that Lewis' intentions were wholly disinterested, and it all fell through." (*Ibid,* p. 570).

jurisdictional quarrels and claims still plagued both federations and could not be easily solved.

One fine day, in the Spring of 1943, Lewis requested of Hutcheson to become his sponsor for readmission into the A. F. of L. The honor and security of Lewis were, from now on, in the hands of a competent strategist and devoted friend. Lewis plan was for Hutcheson, to submit his application for re-affiliation, to be accompanied by a check of $60,000 to be applied to the tax account of the United Mine Workers for the current fiscal period.

On the morning of May 17, Hutcheson, without any fanfare, read Lewis' application at the executive council's meeting. He devoted a large part of his talk to show that there was nothing to fear from Lewis. "I am authorized to make this statement, that any complaints of any character will be adjusted, because I point-blank asked what about District 50, and I was advised that any complaints will be adjusted in conformity with the rules of the Federation. As far as I am concerned, I am quite willing to make a contribution to what we have all been wanting to do, and it seems to me that this is a step in that direction. . . . It is only in conformity with what we have all been trying to do, and it seems to me, we are never going to accomplish the unification of the labor movement, if we do not take this step. ". . . He also advised the Council that" there isn't going to be any further stoppage in the mining industry.'[17]

The Executive Council was not immediately taxed with the application. Unhappy Lewis now stood denuded as though he were a suppliant. To be sure, he was laden with sin, but none of the Council members relented. Vice-President Tobin of the Teamsters wanted to know "what jurisdiction the Miners are coming in on." He spoke of his share of difficulties with Lewis' brother, Denny, "whose catch-all District 50 chartered the Dunnes, 'communists' of Minneapolis. John L. Lewis is a pretty able man, he will fight and he has courage, but he has blundered so bad with his controversy with the government that he may lose some of the things that he might have gotten." There was the Progressive Mine Workers Union (A. F. of L.) which opposed the "dictator of the United Mine Workers coming back into our ranks." Having delivered himself of a vehement speech, President Lloyd A. Thrush warned the Council that he "does not intend to give up any of our jurisdiction or relinquishing any of our rights as stated in the charter of the A. F. of L."

It was obvious to Hutcheson that the attacks on Lewis were well organized. Feeling against the miners' chieftain ran high, and tension mounted. William Hutcheson appealed to reason. "This situation has

---

[17]*Hutcheson's Private Papers* (May 17, August 23, 1943).

been confronting us for several years and it is my belief that every member of this Council has expressed himself as wanting to do everything possible to cement the labor movement. If any one should have any personal feeling in the matter, I perhaps should be one of them, but I want to say here and now that I have none, that I have no personal ambition or desire other than to be helpful to the labor movement. It seems to me that we ought to be diplomatic enough to still find a way to continue further conferences." The fear of District 50 and the dogma of jurisdiction dominated the council members. It was 1:30 P.M. when the "nays" outvoted the "ayes." "Why not have Lewis come back as he left us, not as he is?" pleaded Hutcheson. "Wasn't that the basis for the return of the International Ladies Garment Workers?" The meeting adjourned.

When a year had gone by without any final action on the application, Lewis withdrew it, charging that the Roosevelt administration was responsible for the delay and that the A. F. of L. had become a "political company union," the puppet of a political organization. Lacking the courage to vote on the application or even acknowledge the receipt of the check, Lewis asserted, the majority of the executive council had hypocritically muttered and mumbled and indulged in fearsome incantations over the fallacious and hoary question of jurisdictional rights."[18]

Hutcheson was by temperament an optimist, but he was too wise and old to believe in rapid progress. "The feeling against John was quite understandable to him and it was natural for human beings to develop an aversion for other humans." Weeks, months and even years passed, and the heap of words uttered at successive conferences piled up higher and higher. It was not until January, 1946 after an absence of almost a decade, that the dynamic architect of the C.I.O. was brought back with his 600,000 miners into the Federation. The return of the powerful U.M.W., which had been the backbone of the early C.I.O. organization, brought new hope to the Federation that other C.I.O. groups would follow it in reaffiliation.

Lewis, as he demanded, was elected at once to a vice-presidency of the A. F. of L. The jurisdictional problems presented by the miners' "catch-all" District 50 were to be settled by negotiations with the unions concerned and, if this failed, by the A. F. of L. Executive Council. The return of the miners more than balanced the disaffiliation of the International Association of Machinists, which had withdrawn from the Federation before as a result of a jurisdictional quarrel with the Brotherhood of Carpenters. Exactly a year later, both Hutcheson and Lewis quickly

---

[18]*New York Times,* May 9, 1944.

responded to Philip Murray's appeal "to rise above any petty or personal quarrels to assure completion of a unified program of action on the
part of the three labor organizations: the A. F. of L., the C.I.O. and the
Railway Labor Unions. President William Green, Vice-President Tobin
and Secretary-treasurer Meany completed the personnel of the A. F. of L.
committee to discuss the "question of organic unity." The committee
designated by Philip Murray for the C.I.O. consisted of Walter Reuther
(United Auto Workers), Albert Fitzgerald (leftist United Electrical
Radio and Machine Workers, UE) Emil Rieve (Textile) and Jacob
Potofsky (Amalgamated Clothing Workers).

Nothing happened.

After the spring of 1942, new duties piled on Hutcheson in an ever
increasing load. In that year's congressional elections, labor forces had
suffered a severe setback, as the Republican party, scoring its biggest
victory since 1928, gained nine Senate seats and almost won control of
the House of Representatives. Conservative Democrats from the South,
combining with the Republicans, had created a top-heavy anti-union
coalition able to legislate at will and to override a presidential veto, as the
passage of the Smith-Connally Act in 1943 demonstrated.

Although William Levi Hutcheson was cold toward independent
labor political activity, he bitterly resented the Smith-Connally Act,
whose Section IX restricted unions from making financial contributions
to political parties. He vigorously challenged the Southern Democrats
who combined with Republicans to launch a "vicious attack on labor
unions." He called upon his 400,000 carpenters to defeat H. R. 6790
and H. R. 6792 and other "sinister" bills sponsored by Congressmen
Boren and Wickersham of Oklahoma.

"In one or another of these bills", Hutcheson informed the members,
"provision is made to abolish the 40-hour week, payment for overtime,
the closed shop, collective bargaining, and to suspend, for the emergency,
such vital laws as the Walsh-Healy Act, the Bacon-Davis Act, the eight-
hour law and the National Labor Relations Act.

"All of this mind you, despite the solemn pledge, given by organized
labor to the government of a no-strike policy on defense projects for the
duration of the war. And all of this, too, despite assurance given Congress by the President of the United States. . . . This is no idle talk. This
is deadly serious. The chips are down and our enemies are out to destroy us if they can. We never sought a fight, but by the same token we
have never run from one. And We Are Not Going To Take This Lying
Down."[19] He was profoundly irritated with those in the Republican
Party who "pursue an anti-labor course."

[19]Anti-Labor Bills Before Congress," *The Carpenter,* vol. LVII:4 (April, 1942),
pp. 3-4.

But William Hutcheson did not rest there. Aware of the absence of a feeling of solidarity between the A. F. of L. and the C.I.O., he was quick to appreciate the need to break down the barrier between the urban outlook of most trade unions and the conviction of the small farmer cooperatives and the farm-laborer that they do not have any kindred interest with the workers in the city. This was not a matter of passing resolutions; it was not even a matter of temporary interest in active organization, such as that which produced the Southern Tenant Farmers' Union as a section of the United Tannery Workers of the C.I.O. By 1940, except as precious memories whispered here and there among friends whose bona fides could not be questioned, it was difficult to believe that the necessary unity between labor in town and farmer in the country had retained more than a formal programmatic significance for the C.I.O. leadership.

It was on the achievement of that unity and mutual interest that Hutcheson sought the active aid and support of the Cooperative Farmers' group. With rare patience, he explained to the chairman, James McConnell and to Secretary Clark Brody that farmers' prosperity ultimately depended on the workers' demand for consumption goods. At one of the sessions, Hutcheson inquired if the Cooperative Farmers "accept into membership small farm owners who work on their own farms." As a result of these conferences, Hutcheson secured support in opposing the Hatch-Burton-Ball bill. By August 20, 1946, Hutcheson reported that "the ground-work was laid for a very good understanding between the Farmers' Cooperatives and the American Federation of Labor; that on two occasions they were very helpful when I contacted James McConnell in regards to anti-labor legislation; that we have started on the road for a real cooperative understanding." He urged the A. F. of L. Executive Council "to view them with friendly concern because they could help us in the future on anti-labor legislation.[20]

The anti-union drive achieved more success during the war years in putting legislation on state statute books. Much of this legislation was enacted in the south, west and the southwest, all of which had achieved relatively little industrialization in earlier years, but to which the war had brought both more industrial development and more vigorous efforts at unionization. In 1942, California enacted its "hot cargo" act, prohibiting secondary boycotts, and five other states adopted some form of legislation reflecting dissatisfaction with unionism. The following year, when most state legislatures were in session, a dozen states enacted restrictions, some of them quiet drastic, on union activities.

Another essential point of William Hutcheson's program was his

---

[20]*Hutcheson's Private Papers*, August 20, 1946.

insistence that the A. F. of L. Executive Council set aside the sum of $500,000 to organize the South and to fight this legislation;[21] he urged the Federation to challenge in the courts the constitutionality of some "unconstitutional" anti-labor measures.

At the same time, he viewed with apprehension, the political activities of Sidney Hillman and Philip Murray, under whose leadership the C.I.O. Political Action Committee was then established, to mobilize labor support behind Roosevelt and the Democratic ticket, and to getting out the vote. Other members of the Committee included: Van A. Bittner, Albert Fitzgerald, R. J. Thomas, Sherman Dalrymple, and David J. McDonald. Its declared purpose was not only to mobilize the millions of C.I.O.'s adherents for active participation in state and national elections, but also church and women's groups as well as farmers, consumers and community organizations throughout the United States. Hillman denied that this was a move in the direction of independent political action, for the formation of a third party; rather in theory it was the A. F. of L. traditional non-partisan policy to be applied more vigorously than the Federation had ever contemplated. In practice, the *Pac* was an effort to influence — and, where possible, dominate the Democratic party.

Not unlike Labor's Non-Partisan League, the CIO's previous political department, which vanished with John L. Lewis, the *Pac* attempted to build its organization from the precincts upwards. Its leaders believed that only through favorable governmental policy can the economic interests of labor be protected. To pragmatic Hutcheson, this approach was a fatal error in strategy and unrealistic. It assumed first, that labor can reach agreement within its own ranks, whereas in fact, neither the Federation nor the CIO had as yet discovered a wide area of common interests. All of the A. F. of L's. and Hutcheson's attempts to lay the foundation of common interests rooted in the workers economic status had been frustrated by the C.I.O. throughout the 'forties. Second, the attempts of *Pac* to mobilize opinion behind the Democratic ticket narrowed labor's scope and effectiveness. Third, the *Pac* refused to confront the glaring fact that it was unlikely that the Republican policy would differ in any marked degree from Democratic policy. Hutcheson believed that labor had greater scope if it remained outside both political parties. This envisaged not nonpartisanship but aggressive bargaining with *both* political parties. Finally, Hutcheson believed that the welfare of labor and agriculture are their own concern. Wage earners in both parties could achieve their ends, which they deem good, not through governmental channels but through their own strength and effort.

*   *   *

---

[21]*Hutcheson's Private Papers,* May 15-22, 1946.

During Christmas and New Year of 1943, Hutcheson was back again at his cottage, in the Brotherhood's Home, in Lakeland, Florida, a quiet city of 22,000 surrounded by sparkling lakes. Here he loved to lie in the sun looking out to see the vast grounds of the Home, with its heavy growth of pine, fir, oak, Australian cedar and dogwood trees; or to lounge outside the cottage, reading. Hutcheson longed to take a rest. He needed it. Since the war, additional duties piled on him in increasing load. In Philadelphia, where the Metropolitan District Council of Carpenters celebrated its sixteenth anniversary, the National Broadcasting Company asked him to deliver a nation-wide address in the entourage of Mayor Samuels and Senator James J. Davis. "Labor's Contribution Toward the War" was the subject of an address he delivered on Labor Day.

In San Francisco, he was the guest of Henry Kaiser's Richmond Yards, where the S.S. Peter J. McGuire was launched, named after the father of Labor Day and founder of the Brotherhood of Carpenters. He lashed out at the Smith-Connally team, authors of the Act. He was fierce in his criticism of Republicans who aligned with the Southern Democrats. A member of the Indiana State Chamber of Commerce, he initiated a series of conferences between labor and industry, highlighting the importance of full employment, and collective bargaining as a necessary instrument of industrial government. The Columbia Club in Indianapolis, which is frequented by its most illustrious citizens, invited him to serve on its public questions committee of which Senator Homer E. Capehart was co-chairman. He worked unflinchingly to strengthen the Republican State Committee of Indiana, when the party was "making a comeback struggle."

In Lakeland, Hutcheson relaxed by talking shop, politics, war or — simply playing dominoes or cards. By his side were his elder sister Minnie and his younger brother Bud. Members of the general executive board, including his oldest son Maurice, First Vice-President of the Brotherhood, also gathered about him in this quiet retreat. The mayor of Lakeland often came to visit with the Brotherhood's General President.

By the end of January he was back at his office in Indianapolis. The Brotherhood had become a "giant" among labor unions, having reached a membership of nearly 450,000 with its network of 1900 local unions spreading over forty-eight states and Canada. It nearly doubled its membership since 1940, when the Carpenters Union totalled 297,905. Its most important expansion movement during the war was devoted to organizing the southern "frontier" country and the northwest, and the west. The Brotherhood concentrated all its efforts on keeping war projects supplied with capable carpenters, and the armed services with "seabees." Shortages of trained carpenters at the Hanford and Clinton

Engineer Works were satisfactorily filled through the Brotherhood's comprehensive apprenticeship system.

Hutcheson's cooperation with the War and Navy Departments secured him much praise from Under-Secretary of War Robert Patterson and Navy Secretary James Forrestal. "Your assistance in recruiting skilled mechanics to help build the Clinton and Hanford projects was an important factor in rushing these projects to completion and making it possible to drop the first atomic bomb on Japan. I want to thank the officers and members of your organization for this contribution," wrote Robert P. Patterson.[22]

At the age of seventy, Hutcheson wielded considerable political influence in his own right and through his labor constituency. Magnificos of high corporate rank, serious, rich, influential men coveted his friendship. As mentioned above, Victor Emanuel, President of Avco Manufacturing Corporation, and his nephew Mortimer S. Gordon, Samuel Ungerleider, head of Michael's Furniture Stores, Cecil B. De Mille, noted movie director and producer, newspaper publisher Eugene Pulliam of the *Indianapolis Star* and *News* were part of his social circle. His virtues as a labor statesman, who was credited with rigidly upholding the sanctity of labor contracts, were extolled. Political luminaries of national rank were always in his entourage; Dr. John R. Steelman, assistant to President Truman, former U. S. Conciliator Cyrus Ching, Thomas E. Dewey, Senators Styles Bridges, Homer E. Capehart, Robert A. Taft and Spessard Holland; Congressman George A. Bender (now U. S. Senator from Ohio), Charles Halleck and Joseph Martin of Pennsylvania. He was on friendly and intimate terms with Indiana State Supreme Court Justice Arch L. Bobbitt, Judge Harry Routzohn, an influential figure in Ohio Republican politics and erstwhile U. S. Solicitor General, former Federal District Attorney Charles Tuttle, Fred E. Shortemeier, former Indiana Secretary of State and Secretary of the State Central Republican Committee. U. S. Chief Justice-to-be of the Supreme Court Earl Warren and U. S. Attorney General Herbert Brownell, Jr., were among his friends. Masonry was another of Hutcheson's strong points.

As the election of 1944 dawned, Hutcheson, the labor confidant of the Republican national committee, was going through a rude awakening, which the top-heavy anti-union coalition of Republicans and Southern Democrats had brought in its train since the passage of the Smith-Connally Act in 1943. It was against this background that he embarked upon a great political quest, the achievement of which might secure him not only the Vice-Presidency of the United States on the

---

[22]*Hutcheson's Private Papers*, August 8, 1945.

Republican ticket, but a tactical position within the party which he could use as a vehicle for the attainment of his particular purposes. He began his first skirmish in his own home state, Indiana.

On June 4, a move to put William L. Hutcheson in the second place on the Republican ticket to "win labor back to the party" was started by Judge Harry N. Routzohn, former Republican representative from Ohio and Fred E. Shortemeier, former Indiana Secretary of State. Asserting that the selection of Hutcheson would refute the "smear" that the Republican party is anti-labor, Routzohn said his candidate would carry the "rank and file of the labor votes with him for the Republicans." Other reasons advanced in behalf of Hutcheson's candidacy included the claim that leaders of the A. F. of L. would give their support, that building contractors and a host of other manufacturers throughout the country who have dealt with the United Brotherhood of Carpenters in the twenty-nine years during which Hutcheson had headed the organization, would aid his election, and that support would also be forthcoming from leaders of the farm cooperatives and rural organizations. The choice of Hutcheson would offset New Deal influence in industrial states. It would also furnish a Vice-Presidential candidate from the Middle West.

In an article published in the June issue of *The Republican,* Shortemeier launched an attack on the Republican party for its "failure to grasp the clear opportunity to make an ally of labor in the great duel between economic freedom and economic regimentation. "There is still time to save the situation," he warned the Republican high command. "One of the decisive battles in the struggle to safeguard the American system will be fought in the months ahead — in the presidential elections. We can and must line up labor with the Republican party. If we fail to do so, if we continue blithely to let the New Dealers capture American labor without even a struggle we shall in effect be 'throwing' the election. Worse than that, we shall be throwing the last chance to save individual freedom from being swallowed up by the superstate.

"Have we forgotten that Samuel Gompers, the revered leader of American unionism, found it not only possible but imperative to work together with the Republicans on all crucial issues. In his youth, Gompers was an enrolled Republican but later switched his political loyalties. The Republican Party represents the opposition. As the party that has always been deeply sympathetic with the constructive, conservative, commonsense policies of the foremost trade unions, it can win labor as an ally — provided it tries and tries hard. . . . But the most effective, the most convincing move that we Republicans can make is to select a labor man for high place on our national ticket. The name that comes automatically to mind in this connection, of course, is that of William L. Hutcheson."[23]

The 1944 election was viewed by Hutcheson as "a turning point of human progress." With passion, Hutcheson spoke of the vast social and economic issues that are coming into focus. "Just as this is the year of decision of our great and uncompleted war task, so the choice which the American people will make in the 1944 presidential election will determine the shape and direction of our national economy for at least a generation." Hutcheson believed that labor votes would determine the 1944 election. "As producer, as consumer, as citizen, the American wage earner feels the impact of every throb of our national viewpoint. His viewpoint is that of the whole American economy. Labor speaks with a voice, not of a faction, but of the national interest as a whole."

His platform and program for the Republican party was started with terseness and simplicity. It included: the preservation of "free enterprise," the abatement of bureaucracy, the halt of governmental paternalism, the creation of postwar jobs through private industry, the maintenance of labor's social gains, and finally, the protection of our national interests.

The election of 1944 was indeed novel in one respect. Farmers and wage earners in representative numbers now expected the Republican leaders to treat them as the peers of industry. Labor leaders in the opposition party had been more widely accorded a respectable status and the spokesmen for agriculture were generally accepted as sober middle-class citizens. Combined with industry, both agriculture and labor would form a tripartite interest basis for the Republican party to come to political power.

On July 7, when the Republican national convention met to nominate a new presidential candidate, the Indiana delegation moved to test its strength, battling for recognition. To keep the question of Hutcheson's vice-presidential nomination alive, its delegates distributed Shortemeier's eloquent pamphlet, "The Republican Party and Labor" which appeared in the Republican Party's propaganda organ. A committee composed of three delegates, Shortemeier, Judge Routzohn of Dayton and Congressman Raymond C. Willis then proceeded to the Stevens Hotel to sound out party sentiment and whip up enthusiasm for Indiana's favorite son as vice-presidential choice. Together, they presented a persuasive argument in the national committee headquarters and other influential sections of the party. They pointed out to this inner group that much was to be gained by nominating a labor leader as vice-president. J. Russel Sprague, chairman of the Republican national committee, Governor

---

[23]Fred Shortemeier, *"The Republican Party and Labor,"* June, 1944.

Thomas E. Dewey and John Foster Dulles seemed impressed, but non-committal.

Hutcheson himself felt bound to remain in the background. He then turned for advice to Samuel Ungerleider, of Fenner, Beane and Ungerleider.

Ungerleider was that rare type of Wall Street financier, a man who really cared for labor, no matter where his care for it might take him. He really did believe that Hutcheson the labor leader and author of the Republican party's labor platform would considerably enhance the party ticket. Ungerleider did not doubt that Hutcheson was vice-presidential timber; what puzzled him was the Republican machine's stand toward having a labor leader on its national ticket. He had his doubts about the governor of New York who, unlike Wendell Willkie, his main rival, might not venture forth outside the precincts of the machine. While those doubts were still to be resolved. Ungerleider, one-time supporter of Roosevelt, made some successful moves to strengthen Hutcheson's political stocks. He won over Cecil B. De Mille, who headed the California delegation. Councilman Herman Finkel of the Ohio delegation was persuaded. Charles Tuttle of New York was most sympathetic to the nomination and, of course, there was also John L. Lewis, who undertook to court the West Virginia delegation and those from other coal regions.

As the convention advanced, the inner circle disclosed the name of the presidential nominee. It was Thomas E. Dewey of New York. A conference between Hutcheson's backers and the New York governor yielded no more than silence. A party caucus decided on the choice of Governor John W. Bricker of Ohio as Dewey's running mate. There was but little doubt that Bricker was chosen by the active will of the presidential candidate. With that choice, therefore, there was the renewed hope that the vice-president would retire into that obscurity which, so many Americans curiously considered the vice-president's proper place.

Hutcheson's idyllic era with the Republican Party seemed about ended, when one of Indiana's politicos and well-wishers who supported his nomination, approached him, and urged him to reconsider. On October 26, from the New York studio of radio station WOR, Hutcheson posed six conditions which, he said, the candidates for President would have to meet in order to to qualify for labor support.

1. Take the government straitjackets off collective bargaining and restore it to its former free status.
2. Get rid of the incompetent bureaucrats who are now staffing the Federal agencies dealing with labor, and replace them with administrators who understand labor's needs.
3. Halt the dismantling of the Department of Labor and restore the Depart-

ment to its intended importance under the secretaryship of a man chosen from the ranks of labor.

4. Put a stop to political one-man-rule of labor policies in Washington, and replace it by fair and impartial rule of law.

5. End government favoritism for particular unions, and discontinue the present mischievous White House policies of personal interference in the internal affairs of organized labor.

6. Pledge himself to the general economic policy which will assure labor and the returning serviceman a job at adequate and progressive wage levels in private industry.

He emphasized that the Brotherhood of Carpenters would vote "according to their own free choice" and would, "as in all elections divide their votes among both presidential candidates."[24]

The six demands presented in the broadcast were completely ignored by President Roosevelt and the New Deal campaigners in four months of campaign speeches.

Roosevelt's margin victory, reduced to only 3,100,000 in excess of Dewey's 21,300,000, could not have been gained, C.I.O. political leaders modestly proclaimed, save for the "strength of Hillman's Pac drive." The great turnout, the rise of the *Pac*, the "Hillman Blitz" were "providential for Roosevelt."

The year 1945 was a year of great events. As it opened, the German counter-offensive of the Bulge in the snowy Ardennes was being turned back, while at the other end of the world General MacArthur's troops were storming through the Phillipines. In March, America's troops seized intact a bridge across the Rhine at Remagen, and the path was opened for an offensive across Germany. In April, when the offensive had just reached the Elbe, Franklin D. Roosevelt—who proved himself a masterly war leader died, exhausted by his long labors toward victory; and the massive burdens of the Presidency of the United States fell upon the shoulders of an unassuming Vice-President, Harry S. Truman. Later in the same month there began, at San Francisco, the international conference which set up the United Nations organization. By early May, Mussolini was dead, Hitler was a suicide and Germany surrendered. In July, the first atomic bomb explosion took place in New Mexico. In August, the bomb was used on two Japanese cities, and Japan surrendered—just after Joseph Stalin had belatedly moved his Red army against the Japanese.

The approach of V-J found labor uneasy, for each cutback in production meant immediate joblessness for some war workers and apprehension for the remainder. Henry Wallace's goal of "sixty million jobs" seemed to many business groups, among others, visionary and even dan-

---

[24]*New York Times,* October 27, 1944, p. 36: 2.

gerous, an irresponsible promise of from four to ten million more jobs than the postwar economy was likely to provide, while Director John W. Snyder of the Office of War Mobilization and Reconversion predicted that there would be five million jobless within three months and eight million by the Spring of 1946. To the labor movement, however, a full employment economy was the primary postwar goal.

The Executive Council of the Federation advocated full employment and maximum civilian production as the major goals, urged upward revision of wage rates to provide sufficient purchasing power to wage earners to match the nation's productive capacity. Even before V-E Day, Hutcheson urged the inauguration of a large-scale home construction program in America as an indispensible step towards speeding postwar reconversion and stabilized prosperity. He formulated a series of positive programs "to insure to the nation a complete supply of building trades mechanics and laborers in all classifications of skill in every community to build the volume of housing units so urgently required under the present existing conditions." The program involved nearly 12,000 contractors who had joined with the unions in establishing area-wide programs in 800 communities.

The Wagner-Ellender-Taft General Housing Bill, which embodied a long-range program for housing families of all incomes with a maximum reliance on private enterprise and local initiative was vigorously pushed by him, only to have been blocked by a small and influential lobby in the House of Congress. And when socially-minded Henry J. Kaiser, one of the sponsors of the National Committee on Housing, applied for material assistance to the Executive Council of the Federation, Hutcheson promptly responded by offering to contribute ten thousand dollars if Kaiser would communicate with him at the Carpenters' national office in Indianapolis. He was little disturbed or not at all by the semantics of Mr. Harry Bates, President of the Bricklayers, who noted that the National Committee on Housing was the "brainchild of Mrs. Samuel Rosenman, and one of her more socialistic ideas."

Few things concerned him more, even before the fighting in Europe had ended, than the subject of reconversion to the peacetime needs of the civilian economy. Early in May of 1945, Hutcheson stubbornly pursued his plan for a postwar America, independently of the Executive Council of the Federation, a copy of which he mailed to President Harry S. Truman. This plan, dated May 5, simultaneously presented to and approved by the A. F. of L. Executive Council, so accurately describes Hutcheson's social and political outlook, that it is quoted here in full:

"The deep-grounded determination of the American people that total war, with its horrors, shall not return, justifies the fullest exploration by our nation of the possibilities of an international organization of nations which shall underwrite an enduring peace.

The outlines of such an organization were tentatively sketched at Dumbarton Oaks. At San Francisco, the United Nations will address themselves to the task of filling out the scaffolding of the Dumbarton Oaks decisions, and of embodying them with a workable and acceptable permanent structure of peace.

Upon their success hinges much of the future hope of mankind. Industry, labor and agriculture should full-heartedly support the objectives of the San Francisco meeting.

We are deeply interested and greatly concerned in the attainment and maintenance of a future and permanent world peace. To do this we must maintain and safeguard the economic and political well being of the American people here at home.

Great as are our resources, they are not inexhaustible. There are limitations and restrictions upon our abilities to contribute which, if disregarded, will place an undue strain upon our domestic economy and which, if unheeded, will reflect injury not alone upon ourselves but as well upon those whom we would benefit.

We are, therefore, faced with the prime necessity and requirement of conserving and safeguarding and advancing the economic and social interests of all our peoples and particularly those of America's wage earners. To this end we hold imperative and essential the following program and procedure:

1. Maintenance of a high and ever progressively increasing American standard of living, measured in real purchasing power. This is a basic consideration. It should govern all our domestic and foreign policy relations and decisions.

2. The planning and financing of a vast program of urban and rural housing, and road renovation and re-building, of rural electrification and of long overdue public works is of utmost importance. Such a program will provide the broad economic basis for a successful transition of our national economy from war to peacetime production. It is essential that this program have precedence over any other domestic objective. The implementing of such a program guaranteeing, as it does, a continued period of full employment and of sustained high living standards to the American people, is an obligation we owe to millions of men and women in uniform as well as those returning from factories converting from war to peacetime production, who will return to seek employment after the war.

3. Safeguarding the foundation of our American way of life and of wellbeing by the maintenance of unclosed economic opportunities of our citizens under a system of free enterprise is imperative to the perpetuity of our constitutional social and political order. This policy must continue to guide the American people in the after-war period. The channels of opportunity must be kept open for our returning service men and women and for the youths who are to follow us.

International cartels and international trade controls which tend to limit or restrict the free and full scope of the economic opportunities of our people must be discouraged.

4. Government controls and direction of our life and relations made imperative by war requirements and necessities must insist upon an orderly but

speedy end of the economic regimentation, direction and control made necessary and accepted as an essential expedient during the war period.

5. We will continue to contribute our proportionate share together with other nations in organizing the conditions and providing for world reconstruction and in rendering fullhearted support to policies that will facilitate self-sustaining economic recovery of all nations and thus contribute toward a healthy world economy. We must nevertheless avoid the errors of the 20's in exporting both goods and money to defaulting foreign customers and in extending help to other nations we should predicate such help upon a self-liquidating basis.

6. Ideological infiltration into our American political and economic life by propagandists of foreign nations or directed, subsidized or controlled by foreign sources, must not be permitted. The American people have no intent or desire to interfere with the internal political arrangements of other nations. We must insist that other nations be equally scrupulous in discouraging divisive political intervention by those acting in their behalf in our country. Ideological activities must stop at the nation's boundaries."[25]

On the Executive Council of the Federation, Hutcheson was the sole dissenter who opposed a "no-strike" pledge after V-J Day. Patriotic appeals against strikes in an era of peace had lost their force, precisely at the time that pay envelopes were shrinking due to the loss of overtime earnings. For similar reasons he wanted no further dealings with the National War Labor Board, "which has outlived its usefulness now that peace is here." Cooperation for war production was a patriotic necessity in a time of national emergency, but labor had suffered the most under wartime controls and it could improve its position once the government ceased to fix the terms of the employment contract and became only the policeman. "Continuation of the National War Labor Board will force labor and management to go to the government for the solution of their disputes instead of finding their own solutions through the orderly processes of collective bargaining."

Labor insisted in the Fall of 1945 that employers could afford to increase wages substantially without increasing prices, and that this was necessary to sustain purchasing power and avoid business collapse and large-scale unemployment. The A. F. of L. declared that industry could afford to raise hourly rates twenty percent without material increases in prices. The C.I.O. argued that an even greater pay rise was possible. Labor's position received government support late in October from the office of War Mobilization and Reconversion and from President Truman, who in a radio address declared that weekly earnings of many war workers had been reduced by a fourth because of loss of overtime and "reclassification" to lower-paying jobs. "Wage increases are . . . imperative to cushion the shock to our workers to sustain adequate pur-

---

[25]*Hutcheson's Private Papers,* May 1-9, 1945.

chasing power and to raise the national income." Within the existing price structure, Truman declared, there was room for business as a whole to grant wage increases. This was made possible by the elimination of overtime, increased productivity, high profits, and the prospective elimination of the excess-profits tax. Employers, however, remained unimpressed by all these arguments, whether from government or union sources; wages could rise substantially, management insisted, only if corresponding price increases were allowed.

In this situation, in the late fall of 1945 and the winter of 1946, the government appointed fact-finding boards in a series of major disputes, in the hope that an airing of the facts before the tribunal of public opinion would narrow the area of disagreement and encourage genuine collective bargaining on issues that remained.

Against a background of mounting strikes, the President called a National Management-Labor Conference in Washington. Full delegations represented the National Association of Manufacturers, the Chambers of Commerce of the United States. The delegation of the American Federation of Labor was headed by Hutchson and seven others of the Executive Council. The C.I.O., and the United Mine Workers and the Railway brotherhoods were also represented. In his opening address to the conference Truman pointed out that during war, labor and management had worked together well under government controls, performing a miracle of production. A way had to be found, President Truman emphasized, to resolve differences between labor and management without stopping production. Where collective bargaining produced no results, "then there must be a willingness to use some impartial machinery for reaching decisions on the basis of proven facts and realities, instead of rumor or propaganda in partisan statements. That is the way to prevent lockouts and strikes."[26] If the conference could recommend machinery to prevent or settle industrial disputes, the President declared, it would have made vast progress for industrial peace and laid a foundation for an era of prosperity and security.

The conference, dealing with many of the fundamental and long-range problems in the area of union-management relations, reached agreement on a number of matters of significance. The conferees agreed, under the vigorous leadership of Hutcheson, that grievances under existing contracts should be settled by voluntary arbitration rather than by strikes or lockouts; that the United States Conciliation Service should be strengthened; that during initial bargaining for contracts, strikes should be postponed until all peaceful procedures had been

[26]The President's speech is reproduced in *National Labor-Management Conference,* November, 5-30, (U. S. Dept. of Labor, Division of Labor Standards (Washington, D.C., 1946), Bulletin No. 77.

exhausted. Even more significant was the fact that management and labor representatives made a serious and a strained effort to reach an understanding on how to make collective bargaining function better.

The diminution of collective bargaining in the war years was one of the important factors that precipitated the outbreak of strikes in 1946 in mass production industries. The techniques of collective bargaining had grown rusty through long disuse. When government controls suddenly were removed after the war, management found that it had not developed adequate machinery to be able to cope with the new situation.

Despite these achievements of the conference there remained a number of specific points of disagreement. Hutcheson and other labor representatives objected vigorously to an industry plan for strike notices, cooling-off periods, and the appointment of fact-finding boards where "public health or safety" was endangered. Management, in turn, rejected a labor proposal for a declaration in favor of higher wages to serve as a guide in reconversion wage disputes.

Hutcheson challenged management's proposals that union status be defined by legislation, that labor be made equally responsible with industry under the Wagner Act. Management's proposal that labor give up its immunities under the antitrust laws (the Clayton and Norris-LaGuardia Acts) roused him to opposition immediately. Had he not stood trial in the United States Supreme Court to establish the unions' immunity under those statutes, and won? Hutcheson rejected any legal ruses designed to encourage further governmental intrusion into labor affairs, including jurisdictional disputes, insisting that existing law was adequate and that the right to strike should not be circumscribed.

There was widespread disappointment on the part of many of the participants that the conference failed to reach agreement on machinery to prevent, settle or minimize industrial disputes in the reconversion period. This, despite the fact that progress had been made on a number of matters of significance: that grievances under existing contracts should be settled by voluntary arbitration rather than by strikes or lockouts; that during initial bargaining for contracts strikes should be postponed until peaceful procedure had been exhausted; and that joint meetings of top management and labor officials should be continued, in the hope that an understanding be achieved.

But these could hardly mollify the fears and anxieties of a movement and its leaders whose behavior pattern was largely determined by the mental part of the world of 1919, which passed on unchanged to 1946. The melancholy, grim memories of World War I were not lost by the mere passage of time. On the contrary, they were strongly reinforced by management's clamor that the power of labor unions should be "harnessed" and their "favored position" under the Wagner Act drastically altered. But now that labor was at the peak of its numerical strength and thus strong enough to resist any "open shop" drive, its leaders remained inflexible, insisting that existing law was adequate and that the rights of labor must under no circumstances be circumscribed. It was this inflexibility that paved the way for the 1947 punitive legislation.[27]

It was during this period of adjustment for peacetime conditions, when industry and labor were straining to break the weakening bonds restraining them, that most of the trouble occurred. Nearly every industry felt the impact as unions and management squared off for tests of economic strength. An enormous strike wave engulfed the country, as workers fought for substantial pay increases to maintain wartime take-home-pay and as employers insisted that any pay rises be compensated for by price boosts. At one time, in the Winter and Spring of 1946, great CIO strikes were raging almost simultaneously in the steel, automobile, meat-packing, coal and electrical industries. The strikes themselves were of a sort to arouse extreme public interest and concern — strikes in key industries affecting huge groups of employees and the consuming public very directly.

Never one to wax dramatic, or "hide behind verbiage," Hutcheson viewed the postwar readjustment period as one "that will bring a blitz." "Organized labor," he declared, "is faced with the biggest battle in its history looming on the horizon. This became crystal clear by the time Congress (the Seventy-eighth) laid aside its duties for the Christmas vacation." During the war, he issued similar, highly indignant warnings and manifestoes to labor and the carpenters alike. Now he feared the shapeless tide of public disapprobation, which in a democratic society at least, is the ultimate mover of legislation, and is the element in which labor lives and moves. He had seen this tide run strongly against labor organizations in the 1920's, then turn almost equally strongly in the other direction in the era of the Wagner Act. Now it was turning again. Again he issued a warning.

"There are the Hobbs Bill, the May-Smith-Arends Bill, the President's proposal for an enforced "cooling-off," and a host of others. Individually and collectively they are aimed at one thing and one thing only—compulsion of one kind or another for American workers. The fight for survival of unionism now reaches down to every worker and wage earner who had enjoyed or hoped to enjoy the fruits of organization. It behooves every American worker to be on his toes during 1946 and on."[28]

---

[27]For an extensive and valuable analysis of the Conference, its accomplishments and failures, see George W. Taylor, *Government Regulation of Industrial Relations,* (Prentice-Hall ,1945), Chapter V.
[28]*Hutcheson's Private Papers,* January, 1946.

The A. F. of L.'s educational program did little to improve the general social attitude toward the labor movement. Nor was the effectiveness of Hutcheson's warnings and manifestoes "visible" in the Congressional elections in November of that year. Paradoxically enough, it was while the labor movement was at the peak of its numerical strength, reaching almost the fifteen million mark, of which the Federation had constituted seven million, that the long legislative drive on trade-union rights culminated in the passage of severly restrictive legislation. Just as the callous and irresponsible conduct of many leaders of business who, as we have noted, violated many of the canons of the common morality in conducting their war against the unions and by so doing created a great deal of sympathy for their weak opponent, so the nation-wide strikes that paralyzed the economy in the winter months of 1946 helped to create a climate of opinion, fear and alarm in which the Taft-Hartley Act was possible.

It is hard to say that the community at large has suffered now that the weak bargaining position of the workers has evidently been improved. Nevertheless, popular indignation with labor's postwar claims reflected a feeling that a bargaining position that was once unduly weak had now been made unduly strong. But there were maritime strikes, light and power strikes, the nation-wide telephone strike, and finally the nation-wide coal strike of John L. Lewis' United Mine Workers and the widespread railroad strike that antagonized public opinion in 1946 and led Congress to enact restrictive legislation aimed at labor.

There was, to be sure, "a host of wealthy lobbyists in Washington backing them up with moral and financial support," sadly recorded Hutcheson. The National Association of Manufacturers carried on a vigorous popular campaign against unionism as a monopoly, pointing to industry-wide bargaining, the closed and the union shop, and the secondary boycott as evidence of monopoly power. The N.A.M. also proposed that unions be obligated by law to bargain collectively, that a strike be permitted only where a majority of workers had voted for it by secret ballot under impartial supervision, that strikes not related to wages, hours, or working conditions be outlawed, that mass-picketing and other defenses be prohibited. The Chamber of Commerce advocated a very similar program, likewise proposing a wholesale revision of existing labor legislation, and support for such a move came from many other quarters as well. Much of the press, a number of politicians joined in the debate, attacking labor's abuses and many of the more defensible practices of unions, such as the closed shop and area or nation-wide collective bargaining.

The large number of measures introduced in Congress during wartime to restrict the legal rights of labor or to regulate unions in one way or another became a veritable flood once hostility ceased. There is little doubt that the unprecedented volume and seriousness of the 1946 strike wave aroused Congressional tempers at a time when the peculiar wartime need for national unity no longer existed.

1946 found John Lewis and his miners back in the A. F. of L. through the persistent efforts of Hutcheson. Like Lewis, Hutcheson felt that this move was a step in the direction of ultimate amalgamation of A. F. of L. with the C.I.O. Both believed that the A. F. of L. could serve as the platform from which they could make moves in that direction. Before he and Hutcheson could begin a new drive for "organic labor unity," the Miners' president announced the expiration of the coal contracts. On March 2, he issued his thirty day strike warning, and again developments followed the usual routine: the balking of the operators and the national strike on April 1. As coal supplies diminished, a nation-wide "brownout" was imposed by the government to save fuel, while a creeping paralysis threatened the country's industrial organization. Meanwhile in Congress there was a growing sentiment to declare illegal the collection of royalties by unions and to enact bills sponsored by Representative Francis Case of South Dakota severely restricting union activities. It should be added that Lewis demanded, in addition to the wage-raise, a royalty on each ton of coal mined to finance health and welfare services in mining camps and also insisted on more adequate safety provisions. From the operators' point of view, fringe benefits added to the cost of production just as surely as wages did, and might further jeapordize the industry's position in the postwar competition with other fuels. Moreover, the operators denied that health and medical issues, properly belonged in collective-bargaining negotiations, and objected in principle to turning over a large sum to be spent at the union's discretion.

A two-week truce in May, during which the Miners returned to the pits, afforded temporary relief without settling the issues in the dispute. Shortly before the truce was due to expire, President Truman ordered Julius A. Krug, his new Secretary of the Interior, to seize the mines. Finally, on May 29, Krug and Lewis reached agreements on terms to prevail during the period of government operation. The welfare dispute was settled by the establishment of a "welfare and retirement fund" to be financed by a royalty of five cents for every ton of coal mined. The administration of the fund was to be in the hands of three trustees, one of whom, U. S. Senator Styles Bridges, was appointed at Hutcheson's urging. Furthermore, the Miners received a wage increase of eighteen and a-half cents an hour which, with overtime, meant a daily boost of $1.85; $100 vacation pay; a guaranteed work week of five nine-hour days, with overtime pay after the seventh hour; and a federal mine safety code was to be adopted.

While labor leaders attacked the Case Bill as the "worst type of vengeful and hysterical legislation," and as "punitive and vindictive and un-American legislation," Hutcheson sought to influence his political friends, among whom were Senators Wayne D. Morse of Oregon, Styles Bridges, House Speaker Joseph Martin and Robert A. Taft. At the same time, he fired at the irresponsible conduct of the industrialists who "seemed to be determined to place legislative shackles on organized labor." For a long time business has been talking about the necessity for preserving "free enterprise," Hutcheson declaimed in an address he delivered before the Indiana State Chamber of Commerce. "With this proposition no honest American has any quarrel. But how long can enterprise remain free if all segments of it, workers as well as owners — are not free? Not very long, is the answer. Freedom is an ephemeral thing. Everyone must be free, or nobody is free. Today business is chafing under the ever-increasing amount of federal control. Yet if you will look back a few decades you will find that it was business itself that promoted greater centralization in Washington. It wanted a freer hand to expand across state borders. It got what it wanted and now it is unhappy.

"Now it wants labor shackled. Can it not see that shackles for labor would eventually mean its own shackling? To these I commend the words of Abe Lincoln with a little bit of paraphrasing: *Free enterprise cannot long endure half slave and free free*."[29]

On June 1, by a vote of sixty-one to twenty, the Senate passed its version of the controversial legislation. By that time, however, the immediate emergency had passed, opposition developed from employers, and the measure was allowed to die quietly. "Maybe it is only coincidental that this is an election year, but at any rate the vicious Case anti-labor bill has been smothered in committee in the Senate," Hutcheson proudly reported in April, 1946. "But," he warned, "Let no one be fooled, . . . Anti-labor legislation is not a dead issue. The industrialists have too many hirelings in Washington and too much money in their coffers to lay down. Other anti-labor bills are in the process of being conceived now."[30]

In the meantime, John L. Lewis and his coal miners again took the center of the stage. It opened with a struggle that was to cast him in a role similar to the one in which Hutcheson had found himself in 1940 and 1941 when he was prosecuted by the Department of Justice under Francis Biddle and Thurman Arnold. Accusing the government of having violated the vacation pay and welfare fund provisions of the contract, Lewis declared the contract had been voided and threatened another strike unless a settlement were reached by November 20.

[29]*Hutcheson's Private Papers*, April 15, 1946.
[30]*Hutcheson's Private Papers*, covering A. F. of L. Executive Council meetings, March 25 to April 2, 1946.

Thereafter, the Miners' leader served a set of demands on the Coal Administration, including a substantial wage boost, reduction of hours, and increase in the health and welfare fund. The government refused to reopen the contract on the ground that the Krug-Lewis Agreement of the previous May, covered the entire period of government operation. Lewis argued, on the contrary, that he had properly served notice to terminate under the provision of his April, 1945 contract which had been extended by the Krug-Lewis Agreement and which provided for termination on appropriate notice if there was any change in the government's stabilization policy.

Krug answered, citing a new opinion from Attorney General Tom Clarke, "which rules that you (Lewis) are without power to terminate the contract with the government."

Lewis remained silent as the strike date approached. The press reported a long night conference at the White House and the country fatalistically awaited the coming of the inevitable strike. Suddenly on November 17, the administration announced its order to the Attorney General to fight rather than negotiate a new contract. On November 18, two days before the walkout was scheduled to begin, Attorney General Clarke requested a restraining order against Lewis from Federal Judge T. Alan Goldsborough. Judge Goldsborough issued a temporary order restraining all officials of the union from continuing the contract termination notice in effect. Judge Goldsborough set a hearing on the preliminary injunction for November 27, at which time there was to be a judicial termination of the disputed contract. Lewis refused to withdraw his termination notice as ordered by Judge Goldsborough, and the coal mines of the nation shut down on November 20, with the inevitable effect on railroad operation, steel production, and the nation's economic machinery in general.

On December 4, Judge Goldsborough fined the union $3,500,000, and Lewis personally, $10,000. In an impassioned statement made in court after he was adjudged in contempt, Lewis declared that the restraining order had been issued in violation of both the Clayton and Norris-LaGuardia Acts. The union promptly gave notice of appeal and the government requested the Supreme Court to review the case at once. Union lawyers protested vigorously against the size of the union's fine, which amounted to $250,000 for each day the strike had been in effect. The recommendations of the government counsel, they declared, were part of a political program designed to break the union and empty its treasury. The conviction and the fines dwarfed any financial penalty ever imposed on a union in the history of the country.

Hutcheson's fury knew no bounds. He rallied unhesitatingly to Lewis' corner as it became increasingly clear to him that an outright attempt was in progress to wreck the Miners' Union. Such a deliberate misuse of the injunction weapon both labor leaders commiserated was outlawed by the Norris-LaGuardia Act, which was the subject of court review in U.S. vs. Hutcheson. The Carpenters' general president concluded that his friend Lewis "has been made the whipping boy" of the Truman administration, as was Hutcheson during Roosevelt's third term.

On December 4, when Judge Goldsborough denounced the strike as "an evil and monstrous thing" and a threat to democracy itself, Lewis called Hutcheson by long distance in Indianapolis. After their first moments of stupefaction, Hutcheson urged him to "slap back" and appeal Goldsborough's preliminary injunction. Lewis then inquired if Hutcheson "would hold in safekeeping the U.M.W.'s. certified check of $1,000,000 made out to his name. If you did, I would feel much more secure. Your impressive discretion was never imitated by anyone in our fraternity." Incredulous Hutcheson was happy to oblige a friend under stress and thereupon "he became the unbonded custodian of $1,000,000 of United Mine Workers' money," John Lewellyn Lewis informed the author.

"We felt that our money was just as safe with Bill as if it were deposited in the United States Treasury. When we realized that a plot was afoot to ransack our union treasury, he was the first friend who came to our minds — Somebody to whom we could entrust at least a million dollars for safekeeping. Bill Hutcheson was in the million dollar class as far as the United Mine Workers and I were concerned."[31]

Early in March, the U.S. Supreme Court upheld the conviction both of John L. Lewis and the United Mine Workers, though it reduced the fine levied on the union to $700,000 on the condition that the union purge itself of contempt within a reasonable time. Lewis abided by the court's decision and withdrew his notice to Krug ending their contract.

The Executive Council of the American Federation of Labor, of which Hutcheson was First Vice President, bitterly condemned the Supreme Court's decision. It declared that the most crucial issue was whether an order issued beyond the jurisdiction of the court had to be obeyed, for "if such orders could sustain contempt charges, every labor union would be exposed to financial ruin by the arbitrary caprice of any anti-labor judge in this country. This reprehensible decision of the majority will go down in history as one of the most ignominious decisions ever announced by the Court." The C.I.O. likewise termed the decision one of the "most reactionary and incomprehensible."

As Lewis fought Truman and the Court, Congress, obsessed with its

---

[31]Interview with John L. Lewis, June 15, 1954, headquarters, United Mine Workers of America, Washington, D.C.

hatred for Lewis, began to move in with harsh anti-labor legislation. They were fortified by an antagonized public opinion and other work stoppages and raise demands in the steel and automobile industry.

In November 1946, the Republicans swept the Congressional elections, winning majorities in both the House of Representatives and the Senate. One of the reasons, undoubtedly, for the Republican victory was that many voters were greatly alarmed by the nation-wide strikes. When the Eightieth Republican Congress assembled early in January, 1947, one of the first things the legislators went to work on was the drafting of a new labor relations law, a new code of conduct for unions and management in dealing with each other. The new Congress regarded the election, correctly or incorrectly, as a mandate to them to amend and modify the Wagner Act, labor's "Magna Charta." A large majority of Congress felt that while the Wagner Act was necessary when adopted in 1935 to aid workers in organizing and bargaining collectively, over the years it had given unions an unduly strong bargaining position and advantage over employers. There was no question but that the Eightieth Congress was determined to overhaul the Wagner Act both as a means "of ending abuses of power and balancing the scales of law as between the two elements of the economy."

Early in December, William Hutcheson issued another manifesto, entitled "A Time for Reflection," in which he warned the Republican Party that victory is not a mandate to destroy unionism. Said he, in part, as follows:

"Before the Eightieth Congress convenes, it might not be amiss for the Republican Party to take careful stock of the situation. There is every indication that the landslide vote last month came less from a popular endorsement of the Republican platform and more from a protest against the ever-increasing amount of government control that has grown up during the war years. The people were fed up with price controls that didn't control prices; they were fed up with wage controls that made a mockery of collective bargaining; they were fed up with bureaus and agencies and directives and edicts. When they got the opportunity on November 5, they said so at the polls.

"Clearly the Republican Party received a mandate from the American people to bring to an end the era of government by bureau and edict. However, that is as far as it goes. There are those in the Republican Party who have long pursued an anti-labor course. They have been vociferous and they have been persistent. Unfortunately, they have also ranked high in the Party. Let the Republicans not make the mistake of assuming that last month's victory at the polls was an endorsement of the anti-labor policy these leaders have voiced. Such is not the case. As much as any other group, labor has smarted and suffered under bureaucratic domination of our economy. For five years workers have seen prices skyrocket despite a pledge by the government that they would be held down. At the same time, they have had their wages rigidly controlled during that period. Wage adjustments they have negotiated with their employers have been altered, qualified or denied altogether by one or another of the bureaus or bureaucrats. Labor was thoroughly fed up with controls by November 5.

"Certainly a substantial share of labor support must have been an underlying factor in the Republican victory. That support was forthcoming not because the workers wanted their unions tampered with, but rather because they wanted their unions freed from government dictation which supplanted collective bargaining during the war years. The Republican Party should bear that fact in mind. What support the Party receives from labor from now on will be in direct ratio to the manner in which the Party recognizes that fact. Workers want their unions free and unfettered. Put bluntly, they want politicians kept out of labor relations.

"Not only in the field of labor but also in the whole broad field of social progress the Republican Party should move with caution. Since the Party was last in power, many social gains have been made. The Social Security Act, the Fair Labor Standards Act, and many other basic laws have been written into the books. While some of these acts may have room for improvement, basically they are progressive. Where abuses exist, the Republican Party can add to its prestige by instituting reforms. Where injustices exist the Party can increase its popularity by wiping them out. But the fact should never be overlooked that these things are now a fundamental part of the American Way of Life.

"The fear that is uppermost in the minds of most of our people today is the fear of another depression. The danger is great. A boom is developing which is slowly but surely courting a bust. Since the Republican Party was last in power, the nation has weathered a disastrous depression. That depression taught some bitter but valuable lessons. Through the years since 1932 a number of safeguards have been set up against a repitition of the black days of the 'thirties. While none of these safeguards can stave off a depression if the proper sort of conditions develop, they can and will cushion the shock and decrease the attendant misery if one comes.

"To the little man on the farm or in the city, the threat of another depression is a spectre haunting his every waking hour. Wherever he goes and whatever he does the fear of another depression is never completely out of his mind. He looks to his leaders for assurance that the black days of the 'thirties will not be repeated.

"The task facing the new regime is a tremendous one. The fate of the Republican Party — and for that matter, the fate of Democracy itself — may be hanging in the balance. The people made it clear on November 5 that they want this country to remain free. However, as we have said many times before, freedom is an ephemeral thing; all segments of the economy must remain free or eventually none will be free."[32]

While the Eightieth Congress was manuvering and Hutcheson issued manifestoes warning both the Republicans and management, the most vehement campaign of the National Association of Manufacturers was again testing its old-new recipe for evils in unionism that were eating away at the foundations of the Magna Charta of Labor—the Wagner Act of 1935. Alarmed at the advanced status of labor and unionization during World War II, management sought "equalization" between the rights of unions and employers. Labor's weak position had been strength-

---

[32]"A Time for Reflection" *The Carpenter,* Vol. LXVI:12 (December, 1946), pp. 5-8.

ened, in the process of which the State had taken a part. But industry thought it odious, if not dangerous, that the poor and the excluded could improve their lot in a democracy only by winning power. Actually, labor's "countervailing" power was hollow, strong as it was numerically. It had not learned that victories won on the economic front might be lost in the political arena by a group not oriented nor sufficiently educated to exert maximum political effectiveness.

Ironically enough, the very man who dissented with the concept of the state as umpire in the economic field and in labor-management relations, was entrusted with the task of defending the New Deal which had given organized labor the legal means to carry on large-scale collective bargaining effectively. In his remaining years, less than six, William Levi Hutcheson fought with vehemence and persistence to reverse the trend that threatened to curtail labor's economic rights. He was one of three appointed by the Executive Council of the American Federation of Labor to debate before the House Labor Committee no less than seventeen bills dealing with labor policy that were dropped into the hopper of the House of Representatives. Faced with the problem of freeing labor from the charges of undemocratic practices within the unions, the taint of racketeering, jurisdictional disputes and other "abuses" that had caused a mounting critical opinion against unions and the inconvenience suffered by the public in the great postwar strike wave, Hutcheson had found the formula — "class legislation."

And class legislation it was! It was the weakness of both labor and its leaders who sought to mobilize all political pressure they could to effect the measures being shaped against it, that it could not find a lever with which to turn public opinion against the N.A.M., which is generally credited with fathering the Taft Hartley Labor-Management Act. Neither of the two houses of labor, the A. F. of L. and the C.I.O. could agree which of the two or three weak tools they possessed, they were to use. They suffered, too, from a weakness that was inevitable in a movement which even now in the mid-'fifties had never enjoyed the symbols of power; the leaders were nearly all Democrats, who, in their unsteady enthusiasm, might switch their support from the Democratic to the Republicans and, a little later, from the Republicans to the Democrats.

It was a tribute to the respect shown by or expected of the fifteen Republicans towards Hutcheson, the Republican "master politician" that his manifestoes addressed to the Republicans so profoundly irritated them. In his testimony before the House Labor Committee on February 26, 1947, he gave Congress some straight-from-the-shoulder facts about labor and the vehement agitation for legislation to curb labor activities. Without flourish, calm and collected despite efforts of Congressman Ralph W. Gwinn of New York, and Edward O. McCowen of Ohio, to confuse and befuddle him, Hutcheson chose to debate informally and patiently. He minced no words and he evaded no issues. He bluntly told the twenty-five committee members, among them ten Democrats, what would happen if various bills hamstringing labor were passed. When Congressman Samuel K. McConnell, Jr. of Pennsylvania tried to get him to admit that mandatory open shop principles might not injure the labor movement, Hutcheson recited a little bit of history of the American Plan.

Congressman McConnell: "Mr. Hutcheson, how do you define an open shop, as you know it? Or an open shop as you understand it? That becoming a member of an organization is not a prerequisite to obtaining work in that particular plant?"

Mr. Hutcheson: "Just a moment ago, I think the record will show that I have said at any time the employer needed men that could not be furnished through our regular union channels, it was our position that the employer could hire anyone he liked, and if he, the employer is satisfied with the work that that man performed, then we would be glad to take him into our organization.

"On the other hand, I do not expect you to go so far as to say that you would favor passing a law to compel men to work."

Congressman McConnell: "I have asked you a question."

Mr. Hutcheson: "I'm answering it."

Congressman McConnell: "I said has the open shop principle destroyed unions?"

Mr. Hutcheson: "Let me go a step further. Some of you Congressmen have a habit of making a speech, so you will have to excuse me, if I make a short speech in answering this question.

"I don't mind citing this. You gentlemen probably know something about the Attorney General in the State of Florida, Mr. Tom Watson. Whether you do or not, he got an amendment to the Constitution passed down there, outlawing what he called a closed shop.

"Before that came about, he made an appointment with me and came over to Lakeland, where the home of our organization is located.

"I don't want to bore you, but I think this would give you a little enlightenment. He discussed it with me, and I said to Mr. Watson, "are you of a mind that you are going to pass a law to compel men to work?

"He said, 'no.'

I said, you go ahead and pass this amendment, and if you do, we will proceed in this manner: we will continue to work for our employers, and if your law is such that he wouldn't sign what we call a union shop, we will work for him. But if he hires a non-union man, that is his privilege and he can hire him, but if he comes in there and we solicit his membership and he refuses to join our organization, then we will go to our employer and say, "you have a perfect right to keep that man, but if you do, we are not working with him. There is your choice."

Congressman McConnell: "What do you mean by the American Plan, as you call it?"

Mr. Meany, Secretary Treasurer of the American Federation of Labor (interjecting): The American Plan was the open shop of 1919, 1920 and 1921. It reduced our American Federation of Labor to a skeleton. It wiped out our unions on the Pacific Coast completely."

Congressman McConnell addressing Hutcheson: "You seem to disagree with that statement, Mr. Hutcheson?"

Hutcheson: "I don't agree with George's (Meany) statement that we were wiped out, because we weren't. We fought it out."

Congressman Wint Smith, Kansas: "There are several questions that I disagree with you about, but there is one that I agree with you on.

"I have great respect for one thing you have said here, I would like to make a speech about it, because you are the first man who has come up that I think is fair and open minded, representing as you do a lot of labor.

"When you say you are not a politician, though I want to say: you are a past master. I wish I were as good as you are."

Hutcheson: "Thank you, sir."

Hutcheson questioned the competence of the committee member who he thought had no previous experience with labor. "I came before you with the thought in mind that I did not think you gentleman knew the real picture of labor. It is pretty deep. Now, I do not know what your occupation is, but whatever it may be, I probably do not know a damn thing about it. You get me?

Congressman Max Schwabe, Missouri: "But we talked about abuses this morning, and there has been a lot of testimony before this committee, perhaps not with respect to your union, but various abuses. We named some of them."

Hutcheson: "Congressman, let me inject a thought again: our organization is made up of human beings. Did you ever see a perfect human being in your life?"

Congressman Schwabe: "No, and we cannot make them perfect by legislation. I appreciate that."

Hutcheson: "Now, being made up of average over-all human beings, you cannot expect everyone of them to be perfect. We have good, bad and indifferent, the same as we have in attorneys and doctors and so forth.

Now, in reference to the cooling-off period. I am going to hit the high spots; and I may miss some of them, I will be glad to give you such information as I can. I think that this committee is made up of American citizens, as are the members of our organization. We do not believe in class legislation. We have never had in this country of ours any class distinctions. Therefore being Americans, we do not believe in class legislation. I might say that any legislation that is enacted should be for the majority of all the people of the United States.[33]

While open hearings before the House Committee were held for six weeks, Hutcheson continued to write stirring manifestoes, "Congress, Take Note!" "Legislation Holds No Lasting Answer," "A Declaration," "Class Laws Are unAmerican," the latter of which he broadcast over Station WLW and the National Broadcasting Company, denouncing Congress and demanding justice, for "all classes and creeds and colors must maintain the right of self-determination. We reaffirm our faith in the free enterprise system. We believe that it has produced for us more of the good things of life than any other system invented by the mind of man. However, we must point out that a free labor movement must always be an integral part of the free enterprise system . . . all segments of our society must be free, or eventually none will be free."

Public opinion, management, even the wage earners did not respond. Management refused to follow Hutcheson's reasoning and the House Committee he denounced as useless mandarins attacking an indispensable institution of the community which paid them.[34]

President William Green and Mr. George Meany, Secretary-treasurer, presented the point of view of the A. F. of L. while Hutcheson was entrusted with the dual task of presenting the point of view of the Federation's affiliates and of the Brotherhood of Carpenters. An aging man, fired by righteous indignation, William Green delivered his *piece de resistance*. Hutcheson was the fox, at times evasive and even "philosophical." His main ammunition he prepared for a struggle with his friend, the Senator of Ohio, Robert A. Taft. Philip Murray of the C.I.O. spared no one. He was vigorous in his attack on the House and Senate Committees. His just demand that the Senate Committee Chairman rescind the appointment of Gerald D. Reilly, a highly prejudiced consultant to the Senate Committee was not answered. Lewis was not unduly concerned about the effects of the law, for he believed it would collapse under a boycott of organized labor.

The House Committee, of which Representative Fred A. Hartley, Jr. of New Jersey was Chairman, was ready to act first. Its bill reported favorably to the House on April 11, prohibited the closed shop, restricted collective-bargaining to a company-wide basis, denied bargaining rights

---

[33]"Statement of William L. Hutcheson, President of UBCJA and First Vice President of A. F. of L.," Hearing Before the Committee on Education and Labor, House of Representatives 18th Congress: First Session, Vol. 3, pp. 16-64FF.
[34]Harry A. Millis and Emily Clark Brown, *op. cit.* pp. 367-70.

to unions officered by Communists, provided for a seventy-five-day "cooling-off" and fact-finding period enforced by injunction in the case of work stoppages threatening public health or interest, outlawed strikes unless at least five union-management conferences had been held and the majority of workers in the plant had voted to reject the employer's final offer, regulated internal practices, prohibited the use of coercion or the refusal to bargain collectively by employees, prohibited mass-picketing and secondary boycotts, made unions liable in court under the anti-trust laws, required union registration and annual reports to the Department of Labor, prohibited union contributions in elections involving federal office, required craft unions where a majority of the craftsmen desired, provided that unions might be sued for breach of contract. The final vote for passage of the measure, came before the House on April 15 under a rule that limited debate to six hours. On the 17th the House passed this "tough" measure by a vote of 308 to 107. Only 25 Republicans voted against the bill, while 93 Democrats stood with 215 Republicans voting in the affirmative.

This comprehensive and complicated measure which, according to Chairman Hartley, was "Labor's Bill of Rights," came before the House on April 15 under a rule that allowed six hours for general debate on the measure on a very restricted time, under a five-minute rule, for the proposing and consideration of amendments. In any event, there were not more than three sessions of the House given over to the debate on the measure and the bill was passed on April 17.

On the day that the House passed the Hartley Bill, Senator Taft introduced S.1126 in the Senate. The Taft Bill established unfair labor practices in which unions were prohibited to engage, outlawed the closed and regulated union shop, required a sixty-day notice for termination or modification of a contract, permitted employers to adjust grievances with individual employees, protected craft bargaining units, restricted the right of strikers to vote in bargaining elections, made provisions for decertification petitions by groups of employees, provided for registration and the filing of annual reports by unions with the Secretary of Labor, limited the period in which unfair labor practice charges could be filed, required the Board to give priority to certain charges that could be filed against unions, facilitated damage suits against unions for violations of contract, made the National Labor Relations Board judge, jury, and prosecutor, and provided for injunctions, cooling-off periods and boards of inquiry in strikes affecting substantially an entire industry and imperilling national health and safety.

Of the thirteen members on this committee, eight were Republicans and five were Democrats. In the Senate, the Committee minority split with Senator Taft and his conservative colleagues, asserting that "this bill is designed to weaken the effective problem of labor legislation which has been, with great pains, built over the years. It would be destructive of much that is valuable in the prevention of labor-management conflict. It contains many barriers . . . that can only make more difficult the settlement of disputes. Its principal results would be to create misunderstanding and conflict. . . ."[35]

The Senate amended the Committee's Bill making "coercion" on interference with the rights of employees by unions an unfair labor practice, and denied certification privileges to Communist-led unions. The Senate then adopted the Bill by the overwhelming vote of 68 to 24. The measure that emerged from the committee that reconciled the Hartley and Taft Bills resembled the Taft measure. "There was what might be termed a 'conservative liberal' split in the Committee majority. The Bill as finally accepted by the Senate included most of the provisions desired by Senator Taft, who represented the conservative view on the Committee."[36] Only Senator Morse stood fast. He voted, against his colleagues when the Senate Bill passed.

During this time, Hutcheson was engaged in a last desperate but vain combat to ease and modify some of the more discriminatory and harsh provisions of the Taft Bill. He had hoped to make the *best* of his friendship with Robert A. Taft, whom he had known for twenty-nine years, since the former started his career as assistant counsel to Herbert Hoover. The Senator, William Howard Taft's eldest son knew Hutcheson far better than did most of the other Republican solons on the Committee. He therefore did not underestimate his adversary. Taft was well aware of Hutcheson's intimate association with his father on the National War Labor Board during World War I.

In his laudable enterprise Hutcheson now needed two chief lieutenants to keep him in touch with the Senate Committee course of action. The plan of the campaign was for Judge Harry Routzohn to appeal to Taft, who thus found himself approached on the one side by a powerful Ohio Republican politician and on the other by Hutcheson and Richard Gray, President of the Building and Construction Trades Department of the A. F. of L. Senator Taft was inflexible, and Hutcheson, accompanied by Judge Routzohn and Gray tried a last card. "Your political career as Presidential contender," he warned the Senator, "will be compromised, perhaps fatally, by your conduct as Chairman of the Senate Committee. Any politician with some appreciation of duty to cold facts would hardly seek advantage by utilizing cynically familiar patterns of action and belief . . ." He charged Taft with becoming an autocrat and a crude

[35]*Federal Labor Relations Act of 1947, Minority Views.* 80th Congress, 1st Session, Senate Report 105, Part 2, 1947, p. 1.
[36]Harry D. Millis and Emily C. Brown, *op. cit.,* p. 375.

conservative partisan. "Given the existence of a free economy, an unfettered labor movement will strengthen its capacity for autonomous self-
regulation," Hutcheson told Taft with unconcealed bitterness.

Shocked out of his poise by such candor, Senator Taft retorted
that he would not let this intimidation influence him. He promised,
however, to Hutcheson's chief lieutenants, that he would introduce no
amendments to the Bill designed to outlaw interference by unions with
the rights of employees, secondary boycotts and jurisdictional strikes.

On April 13, ten days before the general debate on the Taft Bill in
the Senate commenced, Hutcheson had his last unpleasant interview
with Senator Taft. The latter had not kept the promise he made to
Judge Routzohn and Richard Gray. In short, he was evasive, insincere
and lacking in his characteristic probity. Bitter remarks were exchanged
between them. "If your father knew what you did, he would turn over in
his grave," Hutcheson told Senator Taft.

The Senator amended the Committee's Bill to make "coercion" of
employees by unions an unfair labor practice, to prohibit the certification of unions officered by Communists and to expressly authorize "free
speech" for employees and employers. However, defeated by a single
vote, was Taft's effort to restrict industry-wide bargaining. The Senate
then adopted the Bill by an overwhelming majority, by a vote of 54 to
17. Favoring the Bill were 37 Republicans and 17 Democrats. Against
it were 15 Democrats and Republicans Morse and Langer. Of the ab-
sentees whose views were announced, 15 would have been in the affirmative and 7 would have been opposed. Here, as in the House, more than
the two-thirds necessary to override a veto had been attained.

On June 5, Senator Taft opened debate in the Senate with a defense
of the conference, asserting that the conference committee measure represented a victory for the Senate, since it was substantially the same as
the version of S.1126 sent to the conference. He expressed regret that
certain ends were not covered at all, or covered inadequately. He stated
that amendments to restrict or outlaw political contributions and expenditures by unions and on strikes of government employees were
reported unfavorably. This was the measure of Senator Taft's liberality.

Summarizing his defense of the Conference Bill, Senator Taft stated
that this Bill was still fair and just and represented workable solutions
to the pressing labor relations problems of the day, since it was for all
practical purposes the same Bill which the Senate had originally agreed
to and which had been based on these premises of "equitableness" and
workability.

Summing up for the opposition, Republican Senator Morse, in a long
speech against the Bill on June 5 declared: "I shall vote against this Bill

Under-Secretary of War Robert Patterson takes time off during World War II to express "nation's gratitude" to the General President of the United Brotherhood of Carpenters, "for members' all-out cooperation."

Exiting from White House, March 8, 1946, after a conference with President Truman are John L. Lewis of the United Mine Workers and William Hutcheson. Following their visit, coal operators agreed to submit deadlocked coal dispute to arbitration.

Initial efforts to wipe out conflict that kept A. F. of L. and C. I. O. in opposite camps, were launched by these 10 labor leaders on May 1, 1937. From left to right; Emil Rieve (Textile), Walter Reuther (UAW), Jacob Potofsky (Amalgamated Clothing Workers), Albert Fitzgerald (United Electrical, Radio & Machine Workers, since expelled from C. I. O.), A. F. of L. President Green, C. I. O. President Phillip Murray, Daniel Tobin (Teamsters), John Lewis (Miners), William L. Hutcheson (Carpenters), and George Meany, the then Secretary-Treasurer of the Federation.

International News Phot

William L. Hutcheson's "buddies" honor the UBCJA chieftain as he voluntarily lays down his chest of tools. Here in round-robin hand-clasp are: the late A. F. of L. President William Green, John L. Lewis, the "president emeritus" of the UBCJA, his successor Maurice A. Hutcheson, and Daniel J. Tobin, president emeritus of the Teamsters.

that has been reported by the Conference Committee because, after careful study, I'm completely convinced that the amendments added in conference make it impracticable and an unadministrable law. Virtually every amendment which has been made threatens the legitimate rights of the American workingman. . . ."

The President had about fifteen days to consider the measure finally approved by the Congress after the conference. During most of the time between his veto message and the passage of the conference measure, the President was away from the White House. Before his departure, the Carpenters' president sought every means at his command to bring pressure on the White House through the President's aide Dr. John R. Steelman, a loyal and warm friend of "Bill" Hutcheson. In vetoing the bill, President Truman branded the measure harmful to the peoples' best interests, avowing that it would send strikes soaring and destroy national unity. Taken as a whole, Truman declared the Bill would "reverse the basic direction of our national labor policy . . . The most fundamental test which I have applied to this Bill is whether it would strengthen or weaken American democracy in the present critical hour . . ."[37]

Unmoved by the President's plea, the House at once overrode the veto by a vote of 331 to 83. This was 55 more votes than the two-thirds needed to override the veto. The Senate did not move so hastily. Debate followed that evening. The banjo-playing Senator Taylor of Idaho gained the floor about 10 P.M. and commenced a "talkfest" with the objective of delaying the vote until the following Monday in order that the sentiment of the country over the President's message might reach the Congress. He was joined by Senators Morse, Pepper and Murray, and despite majority assertions to the contrary, achieved their objectives when the Senate agreed to postpone the final vote until 3 P.M. of June 23rd. These tactics, however, were to no avail. Senator Aiken, the first Senator on the roll call and one of the doubtful Republicans, cast the first vote in favor of the measure and everyone then knew the veto would be overridden. It was, by a final Senate vote of 68 to 25. Thus, the Labor-Management Relations Act of 1947 became law. In both Houses a substantial number of Democrats joined the Republican majority to place the Taft-Hartley measure on the statute books, for the first major revision of our labor relations legislation since the adoption of the Wagner Act twelve years earlier.

*   *   *

In July, 1947 William Hutcheson announced in *The Carpenter: "The Dark Ages Return.* By the time this appears in print the fate of the Taft-Hartley Bill will have been settled. But we are not naive enough to

---

[37]*Daily Congress Record,* 93:7503.

believe that the Taft-Hartley Bill will settle the matter of labor legislation. By now it is clear that the vested interests which authored and
backed the Taft-Hartley measure will be satisfied with nothing short of
complete legislative hamstringing of labor. Their goal is final and ir-
revocable destruction of organized labor. . . . They want to return to
the days of 'rugged individualism' — which is a fancy name for white
slavery. . . ."[36]

It was not only the Brotherhood's press with its many political manifestoes that was active. Hutcheson and a sub-committee of the Executive
Council of the A. F. of L., consisting of Daniel J. Tobin, David Dubinsky, William Green, George Meany and Matthew Woll, were beginning
to use the Taft-Hartley Act as a means of demonstrating their vigilance,
even before the Act became fully effective on August 22, 1947. In a
ringing declaration entitled *"No Compromise With Slavery,"* the sub-
committee called the workingmen and women to "mobilize their economic strength so that they substitute collective action for individual
action." "The material, educational and cultural well-being of all classes
of people depend upon an adequate financial income . . . that means
wages high enough to enable them to maintain themselves in decency
and comfort. This a noble objective. It squared with the American
way of life."

The declaration denounced the N.A.M., which "may function and
serve their respective membership without any interference on the part
of government." With unusual vehemence, the signatories called upon
the Federation's seven million constituents to "concentrate their efforts
toward bringing about the defeat of every member of Congress for re-
election who voted in favor of final enactment of the Taft-Hartley Act."

In an article, *"The Leopard Has Not Changed His Spots,"* Hutcheson assailed the N.A.M.'s policies, criticized Charles E. Wilson, head
of General Motors, who pleaded for the abolition of the forty-hour
week, while General Counsel Robert N. Denham of the N.L.R.B. was
charged with "partisanship," which is incompatible with traditional
American standards of justice and fair play.

The transference of the Taft-Hartley Act from the moral to the political plane which anti-labor Congress deplored, though it realized that
it was inevitable, was now well under way. "Stung to the quick," Hutcheson went to work in politics more actively than ever before. None
of the International unions affiliated with the A. F. of L. or C.I.O.
matched the Brotherhood's financial contribution towards activizing labor
politically. The reports to the House Clerk on expenditures in the 1948
election campaign showed that the Carpenters contributed approximately

---

[36] Dark Ages Return," *The Carpenter*, Vol. LXVII:7 (July 7, 1947), pp. 7-9.

forty percent or $100,000 of $243,024 collected by A. F. of L's. Labor League for Political Education, or fifteen percent of $696,004 of the total collected by six major labor organizations.[37]

"Ohio tees off" was the Brotherhood's answer to Robert A. Taft. Practically every Ohio industrial center was represented at the February 8, 1948 meeting "for a showdown fight against the forces of reaction in both the United States Congress in the Ohio General Assembly." At least 500 Brotherhood delegates from local unions and district councils throughout the state were present. Special buses carried the Brotherhood's delegates. Under the slogan "We are Well Organized in the Industrial Field; Let's do as well in the political field," the Brotherhood's delegates mercilessly attacked the "reactionary forces which seemed bent on emasculating organized labor."

Satire was another weapon which the Brotherhood used against the Senior Senator of Ohio. "Have you noticed that all God's candidates got liberalism these days? Even Taft! We have just noticed a handout from the National Taft-for-President clubs which announced in a newspaper that Taft is a Conservative-Liberal. . . .

"Once, during a certain campaign in the far-off heroic time, a beery sage named Henry Mencken who lived in a place called Balmer Merlin said Republicans can win with a Chinaman.

"It may be that 1948 will prove the words of the prophet true. But if the Republicans try it, he'll have to be a Liberal Chinaman."[38]

"Attention, Senator Taft," "You Are in Politics" and other such provocative headlines aroused the anger of men who three and four years earlier could not be swept off their feet by Hutcheson's verbal action. Now the appeals of the Brotherhood's Non-Partisan Committee for the Repeal and Defeat of Anti-Labor Legislation were stirring enough to arouse the anger of the Carpenters.

On November 2, 1948, in an election in which the Taft-Hartley law was a major issue and the Democratic Party program had pledged the repeal of the Act, the voters returned a Democratic Congress. The Brotherhood took some credit for the results of the elections. In New Mexico the "Right to Work" Bill was voted down by the effect of political work done by its Non-Partisan Committee. The Twin Cities District Council of Carpenters was credited by winner Senator Hubert H. Humphrey with defeating Senator Joseph H. Ball, one of the most vociferous anti-laborites in the Eightieth Congress. The Brotherhood as well as other unions continued their political interest and activity. It was an unavoidable effect of repressive anti-labor legislation, plus

---

[37]*William L. Hutcheson, Private Papers*, October 2-11, 1949.
[38]"Everybody Wants to Get in the Act," *The Carpenter,* Vol LXVIII:8 (August, 1948), pp. 27-28.

lack of action on other vital problems. "The job is not finished," wrote Hutcheson. "Labor will only have thirty-eight tried and true friends in the Senate out of ninety-six. In the House, labor will have some one hundred and seventy-two avowed friends — far less than the two hundred and eighteen needed for a majority. This means that the need for political action is as great as it ever was. We have another date on November 7, 1950."[39]

On December 12, 1947, while Hutcheson was preparing to celebrate Christmas and New Year at the Carpenters' Home in Lakeland, Florida, a telephone call came through from Washington. It was from the White House. Dr. John R. Steelman, Assistant to the President and an old friend, was on the phone. He informed him that President Truman wished him to serve as a member of the new National Labor-Management Panel and, furthermore, he wished to see him as soon as possible. After some further talk seasoned with personal compliments, he told Steelman he would think it over and call him back. Hutcheson did reflect and discuss the matter for two days. On the 18th he went to Washington and the White House to visit the thirty-third President of the United States.

He first went to see John R. Steelman, with whom he had been friends since the time when the latter was appointed Director of the Mediation and Conciliation Service of the United States by President Roosevelt. The President of the United States, received him with cordiality and friendliness. He shook his hand and, addressing himself to Steelman and Hutcheson said: "I have been most satisfied with your consistent opposition to the Taft-Hartley Act, and I wish therefore to acknowledge your ability to fight for what is right, by appointing you a member of the twelve-man Labor-Management Panel." Hutcheson felt a profound sense of satisfaction and thanked the President. He was appointed to this office for a term of one year, expiring on December 18, 1949.

The National Labor-Management Panel was created as part of the Labor-Management Relations Act of 1947 (Taft-Hartley Act). Title II, Section 205B provided for the appointment, by the President, of six men from management and six men from labor, with a duty, "to advise in the avoidance of industrial controversies in the manner in which mediation and voluntary adjustment shall be administred, particularly with reference to controversies affecting the general welfare of the country." Upon request of parties in dispute or upon its own motion, the new agency was to offer its services whenever a dispute "threatens to cause a substantial interruption of commerce." The Director was required to avoid attempting to mediate disputes which would have only

---

[39]*The Carpenter,* Vol. LXVIII:12, (December, 1948), p. 9.

a minor affect on interstate commerce, if state or other conciliation services are available. If the Director was unable to bring the parties to agreement within a reasonable time, "he shall seek to induce the parties voluntarily to seek other means of settling the dispute without a resort to strike, lockout, or other coercion." Handling of grievances arising under agreements was to be engaged in "only as a last resort and in exceptional cases."

Much of this was sound and in accord with practices which had been developed by the Conciliation Service and with recommendations of the Labor-Management Conference of 1945. Hutcheson had served on the Advisory Committee of this policy-making body in 1945. As a top spokesman for the American Federation of Labor, he recommended to the 1945 Labor-Management Conference that the United States Conciliation Service should be recognized as an effective and completely impartial agency within the U.S. Department of Labor. His statements of principles and procedures to make collective bargaining work effectively greatly strengthened the Conciliation Service. All this meant progress and was being developed in close cooperation with industry and labor. But Senator Taft felt otherwise: "As long as the Service was an agency of the Department of Labor it must necessarily take a pro-labor slant and therefore could not be as fair in mediating differences between parties."

There is no doubt that Senator Taft's decision reflected a wish to weaken the Department of Labor, as part of a desired "equalization" sought by the Act. This was another point of contention between Hutcheson and Senator Taft. Hutcheson consistently advocated the principle of placing all government labor activities under the direct authority and responsibility of the Secretary of Labor. However, the new Advisory Committee appointed by the President, in place of the functioning committee was set up in the Spring of 1948. The Panel decided 735 disputes in one year. "It required great discretion on the part of the National Labor-Management Panel, if it was to maintain the needed impartiality and not throw its weight on one side or the other in a dispute."[40] Cyrus S. Ching, the new Director of the Federal Mediation and Conciliation Service leaned heavily on Hutcheson in the setting-up of the Service.

The Carpenters were so impressed with their seventy-four year-old president's performance on the Labor-Management Panel that they did not hesitate to publicly recommend, in the pages of the U.B.'s official magazine, Hutcheson's name for a major diplomatic assignment. "Some months ago we ran an editorial suggesting that a few of our top-flight labor leaders could be used to good advantage in handling our relations

---

[40]Harry A. Millis & Emily C. Brown, *op. cit.*, p. 573.

with foreign nations. The editorial solicited considerable comment — all of it favorable. Men like Bill Hutcheson . . . may not be able to wear striped pants with the proper air of elegance, and they may not be able to crook their little fingers at the proper angle while holding a tea cup, but when it comes to negotiating, bargaining or working out agreements they can hold their own with the best any other nation can offer. . . . However the dead hand of medieval pomp and circumstance still surrounds international relations. Double-talk, protocol and wheels within wheels complicate things considerably. Some straight from the shoulder talk might improve things considerably; and men like Bill (Hutcheson) are just the boys who could inject it into international relations."[41]

When President Truman asked John Steelman to arrange a meeting with Hutcheson, he was convinced that the Carpenters' President would not resort to evasion or refuse to answer blunt questions.

In November of 1946 when Hutcheson paid his first visit to the White House, Truman gave him the opportunity to declare his convictions of the proposed anti-labor regislation that was being drafted by the Republican Congress — and to give his reasons. As they shook hands, Hutcheson said: "Mr. President, I am a Republican as you are a Democrat. But I assure you that I am an American first and always, and a Republican, second. The President replied: "I am sure you are, Mr. Hutcheson." Hutcheson told the President that the proposed new labor relations laws will be impossible of enforcement, certainly in the building and construction trades. He admitted that some overhauling of the Wagner Act is in order; that the "strike situation has been serious during the past year and a-half; but it was due in major part to the aggravations, irritations and injustices. The real way to stop strikes is simple. Let the employers raise wages enough to wipe out the decrease in purchasing power of weekly earnings; at the same time let them lower prices to bring them down to a par with what they were on V-J Day, and the strike situation will be automatically settled. Workers like strikes less than any other one class. They strike only when necessity compels them." He disagreed with the President's own recommendations to prevent jurisdictional disputes, to prohibit secondary boycotts. "There is a misconception that legislation can correct difficulties which stem from basic human relationships. Were this true, the world might be a happier place.

"Mr. President, I have been part of the labor movement for fully a half a century. During these years I have seen ideas, patterns, and theories come and go. But in all this time I have never seen a sound

---

[41]"A Greater Voice in World Affairs," *The Carpenter,* Vol. LXVII:11 (November 1948), p. 27; Vol. LXVI:6, (June, 1946), p. 17

concept of labor relations incorporated into the American way of life but what that concept was based on the fundamental premise that men must be free to work or not to work, to do business or not to do business, to accept or not to accept chances that the vagaries of ever-changing conditions present."

Hutcheson's views of world affairs elicited favorable comment from the President. He was pleased, he recalled, with his eight-point document on the Dumbarton Oaks Conference which John (Steelman) presented to him sometime in 1945. And when the Taft-Hartley measure came up for the President's signature, Mr. Truman sought the advice of Hutcheson. "He (the President) knew that Hutcheson and Taft had been working pretty closely together, but the Carpenters' President was left holding the bag. There is no doubt that Hutcheson's advice to the President influenced his veto."[42]

Hutcheson's Republican political friends were not of much help. Senators Capehart, Bridges and Taft nearly put him out of his wits by their support of the Taft-Hartley Act. He was especially bitter at Taft and the Senator from Indiana, Homer S. Capehart. Hutcheson did however endorse Senator Styles Bridges' candidacy for re-election to the United States Senate in 1948. He gave Bridges his "unqualified support and endorsement."

> "While I have on occasions disagreed with you on certain questions and openly disagreed with you on your position with respect to the Taft-Hartley Act and still do — I have always respected your views.
>
> "Your years in the Senate have proven beyond preadventure your qualifications. We need tried and true representatives in the Senate. The home front consisting of the laborer, the farmer and the Government must be upheld. To deprive the Government of your aid and experience would to my mind be a mistake."[43]

He flayed Senators Capehart and Taft. "The great labor victory at the polls last year went for naught because the Tafts and the Capeharts retained their power. November 1950 offers working people a chance to finish the great job. It will be no easy job to unseat the lords of special privilege in Congress but it is a job that must be done."

When World War II ended, labor leaders expected the bitter struggle of the 1920's to be repeated. This ghost of the past was the real generalissimo directing Hutcheson's postwar strategy. Among the nation's top labor leaders, Hutcheson, the veteran of two grim ordeals, maneuvered himself in anticipation of an economic collapse and a new anti-labor offensive.

---

[42]The above and preceding quotations are based on a lengthy interview with Dr. John R. Steelman in Washington, April 8, 1954.

[43]William L. Hutcheson, *Personal Correspondence*, July 1, 1948.

During World War I, with unionization enjoying the protection of the National War Labor Board, the Brotherhood, as well as the American Federation of Labor, doubled its membership. By 1920 the Federation's membership of 5,000,000 covered 12 percent of the total working force. With the war's end, the industrial truce was replaced by the American Plan (open-shop) offensive. Strike after strike was called, fought out and broken. Within three years the American Federation of Labor lost nearly 2,000,000 members and the Brotherhood percentage-wise almost as many. In 1948 the A. F. of L. had a membership of 7,500,000 and the Brotherhood three-quarters of a million. History had not repeated itself!

Despite fears of a postwar "recession," the latter 'forties and early 'fifties were indubitably prosperous years in every major economic sector. Industry and the farm were called on to fill deferred wartime needs, defense orders and Korean War orders, as well as the normal economic demand. "Full Employment," with minor exceptions, was the rule. As a result of government orders, the national economy was not compelled to meet the test of converting from high wartime productivity to the restricted demands of normal peacetime consumption. Only inflation and a severe housing shortage remained to plague labor, as well as the average citizen. Since the mid-year of 1947, these were superseded in importance by the passage of the Taft-Hartley Act, which had sparked the labor movement's dynamo with a new fighting spirit. For in it lay the unexploded dynamite with its union-busting potential during a period of unemployment, and when a government and Congress hostile to labor might be in power. The inflationary movement clearly had a pronounced impact on the growth of the Labor movement. Certain it is that it has been a potent factor affecting the distribution of income between broad classes of receivers.

The businessmen's prestige had revived considerably since the dark days of the 'thirties and there was a tendency at large to stress *laissez faire* ideas of free enterprise as the Democratic antithesis of totalitarian Communism. Economic individualism was advocated as a basic bulwark against both Socialism of England and Communism of Russia.

During these years there was an imposing growth in the size, authority, and complexity of the federal government superimposed upon the growth that had taken place under the New Deal. To be sure, that growth was nothing wholly new. But the government and the State had been growing almost continuously. The New Deal did accelerate this trend, and the war of 1941-1946 gave it a much stronger push. By 1940, when the New Deal had done its utmost and the war boom was just beginning, the number of federal civil employees rose from six-tenths of a million in 1930 to a little over a million in 1940. By 1945, when the war was ending, it had shot up to more than three and one-half million and in the years following World War II, the number had shrunk only part way. In 1949, some four years after the war, and before the Korean crisis, there were still over two million federal civil service employees.

William Levi Hutcheson now gave himself over almost completely to three major projects: the defeat of the Taft-Hartley Act, "Horizons Unlimited" for the American worker, and the political problem of freedom. However, all these did not form a social-political "philosophy," but rather, a picture. Hutcheson was not vigorously logical, for despite his pronounced individualism, denouncing as he did "free-riders," he pushed with vigor federal social security. Nevertheless, there was a certain unity to the mirage which persisted in his mind. It gave him scope, at the age of seventy-four, to act as a leader of American opinion, using the air waves to oppose "socialized medicine," write editorials urging labor to obtain a greater share in the management of government, and to denounce the "brass." He proclaimed labor's and farmers' right to a greater share in the national income, and he dreamed of universal peace, with a strong American labor movement playing a significant role in its attainment.

He had gladly welcomed his appointment to the Ancient and Accepted Scottish Right of Freemasonry. Generally, on such occasions, a tableau was given, portraying the evolution of humanity according to the Book of Genesis, the Talmud and Masonry. His faith in the existence of God, however, had no other foundations than simple utility and the "social service" of the Methodists. His brother Mason, Reverend Logan Hall of the Meridian Street Methodist Church, Indianapolis, continued to be the recipient of generous contributions "for making it possible to spread Christmas cheer for the indigent and young" in the community. The good reverend appreciated "the privilege of being steward of these funds." He took time off to write a letter protesting the dismissal of a waiter, R. G. Brogiriou from the service of the Washington Hotel, Washington D.C. where he often stayed while attending Executive Council meetings of the Federation. "It has recently come to my attention that you have dismissed Mr. R. Brogiriou from the service of the hotel," he wrote the hotel Management. "This I regret very much, as I am frank to state and admit that he was one of the reasons why I have for years stopped at your hotel."[44] Brusquely he turned down the Republican campaign chairman of Polk County, Florida, who requested a contribution from the residents of the Carpenters Home in Lakeland. "In

---

[44]William Levi Hutcheson, *Private Correspondence,* December 28, 1948 to January 5, 1950.

reply to that inquiry let me say that the occupants of the Brotherhood's Home have no means of supporting themselves, and the expense of maintaining the Home is paid by the International organization. The International is a non-partisan organization. Members are guaranteed that the Brotherhood will in no way interfere with their religious belief and political opinion, and with that policy, of course, the International never makes contributions to any political party."[45]

Every letter he received from his friends, proved to him that he was needed, ailing as he was now. Samuel Ungerleider sought his help to solve a jurisdictional dispute between local 34 of the Retail Clerks International and Local 138 of the Teamsters International. "I would not make this request if it weren't important to me," wrote Ungerleider to Hutcheson on December 3, 1948. Ungerleider requested that Hutcheson intervene with Mr. David Beck of the International Brotherhood of Teamsters. Hutcheson suggested that Ungerleider "contact the Teamsters' representative in New York City, M. J. Cashal, room 712, at 265 West 14th Street." Calumnies and accusations against John R. Steelman at the hands of a "Michigan Republican Senator" aroused Hutcheson's ire and bitter irony. "My main reason of writing you" wrote Dr. Steelman, "is that I have learned you are still 'under the weather.' Not only with my being threatened with jail but more important with many worse problems becoming increasingly serious, I doubly regret that you have been unable to come to Washington. There would be too much to talk over. I note, for example, that some of the coal miners have quit work. It all adds up to the fact that you ought to get well immediately and get back into harness."

Hutcheson welcomed Dr. Steelman's letter, reassuring him six days later that "as usual in the past if at any time there is anything I can do to be helpful, all I have to do is to be called upon . . . The gentleman from Michigan has a certain amount of hot air that he has to expel and get rid of now and then. Beyond that, in my opinion there is nothing to worry. . . ."[46] Despite the fact that his physical condition became discouraging and he suffered from further complications, he participated as often as he could in the strenuous and complex National Labor Management Panel. He recovered to the extent that he would be back in Indianapolis at least part of the time, serving the Brotherhood.

As the presidential political kettle began bubbling again in August of 1948, Hutcheson's name kept cropping up in the news. Dispensers of "confidential" news predicted that he and the United Brotherhood of Carpenters Non-Partisan Committee would jump on one bandwagon or another.

---

[45]*Ibid,* April 10, 1948.
[46]*Ibid,* John R. Steelman to Dear Chief "personal," March 16, 1948.

"All such statements or predictions," Hutcheson announced in the August issue of *The Carpenters,* "are pure conjecture and without foundation of fact. The Brotherhood's Non-Partisan Committee for the Repeal and Defeat of Anti-Labor Legislation is set up for the sole purpose of defeating legislation detrimental to the best interests of all workers in general and organized carpenters in particular. As President of the Non-Partisan Committee, I'm similarly dedicated. In the meantime, stories allegedly giving inside dope about what I am going to do can be treated as pure fiction."[47]

Hutcheson's political strategy in the 1948 presidential election was determined, first, by his all-out opposition to the Taft-Hartley Act, and, second, by his pragmatic political temper. Taft had been singled out as the primary target for what was intended as a mighty demonstration of Hutcheson's wrath, as well as his influence as a national labor leader. There was, indeed, a contrast, between his position in the Republican party in 1948, with the one he held for a quarter of a century during which he was the recognized party functionary, channeling labor intelligence into party activities, composing its labor platforms, and enlisting labor support and influence in Republican politics.

In 1948, the Republicans of Indiana elected Hutcheson as a delegate to the GOP National Convention from the Eleventh Congressional District. Reckoning with the prevailing Republican drift toward the formation of a nation-wide conservative coalition, he battled to strengthen the anti-Taft forces rallying behind Governor Thomas E. Dewey, from whom he sought a clear commitment that the Taft-Hartley Act was unjust. In this strategy he was strengthened by the Democratic party whose program had pledged the repeal of the Act. Dewey won the presidential nomination, accepting most gracefully Hutcheson's support. The latter then jockeyed to obtain the Vice-presidential nomination for Senator Arthur Vandenberg of Michigan, who during the high tide of the Democratic party's success in 1936, urged the party to accept the social aims which the "opposition party had the wisdom to adopt." In nominating Vandenberg, Hutcheson warned the Republicans that their conservatism will bring suicidal consequences. The GOP national convention nominated the liberal Governor of California, Earl Warren, as Dewey's running-mate.

In 1944, Hutcheson spoke under the auspices of the Republican national committee, urging the election of Dewey and Warren. In 1948 he was a critical observer, at times expressing disenchantment with Republican national politics. Governor Dewey was ill prepared to meet Hutcheson's demand that he declare himself outrightly in favor of Taft-Hartley

---

[47]"Much Fiction, Little Fact," *The Carpenter,* Vol. LXVIII:8, (August, 1948), p. 28.

repeal, lest he alienate voters in "Taft's camp." Although, Hutcheson urged Dewey to vie with the Democratic Party's platform, assuring him of his support at the Executive Mansion in Albany, the Republican Presidential candidate did not declare for outright repeal, but promised a fair review.

William Hutcheson felt his political disillusionment keenly and frequently reproached himself for his public zeal.

Early in 1950, when Republican strategists sought his assistance to "revitalize the party and correct some of the mistakes which the leaders make the past few years," Hutcheson exhorted his Republican colleagues to favor labor. Their exchange follows:

Law Offices
BOBBIT, MARTZ & BEATTEY

January 5, 1950

Dear Mr. Hutcheson:

I am advised that Cale J. Holder, Republican State Chairman of Indiana, has recently had a conference with Mr. Meadows and is writing or has written you soliciting your cooperation in the coming campaign.

Mr. Holder is attempting to repair some of the damage to the Party which has been done during the past six years and is making an honest and sincere effort to reestablish the relations between you, your organization and the Republican Party which you and I enjoyed during the time I was Republican State Chairman. I have known Cale for a number of years and can vouch for his integrity and sincerity of purpose.

I shall never forget the valuable assistance and fine cooperation which you and your associates gave me in 1938 and 1940, at a time when the Republican party was making a "come-back" struggle in Indiana and I am thoroughly convinced that without your help the gains which we made through those election years would not have been possible.

I personally am anxious to have you again take an active part in the counsels of the party and I am sure that you will be able to assist Mr. Holder in his efforts to revitalize the Party and correct some of the mistakes which our leaders made the past few years.

With best wishes to you for a most happy and prosperous 1950 and many, many subsequent years, I am,[48]

Sincerely yours,
Arch N. Bobbit

ANB:JM

January 17, 1950

Dear Arch:

In reply to your communication of January 5 will state that I have not heard direct from the new Republican State Chairman, Mr. Cale J. Holder.

Our mutual friend and former co-worker, Fred Shortemeier, wrote me in reference to the matter, stating that Mr. Holder would like a conference with myself and associates, and I advised him that I would be glad to have a

---

[48]William L. Hutcheson, *Private Correspondence*, January 5, 1950.

conference upon my return to Indianapolis, which will be sometime in the latter part of March, but that I would expect from Mr. Holder some very definite commitments as to what the policy of the Republican Party is to be in the future, before he could expect any commitments from me.

I am frank to say that does not only apply to Indiana, but the whole country, and if the Republican Party expects in the future to get any support from organized labor they will sure have to take a definite stand as to what their policy will be, and it will have to be more favorable to labor than it has been for the past few years.[49]

With kindest personal regards, I am,

Very truly yours,

William L. Hutcheson
General President

WL:HG

Couched in identical terms was Fred E. Shortemeier's communication, Hutcheson's early supporter for the vice-presidency in 1944.

Mr. Shortemeier invited Hutcheson to become a delegate to the Republican National Convention in 1952. "We hope," he added, "you will be active as you formerly were in working out the labor cause in our Party." In reply, Hutcheson left no doubt in the mind of his correspondent, that he "will expect some definite statements and commitments from Holder, if he desires to accomplish what you have set forth."[50]

His awakening was both disagreeable and frustrating. Between 1948 and 1952 it took all the art and persuasion of Shortemeier, Indiana State Supreme Court Judge Arch N. Bobbit, Gale Holder, new Republican State Chairman of Indiana and Gov. Thomas E. Dewey to avoid an open break between Hutcheson and the Republican party.

What brought him as a delegate from the Eleventh Congressional district to the Republican National Convention in 1952 was General Dwight D. Eisenhower's explanation of his labor policy to the Hutchesons, which he subsequently reiterated to the American Federation of Labor convention, on September 17, 1952. "I have talked about the Taft-Hartley Act with labor and industry people. I know the law might be used to break unions. That must be changed. America wants no licensing union-busting. And neither do I." With these concrete assurances to labor, it was hard for Hutcheson to stay on the reservation. He was bold enough to ignore the instructions of the State Convention of the Republican party which pledged its delegates to Senator Robert A. Taft. Early in June, he assured General Eisenhower that he and his co-delegate, Mr. Eugene Pulliam, Indiana newspaper publisher, "will declare ourselves in favor of you as candidate for the United States Presidency." His attitude toward Taft

---

[49]William L. Hutcheson, *Private Correspondence,* January 17, 1950 .
[50]*Ibid.*

and his political machine in Indiana was clearly reflected in the following note to the General:

"Mr. Dwight D. Eisenhower,
Detroit, Michigan.

Dear (General) Mr. Eisenhower:

Mr. Eugene Pulliam who is a good friend of mine and a co-delegate to the
Republican National Convention will no doubt give you information in
reference to the political situation here in Indiana.

Both Gene and I are delegates from the Eleventh Congressional District,
and we both have declared ourselves in favor of you as candidate for the
United States Presidency. The State Convention of the Republican party
passed a resolution that all delegates should be instructed to cast their ballots
for Bob Taft as the candidate, both Gene and I have told them to go to - - - -.

We are of the opinion that the State Chairman will back away from the
position that he has been placed in; however we will try to straighten that
out so that we can exercise our American right before we get to the
Convention.

With kindest personal regards and best wishes, I am,

Sincerely,

William L. Hutcheson

General President Emeritus

Perhaps at the bottom of his heart he felt revengeful against Taft.
Certainly he had a grudge against the Senator of Ohio, who while
"brilliant," was unwilling to acknowledge that the concessions demanded
by Hutcheson in 1947 were not at the expense of the entrepreneur.

The Republican National platform favored the retention of the Taft-
Hartley Act, although it urged the adoption of such "amendments to the
Act as time and experience showed to be desirable and which further
protect the rights of labor, management and the public." Democratic
candidate for the Presidency, Governor Adlai Stevenson of Illinois,
declared himself for outright repeal of the Taft-Hartley Act as had
President Truman in 1948. This, together with the passage of the Act
by a preponderantly Republican Congress, finally drove the non-
partisan Federation to action. While the Federation's Labor League for
Political Education tirelessly reiterated Gompers maxim, "to administer
a stinging rebuke to men or parties, who are either indifferent, neglectful,
or hostile, to labor," the 1952 Annual Convention of the Federation assumed a more conspicuous role in the elections by formally endorsing
Adlai Stevenson for the Presidency. Not since 1924 was the Federation
carried so far from its moorings that it officially supported a Presidential
candidate running on the Democratic ticket.

As in 1924, the Brotherhood of Carpenters adhered to the policy of
strict neutrality and "non-partisanship." This judgment was reinforced

by experience, explained Hutcheson in a lengthy declaration to Executive Council. "Because organized labor was politically weak in several of the last elections, anti-union elements fastened an anchor around the neck of the labor movement in the form of the Taft-Hartley Law. Despite valiant efforts to amend it or repeal it, the same elements which passed the law in 1947 had managed to keep it on the statute books intact and unchanged. . . . Organized labor should have no 'alliance' with existing political parties.

"It is the unalterable, unanimous opinion of the General Executive Board of the United Brotherhood of Carpenters and Joiners of America that the traditional non-partisan policy of the Federation must be preserved if the Federation is to render the utmost to its members and affiliates. . . . The non-partisan policy which the Federation has long pursued is the result of no accident — it came about because partisan politics embroiled the Federation in partisan battles which threatened to tear it asunder half-a-century ago."[51]

The election of 1952 exposed the labor movement's weak political position. Despite its greatly increased numerical strength, the labor movement had not made corresponding gains in political influence since the passage of the Act. Seeking assistance, the Federation, like the CIO, turned to the so-called liberal wing of the Democratic party. Labor lacked the means of swaying public opinion, and was too poorly organized as compared with other groups to influence government policy. Its educational program was too parochial in character. Labor was unable to deliver its membership, except in the direction toward which that membership was inclined in a period of prosperity. Consequently, legislators were more responsive to the groups that could more effectively influence elections.

Labor and the Democratic party had been uneasy allies, mutually suspicious of each other. The more labor pushed to the forefront, the more resentful became other Democratic elements. At no time was there a meeting of minds between the labor leaders and the Democratic regulars; nor was there a unified strategy that guided the anti-Conservative forces. The dominant sentiment since 1948 had been clearly to keep labor at arms' length. This feeling was doubtless strongest among the Republicans, but it held for Democrats as well. For labor to align itself with the Democratic party would, in effect, amount to a rejection of social experiment. The dominant concern of the New Deal and Fair Deal elements is not to get more but to preserve the gains of the last twenty years. The unexpected strength of the Democrats in 1948 lay not with Mr. Truman's promise of any great forward steps in eco-

---

[51]William L. Hutcheson's *Private Papers, covering Executive Council proceedings. Council of the Federation, September 15 to 21, 1952.*

nomic policy but in his evident willingness to defend what existed including the measures in the New Deal years.

Such success as the Brotherhood achieved, Hutcheson ascribed to the union's continued devotion to its first principles. Indeed, the United Brotherhood of Carpenters and Joiners of America referred to precedent and tradition when it opposed endorsement of either candidate for the presidency in the election year of 1952. It quoted Section Eight of Article Three, which specifically prohibits partisanship on the part of the Federation. But the Brotherhood was not unaware that, "events of the past decade have made it clear that as far as organized labor is concerned, economic strength can be nullified by political weakness." Hutcheson's and the Brotherhood's creed was that labor must make its influence felt through a two party system. The phenomenon of labor as a countervailing power provided the Carpenters' with a strong justification for labor to look after itself rather than to seek succor from the state.

*　　*　　*

In *"Beware the Siren Song"*, Hutcheson dealt with the problem of power and freedom. He saw the labor movement as threatened from three sides. "First there is the very strong definite threat of the interests. . . . For purposes of their own, special interest groups are anxious to shackle, if not entirely destroy, the American labor movement. However, they are not hard to handle. They are effective only so long as they exert plenty of control in Congress and the State Legislatures. A politically aroused labor movement can soon change all of that. By electing its friends and defeating its enemies, labor can block the current wave of anti-labor legislation."

No less serious to him was the threat of Communism. Though the Russians cited Lenin, Stalin, and other communist apostles for the axiom that capitalism and communism could coexist peaceably, the total picture of the international chessboard was not reassuring. To make matters worse, American communists apparently adopted the new line of the Soviet Foreign Office — that the chief threat to peace was American "imperialism" and that in any war with the Soviet Union true communists would not fight for the United States. This implied the existence of a Fifth Column that bears watching.

"While the number of actual communists in American labor is very small, the amount of destruction they can breed is all out of proportion to their numbers. This is so, only because the rank and file of many unions is too lackadaisical to do anything about the situation, when it arises. . . . To the extent that either the officers or the rank and file members of the union adopt a complacent attitude towards Communism, to that extent they jeopardize the democratic cause at home and abroad.

"With American labor, like America itself, dedicated to world leadership, a tremendous responsibility devolves upon every union officer and every union member; a responsibility to keep our labor movement strong, free and independent; a responsibility to combat the anti-democratic philosophies.

"The great test for America during the Cold War is not only to resist the advance of Russian power, but to preserve intact our own democratic heritage of civil liberty and individual opportunity.[52]

He was critical of President Truman, who in the fall of 1951 asked for authority to permit all branches of the Executive to classify information. "Classify is just another fancy word for censor. To our way of thinking such a move can do national security more harm than any possible leaks which might result from having too much information available to the public." Rather dismaying were the sweeping charges of Senator Joseph McCarthy of Wisconsin, who impugned the loyalty of the State Department, its advisors and other reputable citizens. "How many innocent people get hit seems immaterial. By their own standards, McCarthy and Pegler are the only two 100 percent Americans left in the nation." Hunger, despair and a weak labor movement, not weaknesses in democratic philosophy with its ideas of free enterprise and civil liberty, were the sources of Communist victories in Europe. He urged that the Federation should give financial support to the anti-Communist movement in France led by Jouhaux.

Probably the most fundamental political problem that occupied Hutcheson's attention was the continuous encroachment of politics on economics. Politicizing of human life as was seen most dramatically in the increasing power of the state, in democratic and in totalitarian regimes alike gave him a sense of deep discomfort.

The state power, argued Hutcheson, is there to defend the American way of life against aggression, internal and external; and it must be used legitimately to educate the nation's children, to lay down some minimum standards of life below which its families should not be allowed to fall, and a simple apparatus for social service and relief for the old and the sick and unemployment benefits. Beyond that, he regarded state aid as a method of eroding the responsibilities of the individual. As we place greater burdens on the State, do we not necessitate the creation of something very like the corporative state?

"No Mussolini or Hitler will ever rise in this virile country," he said in 'Beware the Siren Song.' "But the same end results can't be achieved

---

[52]William L. Hutcheson, "Beware the Siren Song," *The Carpenter*, Vol. LXVIII:8, (August, 1948), pp. 8-10.

by too many people falling for the 'something for nothing theory.' Neither this nor any government ever gave away anything without taking back something in return. What government always takes back from the people is freedom, the most precious item of them all." Totalitarian states preach the myth of self-identification of the individual with one organic whole. If democracy means anything, it means the denial of this creed and the assertion of a faith in the individual in his capacity to adapt the environment to his needs and aspirations.

But this too is a myth and even an idle dream unless ways and means can be found for its realization.

He was hard on those who believed in the "something for nothing philosophy," "that the government owes you something or must lead us around by the hand and take care of our problems for us." He objected to the United Nations "free-riders." He opposed the Executive Council's [Federation] endorsement of the North Atlantic Pact, unless "we make it clear that we are not to furnish funds to re-arm those who sign the pact."

Hutcheson's image of the state was reflected in his address delivered before the House of Delegates of the American Medical Association on December 7, 1950. It was part of the AMA's national education campaign to resist both voluntary and compulsory systems of health insurance. As the major opponents of medical reform, they held that there were enough free dispensaries and other health services to take care of practically all poor families. They also stressed the fact that the United States led the world in the number of physicians per capita.

Speaking over a nationwide hookup on ABC's network, Hutcheson denounced "socialized medicine."

"I am against socialized medicine. . . . This probably does not jibe with the feelings of a good deal of the rest of the labor movement, because much of the pressure for "free" medical care is coming from labor organizations. But it does reflect my sentiments and the sentiments of our recent convention. . . . After two years of the National Health Program, London doctors still have preferences as to where they want to practice. By compulsion of one kind or another, somebody is going to have to shoo doctors away from the fancy neighborhoods into the tenement districts or the program will wind up where it started. When the government is given authority to tell one group or one profession where and how its members are to work, no other group or profession can be safe for long. If the day ever comes to America when Uncle Sam usurps the power to dictate to doctors under a health plan, it will be a sad day for carpenters.

"Adequate housing is still an unsolved problem in this country, especially for the poor. If it is logical to nationalize the medical profession to get more medical service for the poor, it is equally logical to nationalize the home construction industry to get roofs over the heads of the lower income groups.

"I do not know much about doctors, but I know quite a bit about carpenters.

They are an independent lot. They want to work where they want too; free to negotiate the terms of their wages and working conditions through collective bargaining. They will retain these freedoms only as long as all other groups retain theirs. Socialized medicine would only be the first bite of our free enterprise system.

"I know that the backers of the national health in this country resent the term 'socialized medicine.' They have all sorts of arguments to 'prove' that doctors and patients will remain free as the air under their program. They make a strong case. Perhaps if human nature were less ornery and less avaricious, an idealistic health program might work out all right. But so long as people have preferences, so long as Park Avenue has more appeal than Hell's Kitchen, there will be an uneven distribution of doctors under any plan that does not contain compulsion. And once compulsion enters the picture, the rights and freedom of all citizens stand in jeopardy."[53]

These bold phrases, which doubtless did justice to the American Medical Association, recall in part the very roots that lie deep in the total circumstance of American history. The rugged individualism of laissez faire was a strong American trait which Hutcheson derived from the self-reliance frontier psychology and his militant Protestant heritage. However, the frontier individualism which he preached had not excluded considerable help from the state.

He denounced the Committee for Constitutional Government as the "arch-foes of all social legislation." To them anything which obligates the government to extend a helping hand to less fortunate citizens reeks of Communism."

On the opposite side of the fence from the reactionaries said Hutcheson, "are the extreme left-wingers who want the government to be all things to all people, who want everybody to be taken care of from the cradle to the grave whether they contribute anything or not. Whether or not such a program can be financed bothers them not a bit," he wrote in October, 1949.

"Fortunately there are not many of these either," he concluded. There are millions upon millions of straight-thinking citizens who believe that the government can and must protect its citizens against the vicissitudes of sickness, joblessness and old age. . . . The idea that the government should not be interested in the welfare of its people is preposterous. Than protecting the welfare of all the people the government has no other excuse for existing. . . . However, what must be borne in mind is that the government can not give anything to anybody without taking from someone else. The government does not have a dime. All it has is the power to tax its people. When it gives one it must take away from another. That fact must be recognized in all social legislation."[54]

53William L. Hutcheson, "Socialized Medicine is No Bargain," reprinted in, *The Carpenter,* Vol. LXXI:1, (January, 1951), pp. 12-14.
54"Which Road," *The Carpenter,* Vol. LXIX:10, (October, 1949), pp. 7-9.

Hutcheson's world of values and attitudes to mid-twentieth century America was reflected in another article, his last, which appeared in the *American Federationist* of October, 1950. He reaffirmed his faith in mass education and the passion of every youth and adult to secure it. He credited the labor movement with "fighting for free education down the years." Today it is still the working people who, through their unions, are constantly demanding and working for bigger and better educational opportunities for all children. The American university of today is a far cry from the stilted, hidebound institution our forefathers knew. Then advanced education was the prerogative of children of wealthy people. Today children of all classes and all creeds rub shoulders in institutions of higher learning. Working one's way through college, has become the traditional badge of accomplishment."

He was especially critical of our educational system that "instills in them (children) a revulsion for manual labor by which a vast majority will have to earn their livelihoods. By the very nature of our economy, seven out of ten youngsters now entering the world will have to gravitate toward more or less skilled labor. Manual skills are considerably more rewarding than office work, both from the monetary standpoint and from the satisfaction standpoint. Through organization, skilled mechanics have elevated their wage scales to the point where the average skilled workman receives considerably more pay per hour than the man who pushes a pen or beats a typewriter."

The article ended with a plea for the educators to recognize the fact, "that we ought to make our education as realistic as possible. We neither want nor need to educate less."[55]

Hutcheson was deeply committed to the happy wedlock of capitalism with democracy. Having grown up together, they have enormously enriched our lives materially and spiritually. Their contribution came from the capacity of capitalism to release and reward initiative, while democracy kept the ultimate power in the community fluid and responsible.

In *"We Have the Formula,"* summarizing his conclusions on free enterprise, Hutcheson postulated that capitalism's achievements "have still only scratched the surface. In the next thirty years we can double our standard of living and permanently banish poverty from our midst. We can do these things if we keep greed out of the saddle."

His formula for permanent prosperity consisted of three parts: high wages, low profits, and tremendous volume. High wages are needed to maintain purchasing power. Low profits are needed to keep prices down so that more people can buy. Large volume is needed so that decent

55William L. Hutcheson, "Education Needs Realism," *The American Federationist,* Vol. 57:5, (May, 1950), pp. 6-8.

returns can be made on investments.[56] Hutcheson's course proposed a completely free market, but one that would be limited by state intervention to minimal terms and primarily for the purpose of arresting the downward spirals of deflation before they have run their course. His judgment was based upon the presupposition that the increasing production of a dynamic, ever-expanding economy would have much ultimate effect on the distribution of income as between the big shares of labor, agriculture and business through the automatic competitive process of a free economy. As a labor leader, he was dedicated to "full employment" and how best to increase the size of the worker's pie, and more especially, of the carpenter's pie. It is not equality as such that troubled him, but poverty. Whether poverty and equality are the same is a moot question. As far as Hutcheson was concerned, poverty will be reduced mainly because of the rise in per capita income due to an over-all rise in the productivity of the American economy. What is left out of this brief account is a factor which contradicts the "Law of love." This is the factor of self-interest, whether in its individuals or in its collective form. Hutcheson described it as "greed." It is precisely this element of "greed," which is inclined to appropriate more privilege to itself than its social function requires, that must avail itself of "coercion" to establish a minimal order.

This, in short, was Hutcheson's image of America.

The same image, which lured his indigent ancestors from the Old World in the early nineteenth century, gave Hutcheson the sombre view and hatred for all restrictions and abridgement of personal freedom, and encouraged his unremitting battles against state coercion of business, industry and labor in the mid-twentieth century.

The whole country, thought Hutcheson, at the age of seventy-six, was pervaded with that image, and it reminded him of his childhood, when he had been "happy" in the Saginaws.

* * *

Nothing could have been more pleasant and gratifying than the respect and admiration of a crowd of eight hundred guests, long-time collaborators, labor leaders, friends, and well-wishers who came from all parts of the country to celebrate Hutcheson's seventh installation for the General Presidency of the United Brotherhood of Carpenters and Joiners of America, on Saturday, April 7, 1951. Although Hutcheson was powerful and happy, he had to follow Mathers' advice and that of the doctor and "stoop" down when he was at the topmost point of his success. His election in September, 1950 was uncontested, as was his authority, in the Brotherhood. Thanks to his unwavering efforts and his

---

[56] "We Have the Formula," *The Carpenter*, Vol. LXVII:6, (June, 1947), p. 12.

team of eleven General Executive Board members, the Brotherhood grew in the thirty-six consecutive years of his stewardship to a membership of 703,649, an increase of 440,254 since 1916. During this period, Hutcheson had achieved a brilliant career as labor leader.

The twenty-sixth convention was very generous to him. It allowed him to retire when he "shall feel free to do so from that office." It created the office of General President Emeritus, for which he received the same yearly salary of $30,000 for "services he may desire to perform." As Emeritus, he remained a member of the General Executive Board to represent the Brotherhood at all labor organizations with which the Carpenters were affiliated. In tribute to his achievements, dogmatic combativeness, audacious leadership, able administration and incredible courage, the delegates passed the following resolution in September of 1950:

". . . Whereas, throughout an entire period, which includes two World Wars, he has unflinchingly fought to uphold not only our work jurisdiction but all of the great principles for which our Brotherhood stands; and

Whereas, throughout his splendid period of service he has displayed those qualities of leadership which have brought our Brotherhood to a position of eminence, not only in the labor world but in all spheres of public life; and

Whereas, our Brotherhood is fully aware of all that has been accomplished under the leadership of General President William L. Hutcheson, we the delegates here assembled at this, our Twenty-Sixth General Convention are desirous of expressing to him the gratitude of the membership . . ."[57]

Such an ardent fighter, indifferent to the pressures of friends and enemies and government "bureaucrats," could not be expected to give up life easily.

These last three years of his life showed all the vehemence of a final appeal to his American contemporaries and of an invocation of posterity. His cherished themes were repeated in his address. He thanked the members, friends, associates and guests for their tributes and pledged that one and all they would continue fighting for a better life "for all who work with their hands or brains for their livelihoods;" that they would see men govern themselves with the least amount of government intervention. He warned that "government *encroachments* upon the lives and rights of citizens must be stopped. Freedom can be lost from within as easily as from without. Every time the government takes it upon itself to regulate the lives and destinies of the people — regardless how noble the motive — a little bit of freedom is lost. If the chipping away process continues for any length of time, the people may eventually find all their freedom gone." He talked of his ideal of "united union as a united nation" as a bulwark against totalitarian inroads. It would be a society of free men, in which democracy prevails. The functions of

[57] U.B.C.J.A.; *Prceedings*, (1950), p. 251.

government must be shared by many political divisions, as well as by trade unions and cooperative associations. For these are the crucibles whence public opinion emerges; they are the dynamos whence flows the voltage to inspire and control the democratic state.

Greater men had reconciled the free enterprise axioms, strict construction of the Constitution and less government doctrines to serve modern industrialism and the atomic age. This creed of Hutcheson may not prove workable, but whether we can find a new one overnight, time alone will tell.

*   *   *

All during July and August of the same year Hutcheson had been ailing. In the middle of August he went to the hospital for a few days check-up. His good and loyal friend, John Steelman, Assistant to President Truman, was quick to write him on August 14, expressing hope that he would soon be back on the job completely recovered. Aging William Green called him to express his regrets and that of the Executive Council of the American Federation of Labor. Victor Emanuel inquired of his health, but never once missed an opportunity to drown Hutcheson with "memoranda," magazine reprints and news digests, all of which he read without the benefit of this new type of corporation executive, who was as friendly with John L. Lewis as he was with George Meany. Emanuel knew that the "new common law" of management-labor relations is beneficial in the long-run to the corporation as well as to its employees, for Hutcheson made him an "honorable member"of the Brotherhood of Carpenters.

Toward the end of August he recovered. The overwhelming and tedious work of the Brotherhood had now become an unpleasant side of his life. Besides being First Vice-President of the Federation, he had to act as arbiter in Lewis' new fracas with the A. F. of L. Countless requests for speech-making and personal appearances from the Brotherhood's local unions, from employer groups and local medical groups, persuaded him to transfer most of his functions to his son Maurice.

In October-November, 1951, he had a violent attack of gout, still another, came in more serious, in October. He could no longer visit the Brotherhood. His nurse vainly coddled him at his home in Indianapolis, which had become a prison of tenderness. Nearing the age of seventy-eight, he felt "old age creeping up his back." On December 4, he finally decided to retire as President of the Carpenters.

On the succeeding days, Secretary of Labor Maurice J. Tobin was joined by John L. Lewis, Senators 'Spess' Holland, the Federation of Grandmothers Clubs of America, Victor Emanuel, Charles H. Tuttle and all the Carpenter locals in the unanimous chorus of tribute to Hutcheson.

The Brotherhood itself made him a life member of the organization, awarding him a citation, which read in part: "the services of William L. Hutcheson have confounded his enemies, and maintained our prestige throughout the world. No man in this nation has contributed to the growth of organized labor, both in the United States and the world, than has William L. Hutcheson."[58]

The testimonial dinner tendered to Hutcheson on May 3rd, 1952 was clear proof to him of his popularity. Six hundred union men, representing every state in the union, including Alaska and the Canadian provinces, filled the ballroom of the Columbia Club in Indianapolis. Among those who came to cheer him and laud his career were: William Green, President of the American Federation of Labor, George Meany, Secretary Treasurer, John L. Lewis, Richard J. Gray, President of the Building and Construction Trades Department, Joseph Keenan, Secretary of the Department, Daniel J. Tobin, President of the International Brotherhood of Teamsters and James Petrillo of the Musicians Union. Tobin acclaimed Hutcheson as "one of the foremost labor leaders of all time. He represented the best there is in the labor movement and makes me feel lonely to know that he is laying down the buckles and sword."

William Green recalled the many occasions upon which Hutcheson defied the forces which "were seeking to reduce American working man and the American Plan of the 'twenties. Charles H. Tuttle described Hutcheson's triumphs in the Supreme Court when Thurman Arnold was "prepared to put a leash on all organized labor through anti-trust prosecution."

The last speaker was John L. Lewis, a companion of the labor struggle for nearly half-a-century. Lewis gave free expression to his praise for Hutcheson's friendship. Hutcheson, he thundered, was a fighter. Ringingly he made the candid admission and boast that, in the dark days of December, 1945, when the United Mine Workers of America was fined the staggering sum of three and one-half million dollars, an obvious move by government counsel to break the union and empty its treasury, he summoned Hutcheson to be his guardian and trustee of one million dollars. He reminded the audience, consisting mostly of carpenters, of Hutcheson's achievements for the labor movement. He outlined the need for greater unity in organized labor. "If we do not achieve it, this growing encroachment of government controls will lead us to disaster," a note that struck a familiar chord to Hutcheson.

There was no doubt that, after all this acclamation, Hutcheson ranked with Samuel Gompers, Peter J. McGuire, although their tem-

---

[58]Regular Meeting of the General Executive Board, *The Carpenter,* Vol. LXXI:7, (July, 1952), p. 23.

peraments and heritages were not identical. But like him, they had deep American roots. No nation had been compounded of so many elements of religious, political, and economic dissent.

Lewis' words moved him deeply.

Sitting under the American flag, nearly bald, with penetrating brown eyes, Hutcheson at the age of seventy-eight still looked the tall, broad shouldered man that he was, but less firm and more placid, though his mind was as vigorous as ever. Up to the last days of his life he kept the "chains" of his friendship clear and shining, according to a favorite Indian proverb he learned in Saginaw, and his heart was filled with solicitude for all persons he had met and loved, and who loved him in return. It was not surprising that he kept a deep and a most constant affection for his friend Lewis, as he had given him his counsel, friendship and admiration. He did not forget John Steelman, whom he mailed a special brochure about the testimonial dinner given in his honor; nor did he forget to send him a box of oranges for Christmas.[59] His mail from Samuel Ungerleider and Victor Emanuel delighted him. He was indifferent and cold to "Homer" Capehart who sought to revive his friendship. He took warm note of Estes Kefauver, the highly competent and adroit Senator of Tennessee who solicited his "counsel and advice on a sound labor program," when he was campaigning for the Democratic Presidential nomination in the spring of 1952.[60] He was happy to see Maurice, his sole surviving male descendant service the Brotherhood. He had never been consoled for the death of his son Delos.

Hutcheson spent his last Christmas with aging brother carpenters in the Carpenters' Home in Lakeland. He became a solitary old man whose quick mind was no longer able to cope with the brutal demands of life and whose friendships flung all over the country, made him vulnerable to attack and praise in many places at once. Now that the night was falling, and his pains became acute, Hutcheson felt he had been cruelly abandoned. Not even the tall trees of the forest surrounding the Home comforted him. Every move he made as he lay in bed was painful to him, and was all the more sharp since he retained the clearness of his mind. He realized perfectly he was dying and that he was alone. He could no longer turn to the past, with all its struggle and all sorrow. As to the future, he felt he had no longer the energy to work: his day was over.

He closed his eyes.

*   *   *

During the winter of 1953 he became increasingly weak. He was seventy-nine on February 7, and had long since drawn upon any re-

---

[59]William L. Hutcheson, *Private Correspondence,* May, December, 1952.
[60]*Ibid,* March 10, 1952.

serves of recuperative power. In the beginning of spring, an improvement was noticeable. He returned to Indianapolis to enjoy the warmth and comfort of his old environment. May had scarcely begun when he left for his lodge in Winchester, Wisconsin. His mood was gentle and relaxed. On the 12th of October he suffered a stroke. He felt the approach of death. A private plane flew him to the Methodist Hospital in Indianapolis. "These pains will soon be over," he jested with the pilot. The pilot agreed, adding that he would see him live many years more. One of the airport employees offered to assist him off the plane, but he gently waved him aside.

The eight short days of October ebbed with the passing of his strength. There was no other sound in the room but the heavy rise and fall of his breathing. Maurice, Joe Plymate, his private secretary, Stella and Myra waited immobile at the opposite sides of the bed; occasionally tears streamed down their cheeks. Hutcheson gropingly fluttered his fingers and eagerly grasped Myra's proffered hand. He held it with pitiful tenacity as though he was fighting with the Angel of Death.

Within an hour, an oxygen tank and a respirator arrived, while the doctors worked over him. Two heart specialists came an hour later. His friend Reverend Dr. Logan Hall, himself suffering from a heart condition flew in from the Flower Hospital in New York. Hutcheson waved his hand through the oxygen tank as Dr. Hall entered the room. "We both looked at each other and it spoke volumes. Both of us are Masons, Hutcheson is a 33rd Degree Mason and I am a 32nd,"[61] related Reverend Logan. On Tuesday, the 20th of October, 1953, the restless heart of William Levi Hutcheson came to a stop.

The Methodist Hospital was filled with the sound of sorrow. The news spread throughout Indianapolis, and soon reached throughout the country. There was a superb funeral ceremony in Indianapolis, at which Reverend Hall officiated. The Carpenters, labor leaders, Masons, politicos, friends all joining to pay him honor.

The man chosen to pronounce the funeral oration was none other than his devoted lifelong friend, John L. Lewis, whom Hutcheson sincerely loved. A saddened and lachrymose Lewis accomplished his task as a devoted friend would have, and the crowd beneath the pulpit—associates, government representatives, labor leaders, spectators and friends, wept at his words. The mourning extended to the Carpenters Home in Lakeland, Florida, where 250 old carpenters gathered on the grounds of the 1940 acre estate in honor of the man who had stood guard over their union for nearly four decades.

---

[61]Interview with Reverend Dr. Logan Hall, March 21, 1954 at the Methodist Church in Indianapolis.

EPILOGUE

Hutcheson, the labor leader can be appraised in terms of the union he led, while other parts of the work he left have been assimilated to the general stream of the American labor movement. The latter frequently become dissociated from the initiator's name and in time are almost impossible to identify.

The fact cannot be gainsaid that Hutcheson's most vital contribution was to the Brotherhood of Carpenters. His success must be appraised by the carpenters' gains in terms of increased income, improved working conditions, and greater job security, which would not otherwise have been attained. He helped reduce the nationwide work week from forty-four to forty and to thirty-five hours while the purchasing power of the weekly envelope increased from $5.50 per day in 1916 to $23.05 in 1952. He gave the Carpenters Union job "control" through the union shop. The union's prestige rose as it increased the share of the Carpenter's total income. As a consequence, it gained social power, and this social power included political and moral prestige.

What Hutcheson did collectively for the labor movement was to help raise its general standard of living, and the recognition that it belongs to the social equilibria of our technical society. He gave impetus to the tendency that the labor movement as a democratic institution operates as an important check on any center of power that is inclined to appropriate more privilege to itself than its social function requires.

Hutcheson cannot be understood in isolation. As we have repeatedly stressed, his approach to the labor movement and his outlook grew out of the clotted experiences of his contemporaries and predecessors, as well as of favorable and unfavorable social forces and conditions. Hutcheson came to the labor movement when American labor relations developed in an economy with rich, open resources. This, in combination with a rapidly growing, expanding economy and fluid class structure, have made the concept of class, no less than the concept of class struggle, largely irrelevant. The two-party system was well entrenched.

The Brotherhood, as well as the trade-union movement developed by continual battle rather than by peaceful expansion. Both fought to win

329

members, the right to bargain collectively and then, the best pay and working conditions possible — and all this against formidable opposition. Labor relations were contractual — that is segmental, limited, not inclusive, and formally voluntary; only the cash nexus, the money wage, controls; the employee was free to quit his job and the employer was free to turn the worker out on the street; not personalized ties nor *noblesse oblige,* but the market bargain was the bond. Thus, the unions acted on "business principles," with labor as its product. Even the newer industrial unions have emulated the old craft unions in that they concentrate upon immediate tangible benefits rather than upon visionary schemes of reshaping the system.

"Business principles" was Hutcheson's initial contribution to the Carpenters' labor strategy, as it was that of Samuel Gompers, Peter J. McGuire, and in our own time, of David J. McDonald, John L. Lewis, Dave Beck, Walter Reuther, David Dubinsky, Patrick E. Gorman, Al Hayes, Jacob Potofsky, Emil Rieve and their colleagues.

During the first few years of his administration, Hutcheson concentrated on the problems of internal control and discipline, two pre-conditions without which the union could neither survive, let alone grow. Unless the rank and file could be relied upon to support his policies the union either remained weak or stationary. These were formidable tasks even for an aggressive leader like Hutcheson. The members' willingness to reelect him seven successive terms was but one manifestation of their desire to avert internal dissension. Most important, however, was the fact that he "brought home the bacon" to the carpenters. Despite the difficulties of his work, his modest salary of $3,000 (1915), he remained at the helm. He not only saw his union through, but showed great capacity to adjust himself to new demands.

While other union leaders acted the hesitant super-patriots during World War I, Hutcheson transformed himself into a fighter. His strength was in his sense of timing, a comprehension of detail, and appreciation of the true conditions of the trade, and the proper assessment of the role of labor in a highly industrializing America. He won the precious right of recognition for labor blessed by the government even if only "for the duration of the war." He helped draw up the "Principles and Policies to Govern Relations Between Workers and Employers in War Industries for the Duration of the War," which brought the National War Labor Board to life. The advancement of the status of labor and unionization during World War II through the establishment by President Roosevelt of a replica National War Labor Board, is a contemporary manifestation of that tendency that can properly be listed under the heading of the Hutcheson legacy. He argued vehemently for it on the Executive Council of the American Federation of Labor.

It is very clear that Hutcheson was an extrovert; and it is plain that his social outlook required definite conception of the labor movement. William Levi tried to correlate the labor movement with a free, unfettered economy. Hutcheson was a thoroughgoing individualist. His concern was to reconcile his individualism with a completely free market system. He conceived this reconciliation in economic (and technological) terms, basing his judgement upon the pre-supposition that the increasing production of a dynamic and ever-expanding economy would increase the size of the workers' pie through the automatic competitive processes of a free economy. He thought in fact that the strength and prestige of modern labor is derived from the inevitable gains through its own intervention in the economic process.

A man of deep convictions and keen insight, he chose to deal in particulars rather than in generalizations. He was biased against social planning, which he disapproved, while he sought dilligently to erect a strong, unified labor movement which would enjoy the freest possible play, unencumbered. Hutcheson conceived the organized labor movement as a neutralizing influence on the coercive power of the employer by the workers developing "countervailing" power of their own.

William Levi focused his major interest on the betterment of the Carpenters, first and always. His activities embraced all of America. He wanted both labor and industry free from the regulating hand of the state. He disliked and fought restraints of any kind. He disliked, indeed, anything that controlled or regulated, but for the minimal provisions of social security and primarily for the purpose of arresting the downward spirals of deflation before they have run their course. But within the limits of his world he dealt with the vital problems of individual freedom, increasing state coercion and economic justice for the worker, in which he showed himself a fighter. His uncompromising opposition to the Taft-Hartley Act, his bias against "socialized medicine," his militant fight in the Supreme Court — U. S. vs. Hutcheson et al (312 U. S. 219, 1940) in which the unions were held substantially immune from Anti-trust legislation, sprang from the same source.

The Northwest formed the social and cultural background out of which William Levi grew. As the years passed, two tendencies appear to be peculiarly identified with Hutcheson, one economic and one political, both of which need emphasis. The economic is that of an open free economy, laying a great deal more stress on economic development rather than on equality itself as an ideal to be striven for in our economic system. Indeed, "redistribution" or slightly planned economy was to him not an important weapon in the abolition of poverty; where economic inequalities and poverty have been reduced it has been mainly because of the rise in per capita incomes due to the over-all rise in the productivity of American industry and technical advancement. Whether this has worked itself out in our contemporary life is not easy to say. The inter-action between technical progress and equality are extremely complex, and not well understood; but the possibility that within limits these objectives may compete with one another cannot be cast aside.

Significant was his role in politics. Dealing only in the broadest and suggestive terms, we may define William Hutcheson's political temperament and role as stable and traditional in approach and practice veering in the direction of those who accept change to the extent of protecting the "usable past" and present. Hutcheson, the General President of the Brotherhood, never saw fit to deviate from the classic doctrine of the Federation: *"Reward your friends, punish your enemies."* He sought the Brotherhood's objectives through economic pressure and negotiation. And when the Federation moved to support the Progressive LaFollete-Wheeler ticket, Hutcheson refused to surrender, consistently adhering to the outlook of aggressive bargaining with both political parties. Nevertheless, he takes his place as one of the heirs of Peter J. McGuire, Gompers, and many others as to make any catalogue tedious. This attitude has been complemented by one which appeared in another form in Hutcheson's work under the title of political.

Since 1920 he played the role of special interest representative and professional party man in the Republican national committee. He filled the useful function of organizing and clarifying the views and aspirations of the wage earners *inside* the Party and influenced party policy. Through his lobbying activities he participated in the task of adjusting conflicting interests and of constructing administrative devices for management. He knew that to be effective, any special interest representative must participate in the process of management itself.

The difference between Hutcheson of the A. F. of L. and Hillman or John L. Lewis of the C. I. O. in 1936, involved, as we have stressed, primarily an issue of *tactics*. Thus far, both federations have been opportunistic and chiefly concerned with concrete gains. Whether union members, any more than employers, will discover a wide area of common interest as the approaching merger draws nearer, is difficult to say. But before labor can be successfully unified and organized and its purposes envisaged, many factors must be taken into account. A great deal will depend on the course of economic development of the country.

Gathering these matters up in summary, we find that William Hutcheson contributed the idea of a neatly rounded, timely outlined tactic; that he accepted the ideas of Samuel Gompers and Peter J. McGuire and, finally, that he saw how thin is the line between "economic" and "political" activities and how questions of power unavoidably confront the labor movement at every turn.

Hutcheson was an heir of Gompers and McGuire and as such exercised a vital influence on the labor movement of our time, than through any influence he may still exert upon the development of the current labor movement. There is one way in which he differed from his predecessors and contemporaries. Not since 1918 has there been a labor representative who acted on the conviction that labor must be treated by government and political leaders as the peer of industry. He was accorded that status by Presidents Wilson, Harding, Coolidge, Hoover Roosevelt and Truman, even though he fiercely disagreed with some of them. His friendship with Congressmen and Senators has not always yielded dividends or concessions to labor and the Carpenters in particular. But here again, he loathed to depart from the McGuire - Gompers strategy: . . . "to stand by our friends and administer a stinging rebuke to men or to parties who are either indifferent, negligent, or hostile to the welfare of labor."

Though he had never ascended to Lewis' oratorical heights, he had ideas which roused attention, prejudice and intense partisanship. He kept abreast with all economic, political and technological developments of the day. He aimed high. He became a labor leader and he knew how to hold his rank. In 1944 he found that the balance of his ranks was not strong enough with the professionals of the Republican Party to make the vice-presidency accessible to him. If he arrived at the top it was simply because he possessed the talents required to organize, lead and administer 800,000 carpenters. He knew how to marshal and channel their emotions. He knew how to negotiate with the captains of the building and construction industry and how to make political deals that would advance the welfare of his charges.

One curious thing about the life and work of Hutcheson is that none of the small coterie of devotee-writers who lavished so much attention on the labor movement and its leaders since the mid-'thirties, made an effort to understand him. It was a case of love for a "new" labor movement which opened their eyes as it blinded them. The result has been a series of labor histories, some widely-quoted, biographies, monographs and popularized journalistic outpourings, which are permeated with strong emotional content, unashamed bias, and confusion of moral judgement, and deliberate perversion of facts. It is doubtful that present-day literate and sober readers will rank them with the works of Professors Commons, Perlman, Taft, Ginsberg and Wolman.

To be sure, they were part of a conditioning whose cultural climate was highly charged with moral tone, which stood either high or low on scales of "goodness." Those were the years of the Great Depression, with laissez faire capitalism reaching its nadir. This period also marked the rise of industrial unionism which, having been stimulated by the state, won its just day. Then, too, John L. Lewis, Sidney Hillman, and eight others parted ways with their old colleagues of the Federation. Henceforth, the devotee-writers sharpened their professional arrows and spears and directed them mainly, if not solely, at the "conservative," "narrow" labor leaders of the Federation, with Hutcheson as their major target.

Actually, it started in 1924, when a few fledgling Communists launched their attack on the well-organized construction and building trade unions, boring from within. But it remained for Messrs. Bruce Minton and John Stuart of *New Masses* memory to set their fires of the inquisition on the "unbelievers" in one-big-union. After careful reading of *Men Who Lead Labor*,[1] authored by the above-mentioned writers and of three typical labor histories subsequently written by Edward Levinson,[2] by Herbert Harris[3] and Charles A. Madison,[4] one can hardly escape the conclusion that Minton and Stuart set the tone for all three of them. In unison, they repeat and rehash almost verbatim charges and allegations, none either *substantiated* or *documented* — that the leaders of the Federation were: gangsters, czars, potentates, embezzlers, grafters, absolutists, tyrants, fascists, red-baiters, ad infinitum, ad nauseam. While no one escapes with a clean bill of health, Hutcheson is surpassed by none in taint, villification and invective. By contrast, the C. I. O. leaders were the militants and the progressives and its organizing energies. Two or three years previously, these same labor leaders had been portrayed by these labor-specialists as leading the way "toward class collaboration."

A documented life-study of Hutcheson, or an objective appraisal of his life and work as a labor leader was attempted by none of the writers in question. The evidence we have painstakingly gathered of his life and work was available to any earnest researcher or social historian who claims an interest in the labor movement and its leaders. An application of technical proficiency, an insight into the movement itself as it had emerged in the course of his lifetime, was cynically avoided by the three of them. We repeat: love for the new movement opened their eyes as it blinded them. The result is that the portraits of Hutcheson unveiled by Levinson, Harris and Madison are not only identical in color — but facsimiles of Minton and Stuart. There is no need to put our finger upon these typical writers who practice the science (human) of writing labor histories.

What we are concerned with especially is the phenomenon of writers and much-quoted labor historians of the type of Dr. Herbert Harris,

[1]Bruce Minton and John Stuart, *Men Who Lead Labor* (Modern Age Books, 1937).
[2]Edward Levinson *Labor on the March*, (Harper & Bros., 1938).
[3]Herbert Harris, *American Labor* (Yale University Press, 1939).
[4]Charles A. Madison, *American Labor Leaders* (Harper & Bros., 1950).

Striking photo showing the late A. F. of L. President William Green beaming his approval as the third largest union in the U. S. and Canada named Maurice A. Hutcheson, General President in 1952. Green still remembered when Maurice, came to work as a clerk in the headquarters of the United Brotherhood of Carpenters and Joiners of America in 1913.

The President of the United States, Dwight D. Eisenhower, poses with Maurice A. Hutcheson, the only International Union Chieftain in the United States who actively supported his candidacy in 1952.

(Photo by Alexander Archer)

U. S. and Canadian Leaders of the United Brotherhood of Carpenters and the International Association of Machinists display satisfaction, as M. A. Hutcheson (front row, third from right) and Machinists' Pres. Al. Hayes (center) sign peace pact designed to end one of the oldest jurisdictional disputes in labor history.

New A. F. of L. President George Meany (right) at Carpenters' convention in Cincinnati, Ohio, Nov. 15, 1954, acknowledges that Maurice A. Hutcheson (center) and Richard J. Gray (left) President of the Building & Construction Trades Department (A. F. of L.) deserved public's accolades for spurring Federation into setting up intra-A. F. of L. no-raiding machinery.

Indianapolis

Increasing U. S. concern with world-wide economic ferments led to establishment of International Development Advisory Board, on which labor is represented by Maurice A. Hutcheson, (top row, first right). Here Pres. Eisenhower poses outside the White House with the entire Board. Left to right: first row: Harvey S. Firestone, Jr., Mrs. Jessie Vann and Eric Johnston. Second row: Joseph P. Grace, Jr., Gardner Cowles, Dr. Robert P. Daniel and Harold Stassen, Foreign Operations Administration Director. Third row: Dr. Wm. R. White, Herchel D. Newsom, Lawrence F. Whittemore and Hutcheson.

Cordial Relations between U. S. Secretary of Labor James P. Mitchell (right) and the Carpenters' General President serve the best interests of the Brotherhood's far-flung membership.

The social whirl — a popular towsome at Washington and cross-country socials of labor, industry and government are Maurice and Ethel Hutcheson. Personal appearance demands from over 2,900 local unions in the U. S. and Canada keep the Hutchesons constantly "on the go."

Charles Madison and the late Edward Levinson, who, equipped with modern techniques of investigation and presumably grounded in technical proficiency, should resort to the propaganda weapons of Minton and Stuart. This is a view which holds favor in certain cultures, or spiritually totalitarian regimes. It is a legitimate function of a historian or biographer to regard, say, the ethical ideas and social values of a economic movement, or the behavior of its leaders, as part of his investigation. Indeed, the historian of social or economic organizations may include his beliefs and judgements as part of his data; they form an essential part of the "universe" with which he is dealing, and cannot be neglected. His ideas of "good" and "evil", of what is "right" or "wrong," of what constitutes "a good movement," "a good union" or a "good union leader" or a "scoundrel" are as much variables of the writer's treatment, as the price of cheese or the vote in an election.

But it is generally accepted, we think, that the writer or biographer should also be a historian; that the moral judgements which he passes on should be based firmly on sound documentary evidence. A social scientist or social historian may be a moralist, but he will be a better one, and also a less dangerous one, if he spells out as clearly as he can his pre-judgements.

It would be fatal to underestimate the cumulative effect and carrying power of such paralyzing attitudes which, we believe, have generated in many influential quarters, in addition to the myths and misrepresentations which have saturated our public mind and academic textbooks.

PART | VI

THE NEW and THE OLD

CHAPTER | **XVIII**

THE NEW AND THE OLD: MAURICE A. HUTCHESON

No matter how deep a social conscience a man has, he will have a hard struggle to lead the masses unless he is one of them by birth. This, despite the fact that the labor movement itself is tinged with ethical coloring, and has attracted a good deal of public support because of it. Workers are suspicious of those who differ from them in social status and speech. In recent years the marked advance in salaries and the less bellicose atmosphere have raised the profession of labor leadership, even in the eyes of the middle-class community. However, for psychological if for no other reasons, today's and even tomorrow's labor leaders will still be recruited from the working class. Labor leadership as a profession is not as yet deemed a thoroughly respectable trade, and few leaders encourage their children to follow in their footsteps.[1] Opportunities in industry, business, finance and the professions induced most of them to escape the ranks of the workers.

A description of the leadership in the Brotherhood found in Chapter XX of this book clearly indicates the father-son pattern. Of the eleven members on the General Executive Board, all are workers' sons. Professor Eli Ginsberg's analysis of the leadership in ten major unions, inclusive of the Brotherhood of Carpenters, clearly reveals that the overwhelming majority of the leaders followed their fathers' footsteps.[2]

Maurice A. Hutcheson, the subject of this chapter, who had chosen to follow in the footsteps of his father, was subjected to a working-class background, acquiring a first-hand knowledge of the frustrations and aspirations of the carpenters whom he was to lead. The evolution of Maurice A. Hutcheson into a labor leader involves a good deal of the

[1]Eli Ginsberg, *The Labor Leader* (Macmillan Company, 1948), p. 51.
[2]*Ibid.*

339

work and activities of his father and of the labor movement which had saturated his outlook. By the time he resolved to follow his inclinations in behalf of labor, he had ample opportunity to think through some of the inconsistencies and confusions—not excluding his own—of the social and political points of view of America's major labor leaders while he moved in the world of the most active and ambitious of them.

In March, 1938, when first vice-president George H. Lakey died after a prolonged illness, Maurice Hutcheson was appointed to fill that vacancy through December, 1940. During that two year period he exhibited a marked disposition to experiment with new techniques. He was an ethusiastic reader of social science, history and politics. He possessed amazing energy — but almost all of it was devoted to the carpenters. His warm personality made him a favorite everywhere. On December 11, 1940, the twenty-fourth convention of the Brotherhood promptly elected him as its second ranking officer.

At the age of forty-three, Maurice A. Hutcheson could point to an unbroken 29-year long membership in the Brotherhood and a record as a journeyman carpenter in Ohio, Virginia, Port Newark and New York; service in the U. S. Navy; a twenty-nine year record as fiscal and general officer and functionary of the United Brotherhood; an intimate knowledge and understanding of labor laws operative throughout the United States and Canada on the regional and national levels, and to added erudition in technology.

From reports based on personal interviews and others who know him, he is somewhat unlike his father; more on the quiet and reserved side, more deliberate and introspective. He is looked upon by his associates as a moderate. He affects a disdain for the autocrat and the crude partisan. Up to this point, Maurice has shown a pronounced aptitude for administration, interpersonal relations, giving every indication of the tactician in the making. He has unlimited patience and had no difficulties in strengthening the ties between his role of general and fiscal officer, and the local union leaders. In brief, he developed into a diplomat and a person able to view all sides of a question with complete objectivity.

A year or two after his election to office, he was confronted with the fact that his father meant to subject him to an intensive practical "schooling" in the organizing intricacies of the Brotherhood, entirely apart from the specific functions of the First General Vice-President. He was assigned to the Pacific Northwest to organize the lumber and sawmill industry, ridden with industrial conflict and jurisdictional disputes. He performed a creditable job in St. Louis, Santa Clara County, California, for the performance of which he was awarded a symbolic gavel. As Fourth Vice-President of the A. F. of L.'s Building and Construction Trades Department, his contribution was impressive. Meanwhile the job that confronted him as a member of the National Joint Board for the Settlement of Jurisdictional Disputes, was enough to try the most seasoned, skilled negotiator in the construction and building trades. He adopted the use of audio-visual aids, a series of four films, in order to define more clearly the Carpenters' broad jurisdiction. They have helped considerably the Brotherhood's organizing efforts throughout the country. The fascinating theme of carpentry featured in these films has been brought to the attention of thousands of adolescents in trade and vocational schools and civic groups. Hutcheson seeks thereby to stimulate greater interest in vocational education and to encourage new labor recruits to enter the skilled trades.

In April, 1945, Maurice A. Hutcheson was one of nine labor leaders in the building and construction trades to visit the European theater of operations, at the invitation of General Eisenhower and the War Department. Though ostensibly studying the "breadth and scope of the operations", he was obviously extending his range of interests. When he returned from Europe in July, he reported the circumstances under which German totalitarianism "was literally gasping its last breath." "And if I live to be a thousand years I will never forget the things I saw."

He saw the European carnage and despair brought on by dictatorships and the emphatic reassertion of historic human rights that were finally defended by Americans on the battlefield. Was it not a melancholy fact, he recorded, that generations of advance in transportation and communication had not made the world kin in spirit but had allowed the growth of violent nationalism and totalitarianism? He envisaged an increasing interdependence of labor throughout the world; that in the current ideological struggle against Communist totalitarianism, the American labor movement, led by a vigorous democratic leadership, could make a major contribution to the economic recovery of Europe.

This European experience threw him upon his own internal resources and for the next six or seven years he strove to involve himself in the overall organization of the Brotherhood. Throughout the 'forties he streamlined the administration of the union. Every one of its 835,000 members has a card on file at headquarters upon which his dues and assessments are registered quarterly. Annually, the Brotherhood pays three million dollars in death benefits. To carry out its operations more efficiently, the union uses I.B.M. machines. In 1951 and 1952 he promoted Raleigh Rajoppi and J. F. Cambiano, two experienced labor leaders who had grown up in the ranks of the Brotherhood, to the general executive board.

By December 4, 1951, when it was clear that his ailing father would have to step aside for good, authority within the Brotherhood automatic-

ally passed on to Maurice A. Hutcheson and for the first time he became
chief officer in fact as well as title. Maurice, now fifty-eight and the oldest
in age of his fourteen predecessors, was elevated to the General Presidency of the Carpenters. Thus entrenched, Maurice did something which
many say — his father would have done and did. "Young" Hutcheson,
with the energetic support of the General Executive Board, made a
lightning move to have it out with the Executive Council of the Federation. The showdown occurred at a meeting, on September 25, 1952
when the Federation moved to endorse Adlai Stevenson as presidential
candidate in the impending national election. Maurice reminded the Executive Council of "the disruptive effect of partisan politics; that only
harm could accrue to organized labor through convention endorsement
of a single party or candidate. . . . It is the unalterable and unanimous
opinion of the General Executive Board of the Brotherhood of
Carpenters and Joiners of America that the traditional non-partisan
policy of the Federation must be preserved if the Federation is to render
the utmost in service to its members and affiliates. . . . Furthermore,
as affiliation with the American Federation of Labor is on a voluntary
basis, the question of endorsement of any candidate should be left to
each individual organization to determine the course they wish to take
and by doing so the Federation would then preserve its traditional policies."

This statement of policy of his new administration was signed and
co-signed by the chief officer and the General-Secretary and copies of
which were circulated among the Brotherhood's entire constituency.

It was not until November 4, when the election results were announced, and Dwight Eisenhower was declared the winner, that Federation
leaders experienced some discomfiture. Introspective Maurice A. Hutcheson, felt vindicated in his belief that the labor movement could not
afford to align itself openly with one political party.

In a post-election analysis, *"Our Sights Need Readjustment,"* he
argued that U. S. labor would enjoy greater scope, effectiveness and
bargaining strength if it remained outside political parties. This implied
not non-partisanship but aggressive bargaining with both political parties. Viewed, however, from the point-of-view of the total social environment, he submitted that, "no one party has a monopoly on either all
the virtue or all the vice that exists in political life. There are good men
and bad men in both parties, a fact which points up the wisdom of the
policy McGuire and Gompers adopted when they made 'elect your
friends and defeat your enemies', their motto. From the election returns, I think it is fairly obvious that a good deal of the labor vote must
have gone to General Eisenhower, despite the exhortations of the Federation. The labor movement must never allow itself to be jockeyed into

a position where it is hanging on the coat-tails of any political party."[3]

To forestall the repetition of such an open alignment, Maurice chided the Federation not to "underestimate" the American workers, "either as to intelligence, independence or ability to make decisions for themselves."

Up to now, Maurice had not acted or spoken like a man who is ready to repudiate the "usable past" and ideas of Peter J. McGuire and Samuel Gompers that could be adapted to modern social and political conditions. Nor had he gone over to the Republican camp. At this point in his career, he made his first important political gesture, after much deliberation and introspection, to give his support, as a key personality in the labor movement, to General Eisenhower. He was now in a position to speak up as the leader of a giant union who had been one of the first to be invited to meet the presidential candidate of the Republican party in July of 1952. Impressed with the interview, Maurice adopted a deferential and loyal attitude toward General Eisenhower. He was quite ready to back him and bolster his pro-labor stand. He asked Eisenhower to support the policy of removing the harsh provisions of the Taft-Hartley Act and the President agreed to help .

His prediction in March, 1954, that a Democratic majority in both houses of Congress, would not seriously press for the liberalization of the Taft-Hartley law, has since been confirmed. This, notwithstanding the fact that its repeal was pledged in the party platform. Nor did he anticipate back in '52, that the election of a Democratic presidential candidate would erase the Taft-Hartley Act from the federal statute books.

However, he does expect the federal government to act positively on behalf of labor and "its general welfare," lest it risk the charge that the political strategy of the dominant party is to place chief reliance upon the business community. The future of both the Republican and Democratic parties, Maurice suggests, lies in its skill at compromise, synthesis "and manipulation." Neither party can afford to alienate business or labor. Both interests must be increasingly considered, since within the last decade or so, questions of economic readjustment and labor's welfare have come to the forefront of politics.

He elaborates on the fact that too many labor leaders, in their present search for an alternative procedure, aim at securing, through a cohesive labor movement, now in its process of formation, the actual balance of power within the Democratic party. Hutcheson maintains, that both major parties can profit by labor's strength without going all the way to the left or the right.

That the Brotherhood's national prestige did not suffer from his re-

---

[3]Maurice A. Hutcheson, "Our Sights Need Readjustments," *The Carpenter*, Vol. LXXII:12 (December, 1952), pp. 7-8.

lationship with President Eisenhower is certain. On the contrary, it added much piquancy to his leadership when the President appointed him to the Advisory Board of the Foreign Operations Administration headed by Mr. Harold Stassen. As its labor advisor, he has been an avid, cultivated participant in its deliberations. He made his presence felt at its meetings. He has given adequate attention and pushed vigorously measures that were calculated to keep the European labor movement free and at the same time assist wage earners in Europe and retarded countries to raise their living standards. "By doing so, we could also keep them from undermining the American market. Poverty is so great abroad that the working population can not absorb our goods. We must do everything to raise their economic position."[4]

Maurice A. Hutcheson's second test of his career came nine months after his ascendancy to the General Presidency, when he was convinced that Mr. George Meany, "freshman" A.F. of L. president had acted the crude partisan to the detriment and neglect of the American Federation of Labor affiliates.

For over a decade, now, the Brotherhood of Carpenters and the Building and Construction Trades Department of the A. F. of L. had repeatedly and urgently pushed the idea inside the Federation Executive Council of formulating a guide, aimed at "minimizing jurisdictional raiding among its affiliates." Time after time, both gazed hopefully, impressing on the consciousness of the Council members and the President, Mr. George Meany, that some effective positive action should be taken about this festering condition, for neither the Carpenters nor the building trades escaped unscathed at the hands of the A.F. of L. raiders. A survey indicated that at least $300,000,000 worth of construction work had been lost to building tradesmen "through usurpation of jurisdiction by non-construction unions," among them the Railway Maintenance of Way Employes, the American Federation of State County and Municipal Employes and even some small Federal Unions dominated by the Federation itself. Early in August of 1953, prior to the meeting of the Executive Council, Mr. Richard J. Gray, representing the Building and Construction Trades, advised Mr. Meany of the seriousness of the situation, restating his views most emphatically: the recognition by the Federation of the "seriousness of the jurisdictional problem, the need for analyzing it as completely as possible, and finally, the setting-up of an impartial umpire to make and decide jurisdictional disputes."

On the morning of August 12, a bill of grievances was submitted by Mr. Gray to Mr. Meany and the Executive Council. Mr. Meany,

---

[4]Interview with Maurice A. Hutcheson in Indianapolis, on March 15, 1954.

while impressed, was not profoundly moved. The new A. F. of L. President tended to deprecate the jurisdictional problems as a necessary evil in the Building and Construction trades even though he made serious advances toward a cohesion of A. F. of L. and C.I.O., of which the no-raiding pact was a *sine qua non* condition to any contemplated fusion of the two rival federations. William L. Hutcheson, First Vice-President of the A. F. of L. and President-Emeritus of the U. B., benevolently called the defiant Mr. Meany to task, repeating the views of Mr. Gray—that it was essential for the Federation to consider the differences between the Federation unions first before attempting to solve rivalries and disputes with the C.I.O. William Hutcheson, complaining of poor health, did not return to the afternoon session of the Executive Council, but instead apprised his son, Maurice A. Hutcheson, of Mr. Meany's defiant words to ease his frustration.

This was a problem serious enough for Maurice A. Hutcheson, the new General President of the Carpenters. For, in judging Mr. Meany's response to trouble, he was bound to fire off a monstrous charge of a military shot and hope that at least something hits somebody. Maurice, motivated by his responsibility for the life of the organization as General President, fulfilling his duty of Vice-President of the Building Trades Department, and with the mark of a good executive sought to insure as far as possible that something would be done about correcting this condition without upsetting A. F. of L. - C.I.O. negotiations. He saw the need for a precision rifle rather than the blunderbuss.

That afternoon he reprimanded Mr. Meany and the Executive Council. In an urgent but moderate epistle handed to Mr. Meany, Maurice notified the Council of "withdrawal from the Federation as of the date." "We have no objection to no-raiding agreements between all organizations, in or out of the A. F. of L.; however if the A. F. of L. is not able to control its own affiliates, our own organization being no exception, we fail to see where there is any benefit to the United Brotherhood of Carpenters and Joiners of America to continue paying per capita tax to the A. F. of L.," wrote the new chief officer of the Carpenters."[5]

Another epistle, no less conciliatory, was added by the General Executive Board on August 19. It reminded the Council and the Federation President of the deteriorating conditions in the building trades. "In view of the unhappy situation on jurisdiction existing within the Federation, it appears somewhat ludicrous to us that the Federation should be worrying about a no-raiding pact with the C.I.O. while its own house remained in such disorder. There is no point in taking on a thousand more jurisdictional cases by embracing the C.I.O. when hundreds

---

[5]*Trade Union Courier,* Vol. XVIII:12 (August 12, 1953), pp. 1-18.

of inter - A. F. of L. suits wind up before the N.L.R.B. each year."

"It seems ironical that the U.B.C.J.A., one of the few A. F. of L. unions which has refrained from raiding as much as possible, should be cast in the role of a union objecting to a no-raiding agreement. The desire to eliminate raiding is the very reason why the United Brotherhood of Carpenters left the Federation."*

The note concluded with an appeal to the Federation "to adopt a more realistic attitude toward jurisdictional raiding among and between its affiliates. Or, the U.B. will have to go it alone. We have no intention of encroaching on anyone's jurisdiction, and by the same token we do not intend to let anyone encroach on ours. For nearly three-quarters of a century we have been a vital part of the labor movement. We are still part of it. Our hand is extended to those who desire our friendship."[6]

By the 8th of September, Mr. Meany was finally convinced by Maurice A. Hutcheson's arguments and proposed that the American Federation of Labor adopt a new policy definitely designed to prevent raids within the organization. Maurice Hutcheson's efforts to bring order out of the chaotic jurisdictional picture paid off. Under these circumstances, collaboration between the Carpenters and the Federation was to be the policy, and the Carpenters were continuing their membership in the American Federation of Labor.

As is always the case with the absentee, the Carpenters who "disaffiliated," were in the wrong. Writers in influential journals and newspapers have pointed to Mr. Meany's behavior bearing on this "incident" as a precedent-setting pattern intended for those leaders in the labor movement who might choose to question the "leadership principle" in a voluntary economic organization.

Wrote Mr. A. H. Raskin, labor specialist of the *New York Times:* "Meany lost no time in letting the world know that he was not going to be pushed around. He took on Daniel J. Tobin of the Teamsters, . . . the "invisible ruler," the late William L. Hutcheson who decided to give Mr. Meany a taste of his power. He sent a letter to the A. F. of L. announcing that the 800,000 member Carpenters Union was seceding because of dissatisfaction with the Federation's policies on jurisdictional disputes."[7]

It should be stated for the record that it was Maurice A. Hutcheson

---

*The only ironic note in the quarrel was that on the very day the Brotherhood withdrew from the A.F. of L., on August 12, 1953, the Carpenters marked their seventy-second birhday, having come to life on August 12, 1881, five years prior to the establishment of the "parent" Federation, which it helped to create.

[6]*Ibid,* Vol. XVIII:13 (Aug. 26, 1953) p. 24.

[7]A. H. Raskin, "New Task for the Blunt Meany," *N. Y. Times Magazine,* Feb. 20, 1955: theme repeated in *Time,* Vol. LXV:12 (March 21, 1955), p. 23.

and not William L. who took issue with Mr. Meany's position. It was Maurice who pushed his idea of establishing machinery for the settlement of jurisdiction with grace and moderation. And, finally, it was the new General President of the Carpenters who reprimanded Mr. Meany in an urgent but conciliatory epistle. His letter of disaffiliation was not of a supplicant, to be sure.

We heartily agree with Maurice Hutcheson that it is not a *necessity* of organization for a leader to exercise power or authority without "checks and balances." One of the objects of a social or economic organization should be to distribute power widely so that nobody has so much that he is corrupted by it. Power by its nature corrupts, it corrupts the goodness.

We are not proposing to write a personal guide through these moral dilemmas. But if this is the general principle of leadership expounded by Mr. Raskin and the anonymous writer of *Time,* then the cost of the merger-to-be of the A. F. of L. and the C.I.O. is too high. Actually, organizations which get into the hands of unimaginative, aggressive personalities do not generally have a long expectation of life. The function of an imaginative personality who has risen to a position of great authority is to receive information, and to transform this information into instructions and not "orders."

Again: "Meany did not wait for the maker of the resolution to finish his sentence" wrote Mr. Raskin with obvious delight. "When a vacancy occurs," (a reference to William L. Hutcheson's resignation on August 12, 1953), "all Vice-Presidents move up one seat, Meany barked. Do I hear a resolution to that effect? Within a minute the proposal was approved unanimously. The Carpenters were out and Hutcheson was out as First Vice President. Three weeks later the giant union sheepishly applied for reaffiliation. Hutcheson never got his job back. But his son was later added to the Council at the bottom of the list of Vice Presidents."[8]

The fact is that William L. Hutcheson was seventy-nine and ailing, and could no longer participate in the Executive Council's deliberations. And as for Maurice A. Hutcheson, his election to the fourteenth Vice Presidency of the Council (one seat ahead of the Machinists' Al Hayes), was in conformity with well-established practices by which Executive Council members are promoted. And speaking of promotions, it is well to bear in mind that evaluation of organizations depends a great deal on the nature of the process by which individuals in them rise to positions of authority. Similarly, the ultimate success of organizations depends on their patterns of promotion and on the type of person who attains leadership in them. Labor organizations are no exception to this rule. This

---

[8] *Ibid*

much, many of us have learned from the social science disciplines.

Hardly had a year passed, when Mr. Meany stood on the dais of the Carpenters' Convention, on November 15, 1954, in the Taft Auditorium in Cincinnati, Ohio and paid his "respects" to Maurice Hutcheson. "I want to pay my respects to Maurice A. Hutcheson and the Building Trades Department and President Gray," recited the sixty-one year old President of the Federation. "They brought this problem to us (jurisdictional disputes) in 1953, spelled it out in great detail, showing what a plague it was on our house and showing the Convention that it was something that had to be dealt with in a more intelligent way than it had been in the past. . . . I want to give credit to Maurice Hutcheson and Dick Gray for the part they have played in that. . . . He [Maurice] knows exactly where he is going at all times, because he follows the simple philosophy that the trade union movement is an instrumentality, to bring benefits to the people that it represents. . . ." [9]

At that convention, the twenty-seventh, Maurice Hutcheson made a skillful and impassioned address. He reminded the listening delegates, that "while we have just cause of being proud of the progress, . . . there are hundreds of thousands of men following our trade who do not belong to our organization. In most instances they are working for wages far below those we have established as just. There is no use in us trying to deceive each other. Every non-union man following our trade and working for sub-standard wages and under sub-standard conditions is a direct threat to the wages and working conditions of every member of our Brotherhood."

He made a savage arraignment of those sectors in the American community who are giving their support to the right-to-work laws, denying trade unions the privilege of protecting their wages and working conditions. "Seventeen states have turned the clock back, "legally" tearing down conditions and standards that generations of union men built up through patience and sacrifice."

His criticism of the coercive nature of governmental agencies and of the concerted effort of Bourbon employers who wish to relegate the individual employee to a permanently inferior status aroused the delegates.

He then moved into the normative plane.

He urged the delegates to dislodge those in a position of power who legislated the right-to-work laws. Labor must never fall behind those democratic institutions which operate as an important check on positions of unequal political power. The vote, in fact, is the wage earners' political substitute for the market. To reduce the "vast pool of unorganized" to an absolute minimum, he told the delegates of the establish-

---

[9] UBCJA, *Proceedings,* November 15, 1954, pp. 9-14.

ment of the office of Director of Organization to "spearhead a stepped-up organizing drive, to organize all the workers who rightfully belong in our organization. This office will advise, offer manpower and financial help, but the initial stimulus must come from local groups." He assured the delegates that the general office will focus its attention firmly on the need for organizing the unorganized, "both for our protection and theirs." He expressed the earnest hope that at the next convention the delegates will represent at least a million members.

The speech ended with a plea that the delegates emulate the fighting spirit of Peter J. McGuire, though he quickly added, aware of how his words would impress his listeners: "These are troubled times. Conditions change quickly. New problems arise overnight. Working together as a cohesive, close knit team, we can meet whatever the future brings with confidence."

Throughout he exhibited a refreshing degree of humility. He was frank to say that the General Executive Board helped him to reach for answers. When he finished, the 1365 delegates rose to their feet shouting enthusiastically. There was no doubt, he was bound to the cause body and soul. He worked for it without flinching. There was no doubt, too, that they had a warm feeling for Maurice. We were there as an observer. Maurice A. won his day. He was elected unanimously General President of the Brotherhood for the ensuing four years.

Before many months passed, Maurice sought to reduce what he thought was a weakness of all large organizations: the difficulty of communication. This grows with the size of the organization since "social distance" between the chief executive and the membership at the end of the line would make it difficult to fulfill the function for which the Brotherhood was intended. Information bulletins, quarterly reports and communications of all types keep the Brotherhood's far-flung outposts throughout the U. S. and Canada well informed on economic, industrial and legal matters germane to the trade. These bulletins are supplemented by others on subjects such as unemployment insurance, old age, social security, and employment. In the field of vocational education, the administration's apprenticeship standard training units, authored by the chief executive, did much to increase the interest of young-adults in the vocation of carpentry. The Union's records for the year 1954-55 show that 30,000 availed themselves of these courses.

The administration's concern with the rise of any inequalities in the union's organism, a second weakness, which has been plaguing many a large, growing organization, has led it to decentralize its operations. The establishment of "district" conferences and regional seminars is a step in this direction. These conferences offer the chief executive and the general executive board an opportunity to establish a closer rapport with the "humble receptors" at the end of the organization. They are also designed to acquaint the members with the problems with which the general office is confronted, and to present plans for "future endeavors to better the opportunities and working conditions of the members."

Ably staffed at the top, the new chief executive is leading his union with subtlety and quiet determination. He seems to possess all the desirable qualities of a leader: he is tall, he has a good heart, and he is moderate in everything, even in the use of his intelligence. He is well adjusted and imaginative. His relationships with his associates, be they in labor, industry, government, or the community, have been pleasant. He is not "driven" by aggressiveness or frustration; nor has he exercised any arbitrary powers. His strongest motive is his willingness to serve as well as extend the Brotherhood's ends. His sensitive spirit will rebel against those inadequate personality types who have risen to positions of great authority in the labor movement.

While Maurice A. Hutcheson's term of office has been brief, his experiences and mature understanding of the economic, technological and political problems, well fit him to cope with the unsolved problems facing the carpenters and labor no less. Peering into labor's crystal ball, he made the following earnest observations in the Spring of 1955:

> "We are now entering the age of the automatic machine-the machine which can think and remember and make choices. Again man stands in danger of falling victim to the machine. The same old ghosts of technological unemployment haunt both his working hours and his dreams. Again his answer must lie in strong democratic unions.
>
> "The coming of the automatic age confronts organized labor with a challenge of unparalleled magnitude. The fruits of the automatic age must be translated into shorter hours, higher living standards and greater security against disease and old age. Only in this way can lasting prosperity be achieved. Only in this way can we remain the master of the machine rather than its slave. Just as organized labor tamed steam and electricity for the benefit of all, so must it henceforth equalize the benefits of automation.
>
> "Through the efforts of organized labor, *a new concept of the working man will be developed—a concept that recognizes him as a consumer as well as a source of labor*. Automatic machines may produce goods faster, but machines can buy or consume nothing. Without consumers, production is meaningless. In the years ahead, organized labor must balance the consumer concept with the source of work concept.
>
> "Based on the achievement of the past 75 years, I predict that American workers, through their union constantly winning for them an ever-increasing share of the fruits of automation, will more than double their living standards in the next half century. I foresee a four-day week within 10 to 15 years. I foresee retirement age reduced to 60, or perhaps even 55, with pensions large enough to provide a luxury scale of living, judged by today's standards."

This is not a text of a naive optimist written in 1955!

Technological unemployment has been feared by labor, and even predicted by responsible thinkers many times since the start of the industrial revolution. It has occurred in parts of the economy where sudden changes have not been accommodated without the loss of jobs. But "full employment" or nearly full employment, has been the usual condition in the 1950's after a century and a half of technological development.

The stock answer to the fear of too few jobs is that technology creates new jobs as fast as it abolishes old ones. It introduces new products, makes old ones cheaper or of better quality at the same price. It increases the purchasing power for these products and widens distribution. Demand thus keeps pace with supply, by and large. Indeed, in periods of inflation demand still exceeds supply and thus drives prices up. Purchasers' wants have never yet been satiated, on a national scale, even in the richest country in the world.

Democracy and technology in combination have, almost intuitively and without ever precisely seeing the problem, edged toward a new solution. They have gone a long way, both toward removing the stultifying type of work from the paid worker, and at the same time gradually absorbing him into a universal leisure class by making it possible for him to be free from the job for longer and longer periods. The process will be completed when automatic devices take the place of operators of repetitive machines, clerical drudges, and workers on assembly lines.[10]

As a thoughtful American labor leader, Hutcheson believes that the position and destiny of American labor is bound up with the salvation of all America, and of humanity.

With these visions and ideals few will doubt the paths along which Maurice A. Hutcheson might choose to trod. His visions of the American economy and of the forces shaping the direction of its change have been neatly summarized by these norms, values and moral certainties.

As a corrective organization, the United Brotherhood of Carpenters and Joiners of America, the world's largest craft-industrial union, has been entrusted into the hands of an imaginative, dedicated leader.

---

[10]Cf. George Soule, *Time for Living* (Viking Press, 1955).

PART | VII

The SAGA of the BROTHERHOOD

CHAPTER | XIX

A CHEST OF TOOLS

The United Brotherhood of Carpenters and Joiners of America
(1881-1954)

"If there is any meaning that can be derived from the per-sistent grouping of men about their tools or within their industry, it is the very clear attempt to reassert human experience, namely, that work must fill a social, a moral, as well as an economic role. The vacuum between the job and the man has proved intolerable ... For the worker, the trade union has been an attempt to escape from this dilemma."[1]

In the Indiana University sector, at the cross-roads of Indianapolis, there stands at 222 East Michigan Street, a modern four-story structure with simple, well-equipped offices of the United Brotherhood of Carpenters and Joiners of America triumphant, with its saints, martyrs and organizers, its stories and its traditions, giving a curious secret strength to its commonplace embodiment. Alongside the job-conscious business-likeness there runs a stream of idealism, expressed in the concept of a "good union man." There have been many unsung sufferers for the cause — carpenters who have suffered the loss of jobs, blacklisting, im-prisonment, and even death because they have believed in the union, not as a means of personal advancement, but as a movement in history for the betterment of the group.

Among its leaders were the self-taught reformer, the ideologue and

---

[1] Frank Tennenbaum "The Social Function of Trade Unionism," *Political Science Quarterly,* (Columbia University, June 1947).

the organizer-executive, but in common they shared a vivid sense of their purpose and their function in the movement. It was this faith which ultimately gave the Brotherhood of Carpenters its initial strength to withstand the attacks of employers and of the State in periods when they have been hostile.

What is it that gives rise to an economic organization such as the United Brotherhood of Carpenters and Joiners of America?

Is its rise the result of a deeply felt need, on the part of those who participate in it? If so, what are those needs which the Brotherhood satisfies in its members?

Considered first from the point of view of economics, the rise of the Brotherhood as a modern union was the result of changes in techniques — i.e., in ways of doing carpentry. As the ancient craft of carpentry began to languish under the impact of new machine inventions and the subsequent development of "substitutes" for the woodworking industry,[2] the carpenter began to feel insecure. As improved machinery has advanced, there was a corresponding diminution in the importance of the craft. Thousands were displaced by the "green-hand" — a woman, an untrained apprentice, an immigrant or child — who could do the work of a score of carpenters at half the wages of one.

The window, doors and other parts of the building which streamed off the machine, standardized, complete, and ready for installation, allowed for a division of labor of the carpenter's work. Carpentry was gradually divided into door hanging, floor laying, stair building, and a score of other special tasks by competing contractors who, paid their "hired-hands" one-half the wage of a fully trained, all around carpenter. With the advent of woodworking machinery still another evil began to threaten the security of the carpenter and his craft: piece work. The production of ready-to-install parts which poured off the new machines were ideally suited to this mode of payment; and piece work, in turn was ideally suited to the speed-up.

In the second place, there were many other aspects and motives which led the carpenters both to join and to support the Brotherhood. A description of the conditions of the carpentry trade as they obtained in July, 1892 are explained to us quite vividly in the Bulletin of the Department of Labor. "Many are the architectural changes and innovations year after year that are making carpenter work more and more scarce. The use of iron and steel and other material to replace wood in building construction in our big cities is working dire havoc in our time-honored craft. Then, too, the general use of the best perfected

---

[2]Kenneth E. Boulding, *The Organizational Revolution,* (Harper and Bros., 1953), pp. 203-204.

woodworking machinery and of cheap mill material made by women and children, the lack of an apprentice system and the easy influx of workmen from other occupations into the carpenter trade, the many fluctuations of business, and the continuous flow of emigration to our shores — all make the lot of the journeyman carpenter much harder, even in the best of times than it was in bygone days long ago."[3] A further glance at the historical background of the carpenter will sufficiently explain how the United Brotherhood of Carpenters and Joiners originated and why it behaved the way it did.

The original American carpenter was an itinerant; he traveled from one isolated frontier settlement to the next, working by contract. He supplied only his skill and a few tools. His customer furnished the materials, lodging, and board. Actually, he was more than a carpenter. He selected and felled the timber which he later fashioned into beams and boards and then installed.[4] He belonged to no association, and to no trade union, since he was both a master and a journeyman.

With the growth of the first colonial towns, the carpenter settled down in the city and opened a shop where, as a combination master carpenter and merchant, he sold directly to a local consumer, turning to the apprentice-journeyman system of England for his labor supply. From March to November, he worked outside on the job; in the winter, he worked inside, fashioning the details of the building. He trained the apprentice who was contracted to him from three to four years until the opportunity to become a master craftsman presented itself. Until the end of the eighteenth century, this system prevailed with but minor variations.

With greatly improved transportation, came a widening of the market. The old nexus was now destroyed by which the artisan made in his own shop, from his own materials, and for his own customers the product the latter desired. The master craftsman, the employer, the worker, capitalist, were no longer a single person. Between the worker and consumer intervened more and more middlemen or speculators, who dominated the building industry. They had capital or knew how to borrow it; they purchased the raw material and made arrangements for its manufacture; they advanced credits to the retail merchant who disposed of the product. Since the speculator-capitalists were competing intently with each other in the growing building industry, they were interested primarily in the cost of production. Only by lowering it could they undersell rivals. The most feasible way was to reduce prices through

[3]Edward W. Bemis, *Bulletin of the Department of Labor,* Vol. IV, 1899 (Washington: Government Printing Office), p. 378.

[4]*U.B.C.J.A. Proceedings* (1936), p. 46; H. C. Mercer, *Ancient Carpenters' Tools and Use in the Eighteenth Century,* passim.

lowering labor costs. Emphasis was placed upon quickness and cheapness in production rather than skill. Greenhorns and journeymen carpenters were employed to do the simple operations and wages were reduced. Thus it came about that the first journeymen's trade union association was organized.[5]

By the middle of the nineteenth century, carpenters associations had existed in most of the larger cities. They were present as far West as Detroit and were active in at least fifteen cities.[6] These associations protested against the factors which were altering their trades. They resented the lower wages, the lowering of the standards of workmanship, and the invasion of their trades by unskilled or semi-skilled competitors. They regretted, above all, that the control of their trade had passed from "members of the profession" into the hands of "capitalists" and "speculators."

Such carpenters' organizations as existed before 1850 were not permanent bodies. They were generally called into existence by some particular grievance, and dissolved when they had succeeded in remedying it or had been defeated.* There were times, however, when the possibility of redressing grievances was favorable. In Massachusetts, carpenters for example raised their wages from $1.10 a day in 1800 to $1.40 in 1850.

From whatever source the wage earner may have come, he was subjected after 1850 to the terms of labor imposed by the railroad and the machine. The extension of the railroad meant that the carpenters from New York competed with those from Chicago. A raise in the wages of a given city meant that a flood of outside carpenters were automatically attracted to that city. Labor agitation, labor practices were no longer the concern of a locality. Thus, there appeared in September of 1865 the New York State Carpenters' Union, but almost immediately after its founding it started to decline, and after 1867 no further evidence of its activities is available.[7]

After the 'seventies, a host of woodworking machine inventions

---

[5]John R. Commons, *A History of Labour in the United States*, (Macmillan Co., 1918-1926), Vol. I, p. 69.

[6]Ibid, pp. 365, 380, 386,488.

*The carpenters originated the ten-hour a day movement, arguing that the ten-hour day could be obtained by reducing the excessive hours of labor during the summer and spreading them through the year. Philadelphia carpenters asserted that a longer day than ten-hours, was physically disadvantageous and gave no time for culture and self-improvement. In Boston, the carpenters who struck for the ten-hour day had been roundly scolded by their employers and by the capitalists who financed construction of that city. The latter viewed with great regret the action of the carpenters. (Edward C. Kirkland, *A History of American Economic Life*, F. S. Crofts & Co. 7, p. 351.)

[7]National Carpenters Union, *Proceedings of the First Annual Convention of New York City*, September 4 to September 8, 1865.

made the carpenter craftsman less essential. For the carpenter it meant a greater dependence upon the contractor, speculator, since his unique skill, formerly acquired by a long apprenticeship, was no longer necessary. Anybody could be taught in a few weeks to tend a machine. A "sander" which smoothed wood as fast as a dozen carpenters and a compound carver, which turned out six wood duplicates and replaced three score carpenters, were but two of a whole series of such inventions which lured handicraft work into the factory and affected a major upheaval in the woodworking industry.[8]

If the piece working system threatened the security of the carpenter through affecting a basic change in the organization of the industry, the rise of the capitalist, middleman and speculator prior to 1850, haunted the carpenter's very doorsteps, literally menacing the status of the carpenter's craft. John Swinton, a journalist with pro-labor sympathies, vividly described this affliction which continued to plague the carpenter since then:

> "Speculators . . . started putting up shoddy houses on 90 day builder's loans. One of the customs in the carpentry work on these shoddy houses is the system of lumping and subletting or piece work. The lumper takes a whole job . . . and sublets it to another, who, in turn, parcels it out to others, who do the work in as rapid a manner as possible . . . they all have to make a profit at the expense of (both) the buyer and the laborer."[9]

There were still other factors that could not fail to leave their imprint upon the carpenter. Seasonality and weather conditions affected the carpenter by depriving him of a large percentage of his normal time, while the contractor found it difficult to plan his completion dates.

All these elements undoubtedly played a part in the carpenters' movement. There was the need for "belonging" in itself; the need of simple fellowship. It was the desire to escape from the feeling of impotence which came over the individual carpenter when he faced the buzzing, impersonal machine. There was also the desire for *status*. The carpenter wanted the dignity of his work admitted and, although he did not insist upon an equality of property and possessions, demanded the equality under the law and the equality of opportunity which a democratic country should afford him.[10]

On Monday, August 12, 1881, thirty-six delegates from eleven industrial cities gathered at the modest Trades Assembly Hall, at 192

---

[8]Frederick S. Deibler, *The Amalgamated Woodworkers' International Union of America*, pp. 32-36.

[9]*John Swinton's Papers* (N.Y.C.) February 17, 1884, p. 4.

[10]Edward C. Kirkland, *A History of American Life* (F. S. Crofts & Co., 1947) p. 356.

East Washington Street, Chicago. In common they responded to an urgent call, penned by Peter J. McGuire, whose object it was to set up a voluntary national union, which was to consist of carpenters, stair builders and mill hands. Few of the delegates had the fares with which to reach Chicago. None had the means to put up at a hotel. All were guests of the Protective and Benevolent Societies of Chicago, the treasuries of which were none-too-bountiful.

They were a physically robust group of men, in their late thirties and early forties. Some, like Gabriel Edmonston, served in the Civil War, while the author of the first platform, Peter J. McGuire was already the unsung martyr of the laboring man. Rejected by his church and his parents, he turned into a full-time missionary of the "weak" and the "underdogs." All were married, had children of school age; were self-educated and passionately concerned with the question of economic justice. They were an aggrieved group of craftsmen, who felt the need for identification with something which was larger and more significant than their own pleasures and pains, and which made demands upon them, even for sacrifices.

At that meeting a preamble was adopted, whose unconcealed concern was to better the position of the carpenter in the community. It read in part:

". . . In the present age, the rapid concentration of wealth in the hands of a few men give them power to control the means of labor and dictate to the workers what they shall receive for the labor they perform . . .

"Our wages are lower than those of other trades which require less skills. Year after year our vocation has lost the proud position it once occupied. It therefore becomes our duty to ask ourselves, shall we willingly permit our craft to sink lower and lower on the social scale? Are we, who have done so much to build the world's wealth, not entitled to a just equivalent for what we do?

"Must we forever be without sufficient means to maintain ourselves and families in comfort and independence, to educate our children?

". . . There is hope for us only in unity and organization. Without unity we must meet our employers at a great disadvantage. The capitalist has the advantage of past accumulations. The laborer unassisted by combination has not. Knowing this, the capitalist dictates terms and waits while his men without funds have no other alternative than to submit . . .

". . . Competition among ourselves intensifies this conflict, reduces wages and renders one workman the victim of another . . ."[11]

Out of these deliberations, lasting four days, came the formal creation of the United Brotherhood of Carpenters and Joiners of America.

It was an auspicious beginning and doubtless a morale builder for the uncertainty and position of the carpenter, although the number thus

---

[11]Frank Duffy, *History of the UBCJA* (MSS.).

affected totaled 2,042, who were unevenly spread in eleven constituent local unions.

A constitution was framed, assigning to the individual locals the right to make their own by-laws so long as they did not conflict with the constitution of the Brotherhood. A benefit system was instituted, paying $250 on the death of a member in good standing. Provision was also made for a "resistance" or defense fund by each local union for the "relief of members and authorized strikes and lockouts." A national card system was introduced to cope with the problem of itinerancy and migratory carpenters newly-arrived from the Continent. Membership dues were set at twenty-five cents per month and one dollar initiation fee. A flat prohibition against piece work was laid down. The constitution provided for the election by the convention of a general president, eight vice presidents, together constituting the general executive board. The office of the General Secretary created in the person of Peter J. McGuire, was the only full-time paid office of the organization.

Contrast this situation with that of 1954. In place of the sparse fauna of eleven local unions and a structurally weak "national" organization, limited to informal contacts by the absence of paid organizers and paid officers, the Brotherhood today is a closely-knit, highly integrated organization, boasting a membership of 823,574 in 1954, 2903 locals distributed over the United States and possessions, including Canada. Its treasury in cash and bonds totaled over 9 millions in 1954. Its members paid an average of $2.32 monthly dues, and an average of $45.16 initiation fees. Few industrial and no craft union outranks it in size, wealth, and influence.

The 1951 Constitution begins by briefly stating the objects, and principles of the organization; then lists its "trade autonomy," which consists of "the milling, fashioning, joining, assembling, erecting, fastening or dismantling of all material of wood, hollow metal or fibre, or of products composed in part of wood, hollow metal or fibre, the laying of all cork and composition, and all other resilient floor covering, all shingles, the erecting and dismantling of machinery and the manufacturing of all wood material, where the skill, knowledge and training of a carpenter are required either through the operation of machine or hand tools."[12]

The constitution provides for a General President, First and Second General Vice-President, General Secretary, General Treasurer, and seven General Executive Board Members, one from each district of the United Brotherhood. The General President is charged with the responsibility of supervising the organizers, negotiating agreements, protecting the

---

[12]*United Brotherhood of Carpenters and Joiners of America, Constitution and Laws,* (January 1, 1951), p. 5.

jurisdiction of the union, and he has considerable and important duties at Indianapolis headquarters. He must decide all appeals, hear complaints, prevent dissension, and see that the 2,903 locals are operating effectively. The General President has authority to appoint a representative "to take possession for examination of all books, papers, and financial accounts of the subordinate group . . . until a complete report has been filed."[13] The chief officer of the Brotherhood is granted power by the Constitution to "subordinate bodies or the members thereof who, in the judgment of the General President are working against the best interests of the United Brotherhood. . . ."[14] In brief, the chief officer is granted authority by the Constitution to "supervise the entire interests of the United Brotherhood, and perform such other duties as the laws may require. He is obliged, however, to "submit a quarterly report to the General Executive Board, and the same shall be published" in the official organ. For all that the chief officer receives a a salary of $600 per week.[15]

The first Vice-President has charge of the label and of the woodworking mills. He also examines and approves the laws of all bodies subordinate to the national office. "In case of charges against the General President, he, in conjunction with the other members of the General Executive Board, shall have the power to suspend said officer pending an investigation." The Second General Vice-President is given no specific authority, but is, in effect a troubleshooter for the General President. His weekly salary prescribed in the union Constitution is $350, a differential of $50 received by the First General Vice-President.[16] There is a $50 difference in the salary of the General Secretary, who is charged with preserving all important documents and papers related to the Brotherhood's business. He receives and keeps records of all monies due from local unions; he compiles all statistical information related to the conditions of the trade. The General Treasurer sees to it that the finances of the Brotherhood are properly managed, and that quarterly audits and accounts are made to the General Executive Board. He is charged with performing "such other duties as the General Executive Board may require." Both, the General Secretary and the General Treasurer are bonded with regular surety companies. The former is bonded for $20,000, the General Treasurer for $50,000.

The General Executive Board has seven district members who are nominated in convention and elected by referendum, but who must belong to a local union in the district which they represent. In addition,

---

13Ibid, p. 9.
14Ibid, p. 10.
15Ibid, p. 10.
16Ibid, p. 11.

all five of the general officers are members of the Board. The General President is Chairman of the Board and the General Secretary handles the secretarial duties. The General Executive Board has charge of all trade movements; it has the authority "to authorize strikes and defend the organization against the attacks of employers, combinations or lockouts. . . ."[17] The General Executive Board acts as a court of appeals on all grievances and points of law, originally decided by the General President, between conventions. Its decisions are binding "until reversed by the Convention."[18] The General President is in direct charge of the activities of the General Representatives (organizers) in their district; it directs organizing drives, has authority to call strikes and aid and assist local unions in the more important strikes. Its members are subject to the beck and call of the General President, and are required "to devote their entire time to the interests of the Brotherhood." For this they receive a prescribed weekly salary of $250.[19]

The most important local unit in the Brotherhood is the District Council, which is formed by all local unions in a clearly defined economic and geographic area. Whenever, in any of these seven areas, there are present two or more local unions, a District Council must be formed.[20] Local unions make and ratify the policies administered by the councils. The District Councils are given jurisdiction over collective bargaining, the framing of work rules for the government of local unions, and local administration of national discipline. This development, largely economic and sociological, has made the District Council President a dominant personality in the Brotherhood. As a result the local unions of the Brotherhood have become largely administrative units.[21] An analagous development has overtaken the International Brotherhood of Teamsters, Chauffeurs, Warehousemen and Helpers of America and the United Mine Workers of America.[22]

The Brotherhood meets quadrennially in a Convention. Representation at the convention is based on five hundred member units in the local unions. For the first five hundred members, two delegates are permitted, for the second, three. Locals with more than 1,000 members are limited to four delegates, and those with 100 or fewer are given one. The District Councils are permitted no voting representation at the Convention.

The rest of the Constitution regulates strikes which "may be sanc-

---

[17]*Ibid*, p. 15.
[18]*Ibid*, p. 15.
[19]*Ibid*, p. 16.
[20]*Ibid*, pp. 21-22.
[21]*Ibid*, p. 21.
[22]Phillip Taft, *op. cit.* pp. 233-234.

tioned by the General Executive Board and financial aid extended
to the extent that it deems adequate." The Constitution deals with finances, benefits, clearance cards, the use of the union label, qualifications
for admission to the Brotherhood, disciplinary procedures, regulations
prescribing a member's conduct on the job, and at union meetings. The
Constitution describes a number of prohibited acts, the violation of
which are punishable by fine, suspension, or expulsion. The union
prohibits members from becoming habitual drunkards, discussing union
business rules; disobeying orders of officers, slandering an officer or
member, the use of profane language, embezzlement of funds, neglect of
duty. While the Constitutional powers granted to the General President
and the National Office are extensive, they are not an adequate guide
to the realities of the Brotherhood's government and the management
of its internal affairs. In its structure, provisions are made for democratic
control by the members. At the same time it is well to bear in mind that
the rights and freedom of union members are influenced by custom,
tradition, and experiences rather than by the written Constitution. But
we shall revert to the subject of union democracy and union discipline
procedure elsewhere in this section.

The union's first five years were marked by aimlessness and considerable floundering. Under Peter J. McGuire's leadership, the Brotherhood of Carpenters and Joiners of America became a protective union,
then a benevolent, then a protective-benevolent society. It experimented
with three different types of executive boards; changed the number of
national officers from a high eleven to a low three; and even the location
of the national offices was moved five times — from St. Louis to New
York, Philadelphia, Cleveland, and Philadelphia. In this fashion, the
early reform leaders sought to draw the carpenter into their union. They
had taken their little "Brotherhood" down a score of administative blind
alleys, when, in May 1886, the eight-hour movement which it initiated,
began attracting a stream of workers to the organization.

For the first five years of the Brotherhood's existence, the general
office consisted of little more than Peter J. McGuire's indefatigable
energies. Wherever McGuire happened to be, there was the general
office. The organizing apparatus of the union was simple. It was limited
in its growth by McGuire's maintaining effective personal contacts
between himself and his "happy family." It meant that Peter J. McGuire,
the Brotherhood's General Secretary left town on the next freight. From
city to city he agitated and exhorted, kept those locals which were alive,
functioning, and brought new ones into being. In the course of a year,
McGuire waged as many as a dozen organizing "drives," timing his
visits with a strike or some other important event. When he was not
on "missionary" work, he wrote. In one year, 1883, McGuire sent out

83,000 communications, circulars, manifestoes. Another means of communication was the Brotherhood's *"The Carpenter,"* which while it reached few carpenters, gave McGuire an opportunity to educate the practitioners on trade unionism, political philosophy, and history. Advertisements offered the carpenters a special cut-rate of the works of Ruskin, Plato, and others.

With this utopian approach, characteristic of an earlier day, McGuire was content to go on producing the immutable product of his personality without any thought of adjusting himself to new and different environments. After five years of arduous work, McGuire claimed 21,423 union members and a surplus of $2,680.12."[23] The structure of the organization remained localized and diffused. Although ten national officers were created, none but that of the General Secretary was paid full time. The General President was a mere figurehead. A General Executive Board, composed of the ten national officers, was created, but no provision was made for it to meet. Since the officers lived at widely separated points, the Board never met.

The financial operations of the general office were also restricted. A strike fund into which each local had to put ten percent of its income, was administered on the local level. The national strike aid had first to be sanctioned by a vote of two-thirds of all locals, on application of a given local for aid. Then the necessary cash was forwarded by each of the various locals directly to the striking local. It never passed through the general office.[24] To a large extent, then, the national union operated a loose type of control and within wide limits the local unions enjoyed considerable freedom in developing their own policies. A "shadowy and nominal national administration" was all that could be had under the circumstances.

It was of little moment to Peter J. McGuire, for he was first and last a reformer, doctrinaire, agitator, and popular philosopher, after his own fashion, and not an administrator or executive. And none could be had. As long as the communications system was limited to formal and informal contacts, the Brotherhood couldn't grow "beyond the number of people who could maintain informal contacts one with another."[25] McGuire administered the union along the lines dictated by his personality and philosophy such as prevailed during the second-half of the last century. The manner in which he and his early co-workers conducted the union can be summed up in these three words: educate, agitate, and organize, without much formal organization. His missionary zeal, with a determina-

[23]Frank Duffy, *op. cit.*
[24]*Ibid.*
[25]Boulding, *op. cit.*, p. 26.

tion to carry the gospel to all carpenters in all parts of America, reflected the nineteenth century pioneering spirit fully as much or more than any religious impulse of brotherhood. Peter J. McGuire, like Samuel Gompers, typified the last of the vanishing tribe of labor leaders, who were teachers, philosophers and organizers all in one!

The labor leader of our own day is in personality structure "other directed," at the risk of drying up his entire inner life. The early labor leaders of the Brotherhood felt that if the workers could be educated first, and then, through the worker, the public, both groups would rapidly come to see the logic in justice of trade union claims. That education might have an effect other than the one intended in a democratically fluid society — to make the worker less content to remain in his existing "station" in life, or that the public might turn against trade unionism — never occurred to them. Similarly, organization was simply a precondition to education, and the union one vast Cooper Union or lecture hall. It was a way of debating and formulating ideas. Organization was first a medium through which to improve the "moral, social and intellectual condition" of the carpenter, and only secondarily, a battle tactic to be employed against the employers.

In his first official act, the Carpenters' General President Gabriel Edmonston, broadcast a circular to the carpenters of the United States in which, "Education . . . is an able assistant to help us obtain the objects of our Brotherhood. We must first understand the rights of labor before we can intelligently defend or discuss its claims. . . . We must, through numbers, impress the dignity of our just demands on the public. If we are confident we are right, let us convince our fellow workmen . . . by cool judgment . . . ."[26]

The harsh realities of the workingman's life stimulated most of his labor union activity — as it allways had. Ten and even twelve hours a day for the carpenters in many cities throughout America, at $2.50 a day in the 'eighties and 'nineties left room for little else but meagre meals and exhausted sleep. The escapes advocated by reformists, that the workingmen . . . "will become contractors, builders, reaping the rewards of his own industry and the profit of his own labor," was natural enough for carpenters who were only a stage removed from the handicraftsman. But practice contradicted anticipation. The carpenter worked ten hours a day, and holidays, and thought there was little use for the union. The leaders of the Brotherhood had to devise some kind of lure to attract the practical carpenter into their reform organization. McGuire and his coworkers struck upon a device which gave the same measure of practical gain—the eight-hour movement, advancing the argument of Ira Steward,

---

26U.B.C.J.A. *Proceedings.* (1890), p. 11.

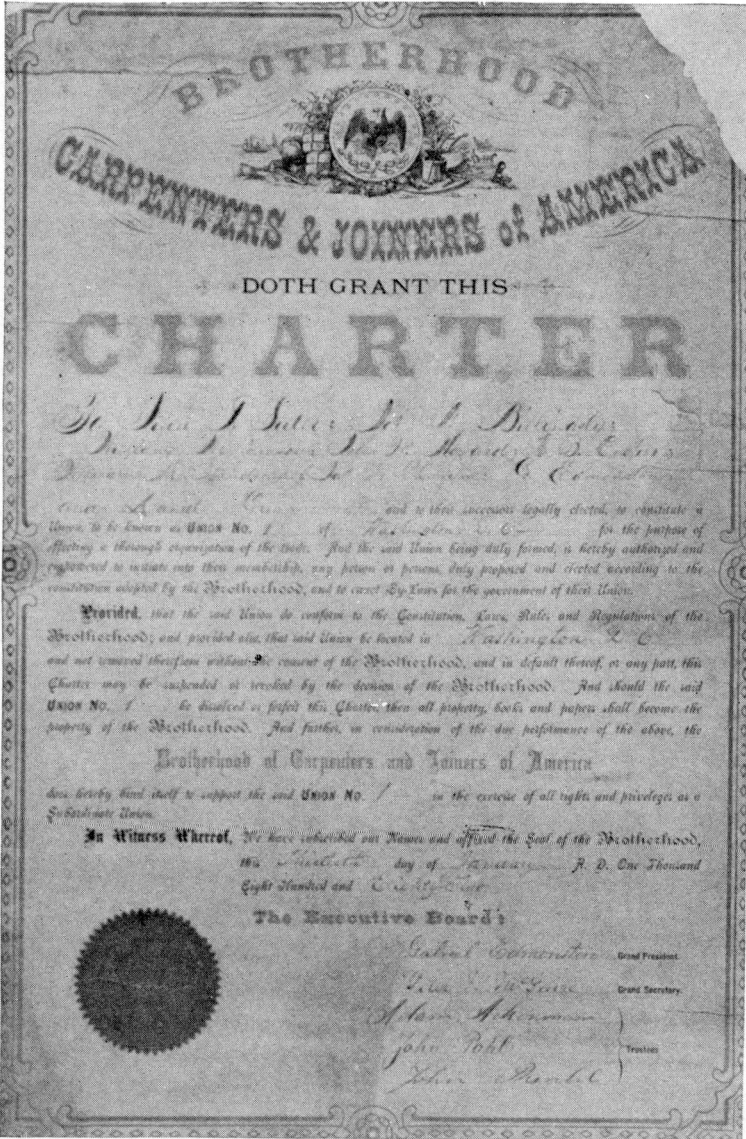

The First Charter! Issued on Jan. 30, 1882, five years before the founding of the American Federation of Labor, it was signed by Gabriel Edmonston, Grand President and by Peter J. McGuire, Grand Secretary of the Brotherhood — both original founders of the A. F. of L. and co-officers with Sam Gompers.

Peter J. McGuire, founder and ideologue of the UBC & JA and its Secretary, 1881-1901, and "father of Labor Day."

Frank Duffy, arbiter and warrior, General Secretary of the UBC & JA, for more than four decades, (1901-1947).

THE BIRTH OF THE BROTHERHOOD

(August 12, 1881)

"In the present age, the rapid concentration of wealth in the hands of the few gives them power to control the means of labor and dictate to the workers what they shall receive for the labor they perform. Every branch of labor is being rapidly monopolized until the vast industrial interests of the world are now almost enslaved to the wealthy and privileged classes, and just in proportion as this state of affairs continues, the power of the capitalist increases and the working people are impoverished and subjected.

"Look at the position occupied by the carpenters and joiners today. Our wages are lower than those of other trades who require less skill and furnish fewer tools. Year by year our vocation has lost the proud position it once occupied. It therefore becomes our duty to ask ourselves, shall we willingly permit our craft to sink lower and lower in the social scale until we are completely enslaved? Are we, who have done so much to build the world's wealth, not entitled to a just equivalent for what we do? Must we be forever without sufficient means to maintain ourselves and families in comfort and independence, to educate our children and qualify them for the duties of life? Shall we be forced by division among ourselves to bow the suppliant knee to capital, and allow our craft to become the prey of the unscrupulous and designing?

"There is no hope for us only in unity and organization. Without unity we meet our employers at a great disadvantage, the capitalist has the advantage of past accumulations, the laborer unassisted by combination has not. Knowing this, the capitalist can dictate terms and wait, while his men without funds have no other alternative than to submit. Competition among ourselves intensifies this conflict, reduces wages, and renders one workman the victim of another. But with organization all this is changed. Hence, we must form a union broad enough to embrace every carpenter and joiner in the land — one that will protect every man in his labor and in his wages. 'Single handed we can accomplish nothing, but united there is no power of wrong we may not openly defy.' Therefore, we, the delegates of various Local Unions of carpenters and joiners in Convention assembled, do hereby establish the 'Brotherhood of Carpenters and Joiners of America,' and we call upon all carpenters and joiners to organize Local Unions as quickly as possible, and connect themselves with our organization.

"The object of our Brotherhood is to rescue our trade from the low level to which it has fallen, and by mutual effort to raise ourselves to that position in society to which we, as mechanics, are justly entitled, and to place ourselves on a foundation sufficiently strong to secure ourselves from further encroachment, and elevate the moral, social and intellectual condition of every carpenter in the land. And to the consummation of so desirable an object, we, the delegates in Convention assembled, do hereby pledge ourselves to sustain the Brotherhood we have formed."

Facsimile of the first page of the preamble to the constitution of the UBC & JA (1881).

At the crossroads of Indianapolis, in the University of Indiana sector, stands the United Brotherhood of Carpenters and Joiners of America building. Militant and triumphant with her saints, martyrs and fighters contributing their life to a great stream of history . . . the American labor movement.

WHERE OLD CARPENTERS GO TO LIVE

The Carpenters Home in Lakeland, Florida, unsurpassed for sheer beauty anywhere in the world. Variegated recreational activities make life pleasant for the men who spent years with hammer, saw and plane and between chores carved out a union scale too. . . .

Golfing — Not for Millionaires!

Mental Relaxation — In the library.

Companionship at the Dinner Table.

Favorite Pastime — Pitching Horseshoes.

Not so strenuous — Shuffleboard

With rod and tackle on beautiful Lake Gibson (on Home grounds).

the "eight-hour monomaniac" of Boston, as justification. Steward asserted the shorter day would aid even the manufacturer. "In the mechanical fact that the cost of making an article depends almost entirely upon the number manufactured is a practical increase in wages, by tempting the workers through their new leisure to unite in buying luxuries now confined to the wealthy, and which are costly because bought only by the wealthy." This shorter work day was to be obtained by an educational campaign in legislation. By 1868, the national government had submitted and passed an eight-hour law for government employees. Such legislation as was secured in the states was worthless.

McGuire propounded his own eclectic eight-hour philosophy, and made the demand for shorter hours the chief immediate goal of the Brotherhood. He felt that if but "10,000 men adopt the nine-hour rule . . . it will require 1,100 (more) men to complete the work now done."[27] The leisure thus afforded all carpenters would create new wants . . . and stimulate a desire for better social conditions. With time to rest and think, the carpenters were expected to educate themselves to the point of view that the free enterprise system adds increase to capital at the expense of labor."[28] The Carpenters' mouthpiece also demanded that "they (the workers) . . . must designate one common day to establish the (eight-hour) system, and let them stand by each other to obtain it."

At this time America's first great labor organization, the Knights of Labor, then nearly 700,000 strong, with over three-fourths of all organized labor, was on the scene. Also present was the youthful but extremely feeble rival, the Federation of Organized Trades and Labor, the incipient A. F. of L., which was beginning a nation-wide campaign for the eight-hour day. McGuire and Edmonston chose the latter, an Association of National Trade Unions, craft in character which the Brotherhood had been instrumental in forming. At the 1884 convention of the Federation, on instructions of the 1882 convention of the Brotherhood, Edmonston offered and succeeded in passing a resolution calling for an eight-hour movement to begin on May 1, 1886. The leaders of the Federation, McGuire, Adolph Strasser and Samuel Gompers of the Cigar Makers continued to feel their way toward a form of organization adapted to American conditions. They had only turned to the eight-hour movement as an alternative to the expiration of their little Federation, a development which, in the depression of 1884 seemed all to imminent. They were depending on the Knights of Labor, which was entering its halcyon years, to effectuate their bold

---

[27] *The Carpenter,* June 1882, p. 4.
[28] *The Carpenter,* July 1882, p. 4.

threat. But the Knights, resentful that the eight-hour movement came from the rival Federation, denounced the projected short-hour movement and advised all Knights to hold aloof from it.[29] Powderly, wedded to political action, expressed distaste for the idea, but the rank and file of the Knights and of other unions and of unorganized workers set the first of May as a deadline for the attainment of fewer hours. Already in April 1886 it became increasingly clear that labor discontent had been channeled in a direction which the great mass of workers considered constructive. During the waning days of April, talk of the eight-hour movement mounted with a grim intensity which was given wide coverage by the press as May Day approached.

May 1 fell on a Saturday and from Boston to Chicago and other great industrial centers the workers turned out. The carpenters in the building trades led the strike in all cities. For all practical purposes, America's industrial centers were in the throes of a general strike. In Chicago, where 80,000 wage earners ceased work it reached its greatest intensity. In that city other factors incited aggressive action. For three months the McCormick Reaper Works, unwilling to be "dictated to" by the unions, had locked out workers and conducted operations with "scabs" and Pinkertons. Finally, there were the anarchists. Although some of their leaders were German immigrants, one, Albert R. Parsons, was an Alabamian, a Confederate veteran, and a Knight of Labor. The anarchists with a small native following frightened citizens by their terroristic language in behalf of the eight-hour day as a class war issue. On May 3, a battle between strikers and scabs at the McCormick Reaper Works was broken up by the police and four strikers were killed. One of the anarchist leaders, summoning a meeting of portent in Haymarket Square for the evening of May 4, included in the appeal, "Working Men, Arm yourselves and appear in full force." In Haymarket Square the dull speeches had worn on into the night and rain had set in when a squad of police advanced to break up the meeting. When one disgruntled speaker protested that this was a peaceable meeting, he was suddenly interrupted by a bomb that rose over the heads of the crowd and exploded among the police. One policeman was killed instantly, seven were fatally wounded.

A wave of hysteria swept Chicago. Under conditions of popular excitement which made a fair outcome of the proceedings unlikely, the leaders of the anarchists were arrested and brought to trial as accomplices to the murder. Although the actual bomb thrower was never discovered and a connection between him and the anarchists was never established, eight men were convicted of murder by a jury; four were actu-

---

[29]John R. Commons, et al, *History of Labor in the United States,* (Macmillian and Co., 1926), p. 419.

ally executed. This injustice to individual men had wider repercussions. Following the Haymarket affair, contemporary labor leaders scurried for cover, uttering hurried disavowals of culpability in order to placate aroused middle-class wrath. Anti-labor legislation was enacted while the radicals were harrassed. Samuel Gompers remarked that the eight-hour movement was set back at least ten years by the bomb discharged at the Haymarket rally.[30] He felt vindicated in his belief that no labor cause could afford the slightest fringe of radicalism.

In terms of immediate and practical gains, the movement was a failure. Employers cancelled the concessions already made to the strikers. In their gratitude to the police, Chicago businessmen raised large purses for them. However, the movement demonstrated that if specific gains were held before the workers, they could be lured into trade organizations. The Brotherhood became the largest trade union in the country, crowding 50,000 practical American carpenters into the union. The eight-hour movement of 1886 "meant a new and very remarkable change in the policy and practice of the labor movement," declared Edmonston.[31]

The eight-hour movement was not only a turning point for the Brotherhood, but for the Knights of Labor and the Federation of Trades as well. The Noble and Holy Order spun into a precipitous decline. A half-million dues-paying members dropped away in two years and by 1893 the Knights had dwindled to 75,000. But the Knights had not yet completely died, and in 1894 they responded to the call for the remote aims of Eugene Debs. The leaders of the trade unions aided and abetted this decline by pointing to Powderly's opposition to, and their own support of, the eight-hour movement.

The leaders of the Brotherhood were cocky about its bolstered strength, and McGuire led an assault of the trade unions upon the Knights immediately after the eight-hour strike subsided. Gompers and Strasser led a similar counter-offensive against the Knights within their Cigar Makers' International Union. McGuire's assault against the Knights was not without some provocation, for the Brotherhood soon after its own birth and later had experienced a considerable amount of jurisdictional trouble with the powerful Knights. After 1887, the attitude of the Brotherhood's leaders toward dual unionism hardened appreciably. Peter J. McGuire's earlier feeling that all unions were members of the labor fraternity working toward the same goals gave way to a feeling that dual unionism was a heresy.

In May, 1886, the Gompers-Strasser-McGuire-Edmonston group

---

[30]Samuel Gompers, Seventy Years of Life and Labor, (E. P. Dutton & Co., 1925), p. 178.
[31]U.B.C.J.A., Proceedings (1888) p. 11.

secured the calling of a convention of the national unions, "to protect our respective organizations from the malicious work of an element who openly boast that trade unions must be destroyed." The proposals drawn up by this convention and presented to the general assembly of the Knights of Labor practically invited the Noble Order to cease organizing trades for which a national union existed and to undo such action in the past. When Powderly failed to react, the stage was set for the formation of the American Federation of Labor. On December 4, 1886, at Columbus, Ohio, McGuire issued a call for a second convention. The convention met and the old Federation of Organized Trades and Labor Unions was dissolved and the American Federation of Labor was born. Gompers was elected First President, McGuire Secretary, and Edmonston, Treasurer. Four years later, as the membership of the American Federation of Labor was going up, it met the membership of the Knights of Labor coming down. The first article of the official creed prescribed organization of labor on craft lines. McGuire had put the case: "Being organized on special trade lines they can act on trade matters all the more intelligently and practically as well as speedily than in mixed bodies."

With a considerably increased membership, the Brotherhood was a force to be reckoned with and it first turned its attention to the United Order of Carpenters and the Amalgamated Society of Carpenters and Joiners. Both of these unions had been in existence longer than the Brotherhood. Since its birth, the Brotherhood had made strenuous efforts to consolidate with the United Order but without avail. The United Order was a district organization with unions in New York, New Jersey and Connecticut. When the Brotherhood was formed, the officers of the United Order chose to remain aloof, and they effectively excluded the Brotherhood's members from the labor market. The United Order controlled the United Building Trades Committees and the Board of Business Agents and was able to force the Amalgamated Society of Carpenters to go along with its anti-Brotherhood policy. However, on May 13, 1888, both the Brotherhood and the United Order merged, the latter agreeing to incorporate the title "United."[32]

Only two crafts actually transplanted their old-country unions to the States. Members of the Amalgamated Society of Engineers and of the Amalgamated Society of Carpenters and Joiners set up their first American branches in 1861 and 1867. The Carpenters were about as strong until after the 1890's, when they increased to some sixty branches and to eight thousand card-holders.[33] After 1890 the much larger rival American unions, the International Association of Machinists and

---

[32] *Workingman's Advocate,* March 23, 1872.
[33] *Amalgamated Society of Carpenters and Joiners,* Annual Report, 1864/5 - 1914/5, *passim.*

the United Brotherhood of Carpenters and Joiners of America sought to absorb their British brothers. In 1913 the Amalgamated Carpenters submitted to the Brotherhood but kept their own benefit system. The Engineers held aloof from the I.A.M. until 1920.[34] The Brotherhood was influenced directly by the benefit system which the Amalgamated Carpenters brought to the United States. To the lack of such a scheme, the collapse of the American Carpenters' national organization in 1872 could be attributed.[35]

From 1886 to 1890, the Brotherhood was perforce little more than a shorter hours organization. And, although a tribute to the personal leadership of McGuire and his co-workers, the growth of the Brotherhood was as much a testimonial to the efficacy of the shorter day's work as a battle standard around which the American carpenter could rally. The dominant motive of the United Brotherhood in its passionate attachment to the eight-hour day was the desire to divide the available amount of employment among a greater number of carpenters. "Multiplication and use of labor saving machines make it our first duty to shorten the hours of labor."[36] The Brotherhood had inspired and agitated for the eight-hour day in 1886 and had given it such leadership as it possessed; the United Brotherhood had become the eight-hour movement of 1890.

The delegates of the United Brotherhood introduced the eight-hour motion at the 1888 American Federation of Labor convention and it was passed. A newer and stronger A. F. of L., however, decided to ride tight rein on this movement in order to prevent another Haymarket Riot. At its Boston convention in 1889, the Executive Council decided that one union would strike for eight hours across the country and it would enjoy the support of the other A. F. of L. unions.[37] On March 20, 1890, the strongest, the largest, and most successful union was chosen "to make the movement for eight hours as a day's work on May 1, 1890" — the United Brotherhood of Carpenters and Joiners of America. The United Mine Workers were to follow next.[38]

McGuire directed the movement personally, hopping tirelessly from one strike point to the next. His tireless agitation was repaid ten fold by the most enormous victory which had ever been won by trade unionism in America. 22,275 carpenters in thirty-four cities gained the eight-

---

[34]Rowland T. Berthoff, *British Immigrants in Industrial America,* (Harvard University Press, 1953), pp. 89, 90.

[35]Theodore W. Glocke, *The Government of American Trade Unions,* (Baltimore 1913), pp. 90-9; S. Higenbotham, *Our Society's History,* (Manchester, 1939), pp. 286-290.

[36]Frank Duffy, *op. cit.*

[37]U.B.C.J.A., *Proceedings,* (1890), p 19.

[38]Frank Duffy.

hour day, and some 32,000 more in 234 cities gained the nine-hour day. A changed United Brotherhood gathered at the Sixth Convention in August 1890 as the last sounds of the successful eight-hour struggle died away. The Brotherhood now had a membership of 53,769 distributed in 697 local unions. McGuire keynoted the Sixth General Convention (1890) on a note of triumph:

> "The number of local unions now under our jurisdiction is 697 . . . with 77,596 enrolled members, and a magnificent roster of 53,769 beneficial members. . . . This places the United Brotherhood in the front rank of labor organizations. It is now the largest and most powerful organization, numerically. . . . In the four years the wages of carpenters in 415 cities were raised from 25 to 75 cents per day. . . . Besides that we have reduced the hours of labor to eight per day in thirty-six cities. . . . This reduction in the hours of labor alone has given employment to 7,300 more carpenters, who had it not been for this movement made by our organization, would be on the streets idle and penniless. These figures speak volumes in favor of the United Brotherhood and its work."[39]

Moving in the relative fluidity of the American class structure, the carpenter and large groups of journeymen and the self-employed had shied away from the Brotherhood. Despite the increasingly heavy capital required for manufacturing machines and their rapid absolescence, many a worker had made the transition from employee to employer and back again not once but several times in their lives. When, after 1886, he crowded into the Brotherhood, he traded his chance to become a boss or self-employed for regular work and better working conditions. To the working carpenter, a shorter day's work meant — a chance to work and regulate conditions under which he worked. Joining the Brotherhood meant also protection against insecurity and other hazards born of the Industrial Revolution.

The Brotherhood also performed the functions of a "friendly society," with benefits for sickness, death and unemployment. Out of his 75 cents monthly dues, the sick carpenter was paid from $3.00 to $5.00 a week, which "made him comparable with the Odd Fellows or the Foresters"*

---

[39]*Ibid*, 189-190.

*Edward W. Bemis, "Benefit Features of American Trade Unions," *Bulletin of the Department of Labor* (Washington: Gov't Printing Office, 1899), p. 381. Reporting on the benefit features of American unions, among them the Carpenters, Mr. Bemis writes: "These sick benefits make the Carpenter comparable with the Odd Fellows, the Foresters, and kindred benevolent fraternities. But these fraternities, to pay the same sick benefits, as those mentioned, collect the same, if not larger, dues than do local unions of the Brotherhood. The Carpenters effect a saving, as compared with the fraternities mentioned, sufficent to meet all the calls upon them for strike expenditures, for death and disability benefits, and the expense of agitating for shorter hours and increased wages. The Carpenters manage all their affairs and disburse their incomes for the objects of the Brotherhood for a relatively smaller percentage of expense than the best accidental association in the world." (*Ibid*, p. 365)

He received $100.00 disability benefits after six months membership; $200.00 after a year; $300.00 after three years; $400.00 after five years, and a wife's funeral benefit of $25.00 after six months membership and $50.00 after a year's membership. In strike benefits he received $6.00 a week. The benefit features are not to be overlooked, these being one of the motives for joining the Brotherhood. Nevertheless, it was the *material aid and psychological advantages which he could gain from the next "trade movement" that were the sum and substance of his membership in the Brotherhood.*

McGuire and Gompers learned much more about "job-conscious" and "pure and simple" unionism from the workers of America than they ever taught them. It is "job-conscious" unionism which has proved by far the most successful, the main object of which is control of jobs through collective bargaining agreements. This type of unionism has survived to date, although motivations other than higher wages have recently been uncovered as reasons for joining a union.[40]

Such success as the Brotherhood of Carpenters had achieved to date can be ascribed to its ability to adjust itself to the constantly changing technical conditions, as well as to the social and industrial environment. After 1880 when the labor force was increasingly recruited from the foreign-born, the Brotherhood welcomed the immigrant carpenters and woodworkers, although it opposed uncontrolled immigration. At the close of the last century and in the first decades of our own, the Carpenters had forty-six local unions consisting of German-speaking immigrants, seven French, four Scandinavian, four Hungarian, one Polish, two Jewish and two Dutch, constituting nearly fifteen percent out of a total of 802 local unions. The Brotherhood's constitution was rendered into four languages: German, Polish, French and Yiddish. Negro carpenters were enrolled in sixteen local unions.[41]

Judged from the point of view of the American folklore of business, the Carpenters' was a dynamic organization, both in structure and in spirit. Its internal morale depended on its ability to maintain rapid rate of growth; workers were attracted to the organization and were willing to serve its ends because it was a growing concern. Local and independent groups of carpenters in Detroit, Connecticut and New Jersey joined up, as did the Knights of Labor Carpenters of Chicago.[42]

Wages had been advanced from $1.50 per day to $2.25 and in

---

[40]See Joel Seidman, Jack London, "Why Workers Join Unions," *Annals of the American Academy* (March, 1951).

[41]U.B.C.J.A. *Proceedings* (1892), p. 16.

[42]U.B.C.J.A. *Proceedings* (1896), p. 26.

the great industrial centers from $2.50 to $3.50.[43] In 1902 the Brotherhood membership in good standing totaled 126,500.[44]

In 1886 the Brotherhood first extended its jurisdiction to include workers other than house carpenters. Planing mills and carpenters running woodworking machines came under the jurisdiction of the Carpenters' Union. This change was made to recognize the increasingly great toll which woodworking mills were taking of carpenters' work, but even more was the extension of the union's jurisdiction over "woodworking machine hands and bench hands in mills."[45] These words were added to "qualifications for membership" in its new Constitution of 1890. This neccessitated the introduction of changes in its structure which modified the character of the organization, shifted the center of power, and affected those unions whose jurisdiction bordered on the Brotherhood of Carpenters.

Early in the development of the Brotherhood, the local union was of great importance. As wages and working conditions were, to a large degree, determined by conditions in the local labor market, the local unions were pretty much self-dependent. Early Brotherhood leaders encouraged local leadership to exercise autonomy. In communities where the union had been firmly established, these were encouraged to bargain, conciliate, and even arbitrate. With a narrow, simple jurisdiction the national union operated a loose type of control. In brief, simple, "grass root" government was the natural outcome.

The extension of the union's jurisdiction, seriously threatening industrial encroachments, greatly improved transportation facilities, in addition to the growth of regional and even national building operations, led to the introduction of a new type organizational unit within the United Brotherhood of Carpenters and Joiners of America. District Councils were established on the basis of the number and location of local unions, trade areas and economic conditions which would present problems requiring common solutions. Their early appearance was modest enough and designed to avoid disturbing any of the vested groups within the organization. The District council was what the name implied, a council of the representatives of the local unions of a given city or locality which was empowered to conduct that portion of local affairs which could best be handled by a body with broader jurisdiction. Not only could it administer and organize local tradesmen, but it could launch organizing campaigns outside the city.

Beginning with the 'nineties, the Brotherhood made it mandatory for the carpenters of any city with two or more local unions to form a district

---

[43]U.B.C.J.A. *Proceedings* (1892), p. 15.
[44]U.B.C.J.A. *Proceedings* (1902), p. 86.
[45]Frank Duffy, *op. cit.*

council. In 1892, McGuire reported thirty-two district councils and they were given all disciplinary power which had previously belonged to the locals. These moves amounted to a mass transfer of administrative and hence of political power from the local unit to the district council. This innovation meant, of course, that the district council became the basic administrative unit of the Brotherhood. District councils attempted to cope with the threat posed by "unfair," country building material, by binding their employers to use only union, city-made materials." But since many of the woodworking mills were operating their plants out of the cities, where they recruited non-native labor, children and women, only an organizational drive with intercity direction could effectively cope with them. A logical step of this development was the use of a salaried "field organizer."[46] A fulltime, paid "field organizer," or walking delegate, as he was called, was an expense which few locals could afford. Hence, the employment of a paid "field organizer" was made possible through the pooled resources of the district council. The original "lecturer" or volunteer, who was fired by the missionary zeal for trade unionism, was now replaced by a paid business agent.*

At first the functions of the business agent were not clearly defined. By 1890, McGuire reported that a full hundred cities had business agents. Doubtless, the number was highly exaggerated. By 1891 the business agent was recognized for the first time as an official person by the Executive Board, when it declared that the business agent could be empowered to "collect dues and etcetera." He negotiated with employers who had previously blackballed the carpenter presenting union demands. The need of a separate official devoting all his time to the union's interests, was found in the rapidly increasing importance of the union working rules. As these rules grew in number, an expert familiar with their nature and with the practice of the trade was necessary to interpret and enforce them. A knowledge of these rules was one of the principle qualifications of the business agent.

Finally, the business agent gradually came into prominence because the subcontracting system operating in the industry made the task of vigilance necessary and difficult. The small employer, lumper, and speculator subjected to intense competition, was often forced, in order to cut costs, to reduce labor standards. Greater watchfulness by the union became necessary. The business agent became the recogni-

---

[46]Frank Duffy, op. cit.

*The "invention" of the "walking delegate" and later professional organizer of the movement has played much the same kind of role as the salesman performs for the business enterprise. Not unlike the salesman, the labor organizer is probably one of the most important developments in the structure of the union relating to the growth of size. Indeed the modern labor leader is acutely aware of the problem of "selling himself," whose personality depends largely on the group around him.

zed officer to protect the union conditions prevailing in the trade.

In view of these requirements, the business agent developed into the union's chief executive officer. His duties consisted of visiting the job to dispose of any dispute that may arise, and to see that none but members of the union are employed; that the jurisdiction is not encroached upon, and that the working rules are not violated. He became in effect, a one man employment agent with a complete knowledge of all new jobs in this casual industry. The knowledge of where the best jobs are to be found, his influence with the employer as to the disposition of these jobs, the special importance which a carpenter attaches to the more important jobs, all of these gave him a tremendous influence with the rank and file of the union members. And the employer also came to realize that the good will of the business agent was a profitable asset, since the business agent represented the union in bargaining with the contractor concerning wages, hours and working conditions. He controlled the labor supply on which the completion of the contractor's project depended. He penalized the contractor for violation of union rules. And his influence extended beyond his own trade. He represented the union in its relations with other labor organizations; he was the spokesman in the central labor councils where he met the business agents of other trades. His greatest influence, of course, as far as the contract or and the workers were concerned, arose from his power to call strikes. The speed with which building operations are carried on and the rapidity with which subcontractors and speculators complete their work on a large project has made the reference of all disputes to the union meeting impractical. The need for quick action, which was demanded by the presence of so many small subcontractors, has given the business agent the right to strike. The sum of the business agent's activities clearly established him as a power on the local level in the United Brotherhood since the 1890's.

The "invention" of the specialized organizer was probably one of the most important developments in the structure of the organization relating to the growth of size. The church, of course, has always employed such professional organizers (missionaries), and it may be that an important element in the growth of Christianity was the "invention" of the missionary. The "walking delegate" or professional organizer in the labor movement and the county agent in farm organizations played much the same kind of role as the missionary of the church. The salesman performs much the same function for the business enterprise.

Improvement in the physical methods of communication had played a similar role in the expansion of the union. One has only to picture the Brotherhood of today operating without, say, telephones and conducting practically all its communication through manifestoes, pamphlets, "lecturers" or the mail to realize the extent to which the telephone, wireless had contributed to the growth of the Brotherhood, and organizations in general. The importance of mechanical aids, recordings, the duplicator, the business machine have had an impact on the structure of the organization. The stereotype of the contemporary executive or administrator as a man with five telephones on his desk may be a little overdrawn, but it at least attracts the attention to the importance of that instrument. Take a look at the Carpenters Union today: it operates a beneficiary pension system for its members. Every one of its 823,574 (1954) members has a card on file at headquarters in Indianapolis upon which his dues and assessments are registered quarterly. In 1953 the Brotherhood sent out 24,430 pension checks to its members monthly, and annually the union pays almost $3,000,000 in death benefits, disability claims to the survivors of its members. To carry out its operations, the union uses I.B.M. machines, and there are 110 people employed in the office. Only six percent of the Carpenters union current income goes for the administration of the national office.[47]

The emergence, in the 1890's, of young local leaders created a more efficient and a stronger trade union. Paid and full time business agents worked under a staff in the district council office. Efficient administrative techniques, able to meet and serve the needs of its members were being applied and molded as the union sought to expand farther in its "environment." A return to "purity" and simplicity of organization in days more violent and dynamic would end the growth of the Brotherhood.

In the summer of 1904 when the Brotherhood's membership reached 160,000, its national office had neither a roll of membership, nor vital statistics of any of its members. The General President of the union had been a mere figurehead. He was not a paid official. A law making the General President full-time and salaried, seating him on the Executive Board as a voting chairman was defeated in 1893. The General Executive Board continued to be elected at large by the convention, and its members were part time and unpaid. Although now and then a "lecturer" was appointed by McGuire, no administrative nexus between the national office and the local bodies was created. No institution or person, other than McGuire existed to coordinate the activities of the various district councils. He and the full time business agents were the sole paid officials of the union.

McGuire, the philosopher-organizer, reformer and radical, who could have walked lightly beside Tom Paine, and creator of the Brotherhood,

---

[47]U. B. C. J. A., *Reports of General Officers and General Executive Board* (1954), pp. 45 seq.

became the "conservative." He favored purity and simplicity in organization, as against the "progressive" elements, the new professional organizers who were more interested in expansion and to meet the needs
of those who composed the union. Indeed, their role became the more
important, as the Brotherhood began to face an increasingly unfavorable
environment, largely due to economic and technological developments.

The revolution in building techniques certainly inflicted hardships
on the United Brotherhood, but it also heightened the already deflated
skills of the specialist carpenter. For example, the modern skyscraper
had ten, fifteen even twenty stories of standardized rooms. Each room
had the same floor, door, window, and wall measurements. It became
an even simpler task for the contractor to hire a carpenter skilled in
only one phase of his task. Consequently, a whole spate of specialist
carpenters' unions cropped up. By 1904 the formation of unions among
locomotive woodworkers, millwrights, shinglers, dock, wharf, and bridge
builders, ceiling woodworkers and carpenters' helpers were reported.
Technological improvements created new crafts such as the sheet metal
workers, plumbers, and electricians, many of whom worked on material
which replaced wood and all of whom, while jurisdictional lines were
fluid, usurped wood work related to their job. With the passage of time,
more and more of the carpenter work disappeared into planing mills.
And to add further to the carpenter's woes, a new competing union,
the Machine Woodworkers International Union stepped into the picture
to claim jurisdiction over these machine carpenters.[48]

The Constitution of 1910 increased the jurisdiction to "cabinet
makers and machine men" in all furniture factories, woodworkers in
furniture factories, the erection of wood, metal and other trim, where
carpenters' tools were used; the building and erecting of all scaffolding,
where carpenters' tools were used, the placing of machinery in factories,
mills, elevators, wharf building. The erection of brackets, plaster board
and arches for floors, where "wood and carpenter tools are used" was
claimed by the Brotherhood; setting up wood mantles, etc.[49]

Each problem raised by the revolution in building techniques was
nation-wide in scope. The new construction companies were nation-wide
in scope thus creating the need for the establishment of a much greater
degree of uniformity in wages and working conditions over the bargaining area. Workmen from other occupations entering the trade led the
Brotherhood to a more formalized apprenticeship system. The new
trades which subsisted on work traditionally belonging to the carpenters
had a broader, if not national, jurisdiction. The invasion by the Machine

---

48*U.B.C.J.A., Proceedings* (1898), pp. 8-10.
49*U.B.C.J.A., Proceedings* (1910), pp. 242-250.

Woodworkers International Union of the Brotherhood's jurisdiction had developed into a contest, from which only the strong could emerge the victor. National problems, and a greatly expanded jurisdiction poaching on the Brotherhood's jurisdiction, an increasingly unfavorable environment demanded solutions on a national scale. The United Brotherhood, more than ever, had to devise policies on a national level which could be put into effect simultaneously in every district council. This, in turn, called for a union with a strong, centralized administration and centrally directed agents, in all localities ready to move at a moment's notice. Consequently, not the least important effect of the revolution in building techniques was to give further economic and institutional substance to the administrative reforms for which the union and the new professionals had been clamoring.

As was stated, the Brotherhood had been made up of a congeries of local unions with the international exercising a very loose authority over its subordinate branches. Such system was the natural outcome of the local nature of the industry in which the union operated, and it made for powerful local leaders who were quasi-independent. However with the development of large area operations, fundamental changes in the union and greater concentration of power in the hands of the international, were being effectuated.

These reforms, long postponed, occurred at a correspondingly accelerated pace. These began with General President William D. Huber in 1910 and continued under James Kirby and William Levi Hutcheson's administrations. Similar developments towards greater concentration were manifest in other key unions.[50]

The movement toward eliminating the barriers to consolidation of the various local unions began in 1910, when the Brotherhood's twelfth General President, William D. Huber merged the locals into a national organization. The next decade witnessed a reorganization of the structure of the Brotherhood. It began with delegating to the General President a greater concentration of power; whereas formerly, he was a mere figurehead without prescribed powers and no regular salary. The Executive Board Members who were elected at large were made full-time and salaried. The latter, hitherto autonomous and free, were made responsible to the General President and through them the General President exercised some control over the locals.[51] The consequences of a more concentrated command in the hands of a chief officer to act swiftly and decisively in times of crisis has been not only increased numerical strength, but an even greater rise in economic power. With a membership,

---

[50]See Phillip Taft, *op. cit.*, pp. 213, 214.
[51]*U.B.C.J.A. Proceedings*, (1916), 42.

in 1912, of 195,499[52] when consolidation was initiated, the Brotherhood grew to 350,391 in 1924.[53]

Under the leadership of William L. Hutcheson, its late General President, the Brotherhood achieved its eminent position. In the year 1950, two years before his retirement, the Carpenters' membership of 710,034 was distributed in 2830 local unions[54]; it had an annual income of $8,824,406.50.[55] Its treasury in cash and bonds for the year 1949 was $7,212,877.36. On the whole, the Brotherhood of Carpenters gained most of its members in occupations recognized as belonging in their traditional jurisdiction, or in areas tenanted by smaller and weaker woodworking unions.[56] The strategic position of the Carpenters has given them a powerful weapon in any jurisdictional controversy with other unions, but so far the weapon has been used against relatively weak opponents, who now enjoy the protection of much greater power and influence than they could themselves mobilize.

Under Maurice A. Hutcheson's leadership since 1952, the number of local unions has grown by 367.[57] The next year or two is likely to witness some developments in the United Brotherhood: an aggressive reaching-out for new members, both in the traditional jurisdictions and on the periphery of the union's jurisdiction. Doubtless, this plan will fill vacuums, organizationally speaking. The absence of organization in some sections of the economy makes the new General President's program feasible. Certainly, it presents an opportunity to an aggressive leadership with adequate finances. At the same time, should large numbers of workers in the same trade be enrolled, especially if the newly-organized have special needs or problems, the relation of the local to the international will inevitably arise. Equilibrium will be maintained only if the workers are allowed to form an organization, exercising a large amount of autonomy in trade matters, but ultimately subordinate to the authority of the President and the Executive Board of the Brotherhood.

---

[52]The Carpenter, Vol .XXXII: 11 (Nov., 1912), pp. 55-66.

[53]U.B.C.J.A., *Proceedings* (1924), p. 30.

[54]U.B.C.J.A. *Proceedings* (1950) p. 142.

[55]U.B.C.J.A., *Proceedings* (1949) p. 113.

[56]"There is a general presumption that improved techniques of organization will have a favorable impact on the rate of betterment, simply because betterment always comes about through organization of some kind, even if it is through the mental and physical bodily organization of a single individual. . . . On the other hand the improved ability to organize has resulted in some cases in the substitution of conflict for coercion, where a coerced group has been able to organize and apply counter-coercion to the coercer. Thus the labor movement has arisen largely in response to the feeling which the individual, unorganized worker has—in the absence of an active labor market — of being coerced by his employer. Its object up to a point has been to neutralize the coercive power of the employer by developing coercive power of its own. (Kenneth E. Boulding, *The Organizational Revolution,* p. 218).

[57]Report of General Officers (1954), p. 41.

The Carpenters have been very tenacious in holding on to their jurisdictional claims, as is shown in chapter XXI. While unwilling to surrender any of the union's jurisdiction, the new administration has entered into an agreement with the Machinists as a preliminary to the establishment of a permanent settlement.[58] The new administration has also introduced a new type of organizational unit within the United Brotherhood. In 1953, its General President Maurice A. Hutcheson, and the General Executive Board called a conference of the First District of the United Brotherhood in Syracuse, New York, which was subsequently extended to the seven districts at large. Each conference concerned itself with the problems of the industry and crafts in the District, but representatives of local unions participated in all districts concerned with any fraction of its members. Each District is an independent unit, recommending to locals having members in the district the policies to pursue. It is likely that the new administration will enlarge the role of the regional conference.

One of the most important questions in union management is the degree of freedom enjoyed by the members. The power exercised over the union by the top officer is also significant. An issue which has aroused considerable attention is the discipline procedure and penalties of the Brotherhood which some earnest students of labor fear, constitutes a "threat to union democracy."[59] Others, still, would determine the level and intensity of democracy of the union by measuring the frequency of opposition in elections to the chief officers. All these issues are of sufficient import, but cannot be treated here in detail. But unless the difference between a labor union and other kinds of social organizations is recognized, the issues raised are likely to be misinterpreted.

Unlike civil society, a union visualizes itself much as a quasi-independent state; it is an organization built around the two poles of service to its members and struggle against the "outside world." The world outside in this case consists of the employer, but also of rival unions and at times the national state itself. A union, as we have seen, is something like a lodge, and something like a church. Yet, it is a single purpose organization. The protection of "jobs" or economic interests of its members is the principal objective of the union. Moreover, in carrying out its tasks, a union must be prepared to take defensive or offensive economic action, involving discipline and sacrifice by its members, in contrast to society at large where there are conflicting interests that must be protected. This does not mean that within the union there are not conflicts, but the

---

[58] U.B.C.J.A. Reports of General Officers, (Dec. 31, 1953), pp. 28-35.

[59] U.B.C.J.A., Proceedings, 1912, 1913, 1914, 1920, 1924, 1928, 1936, 1944, 1946, 1951).

conflicts are subordinate to the chief goal. Because a union visualizes itself as a quasi-independent state, it exercises much more power over its members than a corporation does over its stockholders. Disciplinary penalties for infraction of prescribed rules and agreements are imposed by all unions. To prevent severity and abuse of discretion by their local unions, the national union has established tribunals which review the verdicts of the subordinate units of the organization. The international president who frequently reviews appeals is usually authorized to try a member or to intervene in the affairs of the local. Conditions for both of these are clearly laid down in the constitution of virtually all unions.

Equally noteworthy is the difference between the union president and the business manager. Management's motivation is one of responsibility to the business as such — that is, to keep the organization alive and growing — rather than to the shareholders as a collectivity. There may be some fear of displeasing the general business community; but even this is mild compared with the fierce displeasure which constantly threatens the ineffective union leader.

How do the issues raised above relate to the government of the United Brotherhood of Carpenters and Joiners of America? In its seventy-four-year old history, the Brotherhood elected fifteen general presidents. Of these, four held tenure in office one year each; eight two years each; one fourteen years. The Fourteenth General President, William L. Hutcheson served continuously from 1915 to 1952. In the eight elections for the presidency, rival candidates presented themselves two times, in 1910 and 1914. William L. Hutcheson who served for thirty-six years was opposed only twice. He was succeeded by his son, Maurice A., upon resigning his post in 1952. Opposition did not appear in the conventions of 1946, 1950 and 1954 and all general officers were unanimously elected.

How explain the lack of opposition to Hutcheson? How do we account for the slow rate of change in top union offices in the Brotherhood? Professor Phillip Taft who has examined the election experiences of thirty-four unions between 1900 and 1948, involving the election of 2307 general officers, reveals that the decrease in the number of contests is quite typical for all labor organizations. "The absence of opposition in the national elections of unions is common and tends to develop in almost all well established organizations of labor, irrespective of origin, philosophy, type of control or ideology. Trade union leaders, once they have reached the top or near the top, are seldom removed from office, either by the members, if they are directly elected, or by their superiors if they are appointed."[60] The slow rate of change in top union officers is

---

[60]Phillip Taft, *op. cit.*, p. 41; see table op. p. 41.

also evident outside the United States. Opposition to chief union officers tends to be the rule only in the early formative stages of the union. With the passage of time, followed by the growth of giant corporations, as has been demonstrated elsewhere in this work, contests for office decline. As the union grows and becomes well established, the prestige of the chief officer rises with the organization. It is therefore difficult for members or even district presidents to develop the national prestige necessary to challenge the leaders of the union. The latter who are usually known nationally are likely to have followers throughout the organization, while the reputation of a challenger is likely to be more restricted. The prohibition contained in most union constitutions against issuing circulars without the approval of the chief officer, or against undermining the union or defaming officers, would hinder the formation of formal and organized opposition to chief officers. These are, however, not the principal reasons for the lack of opposition. Even in unions where there are no sanctions against such practices, opposition to those already in office tends to decline. We have reference to Walter Reuther of the United Automobile Workers Union, "where opposition has died off," even though a prohibition against the issuing of circulars is non-existent.[61]

The fact is that elected leaders of the internationals have since about the second decade of our century shown vigorous ability to remain in office unopposed. It is part of the movement of our "organizational revolution." Sidney Hillman, late President of the Amalgamated Clothing Workers of America, was unopposed in office for over twenty-five years. William Mahon, President of the Amalgamated Streetcar and Railway Workers, led Rail Union for over forty years. In the Socialist Brewery Workers Union, the head was never challenged. The Presidential office was never contested in the International Ladies Garment Workers Union. Neither was David Dubinsky since the 1930's. John L. Lewis has been the perpetual leader of the Miners' Union for over thirty years. The Machinists' Union is the only one on record in which a general officer was recalled by a referendum vote.

The attempts to determine the level or intensity of democracy by measuring the frequency or lack of opposition in the elections to the chief officers is unsatisfactory, insofar as the labor movement is concerned. The prestige, performance, acquaintance with membership, and ability of the head of the union may be such that a challenge is not likely to succeed. To an economic organization, regarded as an instrument for the rise of the "lower" groups, democracy unambiguously means control of a responsible leader by the whole rank and file. That requires a cohesive

---

[61]*Ibid*, p. 37; Wright Mills, *New Men of Power* (Harcourt, Brace and Co., 1948), pp. 62-65.

organization that forces the leader to remain alert to the wants of the members; that keeps him responsible. In almost all cases of long tenure, the labor leader in power has been sanctified by some battle through which he successfully led the union. He led a large strike, or organized vast numbers of new workers. In most labor organizations, an analogous process operates.

There is little doubt of the identity of mental processes between William L. Hutcheson and the Carpenters' thinking; it came about as a result of Hutcheson's doing what the members were interested in and what is to their interest. His major accomplishments for the Brotherhood and particularly, his successful battles with the State "sanctified" him. As Professor Taft points out: "Who is there in the Coal Miners Union with the prestige and ability of John L. Lewis; or in the Auto Workers Union to compete with Reuther; or with a Hutcheson in the Carpenters Union, a Dubinsky in the Ladies Garment Workers Union, or a Petrillo among the Musicians? Even in an organization like the C.I.O. Textile Workers Union, the leader of the opposition had to dissociate himself from the charge that he was seeking the post of the President, Emil Rieve."[62]

As was noted, in addition to the exercise of rights within the union, members are subject to intra-union discipline which is often essential for effective dealing with thoroughly autocratic big business institutions. The managers of corporations are not democratically elected by the stockholders to represent their interests. The disciplinary procedure in labor organizations are designed to allow the union to function efficiently in order to insure unity of action. Trial and penalties have been established to compel obedience or to impose punishment of members, if they are found guilty of violating their obligations. Appeals and tribunals are set up in all unions to review the decisions of the locals or their trial committees. In all organizations of labor, more than one tribunal for appeals exists so that a member dissatisfied with the decision of the first appellate body can carry his case to the next one.

The Brotherhood Constitution describes in detail the procedure to be followed in bringing a member to trial. It requires that charges against union members must be made in writing, and "must specify the offense or offenses under the Section of the Constitution and Laws of the United Brotherhood so violated, and be signed by the member or members making such charges." The charges must be read at the local meeting and laid over until the next meeting. In the meantime, the accused must be notified of the charges by registered mail. A trial committee of five is selected out of eleven nominees, the accuser and the

---

[62]Phillip Taft, *op. cit.*, p. 240.

accused each having the right to three challenges. The trial committee of five hears the testimony and examines whatever documents
are submitted. It finally submits its decision to the local membership
which, by a two-thirds vote, can decide the penalty.

A trial at the local level is only the first step in the Carpenters
Brotherhood judicial system. A member who has a grievance or had an
injustice done in any way, or any local union having a grievance
may appeal to the General President for redress, subject to further appeal
to the General Executive Board, and a final appeal to the General
Convention, except violations of trade rules. In the six year period
ending in 1946, the General President considered 431 appeals, 37 of
which were subsequently carried to the General Executive Board. Six
appeals were finally taken to the convention. The appeals to the convention involved: the order that a local affiliate with the district council;
two denials or disability claims; and three fines.[63]

In the four years between the 1946 and 1950 conventions, William
L. Hutcheson handled 264 appeals, 17 of which later appealed to the
General Executive Board, and 5 were appealed to the convention. The
annual average of appeals in the six-year period, 1940-1946, was 71,
and for the subsequent four-year period, 66. In the four-year period
ending October 1954, the Brotherhood averaged 150 appeals each year.[64]

The number of appeals is sufficiently large and stable to indicate
that members and officers of subordinate bodies regard the appeals
tribunal as fair and equitable, and that it is one in which differences
and disputes between locals and district councils and members can be
equitably reviewed. In passing, it should be mentioned, that the absence
of many appeals to the General Executive Board is not important because the General President, has gone over the cases, examined the trial
minutes and the statements of both parties, the plaintiff and the appellant.

In one consecutive eleven-month period in 1952, forty-six appeals
were submitted to the General President of the Carpenters Union.* The
following is a typical list of the number of issues involved:

Violation of Trade Rules. — 8
Working on Saturdays afternoon, overtime or holidays
without permission 8
Failure to procure working permit. — 6
Failure to perform duties as business agent. — 5
Improper assignment of work. — 3
Challenged election. — 3

---

[63] U.B.C.J.A., *Proceedings* (1946), pp. 231-232.
[64] U.B.C.J.A., Reports of General Executive Board (1954), p. 11.
*Cited in Philip Taft, *The Structure and Government of Labor Unions,* (Harvard
Univ. Press, 1954), pp. 143, 144.

Fighting on job. — 1
Labor contracting. — 1
Piece work. — 1
Working with non-union craftsmen. — 1
Working below scale. — 4
Interfering with business agent. — 1
Making false charges. — 1
Crossing a picket line. — 1
Not paying on company time. — 1

One appeal was withdrawn before the decision was rendered by the General President: three of the appeals were by members who objected to the exoneration of officers or members upon charges brought by the appellant; three cases involved the elections, and the remaining thirty-nine cases concerned fines imposed by locals and district councils. The forty-five cases came from thirty separate locals and district councils, and only one district council had as many as three appeals. Three were out of one situation. In other words, while technically there were three appeals to the General President, all the appeals arose in one context and involved a single issue. It was therefore obvious that appeals against a penalty or the conduct of an officer are made from many separate quarters and all segments of the Carpenters union *are aware of their rights and have faith in the integrity of the appellate tribunal.* Of the thirty-nine cases in which fines were imposed, eleven, or 28.2 percent, were reversed and the verdict in seven, or 15.4 percent of the cases was upheld, but the penalty reduced.

A cursory examination of the type and number of appeals that are annually submitted to the General President of the Brotherhood and the General Executive Board, demonstrates the effectiveness with which appeals and grievance procedure protects the rights and interests of its members. Our own review of the practices, procedures and the appellate tribunals in the Brotherhood of Carpenters, are confirmed by the conclusions reached by Professor Taft: "The large ratio of reversals of penalties, their modification when they appear excessive, the number of appeals submitted, the character of the cases and wide dispersion of locals and district councils from which they arise, the insistence upon due process, and number of charges brought against local officers all demonstrate the fairness and the honesty of the appellate procedure of the Carpenters Union. . . . The issue is not how one would rule if deciding a specific case, but whether the procedure is fair and adequate; whether evidence is carefully reviewed; and *whether the rights of defendants are amply protected* (emphasis ours). On all these points, it is our opinion that the Carpenters union does an exemplary job. . . . . It would appear that the union not only does not require the aid of well-intentioned people or governmental agencies, but is an example of an autonomous group well able to handle difficult problems fairly and equitably."[65]

Is it conceivable that the members of the Brotherhood would present hundreds of appeals annually if they believed that such a step was vain and useless? There is no proof whatsoever that members hesitate to protest the conduct of their officers. How can one explain the 153 appeals taken against the decisions of William L. Hutcheson to the General Executive Board and to the conventions? In 1924 the Committee on Appeals and Grievances considered 12 appeals taken against Hutcheson, two against the General Treasurer and the General Executive Board.[66] Four years later, nine appeals were taken against the General President and the General Executive Committee;[67] in 1946 six appeals were taken against the General President;[68] in 1950 seventeen appeals were taken against the chief officer and the General Executive Committee; five of the seventeen were appealed to the General Convention.[69]

While the primary function of an appeal is to redress a grievance or dissatisfaction with a local union's or district council's decision, it fulfills another closely allied function, almost as important, that of providing a ready channel of communication upward. The right to communicate with the Carpenters' General President is inextricably bound up with status. The right of the carpenter to talk back, to seek redress from the chief officer, is a partial criterion of the member's equality with him. As the Brotherhood continues to grow in size, the distance between the individual member and the top may widen and communication may become a problem for each. Nevertheless, the prescribed elections in the locals, the numerous complaints of various kinds against officers, appeals to the General President are not only a kind of listening post for the wants and needs of the members, but manifestations of democracy at the "grass roots" level, where it is of most importance. Constant communication and intercommunication, as well as national programming will doubtless heighten the interest of the membership.

65*Ibid*, p. 149.
66U.B.C.J.A., *Proceedings* (1924), p. 354.
67U.B.C.J.A., *Proceedings* (1928), p. 231.
68U.B.C.J.A., *Proceedings* (1946), p. 238.
69U.B.C.J.A., *Proceedings* (1950), pp. 83, 230.

CHAPTER | XX

LEADERSHIP IN THE BROTHERHOOD

". . . The man who is possessed of authority, private or public, is always likely to be more conscious of the checks and reins on his decisions than of his power to reach them. . . ."

Twelve men, inclusive of the General President, largely run the Brotherhood's affairs of 823,574 carpenters in the United States and possessions, and Canada. These twelve men constitute the core of the United Brotherhood of Carpenters and Joiners of America. It is they who decide questions of policy, organize, plan, collect funds, focus attention on the "collective" aspects of collective bargaining, turn "fight" situations into "problem solving" situations, and act in the role of "bonnie fechter" to the constituency. Clearly, the power and influence of this inner core is great.

Of course, there is another side to the picture. The very nature of the leadership is also a product of the needs of the people in the Brotherhood itself. The leaders of the Brotherhood are as much creatures of the trade, as they are of their roles. The role of the labor leader is to get things for the workers. So the Brotherhood's members of the General Executive Board must in the long run not only reflect the Carpenters' needs but also make gains if they are to persist as leaders.

Some observers have said men become union leaders and aggressive because they are not accepted in American society. Some caricatures depict the union leaders as "frustrated" men, who gravitate naturally and quickly to the trade union movement as an easy outlet for their frustrations.

First of all, we have observed no personality type whatsoever among the leaders of the Brotherhood. It is true that all the members of the General Executive Board have leadership qualities in common. They are mostly middle or long service, in their late fifties to the mid-sixties, self-assured, outgoing people who like to deal with others and who can talk convincingly and with knowledge about union affairs, national and international as well. The majority are "joiners" of civic, fraternal and communal organizations.

Secondly, their motives for becoming leaders are also highly varied, though here we have a more clearly defined pattern: all are motivated by a basic desire to advance the cause and welfare of the working man. This humanitarian motive is a most powerful and dominant one; it is important and must not be overlooked. Of course, it may be mixed with other motives. Some seek self-expression, the chance to talk, to lead, to decide, to influence and to dominate. Some seek to right a wrong they or their father experienced as a worker. Others became union leaders because their parents were.

There is a thrill in competition and in strategy — to guide and lead a large army of 823,574 divided into seven districts. Some simply enjoy the politics of union leadership as a sheer engrossing game like a boxing match, a ball game, or a horse race. We are convinced that this "game mindedness" is a significant motive for some leaders. None seeks to vent a grudge against management, which to the psychologists may be one manifestation of frustration. These motives we have listed are not isolated, of course. They will be found in varying combinations among the different leaders. To understand them, let us take a brief look at the men who have led the Brotherhood in recent years.

Take First Vice-President *John R. Stevenson*. Stevenson is of medium height. He makes a good appearance, is an old-timer, a skilled carpenter and a Scot from Glasgow — and a superb raconteur. He has been a trade union member all his life. Before coming to America, after the San Francisco earthquake, he was a member of the Amalgamated Society of Carpenters and Joiners whose share of influence in the early American labor movement was not insignificant. America required a direct transfer of such British experience as Stevenson brought with him to America. Stevenson rose from the ranks, starting first with his chest of tools in the Chicago Carpenters Local Union 80, in which he served as President. For a decade, he served as business agent for the strategic Chicago District Council, and for three years as its president.

In the roaring 'twenties he challenged the anti-union demagogues and the dangerous post-prohibition "racketeers", who made inroads into Chicago's labor movement. While an orator, he is also a logician. Although many of his large assembly in the district council were at times inert and susceptible to buncombe, he fired off speeches which focused upon the issues of vital concern to labor. His candidness, sincerity and devotion gained the workers' allegiance to the union. Stevenson is a professional unionist in that he knows the history and the objectives of the American union movement and thoroughly believes that it is part of our social and industrial life. In this, he has been somewhat influenced by the social philosophy of the British trade unionists. He is strongly motivated by a desire to help his fellow craftsmen and to bring about a better social and industrial order. He finds that union leadership is a way of fulfilling this motivation. Early in 1941, he was appointed to the office of Second General Vice-President. Five years later, he was elected to the post of First General Vice-President. Stevenson has several talents and outside interests such as croquet and golf. He is an active Mason.

O. William Blaier, Second General Vice-President. He is one of the most astute, intelligent, urbane leaders in the Brotherhood of Carpenters. He is smooth-spoken, affable and yet aggressive. Doubtless, his behavior and personality played determining parts in his becoming the organization's trouble-shooter since 1948, when he was first elected to the General Executive Board. For five years, from February, 1942 to 1947, he was the "governor," or the eye for the organization in the building trades on the Wage Adjustment Board (WAB) in Washington. The son of a Delaware worker, Blaier moved to Philadelphia to enter Central High School, with a fixed ambition of becoming an architect. Economic conditions at home led him to the pursuit of woodworking instead.

At twenty, he joined Local 359, of which he was financial secretary for seventeen years. At the height of the depression he was appointed business agent for the Philadelphia District Council, marshalling thousands of unorganized carpenters. He was not yet forty when the Brotherhood's General President assigned him to the formidable task of organizing the lumberyards and the highly volatile residential housework carpenters in Greater Philadelphia. Earlier in the war, Blaier operated at Fort Dix from a shanty made of pine, where he won strong union allegiance of hundreds of skilled carpenters who built the barracks for the government. Blaier has many strong ideas and convictions about economic and political matters such as the Taft-Hartley Act, state laws curbing the union-shop, "prevailing" pay scales on public works and the tariff issue and is glad to expound them at length. Likewise, he battles consistently against "cheap foreign importations which tear down union millmen's wages." He always seems to use good judgment. His reasoning is clear and his self-assurance does not waver. Among other motives, we think he is one who thoroughly enjoys the game of union politics, about which he is well-informed. He has shown a sharp insight into issues, a quick perception to weigh evidence, to criticize, to form conclusions. He is willing to sacrifice much of his time and convenience to advance the cause of the organization in which he so evidently believes.

Albert E. Fischer, General Secretary, is highly personable and in his fifties. Before coming to the Brotherhood's national office in the mid-forties, Fischer had been Secretary of the Carpenters District Council of Cincinnati. He has been an active trade-unionist all his life. A successor to Frank Duffy since August 23, 1948, Fischer has served in the role of optic nerve between the receptors and the executive. Through him the Brotherhood has been able to narrow the "social distance" which separates the members of the General Executive from the "humble receptors" at the end of the line. He registers the discontents of the members for the executive, otherwise the executive would not receive a realistic picture of conditions, and especially, it would not know whether or not its actions are taking effect. Fischer has a bundle of roles tied up together with communications. He is a dispenser of vital information as well as its recipient.

Frank Chapman rose to the position of treasurer in the fall of '54, after an 18-year-long organizing record in the northwest lumber industry. His career with the U.B. began during the turbulent 'thirties, when dualism swept the labor movement and spread to the lumber and sawmill industry. Cast in the role of a General Representative of the Brotherhood and later as 4-State Co-ordinator, his persuasive logic helped to convince thousands of unorganized workers that the U.B. was more ideally equipped structurally to advance their economic interests. He went to work at an early age in a sawmill at Snoqualmie, Washington. Most likely it was his dissatisfaction with advancement and recognition that led him toward union leadership. Prior to his elevation to treasurer, he was assigned by General President M. A. Hutcheson to the directorship of the U.B.'s newly-created Department of Organization, which was part of the streamlining process developed through the regional conference.

Charles Johnson, Jr., member of the General Executive Board. He is a strong personality, a dynamic, crowd-exciting speaker and possessor of a quick, retentive mind. He bears within him the stuff and fibre of which leadership is made. Johnson, Jr. was born in New York. A native son of a Swedish immigrant, he was early exposed to the industrial, social tensions of the big metropolis — and to economic insecurity. For over three decades, he has been President of the Dock and Pier Carpenters Local 1456, of which Johnson, Sr. was both organizer and treasurer from 1898 to 1946. He is a voracious reader of serious tracts on history, economics, logic and prudence — such words are in his vocabulary. He is a quick fighter for minority rights. Politics fascinates him, but he finds leadership in the union a natural outlet for his tendencies in this sphere. The forces moving him seem to be a desire for self-expression, to help his fellow workers and to bring about a better industrial order. Johnson is proud of the role he and Charles Hanson (president of the N. Y. Carpenters District Council) played in 1953, when they obtained an all-time high increase of 32 cents an hour for the New York car-

penters, paving the way for a similar increase for some 200,000 other
construction workers. He himself gives one other motive for his own union participation: "My father was a union man, so I have been one
too, all my life." Other labor leaders who have known him many years
say about him: "Johnson is progressive. He always comes forward with
highly constructive ideas." He follows the Gompers line politically, believing that organized labor should keep one foot inside the door of both
political parties. He has strong opinions and is aggressive. His life was
considerably influenced by his father, who was a Social Democrat.

Harry Schwarzer rose from the Presidency of Local Union 1108
in 1914 to the General Executive Board of the Brotherhood in April,
1929. He is a quiet, but firm man and undoubtedly one of the most
conscientious, hard workers in the Brotherhood. Like the others, he
started at the bottom, having joined the Carpenters Local 1108 at the
age of seventeen. For a while he drifted and, after an absence of two
years, spent in the U. S. Army, he returned to the occupation of carpentry in 1911. Schwarzer is smooth-talking, fluent, college educated,
with a law degree from Cleveland Law School. In 1911 he was elected
delegate to the Carpenters District Council of Cleveland. Ten years later,
he became its secretary. Schwarzer has but one outlet for his obvious
leadership ability — to serve and advance the welfare of the Carpenters. With the enthusiasm characteristic of a dedicated man, he informs
you that the carpenter receives twenty-five dollars a day in wages for
forty hours a week. Schwarzer is a Democrat and he feels strongly
about politics. He points out that William L. Hutcheson never interfered with his political allegiance.

Henry W. Chandler is an affable, highly intelligent, well-read and
long-service skilled carpenter. A tall and handsome Georgian, he has
been a professional unionist for thirty-three years. He is a good
speaker and takes a forthright stand on inter-racial relations. It is
likely that dissatisfaction with advancement in the South and a lack of
recognition of trade unionism led him toward the union and leadership. For seventeen years he led Carpenters Local 225 in Atlanta,
Georgia. He has had some college education in the technical schools of
Chicago. For eleven years he inspired the loyalty of the Georgia Federation of Labor, of which he was Secretary, and for seven years administered the affairs of the Brotherhood's Georgia District Council. He
resents bitterly the "right to work" law. But he is strongly motivated by a
desire to eliminate all blocks that impede advancement of the workers
in the industrializing South. The Brotherhood gives him protection and
a place in the sun.

Raleigh Rajoppi has about 20 years of service in the Brotherhood.
He is a union man first, through and through. Undoubtedly trade un-

ion enthusiasm has entered into Rajoppi: he is articulate, highly intelligent and gives a polished appearance. Before coming to the Brotherhood, Rajoppi had political ambitions, but his spirit of independence made his adjustment difficult. His motivation is surely one of self-expression, but one also of bringing about a better social and industrial order. He has the Second District's allegiance, and like the others, finds leadership in the Brotherhood a natural outlet for these tendencies. A deft negotiator, his bargaining skill has served the Brotherhood in good stead. Union leadership was a natural step for him.

R. E. Roberts, a vigorous and stalwart representative of the U.B. He is a skilled carpenter and his interest in the union dates back to 1910. He is deliberate and popular. At the age of twenty he joined Local 198, in Dallas, Texas. He has been a very active unionist for years, organizing the Southlands. He is well-respected as a union man and is an able, adroit negotiator. Both management and labor have praised his "human relations" techniques. Roberts also wants an outlet connected with his life work and in that community where he spends half of his waking hours. Under the circumstances, that he should seek this outlet in the Brotherhood leadership is the most natural thing in the world. A southwesterner, Roberts has remained a "rugged individualist."

J. F. Cambiano, a seasoned, battle-tested labor leader, with a flair for the dramatic. He has a strong personality and natural leadership abilities. He is strongly motivated by a desire to help his fellow workers. He has many strong ideas and convictions about economic and political matters. In the crucial 'twenties he helped chart the Brotherhood's strategy when employers sought to relegate labor to the pre-war system. The methods he employed in attacking the "American Plan," which almost wholly suppressed the Brotherhood by coercion on the West Coast, have furnished convincing evidence of his aggressive leadership qualities. He moves cautiously to avoid defeat. For two decades, he has been President of the State Carpenters Council of California, with a membership of 100,000 the largest in the country. He is particularly proud of inaugurating the area-wide agreement system, by which all building tradesmen in this vast sprawling jurisdiction receive a uniform scale of wages. Cambiano prefers the independent lot of a trade-union leader. His motivation is surely one of self-expression, but also one of bringing about economic reform.

Andrew V. Cooper is an affable, mild-mannered, highly intelligent, well-read and long-service sawmill worker. He has been actively identified with the Canadian labor movement from its early days. For years he has faithfully represented the sawmill workers and has been increasingly successful in organizing many sections of the huge area of the

Dominion of Canada. According to Claude Jodoin, President of the Canadian Trades and Labor Congress, "Andy" Cooper is a seasoned labor organizer, an adroit politician and a highly potent force in the Canadian labor movement. A hard worker, it is not surprising that he has inspired loyalty from among thousands of Canadian carpenters. For years the communists fought him until they capitulated in 1949. He is an orthodox trade unionist, convinced, and sincere. He resents the checks on advancements, which he and Canadian labor face everywhere. He is a calculating fighter and a professional unionist with an abundance of ideas on how to advance the cause and welfare of Canadian labor. The forces moving him seem to be a desire for self-expression and service.

We have seen eleven key leaders of the United Brotherhood of Carpenters and Joiners of America, people of both political parties. As a group, they by no means conform to the people in the caricatures. Nor are they frustrated. Each one of them has several talents and even outside interests. Of course, personal ambition and craving for powr strongly motivate a few, but none tends to distort the definition of "welfare of the carpenter." Their basic desire to advance the cause and welfare of the Carpenters is the significant force that helps explain why these men wanted to become union leaders.

All of the eleven we have discussed are equally active in union participation. None could afford to lapse into inactivity. Their activities are under constant scrutiny by their invisible rooters, whose mighty presence is there nevertheless. There is always a desperate necessity to win something. The union leaders of the Brotherhood are acutely sensitive to their constituency. There is constant interaction as well as inter-communication between the leaders and the led; direct communication between the lower and upper grades. Indeed, our spot-observation of the attitudes, conduct, working habits, motivations of the leaders, and on the other hand, of attitudes — to leaders by the rank-and-file carpenter shows a high association between the two.

CHAPTER | XXI

PROTECTING THE "JOB"

". . . It is the protection of the "job" more than any sense of incomes which is the driving power behind the organization (union)...."[1]

What "living space," *Lebensraum,* is to a state, the *job* is to a union. In truth, the two hundred national and international unions in the United States can be thought of as quasi-independent states, all of them surrounded by Alsace-Lorraines. The story of jurisdictional strife is an oft-lamented one; nevertheless it is highly understandable when we see the union as an organization of jobs, — or, one should say, of men in their capacity as the occupiers of specific jobs. Only a certain sense of "class" unity, sometimes like a "Holy Alliance," keeps the jurisdictional struggle in check. Whether the fusion or integration of the two federations as presently contemplated will solve the real and bitter jurisdictional struggles between the affiliates seems at this time problematical. If jurisdictional troubles have been less prominent in the C.I.O., it is largely because the separate unions have been carving "empires" for themselves of the virgin territory of the unorganized, and hence have not bothered much about boundaries between them.

It would be a mistake to assume, however, that industrial unionism has been free of jurisdictional troubles. Although disputes over jurisdiction have not been as numerous in the C.I.O. as in the A.F. of L., quarrels over jurisdiction took place, and do take place between industrial unions. As early as 1945 the C.I.O. Executive Board found it necessary to establish a Jurisdictional Committee, which took as its first assignment a dispute between the Department Store Workers and the Longshoremen. The Amalgamated Clothing Workers and the International Ladies Garment Workers Union have had their conflicts over

---

[1]Kenneth E. Boulding, *The Organizational Revolution* (Harper and Bros.), p. 111.

mannish-type women's clothes. The CIO Farm Equipment Workers, before they were swallowed up by the United Automobile Workers charged the latter with raiding agricultural equipment plants. The United Electrical, Radio and Machine Workers Union came into conflict with the UAW, as did the Transport Workers Union. Inside the A.F. of L., Local 91 of the International Ladies Garment Workers Union has been charged with luring away plants engaged in the production of "snowsuits" from the high wage Cloak and Suit locals in the same "industrial" international. The New York locals of the Bakery and Confectionary Workers came into open conflict with each other over the fancy cakebakers.

The "closing of the frontier" may well witness the spread of internal jurisdictional problems, especially as there are fewer "natural boundaries" between the industries than there are between the crafts in the American Federation of Labor unions. The expulsion of the Communist-dominated unions from the C.I.O. has opened up an area of severe jurisdictional strife, though its sources are ideological rather than simply jurisdictional. The United Mine Workers' catch-all, District 50, involves it in jurisdictional conflicts with a great many unions.

Because the workers' life is involved so intimately with his "job" and with the conditions of "sale" of his labor, protection and control of these conditions has dominated the entire labor movement. It should surprise no one, therefore, to find that the struggle against rival unions or claimants to specific jobs, is frequently much more real and bitter than the struggle against the employer, without whom unions could not possibly exist. This dilemma is particularly acute for the labor leader and his union. It is a dilemma no less acute which faces all organizations. Almost every organization exhibits two faces — a smiling face which it turns towards its members and a frowning face which it turns to the world outside.

The fraternity which cherishes brotherhood and solidarity within its walls seems like a home of prejudice and snobbery to those who are excluded. The church which tenderly nourishes the spirit of its members burns the heretics without — with words if not with fire. The union which builds up a spirit of solidarity among its members, and breaks down religious and racial barriers among them, under the splendid banner of "each for all and all for each" presents a somewhat different face to the employer, to its rival union, or to the obstinately non-union man; it will defend its claim to specific jobs for its members and, if necessary fight encroachments and strike first as a matter of self-defense. The corporation which is viewed by its "insiders" as a great empire of enterprise, to the "outsider" — presents a face of much less friendly character to its competitor.

In a world of competing contenders for specific jobs, the labor leader is continually beset by moral dilemmas. On the one hand, he is drawn toward identification with the movement and toward giving himself wholeheartedly toward its life and activities, as expressions of solidarity which to him is one of the chief ends of man. On the other hand, he is tormented by the fact that the defense and protection of his charges so often seem to mean the breaking of the wider solidarity; and yet how do we include the wider solidarity without breaking the inner solidarity? Woe to the elected representative who is tempted to act deliberately in the widest possible public interest rather than in the interest of those he represents. This is true of a director of a corporation elected by the stockholders; the trade union leader elected by the members, or an executive or legislator of a nation elected by a popular vote. He is all too liable to find himself out of a job.

Holding up their union's side in a jurisdictional dispute is what the rank and file of the membership demand from their leader. "When elections come around, no fact in a candidate's record for re-election is more potent in [many] unions than his ability to win for his union in jurisdictional controversies with other unions."[2] While hardly a paragraph was being devoted to Hutcheson's achievements since he assumed the General Presidency in 1915, the major portion of General Secretary Frank Duffy's nomination speech for William L. Hutcheson, was on the theme, in Duffy's words that "General President Hutcheson has been successful in settling jurisdictional disputes of the Carpenters with other trades."[3] He then began to enumerate a whole series of jurisdictional disputes which Hutcheson had been successful in settling since 1915. "Here are some of them," recited Duffy, who had been serving as the Brotherhood's General Secretary since 1901.

"You remember the Sheet Metal Workers' dispute was on for 20 years in the American Federation of Labor and was never properly settled? When he (Hutcheson) became the President that was one of the things he had in mind, to settle it if it could be settled. He called John Hynes, President of the Sheet Metal Workers, and the members of his Board to meet with him and a committee of the Board of the United Brotherhood, to see if we could adjust matters, and after three meetings, we came to an understanding. That understanding still exists and we don't have to bring anything like that into the A. F. of L. anymore. And that is to the credit of Bill Hutcheson."[4] The Carpenters defended themselves against the plumbers relative to the setting up of cabinets in bathrooms and in toilets. "We met them and through the General President we

---

[2]Jack Barbash, *Labor Unions In Action* (Harper and Bros., 1944), p. 34.
[3]U.B.C.J.A., *Proceedings* (1946), p. 14.
[4]*Ibid.*

came to an understanding." The Brotherhood has had its troubles with the Painters, who claimed the right to put on the chair rail or put up the picture molding. In 1920, disputes existed with the Coopers and the Maintenance of Way and Railroad Shop Laborers. In 1914-1915 the Carpenters had differences with the Roofers and Bricklayers as well as with other unions over cork installation and shingling; with the German-speaking framers, the United Order of Box Makers. In 1939 the Brotherhood advised the Upholsterers International Union of North America to refrain from competing for furniture workers, casket makers and general woodworkers. Most of these disputes were either compromised or settled by Hutcheson; one or two continue to fester and remain unsettled. But none was lost.

The whole problem of inter-union strife over jurisdictional claims provides in a real sense, a "watershed" for the historical development of the United Brotherhood of Carpenters and Joiners of America. The reason is simple enough, for the carpenter was almost first to be victimized by the inventions following the so-called Industrial Revolution and subsequently by the technological innovations which continued to endanger his health, destroy his skill, lower his wages, and cause technological unemployment. He could hardly be expected to sit idly by, when with time he became cognizant that his skill was being rendered worthless and his status imperiled by resulting unemployment. But rather than resist technological innovations, he sought to substitute organized measures of bargaining with employers to lessen the impact of tragedy of displacement, and consistently demanded the equivalent "job" for those engaged in the carpentry craft who have been displaced. Thus it was that jurisdictional disputes not only influenced and sometimes dictated the structure of the Brotherhood of Carpenters, but determined its behavior with other building trades, with its employers and the government as well.[5]

The cause of all this was the Industrial Revolution in the building trades which started in the 1880's, reaching full bloom during Hutcheson's first administration. Since then, there has not been a year without the introduction of some new material for, and some new method of constructing the nation's office buildings, homes, docks, piers and ships. With each technological innovation, a mad scramble for jurisdiction ensued.

The fact that disputes arising out of these technological innovations were not, either in the 1880's, in the ensuing decades and in Hutcheson's time handled in as orderly a fashion as they might have been, can be laid

---

[5]National Resources Committee, "Technological Trends and National Policy" (U.S. Gov't. Printing Office, 1937), Sections IV, V.

upon the doorsteps of the highly complicated building industry.* The very disorderliness, planlessness, the power of the dominant industrial group, changes in techniques had given rise to the union, and the union being an agency for job protection is an agency for jurisdictional preservation as well.

However, for all its troublesome ramifications, technological, socioeconomic and even communal, the Industrial Revolution in the building trades found the journeyman, a handicraftsman. Had its impact been sufficiently far-reaching as to render the handicraftsman useless and unprofitable, the jurisdictional disputes might never have seen the light of day; and buildings and offices like airplanes and automobiles, might be made in factories. But the Industrial Revolution had left the carpenter as essential, though not to the degree as it had found him. On any job, however large, small and up-to-date, the basic tools of the carpenter are still the saw and hammer. The Brotherhood is the major source for recruiting and training these craftsmen. Its meticulously worked-out apprenticeship standards not only tend to replenish the carpenter population but to "professionalize" the craft it as well. In actual practice, the graduate obtains almost the equivalent to a certificate of fitness to do carpentry work. Its membership card is a badge of skill and is regarded as such by its possessor. Its slogan of an "honest day's work for an honest day's pay" is not to be taken lightly. Its "Craft Problems," a regular monthly feature appearing in the *Carpenter,* has done something to foster pride in the craft and in doing a workmanlike job. In the field of constructive union-management relationship, the Brotherhood did much to increase the sense of significance in the work. Thus another need for the Brotherhood of Carpenters, for the craft; thus, an additional source of jurisdictional jealousy and conflict.

For the above reasons and doubtless many others, specifically characteristic of the building trades, the Brotherhood has had comparatively more jurisdictional disputes than other unions. A large share of the blame must, we repeat, rest with the Industrial Revolution.

As late as 1916, the Carpenters did the lion's share of the work of erecting a building. Only gradually did new methods and materials ease out the old. The carpenters having the most work to do, stood to lose the most work with the advent of new trades and new techniques. And few were the new building trades that did not encroach upon their jurisdiction.

Technological changes have not moved them, at any time, to abandon what they thought was their rightful claim to their ever-evolving car-

---

*For a most comprehensive study of the complex construction industry. See William Haber, *Industrial Relations in the Building Industry,* (Harvard Univ. Press, 1930).

penters' jurisdiction, nor have they relaxed their vigilance. Their desire to keep, protect and preserve their jobs, which, as American workers, they place before all considerations has been fixed and constant; and the protection of their "job" has been the primary function of the union and the elected chief officer.

It was this determination which has embroiled the Brotherhood in major and minor jurisdictional disputes with a degree of regularity. Disputes over wood and metal materials were the two most important types; both were illustrative of the degree to which the Brotherhood was affected by the Industrial Revolution and technological evolution. These occurred chiefly with the Sheet Metal Workers, the Iron Workers, and the International Association of Machinists.

We shall come back to them in a subsequent part of this chapter. Together, they will explain another element of the virulence of jurisdictional disputes in union behavior: craft pride.

The principle dual-union dispute engaged in by the Brotherhood, that of the Amalgamated Woodworkers International Union, was caused by the introduction of machinery. The revolving plane was successfully introduced in the early 1840's, and great economy in the smoothing of lumber resulted. This was followed by the introduction of other woodworking machinery, with the result that part of the work formerly done by the outside carpenter, such as the finishing of sashes, doors, window frames, etc., was now transferred to the factory. Although the Carpenters realized that this was an encroachment upon their field, they were unable, having no "national" union, to make an effective protest. Furthermore, they did not fully realize—and none in the building trades could—the extent to which these new workmen would compete with them. In the meantime, the Cabinet Makers, mostly German immigrants, formed a national union and were beginning to admit this new class of workmen. Between 1889 and 1890, the Brotherhood was further surrounded by a second and third union: the International Furniture Workers, and the Machine Woodworkers. A year later, a queer twist was given the situation, when the latter two merged into the Amalgamated Woodworkers International henceforth claiming the combined jurisdiction over all the machine workers in all factories. Continued strife with the Amalgamated, varied by several futile attempts to adjust the difficulty in a manner satisfactory to both sides, finally brought the matter to the attention of the A. F. of L.

The Amalgamated asked for recognition of its right to "full and sole jurisdiction" over the factory woodworkers, whether employed in a planing mill, piano, cabinet, or interior finish factory. The Committee of Grievances, to which the matter was referred, recommended that the Federation defer action until the two parties in question had made further attempts to settle their difficulties. In April, 1902, however, the Executive Council of the Federation decided that the Amalgamated had exclusive jurisdiction over Cabinet Makers and Machine Factory Workers.[6]

With the A. F. of L. behind them, the Woodworkers went on the offensive to win back the disputed workers. This did not relieve the already strained relations with the Brotherhood. Complaints from cities south to Savannah and west to San Pedro poured into the 1902 Convention of the Brotherhood. The delegates issued a ringing resolution, accusing the Woodworkers of cutting rates in order to organize woodworkers and openly calling it a scab organization. The Brotherhood then adopted a resolution reaffirming its jurisdiction over all carpenters and woodworkers, refusing to recognize the decision of the A. F. of L. A copy of the resolution was sent to Gompers personally.[7]

The Woodworkers again took the dispute to the Executive Council of the American Federation of Labor at the 1902 convention. First the convention disposed of the request of the Brotherhood that the Amalgamated's charter be revoked, refusing it on the grounds that the primary cause of the trouble had been a change in policy on the part of the Carpenters. With the consent of the Carpenters, provision was made for the appointment of an umpire to settle the dispute. The Carpenters nominated Sam Parks of the New York Building Trades, as arbitrator, and the Woodworkers, one of their own officers, P. I. Downey. Through some mix-up in the Carpenters' delegation. Downey was elected by six to four votes.

On March 11 of the following year, Downey rendered his decision which gave the Amalgamated complete jurisdiction "over all the Woodworkers in plaining mills, furniture and interior factories," but granted the Carpenters jurisdiction "over all the work on new and old buildings and the putting up of store and office fixtures."

The Carpenters refused to live up to the award, claiming that Downey was ineligible to arbitrate because he previously had been on an A. F. of L. Grievance Committee which heard the dispute. Further, said President Huber, he had agreed only to confer, and even though he had accepted Downey an arbitrator, he was not bound to accept the award. Many letters and resolutions urging the withdrawal of the Brotherhood from the A. F. of L. were received at the general office. While the Brotherhood did not take this stand, it did renew its campaign for one and only one union in the woodworking industry, resolutely ignoring the Downey decision. At the 1903 convention of the A. F. of L.,

---

[6]Frederick S. Deibler, *The Amalgamated Woodworkers International Union of America*, p. 17.

[7]U.B.C.J.A., *Proceedings* (1902), p. 44.

the Amalgamated reopened the matter by demanding that the Carpenters recognize the Downey award. The Carpenters countered with a request that the decision be annulled, on the ground that they had not been notified to appear and present their reasons for refusing to live up to it. They also accused the Amalgamated of unfairness in having made an agreement with the New York Manufacturers Association calling for a nine hour day. The Amalgamated replied that this action was simply retaliatory, the Carpenters having refused to abide by the Downey decision.[8] The Federation adopted a Committee Report recommending that the Downey decision be sustained — which the Carpenters disregarded.

Ensuing attempts on the part of the Federation to bring the two organizations into a conference failed, and the 1904 Convention of the Federation recommended to the Executive Council that the Carpenters be suspended unless they accepted the Downey decision.[9] At the 1905 Convention of the Federation the Executive Council reported that revocation of the Brotherhood's charter would not accomplish the desired result, and that it had not acted, therefore, in accordance with the recommendation of the 1904 Convention.[10]

The next few years witnessed many fruitless attempts to reach some sort of agreement. The Amalgamated held out for the Downey decision, while the Carpenters insisted that the only solution agreeable to them is "that we should have but one organization of Carpenters in this country, and they be under the banner of the United Brotherhood of Carpenters and Joiners of America." Finally, at their 1909 Convention the Woodworkers adopted an aggressive policy, which was really their last resort. The ranks of the Amalgamated had suffered greater and greater depletion; in 1908 there was but one-seventh of the number there had been in 1904. The Brotherhood's attractiveness in terms of benefits was having its effect, and the Amalgamated, having failed to gain its ends, now decided to meet war with war. Never again, unless the Carpenters recognized their jurisdictional claims, would members of the Woodworkers' union discuss peace terms with members of the Brotherhood. This decision, made at the 1909 Convention of the Woodworkers, was really a challenge to the Brotherhood, and the Brotherhood accepted it as such. The refusal of the Woodworkers henceforth, to discuss amalgamation lost them still more members.

At the 1909 A. F. of L. Convention, after again failing to get the rivals together, Gompers produced his own plan of amalgamation. It

8U.B.C.J.A. *Proceedings* (1904), p. 139.
9A.F.L. Convention *Proceedings* (1903), p. 85.
10A.F.L. *Proceedings* (1905), p. 72.

stated that "amalgamation shall take place one year from November 1, 1909, under the pain of expulsion on dissenting parties. . . ."[11] The resolution was passed by a spanking majority. The Woodworkers, although growing weaker and weaker as the conflict continued, paid no heed to this decree. The Executive Council of the Federation, for its part, was reluctant to use the implied powers of expulsion granted by the previous Convention. At the Federation's 1911 Convention, held in Atlanta, they were again ordered to amalgamate with the Brotherhood.[12] By a 15,374 vote to 409, the Convention had ordered amalgamation or expulsion for the determined but weakened Woodworkers. In the war, lasting almost six years, the Amalgamated reported a loss of 19,000 members. Before long the two rivals met in conference, and the Brotherhood dictated the terms of the agreement which finally brought to a close perhaps the bitterest dual-union dispute in the history of the American trade union movement. The merger plan went into effect on January 10, 1912. The terms provided complete membership for Woodworkers' members, both individually and as locals. The Amalgamated was thus completely absorbed by the Brotherhood.

Second in importance to this controversy was the Brotherhood's dispute with the British-transplanted American Society of Carpenters, which set-up its first American branches in 1867.[13] In the early days the two organizations were held together by a strong bond of sympathy: common language, trade union experience, and the idea of collective action. But soon rivalry developed between the two which was productive of disputes and conflicts injurious to both sides. Here rivalry and conflict started after the 1890's, when both sides claimed jurisdiction over practically the same artisans. Trouble had for some time been seething under the surface, and frequent and bitter were the quarrels and feuds in the ensuing years. Although both organizations realized that their own interests were endangered by the recurring opposition, they seemed unable to bring about a consolidation. The Amalgamated Society favored an equal union; the Brotherhood demanded complete absorption of the Amalgamated Society. After many bitter conflicts resulting in disorganization of the workers in many places, notably in New York City, San Francisco and Denver, the controversy was finally referred to the A. F. of L. The Atlanta Convention recommended a conference between representatives of the two organizations, and in case no agreement could be reached, submission of the whole controversy to the Executive Council of the A. F. of L., whose plan for

---

[11]U.B.C.J.A. *Proceedings* (1906), p. 31.

[12]A.F.L. *Proceedings* (1909), pp. 290-292.

[13]U.B.C.J.A. *Proceedings* (1912), pp. 128-130.

amalgamation both sides must accept. The conference of representatives having proved fruitless, the Executive Council met and rendered a decision requiring amalgamation upon the terms proposed by the Brotherhood. The Amalgamated refused to accept the decision and in consequence was suspended from the Federation. Finally, in 1913 the Amalgamated submitted to the Brotherhood but kept their own benefit system. In 1915 the Amalgamated Society of Carpenters and Joiners came to life again. Its *Monthly Report* saw fit to warn its "members against German conspirators."[14] In his report to the 1924 Convention, President Hutcheson had called attention to the organizing activities of the Amalgamated. "There was an apparent effort on the part of those active in the interest of the Amalgamated, not only to continue to take exception to the provisions of our Constitution, but they endeavor to organize and install new local unions under the Amalgamated banner."[15]

Hutcheson charged that in the early part of 1923 the Amalgamated Society in America and Canada had taken steps to form a new organization; that the local unions of the Amalgamated section of the Brotherhood had been notified that the time had come for the Amalgamated again to function as an independent organization, and that the agreement entered into with the Brotherhood in 1913 should no longer be recognized. This the Brotherhood accepted as a renewal of open hostility, and sent letters inviting them to have full membership in the Carpenters union. Subsequently, "all locals of the Amalgamated in the 'States took advantage of the dispensation, availing themselves of the opportunity to become full members of our organization," Hutcheson announced during his third term in office.

Apart from the Amalgamated Society, there still remained the small English-transplanted rival of the Amalgamated Society of Woodworkers. Most of their members were men who, having belonged in the old country, clung to their share in the benefit funds for sickness, unemployment, old age, and death. Obviously the union was restricted to British artisans. But the Brotherhood objected to the English less because of their sudden mass-appearances during the spring, than because they worked for "whatever wages they could get."

Hutcheson's great ambition to build up "one great big organization of Carpenters and Joiners of America" took him to Manchester in August of 1924. There he conferred with the Executive Committee of the Amalgamated Society of Woodworkers. The Chairman, Mr. Frank Chandler, decried the fact that there was friction between the two organ-

---

14Amalgamated Society of Carpenters and Joiners, *Monthly Report September,* 1915, pp. 4-5.
15U.B.C.J.A. *Proceedings* (1906), p. 31.

izations in America and in Canada. Hutcheson replied that his desire to meet with the officers of the parent body was "to bring about a closer affiliation, make for unity of action and prepare to combat the unscrupulous employer more than any one thing." He expressed confidence that as members of the "two greatest woodworking organizations extant, some plan and some understandable method could be worked out whereby a happy solution might be consummated."[16]

A general discussion ensued in which the members of the Executive Committee voiced the sentiment that "there should be one organization of Carpenters in America, and that if any other organization attempted to get into England it would soon put them out of business." The subject of benefits for the old, and death benefits was also discussed. Hutcheson replied that this could be worked out to the satisfaction of the Amalgamated, adding at the same time that "he was something of an opportunist and could not let this matter go without first trying to ascertain if something of a concrete nature could not be put forth, so that both organizations would have some basic principle to work on."[17]

Dual union rivalries seemed to be over for the Brotherhood. All of the three disputes were finally settled to the satisfaction of the Carpenters. Viewed from the point of trade-unionism, the only possible solution of rival unions in the same craft is amalgamation. The American Federation of Labor has consistently refused to charter a new union in a trade which has an affiliated union. In harmony with the Federation's policy, the Brotherhood has from the outset maintained that there must be one national union in the carpentry trade. To this policy the Brotherhood has adhered, and it is hardly likely that a rival dispute will develop with the International Woodworkers of America, a C.I.O. union in existence since 1936. At this writing, good will, and the arts of consultation, conference and discussion have displaced much of the rawness and bitterness that prevailed between the two rivals in the Northwest. In consonance with General President Maurice A. Hutcheson's desire, procedures for resolving conflicts are contributing in a significant way towards a *modus vivendi* between the two organizations. "Attempts to develop proper conduct so that our future activities will demonstrate that a merger is of benefit to the workers who are members of both organizations," have been announced by the General President of the Brotherhood.*

---

[16]U.B.C.J.A. *Proceedings* (1926), p. 46.

[17]Amalgamated Society of Woodworkers, *Minutes*, Tues., Aug. 29, 1922 — Sat., Sept. 23, 1922.

*See *Trade Union Courier*, July 5, 1955.

CHAPTER | XXII

THE BADGE OF SKILL

Early in the century, the carpenter envisaged himself as the possessor of:

"A basic trade that was one of the most general and complete trades which a man can learn. The carpenter foreman who takes care to see that the excavation stakes are properly set; who sees that the foundation is properly laid; who sees that the proper openings are left; who attends to scaffolding for the painter, the electrician, the lather and plasterer. In fact, he is usually the superintendent of the job, and on his shoulders falls all the responsibility to see that the work is carried forward promptly and properly. He must be able to read blueprints, detailed plans and specifications, not only for his own work but for every building trade that comes on the job. To do this and to do it properly, it is necessary that he have a wide learning, and a general knowledge of the diversified work which he comes in contact with."[1]

How could this American carpenter with such professed versatility be dismayed in the face of American technical progress?

How could this American craftsman, whose skill was his only capital, be discouraged by American employers who were seemingly emancipating themselves from skilled craftsmen by machinery since 1885?

It was the failure to recognize craft pride, the certificate of fitness, or the "sentiments" of workmanship rather than the organization of the mass production industry, that accounted for Hutcheson's opposition to the organization of workers under the banner of one big union. The deprivation of status and self-esteem have been, beyond question, prominent in industrial conflicts in this and other countries, Craft pride, the pride of a man who has mastered an intricate job through long and arduous application, was as present in the 1880's, as it was in 1935, when the labor movement split into "craft" and "industrial" blocs.

---

[1] U.B.C.J.A., *Proceedings* (1910), pp. 67-68.

While modern industry has made hash of craft distinctions, the badge of skill of the craft unionist is still with us in the year 1955. As between the "craft" unions of the A. F. of L. and the "industrial" unions which comprise the CIO, the situation seems to favor the former. The holder of a craft union card, the specialist or skilled worker rather than the industrial worker will be given priority to specific job claims. The craft unionist is a specialist in a particular field, and most industries have need of the skills he offers. Membership in a craft union is of considerable importance to the individual worker. The holder of a craft union card can go to any employer in any industry with a feeling that he has something to offer because of his membership in the union. With the industrial type of union, however, this situation is quite different. Here the union membership card is no particular guide to the skill of the holder. It merely indicates that he is a member of a particular labor organization, be it the Steel Workers, Rubber Workers, or Automobile Workers.

The decade-long *leveling process* encouraged by C.I.O. bargaining for increases in flat cents-per-hour terms, has telescoped the percent differentials between the skilled and the unskilled." In company after company, this has aroused the skilled workers to wrath. One result has been that the C.I.O. Auto Workers Union and the C.I.O. Electrical Workers were forced to establish skilled trades departments to assure their skilled workers of preferential treatment at the bargaining table.

"Dissatisfied skilled workers in C.I.O. industrial unions are looking for economic salvation toward the A. F. of L. craft unions representing only one sort of a job. The theory is that C.I.O. bargainers hold their wage rates below the levels a craft union could achieve,"[2] writes an observer of the current labor scene.

Hutcheson foresaw this development in 1935, when he debated with the founders of C.I.O. the merits of a "modified" type of industrial union as against the all-inclusive kind, in which skilled craftsmen could retain their own identity, as well as their strategic bargaining position, instead of "getting lost in the shuffle" among an army of assembly-line workers.

In the 1880's, the Brotherhood's claim included all competent carpenters and joiners engaged in woodwork, stair building, millwrights, planing-mill bench hands, cabinet makers, furniture makers, and carpenters running woodworking machinery. Had the carpenter industry remained stationary, these claims, once proclaimed, would, to a large extent, have prevented jurisdictional strife. But American technical progress, the introduction of new machinery, methods and wood substitutes, have been depriving the carpenters, in common of course with other

---

[2]Stephen K. Galpin, "The Lower Paid Worker No Longer Gains the Most in Today's Pay Setting Trend," *Wall Street Journal,* June 24, 1955.

craftsmen, of work which was formerly theirs; and they have had to
to be continually on their guard to keep work from being taken away
from them. Hence, as changes in the industry have developed, the
Brotherhood came forward to put in its claim, invoking this omnibus job
description. What is true of the Carpenters is, of course, true of other
crafts. But the Carpenters, as was repeatedly stated, have had their
peculiar difficulties in maintaining their versatile jurisdictional claims,
and in consequence have been a party to many trade jurisdictional
quarrels.

If the Carpenters have applied any single test to the determination
of what their specific jurisdictional claims should be, that test has been
the job description of a carpenter. Although the results of the application
of this definition may appear to be inconsistent, the underlying motive
has in every case been the same. Whatever the grounds of the Carpenter's jurisdictional claims, in reality they have applied but one test—
the professed versatility of the carpenter, which "is one of the most
general and complete trades a man can learn."[3] Thus in 1916 President
Hutcheson defined the Carpenter's trade autonomy to include "milling,
manufacturing, fashioning, joining, assembling, erecting, fastening or
dismantling of all material of wood, hollow metal or trim, or of material
composed in part of wood . . . and the erecting and dismantling of machinery, *where the skill, knowledge and training of a carpenter is required,
either through the operation of machine or hand tools.*"[4] Here the type
of training and the Carpenter's equipment or skill required is the test.
Again in 1928, General President Hutcheson described the Carpenters'
job claims to be based "not upon the character and nature of the material used, but upon the skill, knowledge and ability required to properly
erect or install the material."[5]

At the same time, he cautioned the delegates at the Twenty-second
Convention of the "advisability and necessity of uniform action." "We
find," he said, "that in some localities our membership are alert and
insist upon strict observance of the jurisdictional claims of our Brotherhood, while in other localities they seem to be lax in their demands and
permit other building tradesmen to encroach upon our jurisdiction.
Whether that is through lack of interest, or a desire to avert controversy
or whether it is because of local environment and conditions, it is hard for
one to determine; but in any event the members should put forth every
effort to see that our jurisdictional claims, set forth in our Constitution,
are closely and strictly adhered to."[6]

---

[3]U.B.C.J.A., *Proceedings* (1916), p. 144.
[4]U.B.C.J.A., *Proceedings* (1928), p. 53.
[5]*Ibid.*
[6]U.B.C.J.A. *Proceedings* (1910), p. 67.

The same forces which caused difficulties with the Woodworkers also created them with the metal trades. The dispute with the International Association of Sheet Metal Workers arose when metal trim replaced wood trim; that with the International Association of Machinists when metal was substituted for wood in the construction of heavy machinery.

The trouble with the former began in 1909 with the introduction of metal trim. It was rudely called to the Carpenters' attention by a New York City building ordinance prohibiting the use of wood in a building higher than fifty-nine feet.[7] The Carpenters claimed the new kind of work on three grounds: (1) That to put up metal cornices required the same kind of skill as to put up wooden ones; (2) That the trim metal work simply replaced the woodwork; (3) That carpenters' tools and knowledge are used to put up metal trim. The Sheet Metal Workers based their claim on the ground that the material used was that over which they had always claimed jurisdiction. The result was continued strife between the two unions and increasing bitterness as the struggle became more intense. A number of attempts to come to an agreement having failed, the two organizations finally agreed to submit their specific claims to a third party. On April 23, 1909 Judge William J. Gaynor of the New York State Supreme Court handed down a decision in favor of the Carpenters, to which the Sheet Metal Workers immediately objected. Judge Gaynor said that the difference over new material was only a question of molecular distribution, and that, although the new trend was not wood, the work required the skill of a carpenter rather than a machine metal worker.

The Building Trades Department of the A. F. of L., to which the Sheet Metal Workers carried the dispute, took the matter up at its 1909 Convention, held in Tampa, Florida. The Sheet Metal Workers contended that Gaynor had been asked to decide only the question of which union did most of the work and which should do it; and that the judge was technically unfit to render a decision. The majority report of the Adjustment Committee, to which the matter was referred, upheld the Gaynor decision,[8] but the minority report recommended the awarding of metal trim and doors to the Sheet Metal Workers. After a heated discussion, the minority report was adopted, and all parties affiliated with the Building Trades Department were ordered to abide by the decision of the Convention.[9] The Brotherhood refused to yield. After numerous requests that the Brotherhood accept the decision of the Convention, the

---

[7]The Carpenter, April, 1909, p. 28.
[8]Building Trades Department, Proceedings (1909), p. 8.
[9]Ibid., pp. 83-84.

latter was suspended from the Department. The Building Trades Department then asked President Gompers of the A. F. of L. to suspend the Brotherhood. Gompers replied that not only would he not oust the Carpenters, but he would order the Building Trades Department to reinstate them. During 1912, the Brotherhood reaffiliated.

Nothing was achieved in the way of a settlement between the two jurisdictional rivals. The problem still to be solved was: Should the manufacture of hollow-metal trim be conceded to the Sheet Metal Workers; its erection to the Carpenters. To it were added highly emotional overtones, charges, countercharges, recriminations. By the time Hutcheson reached the position of the General Presidency, the whole situation had come to be viewed in a distorted perspective. "Unfair competition" of the Carpenters, charges of "scabbing" and other readily available contentions and accusations hardly cleared the air for an objective evaluation of the contenders' claims.

Exasperated Hutcheson was determined not to yield. To strengthen the Carpenters claims, he cited the expert testimony of the professionals and the manufacturers. "Also the architects and the manufacturers of metal trim, all of whom testified and submitted evidence to show that the carpenter is the logical mechanic to erect metal trim." At the same time, he reassured the membership that your General Officers "have put forth every possible effort to prevent the jurisdiction of this branch of our trade from being encroached upon and while I would like very much to see this matter amicably adjusted, yet I do not believe we should be too anxious or hasty in giving up any work that rightfully belongs to the membership of the U.B."[10]

Hope of settlement was renewed when the Building Trades inaugurated a new and original scheme for the settlement of jurisdictional disputes. The plan as first advanced by a group of contractors, encouraged by John B. Lennon, conciliator of the Department of Labor, called for the formation of a board to settle jurisdictional disputes in the building industry. At a general conference of international presidents and prominent contractors, held in March, 1919, a definite plan was formulated.[11] At a later conference this plan was adopted, and when submitted to the Building Trades Department at its 1919 Convention was also adopted by that body.

It was inevitable that the Carpenters' dispute with the Sheet Metal Workers should reach this National Board of Jurisdictional Awards. The Sheet Metal Workers presented the case, and on December 4, 1920, the Board renderd its decision: "In the matter of the controversy be-

10U.B.C.J.A., *Proceedings* (1916), p. 45.
11U.B.C.J.A., *Proceedings* (1920), pp. 450-453.

tween the Sheet Metal Workers and the Carpenters over hollow sheet metal frames and sash, it is decided that the setting of the hollow-trim metal window frames and the hanging of hollow-metal sash, when such frames and sash are made of number ten gauge metal or lighter it is the work of the Sheet Metal Workers.[12] The conditions of the dispute were once more reversed, and the Brotherhood refused further to participate in the activities of the National Board of Jurisdictional Awards.

Several attempts were made to reopen the case, but all ended in failure, primarily because the National Board for Jurisdictional Awards refused to grant a hearing until the Brotherhood was reaffiliated with the Building Trades Department. The Brotherhood declined to reaffiliate until a hearing had been granted.[13] Finally, the Brotherhood had adopted the position that it would not again reaffiliate until the Department had severed all relations with the National Board of Jurisdictional Awards, whose "awards were hostile to the interests of the Brotherhood and were largely responsible for the prolongation of the metal trim dispute with the Sheet Metal Workers. After prolonged bitterness between the two organizations, a satisfactory settlement of the controversy over the erection and installation of metal trim was reached in March, 1928.

> "The consummating of this agreement will end a controversy of many years standing, and while there have been times that our organization was criticized and censored by other building trades organizations, contractors and the building public, the consummating of the agreement clearly demonstrated the justification of our claims, and shows what may be accomplished if our membership will insist upon the jurisdiction of our organization being recognized."[14]

What is it that Hutcheson gained for the Carpenters? The right for the carpenter to do the metal work, of course. Maintenance of the standard is one of the advantages of what the Carpenters gained, since employers will not be so anxious to engage workers other than carpenters; but when two rival unions are concerned, added difficulties are involved in maintaining the standard rule. But more important than that, even granting that the rate is maintained, the fact is not altered that if the Sheet Metal Workers Union obtains the metal work which has taken the place of woodwork, the amount of carpenter work has been decreased; the number of carpenters remaining the same, unemployment for carpenters will result to the extent to which that work has been decreased. It is, therefore, to the interest of the Carpenters to obtain jurisdiction over work that has displaced carpenter work, and

---

[12]Building Trades Department, *Proceedings* (1921), p. 37.

[13]Building Trades Department, *Proceedings* (1921), pp. 124-125.

[14]U.B.C.J.A., *Proceedings* (1928), p. 51.

to the extent that they obtained such jurisdiction to that extent they have gained.

Another gain to the Brotherhood from its jurisdictional quarrels has been suggested by President Gompers:

"None will dispute the fact that with you I deeply deplore the jurisdictional controversies, and particularly when they assume an acute and often bitter antagonistic attitude; but that they have developed a high order of intelligence in discussion among our unionists, keen perception in industrial jurisprudence, is a fact which all observers must admit. That these acquirements and attainments will be of great advantage in the administration and judgement in industrial affairs, no thinker dare gainsay."[15]

Hutcheson's application of "industrial jurisprudence" was demonstrated by the claim the Brotherhood made to millwright work vis-a-vis the International Association of Machinists.

"We feel that a proper demonstration of the justice of our claim really resolves itself to two main propositions: (a) our claims to millwright work are not arbitrary and capricious; they are based on the natural evolution which has effected all trades. To demonstrate this point, we propose to show, that the millwright is and has been a recognized craftsman for many generations; that in the earliest years of the labor movment his skill and duties made natural his becoming a part of the Brotherhood of Carpenters and that he did so become since the 1890's; that as in all fields, millwrighting has changed with a changing technology; but so has the millwright changed and adapted himself to the new conditions. Finally, the erection of all conveyors is properly within the scope of the millwright."[16]

The Brotherhood's major dispute with the International Association of Machinists when metal was substituted for wood in the construction of heavy industry; or that of the International Association of Iron Workers as iron replaced wood in piles, docks and window frames are manifestations of the same incessant flux of modern industry.

It took forty-one years of intense jurisdictional struggle, followed by litigation, for the Brotherhood and the former to arrive at a settlement over installing machinery equipment. Here again compromise and conciliation by both rival unions took the place of a prolonged paralyzing conflict. It is conceivable that the Carpenters' new General President, Maurice A. Hutcheson, will develop and establish a new code and relationship that might ultimately result in abolishing jurisdictional warfare. At the same time, it is hardly conceivable how the International Association of Machinists could contribute in any way toward the prevention of jurisdictional conflicts in the light of its own criteria for trade demarcation. Possibly no organization defines its jurisdiction in greater detail

---

[15] A. F. of L. *Proceedings* (1905), p. 23.
[16] "Our Case in a Nutshell," *U.B.C.J.A. vs International Association of Machinists.*

than the International Association of Machinists. After marking out its "boundaries" in more than sixteen hundred words, this union made certain that nothing to which it is (or will be) entitled is left out by adding: "all the foregoing and all in addition thereto any other work which it does now or in the future may, as industry develop fall naturally within the scope of the jurisdiction of the International Association of Machinists."

Hutcheson's claim to specific jobs in the cooperage industry was based on similar grounds. To the charge by President Burke that the Brotherhood of Carpenters was invading the Coopers' International Union of North America, Hutcheson made use of his knowledge of the cooperage industry, promptly deducing that the term "cooper" does not refer to "tanks which members of our organization have made and erected for years." "In looking over a city," he explained, "you will see tanks on top of a building for fire hazards, like a wood cistern, and water tanks along railroads. They are made in carpenter shops, made of trim, that is where the contention comes from. There is no one in our organization making kegs or tight cooperage. It may be true in taking over the lumber workers in the Northwest in some instances in connection with sawmill work, they do make a container. It is cone shaped, holds about half a bushel, used for vegetables. It is made out of wood and cut off with a knife — hamper is the real term. We do not look upon that as cooperage. We have no men in our membership who make barrels for containing whiskey and beer, we do not consider the other work cooperage work."[17]

The year 1928 saw the settlement of a principle jurisdictional quarrel between the Carpenters and the Wood, Wire, and Metal Lathers International Union. The principle point of the quarrel: the installation of Celotex material and a light sheet metal with holes (or wire cloth).

The Lathers had in the past encroached upon the Brotherhood's jurisdiction by claiming the installation of "Celotex," and similar materials. The Brotherhood claimed the right to the erection of all Celotex material other than "lathe." Hutcheson, weary of fighting, and desirous of being on good terms with the building trades, pointed with pride to the settlement of jurisdictional disputes as indicative of his "willingness to enter into agreements in reference to jurisdictional disputes. These agreements are evidence of our fairness and also show that our stand in regards to our jurisdiction and the right of our members to do the work is coming to be recognized by other trades as justifiable."[18]

Unquestionably the cost of these jurisdictional disputes has been

---

[17]*Hutcheson's Private Papers*, (January 9, 1936).
[18]*Ibid, p. 52.*

high to the Brotherhood and the rival claimants to specific jobs, which once belonged to the Carpenters. Has the Brotherhood's gain been sufficient to warrant the expenditure?

The Brotherhood's gains cannot, of course, be measured in terms of money, or even estimated with any degree of accuracy. It goes without saying, that the maintenance of a policy of standardization is essential to the success of trade unionism, and that if there are two rival unions in the same craft, it is difficult, even impossible to maintain such a policy. It is, of course, for this reason that the American Federation Labor has from the beginning opposed dual unionism. As was indicated above, there are now two unions in the sawmill and woodworking industry. The amalgamation of the two is therefore to the interest of the members of both, provided the rival is permitted to amalgamate on terms which do not deprive them of their benefits. And such terms were usually granted by the Brotherhood of Carpenters. While it may be true that the Brotherhood would have developed faster, if it had not been for these disputes, the fact remains that during and following them it steadily increased in membership. The Brotherhood has been unusually successful in maintaining its policy of standardization; and the elimination of rival unions, whose presence greatly hampered the enforcement of this policy, was without a doubt a factor in the success.

The issues involving demarcation disputes between the Brotherhood and competing claimants becomes clear, only if we visualize the union as an organization of jobs, which is very jealous of its "territorial" integrity, resisting strongly any attempts on the part of other unions at invasion. That the Carpenters have been very tenacious in holding on and defending their "job" and "territorial" integrity is clearly shown by their long controversies with other unions. They have refused to surrender their stake in the carpenter trade, which is to them "cumulative, unique, tangible and recognized."

It is well put by Robert Hoxey:

"The aim of the union is primarily to benefit the group of workers concerned, rather than the workers as a whole or society as a whole; its theories which attempt to explain determination of wages, hours, conditions of employment, etc., are not generally but primarily group theories. The principles of action which it lays down are primarily group principles and its economic policies, demands and methods are primarily intended to protect and benefit the group of workers concerned."[19]

These are the objective conditions governing the trade-union movement in the year 1955. Workers have established something definitely resembling a "property right" in their job.[20] If the Carpenters, the very

---

[19]Robert Hoxie, *Trade Unionism in the United States* (1922) p. 282.
[20]Robin M. Williams, Jr. *American Society* (Knopf, 1952), p. 195.

real human beings who make up the Brotherhood made their job into a property right, it is simply because they were the first whose "security" had been threatened. The protection of this security is the primary function of the Brotherhood and its elected officers. Hutcheson's "zealousness" in stoutly protecting the job interests of those who made up the Brotherhood of Carpenters incurred much wrath of rival unions. Hutcheson harbored no illusions that a new code for the settlement of jurisdictional disputes will be easy of immediate attainment. "Even men in the Brotherhood," he complained, "say to me, Bill, why don't you settle them?" I say, "how?" Tell me how? There is one way to settle them and only one—give up work carpenters have always done and are entitled to do. Is that what carpenters want?"[21] This was Hutcheson's moral dilemma.

The role jurisdiction has played in the American labor movement can in part be attributed to the same individualism and the same high valuation of property rights which has characterized the American community generally. The role of jurisdiction in the labor movement, is a reflection of our basic mores.

---

[21]*Fortune,* April, 1946, p. 121.

CHAPTER | XXIII

WHERE OLD CARPENTERS GO TO LIVE

Cast me not off in the time of old age;
when my strength faileth,
foresake me not.

Psalm 71:9

The fresh, mild and vari-colored autumn welcomed us to Lakeland, Florida. Compared with the great city we had recently left, with all its noise and brutal contrasts, this little city, surrounded by lakes and steeped in solitude, seemed like Paradise. Two miles from the city are the rolling hills of Polk county. Here are the shores of Lake Gibson calmly spreading their shoulders toward land which is regarded as some of the finest citrus and trucking lands to be found anywhere in Florida. It was late November, 1954 slightly past the "dinner" hour (lunch time for us), when we arrived at the Home of the United Brotherhood of Carpenters and Joiners of America.

As we rode leisurely along the driveway we felt as though we were getting set to spend the day at one of the more sumptuous country clubs in Westchester or Connecticut. Soon, we came to a stop in front of a handsome three-story white stucco building of Spanish architecture, surrounded by a forest of pines, Spanish moss, palms, Australian pines, dog-wood trees, shrubbery and an endless view of velvety green grass. On the porch projecting from the main entrance sat aging men, protected from the rays of the penetrating sun, marveling at the breath-taking grandeur of the scenery for miles around. "Fleets" of ray-birds and red-iron blackbirds fluttered, hopped and skipped about, competing with the thousands of industrious little squirrels for the "left-overs" tossed out with regularity after each noon-day meal by their old reliable friends — the carpenters.

Superintendent C. Marshall Goddard invited us in. As we entered the main building, we found ourselves in the Home's main lounge which

416

closely resembles the huge lobby of a big residential club or hotel in Boston or midtown Manhattan. It is furnished with big, overstuffed chairs and couches, all finished in genuine red leather. Here, the aging carpenters pass part of their time reading, smoking, talking, listening to the radio or viewing television. The main building is 331 feet in length and 205 feet deep, it also takes in three other enjoining smaller buildings to complete the main unit at the Home. These are the laundry, power plant and water system. The main building is constructed in the shape of a huge "E" with north and south wings and the auditorium, comprised of a central extension. The wings and the main part of the building are three stories high, two of them devoted to occupants' rooms and the third furnishes space for the hospital.

Conspicuous to the visitor are the many plaques, which identify the donors who have furnished and equipped the home. Here is the plaque of the Chicago District Council of Carpenters, proudly announcing its share in the furnishing of the lounge. St. Louis local unions provided the pipe-organ for the auditorium. The New York carpenters equipped the dining room. Others provided the furnishings for individual rooms.

On the main floor is the auditorium, which has a seating capacity of 900. It contains a modern motion picture projection apparatus, complete with sound, also the pipe-organ. Here old carpenters congregate each Sunday for religious services. Assemblies, celebrations of national and religious holidays, Christmas and New Year, concerts as well as funeral services are conducted here. Current motion pictures are shown twice weekly. On the cornice is the emblem of the Brotherhood, "Labor conquers all," which is accompanied by the symbols of Masonry.

To the right of the auditorium, is a huge dining room, equipped with refrigeration, and an up-to-date kitchen. It is supervised by experienced personnel. The waiters are courteous, patient and friendly.

Although the number of residents at the time of our visit totaled 287, the Home can accomodate 350. Apparently, the number of applicants could be increased, were the Brotherhood to relax its admission requirements. Each room houses two occupants. The rooms are simply, and adequately furnished with twin beds, desks, easy chairs, a washroom, and individual closets. The floors are covered with small scatter-rugs.

While all rooms are furnished uniformly, the personality of the occupant is reflected in each. In some, one finds a picture of loved ones on the wall; in others, decorations and trimmings have been placed around to give the room a homey atmosphere. The use of strong beverages and liquors is prohibited. The physically handicapped and semi-invalids occupy the first floor. Hence they can walk to the lobby, dining room, auditorium, reading rooms, library and most other places without using the stairways.

When the retired carpenter enters the Home, he is provided with all necessities and accoutrements. He is supplied with two new suits each year, two pairs of shoes, shirts, underwear and shaving equipment.

Meals, served three times daily, consist of the following "typical" menus: breakfast — bacon and eggs, toast and butter, fruit, milk, tea or coffee, alternating with wheat cereal, egg toast, fruit, coffee, tea or milk; dinner — baked ham, sliced pineapple, coffee, tea or milk; supper — bean soup, cold cuts, carrots, crackers, bread, butter, mixed jelly cake, milk, coffee or tea.

Diabetics are served special diets; semi-invalids receive individual attention. The cost per meal, according to Mr. Joe Rogers, the dietician, is approximately thirty-five cents. Potatoes, cabbage, tomatoes and vegetables grow in the Home's own garden of ten acres; cream, milk and meat come from its own dairy farm and cattle raising; citrus and other comparable fruits grow in abundance in its own groves.

In the field of recreation and vocational skills, the Home offers a variety of activities to its occupants. There is the "country club", "Florida's Finest Eighteen Hole, Golf Course," which is the Home's own. and which the occupants memorialized many years ago in William Hutcheson's honor. While the residents of the Home have free use of the course, all other Lakeland residents, visitors and tourists pay a fee of $1.50 per day and fifty dollars for the season. The proceeds from the golf course go toward the Welfare Fund, which provides for all the delicacies, holiday celebrations, national festivals and gifts.

There are enough stretches of level ground for games of croquet, lawn bowling, shuffle board and other outdoor sports. Fishing on beautiful Lake Gibson is one of the most popular pastimes, while other favorite diversions are, checkers, chess, dominoes, billiards and television. A workshop has been outfitted in the basement of the building, where the retired carpenters can work and construct whatever their fancy dictates. Some of the more enthusiastic craftsmen have their own work shops in other buildings on the grounds. All work is done by hand — there are no power tools in the workshop. Canes are popular items of manufacture. Some are made from the Florida-produced bloom spikes of palm tree. These stout, knobby, wide canes are often seen in the hands of home residents. Many have built their own articles of furniture. They construct chairs, tables, foot stools and even cradles.

Although motion pictures are shown each week, more popular entertainment, community singing and musicales would prove a boon to the members. Several television sets have, however, considerably enlivened the residents. The Home offers generous reading matter in 35 popular magazines, to which it subscribes. Definitely among the minority but keenly perceptive of native trends and social values, are those who read

the *New Statesman and Nation,* the *New Republic* and other liberal
journals of opinion. The Home's library contains 3025 volumes. It is
open on Tuesdays and Fridays. The number of readers on those days
averages 30 to 40. A special Hutcheson fund has been set aside for the
purchase of new books. Our impression is that a well-worked adult educational program would give a chance to those who had little education
in their youth. Discussions on current problems, American history, social
science, have been particularly popular among the older men. Education
is an anti-age specific. It has therapeutic values, breathing new spirit and
vigor into aging bodies. Minds intent on acquiring new funds of knowledge are too busy to concentrate on aches and pains.

The Home is in no sense an institution of involuntary confinement,
for the occupants are free to come and go at will. On Sundays, they
are furnished with free transportation. Each resident is allowed ninety
days per year to visit relatives, friends, or simply give vent to a wanderlust to recapture lost days. . . .

The Home is non-sectarian. Denominationally, the occupants are almost evenly divided between Protestants and Catholics. It had been the
practice of the Home to provide each group with a priest and pastor —
who conduct services once every week. Transportation is provided for all
those who attend the church of their denomination. At least a fourth of
the occupants have demonstrated an active interest in local church
activities. The pastors and priests of the Lakeland community encourage the Home's residents to take part in church activities and Bible
classes, thereby giving them a feeling of belonging, participation and
responsibility.

Age classifications range from 65 to 101 at present; those in the
mid-seventies predominate, with a tapering number in the late sixties and
even eighties.

The Home maintains a hospital for the chronically ill and infirm.
Bedtime check-ups are conducted daily by the permanent staff, consisting of Dr. Paul Bird and Mrs. Cecile Miller, superintendent. Occupational diseases, arthritis and rheumatism account for well over 90 percent of the patients. Cardiacs and diabetics constitute the remaining 10
percent out of a total of 50 patients. The hospital is well-equipped to
take care of the chronically ill as well as those stricken with temporary
ailments. The use of outside doctors is permitted. Expensive medication,
inclusive of surgery is furnished without cost to the indigent. No one is
neglected. Meals are brought up directly into the hospital in heated carts
for those who cannot leave. In addition to Mrs. Miller, a graduate nurse,
there are seven aids and nine orderlies, who are respectful, maternal and
tender in their care of those who suffer and need healing. The service
is almost personalized. Reflective of the entire spirit prevailing in the

hospital is the Oath of Maimonides [famed Jewish physician and philosopher of the twelfth century], which is prominently displayed in the office of Mrs. Miller, and which reads:

> The eternal providence has appointed me to watch over the life and health of thy creatures. May the love for my art actuate me at all times; may neither avarice nor miserliness, nor thirst for glory, or for a great reputation engage my mind; for the enemies of truth and philanthropy could easily deceive me and make me forgetful of my lofty aim of doing good to thy children. May I never see in the patient anything but a fellow creature in pain. Grant me strength, time and opportunity always to correct what I have acquired, always to extend its domain; for knowledge is immense and the spirit of men can extend infinitely to enrich itself daily with new requirements. Today he can discover his errors of yesterday and tomorrow he may obtain a new light on what he thinks himself sure of today. O,God, Thou has appointed me to watch over the life and death of Thy creatures; here am I ready for my vocation, and now I turn unto my calling.

Since its inception in March of 1929, the Brotherhood shouldered willingly the responsibility of housing, feeding, clothing and healing 1200 ageing, chronically ill and infirm carpenters. To take care of 1200 human beings is a mighty industry for any institution — eleemosynary, fraternal, state or trade union. In compiling this report, we find this number so distributed as to age, geography and other factors, as to be representative of the body of men now sheltered in the homes for the aged. Of the 1200 occupants since 1929, 50 per cent were between the ages of 70 and 79; 30 per cent were between 65 and 69; 15 per cent between 80 and 89, and 5 per cent above 90. Of the 1200, 700 had children living, 200 had wives, while 300 had neither wives nor children.

There were twelve hundred homes for the aged in the year 1929. Of these, more than a third or 442 were maintained by religious and "nationality" groups; 305 were eleemosynary, 101 fraternal, 46 state, 9 military, 35 miscellaneous; 6 were operated by trade-unions.

Admission requirements to these homes varied, but almost all had age requirements; many had monetary requirements, area restrictions, homogeneity and many others.

Typical were the homes maintained by the fraternal orders and social organizations. Invariably, inability to support one self due to age, indigence, sickness and infirmity was a requirement for admission, and length of membership. At least 40 of 101 required transfer of property; others required minimum monthly payments of twenty dollars.

Comparable to the homes founded by the fraternal orders are those of the trade unions. But compared to the former with 101 homes, only six trade unions pioneered to look after their aged, infirm and disabled members in the late 'twenties. While the problem of caring for these workers was one that caused a good deal of concern to the organized labor movement, union leaders preferred to fight for higher wages, shorter hours, as the chief solution to the social risks of the workman. Some unions strove to inaugurate a choice between pension and shelter while others felt their obligation to the membership fulfilled through a pension fund alone.

Broadly speaking, three types of unions showed an interest in looking after their superannuated, infirm members: railroading, those engaged in machine production and the hand occupation of carpentry.

As early as 1891, the Home for Aged and Disabled Railroad Employees was established by the four train-service brotherhoods — Locomotive Engineers, Firemen and Enginemen, Trainmen, and the Conductors. In 1927 the Railway Conductors established their own Home in Savannah, Georgia. The Pressmen's Home, maintained by the International Printing Pressmen and Assistants' Union of North America, was founded in 1909. The International Typographical Union had built a hospital and sanitarium for the aged and disabled members in Colorado Springs, Colorado. The International Stereotypers and Electrotypers Union of North America dedicated the Costello Tuberculosis Sanitarium in 1924. The Home for Aged Members of the United Brotherhood of Carpenters and Joiners of America was constructed and dedicated on October 1, 1928.

All six homes range in size from a capacity as low as five to three-hundred and fifty. The Home for the Aged and Disabled Railroad Employees has a capacity of over 135; the Railway Conductors' Home, 75; the Pressmen's Home, 200; the Costello Home, 5; the United Brotherhood of Carpenters, 350; the Home for Aged and Disabled Railroad Employees, 200. None of them have religious or monetary restrictions.

Requirements for admission to the Brotherhood's Home are four: A member must be at least 65 years of age; he should hold a continuous membership for not less than thirty years; a member unable to command at least fifty percent of the minimum rate of wages is entitled to admission; a member admitted to the Home relinquishes all claims for donation.

When the Home for Aged Members of the Brotherhood of Carpenters was dedicated in 1928, enthused James J. Davis, U. S. Secretary of Labor, was moved to deliver the following words of praise: "I have no hesitation in saying that this Home is one of the most beautiful and best homes for the aged I have ever seen, and I may say after visiting many of them in all sections of our country, that in erecting it, you have been permeated with the spirit of the Divine Carpenter of Galilee." After a week-long visit of our own, we can hardly refrain from offering a more earthy and this wordly counterpart to Mr. Davis — that the aged carpenter has the equivalent of a magnificent Florida resort, if only he could make use of all the facilities that he had dreamed of in his rural or city youth. The plain fact is that the man who brought this project to fruition not only felt a profound sense of obligation to the carpenters, but even more deeply a sense of appreciation and understanding of the vicissitudes of old age.

Enough has been said of the impulses that actuated Hutcheson to establish a Home for the Aged.

The man who deserves mention as the early proponent of the Home was Hutcheson's predecessor, James Kirby. In 1914 he reminded the delegates that "we are growing older day by day, and sooner, perhaps, than we realize, will reach that period in life when we will find that securing employment is an uphill proposition." Kirby's address may or may not have stirred the delegates in 1914, but the desire of an increasing number of aging carpenters for a home continued. In 1920, when the Brotherhood had on its rolls four thousand carpenters, ages sixty-five and over, Hutcheson debated over and over again the founding of a home for the aged and infirm "brothers."

Making use of his gift for sarcasm, Hutcheson set out to convert words into deeds, shocking those who were either indifferent or unaffected because of age differentials. Addressing himself to the Brotherhood's constituency in a special bulletin, Hutcheson wrote:

"For more than twenty years the question of establishing, First: A Home for the Aged Carpenters; Second: An Old Age Pension, have been discussed through the columns of our official monthly journal "The Carpenter." The subject has been considered, debated and passed upon by our General Conventions. . . . No definite propositions came from any quarter to work upon, and many thought both propositions were abandoned. However, the old-time members of our organization wanted to know, and still want to know, if, after a lifetime of struggle as trade unionists, they are to be thrown on a "scrapheap" in their old age, uncared for and unprotected, to die in poverty or in the workhouse. They feel this is poor recompense for the battles they fought in the past to establish better working conditions, better pay, and shorter hours for the younger men coming after them. So they still insist, and rightly so, that something be done in their behalf."

For carpenters who hoped for a program of action to meet the problem of the aged and infirm carpenters, an ambitious, ready-made plan began to unfold at the hands of Hutcheson in July of 1923. He reported the purchase of a tract of land in Lakeland, Florida, the cost of which was $632,393. Nearly 600 of its 1684 acres, at $375 per acre, was in groves of oranges, grapefruit and tangerine trees. The balance was citrus and vegetable land with approximately one million feet of standing merchantable pine. Since then three hundred acres were added to the Home.

The Economic Survey of 1923 described Lakeland as the center of the citrus industry of Florida. With careful planning, therefore, the Home itself was to become almost completely self-supporting. The City of Lakeland agreed to supply electric power at one-half the regular rate, as well as construct hard surface roads to the property without cost to the Brotherhood.

Since the program for the Home largely depended upon financing, Hutcheson experimented with the sale and distribution of the citrus fruit, with the local unions serving as sales agents. Each local union was expected to sell the membership fruit boxes, which were delivered to any part of the country at a saving to the purchaser, thereby yielding the Brotherhood an increased revenue over what would be derived by selling directly to packing houses. But this method was found wanting. The disposal of a large quantity of produce required a much wider market than the Brotherhood constituency could furnish. Accordingly, arrangements were made to sell direct to canning factories and packing houses. Today, the label "The United Brotherhood of Carpenters and Joiners of America Home Brand", is still to be seen on thousands of crates that are sent throughout the country.

During the first year of its operation, the Brotherhood's Home suffered heavy yearly deficits, which were covered by the union's general fund. Since 1937, the Home has become self-supporting.

In administering the Home, the Brotherhood has taken into consideration most of the basic needs of its occupants — physical, emotional and spiritual. Here, retired carpenters are shown sympathy, affection and tenderness; they are provided with work projects, hobbies and activities. Religious and educational interests are encouraged. Most important, the occupants derive a good deal of satisfaction from the knowledge that the Home is the Carpenters' own.

Although medical science has succeeded in extending the average life of Americans by eighteen years since 1900, the U. S. still trails far behind most north and west European countries in the care of our aged and infirm. In the 'twenties, except for paraphrasing the individualistic language of that period — "the unions would look after the workers!" — few labor union heads made any serious effort to protect their infirm and super-annuated members. As late as 1928, only eleven unions adopted a pension system, the U. S. Bureau of Labor Statistics reported. The United Brotherhood of Carpenters and Joiners was one of them. It was also one of only six unions to make proper provision for its aged and infirm members.

It was not until the 'forties that an increasing interest was focused upon "geriatric" treatment, dealing with problems of aging and chronic degenerative ailments. Postwar years saw unusual progress in public health. The increasingly successful war against infectious diseases brought about during this period a great increase in the number of old people, and a lively interest in pension plans.

The growing tendency among unions, since the end of World War II to provide in their collective bargaining agreements for welfare and pension benefits — in lieu of raises — has led several of them to investigate recently the desirability of establishing Homes or 'villages' for their retired members, modelled after the Carpenters' Home in Lakeland, Florida.

Interestingly enough it was Hutcheson, the individualist and opponent of governmental paternalism, who provided not only a modicum of security for the retired "brothers" but set a standard for such 'homes' well worthy of imitation. Here, in a setting richly endowed with the wondrous handiwork of nature, the aging members of the Brotherhood, of varying faiths and denominations dwell happily and contentedly together.

INDEX

- A -

Adams, William F., cited, 7.
Alinsky, Saul, X, quoted, 204.
Alexander, Moses (Governor), 226.
Altgeld, Gov. John, 52.
Amalgamated Clothing Workers, X, 140, 186, 383, 395.
Amalgamated Streetcar and Railway Union, 383.
American Federation of Labor, XII, 49, 92, 115, 119, 121-126, 129, 134, 150, 154, 155, 158, 160, 172, 174, 177, 178, 182, 185, 187, 189, 190, 192, 194, 196, 200, 206, 207, 208, 210, 215, 216, 222, 223, 254, 256, 259, 260, 263, 264, 269, 271, 273, 274, 275, 283, 285, 286, 289, 290, 293, 304, 310, 317, 332, 344-345, 346, 367.
American Federationist, quoted, 146-147, 322.
American Federation of Musicians, 326.
American Federation of State, County & Municipal Employees, 344.
America First Committee, 254, 256-259.
American Labor Party, 212.
American Medical Association (AMA) 320, 321.
American Newspaper Publishers' Association, 174.
American Plan, The, 121, 126, 144-156; effect on labor, 144-147; Hutcheson's measures, 149-153.
Anti-trust laws, 247-250.
Arnold, Thurman W., 237, 240-244, 247; U. S. versus Hutcheson, 239-250; significance of, 247-250.
Astor, Jacob, 22.

- B -

Baker-Gompers Agreement, 91, 92, 94, 97, 99, 101-104, 124.
Baker, Newton D., XV, 84-86, 87, 91, 92, 96, 97, 99, 226.
Bakery & Confectionery Workers International, 396.
Bard, Ralph (Ass't. Sec'y. U.S. Navy), 264, 265.
Barkley, Alben, 169.
Bates, Harry, 192, 265, 266, 269, 283.
Beck, Dave, 312, 330.
Bender, George A., 278.
Bing, Alexander M., cited, 83.
Berthoff, R. T., cited, 3.
Berry, George L., 169, 210, 218, 221, 222, 223. See also Labor's Non-Partisan League.

Beveridge, Sir William, 171.
Blaier, O. William, XV, 267, 390-391.
Bobbitt, Hon. Arch L., XV, 278, 314-315.
Boulding, Kenneth E., cited, 66, 86, 356.
Bowen, W. J., 109.
Brandeis, Louis, cited, 123.
Bricker, John W., (Sen., Ohio), 281.
Bricklayers, Masons & Plasterers Union, 109, 266.
Bridges, Harry, 229, 268, 290-291, 309.
Bridges, Styles, 269-278.
British Trades Union Congress, 124, 170.
Brotherhood of Locomotive Engineers, 140.
Brotherhood of Carpenters and Ku Klux Klan, 153-154.
Brownell, Herbert, Jr., 278.
Building and Construction Trades Dep't, A.F. of L., XVI, 69, 97, 301, 341, 344, 409-410.
Building Trades Employers' Association, 69, 71, 73-74.
Butler Daniel J., XV.

- C -

Cahan, Abraham, XI.
Cambiano, J. F., XV, 150, 341, 393.
Canadian Historical Association, XVI.
Capehart, Homer E., 277, 309, 327.
Carey, Mathew, quoted, 18.
Carpenters Home, 156, 277, 327, 416, 424.
Carpenter, The, 67, 72, 89-90, 93, 97, 100-101, 104, 108, 174, 233, 243, 304, 306, 308.
Carnegie, Andrew, 6.
Carson, Joseph, 152-153, 232.
Chandler, Henry W., XV, 392.
Chapman, Frank, XV, 391.
Chicago Historical Society, XVI.
Chicago University, XVI.
Chicago Public Library, XVI.
Ching, Cyrus S., 261, 307.
Chippewa Indians, 22, 23.
Cigar Makers Union, 44.
Civilian Conservation Corps (CCC), 189.
Clayton Act., 246-248, 250, 287.
Cleveland, President Grover, 52, 54-55, 247.
Collins, William, 216.
Committee on Emigration from the United Kingdom, cited, 8.
Commons, John R., cited, 8.

Communist Party, 159, 161, 208.
Congress of Industrial Organizations,
  XII, 201-217, 222-223, 227, 233,
  236, 254-256, 260, 269-270, 273-274,
  285-286, 290, 304, 317, 332, 344-345.
Coolidge, President Calvin, 122, 131,
  133, 135, 169.
Cooper, Andrew, V, XV, 393-394.
Coopers' International Union, 413.
Cornell University, XVI.
Coughlin, Father Charles F., 215-216.
Criteria of Writing labor histories, 335.
Cummins, E. E. cited, 77, 158.

- D -

Daily Worker, The, cited, 163.
Dallas News, 111.
Danbury Hatters' Case, 247.
Daniels, Joseph (Sec'y of War), 97.
Davis, William, 261-262.
Detroit Free Press, quoted 29.
Detroit Unionist, quoted, 42, 43.
Debs, Eugene V., 52, 54; pardon of,
  Hutcheson's intervention in, 119, 135-
  136.
Democratic Party, 125, 134, 211, 236,
  317, 343.
DeMille, Cecil B., 278, 281.
Dewey, Thomas E., 24, 278, 280, 281,
  313, 315.
District Council of Carpenters New
  York, XV.
District Council of Carpenters, Cook,
  Lake and Dupage Counties, Illinois,
  XV.
District 50 (UMW), 273.
Dougherty, C. H., cited, 185.
Dubinsky, David, 67, 162, 192, 205,
  212, 214-215, 271, 304, 330, 383-384.
Duffy, Frank, XIV, 70, 72-73, 102, 142,
  157, 162, 164, 166, 397.
Dunlop, John D. cited, 267.
Dulles, John F., 281.

- E -

Eight Hour League, 41.
Eisenhower, President Dwight, 315-316,
  343.
Elizabeth Culver, (mother of), 34-35.
Elks (B.P.O.E.), 137.
Emanuel, Victor, 278.
Emspack, Julius, 269.
Evening Mail, The, 105.

- F -

Farley, James, 210, 218.
Farmers Cooperatives, 275.
Faulkner, Harold V, cited 65.
Fischer, Albert E, XIV, 390-391.
Fitzgerald, Albert, 274, 276.
Florida, Lakeland, XV, 156, 306.
Ford, Henry, 81, 139.
Forrestal, James (Navy Secretary), 278.
Fortune (Magazine) quoted 414.

Foster, William Z., 119-121, 160-161,
  221.
Frankfurter, Felix, 116-117, 249.
Frey, John P, XIV, 170, 199, 202.

- G -

Gailbraith, John K., cited, 209, 425.
General Motors, 212-213.
Ginsberg, Eli, cited 339.
Globe, The, 105.
Goldsborough, Alan T., Judge, 292.
  Story of one million dollar check,
  292-293.
Gompers, Samuel, 3, 43-47, quoted 50,
  84-87, 91-93, 96-98, 102, 109, 119-
  124, 126, 129, 145-147, 226, 248,
  326, 330, 332-333, 342, 367, 370.
Gorman, Patrick E., XV, 330.
Graham, Frank T., 26.
Granger, Party, 51.
Gray, Richard, 301-302, 326, 344, 345,
  348.
Great Depression, Effects of; on Broth-
  erhood of Carpenters, 172-173, 187;
  labor, 186.
"Great Lakes Country," 18; Western
  movement, 24-30.
Green, William, 58, 157, 169, 177, 185,
  187, 190, 193 196 202-203, 205, 210,
  212, 255-256, 269, 299, 304, 325-326.
Greenback Party, 41, 51, 267.
Greenwood, Thomas, cited, 16.

- H -

Haber, William, cited 75.
Hall, Dr. Reverend Logan, XV, 311,
  328.
Halleck, Charles, 278.
Hansen, Marcus Lee, cited 5, 15.
Hanson, Charles W., XV, cited 70.
Harding, President Warren G., 120-121,
  125, 132-136, 169, 333.
Harris, Herbert, cited, XII, cited 162,
  334.
Harrison, President Benjamin, 51, 54.
Harrison, George, 192, 226, 261.
Hartley, Fred, 299-300.
Hayes, Al, IX, 330, 347.
Herring, Peddleton, cited, 133.
Hillman, Sidney, X, 67, 210-213, 217,
  221-222, 237, 271, 76, 282, 332, 383.
Hillquit, Morris, 76.
Historic Michigan, cited, 44.
Historical Society of New York, XVI.
Hobbs, Bill, 88.
Hoover, President Herbert, XVI, 125,
  146, 169-170, 176-177, 190, 301.
Home for Aged Carpenters, 416-424.
Horn, Stanley F., cited, 225.
Houghton, Dr. Douglas, 23.
Hoxey, Robert, cited 414.
Hubbard, Bela, quoted, 21, 22.
Huber, William D., 68.
  186, 223, 228, 229.

Humphrey, Hubert (Sen. Minn.), 305.
Hurley, Edward N., 97-98, 100-101, 103-106, 110.
Hutcheson, Mrs. Bessie (King), XV, 48, 61.
Hutcheson, Bud, XV, 19.
Hutcheson, Campbell, Mary, (grandmother), 4, 7-16, See Hutcheson's Origins.
Hutcheson, Daniel O., (father of), 4, 8, 12, 16, 18-28, 36-38, 42-46.
Hutcheson, Mathilda, 19.
Hutcheson versus Coughlin, Charles, F., 215-216.
Hutcheson, Maurice A., (son of) IX, XI, XIII, XIV. 29, 56, 61, (works with George Meany on Defense Job) 190, 231-232, 267, 327, 339; background, 340-342; inspection of European theatre of war, 341; efficiency in administration, 341; his political program, 342, 343; supports General Dwight Eisenhower, 343, 344; appointment to Advisory Board of Foreign Operations Administration, 344; influences A. F. of L. on Jurisdiction, 344-348; elected general president, 348, 349; his program for the Brotherhood of Carpenters; his structural changes in organization, 349, 350; his ideas of future, 351; for labor 351, 380-382, 405.
Hutcheson, Minnie, 19.
Hutcheson, Myra (daughter of), 142, 328.
Hutcheson, Stella, 143.
Hutcheson, William Levi, object of this work VII, VIII, XI, XII, XIII, XIV, XV; origins 4-10; birth, 35-36; childhood, 36-37; at school, 38; his taste for reading, 38; father seeks trade for, 40; early conditionings, 40-45; his instinct for leadership, 46; as carpenter apprentice, 47; determines to leave Saginaw, 47; goes to Auburn, Michigan, 47, 48; marries Miss Bessie King, 48; early travels, 48, 49; Depression of 1893, effects of, 49-55; other influences on, 50, 55; beginnings of his career at Dow Chemical, 56, 57; on blacklist in Midland, 58; business agent in the Saginaws; improves conditions in the Saginaws, 59, 60; delegate to United Brotherhood of Carpenters, 60; his program for Michigan Carpenters and industrial hazards, 60, 61; Election to office of second general vice-president, 61, as general president, 61; first challenge as general president, 65-79; his views regarding leadership, 80, 81; "demand" for leadership, 65, 69; labor equality vis-a-vis the State, his views on during

World War I, 87-111; public opinion aroused against him, 104; Billy Sunday's tirade of, 105; receives appointment from President Wilson to National War Labor Board; his influence on William Howard Taft, 114, 116; beginnings of a political program, 131; his recognition as special interest representative inside the Republican party, 131, 133; his relations with President Warren G. Harding, 132, 135-6; his reaction to "welfare capitalism" of 1920's; as "joiner," motivations, 137, 138-142; gains admittance to Masons, Elks, Indiana Chamber of Commerce, 137; his family, 142, 143; his strategy in drives against American Plan, 144-153; his stand against third party, 129, 130, 156-158; Communists in the Brotherhood of Carpenters, 159-166; his relations with President Hoover, 169, 170; advocates public works program and thirty-hour week, 173, 174; formulates labor plank for Republican National Committee, 176; investigates labor record of Governor Roosevelt, 177, 178; opposition to President Roosevelt, 187-189; Elected delegate of A. F. of L., to International Labor Organization in Chile, 190; White House opposition to appointment, 190; favors organizing the unorganized in mass production, 197-206; bout with Lewis, 204, 205; legends and anecdotes of his detractions, 204, 206, 221-222; opposition to Labor's Non-Partisan League, 213; opposition to Father Charles F. Coughlin, 215, 216; in role of political non-conformist, 237; his "politics of policy," 237; composes Willkie's labor platform, 235, 236; prosecution by Department of Justice, 241-47; victory in Supreme Court, 249-250; World War II, attitude of; his declaration to Roosevelt, 258, 259; advocates revival of National War Labor Board and union security, 259-264; as peacemaker between A. F. of L. and C. I. O., 268-270; writes of technological developments in television, 267; chief negotiator between A. F. of L. and Lewis, 272, 273; slanders against, 273; his efforts to organize cooperative farmers' groups, 275; his ideas of labor's political action, 276; receives recognition from War and Navy departments, 277, 278; his quest of Vice-Presidency (U.S.), 279-282; his disenchantment with Republican party, 281, 314-315; his national program, 283-288; as friend in need, 292, 293; warns Republi-

cans in Congress, 294, 295; leads in
fight of Taft-Hartley Act, 296-300;
his strategy with Senator Taft, 301;
his appointment to National Labor-
Management Panel, 306; his meetings
with President Truman, 306, 308-309;
admitted to Ancient and accepted
Scottish Right of Free Masonry, 311;
his civic activities, 311, 312; his
friendships, 312; supports presidential
candidate Eisenhower, 315, 316;
political role of labor, 317, 318; his
ideas of the state; relation to freedom 319, 320; responsibility for welfare, 320, 321; danger of communism,
318; politics, encroachment on economics, 319-323; justice in free market (laissez faire), 321-324; end of his
career, 324-327; his last months, 327;
death, 328; funeral services, 328; review of his achievements, 328-335.

- I -

Independent, The, 150.
Indianapolis News, 278.
Indianapolis Star, 278.
I. W. W. (Industrial Workers of the
World) 121, 126, 223-225.
Inter-Church World Movement, 120.
International Association of Machinists,
97, 173, 273, 347, 370, 384, 409, 412.
International Brotherhood of Boil-
makers, 179.
International Brotherhood of Electrical
Workers, 205.
International Brotherhood of Teams-
ters, 180, 312, 363.
International Labour Office (ILO),
XVI, 124, 190-191, 264.
International Ladies Garment Workers,
186, 206, 214-215, 273, 383-384,
395-396.
International Longshoremen's Associa-
tion, 212.
International Union of Bookbinders, 97.
International Union of Operating En-
gineers, 44.
International Union of Ship Carpenters
and Caulkers, 41.
International Woodworkers of America,
229-230, 405.
"Iron Law," 86.

- J -

Jewell, B. M., 170.
Jodoin, Claude, 394.
Johnson, Charles, Jr., XV, 391-392.
Johnson, Gen, Hugh, 187.
Josephson, Matthew, X, quoted 210.

- K -

Kaiser, Henry J., 283.
Kefauver, Estes, 327.
Kennedy, Thomas, 261.
Kenny, Ted, XV.
Keyserling, Leon H., XV, 268.

Kirkland, Edward C., cited 358.
Knights of Labor, 36, 41, 43-44.
In Saginaw Valley, 45, 207, 213, 216,
367-369, 370, 373.
Krug, Julius A., 290.
Ku Klux Klan, 153-154.

- L -

Labor's Non-Partisan League, 210, 212,
221, 232, 276.
LaFollete, Robert M. (Senator), 157,
257.
LaFollete-Wheeler Ticket, 156, 158.
Landis, Judge K. M. (Landis Award),
151-152.
Landon, Alfred M., 212, 219.
Landon, Fred, cited 22.
Lapham, Roger D., 261.
Laski, Harold, quoted, 237.
League of Nations, 123.
Levinson, Edward, cited XII, 162, 334-
335 see *PAC*.
Lewis, Denny, 271-272.
Lewis, Kathryn, 257, 271.
Lewis, John L., X, XIV, 50, 65-67, 81,
105-106, 124-125, 137, 186, 192, 196-
201, 203-213, 217, 220-222, 229, 233,
236-237, 255, 257, 262, 267-269, 273,
276, 281, 289-291, 293, 325-328, 330,
332, 383-384.
Lincoln, President Abraham, 28, 111.
Lippman, Walter, cited 129.
Long, Huey, 172.
Longworth, Alice Roosevelt, 257.
Lumber and Sawmill workers, 223-232.
Lumberjacks, 29-33.

- M -

Macy, Everett M., 102-103.
Madison, Charles A., cited XII, 162,
334-335.
Management-Labor Conference, 286.
Manifestoes to Republican party, 294.
"Statement of William Hutcheson,"
299.
Martin, Joseph (Cong. Pa.), 278, 291.
Masons, 137.
Meadows, Sturges, 169.
Meany, George, 143, 199, 212, 261,
269, 274, 298-299, 304, 327, 344-347.
Metal Trades Department (A. F. of L.),
cited XIV, 97, 108.
Methodist Church of Indianapolis, XV.
Methodist Historical Society, XVI.
Michelson, Charles, 176-177.
Michigan, Detroit, 17; Saginaw county,
21-27; Auburn, 47.
Michigan Federation of Labor, 43.
Michigan Historical Commission, XV.
Michigan Historical Society, XV.
Michigan State Library, XV.
Millis, Professor Wright, cited XI.
Mine, Mill and Smelter Workers, 201.
Minton, Bruce and Stuart, John, cited,
XII, 166, 334.

Mooney, Tom, 150.
Morse, Wayne D. (Sen. Oregon), 291, 301-302.
Muir, Abe, 148, 150, 226-227, 229.
Murray, Philip, 208-209, 236, 261, 269-271, 274-276.

- Mc -

McCarthy, Joseph R., (Sen. Wisc.) 319.
McCormick, James J., 22.
McDonald, David J., 276, 330.
McGuire, Peter J., 159, 326, 330, 332-333, 342, 349, 360, 363-365, 369-370, 377.
McIntyre, M. H., Secretary to President Roosevelt, 268.
McKinley-Bryant, presidential campaign, 53-54.
McSorley, William J., XIV, 170.

- N -

National Association of Manufacturers (NAM), 146, 185, 260, 286, 289, 296, 304.
National Industrial Conference Board, 112.
National Erectors Association, 146.
National Founders Association, 146.
National Labor Party, 123, 129, 160.
National Labor Union, 41.
National Maritime Union, 208.
National Metal Trades Association, 146.
NRA, 182-188, 192, 194, 211.
National Union for Social Justice, 215.
National War Labor Board, 111-112, 260-262.
New Masses, The, 166, 334.
New Republic, cited 115.
New York Central Trades and Labor Council, 212.
New York Public Library, cited XVI.
New York State Federation of Labor, 212.
New York School of Industrial Relations, cited XVI.
New York Times, quoted, 190, 213, 235.
New York World, 105, 177.
Niebuhr, Prof. Reinhold, cited 86.
Norris-LaGuardia Act, 185, 246-247, 249-250, 287, 292.

- O -

Ontario Historical Society, cited XVI.
OPA (Office of Price Administration), 264.
Operative Plasterers' International Association, 267.

- P -

Padway, Joseph A., 240.
Patterson, Robert F.,(Under Secretary of War), 264-265, 278.
Pegler, Westbrook, 319.
Perkins, Frances, 180, 190, 192, 212, 264-265.
Petrillo, James, 326, 384.

Pinkerton Detectives, 45.
Political Action Committee (Pac), 276.
Political philosophy, Brotherhood of Carpenters, The, 150-155, 315-318.
Potofsky, Jacob, 274, 330.
Progressive Mine Workers Union, 272.
Pulliam, Eugene, 278, 315.

- Q -

Quebec Aid Society, 9.
Quigley, Daniel, cited 70.
Quinn, Arthur A., 61.

- R -

Railroad Brotherhoods, 286.
Railway, Maintenance of Way, Employees, 344.
Rajoppi, Raleigh, XV, 341, 392, 393.
Raskin, A. H., quoted, 346-347.
Red Labor International, 159.
Republican Party, 115, 131, 133, 174, 176, 190, 219, 236, 317, 333, 343.
Reuther, Walter, 199, 274, 330, 384.
Riesman, David, cited, 65.
Rieve, Emil, 274, 330.
Roberts, R. E., XV, 393.
Rockefeller, John D., Jr., 125, 140.
Rooney, John E., 267.
Rosenman, Samuel, Mrs. 283.
Roosevelt, President Franklin D., cited XV, Library, National Archives, Hyde Park, XVI, 97, 99, 108, 125; Cox-Roosevelt ticket, 157, 176, 179, 180-181, 183, 189-190, 205, 209-213, 217-222, 232, 234-236, 254, 256, 258, 262, 266, 270, 271, 282, 333.
Roosevelt, President Theodore, 111, 183, 257.
Rose Alex, 212.
Routzohn, Harry, 278-279, 301-302.
Rubber Workers, 197, 202.

- S -

Saginaw News, cited 60.
Saginaw Public Library, cited XVI.
Saginaw Valley Lumberjacks, 45.
Schlesinger, Arthur, cited, 181.
Schwartzer, Harry, cited XV, 157, 392.
Scots Ancestry Research, cited XVI.
Scottish-American Journal, cited, 8, 41.
"See where Old Carpenters Go to Live," 415-424.
Seidman, Joel, cited 105.
Siegfried, Andre, cited XII, quoted 20-21.
Sheet Metal Workers International Association, 124, 266, 397, 409-411.
Sherman Act, 52, 246-247.
Shishkin, Boris, 263.
Shortemeier, Fred, 278-279, 315.
Sinclair, Upton, 172.
Smith, Alfred E., 169, 177.
Snyder, John W., 283.
"Socialized medicine," 320-321.
Social Security Act, 192-193.

Socialist Party, 129.
Sprague, Russel J., 280.
Stassen, Harold E., cited XIII.
Steelman, Dr. John R., cited XV, 106, 260, 262, 268, 278, 303, 306, 308-309, 312, 327.
Steelworkers Organizing Comm., 236.
Stein, Emanuel, cited, 181.
Stevenson, Vice-Pres. Adlai, B. 52.
Stevenson, Adlai E., 342.
Stevenson, John R., cited XV, 389-390.
Stolberg, Benjamin, cited, 220.
Stuart, John, cited XII, 162, 166, cited 334.
Sunday, Billy, 105-106.

- T -

Taft, Charles P., 115.
Taft-Hartley Act, 296, 311, 316-317, 331, 343.
Taft, Philip, cited 70, 75, 78, 162.
Taft, Sen. Robert A., cited XVI, 116, 278, 291, 301-302, 305, 307, 309, 315.
Taft, President William Howard, cited XVI, 112, 115-116, 267, 301.
Tennenbaum, Frank, cited 66, 355.
Terzick, Peter, cited XV, quoted 225.
Thomas, Norman, 257.
Time (magazine), 347.
Thrush, Lloyd A., 272.
Tobin, Daniel J., 179-180, 210, 218, 269, 270-272, 304, 326, 346.
Townsend Old Age Plan, 172.
Toynbee, Arnold, cited IX.
Trade Union Courier, quoted, 345, 405.
Trade Union Educational League, 161-162.
Transport Workers Union, 208, 396.
Trevellick, Richard, 41, 44.
Truman, President Harry S., cited XV, 282-283, 285, 293, 308, 316-317, 325, 333.
Tuttle, Charles H., cited XV, 241, 244, 250, 278, 281, 325-326.

- U -

Ungerleider, Samuel, cited XV, 136, 278, 281, 312, 327.
Union Labor Life Insurance Co., 155-156.
Union League Club, 125.
Unions, Industrial, Basis of, See Chapter XIV.
United Association of Plumbers, 205.
United Auto Workers, 197, 208, 396, 407.
United Brotherhood of Carpenters and Joiners of America, The, as economic social organization, 335, 336; technical changes, and psychological factors, 356, 357; the carpenter in America, 357-360; founding of Brotherhood and its administration, 360, 361; Brotherhood today, 361-364; its early career, 364, 365; Peter J. McGuire,

364; type of leader; the eight hour day, 366-369, 371; other motivations for joining, 372; adjustments of, 373-375; the "invention" of "walking delegate," 375-380; level of democracy in unions, 381; in Brotherhood, 382-387; Leadership in, 388; motivations of, 389; subject to scrutiny, 384; two-sidedness of labor unions, 396, 397; of Brotherhood, 397-399; effect of technological innovations on carpentry, 398-400; jurisdictional dispute; with Woodworkers, 400-403; American Society of Carpenters, 403-405; job description of carpenter, 406; application of, 408-414; role of jurisdictional claims, 415.
United Electrical, Radio and Machine Workers, 208, 274, 396.
United Mine Workers of America, cited XIV, 106, 115, 162, 186, 208, 211, 262, 272, 286, 289, 291-293, 326, 363, 371, 396.
United States Chamber of Commerce, 260, 286, 289.
United States Commissioner General Immigration, cited 5.
United States Department of Labor Library, cited XVI.
United States Steel, 120, 140, 183, 213.
University of Michigan, cited XV.
Upholsterers International Union, 398.

- V -

Vandenberg, Arthur, 235, 313.
Villard, Oswald Garrison, 257.

- W -

Wagner, Sen. Robert F., 192-193, 211.
Wagner Act, 192-194, 287-288, 294.
Walsh, Frank, 112, 115.
Warren, Earl W., (Chief Justice, U. S. Supreme Court) 278, 313.
Wehle, Louis B., cited XV, 89, 91-92, 96-98.
White House Intrigue, 221, 222.
Willis, Cong. Raymond C., 280.
Willkie, Wendell L., 213, 235-237, 256-257.
Wilson, W. B., 111.
Wilson, President Woodrow F., cited X, XV, and Hutcheson, 107-108, 110-112, 117, 120, 122, 134, 179, 213, 267, 333.
Woll, Matthew, cited XIV, 180, 192, 271, 304.
Wolman, Leo, cited, 172.
Wood, Gen. Robert E., 256, 258.
Wood, Wire and Metal Lathers International Union; cited XV, 413.
Workingman's Advocate, cited, 38, 40, 42.
World War II, attitude of labor, 254, 255.
WPA, 188, 232, 233.